ETHIOPIA

Titles in ABC-CLIO's *Africa in Focus Series*

Eritrea   Mussie Tesfagiorgis G.

Ethiopia   Paulos Milkias

Titles in ABC-CLIO's *Asia in Focus Series*

China   Robert André LaFleur, Editor

Japan   Lucien Ellington

The Koreas   Mary E. Connor, Editor

ETHIOPIA

Paulos Milkias

ABC-CLIO

Santa Barbara, California • Denver, Colorado • Oxford, England

Library of Congress Cataloging-in-Publication Data

Milkias, Paulos.
  Ethiopia / Paulos Milkias.
    p. cm. — (Africa in focus)
  Includes bibliographical references and index.
  ISBN 978-1-59884-257-9 (alk. paper) — ISBN 978-1-59884-258-6 (ebook)
1. Ethiopia—History. 2. Ethiopia—Politics and government. 3. Ethiopia—
Economic conditions. 4. Ethiopia—Social life and customs. I. Title.
II. Series: Africa in focus.
  DT381.M63 2011
  963—dc22   2011000407

ISBN: 978-1-59884-257-9
EISBN: 978-1-59884-258-6

15 14 13 12 11   1 2 3 4 5

This book is also available on the World Wide Web as an eBook.
Visit www.abc-clio.com for details.

ABC-CLIO, LLC
130 Cremona Drive, P.O. Box 1911
Santa Barbara, California 93116-1911

This book is printed on acid-free paper (∞)
Manufactured in the United States of America

The publisher has done its best to make sure the instructions and/or recipes in this book are correct. However, users should apply judgment and experience when preparing recipes, especially parents and teachers working with young people. The publisher accepts no responsibility for the outcome of any recipe included in this volume.

To my late brother, Wengielu Elias Amaya, who was eager to read this book but suddenly passed away at his home in Melbourne, Australia barely months before it was issued.

Contents

About the Author

Paulos Milkias, who received his PhD (Dean's Honor List) from McGill University, has taught humanities and political science at Marianopolis College and Concordia University in Montreal, Canada, for more than two decades. Under the government of emperor Haile Selassie, he served as history and information expert in the administration department of the Ministry of Defense. Dr. Paulos has published scores of scholarly articles in prestigious refereed journals such as *African Studies Review, Journal of African Studies, Journal of Educational Thought*, and *Studies in Comparative International Development*. His seminal work, *Ethiopia: A Comprehensive Bibliography*, published by G. K. Hall/Macmillan (extensively cited in the *Oxford Guide to Library Research*, Oxford University Press, 2001), has remained a major reference material for Ethiopianist, Africanist, and Third World scholars since 1990. The author was co-editor of *Northeast African Studies* (Michigan State University). Currently, he is associate editor of *Horn of Africa Journal* (Rutgers University). Dr. Paulos is a renowned encyclopedist and anthologist. He was a contributing editor to the *World Education Encyclopedia* and is coauthor of a lead article on Ethiopian government and politics in *Encyclopedia Aethiopica* (Hamburg University, 2006). Dr. Paulos is an associate editor of the highly acclaimed *Nelson's New Christian Dictionary* (Thomas Nelson, 2001). He co-edited *The Battle of Adwa: The Historic Victory of Ethiopia over European Imperialism* (Algora Publishing, 2005). He has also authored, inter alia, the following monographs: *Haile Selassie, Western Education and Political Revolution in Ethiopia* (Cambria Press, 2006), *Developing the Global South: a United Nations Prescription* *for the Third Millennium* (Algora Publishing, 2010), *Education, Politics and Social Change in Ethiopia*, (Tsehai Publications, Loyola Marymount University, 2010), and *Paulos Milkias Dictionary of Ethiopian Christianity* (University Press of America, 2010.).

Preface

All members of the human race are Ethiopians. With the revolutionary ideas entailed in the Eve hypothesis, this has been ascertained beyond any reasonable doubt. Ethiopia is unique. It is the birthplace of human beings' ancestor Lucy, who lived 3.2 million years ago; an older ancestor, Ardi, who lived 4.4 million years ago; and the even older ramidus who lived 5.8 million years before humans' known written history. A cursory look at Hadar, where Lucy and other 3-million-year-old fossils have been located, could give anyone with some imagination a feeling of how his or her ancestors lived eons of year ago. The fossil of the oldest human species, *Homo sapiens idaltu*, dating back 160,000 years, was also from there. One is bound to ask what this early human's life was like.

As anthropology students know, the history of the human race has been interspersed by some major revolutions in technology and know-how, such as the breakthrough invention of stone implements, the cultivation of crops, the domestication of animals, and the skill to kindle fire. Very few people know that several of these early breakthroughs took place in Ethiopia. The discovery in Ethiopia of human-made stone tools, dating back 2.5 million years—older than the coup-de-poing, a lower Paleolithic stone hand axe, by millions of years—makes the country unique. It was in Ethiopia that donkeys and camels were first domesticated. The Ethiopian highlands are major centers of plants and crops, where according to some specialists, cereals such as teff (*Eragrostis teff*), wheat, barley, and finger-millet (*Eleusine corocana*, known locally as *dagusa*); oilseeds such as nug (*Guizotia abyssinica*); and the world-famous coffee were first domesticated.

This book is intended to shatter the deep-seated stereotype of Ethiopia that has been fueled by contemporary media, which uses graphic pictures of underfed adults and children in order to project Ethiopia as a country on the edge of a chasm—a colossal basket case that is condemned to perpetually struggle for survival in futility and anguish. It is true that owing to the drought and famine that has periodically devastated its people, Ethiopia has frequently appeared across newspaper headlines and on television screens during the past half century, only to fade away when the immediate crisis has elapsed. The images that remain etched on the minds of foreigners are those of the 1984–1985 famine, including images of starving babies suckling the breasts of their dead mothers, which flashed across television screens in living color, followed by the generous response of Britain's Bob Geldof and a group of U.S. rock stars who coined the famous phrase "we are the children" and launched a campaign that raised over US$100,000 for the victims. The latter included among others: Ray Charles, Bob Dylan, Lionel Richie, Stevie Wonder, Michael Jackson, Tina Turner, Diana Ross, Dionne Warwick, Cyndi Lauper, Bruce Springsteen. Ethiopians have remained extremely grateful for this humanitarian gesture. But the name Ethiopia has since become almost synonymous with famine. That being the case, what this clichéd image glosses over is the clear sky, the breathtaking mountains, the precipitous escarpments and valleys, the panoramic scenery, the glorious sunshine and climate of perpetual spring, the wealth of foliage and flowers, and the pristine lakes, rivers, and forests teaming with wildlife, most of which are endemic. In Ethiopia, there is diversity and grandeur unique in the African continent. Ethiopia is not only the origin of humankind and the first Stone Age civilization. It is also a land of people with unsullied spirit of freedom and valor, of heroes and heroines who kept the country independent for thousands of years against great odds. Learning about the achievements of the Ethiopian people is in fact like watching a captivating drama of eons of years gone by.

Only the initiated know that 4,000 years ago, the Egyptian pharaohs considered Ethiopia "the land of the Gods"; in the eighth century BC, Homer referred to its people as "the blameless Ethiopians"; and in the sixth century AD, the Prophet of the Islamic religion, Mohammed, described Ethiopia as the land of the "just." For centuries, Ethiopia slipped out of the world's attention only to reappear and elicit romantic fascination from Westerners. Being a bastion of Orthodox Christianity as well as Islam, and being distant and inaccessible, she carried the charm of mystery and was treated with awe. But until the Italo-Ethiopian war of 1936–1941, there was no stock of reliable and comprehensive knowledge about the country that could satisfy and sober the West's curiosity. Where information existed, it was to a large extent sketchy, and it tended, with few exceptions, to be distorted, with piquant portrayals of and attention to Ethiopia's enthralling legends and charismatic leaders such as Tewodros, Menelik, and Haile Selassie.

Those who delve into this book will learn that the magic the country swayed on the ancients is still there, for even today, its inhabitants are some of the most hospitable on the entire planet, its historical relics captivate any visitor, and its scenic landscapes are breathtaking.

Looking at it from a geographic point of view, Ethiopia is a land of contrasts. Its landmass is one of the planet's earliest formed, with much volcanic activity still lurking on the eastern rim of the Danakil lowlands. The country has dazzling physical features—deep gorges that dwarf the Grand Canyon; high moorlands and plateaus; and long, winding rivers, including the Blue Nile, which provides 86 percent of the water and almost all the silt that Egypt requires for its own survival. Near Bahr Dar, there is the pristine Lake Tana and the awe-inspiring Blue Nile falls called Tis Issat (Smoke of Fire). Ethiopia has savannah grasslands, vast wetlands, lush lowland meadows, parched deserts, pristine lakes overlooking the magnificent panorama of the Bale Mountains. and grand valleys. The country has snowcapped mountains juxtaposed against the Afar depression, with the hottest weather recorded on the planet; and in the Daga highlands where most people live, there is a year-round congenial climate with alpine cool weather and tropical sunshine. All these exist within a territory of 471,776 square miles.

Probing readers here have an opportunity to discover the incredible variety of the traditions of Ethiopia's inhabitants, its people's lore, and its land's biodiversity. Ethiopia's endemic plants, of which there are thousands, are found in a jigsaw puzzle of geographic relief sandwiched between towering mountains, sharp escarpments, and immaculate Rift Valley lakes. The myriad species of Ethiopian birds and mammals would draw awe and admiration from any curious soul. Indeed, wherever one sets foot in this ancient land, there is always something mysterious, something to enjoy and marvel at, such that exploring it in real time is like passing through splendor projected by nature until eternity.

Today, there is a dearth of texts dealing with Ethiopia in its entirety. The only one that comes near to achieving this is Edward Ullendorff's *The Ethiopians: An Introduction to Country and People* (Oxford University Press), but it is dated, having been published in 1973. Other texts on Ethiopia include coffee table books, many of which carry useful information in addition to being emblazoned with a plethora of gorgeous pictures. Unfortunately, such travelogues, although fine for tourists, fail to make an in-depth look at the history, politics and economics of the country. This all-encompassing global handbook as part of the series—Africa in Focus, tries to fill that void in a very ambitious way.

What one sees in Ethiopia today is testimony to the great civilization the country developed during antiquity and products of Ethiopia's unique architectural tradition; thus, for scholars of antiquity, Ethiopia offers a site rich with early human technological advancement. Archaeological finds, monuments, and inscriptions dating from the sixth century BC demonstrate that a succession of civilizations existed in the country for thousands of years. Yeha and Axum are just a few of the centers that continue to yield rich artifacts and edifices from that period. In Aksum, one can gawk at the massive blocks of granite stelae considered by the United Nations Educational, Scientific and Cultural Organization (UNESCO) to be the tallest single stone monument in existence; they were cut and dragged from miles away and erected without the help of any machine more than 2,000 years ago. The stelae are carved to represent floor levels, cross-beams, doors, and windows, resembling a style of timber, mud, and stone architecture still being used in villages in northern Ethiopia. Recently, palaces several stories high have been unearthed near Axum. It is not surprising therefore that Peter James and Nick Thorpe's *Ancient Inventions*, (New

York: Ballantine Books, 1994, pp. 203–204) credits Ethiopians, not New Yorkers, as the earliest designers of "sky-scrapers." Indeed, one cannot help but admire the full glory of the extensive fortresses, promenades, palaces, shrines, royal baths, ancient inscriptions written back and forth in ox-like motion on vast stone slabs, and mammoth burial places, statues, tombs, and churches of northern Ethiopia. Coins of the emperors of Aksum, among them Endybis, Aphilas, Ousanas, and Ouazebas, kept in safes in the Ethiopian national museum in Addis Ababa, are from the early Christian era and were minted in bronze, silver, and gold. Even the castles of Gondar, which were constructed during the age of discovery in Europe, still look majestic; they may have some Portuguese influence but were the product of local Ethiopian craftsmen.

In Lalibala, one can see and admire the 11 elaborately carved churches all dug from a single block of rock more than 800 years ago. It was for the Ethiopian Orthodox Tewahedo Church that these magnificent monuments were constructed by Emperor Lalibala as a solace for both the devout and the sinner. The church has been the custodian of the country's history, independence, and culture. It even claims to be the warden of the original Ark of the Covenant, which disappeared from Jerusalem following the destruction of king Solomon's Temple. All of these points of interest—described in some detail in the book—ought to be visited and studied because they are some of the few special monuments of human achievement in existence.

No informed citizen of the world today can afford to be oblivious to the growths as well as the trials and tribulations of Ethiopia in a continent that directly impacts world peace and security of navigation, with pirates from Ethiopia's nearest neighbor, Somalia, wreaking havoc on the Gulf of Aden. Even though Ethiopia was the only country in Africa that succeeded in remaining independent during the time the continent was parceled off by the European colonialists, it has played a pivotal role in one of the most remarkable renaissances the world has ever known, which is the bringing together of an entire African continent, of which Ethiopia is an integral part. The decision by the continent's leaders to make Addis Ababa the capital of independent Africa in 1964 was a triumph for Ethiopians young and old who wanted to see their country be a center stage in forging alliances that would rid the continent of lingering colonialism and the racist policy of apartheid. Knowing more about Ethiopia and following what has transpired there will help readers to get at least a glimpse of the momentous events that took place in Africa during the Cold War, given that most of the decisions of the continent's leaders were made at the Organization of African Unity and African Union conference halls in Addis Ababa.

U.S. citizens reading this book may take solace in that whereas they may be heckled by many Latin American citizens who are afraid of their country's enormous economic and military might, Ethiopian youth now openly remark, "America Woim Mot" which means "America or death!" Americans will also benefit in knowing how much the West in general and the United States in particular have been diplomatically tied to Ethiopia. Modern Ethiopia opened itself up to the West more fully during the reign of Emperor Menelik II at the end of the 19th century, a relationship that was bolstered by the Ethiopian monarch's decisive victory over the Italian colonialists at the battle of Adwa in 1896. The French cemented their connection to Ethiopia by building a railway line from their colony of Djibouti to the Ethiopian capital. The British kept an embassy in Addis Ababa through which they cultivated excellent relations with Haile Selassie and his family even before he became a regent in 1916.

Barely five years after Haile Selassie ascended the throne in 1930 and started to carry out his modernization drive, however, Benito Mussolini, who wanted the avenge Italy's defeat at Adwa, deployed half a million soldiers armed with tanks and war planes in strategic places in the Horn of Africa. He soon invaded the only country that had remained fully independent in all of Africa, by employing poison gas, among other things, against peasant Ethiopian fighters equipped only with old firearms, spears, and clubs. Although the invaders succeeded in occupying Addis Ababa, the Ethiopian people's resistance continued. Large parts of the country remained outside Italian control. During the Fascist occupation, the United States, Canada, and New Zealand were the only three countries that refused to recognize Italian sovereignty over Ethiopia. Initially, the British and French acquiesced to Mussolini's occupation of Ethiopia with the hope of placating the Italian dictator, who they were afraid might join arms with their arch enemy, Hitler. But following Mussolini's declaration of war on France in 1940, the British and Commonwealth armies came to the aid of Ethiopian patriots who had been waging a very successful guerrilla war during the five years of occupation. As a result of this joint effort, full Ethiopian independence was restored in 1941. From this date on, Ethiopia struggled to guard and maintain its hard-won sovereign political survival and to pursue the policy of modernization cut short by five years of Fascist invasion.

Early during his reign, Haile Selassie had moved his country's orbit from Britain to the United States because America had always wanted trade relations, not direct colonialism, on the continent of Africa. The British, on the other hand, were there to expand their empire. As early as 1923, prior to being crowned as emperor, Haile Selassie had written a letter to President Harding indicating that he wanted to transfer his own personal money from a British bank to an American one. Also before the invasion, Haile Selassie had commissioned an American adviser, the Sorbonne-educated international law expert John Spencer, who remained with Haile Selassie to the waning days of his regime. After the ejection of the Fascists from Ethiopia in 1941, Haile Selassie made some bold moves. Although he benefitted from his diplomatic and military connection to the British, he did not want them to dominate Ethiopian education. Thus, he invited French Canadian Jesuits to come and train his youth. The French Canadians accepted the emperor's call and laid a foundation for the country's first Third Level institution. As former Canadian Ambassador to Ethiopia points out:

> Canadian Jesuits were invited to Ethiopia by the Emperor and taught at and administered the Tafari Makonnen school in Entoto until the 1970's. In 1950, at the request of the Emperor, the Canadian Jesuits founded the University College of Addis Ababa with Father Matte as the first rector. Western education, culture and artefacts were regarded in Ethiopia as in much of the rest of Africa, as a magical elixir which would bring instant progress. The Jesuits wrongly believed the very exotic nature of Western education would avoid any contamination of traditional

Ethiopian society; and like oil and water, the two would remain separate and that Western education would not change Ethiopian society. (Aubrey Morantz. 2011. "Canadian Jesuits and Ethiopian Education," Ottawa. January 20.)

Indeed, much to the chagrin of the Emperor and the French Canadian Jesuits, the seeds of the Ethiopian revolution were sowed at the University College of Addis Ababa when the United States entered the fray. Haile Selassie also tuned down diplomatic and military relations with the British and invited the United States to train not only his youth but also his army. From the 1940s to the early 1970s, the United States gave more aid to Ethiopia than to the rest of the African countries combined. The close relationship between the two continued unabated until the emperor's overthrow in 1974. After a hiatus of 17 years spanning the Derg period, when Marxism-Leninism was paid lip service by Mengistu Haile Mariam, the U.S. government returned to its former relationship with Ethiopia, such that today, it gives $1 billion per annum in the form of bilateral aid to the government of the Ethiopian Peoples' Revolutionary Democratic Front (EPRDF). There are good reasons for such increased interest in Ethiopia by U.S. policy makers. In an increasingly important continent, Ethiopia has the second-largest population; is at the crossroads between Semitic, Hamitic, and Nilotic peoples of the region; and is the headquarters of the African Union and the UN Economic Commission for Africa. For Americans, there are additional geopolitical reasons to care about Ethiopia. The U.S. war on terrorism is more and more moving toward targeting Ethiopia's neighbor—anarchic Somalia, where members of Al Qaeda who bombed Washington, D.C.'s embassies in Nairobi and Dar Es Salam are holed up. When the Ethiopian prime minister, Mr. Meles Zenawi, intervened in Somalia in 2006 in order to prop up the provisional government that was being threatened by El-Shabab, a radical Islamic group tied to Al Qaeda, he was doing it not only to fight against irredentists who were threatening Ethiopia's sovereignty and territorial integrity but also as an ally of the U.S. government, which was reluctant to enter into a potentially bloody war and see its soldiers mauled and dragged on the streets, as in the Black Hawk Down case in 1993.

I have traveled the length and breadth of Ethiopia and have gathered primary data for several of my previous books as well as this one. I am also a former student leader and government officeholder who was fortunate enough to meet and talk with Emperor Haile Selassie. Many of my reflections on the history, geography, politics, and economics of the country as portrayed in this book have been enriched by those experiences.

The book is thematically divided into narrative, contemporary issues, and reference parts. Being Ethiopian-born, I have tried to provide readers with accurate and fair information in the narrative section, not based merely on readings but enriched by personal knowledge. In fact, given my own personal experience of living in both the rural areas and the capital city of Addis Ababa and of being a member of the young educated elite that was rising in the country after its liberation from the Italian Fascists, I have tried very hard to integrate my own experiences with the scholarship in all of the topics addressed in the narrative and contemporary issues sections.

Author Paulos Milkias, center front with a bow tie, pictured with Emperor Haile Selassie, to the left with an imperial cape, a few years before the 1974 Ethiopian revolution. (Courtesy of Paulos Milkias.)

Ethiopia is intended for a worldwide audience, including international organizations, foreign missions, tourists, businesspeople, and instructors at all levels of educational institutions, including elementary and high schools and colleges and universities. I envision the monograph to be a reliable source for libraries, educators, potential tourists, and anyone curious enough to dig into the background of this mystical ancient land.

This book also may benefit Ethiopians who have migrated outside their country not because they wanted to but because of the political and social adversity of the last few decades. Many attempt not to relive the hardships they experienced under Ethiopia's military junta and instead want to concentrate on creating a more secure life wherever they now find themselves. Indeed, who wants to remember the bloody red terror that decimated a whole generation of educated Ethiopian youth, including their loved ones? Who wants to evoke memories of the gruesome deeds of the Derg's security police and vigilantes who terrorized the country by herding tens of thousands into killing fields, who drove multitudes of others into interrogation camps where they were physically and mentally tortured, sometimes with nerve-racking mock execution sessions? Many just want to close this chapter completely from their minds. Others have made a resolve to bring up diaspora-born children as Americans,

Europeans, or Australians, for example, oblivious to their rich heritage. The good news is that many have now come around; they want to expose their progeny to the millennia-year-old Ethiopian history and culture. This book is, I hope, a place to start to retrace their past.

My ardent desire in launching this book is to describe to all its readers Ethiopia's remarkable history; its unique culture; and the valor, resolve, and endeavors of its inhabitants. The volume includes narrative chapters on Ethiopia's geography, history and economics, institutions, and society as well as contemporary issues. And in general, I have attempted to provide a readable survey of Ethiopian culture from the earliest beginnings in its diverse branches: religion, language, Ge'ez and Amharic literature, music, architecture, painting and the applied arts, education, cinema, film, and sport. No book could provide a complete understanding of all aspects of a country's culture, but this monograph can be a useful tool for readers who may develop an ambition to begin to understand this complex ancient society.

In a survey that covers so much, it is inevitable that many points will be glossed over. I am conscious of these imperfections, but I offer this book in the sincere belief that it will initiate the uninitiated to the geography, history, economy, and society of Ethiopia and various aspects of the cultural life and national achievements of the indomitable Ethiopian people. The narrative incorporates vital information on the hundreds-of-years-old schools of music, poetry, theology, history, and philosophy. I hope these details will provide foreigners and Ethiopians alike some of the pleasure I have derived from writing the monograph.

Knowing that many readers of this book may at some stage travel to Ethiopia, I have included introductions to the country's working language, Amharic. Currently, Ethiopian Americans, mostly living in the capital area and on the West Coast, number more than 1 million. Although still a small percentage of the overall U.S. population, Ethiopians now constitute one of the fastest-growing immigrant groups in the United States and have become an integral part of the American culture. A cursory survey shows that as of late, Ethiopian restaurants are increasingly populating the American urban landscape. In fact, due to Ethiopian Americans ubiquitous presence in the Washington, D.C., area, the Ethiopian national language, Amharic, has already been accorded official status by the legislators of the District of Columbia. I have also appended a few useful words and phrases in the majority language of Afaan Oromo, as well as the historically and culturally important medium Tigrigna. Mindful that many will ultimately interact with Ethiopians in their home country or in the diaspora, I also have carefully elucidated the practical subjects of food and etiquette.

In the reference section, I have incorporated several sections of key information, including web sites for national and international organizations, business establishments, and cultural, educational, economic, and tourist organizations. Also included are records of the unique Ethiopian alphabet; the special national calendar; brief descriptions of historical figures and famous people, places, and events; and a comprehensive annotated bibliography, to aid more in-depth research.

Acknowledgments

I am indebted to the Central Statistical Agency of Ethiopia as well as the Ethiopian Mapping Authority whose massive database I have tapped into and whose informative atlas I have consulted in constructing my maps and compiling the book's geography section. I thank Dr. Kim Kennedy-White, developmental editor at ABC-CLIO, who worked closely with me in suggesting changes and editing the manuscript at the initial stages. The people at Apex and Erin Ryan helped in editing the manuscript and choosing the images for the book respectively. I express my gratitude to them. Special thanks go to Ms. Anneliese Papaurelis, editor of the Marianopolis periodical, *Alma Matters* who most generously highlighted my scholarly endeavors and ignited the admiration of thousands of my former students many of whom have sent me congratulatory words via email and Facebook. I thank my friends Worku Sharew, Mahir Ahmed and Yetenayet Akalehiywot who were kind enough to share with me some of the images used in the book.

I am indebted to Kyla Wells, a courageous and intelligent young woman who raised my spirits at the time I was overworked struggling to collect data for the multifaceted topics of this book. Kyla has a plethora of good habits that someone under pressure needs and she taught me some; for that I thank her wholeheartedly. Ms. Sanam Hajilou has looked over the monograph and has given me useful suggestions for which she deserves special mention. I also wish to thank Sister Anna Mary Breen, former president of Marianopolis College, Ms. Norma Raimondo, director of human resources and professional development at Marianopolis College, Dr. Leslie Cohen of Concordia University who is chair of our professional development association, Dr. Karen Ray and Dr. John Hill of Concordia University, Dr. Nancy

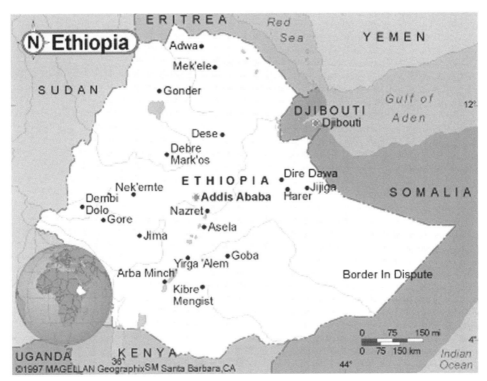

Ethiopia. (Courtesy of Magellan Geographix.)

Berman of Marianopolis College, Professor Toby Morantz of McGill University, Ms. Jeannie Krumel, administrator of the Department of Political Science of Concordia University, who were always supportive of my research endeavors.

I am privileged to have received words of encouragement from Ms. Kathy Assayag, vice president of Concordia University, and Dr. Laurie Bettito, host of the CJAD radio program *Passion* both of whom were at one time my star students but are now my best friends and mentors.

My longtime friend and former classmate Mr. Shiferaw Jamo helped me tremendously by volunteering to read the entire manuscript and by giving me crucial suggestions, particularly pertaining to the economics section, which is his turf. I thank Mr. Shiferaw enormously.

Dr. Guta Zenebe was a friend who stood with me steadfastly as I was struggling to shape this book to form. Mr. Robi Redda was kind enough to help me locate geographic data as well as important maps without which the first chapter of this book would not have been complete. My friend Mr. Abebe Brehanu was helpful in procuring some images I needed to include in the book.

Despite the tremendous amount of support I received from individuals and institutions in writing this book, I take full responsibility for all its faults.

Paulos Milkias Montreal, September 14, 2010

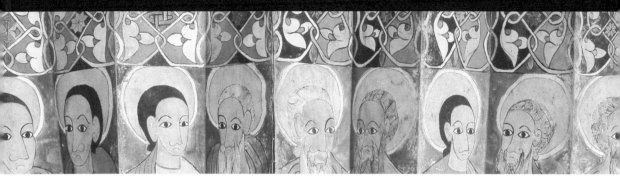

CHAPTER 1

Geography

ETHIOPIA AS THE ROOF OF AFRICA

Science has taught us that the cataclysmic events that set the stage for human life four-and-a-half billion years ago arose from a seething mass of molten rock, lava, and ash that can still be observed not far from Hadar, Ethiopia, where the remains of the earliest hominids were unearthed. The staggering forces that shaped our planet and brought us forth are still active in Ethiopia, dubbed by many as the roof of Africa, given that 50 percent of Africa's mountains are located there.

In Ethiopia, hills suddenly ride up within a few generations, chasms get engrossed with speed, and lakes expand or contract with briskness. Observing Ethiopia over the course of one's lifetime is like watching the mighty forces that forged this unique and marvelous planet, with its inimitable life forms and pristine environment, billions of years ago.

The movement of the earth that brought forth the continental block in the eastern region of African was spawned by extensive volcanic activity forming basalts of hard plateau. These in turn produced what are known as *ambas* in Ethiopia—large areas of flat surfaces that characterize the Ethiopian Highlands. As an example, the Bale Mountains in eastern Ethiopia form the largest area of land above 3,281 feet on the entire continent of Africa.

Ethiopia is at almost the central point of the Great Rift Valley, and the Fantale Volcano, not far from the capital Addis Ababa, is the crux of the valley. This gigantic crevice in the earth's crust meanders with graceful curves and turns from its lowest location near Lake Malawi in southern Africa northward through the interior of Ethiopia. The rift abruptly forks at a right angle in central Ethiopia. The eastern

Lava lake at Erta Ale's active volcano in the Afar region of Ethiopia. (Courtesy of Paulos Milkias/Filippo_Jean, Geo_Decouverte.)

section crosses the Gulf of Aden, and the northern branch ends up becoming the Red Sea.

At the apex of the split in the Awash valley, the earth is split into three giant land masses: the African plate, the Somali plate, and the Arabian plate. Awash is in a real sense the center of the inexorable thrust of the earth's crust. It is from the crater of the Fantale volcano in the Awash valley that one sees the great font from which the planet's molten depths spring forth. This locale, green with lush vegetation, is a veritable isolated garden of Eden. But green and idyllic as it may seem, danger lurks just below the surface. A glance toward the eastern rim reveals steam still rising from the remains of the volcano's last eruption in 1820.

ETHIOPIA'S GEOPHYSICAL MOSAIC

Ethiopia is the land of extremes. It is a country of vast geographical differentiation, with live volcanoes, snowcapped peaks, and torrid deserts. It hosts fresh and saltwater lakes. It has high, rugged mountains; flat-topped mountains; deep ravines; sharply cut river valleys; and wide plains. Altitudes range from the highest peak at Ras Dashen, 14,927 feet above sea level, down to the depression of the Kobar Sink, 377 feet below sea level in Afar. Erosion, volcanic eruptions, tectonic movements, and the sudden collapses of earth formations into caverns have led to accentuation of the unevenness of the surface.

Canyons in the Gondar highlands, east of Ras Dashen. (Getty Images/Michael Poliza.)

Ethiopia is a land of blue skies speckled with cottony clouds touching the horizon. It has a special charm and breathtaking panorama. As a human habitat, it is old beyond imagination. Lucy, the oldest hominid, lived 3.2 million years ago in its remote and wild terrain.

This ancient country, located in northeast Africa, covers 435,186 square miles and borders five African countries—Eritrea, Sudan, Kenya, Somalia, and Djibouti.

Ethiopia is mostly made up of high plateau and mountain ranges with steep edges, sliced up by torrents of rivers and brooks, the tributaries of major waterways such as the Abbay, Takaze, Awash, Omo, Wabi-Shebele, and Baro-Akobo. The western and the southeastern highlands are dissected by the Great Rift Valley. As seen from all sides—the west, the east, and the south—the highlands yield their majestic heights to vast semiarid lowlands.

The western highlands are vast in size and reach between 656 and 8,202 feet in height. The highlands are bisected by deep escarpments curved over the millennia by mighty rivers that flow down from the mountains to the lowlands. En route from Addis Ababa to Dabra Marqos in Gojam, there lies the famous Blue Nile gorge, which dwarfs the United States' Grand Canyon. At the bridge that connects the provinces of Shoa and Gojam, the riverbed is a staggering 4,921 feet below the general level of the plateau. Many of the mountains here are higher than most in the Western massif.

The southeastern mountains are, to a large extent, made of volcanic rocks, but where the rivers cut the terrain deep, crystalline formations predominate. On their western rim are high mountains, including Batu (1,433 feet), stretching to the southeastern lowlands. The rivers Wabi-Shebele and Ganale together with their tributaries

The weathered mountains in the Ethiopian Highlands. (© Nigel Pavitt/JAI/ Corbis.)

dissect the southeastern highlands. Rivers gushing east from the western highlands, together with westward-flowing streams from the eastern plateau, restock the waters of the pristine upper Rift Valley lakes. The rocks are sedimentary rocks covered by recent lava culminating at Mount Musil at an altitude of 6,729 feet above sea level.

The outer lowlands are located west of the western highlands and to the east and south of the southeastern highlands.

GEOLOGY

The oldest rocks in Ethiopia are Precambrian; they are more than 600 million years old and are covered by younger formations. Major placer deposits have been discovered along riverbeds. These placer deposits came about as a result of leaching of the rocks by saline solutions. The amount of their presence indicates the original existence of marine life-forms in sediments that were buried after the sea subsided. Geologists have determined that rocks of this nature in southern Ethiopia contain not many favorable structures for oil because they are only weakly folded.

Blue Nile Gorge at a distance. (Courtesy of Paulos Milkias.)

THE OCEAN IN FORMATION

It has now been determined that a 35-mile crevice that recently emerged in the Rift Valley basin is slated to become a new ocean. Seismic data from 2005 indicate that a volcano named Dabbahu, located at the northern extremity of the rift, erupted first. Then magma oozed out through the middle and began unzipping the crack in both directions, tearing open a 35-mile long slit. An international team of scientists reported in the journal *Geophysical Research Letters* in 2009 that the active volcanic frontiers alongside the brinks of the tectonic marine plates will in the end break apart in large sections. The Red Sea, they elucidated, will eventually discharge into the new ocean, which is bound to connect to the entire body of water between Arabia and the Horn of Africa. The good news for Ethiopian nationalists who lamented the loss of a coastline when Eritrea declared independence in 1993 is therefore that the country will once again become a maritime power. The bad news is that this will happen a million years from now when instead of 192 sovereign entities, there could be only one universal nation on the entire planet!

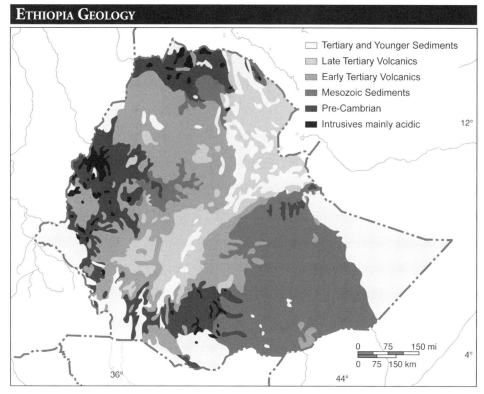

ETHIOPIA GEOLOGY

☐ Tertiary and Younger Sediments
▢ Late Tertiary Volcanics
▨ Early Tertiary Volcanics
▩ Mesozoic Sediments
■ Pre-Cambrian
■ Intrusives mainly acidic

Ethiopia Geology. (Courtesy of Jeff Dixon, www.jeffdixon.ca.)

ETHIOPIA AS A WATER TOWER

Ethiopia is a country of rivers, with major ones such as the Abbay, known to outsiders as the Blue Nile, traversing its national borders. The countries through which these rivers flow are arid and get not only water but also rich soil that is washed down from the mountains during the rainy season. Because Ethiopia divides the rivers flowing into the Mediterranean and the Indian Ocean, it is often referred to by geographers as "the water tower of northeast Africa."

The western highlands slope toward the Sudan, so the rivers on that side, which include Abbay, Takaze, and Baro, flow into the Mediterranean. Rivers on the eastern side, including the Ganale, flow directly into the Indian Ocean, though the Awash and the Wabi-Shebele simply disappear into the arid sands on the borders of Ethiopia and Djibouti. The major southern river, the Gibe, also called the Omo, flows into the Rift Valley lakes.

Ethiopian rivers have dug deep gorges that are 3,280 feet deep in places and interrupted by rapids, making them un-navigable. Only the Baro on the west is navigable during the rainy season.

Ethiopia has a lot of potential if it is able to harness what its rivers offer. The Abbay (Blue Nile), with its great potential, is still underutilized, perhaps mainly because Egypt is almost totally dependent on Ethiopian waters and silt. Egypt has

The Blue Nile Falls. (Courtesy of Paulos Milkias.)

One of the islands of Lake Tana. (Courtesy of Paulos Milkias.)

The Omo River is an important river of southern Ethiopia. (Getty Images/Buena Vista Images.)

lodged complaints that interrupting the natural flow of the Blue Nile would lead to the drying up of Lake Nasser, which would be detrimental to Egypt's survival given that Egypt, unlike Ethiopia, has no rain whatsoever throughout the year.

TEMPERATURE

Ethiopia's temperature is directly related to its relief. Ethiopia also has areas of land that are below 1,640 feet contour line, though they are relatively small in size. Temperature conditions in Ethiopia are also governed to a significant degree by altitude, humidity, and wind factors. Tropical temperatures are not observed in many places because of high elevation. Hot temperatures are found in isolated places of the lowland areas located at the periphery. In the highlands, which form the heartland of the country, the temperature, influenced by altitude, decreases toward the interior. Mean annual temperature varies from over 30°C in the lowlands to less than 10°C in the Daga with very high elevations. Altitude is therefore the key temperature controlling factor in Ethiopia.

In most places, the highest temperatures occur during the high sun period between March and September. Temperatures in different areas depend on the relative position of the shifting sun. Southern Ethiopia experiences its highest temperatures when the sun is vertically overhead; this is in autumn and spring. In the southern and southwestern parts, where there is high humidity and where cloud cover is regular, the temperature falls to a significant degree. Here, the highest temperatures are

Ethiopia, Kuch, Blue Nile river valley, elevated view. (Getty Images/Andrew Holt.)

experienced when the sun is vertically overhead. In some mountainous regions, temperature variations are determined by the direction of rain in relation to the position of slopes as well as the leeward or windward side winds.

Temperatures in Ethiopia, dictated by topography and relief, are as follows: (a) Wurch: very cold area found in highlands above 11,482 feet; (b) Daga: cool highland areas above 8,202 feet; (c) Wayna-Daga: warm areas of land between 4,921 and 8,202 feet; (d) Qolla: hot areas found in regions of the country below 4,921 feet; and (e) Harur: the hottest lowlands below 1,640 feet mostly located in the Afar depression.

Ethiopian towns have temperatures corresponding to their altitude and latitude and their daily range is large. Temperature is high during the day and rises to over 40°C in some places, but is cool to cold at night. The annual range of temperature remains roughly the same throughout the year, regardless of time of year.

One way of classifying the Ethiopian climate is by annual and monthly means of temperature, rainfall types, and local vegetation. It also has tropical-savannah, rainforest, warm-temperate, and cool-highland temperatures. There are highland and lowland regions with elevations ranging from 360 feet below sea level in the Dallol Depression, which is extremely hot, to 14,927 feet at Ras Dashen in the Simen Mountain range, where it is very cold and the elevated peaks host short seasonal snow.

THE NILE

The Nile, which is the longest river in the world, has been providing life to the inhabitants in its basin for tens of thousands of years. The Blue Nile, which joins the White Nile in Khartoum, carries a huge amount of silt washed down from the Ethiopian highlands by torrential rains and deposits it in Egypt. In 1959, Egypt ignored Ethiopia, where 86 percent of the waters of the Nile originate, and signed a bilateral agreement with the rulers of the newly independent country of Sudan for "the full utilization of the Nile waters." It is clear that "full utilization" meant that the other riparian countries such as Ethiopia will have no right to use it. Egypt, which has almost no rain, gets almost all of its fresh water supplies for agriculture, industry and domestic uses, and electric power generation from the Nile. In the case of Ethiopia, spiraling population growth and recurrent drought conditions has underlined the need to achieve food security, which can be fulfilled only by irrigating the Ethiopian highlands and preventing millions of tons of rich topsoil from being washed downstream by the heavy monsoon rains. Ethiopia claims to have every right to develop its own natural resources. But Egypt claims that such actions on the part of Ethiopia would constitute a direct threat to Egypt's people's livelihood and would thus force Egypt to resort to war in self-defense. To show its resolve, Cairo gave stern warning to Ethiopia when the latter tried to utilize Israeli water engineers and surveyors in 1989. In fact, as Jan Luijendijk, a Dutch water engineer working for UNESCO (United Nations Educational, Scientific and Cultural Organization), once said, "if Ethiopia decided to build a dam [on the tributaries of the Nile], then that would mean war with Egypt immediately." Ethiopia's claim that it has an absolute right to use its own waters has international precedents. Turkey's president, Suleiman Demirel, has in fact gone on record as saying that Iraq and Syria had no more right to claim Turkey's water than Turkey had to lay claim on their oil.

But the future is not necessarily bleak. Fear of the consequences has created an incentive for cooperation. In 1999, all 10 Nile basin countries, supported by UNESCO, had created an initiative to "achieve sustainable socio-economic development through the equitable utilization of, and benefit from, the common Nile Basin water resources." Hopefully, this will resolve the zero-sum game both Cairo and Addis Ababa previously envisaged. Egypt cannot totally monopolize the Nile. Nor can Ethiopia deny Egypt's fair share of the resources and bounty of the Nile. They will have to compromise to the detriment of both countries and the remaining riparian nations.

The Ethiopian climate has eight categories, though in short one can simply identify dry, rainy, and tropical . The nine are the following:

1. *Hot arid climate*: This is barren and has sparse vegetation. The mean annual temperature here is between 27°C and 30°C; and mean annual rainfall is less

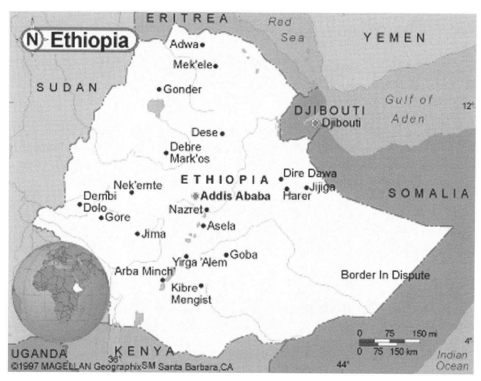

Ethiopia Topography. (Courtesy of Jeff Dixon, www.jeffdixon.ca.)

RELIEF

An extended period of abundant rainfall during the Pleistocene Epoch of Africa, which was comparable with the Ice Ages of Europe, was responsible for producing the deep gorges that dissect the flat-topped Ethiopian plateau. The Ethiopian relief includes a range of altitudes stretching from under sea level to nearly 4,600 meters above sea level, where seasonal snow is spotted. Ethiopian landscape connected with the broader categorization into ecological zones refers to the country's relief as (a) Woorch, constituting the coldest highlands above 3,500 meters; (b) Daga, comprising the cool highlands above 2,500 meters; (c) Wayna-Daga, which includes warm areas between 1,500 and 2,500 meters; (d) Qolla, comprising the hot, relatively low-lying lands below 1,500 meters; and (e) Haroor, the hottest lowlands, located below 600 meters. Being rock-ribbed and lined by steep escarpments, precipitous gorges, torrential rivers, savannah grasslands, semi-desert regions, and fertile green fields, Ethiopia is naturally endowed to produce practically any type of crop imaginable.

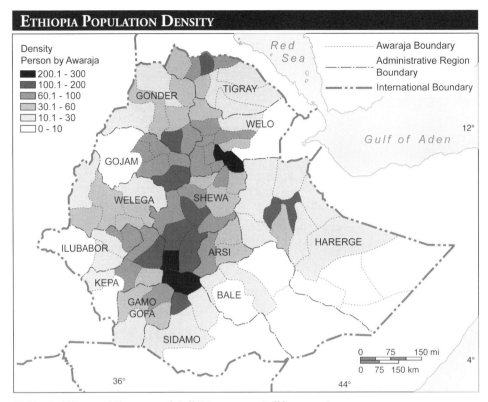

ETHIOPIA POPULATION DENSITY

Density
Person by Awaraja

- 200.1 - 300
- 100.1 - 200
- 60.1 - 100
- 30.1 - 60
- 10.1 - 30
- 0 - 10

Awaraja Boundary
Administrative Region Boundary
International Boundary

GONDER · TIGRAY · WELO · GOJAM · WELEGA · SHEWA · ILUBABOR · ARSI · HARERGE · KEPA · BALE · GAMO GOFA · SIDAMO

Red Sea · *Gulf of Aden*

12°

4°

0   75   150 mi
0   75   150 km

36°   44°

Ethiopia Climate. (Courtesy of Jeff Dixon, www.jeffdixon.ca.)

than 450 millimeters (mm). It has strong winds, low relative humidity, and meager cloud cover. In places, it has heavy evaporation which is 20 times in excess of rainfall.

2. *Hot semiarid climate*: This has steppe-type of vegetation, with mean annual temperature ranging between 18°C and 27°C. The rainfall is highly unpredictable. Because of the fact that it has more evaporation than rainfall, it does not generate permanent streams. The grasses are short and bristly during the dry seasons, and are unpalatable to wild game and cattle. Thus, in those seasons, the animals graze on the tender fresh grasses that grow along water courses.

3. *Cool semiarid climate*: The highlands of Tigray have steppe-type vegetation. The mean annual temperature here is 12°C to 18°C, and the mean annual rainfall is between 400 and 620 mm. There is less evaporation here because of the low temperature of the region.

4. *Tropical climate I*: This region experiences dry weather in winter. The mean temperature of the coldest month is above 18 degrees and the mean annual rainfall lies between 680 and 2,000 mm. Such climate is found up to an elevation of 5,741 feet above mean sea level. The lengths of the wet and dry periods vary. This region has few trees but some bush and lots of tall grasses blending together,

5. *Tropical climate II*: This refers to Ethiopia's tropical rainforest weather, where the temperature of the coldest month rises above 18°C. This region supports

an evergreen rainforest and prevails up to elevations of 5,741 feet above mean sea level.

6. *Warm temperate climate I*: This climate has dry months in winter, with the mean temperature of the coldest month going below 18°C. For more than four months, its mean temperature is just above 10°C. This area exists at an elevation of 5,741 feet to 10,498 feet above sea level. The region has adequate rainfall, and its climate is suitable for abundant forest cover.

7. *Warm temperate climate II*: This has a lot of soil moisture. It is humid and temperate without a dry season. The mean temperature of the coldest month here is less than 18°C. The region has adequate rainfall and its climate is suitable for abundant forest cover;

8. *Cool highland climate*: This climate is found at altitudes more than 10,499 feet above mean sea level, most often in small isolated mountain areas. It has dry weather in winter and its mean temperature is 10°C. The annual rainfall is between 800 and 2,000 mm.

VEGETATION AND LAND USE

Intensively Cultivated Land

Land on which peasant mixed agriculture and private modern farms exist are highly cultivated. The peasant mixed agriculture area covers about 10.3 percent of land where grains as well as sedentary peasant livestock grazing exists. These areas are on the highlands of Tigray, Gondar, Gojam, Wallo, Shoa, and Arsi, as well as highland Hararge, central Wallaga, and northern Bale. About 70 percent of the land in this region supports crops during the rainy season. Twenty-five percent of the rest is fallow land and is used for grazing animals. Because of the overstocked nature of grazing in the area, tree cover has almost disappeared.

Moderately Cultivated Land

Moderately cultivated land encompasses 12.5 percent of Ethiopia. It includes rain-fed land on which peasants cultivate grains, livestock grazing, and perennial crop cultivation of coffee, Enset (false banana roots rich in starch which are staple food in Southern Ethiopia) and Chat (also spelled *Khat* which are leaves of the shrub Catha edulis chewed in Ethiopia and Arabia with the effect of a euphoric stimulant). Here, there are patches of natural forest and bushes. This type of land is used for annual crops during the rainy season. About 40 percent of it is fallow or has natural vegetation used for livestock grazing.

Southern Shoa, parts of highland Hararge, southern Wallaga, Ilubabor, Kafa, northern Sidamo, and Gamo Gofa have more perennial crop cultivation than other parts of the country. Here, only about 25 percent of the land is under annual crop production during the summer and winter rainy seasons

Afro-Alpine and Sub-Afro-Alpine Vegetation

These are in the Simen highlands of Gondar, parts of southeastern Wallo, parts of central Arsi, and northern Bale. They cover 0.2 percent of the total area of Ethiopia and are in the range of 10,499 feet in altitude. Short shrub and heath vegetation abound and are used for sedentary grazing. In some places, barley is widely cultivated.

High Forest

The high forest region constitutes 4.4 percent of Ethiopia and is located in the south and southwest. Coniferous high forests are present in sections of the central, southern, and southeastern highlands. There are also mixed high forests in the southwest. Mixed high forests mostly of broad-leafed species are found where the mean annual rainfall is about 2000 mm and is generally humid. In some areas, about 80 percent of the land is under forest, but most of it has given way to human habitation. The flora and fauna of the woodlands region vary. On the drier periphery of the high forest in the south and southwest of the country, there are more dense woodlands. Nearly 50 percent of this region has grassland.

A close-up view of the Simien mountains in the northern Amhara region (© Diego Lezama Orezzoli/ CORBIS.)

Woodland

The woodlands have alternating canopy and smaller trees than the high forest region. In total, they comprise 2.5 percent of the Ethiopia. The flora and fauna of the woodlands region vary, and cultivated land interrupts their continuity. On the drier periphery of the high forest in the south and southwest of the country, there are more dense woodlands.

In this area, 40 percent of the land has patches of forest and the main occupation of the people inhabiting this area is livestock grazing and engaging in rain-fed peasant mixed agriculture. Open woodland with tall grass undergrowth are found in western Ethiopian highland areas, in the west, and parts of the south and southeast. Nearly 50 percent of this region has grassland and therefore livestock breeding is very dominant. Planted eucalyptus trees around settlements are included in the woodland region. The capital Addis Ababa has the largest of such forest.

Riparian Woodland and Bushland

These are found along the banks of major rivers and on floodplains. They are important in the semiarid and arid parts of Ethiopia where they are used for cattle and scattered seasonal farming.

Bushland and Shrubland

These cover about 21.4 percent of Ethiopia. They are in the intermediate sector sandwiched between the semiarid parts and humid parts. Pastoral livestock grazing and incense harvesting are some of the activities here.

Grasslands

The grasslands region covers 30.5 percent of Ethiopia and is found in the western, southern, and southeastern semiarid lowlands of the country. Here, grass covers 90 percent of the area. In about 70 percent of the zone, where conditions are less humid, the activities of the inhabitants include raising livestock, incense, tree cultivation and honey harvesting.

Exposed Rock or Sand Surface

This covers some 15.8 percent of Ethiopia and is common in northern Hararge and the Afar lowlands. Some rock and sand surfaces are also abundant in parts of Bale and the Hararge lowlands, in the southeast, and the lower course of the Omo River. The area is characterized by recent lava flows with speckled small patches of scrub and shrubs. In places, it consists mostly of alluvial fans and depressions. In other places, it is overgrazed. The salt rocks account for about 0.5 percent of the country and are most common in the Afar lowlands.

Swamps and Marshes

Swamps and marshes are found near lakes and in valleys and lower depressions. In total, they cover 8 percent of Ethiopia. The largest sector is in the Baro-Akobo lowlands in Gambela state. Swamps and marshes are perennial and host scattered trees, grasses, and sedges. Because of this, they are key grazing areas and wildlife sanctuaries. Seasonal swamps and marshes also exist and are used for livestock during the dry season. In the Tana area, dried up marshlands are used for cultivating crops after the floodwaters dry up.

Urban and Built-up Area

This is only for Addis Ababa since the others are very small in size. The entire built-up land is estimated at about 497 square miles, which accounts for 0.05 percent of Ethiopia.

RAINFALL

The direction of winds causes rainfall in Ethiopia to be unpredictable and seasonal. In general, the mountainous areas experience heavy rainfall whereas in the lowlands, it is light. Southwestern Ethiopia always has heavy rainfall. It is the wettest region and experiences a mere two to four dry months per year. The mean annual rainfall of this region is about 1,500 millimeters (mm). In some localities, however, it is even higher. Limu in Jimma, western Arjo and Gimbi, Wallaga, southwestern Gore, Buno-Bedele, Sor and Gaba in Ilubabor, and Gimira in Southern Ethiopia, experiences more than 2,800 mm of rain a year.

In the east and northeast, mean annual rainfall decreases. Central and north central Ethiopia have a moderate rainfall of about 1,100 mm. But in some localities such as western Agaw Midir, southeastern Metekel, and the north central parts of Kola and Daga Damot in Gojam, it passes 2,000 mm. Also, in central Wagara and central Simen Awrajas, in north Gondar, mean annual rainfall passes the 1,600 mm mark.

Southeastern Ethiopia experiences a mean annual rainfall of about 700 mm. Here again, there are variations. In northern Jemjem, it is more than 2,000 mms, and the same is true in parts of Sidamo where it is more than 1,200 mm. In Ganale and Dolo areas of Bale and northeastern Wagara, in Hararge, and the Ogaden, it is less than 400 mm. Tigray, in northern Ethiopia, has a mean annual rainfall of 500 mm, though in some regions it rises to 800 mm.

In general, there is Keremt—long heavy summer rain—and there is Belg, which is the little rainy season. The latter is the short moderate rain falling in spring, autumn, and winter.

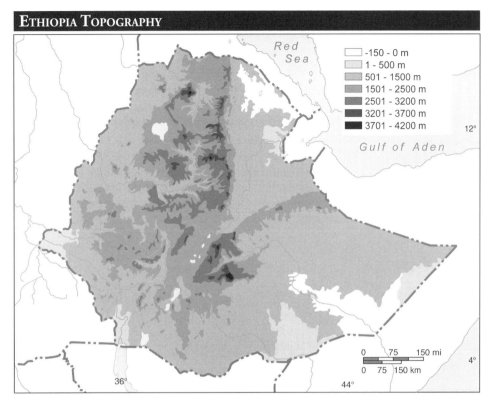

Ethiopia Rainfall. (Courtesy of Jeff Dixon, www.jeffdixon.ca.)

Almost all parts of Ethiopia get rain from the southwest equatorial westerlies and southerly winds from the Indian Ocean. These winds start in the South Atlantic Ocean, pass over the humid regions of the Gulf of Guinea, the Congo basin, and across Central Africa. As such, they have heavy moisture on arrival in highland Ethiopia, causing very intense downpours in Ilubabor, Kafa, Gamo Gofa—all of which are located in southwestern Ethiopia.

Rainfall decreases in the northeast. Forty percent of the rain in southwestern Ethiopia falls during the period of sowing and reaping—locally referred to as Mahar. Unlike in the southwest where rains are heavy and fall for eight or more months a year, the Tigray state has two to three months of very short rains.

The southerly winds traversing the Indian Ocean lose their moisture as they pass over the East African highlands. Consequently, a rain shadow is cast over the eastern escarpments of the northwestern plateau and nearby lowlands, thus making rain there very scanty.

In winter, a large part of Ethiopia is influenced by continental air currents that flow from the north and northeast. These winds start in north African and west Asian high pressure centers. They are cold and dry, and do not carry much rain. The southwest equatorial westerlies pass over southwestern Ethiopia, providing moderate rain. Overall, winter is the season of lowest rainfall in Ethiopia.

In spring, a strong cyclonic cell builds up over the Sudan, a lowland country. This cyclone attracts winds from the Gulf of Aden and the Indian Ocean that pass across central and southern Ethiopia. The damp easterly and southeasterly winds generate big rains in southeastern Ethiopia and the little rains of spring to the east-central part of the northwestern highlands. When the little rain occurs in Belg, it becomes the second most important sowing season.

Spring is the main rainfall season for the southeastern highlands and nearby lowlands such as the Ogaden, Borana, the southern Sidamo, and Gamo Gofa. The second rainy season occurs in autumn. The annual total for the towns of Moyale and Kalafo is 1,000 mm and 500 mm respectively for the two seasons. They experience 50 percent and 60 percent of rain in the spring and 37 percent and 33 percent in autumn.

POPULATION DISTRIBUTION AND DENSITY

In 2007, the population of Ethiopia had reached 73,918,505, making the country the second most populous in Africa. Of these, 80 percent live in rural areas, their density being determined by possibilities for farming or cattle herding, factors that are shaped by the environment. Climate relief, rainfall, and land fertility have a lot to do with the uneven distribution.

In most countries, river valleys were the locus of heavy human settlement and civilization as in Egypt, Iraq, China, and India. In Ethiopia, it is the direct opposite. People tended to settle away from river banks and river valleys because of their high temperatures, inadequate rainfall, and presence of deadly diseases such as malaria.

Physical factors of the land play a large role in the distribution and density of population in Ethiopia. Soil conditions encourage or discourage population settlement, particularly on the highlands. The reddish-colored volcanic soils that are characteristic of the highlands, and it is here that most people live and cultivate the land. The lowlands comprise of half the entire country but host only 19 percent of the people.

The rainfall, which is influenced by relief, determines where people tend to settle. However, that rule does not apply to Daga areas that are above 9,843 feet. In the Daga highlands, cold temperatures predominate so there is less population density there. It is in the Woina-Daga, which is between altitudes of 3,281 to 9,843 feet above sea level that most people live. Here, there is enough rainfall and other fitting natural conditions for cultivation of crops. Settlements are evenly distributed on the plateau. On the other hand, settlements are widely dispersed on the jagged and craggy Daga mountains.

Shifting cultivation and nomadic life are common in the lowlands and along the river valleys. Here, there is light rainfall together with high temperature levels, and there are problems with diseases such as malaria. Owing to this, a large part of the lowlands is sparsely populated. Population concentration is more intense in urban centers, particularly in Addis Abeba Dire Dawa and Harar.

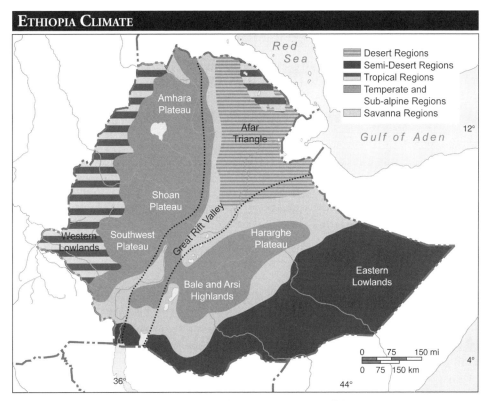

Ethiopia Population Density. (Courtesy of Jeff Dixon, www.jeffdixon.ca.)

The average population density for the nation as a whole is about 17 per square mile. Average density by regions varies considerably. It varies from 3.9 per square mile in Bale to 47.3 per square mile in Shoa. Kambata in the southern part of the country has 100 to 150 people per square mile, making it the most densely populated region outside the urban areas. The highest rural population densities are also found in Hadiya and Walaita—again in the southern state classification. The same is true in the central zone of Shoa, rural Dassie, and Qalu in Wallo. These areas have an annual rainfall ranging between 1,000 and 1,200 mm. They have relatively fertile soil and moderate temperatures between 15°C and 20°C. In general, good climate and fertile soil attract settlement and therefore creates high population density. This is characteristic of the highlands below 9,843 feet. By contrast, the lowlands, which have less fertile soil, hot temperatures, and tropical diseases, have very low population density.

DROUGHT-PRONE ZONES

The arid and semiarid areas of Ethiopia are drought-prone zones. Here, rainfall is either too low or unreliable for sustained crop cultivation or grazing of animals.

ARDI SURPASSES LUCY

In December 2009, the prestigious scholarly journal *Science* dubbed the finding of Ardi, the ossified frame of a feminine hominid who lived in Ethiopia 4.4 million years ago, the biggest scientific breakthrough of 2009. The discovery of Ardi, which changed the way we think about early human evolution, involved 15 years of meticulous concerted effort by 47 scientists of diverse expertise from 9 countries who meticulously examined 150,000 specimens of ossified animals and plants in the locality where Ardi was discovered. Scientists have now determined that *Ardipithecus ramidus* was a representative of humans forming a primate branch. and predates the now world-famous Lucy, also found in Ethiopia in 1974, by more than 1 million years. Ardi is the closest to the final ancestor shared by humans and chimpanzees some 6 million years ago.

The criteria used to distinguish the drought-prone zones from the more humid zones of the country is when it is observed that the region experiences a growing period of 120 days at 70 percent reliability level in about two years out of three. Clearly, where there are 120 days of consistent rain it is a humid area, and where they are less than that it is a drought-prone area. In general, records consistently show 700 mm mean annual rainfall in northern Ethiopian and 775 mm in the northeast and east.

In the south and southeast there are two rainy seasons—one in spring and the other in autumn, the length of the growing period is 120 days at 70 percent reliability level. It is considerably less in the drought-prone zones. There are four of these drought-prone zones.

Zone 1 is mostly arid and encompasses about 26 percent of the total area of the country. The inhabitants here are basically nomads.

Zone 2 covers about 13 percent of the total area of Ethiopia and is semiarid or arid. It is again the locale for nomadic pastoralism. There are few pockets of cultivated areas in this zone where there is adequate seasonal moisture and relatively fertile land. Because in two years out of three the length of the growing period is 30 to 75 days, the only main occupation here is pastoralism. About 6 percent of the total rural population of Ethiopia lives in this zone.

Zone 3 covers about 16 percent of Ethiopia. Roughly 13 percent of the total rural population lives here. The proportions that live in this zone are as follows: Tigray 34 percent, Wallo 20 percent, Ogaden 26 percent, Bale, 39 percent, Sidamo 9 percent, and Gamo Gofa 16 percent.

Zone 4 is clearly drought-prone and accounts for nearly 55 percent of the total area of the land. Drought-prone zones make up 90 percent of Somali State, 80 percent of Bale and Sidamo, 70 percent of Tigray. 65 percent of Wallo, and 45 percent of Gamo Gofa. Close to 25 percent of the total rural population of Ethiopia live in drought-prone zones. The proportion of rural inhabitants who live in drought prone zones is as follows: Tigray 55 percent, Wallo 30 percent, Bale 65 percent, Sidamo 10 percent, and Gamo Gofa 25 percent.

RURAL FOOD SHORTAGE AND FAMINE

Drought conditions have brought about famine in Ethiopia throughout history. In the distant past, there were a series of famines due to lack of rain or locust infestation. These include seven famines from 1257 to 1288, then from 1547 to 1759. The most documented in the recent past were the general famine of 1888, the Tigray famine of 1958, the Wag-Lasta famine of 1966, the Wallo famine of 1973, and the disastrous northern famine of 1984–1985.

One important thing to note is that contrary to popular belief, Ethiopia is not a country that is condemned to experience famine indefinitely. Many parts of the drought-prone zones have large tracts of marshland or swampland, and others have riparian locations. Thus, the inhabitants have enough sources of moisture other than rainfall that they can harness under the right conditions. Such regions include parts of Galab and Hamar Bako in Gamo Gofa, Maji and Goldiya in Kafa, Elkere and Dolo in Bale, Gode, Chercher, Qalafo, Qebri Dahar, and Degehabur in Somali State, Raya and Kobo, and Awasa and Qalu in Wallo.

To dispel doubt about Ethiopia's potential to defeat famine, one should see studies conducted by world experts. Global Environment Facility (GEF) scholars

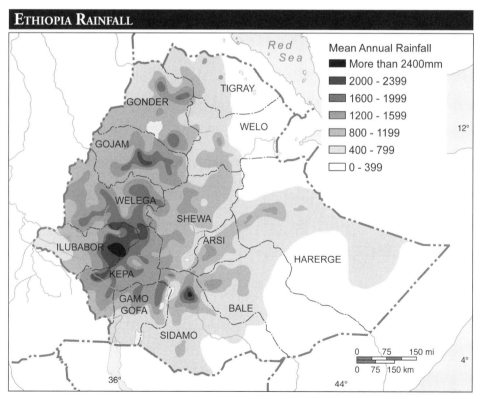

Ethiopia Food Crop Production. (Courtesy of Jeff Dixon, www.jeffdixon.ca.)

have pointed out in 2001, (Global Environment Facility, 2001, p. 1) that though it may sound unimaginable, drought prone Ethiopia can be considered for the world's seed basket! It is true that the very mention of Ethiopia reminds one of starving babies, starving children, of men and women lacking the bare necessities of food, clothing, and shelter, but the Global Environment Facility's report confounds this notion.

Over 85 percent the Ethiopian population lives on the highlands with almost 90 percent of them depending on agriculture. The Ethiopian highlands cover 50 percent of the total area of the country. They are also the engine of 90 percent of the economy and 95 percent of the staple foods and cash crops produced during the rainy season. The ecological heterogeneity of Ethiopia offers suitable conditions for a wide range of flora and fauna. The environment of the plateau shows vast biodiversity, with about 7,000 higher plant species, of which 840 are endemic. It should be mentioned that Ethiopia is the origin of coffee and home to a diversity of cereal grains such as barley, 277 species of mammals, of which 31 are endemic and about 861 species of birds, of which 16 are endemic.

Water covers 7,400 square kilometers of Ethiopia, with 11 major lakes. Annual surface flow from 12 major river basins is about 110 billion cubic meters, of which 43 billion cubic meters are found in the Amhara Region where famine is recurrent. Nearly 75 percent of the water drains into the neighboring countries of eastern Africa, signifying that Ethiopia is surely a water tower of Africa.

Ethiopia has good agricultural soil of the tropics that are essential for bumper crop production. However, it is ironic that while it suffers from food shortage almost every half decade, Egypt, with literally no rain dropping on its territory, harnesses the Nile, getting 86 percent of its waters and almost all the silt that makes it exceedingly fertile from the tributaries of the Abbay originating in the Ethiopian highlands. As a result, it is a major producer and exporter of cereal grains, particularly beans. Furthermore, just about half a century ago, China and India were known internationally as economic basket cases; but now, through good agricultural development strategies they have become net food exporters while at the same time feeding ¼ of humanity in their own countries. Indeed, if prudent policies are charted, sustainable development is adhered to, and implemented with substantial assistance from the international community, particularly from the wealthy and technologically advanced Western nations, Ethiopia—now known as the land of perpetual famine—can in the future become the breadbasket of Africa and the Middle East.

REFERENCES

Abate, S. 1994. *Land Use Dynamics, Soil Degradation, and Potential for Sustainable Use in Metu area, Illubabor Region, Ethiopia.* Berne: University of Berne Switzerland, Institute of Geography.

Abul-Haggag, Y. 1961. *A Contribution to the Physiography of Northern Ethiopia.* London: University of London Athlone Press.

Albategius and C. Alfonso. 1969. *Al-Battåanåi sive Albatenii Opus astronomicum.* Frankfurt, Minerva.

Vigilant, L. and M. Stoneking. 1991. "African populations and the evolution of human mito-chondrial DNA." *Science.* Vol. 253 Issue 5027. P.1503.

Amin, M., et al. 2004. *Journey through Ethiopia.* Nairobi, Kenya: Camerapix.

Amin, M., D. Willetts, et al. 2001. *Ethiopia: A Tourist Paradise.* Nairobi, Kenya: Cam-erapix.

Atkins, H. 1970. *A Geography of Ethiopia.* Addis Ababa, Ethiopia: Sim Print.

Ayele, Bekerie. 1997. *Ethiopic: An African Writing System, Its History and Principles.* Law-renceville, NJ: Red Sea Press.

Baker, J. 1986. *The rural-urban dichotomy in the developing world: a case study from northern Ethiopia.* Oslo: Norwegian University Press.

Balletto, B. L. 2001. *Spectrum Guide to Ethiopia.* Nairobi: Camerapix Publishers Inter-national.

Belai, Giday. 1980. *Axumite Coins: Money and Banking in Ethiopia.* Addis Ababa: Personal Publication, Ethiopia.

Berg, E. 1999. *Festivals of the World: Ethiopia.* Milwaukee, WI: Gareth Stevens.

Berg, E. 2000. *Ethiopia.* Milwaukee, WI: G. Stevens.

Berhane Asfaw, Tim White, Owen Lovejoy, Bruce Latimer, Scott Simpson, and Gen Suwa. 1999. "Australopithecus Garhi: A New Species of Early Hominid from Ethiopia." *Science,* 284: 629–635.

Birkby, C. 1942. *It's a Long Way to Addis.* London: F. Muller.

Briggs, P. 2005. *Ethiopia*: Giulford, CT: Bradt Travel Guide.

Britton, T. L. 2002. *Ethiopia.* Edina, MN: Abdo.

Browder, Anthony. 1992. *Exploding the Myths: The Nile Valley Contributions to Civilization.* New York: Institute of Karmic Guidancee.

Bunney, Sarah. 1994. "Prehistoric Farming Caused 'Devastating' Soil Erosion." *New Scientist* 143(1945): 16.

Butzer, K. W. 1971. *Recent History of an Ethiopian Delta: The Omo River and the Level of Lake Rudolf.* Chicago: University of Chicago.

Cann, Rebecca L., Mark Stoneking, and Allan C. Wilson. 1987. "Mitochondrial DNA and Human Evolution." *Nature* 325: 31–36.

Carr, C. J. 1977. *Pastoralism in Crisis: The Dasanetch and Their Ethiopian Lands.* Chicago: Department of Geography, University of Chicago.

Darwin, Charles. (1859) 2003. *The Origin of Species.* New York: Signet.

Di Lauro, R. 1949. *Come abbiamo difeso l'impero.* Roma: Edizioni l'Arnia.

Diodorus Siculus. 1653. *The History of Diodorus Siculus. Containing All That Is Most Memo-rable and of Greatest Antiquity in the First Ages of the World until the War of Troy.* London: John Macock.

Dixon, A. B. 2003. *Indigenous Management of Wetlands: Experiences in Ethiopia.* Aldershot, UK: Ashgate.

Englar, M. 2006. *Ethiopia: A Question and Answer Book.* Mankato, MN: Capstone Press.

Ethiopia, Government of. 1956. *Empire of Ethiopia, Provinces and Awrajas*. Addis Ababa, Ethiopia: Mapping and Geography Institute.

Ethiopia, Government of. 1981. *National Atlas of Ethiopia*. Addis Ababa: Geography Division of Ethiopian Mapping Agency.

Ethiopia, Government of. 2000. *Agro Ecological Zones of Ethiopia*. Addis Ababa, Ethiopia: Natural Resources Management and Regulatory Department.

Farb, Peter. 1968. *Man's Rise to Civilization as Shown by the Indians of North America from Primeval Times to the Coming of the Industrial State*. New York: E. P. Dutton.

Fassil, G. K., and Organisation for Social Science Research in Eastern Africa. 1985. *Challenging Rural Poverty*. Trenton, NJ: Africa World Press of the Africa Research and Publications Project.

Fattovich, R. 1988. "Remarks on the Late Prehistory and Early History of Northern Ethiopia." *Proceedings of the 8th International Conference on Ethiopian Studies* (1): 85–104. Addis Ababa: Institute of Ethiopian Studies.

Gee, Henry. 1993. "Why We Still Love Lucy." Nature 366: 207.

Gillespie, C. A. 2003. *Ethiopia*. Philadelphia: Chelsea House Publishers.

Gish, S., W. Thay, et al. 2007. *Ethiopia*. New York: Marshall Cavendish Benchmark.

Goldman, Phaon. 1989. "The Nubian Renaissance." In *Egypt Revisited*, 2nd. ed. New Brunswick, NJ: Journal of African Civilizations, 261–270.

Gozalbez, J., and D. Cebrean. 2006. *Touching Ethiopia*. Addis Ababa, Ethiopia: Shama Books.

Greenfield, Richard. 1965. *Ethiopia: A New Political History*. London: Pall Mall Publishers. 375–418.

Heine, B., and D. Nurse. 2008. *A Linguistic Geography of Africa*. Cambridge: Cambridge University Press.

Helldén, U., and L. Eklundh. 1988. *National Drought Impact Monitoring: A NOAA NDVI and Precipitation Data Study of Ethiopia*. Lund, Sweden: Lund University Press.

Holden, Constance. 1995. *Science* 267(5198): 618.

Hudåud al-åalam. 1980. *The Regions of the World: A Persian Geography, 372 A.H.–982 A.D.* Karachi: Indus Publications.

Huntingford, G. W. B., and R. Pankhurst. 1989. *The Historical Geography of Ethiopia: From the First Century AD to 1704*. New York: Published for the British Academy by the Oxford University Press.

Imperial Ethiopian Mapping & Geography Institute. 1960. *Ethiopia: Major Rivers*. Addis Ababa, Ethiopia.

Imperial Ethiopian Mapping & Geography Institute. 1965. *Ethiopia: Coffee Regions*. Addis Ababa, Ethiopia.

Ishaq, Ibn. 1955. *The Life of Muhammad, a Translation of Ishaq's Sirat Rasul Allah*. London: Oxford University Press.

Jackson, R. T., T. P. J. Russell, et al. 1969. *Report of the Oxford University Expedition to the Gamu Highlands of Southern Ethiopia, 1968*. Oxford: University of Oxford School of Geography.

James, Peter, and Nick Thorpe. 1994. *Ancient Inventions*. New York: Ballantine Books.

Johannes Hendrik, Kramers, ed. 1965. *Ibn Hawqal, Abâu al-Qåasim Muòhammad, Configuration De La Terre,* Beyrouth: Commission Internationale Pour La Traduction des Chefs d'âoeuvre.

Kebbede, Girma. 2004. *Living with Urban Environmental Health Risks: The Case of Ethiopia.* Kings SOAS Studies in Development Geography. Aldershot, UK: Ashgate.

Kebbede, Tessemma. 1969. *Yetarik Mastawesha.* Addis Ababa, Ethiopia: Artistic Printing Press.

Kurtz, J. 1991. *Ethiopia: The Roof of Africa.* Toronto: Dillon Press.

Lassieur, A. 2004. *Ethiopia.* Mankato, MN: Capstone Press.

Ludi, E. 2004. *Economic Analysis of Soil Conservation: Case Studies from the Highlands of Amhara Region, Ethiopia.* Berne: University of Berne Switzerland, Institute of Geography.

MacDonald, J. F. 1957. *Abyssinian Adventure.* London, Cassell. pp. 207–208.

Masaaudai, S., M. Ahmad, et al. 1960. *Al-Masâudâi: Millenary Commemoration.* Aligarh: Indian Society for the History of Science.

Masudi, P. 1989. *The Meadows of Gold.* London: Kegan Paul.

Mesfin, W. M. 1970. *An Atlas of Ethiopia.* Addis Ababa: Haile Selassie I University Press..

Mesfin, W. M. 1971. *Welenkomi: A Socio-Economic and Nutritional Survey of a Rural Community in the Central Highlands of Ethiopia.* Berkhamsted: Geographical Publications.

Mesfin, W.-M. 1964. *The Background of the Ethio-Somalia Boundary Dispute.* Addis Ababa, Ethiopia: Berhanena Selam P.P.

Mesfin, W.-M. 1972. *An Introductory Geography of Ethiopia.* Addis Ababa, Ethiopia: n.p.

Mesfin, W.-M. 1986. *Rural Vulnerability to Famine in Ethiopia, 1958–1977.* London: Intermediate Technology Publications.

Mesfin, W.-M. 1991. *Suffering under God's Environment: A Vertical Study of the Predicament of Peasants in North-Central Ethiopia.* Berne, Switzerland: African Mountains Association, Geographica Bernensia.

Michels, J. 1990. "Regional Political Organization in the Aksum-Yeha Area during the Pre-Axumite and Axumite Era." *Proceedings: Tenth International Conference of Ethiopian Studies.* Paris: Institut de France.

Morantz, Aubrey. 2011. "Canadian Jesuits and Ethiopian Education," Ottawa. January 20.

Morris, N. 2004. *Ethiopia.* Chicago: Raintree.

Munro-Hay, S. C. 1986. *The Munro-Hay Collection of Axumite Coins.* Napoli: Istituto Universitario Orientale.

Nettler, Gwynn. 1957. "A Measure of Alienation." *American Sociological Review* 22(6): 670.

Neville, E. 1906. *The Tomb of Hotshopsitu: Her Life and Monuments.* London: Methuen.

Nolen, B. 1971. *Ethiopia.* New York: F. Watts.

Pankhurst, A. 2001. *Natural Resource Management in Ethiopia: Proceedings of the Workshop Organised by Forum for Social Studies in Collaboration with the University of Sussex, Addis Ababa.* Addis Ababa, Ethiopia: The Forum.

Pankhurst, R. 1984. *Let's Visit Ethiopia.* London: Burke Pub.

Pankhurst, Richard. 1965. *The Ethiopian Royal Chronicles.* London: Oxford University Press.

Pankhurst, Sylvia. 1942. "Ethiopia" *New Times and Ethiopia News* 17(1): 1–2.

Perl, L. 1972. *Ethiopia, Land of the Lion*. New York: Morrow.

Phillips, Jacke. 1997. "Punt and Axum: Egypt and the Horn of Africa." *Journal of African History* 38(3): 423–457.

Pieroni, Piero. 1974. *L'Italia in Africa*. Florence: Vallecchi.

Pierotti, Francesco. 1959. *Vita in Etiopia, 1940–41*. Bologna: Cappelli.

Pirenne, Jacqueline, ed. 1986. *Académie des inscriptions et belles-lettres*. Corpus des inscriptions et antiquités sud-arabes II Le Musée d'Aden, Fascicule 2, Antiquités, 2(20). Louvain: Editions Peters.

Procopius and H. B. Dewing. 1953. *Procopius, with an English translation*. Cambridge, MA: Harvard University Press.

Quintana-Murci, Luis et al. 1999. *Nature Genetics* 23(4): 437–441.

Rainey, Paul. 2003. "Evolution: Five Big Questions: Is Evolution Predictable?" *New Scientist* 178(2399): 37–38.

Ritler, A. 2003. *Forests, Land Use and Landscape in the Central and Northern Ethiopian Highlands, 1865 to 1930*. Berne, Switzerland: University of Berne, Institute of Geography.

Rosenthal, E. 1941. *The Fall of Italian East Africa*. London: Hutchinson, 81–82.

Rothman, J. 1994. "Mechanisms of Intracellular Protein Transport." *Nature* 372(6501): 55–63.

Ruhben, Barrett. 1998. "Where Do Languages Originate?" *Etymology* http://itsmagic.tripod.com/ETYMOLGY.HTML/ Accessed January 3, 2000.

Sander, E. 1929. *Das hochland von Abessinien Habesch: Eine länderkundliche monographie*. Heidelberg: C. Winter.

Scheffer, Brigette. 1995. "Dark as Hell, Strong as Death, Sweet as Love—How Coffee Conquered the World." *New Internationalist* 271: 22.

"Selassie Pledges Unchanged Rule." 1960. *New York Times*. December 21.

Simonson, J. 1968. *Come Along to Ethiopia*. Minneapolis: T. S. Denison.

Simoons, F. J. 1960. *Northwest Ethiopia: Peoples and Economy*. Madison: University of Wisconsin Press.

Soil Conservation Research Programme Ethiopia, Ya'Ityopya karta sera derejet., et al. 1995. *Ethiopia Agroecological Belts*. Addis Ababa, Ethiopia: Soil Conservation Research Programme.

Stanley, Henry Morton. 1896. *The Abyssinian Campaign*. London: S. Low Marston. 140–141.

Steer, G. L. 1942. *Sealed and Delivered: A Book on the Abyssinian Campaign*. London: Hodder and Stoughton.

Stoneking, Mark. 1994. "In Defense of 'Eve'—A Response to Templeton's Critique." *American Anthropologist* 96(1): 131–141.

Stringer, Chris. 2003. "Human Evolution: Out of Ethiopia." *Nature* 423(6941): 692–695.

Sykes, C. 1959. *Orde Wingate: A Biography*. London: Collins.

Tabarâi, Donner, and Fred McGraw. 1993. *The Conquest of Arabia*. SUNY series in Near Eastern studies. Albany: State University of New York Press.

Tannenbaum, D. 2008. *An Ethiopian Album: A Photographic Journey through Nature and Culture*. Blurb.

Thomas, R. S., and D. J. Patton. 1964. *Focus on Geographic Activity: A Collection of Original Studies*. New York: McGraw-Hill.

U.K. Government. 1943–44. *House of Commons Debates* 398: 220.

United Nations Economic Commission for Africa. 1967. *Vegetation and Agricultural Zones of Africa*. Addis Ababa, Ethiopia: UNECA.

UNDP, Global Economic Facility. http://www.undp.org/gef/ accessed March 20 2003.

U.S. Central Intelligence Agency. 1999. *Ethiopia*. Washington, D.C: Central Intelligence Agency.

U.S. Central Intelligence Agency. 2000. *Eritrea and Northern Ethiopia*. Washington, D.C: Central Intelligence Agency.

U.S. Government. 1960. *Letter by the Ambassador of the U.S. to Secretary of State, Monrovia*. December 15. SD 775.11/12–1560.

U.S. Government. 1960. *Letter by Richards to Secretary of State, Addis Ababa*. December 16. SD 775.00/12–1660.

U.S. Government. 1960. *Letter by Richards to Secretary of State, Addis Ababa*. December 17. SD 773.11/12–1760.

U.S. Office of Geography and U.S. Board on Geographic Names. 1950. *Ethiopia, Eritrea, and the Somalilands; Official Standard Names Approved by the United States Board on Geographic Names*. Washington, DC: Government Printing Office.

Vantini, G. 1975. *Oriental Sources Concerning Nubia*. Heidelberg: Warschau. 73.

Weigel, G. 1986. *The Soils of the Maybar/Wello Area: Their Potential and Constraints for Agricultural Development: A Case Study in the Ethiopian Highlands*. Berne, Switzerland: University of Berne, Institute of Geography.

Wilford, John Noble. 1995. "Believers in African Eve Think They Have Found Adam." *New York Times*, May 26.

Wood, A. P. 1975. *Migration and Settlement in the Forest Fringe, Illubabor Province, Ethiopia*. Liverpool, UK: Liverpool University, Department of Geography.

Woods, H., and G. Woods. 1981. *The Horn of Africa: Ethiopia, Sudan, Somalia, and Djibouti*. New York: F. Watts.

Zachariah. 1899. *The Syriac Chronicle of Zachariah of Mitylene*. London: Methuen & Co.

Zeleke, G. 2000. *Landscape Dynamics and Soil Erosion Process Modeling in the North-Western Ethiopian Highlands*. Berne, Switzerland: University of Berne, Institute of Geography.

Zewde Gabra-Selassie. 1976. *Eritrea and Ethiopia in the Context of the Red Sea and Africa*. Washington, DC: Woodrow Wilson International Center for Scholars. 6–30.

Zuehlke, J. 2005. *Ethiopia in Pictures*. Minneapolis: Lerner Publications.

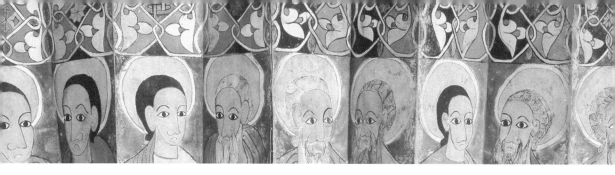

History

ETHIOPIA: THE MYSTICAL LAND OF ANTIQUITY

Ethiopia's name stems from the Greek words *aitho* and *ops*, which together mean "burnt face." This was a Hellenic designation for the dark-skinned people of northeastern Africa. In the conception of ancient historians, Ethiopia consisted of a vast expanse south of Egypt and has been known as a mystical land with highly cultured, hospitable, and extraordinary inhabitants.

ETHIOPIA: THE CRADLE OF HUMANKIND

Ethiopia's history is the history of humankind because we are all Ethiopians, regardless of whether we are of African, Asiatic, European, Oceanian, or Amerindian origin, because scientists have now ascertained that Ethiopia is the cradle of humankind. Fossils of human predecessors known as *Australopithecus afarensis*, which have been found to be as old as 5.5 million years, have been unearthed in the Awash River basin located within the wilderness of Afar in eastern Ethiopia. The latest specimen, found in the same area, adjoins another 4-million-year-old forebear to the human family tree. At the time of its discovery, the structure of the fossil was found to be so much like humans that investigating scientists were astonished; they thus coined the specimen "surprise." Then in 1974 came the remains of "Lucy," a humanoid female who is estimated to be 3.5 million years old, and just recently, modern human remains estimated to be 160,000 years old were found in the same area. The discovery of what has now been named *Homo sapiens idaltu* (*idaltu* meaning "the elder" in the Afar tongue) was a bombshell that rocked the world of contemporary scientists who were investigating the origin of man. Scientists believed for a long time that modern humans are no older than 100,000 years, but this fossil, which surpasses this estimate by 60,000 years, turned out to be the oldest human ancestor ever unearthed. Paleoanthropologists now conjecture that the *idaltu* fossil closes a crucial gap in humans' distinctive breaking away from primates. In general, it also further advances the theory that modern humans evolved in Ethiopia starting around 200,000 years ago and soon after spread across the rest of the planet.

OLDEST HOMINID HABITAT—AFAR, ETHIOPIA

The Ethiopian fossil's theoretical importance as a missing link in the evolution of humankind was also confirmed by scientific studies of linguistic progression and genetics, which have become important tools in investigating man's past, and other linguists have traced some basic words to the Proto-Afro Asiatic or Hamitic languages of East Africa. For example, in both Oromo and Somali, *tak* means "one," and a derivation of the term *palam* refers to "two." These words with the same connotation have been found in Asia (Sino-Tibetan and Jeh), Europe (Zyrian and Votyak), North America (Eyak and Wintun), South America (Aguaruna and Colorado), and Oceania (Proto-Karonan and Proto Australian). The scientific conjecture is that when *Homo sapiens* developed larger brains in Ethiopia, they also evolved a language, which, according to Noam Chomsky, has become a genetic blueprint of humanoids, and some of them went on a sojourn to other lands equipped with what can arguably be said to be the most efficient means of communication.

Tracing the most basic female genes in humans and looking at their roots further bolsters the paleoanthropologists' theory. In a highly acclaimed scholarly article published in the journal *Nature*, Rebecca L. Cann, Mark Stoneking, and Allan C. Wilson (1987) demonstrated a genetic blueprint that proves that Ethiopia is undoubtedly human beings' ancestral homeland. Their study illustrates that the unique patterns of the female-borne genetic element (mitochondria) that is passed on from mother to daughter traces our biological roots as well as dispersal patterns across the globe, the logical conclusion being that all of humanity can trace its family roots back to a single woman in Ethiopia.

This last point, now known as the "Eve hypothesis," has become a hot issue among paleoanthropologists. A study by Stephen Jay Gould (1992) of Harvard, who analyzed the fundamental meanings of the "Eve hypothesis," suggests—and this corroborates what the human fossils have shown—that the female-borne gene of all modern humans has a common origin in Ethiopia some 200,000 years ago. If taken as proof, Gould's findings have a significant impact on the study of human origins and further propel the theory that Ethiopia is in fact the birthplace of *Homo sapiens sapiens*.

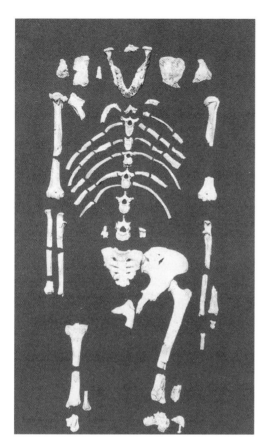

Lucy's fossil, known in Ethiopia as Dinkinesh, is a hominid of the Australopitecus Afarensis *genus discovered in Hadar, Afar region (3.2 million year old). (Courtesy of Paulos Milkias.)*

THE EVE HYPOTHESIS

It was around the closing decades of the 20th century that Dr. Allan C. Wilson, considered to be the leading molecular evolutionist of the 20th century, introduced what is now known as the "Eve hypothesis." The scientific work was funded by the Macarthur Foundation Fellowship, and the "Genius Award" was awarded to Wilson in 1986. His team collected mitochondrial DNA from 147 people from five disparate geographic areas and then analyzed the DNA with restriction mapping. Using the study, the scientists proved that all the samples of human mitochondrial DNA stemmed from one woman who lived in Ethiopia about 200,000 years ago. Wilson published the results of the study in the prestigious scientific journal *Nature*, in which he presented empirical evidence that the most recent maternal ancestor of all living humans was a woman living in Ethiopia about 200,000 years ago. A second group of scientists using restriction mapping of mitochondrial DNA from 3,065 humans in different parts of the world also came to the same conclusion, attesting to the common origin of humans in Ethiopia.

ETHIOPIA AS THE CRADLE OF HUMAN CIVILIZATION

Because scientific works have so far traced and established human biological roots to Ethiopia, our next task is to try to trace humans' cultural development. The blueprint of a civilization is essential in understanding the essence of human history. But what do we mean by "civilization"? Civilization implies peoples' progress in the struggle between humanity and nature. Animals and humans use tools to control nature, but whereas animals do what they do by instinct (e.g., a beaver building dams or bees producing honey), humans consciously manufacture tools to control nature. And it is for this reason that humans are called *Homo faber* (i.e., "man the maker"). Richard Greenfield (1965) accurately stated, "The history of mankind has been punctuated by several major breakthroughs in skill and technology such as the discovery of how to make and improve bone and stone implements; how to control and create fire; how to cook and make pottery; how to domesticate animals (previously only hunted), and how to cultivate plant life (previously only collected) . . . It is not always remembered, however, that several of the earlier discoveries . . . occurred in Africa and were made by Africans" (p. 14).

Because logical assumption based on scientific investigation leads one to believe that human life developed in Ethiopia, one is also bound to believe that many of the most significant instances of progress and critical elements in the maturation of the human species and civilization also arose in Ethiopia. These developments include nurturing the earliest stages of agriculture and people's control of fire.

The earliest case of human ancestors using tools has been traced to Ethiopia. Furthermore, scientists have proven that millet, sorghum, cotton, coffee, soft wheat, and camel were domesticated in Ethiopia and then were introduced to South Arabia and from there to the rest of the world more than 10,000 years ago.

Ethiopia evolved its own writing system starting at about 2000 BC. And it may be a great surprise to New Yorkers to learn that Ethiopia, the present land of thatched-roof *tukuls*, is the origin of high-rise buildings!

ETHIOPIAN HISTORY: SEMITIST VERSUS AFRICANIST PARADIGM

Notwithstanding ample historical corroboration, for hundreds of years, there has been an attempt to dislodge Ethiopian civilization from Africa by tracing everything from its language and culture to its agriculture and architecture to a distant source: South Arabia. This effort to dislodge the African root of Ethiopian civilization has been advanced in many forms.

One argument is that not only is Ethiopian history an offshoot of Arabian history, but that the Africans also were culturally dominated by a more advanced civilization from across the Red Sea. The scholars advancing this view ignore the connection between Egypt and Ethiopia during the pre-Sabean period. Even after that time, the nation of Axum was more connected to Nubia—a sister nation state just south of

Egypt than to South Arabia across the Sea. For a long period after the implosion of the Cushitic empire, which existed 5,000 years ago, one Cushitic state Axum, that had an upper hand dominated the political landscape in northeast Africa. Even as late as the 10th century BC, Axum ruled over Nubia. Al-Batani, the astronomer, who died in 929 AD, retells information from Ptolemy and mentions "Ksumi, (Axum)" as the country of "the king of Cush" (Nallino, 1907, 20:47).

Axum itself, which is now associated with the Tigary region, was at first situated in the western part of the Semitic-dominated Ethiopian kingdom, much nearer to Nubia than to Arabia. Recent investigation in the Kassala region of the north conducted by Italian archaeologists has hinted that some specific aspects of Axumite culture came from the western lowlands long before the similarities between Sabean and Ethiopian artifacts could be discerned. Archaeologists have also observed characteristics of pre-Axumite pottery that resemble those of the Nubians. Carvings, erected stelae, and funerary customs in northern Ethiopia have all been found to be characteristics that Axum shared with the nations that established the civilization of the Nile—namely Nubia and Egypt—not with South Arabians. And no one can contest the assertion that there is not any evidence of South Arabian civilization in Ethiopia 5,000 years ago. But there was a flourishing Ethiopian civilization in the Horn of Africa then.

A careful study of the artifacts in northern Ethiopia and present-day Eritrea—now numbering 90 in total—has been conducted in the area of Hawelti-Melazo. These sites include a well-known sanctuary and other structures and burial places of Yeha. The historical sites here clearly exhibit distinct characteristics of the Nile Valley. Furthermore, some of the writings found in northern Ethiopian sites bear names that have no resemblance to South Arabian designations.

ETHIOPIAN WIFE OF MOSES

As recounted in the Old Testament (Numbers 12:1), when the Jewish patriarch Moses wedded an Ethiopian woman, his sister Miriam and his brother Aaron admonished him for marrying a Gentile. In his book *Antiquity of Jews* (book 2, chapter 10), Josephus, the great Jewish historian (AD 37 to 100), wrote that while Moses lived in Egypt, he commanded the Egyptian army in a war against Ethiopia and that it was during this sojourn that he married an Ethiopian woman. According to Josephus, Tharbis, who was the daughter of the king of the Ethiopians, saw Moses as he led the army near the walls and fought with great courage. Admiring his exploits, she fell deeply in love with him. She soon sent to him the most faithful of her servants and suggested a marriage. He accepted the offer, on the condition the she would procure the delivering up of the city. She agreed. With her complicity, Moses succeeded to subdue the city of the Ethiopians and kept his promise and married Tharbis. He then led the Egyptians back to their own land.

One archaeologist writing about the finds of an expedition he conducted in northern Ethiopia, particularly in Yeha, stated that the shape of the jars there bears close resemblance to an Egyptian artifact. Quite possibly, Egypt copied the Ethiopian art form, or Ethiopia copied its neighbor's, but the similarity makes perfect sense because there is close affinity in the civilizations of the Nile Valley. It is important to add here that local tradition has it that Yeha, where these artifacts were found, was the Queen of Sheba's capital. One common fixture in Ethiopian history is the locale of her legendary kingdom. Ethiopian monarchs, including Haile Selassie, have claimed descent from Makeda (the Queen of Sheba) and King Solomon. The claim to this ancestral background is found in two Ethiopic books, *The Kebra Nagast* (Honor of the Kings) and *The Fiteha Nagast* (Law of the Kings), originally written during the Middle Ages by church scholars who had reliable records from the Arab world available to them. Because biblical sources are silent on this issue, historians have been divided as to whether, as recounted in the first book of Kings and second book of Chronicles, the Queen of Sheba was really from the region of Axum in northern Ethiopia or from Himyar in South Arabia.

The Stela of Axum (ca. second century BC to fourth century AD). (Courtesy of Paulos Milkias.)

Though contemporary Western scholars such as Edward Ullendorff (1973) discount the claim, the Egyptian Coptic church and the Orthodox Church of Ethiopia are categorical in advancing the idea that Sheba was from Africa, not Arabia. The Coptic and Ethiopian historiographical assertion was supported in antiquity, as early as the first centuries of the Christian era. Among those who accepted the Egyptian and Ethiopian version that the Queen of Sheba was from the region of Axum in northern Ethiopia were the noted Jewish historian Flavius Josephus, famous early theologian of the Christian church Origen, and St. Anselm and St. Augustine. In modern times, noted Orientalists and biblical scholars such as Ephraim Isaac and Cain Felder have supported this line. But no matter which version is advocated, the African paradigm is strengthened by the fact that the Ethiopian Hamites and Semites residing in northern Ethiopia, from which the Ethiopian royal family originates, ruled South Arabia for centuries before and after the Christian era, and the situation has never been the other way around.

Richard Greenfield, who is an astute observer and a meticulous scholar of Ethiopian history, states that until recent years, it has been a characteristic of research workers in Africa to attribute almost every African achievement to one "foreign influence" or another, and Ethiopia has been no exception to this. Several fragments of s stone inscriptions on stone slabs exist, and one inscription discovered near Yeha in 1955 was determined to be older than any other then known, including those found in Arabia. Other stone inscriptions show distinct features of local Ethiopian origin.

Crowns of Axumite Emperors (2nd century BC to 10th Century AD.) (Corel.)

Between the first and third centuries AD, the Axumite monarchs played a pivotal role in inter-state clashes in South Arabia. But by the fourth century, evidence abounds that Axum had extended political suzerainty over areas ranging from Kasu and Noba in the Sudan to the Cushitic Bejas in the North. At that time, Axum had appropriated the imperial role of its sister ancient Ethiopian states—Meroe and Napata. The Central Cushitic people of Agaw also became subjects of the rising Axumites. Through its port at Adulis, the Axumites sent goods obtained from their vast East African empire to the world market. This enabled the rulers of the new Ethiopia to take control of the rich trade centered in the Arabian Peninsula. To bolster their position, Axumite leaders employed skilful diplomacy and befriended the Romans, who had a huge empire just outside Ethiopia itself and who became their trading partner.

ETHIOPIA AND THE EGYPTIAN PHARAOHS

Thanks to the well-known tradition of the Egyptian pharaohs of putting into record every major event that took place during their reign, there is ample evidence that Ethiopia history is firmly rooted in Africa, not Arabia, though Ethiopian conquest of the latter created a new connection after AD 330. The Egyptian visitors marveled at the fabulous riches of Ethiopia during the reins of Queen Hatshepsut (1479 1458 BC) and the Ptolemies (285 to 246 BC).

Hatshepsut's Mortuary Temple in Der El-Bahry Egypt describes her subjects' expedition to the Land of Punt located in present day Ethiopia (1473–1458 BC) (Corel.)

ETHIOPIA AND THE EGYPTIAN PHARAOHS

Egyptian pharaohs sent expeditions to Ethiopia, known to them at that time as the land of Punt, to acquire gold, ivory, and myrrh. The first recorded contacts were during the First and Second Dynasties (3546–3190 BC). Egyptian hieroglyphics also report that during the Fourth Dynasty (3100–2965 BC), the son of Cheops, the builder of the Great Pyramid, was in possession of a servant from Punt. King Sahure (2958–2946 BC), of the Fifth Dynasty, sent his navy to Punt, and it later returned with myrrh, gold. and logs. King Pepy II (2738–2644 BC) of the Sixth Dynasty also recorded that he had a *tenq* (midget) servant from Punt. More expeditions were made during the rule of the Eleventh Dynasty pharaoh, Mentuhotep IV (2242–2212 BC). The most famous Egyptian expedition to the land of Punt was commissioned by Queen Hatshepsut (1501–1479 BC), who recorded the details of the trip with extensive hieroglyphic stone inscriptions at her temple in Dair el-Bahri in the city of Thebes. The tomb of a high Egyptian official at Thebes, during the reign of King Amenhotep II (1447–1420 BC), shows the arrival of two chiefs of Punt, bringing gold, incense, ebony trees, ostrich feathers and eggs, skins, antelopes, and oxen from their country. The stone inscriptions of Pharaoh Ramses III (1198–1167 BC) tell of Egyptian ships returning from the land of Punt with many products. Later expeditions by the Greek royal families of Ptolemys in Egypt were recorded at the beginning of the fourth century BC. The major reason for the Ptolemy's interest in Ethiopia was acquisition of domesticated elephants to use in war. The first Ptolemy king to take elephants from Ethiopia was Soter (305–285 BC), who sent an expedition along Ethiopia's eastern coast, under the command of a captain by the name Philos, who wrote a book titled *Aethioica*. Then another expedition was organized by Ptolemy II, known as Philadelphus (280–246 BC), who was very passionate about hunting for elephants in Ethiopia. In fact, the pharaoh gave rich rewards to those who succeeded in capturing the most powerful elephants. He requisitioned so many elephants from Ethiopia that special elephant parks were created in the cities of Thebes and Memphis. Hunting for elephants continued during the reign of Eurgetes I (246–221 BC), during which time some of his men described visiting the famous Axumite port of Adulis, where they left an inscription.

In 1472–1458 BC, the Egyptian Queen Hatshepsut sent five vessels to the land of Punt, as they called Ethiopia at the time. The expedition was under the command of a black Egyptian captain named Nehasi, who was described as Prince Chancellor, First Friend Wearing the Collar, meaning that he was among the highest-ranking ruling-class persons under the queen.

Again in 305–385 BC, the first Greek dynasty pharaoh of Egypt, Ptolemy Soter, sent an expedition to Ethiopia under the leadership of a captain named Philos in order to procure elephants to use in battle against the Babylonian army. Philos subsequently wrote a book called *Aeithiopica*, in which he described his journey. In 280–286 BC and

Imperial tombs (Early sixth century AD). (Courtesy of Paulos Milkias.)

246–221 BC, Ptolemy II Philadelphus and Ptolemy III Euergetes, respectively, sent expeditions to Ethiopia to procure elephants. Egyptian ships of the period visited the Axumite port of Adulis, and one of the Ptolemies left an inscription on a stone monument in his own memory. Depots were constructed along the coast of the Red Sea, and ivory, skins, ostrich feathers, and live elephants collected from the interior of Ethiopia were housed there. A stele inscribed with hieroglyphs, put up in Egypt during the reign of Ptolemy II and found at Pithon, refers to the king founding the city of Ptolemais Theron on the coast of modern-day Eritrea, which used to be part of ancient Ethiopia. The ruins found here, Philos conjectures, are part of the territory of Punt. In brief, Ethiopian civilization was uniquely African and was thriving long before South Arabia had anything tangible in the form of civilization and definitely long before the Greco-Roman influence engulfed the planet with Macedonian and Roman invasions.

THE CUSHITIC KINGDOM OF DAMOT

Around 2000 BC, the kingdom of Damot flourished in northern Ethiopia. The Blen people who now reside in northwestern Eritrea are descendants of the Damot. The Cushitic state of Damot, written as Tiamo or Tsiyamo in the still-surviving stone slabs near Axum, had already been established by the second millennium BC. And as additional s stone inscriptions in northern Ethiopia show, Damot had extended its dominion over South Arabia, and its ruler was called "mukarrib of Damot and Saba" (Caquot and Drewes, 1955, 26–32, 197; Drewes and Schneider, 1967, 91

Just around 500 BC, the center of political power for the Semitic-speaking people of northern Ethiopia became Mezbir. Between 400 and 250 BC, the center of political power moved first to Hinzat and then to Yeha. The next and most important settlement then became Axum, when a great city was established.

ETHIOPIA AND THE ANCIENT GREEKS

The Hellenic people, who sojourned up the Nile from Egypt and found the inhabitants of the area to be dark, opined that their skin was burned when the golden chariot of the Greek god Phoebus circling the equator came too near to their faces. Greek writer Strabo (63 BC–AD 24), however, wrote that the Ethiopians became dark because of "the sun and its scorching." Homer, in his book the *Odyssey*, described Ethiopians as the furthest living humans. Herodotus (490–425 BC), known as the father of history, also believed the Ethiopians inhabited the ends of the earth. He reported, "I went as far as Elephantine (i.e. Aswan) to see what I could with my own eyes. I was told, south of Elephantine the country is inhabited by Ethiopians . . . Beyond the island is a great lake, and round its shores live nomadic tribes of Ethiopian. . . . The Ethiopians are said to be the tallest and handsomest men in the whole world." The great Greek playwright Aeschylus, who was Herodotus's contemporary, also suggested in "Prometheus Bound" that Ethiopia was a country of "black men" who lived in "a land far off . . . by the fountain of the sun where there is a river called Aethiops." By all accounts, the ancient Greeks held Ethiopians in awe. Homer refers to them in the *Iliad* as the "blameless Ethiopians." He wrote that they were visited by the king of the gods, Zeus, as well as by the goddess Iris, who traveled to their land to share their sacrificial rites, and by Poseidon, the sea god, who was delighted by their feasts. In the first century BC, another Greek writer, Diodorus Siculus, stated that the gods Hercules and Bacchus were "awed by the piety" of the Ethiopian people, "whose sacrifices . . . were the most acceptable to the gods."

THE RISE OF AXUM

The Semitic-speaking Ethiopians' first capital was Yeha, where a magnificent temple was built in 600 BC. Yeha was situated about 12.43 miles north of Axum. The latter became a fixed capital for all Ethiopia around 300 BC. An empire soon expanded and flourished from this center.

By AD 50, the Axumite realm originating in northern Ethiopia had spread to the Red Sea and Indian Ocean littoral and along the valleys of the rivers Ansaba, Barca, and Marab. By AD 100, as the Peripulus of the Eritrean Sea used by merchants of antiquity recounts, Aksum had become one of the four greatest powers in the world (together with Rome, Persia, and China). It was during this time that King Zoscales of Aksum developed extensive foreign trade through the Red Sea Port of Adulis.

Axum's control of South Arabia was momentous and prevailed for a long time. By AD 200, as indicated by stone inscriptions in Yemen that were carved at the Mahram Bilqis, the Axumite kings Gadarat and Adhebah had established garrisons in South Arabia. In fact, whenever there was conflict among the Arab states of the period, they called on Axum for support against a rival. For example, an early third-century stone inscription found in South Arabia depicting a treaty between several kings—the king of Hadhramawt as well as Yada'ub, Gaylan, and the king of Axum, Gadarat—states, "They agreed together that their war and their peace should be in unison, against anyone [who] might rise up against them, and that in safety and in security there should be allied together, Salhen and Zararan and 'Alhan and Gadarat."

According to South Arabian stone inscriptions, between AD 200 and 230, Zafar, the capital of Himyar, was occupied and garrisoned under the authority of Baygat, the son of the *nagashi* (a derivation of *negus*, for king) of Axum. Also, stone inscriptions in al-Mis'al in Yemen clearly mention two kings of Axum named Datawnas and Zaqarnas who extended their rule over Arabia between AD 260 and 270. Other stone inscriptions in the same area also clearly show that between AD 100 and 400, through political alliance, naval power, and military muscle, Axum exerted control over Arabia from Hadramawt in South Arabia to Najran in modern Saudi Arabia. Just a few years before the birth of Islam, Ethiopian power was so important in the Middle East that emissaries came to pay their respects to the Axum domiciled kings. An interesting sixth-century Islamic history, translated by a Chinese historian named T'ien-fang Chih-sheng shih-lu between 1721 and 1724 and published in 1779, recounts Mohammed's biography titled *True Annals of the Prophet of Arabia*. According to the book, in 577, when Muhammad was just seven years old, the Axumite Najashi [Nagasi] (king) Saifu came to the throne of Ethiopia.

Whereas the kings of Axum used the royal title that included South Arabian kingdoms, none of the South Arabian monarchs ever mentioned political suzerainty over Axum or Ethiopia. Furthermore, starting from the reign of Emperor Endubis, Axumite kings minted coins in gold, silver, and bronze for use both in East Africa and in Arabia. No South Arabian coin had currency in Ethiopia and northeast Africa. Nor have written South Arabian records been discovered in Ethiopia or anywhere else in the Horn of Africa claiming suzerainty over Ethiopia.

Scholars who perform rigorous research are already inclined to accept the premise that the civilization's movement was from Ethiopia to South Arabia, not the other way around. Among these bold scholars is Jacqueline Pirenne, who concludes that civilization did not expand from Yemen toward Ethiopia, but very likely was the other way around, from Ethiopia toward Yemen (Peters, 1986, 30). Western scholars such as Michels, however, continue to claim that the trace of South Arabian influence in Ethiopian artifacts proves one thing: the South Arabians mustered a highly advanced culture and thus extended subjugation over Cushitic Ethiopians and, with political supremacy, forced them to adapt their culture. Most of the Ethiopian artifacts had in fact no resemblance to those from South Arabia. The Ethiopians themselves ingeniously crafted them. And instead of South Arabian rulers or kings leaving their imprint in Ethiopia, it is Ethiopian rulers who left their imprint in Arabia.

When Cosmas Indicopleustes, who wrote *Christian Topography*, went to Axum in the sixth century AD, he observed a multistoried palace and four elaborately carved figures of unicorns, none of them related to contemporary relics in South Arabia. Then the governor of Adulis, on the specific orders of Emperor Kaleb of Axum, asked him to transcribe an inscription on a marble chair at the Axumite port of Adulis, which had been erected several centuries before by an unknown king of Ethiopia. This pre-Christian Ethiopian king claimed to rule northeast Africa as well as South Arabia. The inscription states in part, "I sent a fleet and land forces against the Arabitae and Cinaedocolpite who dwelt on the other side of the Red Sea and having reduced the sovereigns of both, I imposed on them a land tribute and charged them to make travelling safe both by sea and land" (Pankhurst, 1967, 3–7). One would presume that a superior civilization would be reinforced by political power. But it is important to note that no parallel records showing this have ever been found in South Arabia.

Ezana, the first Christian emperor of Ethiopia, who reigned in the fourth century AD, wrote on one of his stone inscriptions; "Ezana, king of Axum and of Himyar and of Raydan and of Ethiopia and of Saba . . . king of kings." Another inscription reads, "Ezana, the son of Ella Amida, of the family of Halen, king of Axum and of Himyar and of Raydan and of Saba and of Sahlen." In a third inscription that dated to the period after his conversion to Christianity, Ezana wrote, "By the power of the Lord of Heaven who is mightier than everything which exists in heaven and or on Earth, Ezana, the son of Ella Amida, of the descent of Halen, king of Axum and of Himyar, Raydan, Saba, Salhen" (Pankhurst, 1965, 1–7). In all statues Ezana erected, the imperial claim is that the monarch was the king of Himyar and Raydan, both of which were in South Arabia. No South Arabian king has ever claimed to rule Ethiopia.

Christianity came to Ethiopia in AD 330, when Frumentius, a Syrian monk, converted Emperor Ezana and was consequently ordained by Athanasius, Patriarch of Alexandria, as the first Orthodox Christian bishop of Ethiopia. Following the emperor's conversion, Christianity spread rapidly, and as Cosmas Indicopleustes wrote, by the beginning of the sixth century, there were Christian churches throughout the empire.

Saint Mary of Zion church in Axum, believed to host the true Ark of the Covenant Moses received on Mount Sinai. (Franco Taddio/Stockphotopro.)

In AD 523, upon the request of the Byzantine Emperor Justin I, Emperor Kaleb of Axum sent a military expedition to southern Arabia and rescued the Christians of Nagran from the persecution of Dhu Nuwas, the last Himyarite ruler of southern Arabia. And more than half a century prior to the birth of Islam, Kaleb's viceroy in southern Arabia, Abraha, was attempting to expand the realm of the Axumite Empire as far North as Mecca.

AXUM AT THE TWILIGHT

Even after the momentous events of Axum's conquest of South Arabia, when the Persians took over South Arabia and Islam spread in the region, pushing the Christian empire further west into the mountains, Ethiopia's importance in the region continued unabated. A well-known essay titled "Hudud al-Alam" (1980) authored by a Persian writer in AD 983, for example, states, "This country [Ethiopia] has a very mild climate. They obey their own king. Merchants from Oman, Hejaz and Bahrain often go to that country for trade purposes" (372).

A historian at the time named Al-Ya'qubi described Axum during the last decade of the first millennium as follows: "[Axum is] a vast and powerful country. They have big cities and their seacoast is called Dahlak. The largest of their kingdoms is the kingdom of the Najashi, who is a Christian. Their capital is called Kafar [possibly Ankobar]" (Khalidi, 1975, 29).

Yet in another work, Al-Mas'udi provides interesting information about the reach of the Axumite Empire on the Red Sea coast. In his geographical text "Muruj al-Dhahab" (Meadows of Gold), he comments, "The principal city of the Habasha [people] is called Ku'bar [Ankobar], which is a large township and the residence of the Najashi [king], whose empire extends to the coasts opposite the Yemen . . . [and] possesses such towns as Zayla', Dahlak and Nasi" (Al-Mas'udi, 1841, p. 10).

After the Persians replaced the Axumites in Arabia, one notable development was documented in Islamic history. Islamic records in Hadith (which is a tradition based on reports of the sayings and physical activities of the Prophet Muhammad and his companions) point out that Armah, emperor of Aksum, provided refuge to the first generation of Mohammed's followers when they faced severe persecution in Mecca in AD 615. And among the more than 100 refugees who participated in what is known in the Muslim tradition as "the First Hejira," were Mohamed's son-in-law and successor Uthman Ibn 'Affan; the prophet's daughter, Ruqayya; his cousin, Jafar bin Ali Talib; and two of the prophet's wives, Umm Habibah and Umm Salma. Notwithstanding the prophet's directive not to attack Ethiopia, however, several jihads were conducted against the country, and the lowland areas to the north and east of the empire were Islamized. This led to the almost total isolation of the Christian empire for over a thousand years. The original home of this dynasty was Agaw, located in Lasta district—a Cushitic society that preceded the Semites of northern and central Ethiopia. They frustrated the attempt of the Fatimid caliphs of Egypt who tried to put Ethiopia under their own sphere of influence. They expanded the Christian empire beyond the Muslim sultanate of Shoa and exerted direct sovereign control over the Dahlak Islands in present-day Eritrea.

St. George's Church, hewn in the image of a cross from a single block of rock (ca. 10th to 13th centuries AD). (Courtesy of Paulos Milkias.)

The most important legacy of the Zagwés, who ruled Ethiopia for a century and a half, was their imprint in the construction of magnificent churches around their capital at Adefa (later named for King Lalibala). Furthermore, the influence of the Zagwés in the Near East was so prominent that in 1178, Sala al-Din, the sultan of Egypt and Syria, granted Ethiopia the use of the Church of the Holy Sepulcher and the Chapel of the Invention of the Cross, as well as a station in the Grotto of the Nativity in Bethlehem.

One of the rock-hewn churches of Lalibala (12th to 13th centuries AD). (Courtesy of Paulos Milkias.)

PRESTER JOHN

The man known in Ethiopia as Yimrahanna Kristos was referred to in Europe during the time of the Crusades as "Prester John" (Latin: Prete Anie). Yimrahanna Kristos was the first of the four emperor-saints of the Zagwe dynasty, and he ruled Ethiopia for 40 years. The emperor was devoted to the church, and besides, his imperial duties, he used to serve as a priest. He was the only Ethiopian emperor who was priest-king. His first appearance in historical documents was in the *Chronicle* of Otto Freising, who had heard word of a powerful Christian sovereign reigning in the East in 1145 from a Syrian bishop who had arrived at the Papal Court in Viterbo. During the Fifth Crusade, which took place at the beginning of the 13th century, information about Ethiopia trickled to Europe. The European report suggested that Prester John was a devoted priest as well as a great monarch. European writers soon started to depict Prester John as a great monarch who resided in a grand palace, carried an emerald scepter, was attended by hundreds of princes, and had an archbishop as a butler and a king as a chief cook. Others gave their imaginations free rein. Prester John, they wrote, had a magic mirror through which he could glance at every corner of his vast empire; his robes, washed only in fire, were woven by salamanders. Ludivico Ariosto, the famous early Renaissance poet, was inspired by these fantasies to describe the land of Preteianni (Prester John) as a place where one could find golden-chained drawbridges with solid crystal columns; musk, balsam, and umber in every corner; and a palace whose walls and ceilings were studded with pearls and whose rooms differed from each other in that the floors of some were made of rubies whereas others were covered with topazes and sapphires.

THE RESTORATION OF THE SOLOMONIAN DYNASTY

There was a great deal of achievement during the reign of the Cushitic Zagwé dynasty, but the Semites who believed that the Agaw people had usurped the throne were working hard to overthrow them. The Semites ultimately succeeded in their aims and installed Yekuno Amlak (1270–1300), who claimed descent from King Solomon and the Queen of Sheba, in place of Neakuto Le'ab.

Depicted in the Old Testament (Kings 10:1–13), the connection between Yekuno Amlak's dynasty and Solomon and Sheba also was elaborately narrated in the *Kebra Nagast*, which appeared in tandem. Menelik, it was also claimed in the *Kebra Nagast*, brought to Ethiopia the Ark of the Covenant, which was given to Moses by God. But there were claims and counterclaims to the throne that led to a drastic solution: all claimants of the throne had to be imprisoned on an escarpment of Gishen, with literally no possibility escape except for one entrance that was heavily guarded. The rise of the Solomonian dynasty in the thirteenth century signaled the ascendancy of

The castle of Emperor Fasilides (1632 to 1667). (Courtesy of Paulos Milkias.)

The castles of Gondar (17th century). (Courtesy of Paulos Milkias.)

the Amhara ruling classes, who controlled power until the time of Emperor Haile Selassie and the Derg's overthrown by the Tigray People's Liberation Front in 1991.

THE ERA OF THE PRINCES

When Iyoas, an Oromo-speaking emperor, took over power and ruled from 1755 to 1769, Ras Mika'el Seul of Tigray was summoned by traditionalists in Amhara to aid in resisting the Oromos leadership of the empire. Mika'el made his move at a time

Emperor Fasilides's castle (17th century). (Courtesy of Paulos Milkias.)

when two dowager queens were fighting to control state machinery in the name of their imperial sons, both with the support of different Oromo warlords. After removing the Oromo kingmakers, Mika'el dictated policy decisions in Ethiopia for a period of 25 years while acting as a regent of a series of weak emperors.

Initially, Emperor Iyoas attempted to get Mika'el assassinated. But Mika'el survived, purged the emperor, and handpicked the next three emperors: Yohannes II, Tekle Haimanot II, and Tekle Giorgis I.

During the Zamana Masafint [Era of the Princes], the power of the emperors had waned, and the regional kings of Shoa, Gondar, and Gojam were in full control of political power in their territories. After 25 years of being a power broker in Gondar, Mika'el Sehul's influence ultimately came to an end when the Oromos regrouped and defeated him.

During the heyday of the Zamana Masafint, the princes running their autonomous regions were subject to raids from other warlords who coveted an additional

MARKANISH

Markanish (Bint Karbinal) was a 13th-century celebrated Christian queen who ruled her dominion in the area of Harar. According to the Fath Madinat Harar, an unpublished chronicle of Harar from the 13th century, Markanish was a sovereign of the Christians who fought against Abadir 'Omar ar-Rida the Harari spiritual and secular leader and his disciples. The Fath indicates that she took the throne from her brother Jurniyal in 1253, following his conversion to the Islamic religion. When he challenged her rule, Markanish engaged him in battle, where he died in 1257, unfortunately; Markanish herself was martyred by the forces of Abadir in 1290 in an Oromo village near Argobba.

ZARA YAQOB

Emperor Zara Yaqob (the name means "offspring of Jacob") ruled Ethiopia for 34 years (1434–1468). His reign was one of the most eventful during the middle Ages. He conducted an unsuccessful military campaign to convert the Falasha (Beta Israel) community in Gondar province, which practiced a non-Talmudic form of Judaism, to Christianity. His major passion was, however, to achieve national unity and to break Muslim encirclement. He was a reformer of the Church as well as the social and religious life in his domain. He had to wage a series of wars against Muslim potentates on the periphery, and three of his brothers died in that struggle. The emperor dealt Ifat, one of the most powerful Muslim kingdoms on the periphery, such a crushing military blow that their the latter's hegemony passed to the sultans of Adal in Harar province. Zara Yaqob believed in uprightness, both religiously and in social life. In this, he did not distinguish between the nearest of kin and others. If he felt that a law had not been followed, he took severe action to punish those accused of the act. Zara Yaqob had his wife flogged to death when she attempted a palace coup in favor of her son. He also executed three of his daughters for worshiping idols. As a learned Dabtara prince, Zara Yaqob followed theological trends at home and abroad. He dispatched delegates to the Council of Florence (1431–1445). He also created links with the Western churches, including Rome. His wrote religious tracts extensively. Among the major ones he left behind when he died were the creed of the Ethiopian church and five other theological treatises. Zara Yaqob encouraged the development of literature at every level. He reformed the administration of the Church and reformulated the Church calendar.

---

realm. During that time, many peasants stopped farming the land. Unpaid soldiers and *shiftas* ("outlaws") made their normal life very difficult. There was a continuous civil war and a series of bloody conflicts such that as many as six rival emperors claimed the Solomonian throne in 1800.

The last kingpin of the Zamana Masafint was in fact an Oromo warlord named Ras Ali who was defeated by Emperor Tewodros—an Amhara emperor who ended the era of state anarchy in Ethiopia. Though he united his realm under a centralized state machinery, the new emperor faced a series of rebellions, one of which was directed by the ambitious young Menelik, who escaped from the imperial prison at Magdala and raised his own army in his father's kingdom of Shoa, where he had crowned himself king.

THE REIGN OF EMPEROR TEWODROS, 1855–1868

Despite the rebellions from every province and from the church, which opposed his interference in their control of large estate holdings, Tewodros succeeded in setting up a modern-style system. He established a salaried military and administrative,

---

ZA-DINGIL

Za-Dingil was the emperor of Ethiopia (1603–1604) who converted from Orthodox Tewahedo to Catholicism under the influence of the Jesuits. Za-Dingil was eager to announce his conversion even against the urgings of his Jesuit friend Pedro Paiz. Opposing the Ethiopian Orthodox tradition, he published a proclamation ordering that it was henceforth illegal to keep the Jewish Sabbath as a holiday. He instructed that only Sunday be celebrated, in keeping with Roman Catholicism. Za-Dingil wrote in a letter dated June 26, 1604, to Pope Clement VIII of the Vatican that as emperor of Ethiopia he acknowledged the Pope's ecclesiastical supremacy. This brought about the Emperor's excommunication. He was confronted in battle by Orthodox Christian zealots led by Ras Atnatewos of Amhara, who, supported by the Ethiopian clergy, had already passed a death sentence on him. To make matters worse for him, his army, which was almost wholly Orthodox, deserted. When defeat seemed inevitable, he marched south and took refuge in Enarya (near present-day Jimma in the Kaffa region). In his absence, the dissidents stormed the treasure house of Gishen and impounded the entire imperial wardrobe, with 12 cases of gold chains and ornaments. Then in hot pursuit, they crossed the Abbay and followed Za-Dingil to Enarya. The emperor, who was guarded by a Portuguese contingent and few thousand loyal troops, decided to engage the rebels. Camping on the plain of Barcha, on the evening of October 14, 1604, he faced enemies head on. Two hundred Portuguese carrying muskets were sure that Ze-Dingil would win, but that was not to be. As the battle progressed, his army was decimated. The emperor was unhorsed, encircled, and speared. The coup de grace was delivered by Ras Za Selassie, governor of Dambia, with a lance hurled from a distance. He was then beheaded. The body of the emperor was exhumed from the field of battle a few days later and moved to the monastery of Daq Estepha on Lake Tana. The winners then restored the deposed Emperor Yaqob in his place after the latter swore to be loyal to the country's Miaphysite faith.

---

judicial, and civil service contingents to protect the country against foreign invasion and to run state affairs smoothly.

Tewodros's fall came when, slighted and angered by the British government's failure to promptly answer his request for a bilateral alliance against the Ottomans and a supply of European technicians, Tewodros imprisoned the British consul in his realm, as well as the special envoy of Queen Victoria and several European missionaries. As a result, the British dispatched to Ethiopia a military expedition under the command of General Napier.

Prior to attempting the march through the difficult terrain of Ethiopia, Napier made clear to the country's feudal lords, who were rivals to Tewodros, that the British government's intention was solely to secure its nationals and other foreigners who were illegally imprisoned. The British consequently succeeded in negotiating the difficult mountainous terrain of Ethiopia and in joining battle with the emperor at Makdala. Tewodros's army, clearly no match for Napier's well-armed military force, was speedily defeated, and the Ethiopian emperor, in order to avoid the indignity of

An engraving from the Illustrated London News *showing Emperor Tewodros (Theodore) II of Ethiopia committing suicide on April 13, 1868 as British troops arrived to free more than 40 European prisoners, including the British Consul Charles Duncan Cameron and his retinue, at the mountain fortress of Magdala in central Ethiopia. (© ANDREW HEAVENS/X01805/Reuters/ Corbis.)*

capture by his enemies, committed suicide with a pistol previously given to him by Queen Victoria. Hundreds of illuminated manuscripts that are now deposited at the British Library and the Royal Library in Windsor Castle, among other locations, are remnants of this war booty.

THE REIGN OF EMPEROR YOHANNES IV

An intense power struggle ensued following Tewodros's death. A Zagwé descendant named Takla Giorgis crowned himself briefly but was soon overthrown by Dajazmatch Kassa Mircha of Tigray, who had helped Napier in the anti-Tewodros campaign and in return received plenty of firearms, including artillery pieces, with which he subdued his rivals. Kassa was crowned emperor in 1872 under the throne name Yohannes IV.

Emperor Yohannes had to defend Ethiopian territorial integrity against a series of foreign invading forces. The Egyptians' attempt to conquer Ethiopia and thus secure the headwaters of the Blue Nile, which is a primary source of their livelihood, was also frustrated when, twice in 1875 and 1876, the armies of Khedive Isma'il faced crushing defeats. With the tacit approval of the British, the Italian colonialists usurped the formerly Turkish- and Egyptian-occupied Ethiopian seaport of Massawa in 1885. They

THE ZEMENE MESAFINT (OR "ERA OF THE PRINCES"), 1706–1855

This was a time in Ethiopian history when autonomous regions under independent warlords proliferated outside the political control of the central imperial government. Zamana Masafint started with the assassination of Iyasu the Great, which led to a gradual decline of the Solomonian dynasty. What followed was a power struggle between his mother, Empress Mentewab, and his widow, Wubit. Rivalries also intensified among Oromo, Amharas, and Tigre warlords. Iyasu's son Iyoas, who was brought up by his Oromo cousins, took the throne as a child and made Afan Oromo the court language of Gondar. This enraged the Gondar Amharas. The young emperor also openly favored his Oromo cousins. For example, on the death of the ruling *ras* (duke) of Amhara, Iyoas appointed his uncle Lubo as governor. As the conflict between the Oromos and the Amharas in Gondar intensified, Ras Mikael Sehul of Tigray, who had accumulated firearms through the port of Massawa, found an opportunity to intercede. He immediately took power and purged the Oromo warlords, basing his power on an Amhara–Tigre coalition. When the young emperor raised his Oromo uncle Fassil to power, Mikael Sehul deposed and then assassinated Iyoas. From the Wahini jail, where all imperial contenders were incarcerated, Mikael brought out and crowned Yohannes II, a prince who was very old and not interested in political power. When Mikael's plan to have Yohannes marry his daughter was rejected, Mikael had Yohannes assassinated. Mikael Sehul was in the end defeated by Oromo warlords. He was allowed to retreat to Tigray, thereby leaving the control of the imperial throne to the Oromos one more time. The Oromos continued to be kingmakers until Kassa of Gondar from the Amhara region of Quara, who had no claim to the Solomonian dynasty, fought his way up and crowned himself Emperor Tewodros II in 1855.

then embarked on an aggressive expansion campaign further into the highlands, only to be decisively defeated by Emperor Yohannes at the battle of Dogali in 1887.

That same year, the Messianic Islamists of Sudan known as the Mahdists encroached on Ethiopian territory. After defeating King Takla Haimanot, the regional king of Gojam and Begemder, the Mahdists' forces devastated the old Ethiopian capital of Gondar. In retaliation, Yohannes moved in full force against the Sudan. Before his death, Yohannes commanded his able general Ras Alula to crown the emperor's son, Ras Mangasha.

EMPEROR MENELIK AND ETHIOPIA'S HISTORIC VICTORY AT THE BATTLE OF ADWA

Despite Yohannes's strong wish to pass on the crown to his son, the emperor's Amhara rival Menelik of Shoa, who had for a long time aspired to climb the Solomonian throne, came forcefully. In fact Menelik had not recognized Yohannes as emperor until 1878–1879 when the Shoan negus faced a military defeat in a struggle between the two monarchs.

Throughout the next decade, Menelik engineered Ethiopia's return into the southern and western regions that had been abandoned in the 17th century when the kingdoms of Ifat, Dawaro, Fatagar, and Damot were swept away by the swift tide of Oromo warrior-age groups known as Lubas. By waging numerous wars with the new weapons he had acquired from Europe, Menelik succeeded in incorporating within his domain all major Oromo confederacies and sovereign territories, including those of Arsi, Harar, Jimma, Limu, and Wallaga, and several other kingdoms and states of southern Ethiopia such as Kaffa, Walaita, Sidama, and Janjaro. In their conquest of the south, Menelik and his followers were inspired by the idea that they were regaining lands that had once been part of the Christian empire. For them it was a holy crusade to restore Ethiopia to its historic grandeur.

Menelik, who feared that Yohannes's son Mangasha, supported by the famous imperial army general Ras Alula, might try to follow his father to the throne, made a pact with the Italians in 1888. The Italians in turn provided Menelik with plenty of firearms.

In the meantime, Menelik attempted to unify the empire and introduce modernization. Through diplomatic negotiations with France, he succeeded in having a railway built, thus connecting his capital city of Addis Ababa to the Red Sea coast of Djibouti. He opened the first Western-style school as well as the first modern hospital. He introduced the conveniences of the telegraph and electric power into his empire. He established the printing press and launched a relatively liberal newsmagazine, *A'imiro*, where freedom of the press was for the first time exercised by his newly educated elite.

The Shoan monarch's agreement with the Italians resulted in an intractable squabble when the Italians interpreted article 17 of the Treaty of Wuchale (Uccialli), concluded in 1889 by the Italians and Menelik, as giving Italy a protectorate status over Ethiopia. Though it was utterly inconceivable that Menelik would have agreed to his historic country becoming a protectorate of Italy or any other power, the new emperor soon learned that the Italian interpretation concocted by the Italian envoy Count Antonelli was slowly gaining ground in Europe.

The Italian colonialists, who had by 1890 established themselves along the Red Sea coast in an area they had named the colony of Eritrea, soon risked a major confrontation with Menelik's army, only to be soundly defeated by a hastily mobilized Ethiopian peasant army in one of the greatest battles in the history of the world—the Battle of Adwa of March 1, 1896.

Historically speaking, Adwa was the most major military operation between the Africans and the Europeans since the time of Hannibal in 200 BC. For Ethiopia it was the most triumphal; for Italy it was the most disastrous. The Italian colonialist invaders were defeated totally. All their artillery pieces were captured. One out of four of their generals was taken prisoner. Two of the remaining generals as well as half of their staff officers were killed. Following the victory, Italy and the European powers categorically recognized Ethiopian sovereignty, and Menelik returned back to Addis Ababa to carry out the consolidation of his empire and the modernization drive he had started. His age advancing, the emperor died following a long illness in 1913.

LIJ IYASU AND THE VACANT THRONE

Following Menelik's death, a power struggle ensued between his grandson, Lij Iyasu, and the Shoan nobles led by Ras Tafari Makonnen, later to be crowned Haile Selassie I. Citing the civil war that had engulfed the country during the previous two emperors, Menelik announced prior to his death that he had chosen his 12-year-old grandson Lij Iyasu—the son of Menelik's daughter Princess Shawaragga and the Oromo ruler of Wallo, Ras Mika'el—to succeed to the Solomonian throne.

The need to assure safe succession was underscored by the fact that during Menelik's last days of long illness, the major European powers Britain, France, and Italy had signed a tripartite agreement that clearly infringed on the sovereignty of the country. By that agreement, which did not involve Ethiopia, the three colonial powers demarcated their spheres of influence over Ethiopia—Britain claiming to control the headwaters of the Nile, France dominating the territories through which its railway line from Djibouti to Addis Ababa passed, and Italy claiming control over the rest.

When the dying monarch's consort, Empress Taytu, tried to dictate state matters from her husband's palace in Addis Ababa, the Shoan aristocracy, with the support of the Mahal Safari, or Imperial Bodyguard, rebelled and banished her to Entoto.

Empress Taytu Bitul, consort of Menelik and hero of Adwa. (1844–1918) (Hulton/Archive by Getty Images.)

The young prince, now beyond the control of his guardian, got into daunting political trouble. His attempt to woo Ethiopia's Muslim population and his close relationship with Germany and Turkey, which were enemies of the Allied powers during World War I, led to a plot to overthrow him. The move succeeded with the support of the Church, which had excommunicated the young monarch for flirting with the Muslims. Thus in 1916, Empress Zawditu, the daughter of Menelik, was chosen to take her father's throne, and Ras Tafari Makonnen (later Haile Selassie) was named regent with full political powers to rule the country.

When his excommunication and overthrow was announced in 1916, Iyasu tried to rally his supporters to march on Addis Ababa, but his army faced a resistance led by Haile Selassie's supporter Fitawrari Takla Hawaryat, who had modern military training from a famous Czarist Russian military academy. Though Iyasu was initially successful in battle, he was ultimately defeated at the Battle of Sagale, a few miles north of Addis Ababa, and was captured after living as a fugitive for a few years; then, he was kept in custody until his death.

THE HAILE SELASSIE PERIOD I: RAS SAFARI'S REGENCY AND EMPERORSHIP, 1916–1936

Iyasu stayed at large among Muslim sympathizers in the districts of Afar for about five years but was ultimately captured and put in jail. In the meantime, Fitawrari Habte Giorgis, a trusted official of Menelik who supported Ras Tafari in his bid for the regency, wielded power behind the scenes. But his death in 1926 allowed Tafari to practice what his title denoted: "Crown Prince and Regent with unlimited political powers."

In 1928, Ras Tafari was crowned negus, and at the empress's death in 1930, he was crowned emperor as "Lion of the Tribe of Judah, Elect of God and king of kings of Ethiopia."

In the years prior to the Italian–Ethiopian war of 1935–1936, Haile Selassie became a champion of modernization, generally known in Ethiopia as Me'irabawi Seletane (Western civilization). In 1920, he commissioned a group of legal pundits to develop modern bureaucratic procedures and legal rules by consulting codes from western Europe. Tafari was a reformer par excellence. He abandoned reliance on a peasant fighting force and created instead a modern army trained first by the White Russians (who were loyal to the overthrown Romanoff family and were opposed to and fought against the Bolsheviks led by Lenin in the early 1900s) and then later by the Belgians. He promulgated the country's first constitution. And in July 1931, he established a bicameral parliament.

While carrying out his administrative reform, Haile Selassie was careful to reserve for himself absolute power, suggesting that political power emanated from divine will. One of the clauses of the Constitution (article 11) stated, "The person of the emperor is sacred, his dignity inviolable, and his power indisputable." Other clauses reserved for the emperor exclusive prerogative over central and local government, the legislature, the judiciary, and the executive as well as the military establishment.

Starting in 1930, Ras Tafari secured the cooperation of various international banking institutions and established the Bank of Ethiopia, which starting in 1931 issued an Ethiopian currency. He introduced the first airplane into the country. More were added later, until Ethiopia was being served by a dozen airplanes just before the Italian invasion in 1936.

To enhance the dissemination of information and general knowledge, Tafari founded the Berhanenna Selam Printing Press and established the first radio station in the country. He expanded Western education and established the first secondary school in the country. He also sent hundreds of young Ethiopians to study abroad.

By befriending the West, which was set to fight against both Fascism and Communism, Haile Selassie quickly secured reliable allies abroad. To join the family of modern nations, Ras Tafari abolished slavery and by that act succeeded in getting Ethiopia accepted into the League of Nations. Additionally, because of great pressure from the European powers that had colonized the rest of the continent, Ras Tafari signed the Arms Traffic Act with Britain, France, and Italy. But the regent did not sign the agreement until he had secured legal guarantees that the Ethiopian state could procure arms to guard against external aggression and to maintain internal order.

In 1925, Tafari invoked Ethiopia's membership in the League and frustrated a British–Italian agreement to encroach on Ethiopian sovereignty; without consulting Addis Ababa, the nations had agreed that Italy would build a railway through Ethiopia, connecting its colonies of Eritrea and Somalia, and that Britain would build a dam on Lake Tana. Tafari expanded the number of roads, schools, and hospitals in the country and sent hundreds of Ethiopian youth to study abroad and then return back to serve in the modern bureaucracy he created.

Tafari also weakened the position of the traditional nobility. The only thing he did not do, which was to become his undoing later during his imperial reign, was try to address the intricate problem of land tenure, which was linked to the traditional political order, the royal family, the feudal nobility, and the Church.

FASCIST INVASION AND THE ETHIOPIAN RESISTANCE

Barely five years after Haile Selassie was crowned, Mussolini, who wanted to avenge the Italian defeat at Adwa and to revive the Roman Empire, launched, in October 1935, an invasion force of 500,000 men, well-trained and armed with hundreds of tanks and fighter planes, against an Ethiopian feudal army equipped only with old guns, spears, and clubs. Despite the odds against them, the Ethiopian fighters put up a stiff resistance for six months, and Mussolini's troops succeeded in entering Addis Ababa only after brutally spraying poison gas, which was prohibited by the Geneva Convention, on soldiers and civilians alike. Haile Selassie went into exile in England after making a final and futile plea to the League of Nations in Geneva.

Ethiopian freedom fighters, however, did not give up. They continued their struggle by reverting to guerrilla warfare. As soon as the last conventional defense was broken, the Western-educated youth, most of whom had initially been conscripted

Ras Tafari (later Emperor Haile Selassie), who was Regent of Ethiopia from 1916–1930, wearing traditional attire, riding a mule, and being escorted by armed retainers. (Library of Congress.)

Haile Selassie, emperor of Ethiopia, 1930–1974. (Library of Congress.)

Emperor Haile Selassie invoking the conscience of the world at the League of Nations in Geneva following Mussolini's invasion of his country in 1936. (Library of Congress.)

into the Imperial Bodyguard, regrouped themselves into guerrilla units and founded a political party, the first of its kind in Ethiopian history, known as the Tekur Anbassa (Black Lion). Other Western-educated Ethiopians, in collaboration with their traditionally educated cohorts, later formed the "Committee of Union and Collaboration against Italian Fascism" and disseminated information and propaganda against the occupying force (Taddesse Macha, 1950, 1–71).

The Italians continued their merciless bombings and poison gas attacks against villages occupied by members of the resistance.

Mussolini, in the meantime, had poured into Ethiopia about a quarter of a million Italian settlers, believing that the country was peaceful enough for systematic colonization by whites. However, patriotic resistance continued. The Fascists' attempt to disarm the people helped the cause of the liberation struggle, for Ethiopians would rather sacrifice their lives than lose their guns. Hundreds of thousands thus joined the ranks of the patriotic fighters, and Mussolini soon found that his white settlers, or colonists, had to be protected by an army almost twice their number.

After Italian Blackshirts slaughtered tens of thousands of Ethiopian civilians in the city of Addis Ababa and the Monastery of Libanos, the Ethiopian guerrillas, bolstered by enthusiastic new recruits, moved to within 24 miles of Addis Ababa and harassed the Italians who ventured outside the fortified central city limits. The patriots avoided engaging the Fascist army wherever they had superior forces. They attacked only when they felt that their numbers as well as their arms were equal

Mussolini's fascist army and askaries (Eritrean native soldiers) on the march to invade Ethiopia (1935). (Hulton-Deutsch Collection/Corbis.)

to or better than their enemy's. They raided military convoys. As time passed, the patriots expanded the theater of war to such an extent that the Italians could supply the outposts outside Addis Ababa only by air.

According to eyewitness reports from a correspondent for the Luxembourg newspaper *Escher Tageblatt*, during the final months of 1937, the Italians were in control of only the major cities and towns. The correspondent adds that it was impossible to travel on any motor roads in Ethiopia without being escorted by armed convoys. This military situation was confirmed by a reporter for the *London Times*. At the end of 1937, battalion-level Fascist military units had met a series of defeats at the hands of the Ethiopian forces, which were armed with weapons captured in previous engagements. In Gojam and Begemder, in particular, there was no Italian presence except at a few isolated fortified spots, where they were virtually surrounded and received food and ammunition by aircraft. According to a British reporter, at the beginning of 1938, "Wounded and sick Italian soldiers arriving in [Port Said] revealed that bands of Abyssinian warriors are constantly attacking military outposts throughout the country and inflicting mass destruction" (*The Evening Standard*, February 4, 1938, 1–2). Correspondents for major British newspapers also reported that in mid-1938, trainloads of wounded Italian soldiers were constantly shipped through Djibouti.

The Italians themselves had started to recognize the success of the Ethiopian guerrillas' new tactics. They clearly recognized the expertise of Ethiopian fighters in the art of surprise and attack and the Italians were far from controlling areas outside the urban centers. According to one high Fascist official in Ethiopia, Raphael di Lauro, "in many areas . . . as close as the suburbs of Addis Ababa, the Italians could not restore public order" (di Lauro, 1949, 126–303).

During the final years of the occupation, power was slipping out of the hands of the Fascists, who were surrounded by Ethiopian guerrillas.

Garasu Dukki's 12,000-guerilla force, well armed with war materials captured from the Fascists, had surrounded the city of Jimma and put it under siege. As the Italian officer on the spot wrote, the city was "in peril," and Italian soldiers and civilians "rarely slept" at night (Pierotti, 1940–1941). In the suburbs of Addis Ababa where Abebe Aregay's force of 30,000 constantly harassed the invaders, 35 main forts connected with a network of barbed wire were constructed. Even hotels where the Italians stayed, such as the Albergo Imperiale, were fenced in with barbed wire. Consul General Bonacorsi, commander of the Fascist Blackshirts in East Africa, thus reported to Rome, "If at any point . . . a detachment of English or Frenchmen were to enter with a banner unfurled, they would need little or no troops for they would find the vast mass of the Abyssinian population would unite themselves . . . and eject our forces" (Steer, 1942, 41–42).

It was on July 12, 1940, when Mussolini declared war on the Allies by approving the invasion of France by the German Nazis, that the UK government officially declared it would support the anti-Italian Fascist struggle in Ethiopia. Thus, Emperor Haile Selassie, who was in exile in Britain, was flown from his exile residence in Bath, England, to Khartoum, Sudan. Ethiopians in exile in the Sudan and Kenya were subsequently provided with military training under General Orde Wingate and were equipped with 10,000 Springfield rifles and Bren guns.

Wherever they had fortified themselves, and whenever they moved on the roads, the Italian armies were ceaselessly harassed by the growing patriotic force now bolstered by British support. On April 13, 1941, a Fascist cavalry regiment of 450 troops was moving from Addis Ababa to Addis Alem when they were ambushed by the patriots; "only 50 got away with their lives" (Birkby, 1942, 239–240). In Gojam the strong Italian fortification at Bure was besieged by the patriots, and several attempts to break out were repulsed. The morale of the Italian colonial troops soon plummeted, and mass desertions ensued.

In the north-central front, the Italians reported that a ferocious war had broken out at Debark, Gondar, and 400 Italian troops were killed by the patriots. Sakotta was under the control of patriot forces led by Wagshum Wossen Hailu, and the Italians had failed to recapture it during the previous five years. Gayint and Iste were taken by Yohannes Iyasu (son of the deposed Emperor Lij Iyasu). Patriots had likewise captured Debre Zeit, Makdala, Debre Tabor, and Azezo. Gondar, one of the most important historical cities, was also captured by the patriots, who "crept up astonishing precipices unexpectedly by night and cut the road" leading to Wolkait (Government of the United Kingdom, 40–60, 140–141). Ras Seyoum Mengesha of Tigray raised an army of 20,000 men and, together with Wagshum Wossen Hailu, attacked the Italian army that was entrenched at Amba Alagie and then attacked General Frusci's headquarters near Mai Chew.

According to Birkby, who was an eyewitness to this engagement, the victory was achieved through hand-to-hand fighting, and "every bomb the Patriots threw was stamped 'Made in Italy'—captured from the enemy. The Patriots fought with open eyed bravery and they suffered fairly heavy casualties" (Birkby, 1950, 290). Guerrilla bands supported by the local inhabitants, armed only with obsolete guns and spears, also captured Quoram.

Di Lauro attributes Italian defeat at Kombolcha to the patriotic forces that scaled the precipices "like squirrels" and attacked the Italians day and night. "The battle of Kombolcha," he adds, "was the battle of bandits and was won by them" (Di Lauro, 1949, 259–260). Dajazmatch Negash's Gojam guerrillas also engaged the Italian army moving from their Bure and Debre Markos forts and defeated them. At Motta, AnDergatchew Messai and Wagshum Wossen Hailu attacked and captured the Italians in their forts. Dangila and Injibara also fell to the Ethiopian guerrillas after heavy fighting.

In the south, Ras Mesfin Sileshi's fighting force had defeated the Italian army commanded by General Gazera at Bunno Beddelle. Fitawrari Olana's patriotic fighters captured the Italian military garrison at Yubdo, Wellega, with valuable stocks of arms and ammunition. It confiscated hoarded Maria Theresa dollars (the Austrian minted currency). Of particular importance was the value of the Thaler, which is made of pure silver and was used and coveted in the entire Middle East and Horn of Africa because of its value. They also neutralized and captured 26 Italian Blackshirt battalions (Steer, 1942, 162). If these forces had not been put out of action, they could have been used against the British in Keren, Eritrea, where the last major encounter between the Commonwealth forces and the Italians occurred.

It was in the wake of these events that South African, Southern Rhodesian, and Belgian forces arrived and found the enemy in retreat wherever military engagements between the British and the Italians were made. The patriots were used as a support force, either for initial attack or in mopping up operations. According to Di Lauro, when the South African army went to attack the Italian army near Ankober, they successfully employed 6,000 Ethiopian guerrillas carrying 20 portable cannons at the front. At Kombolcha the patriots, who were assigned to fight on the flanks by the South African army, occupied two very important mountain heights and "rushed in fearlessly and mercilessly at the climax of the battle," following which the "broken" Italian soldiers fled (Government of the United Kingdom, 116–117). The stamina of the wiry Ethiopian mountain warriors astonished the South Africans. Birkby commented, for example, "[The Ethiopian fighters] had legs and arms like Matchsticks but they . . . could run with a [27 kg.] case of mortar bombs, where we could barely stagger" (Birkby, 1950, 237).

As for the Fascist soldiers, they tried to avoid capture by the patriots, fearing retaliation for the atrocities they had committed, and felt relieved when the British forces appeared on the scene. According to J. F. MacDonald (1957), the Italian soldiers near Lake Abaya and Shashamane were "too glad to surrender [to the British]. For weeks, they had trudged over rain swept inhospitable hillsides, constantly harried by Shifta [guerrillas] who gave them no rest at night and hung on their flanks all day" (207–208).

As a matter of fact, the British strategy for demoralizing the Italian soldiers was to threaten to let loose the Ethiopian patriots on their fortifications. At Dera, when 14,000 Italian troops stubbornly continued to fight against Gideon Force and Ethiopian patriots, Wingate ordered a lull on the attack and then threatened to let the patriots storm into the fort and capture the Blackshirts. The Italians immediately surrendered when they were informed of the threat.

There can be no doubt that even without British intervention, the patriotic forces that already numbered about half a million by 1940, despite their initial lack of coordination, could have ultimately liberated Ethiopia from the Fascists. But the disintegration of the Italian army within a span of a few months was achieved partly through British and Commonwealth engagements at major Italian army concentrations at Amba Alage, Debre Markos, Dembidollo, Megga, and Keren, where aircraft, artillery, and tanks—not available to the Ethiopian guerrillas—were effectively employed.

A number of the British officers and civilians who participated in or watched the war at close quarters fully agree on one point: the patriotic struggle was crucial in bringing about a speedy Fascist defeat. But when one British author went to the extent of suggesting that it was the Ethiopians and not the United Kingdom who defeated the Italians in 1941, the remark rekindled the nationalistic pride of some members of the British government. Thus, Mr. Brendan Bracken, who was Minister of Information, speaking on behalf of Winston Churchill's ruling Conservative party in Britain commented:

> The author is trying to champion Ethiopia by blackening the name of this country. But I think that the record of British military achievement in Ethiopia and of our subsequent dealings with that country can stand up for themselves. This paper contains attacks on England which are worthy of Goebbels. It has insulted the British troops who have rescued Ethiopia, and in my opinion it is a poisonous rag. (Steer, 1942)

Notwithstanding the British official position, the defeat of the Italians in Ethiopia was in fact achieved mainly by the Ethiopian patriots. Sylvia Pankhurst (1960) states, "Throughout the campaign, the Patriots fought in the mountains; Generals Platt and Cunningham advanced by the roads from which they scarcely departed. Everywhere these Generals received Patriot support. A force of 200,000 Italians was destroyed, 40,000 were vanquished by the Emperor's army, 35,000 by other Patriot forces, 85,000 by General Platt, with . . . Patriot assistance, 40,000 by General Cunningham and Patriot assistance" (377). In any case, the end of occupation of Ethiopia with the intervention of the British did not mean—as many patriot leaders, particularly Belay Zelleke, had feared—the immediate independence of the country. It rather marked the beginning of a diplomatic tug of war between the negus and the United Kingdom, for no sooner had the total defeat of the Fascist forces in the Horn of Africa been achieved than British military commanders openly exhibited their ulterior motive:

they did not come in to help in the liberation of the country and then simply make an exit; they were there to stay.

THE HAILE SELASSIE PERIOD II: 1941–1974

After overcoming some British military personnel's initial ambitions to declare Ethiopia a British protectorate, Haile Selassie resumed the modernization of his feudal autocracy. He reopened the educational establishments the Fascists had closed down and built many new ones throughout the empire. Secondary schools were opened in the major cities of Addis Ababa and Harar. In 1950, the University College of Addis Ababa was opened to accommodate the graduates of the new academic high schools. This became the base around which the Haile Selassie I University (later renamed Addis Ababa University) was established at the palace the emperor donated. The university brought together the colleges of public health, agriculture, engineering, building, and theology. Other faculties and colleges were later added in the fields of medicine, education, law, social work, Ethiopian studies, and business administration.

Teaching hospitals were created to produce nurses and dressers for the hospitals and health centers established throughout the empire. Roads built by the Italians were expanded. A modern air force training center was opened, and one of the most successful crown corporations, Ethiopian Airlines, was established. A modern telecommunications center was opened. Economic development was taking place at a respectable rate of 4 percent, which was higher than for the rest of the African countries combined. Under Haile Selassie's leadership, Ethiopia became a founding member of the United Nations in 1945, and Eritrea was federated with its mother country in 1952 following a very successful diplomatic move at the United Nations. The world body was persuaded to station its Economic Commission for Africa in Addis Ababa. Using his stature as the eldest statesman of Africa, Haile Selassie also convinced the African leaders to choose Addis Ababa as the capital of the Organization of African Unity (later the African Union) at its founding in 1963.

Despite these commendable achievements, Haile Selassie refused to bring about the political reforms agitated for by the educated Ethiopians his modern school system had produced. Absentee landlords, the Church, and the royal family still controlled 90 percent of the land, and peasants paid up to 75 percent of their produce to their landlords. The bicameral parliament Haile Selassie instituted kept the Senate appointive (by him), with the Chamber of Deputies being elective. But the emperor still held veto power over the decisions of both. Furthermore, the Revised Constitution of 1955, far from limiting the power of the emperor, still referred to Haile Selassie's person as "sacred."

Haile Selassie also applied his policy of *shum-shir* (appoint-demote) against those who espoused rapid social and political reforms. He made them senators—a position with prestige but no authority—stationed them as ambassadors abroad far

away from domestic affairs, or even dismissed or incarcerated them if they were bold
enough to challenge the policies to which he had clearly committed himself.

THE STATUS OF THE EMPEROR
IN THE CONSTITUTION

The Constitution of 1931 simply reasserted the emperor's status as recognized by the
Ethiopian Orthodox Church and the age-old tradtion of the country. It reserved imperial succession to the line of Haile Selassie and declared in article 11 that "the person
of the emperor is sacred, his dignity inviolable, and his power indisputable." The revised constitution of 1955 did not revoke this: it simply reiterated it. The governmental
structure was tailored to hold institutions characteristic of modern Western-style states.
A prime minister was appointed by the emperor to manage the governmental process.

For all practical purposes, command over central and local government, the legislature, the judiciary, and the military remained with the Negus. As head of state
and government, Haile Selassie held supreme authority to conduct *shum-shir* to keep
control over the new nobility that kept the system going. He could declare war, state
of emergency, and martial law at will.

JAPANIZATION AND ETHIOPIA'S NEW
POLITICAL STRUCTURE

Japanization—which meant following the Japanese example in introducing Westernization to a feudal order—was launched at the urgings of the new political elite. In
Japan, power was centralized, but the Samurai group that constituted the mercan-
tile class enjoyed a high degree of respect from the populous even before the 1868
Meiji restoration; its members held prestige and power but did not hold property
in land because the Meiji land settlement had freed the peasants from servitude to
their landlords by compensating the latter with government bonds. Haile Selassie's
Ethiopia had, by contrast, no such class. The regional and local administrative units
remained archaic, and the purpose of the new parliament, which was not elected and
could therefore not claim popular representation, was to be a palliative for enlight-
ened despotism and centralization, not a source of delegation of authority, which is
a precondition for contemporary liberalism and civic society.

THE NATURE OF THE POLITICAL
SYSTEM AFTER 1941

Haile Selassie's modernization efforts were temporarily halted with the Fascist invasion of 1936 but were resumed after liberation in 1941. Starting in 1942, the emperor
sought to secure control over local government by placing it under a new centralized
administration. Following the rise to power of the Ethiopian People's Revolutionary Democratic Front (EPRDF) in 1991, the number of Waradas (districts) reached
600 (see table 2.1)

TABLE 2.1 Total Population of Ethiopia in Thousands by Region, Urban–Rural Divide, and Sex (Based On 2007 Population and Housing Census)

Kilil (State)	Urban			Rural			Male (Total)	Female (Total)	Male and Female (Total)
	Male	Female	Total	Male	Female	Total			
Tigray	440	452	892	1,811	1,862	3,673	2,251	2,314	4,565
Afar	76	61	137	727	585	1,312	803	646	1,449
Amara	1,203	1,205	2,408	8,857	8,871	17,728	10,060	10,076	20,136
Oromia	1,929	1,936	3,865	12,079	12,123	24,202	14,008	14,059	28,067
Somali	431	373	804	2,013	1,743	3,756	2,444	2,116	4,560
Benishangul-Gumuz	34	33	67	296	293	589	330	326	656
Southern Nations/ Nationalities and Peoples	697	704	1,401	7,134	7,210	14,344	7,831	7,914	15,745
Gambela	26	25	51	106	102	208	132	127	259
Harari	67	64	131	40	38	78	107	102	2,091
Addis Ababa City Administration	1,511	1,636	3,147	0	0	0	1,511	1,636	3,147
Dire Dawa City Administrative Council	161	161	322	53	53	106	214	214	428
Total	6,575	6,650	13,225	33,116	32,880	65,996	39,691	39,530	79,221

Source: Central Statistical Authority of Ethiopia, August 2008.

It is true that Haile Selassie did attempt to strengthen the national government by recruiting a new generation of educated Ethiopians who were put in key positions in the ministries with clear-cut job descriptions. Haile Selassie also instituted a new judicial system, but the judges were again directly appointed by him, did not enjoy political immunity during good behavior, and could be removed at will by imperial order.

THE REVISED CONSTITUTION AGAINST A BACKDROP OF A MODERNIZING FEUDALISM

After Eritrea was federated with Ethiopia in 1952, the emperor promulgated the Revised Constitution of 1955 in which the Senate remained appointive, but the Chamber of Deputies was elected. However, no proper census was taken, political parties were banned, 96 percent of the people were still illiterate, and the economic supremacy of the landed nobility in the countryside remained untouched. It was under these circumstances that the anti-feudal, frustrated educated youth, mostly students and teachers who could not channel their grievances in any other manner because there was no political party, instigated a Marxist revolutionary upheaval.

THE ABORTIVE COUP D'ÉTAT OF 1960

The abortive coup d'état of 1960 was instigated by Germame Niway, a graduate of Colombia University in New York. This was the first open challenge against the feudal regime—a prelude to the ancien régime's eventual downfall. By launching the coup while the emperor was on a state visit to Brazil, the rebels hoped to appease the conservative rural populous who could never imagine a challenge to a person they had known for long as "the Conquering Lion of the Tribe of Judah." General Mengistu Niway, the brother of Germame, forced the crown prince Asfa Wossan to read a proclamation castigating the Haile Selassie regime for all the ills of Ethiopia and proclaiming that he had ascended his father's throne as a constitutional monarch dedicated to the rule of law and justice.

But a loyalist army led by two prominent generals, Merid Mengesha and Kebede Gebre, ordered an attack against the rebellious Imperial Bodyguard. Intense fighting with armored vehicles, tanks, and mortars started to rage. The police commando known as *Fetno-Derash* under the command of General Tadesse Birrou joined the loyalists, increasing their chance for success. The fighting spread like wildfire until the city of Addis Ababa, from the airport to the imperial palace, had become a major battleground. Air force jets then swooped from the clear sky and showered machine gun fire on rebel headquarters. They also broke sound barriers to create noise to frighten the already demoralized body guard soldiers. The war was decisively won by the loyalists within three days of the start of the confrontation.

The battle was lopsided right from the start; 10,000 Imperial Bodyguard soldiers were pitted against the army's 30,000 men, backed by thousands of Fetno-Derash defectors from the police force. General Merid's loyalist soldiers also enjoyed air support that ultimately became crucial, because not only did the latter fight on the side of the national army—they also transported loyalist soldiers to the capital.

It is important to note that the Americans had played a key role in saving the Haile Selassie regime. Technical help was given to the loyalists by the U.S. Air Force and its international communications network. When he made a stopover in Liberia, the emperor used American facilities at Robertsfield Airport to contact his loyalists in the city of Asmara in Eritrea. And during the night, while Haile Selassie was flying back to Ethiopia via Khartoum, Sudan, his loyalists, flanked by American military advisers, were deployed in key positions around Addis Ababa, ready for an early morning attack on the dissidents.

U.S. advisers were with the army wherever they went and their air force attaché was at the airport helping to establish radio contact with the Imperial plane, which had just taken off from the American base of Fort Lamy. On his triumphant return to Addis Ababa, the emperor called over Arthur Richards and his two military attachés. He then "expressed sincere gratitude" to the people of the United States and its president. (Richards, SD 773.11/12-1760)

The emperor pardoned the crown prince but he was ruthless against those who led the abortive coup. Germame Niway, the leader of the rebellion, Workineh Gebeyehu and other Western-educated intellectuals such as Germame Wonders, who formed the leadership of the Revolutionary Council, committed suicide to avoid capture, but their bodies were brought by convoys of jeeps to the center of Addis Ababa, near Emperor Menelik's triumphal statue, and hanged to show Haile Selassie's resolve that he would not tolerate any such rebellion in the future. General Mengistu Niway, who was captured after receiving a bullet wound to the eye, was tried and hung at a church square in the marketplace. Other rebel officers, some dead and others alive, were also hanged, or their bodies strewn on park meadows for people to see. That was, in fact, the fate of the commander of the police force, General Tsige Dibu, who died fighting for the rebel cause.

To those who hoped that this bloody revolt would have a shock effect on the emperor and would induce him to bring about rapid reform including the abolition of feudal landownership, Haile Selassie's answer was the opposite. He announced to a group of British, American, and other foreign journalists, "there would not be the slightest deviation from the path we have followed in running Ethiopia . . . there will be no change in the system of Government or in the Government's programs"(*New York Times*, December 21, 1960).

The abortive 1960 coup d'état had sounded a clarion call for change. But Emperor Haile Selassie refused to implement reforms that even foreign advisers were urging him to adopt. This was to change 14 years later, due to unabated and continuous student upheavals and the revolt of the army.

THE ETHIOPIAN REVOLUTION OF 1974

The failure of the coup proved to be a pyrrhic victory for the Negus because student demonstrations demanding reform and political liberalization became even more intense. But Haile Selassie's failure to dismantle feudalism, rising inflation, corruption in high places, and famine that claimed the life of hundreds of thousands of peasants, but was concealed from the outside world, provided the backdrop against which the Ethiopian revolution of 1974 began to unfold. Teachers opposed to the World Bank sponsored the Education Sector Review, which recommended unpopular curriculum changes in the schools, and went on strike. Taxi drivers who could not absorb the steep increase in gasoline prices stopped their services to the public. Workers in the few factories that had been created since the liberation from fascism who were not allowed the right of collective bargaining went on strike. The military contingents in conflict areas such as Eritrea and Sidamo complained of maltreatment by governing authorities. They subsequently mutinied and arrested their officers. The latter, with other armed forces personnel, created a committee called the Derg and started to chart the political course of the country. This military committee appointed the Oxford-educated aristocrat Endalkatchew Mekonnen as prime minister, but he was removed within five months of taking office. Another Oxford-educated aristocrat, Mikael Emeru, was then appointed but was also removed to give way for a full-fledged military takeover of the country. Haile Selassie was then dethroned and was died mysteriously while under palace arrest.

THE DERG REGIME

The students and the teachers who spearheaded the revolution and their proletarian supporters could not form a government because they had no guns. So medium- and lower-ranking military officers saw a chance to fill the power vacuum that had suddenly emerged. In time, this group of officers became the Provisional Military Administrative Council (PMAC), referred to simply as the Derg which is an Ethiopic word for "committee."

The new junta assassinated Emperor Haile Selassie in 1975 and buried him in a secret grave on the palace grounds. Mengistu told his Derg colleagues that eliminating the monarch was a must because the loyalists could galvanize support against the revolt and ultimately eliminate them.

To purge the civil service of feudal and conservative elements, the military government sent many professional bureaucrats to the Soviet Union, Eastern Europe, and Cuba, where they received intensive ideological indoctrination. Civil servants were governed by a Stalinist-style *nomenklatura*, which meant that the government's political cadres had the dubious job of keeping secret files on all government functionaries. The Congress, which elected members of the central and standing committees, was invested with supreme authority to ratify whatever was decided by the higher bodies.

MENGISTU'S ASCENT

As the Derg progressed into the control of all levers of power, Majors Mengistu Haile Mariam and Atnafu Abate, who had been radicalized by progressive student

The Jubilee Palace of Emperor Haile Selassie built in 1955 to commemorate his 25th year of Imperial Rule. (Courtesy of Paulos Milkias.)

leaders, became chairman and vice chairman, respectively, of the PMAC. Not long after, Aman was assassinated. Aman was a committed Ethiopian nationalist, but his suggestion that the military cabal be reduced and the Eritrean war be solved politically rather than militarily, played into the hands of Mengistu, who was preparing to usurp the top position. Aman was subsequently assassinated by the Mengistu clique. Another high ranking general, Tafari Benti replaced Aman but was also assassinated. After that, Colonel Mengistu Haile Mariam assumed total military, administrative, and political control of Ethiopia.

After the Derg came to power, the Ethiopian students' primary slogan "land to the tiller of the soil" was implemented.

Though removing Haile Selassie gave the Derg a respite, civil war raged all over the country. In addition to the Eritrean Liberation Front, which had been active since 1961, many guerrilla bands were organized in Tigray, Gondar, Wallo, Ogaden, Bale, Wallaga, and other provinces.

RADICAL CIVILIAN PARTIES: WHITE AND RED TERROR

Although it subsequently abolished the monarchy, the road was not smooth for the Derg. A half-dozen Marxist parties, two of which were prominent—Ethiopian People's Revolutionary Party (EPRP) and MEISON (All Ethiopian Socialist Movement)—emerged to challenge its power. The EPRP was ruthlessly crushed during the time the Derg launched the Red Terror, which gave license to its followers to capture and kill the rebels. MEISON, led by Haile Fida, initially gave critical support to the Derg with the hope of ultimately taking over power, but when MEISON, in collaboration with the military had initially organized the *qebeles* (urban dwellers' associations) and peasant associations that decimated the EPRP, saw that the Derg, with Mengistu Haile Mariam at the helm, was trying to bypass it by sponsoring two Marxist parties known as Waz League and Sadad, it began to act independently and to influence the command of the newly mobilized peasant militia, which was created in response to Somalia's invasion of the Ogaden province and the ascendancy of Eritrean and Tigrayan insurgents (Eritrean Liberation Front and Tigray Liberation Front, respectively). MEISON'S move threatened the Derg's dominance of local governments throughout the country, whose leadership it had supplied unchallenged during the bloody encounter with the EPRP. Consequently, MEISON too was decimated, with its leaders killed in combat or executed after being captured.

In order to mollify the Soviets, who had been trying to cultivate the amalgamation of civilian Communist parties under the umbrella of MEISON, which was planned to act as a vanguard party, and fearing the dangers of a political vacuum that would be left as a result of the purging of MEISON, the Derg, in 1978, promoted the union of several Marxist-Leninist organizations into a single umbrella group called EMALEDEH (an acronym for the Amharic name, translated as the Union of Ethiopian Marxist-Leninist Organizations). The birth of EMALEDEH was the culmination of the Derg's victory in purging all its leftist opponents and consolidating state power. It had factions that competed for power and influence. The largest one, subsumed under the banner of "Seded," was socialist and Ethiopian nationalist in orientation and was led by Mengistu Haile Mariam.

As Mengistu positioned himself to monopolize power, many purges were aimed to unseat him. One was by the commando leader General Getachew Nadew, a failed attempt, and another was by captains Alemayehu Haile and Moges Haile Mikael, members of the military committee who used their position to remove Mengistu from the key position of the Derg. In this mini-*pustch*, they piled political prerogatives on the late Aman's successor, General Tafari Benti. Like with General Aman, the faction-ridden conspirators chose him to be a nonpartisan moderator of the military committee. The Alemayehu-Moges scheme was crushed by Mengistu and his loyalist security chief, Daniel. All the ringleaders, including General Tafari Banti, Alemayehu, and Moges, were summarily executed. At the top state governing level, the first victim of the purge conducted by Mengistu was the leader of Coordinating Committee of the Armed Forces, Police and Territorial Army, Colonel Alem Zewd Tesemma. Second was the highly popular Eritrean-born First Head of State General Aman Mikael Andom, who was proclaimed president. Third was Aman's replacement, General Tafari Benti.

This left a clean slate for Mengistu Haile Mariam. The last obstacle remaining was the group known as the Nius Derg Junior Derg, which controlled most political power outside the capital and became a parallel government. Colonel Mengistu Haile Mariam then assumed the key position of power in the Derg after that particular purge, which took place in 1977. From this time on, he went on to create a new power structure on the Soviet model—a chairman, a 16-member politburo (ruling cabinet), a 32-member Central Committee, and a Congress of the entire Derg membership. To perfect his Stalinist control, Mengistu had Captain Berhanu Kebede, an Ethiopian version of Beria (Stalin's security chief and henchman), head an interrogation team, torturing and killing any individual he fancied in the name of counter-revolutionary activity.

Mengistu then turned his attention to the civilian parties that were becoming obstacles to his goal of unchallenged control of the state. The IMALEDIH coalition of left-wing parties was dissolved. Even Colonel Mengistu's Seded, which had enjoyed state protection, was legally disbanded. Many of the leaders of these parties were executed. When Mengistu set out to create the Ethiopian Workers' Party, membership was individual, and loyalty to the dictator was the major criterion for acceptance. In fact, thereafter, Mengistu became the party itself.

GUERRILLA CHALLENGE

Parallel to Mengistu's rise to power and his ruthless methods of political control, the Eritrean Liberation forces that had been fighting for independence since 1961 galvanized support among the population of the province and intensified their attacks against the Ethiopian regime. Other liberation fronts arose and grew rapidly, two of which were crucial: one in Tigray, the Tigrayan People's Liberation Front, or TPLF; and the other in Oromoland, the Oromo Liberation Front, or OLF.

LAND TO THE TILLER AND
MASS ORGANIZATIONS

As noted previously, after the revolution, radical students' demand for "land to the tiller" was put into effect, and all lands, rural and urban, were nationalized and run by *gäbäré mahbärs* (peasant associations) and *qebeles*. The Derg also gave the *qebeles* and peasant association leaders the power to collect taxes. The law and order powers of the *qebeles* were expanded when Mengistu Haile Mariam, who by now had become the Derg's strongman, gave a directive for "free action," which meant they could extra-judicially kill government opponents. The new regime, which initially started with the slogan "Etiopia Teqdäm" ("Ethiopia First") and advocated *hebrätäsäbaw-inät* (socialism), came in contact with radical student leaders from Ethiopia and from abroad and immediately announced the ascendancy of a Marxist system or "scientific socialism" under the command of Mengistu Haile Mariam. It may be useful to note here that "scientific socialism" was first mentioned by Friedrich Engels to distinguish the doctrines that he and Karl Marx developed to show how societies move through several stages, including feudalism, until they usher in capitalism, which is inevitably destined to give way to socialism, where the absolute equality of citizens would be guaranteed.

ETHIOPIAN WORKERS' PARTY AND MARXIST POLITICAL STRUCTURE

To ensure Soviet bloc support, the Derg created the Commission to Organize the Party of the Workers of Ethiopia (COPWE), and at the commission's second Congress, on September 12, 1984, COPWE was replaced by a civilian communist party named the Workers' Party of Ethiopia (WPE).

Subsequent to its consolidation of power, the Derg devised a new national constitution that became instrumental in the birth of the People's Democratic Republic of Ethiopia (PDRE). The Constitution was promulgated on February 22, 1987, and the People's Democratic Republic of Ethiopia was proclaimed, after which the PMAC was formally abolished. As a Marxist-oriented party, the WPE now set its development within the framework of what was called the National Democratic Revolution Programme (PNDRP). The new constitution was literally a carbon copy of the 1917 Soviet constitution, except that it conferred extraordinary powers on the president (in this case, Mengistu Haile Mariam), who had succeeded the assassinated head of state, General Tafari Banti. This was in direct contrast to the Soviet system, which was characterized by regional federalism. The principal organs of state power at the local government level were regional *shangowoch* which were responsible primarily for executing the central government's proclamations and decrees.

The Workers' party was ostensibly mass-based, but in reality, more than half of the members of the politburo, the secretariat, and the central committee were military men. In regional administrations also, there were parallel appointments, one civilian and the other a Workers' party political cadre, the latter enjoying immense political influence. More than 50 percent of the Party Congress was also composed of military personnel. So for all practical purposes, the seemingly civilian Ethiopian Workers' Party served the Derg only as an instrument of political control. Such an unchallenged and overbearing stance enabled the military regime to transform the very structure of rural Ethiopia, which was home to 90 percent of the country's population.

It was clear to any political observer that because of the priorities of the regime, the country's resources were heavily drained by civil war, which continued to sap the economic vitality of the Ethiopian state.

CLOUT OF POLITICAL CADRES

On the general political landscape, there was a blurring of lines between party and state given that party cadres tended to interfere freely in the fields of administration and government policy. As an example, party operatives had major political and intelligence-gathering roles in the workplace.

Political cadres could audit the accounts of any government institution, mass organization, or private citizen.

THE RISE OF THE EPLF AND TPLF

After years of struggle, in early 1988, two Marxist-oriented insurgent groups, the Eritrean People's Liberation Front (EPLF), and the Tigrayan People's Liberation Front (TPLF), began to coordinate their attacks against the Derg. At this time of total desperation, the Derg's strongman, Mengistu Haile Mariam, who desired rapprochement with the West, announced the end of socialism.

THE END OF THE DERG AND THE BEGINNING OF A NEW ERA

Initially, Mengistu Haile Mariam had bragged that he would crush all the guerrilla bands that arose throughout the country with brute force. However, that was not to be. The insurgents got stronger and stronger as Mengistu got weaker and weaker. He began to blame others for his losses and to plot his personal survival. The fall of the Derg regime and the rise of the ruling EPRDF had actually become almost inevitable when the Soviets under Gorbachev told Mengistu Haile Mariam that they would not support the Derg any more because the Cold War was over, and a new policy of liberalization had been adopted by Moscow. Concerned officers then tried to stage a coup. But eavesdropping East German security personnel intercepted the plot and warned Mengistu about the danger that was looming. While Mengistu was away, his supporters successfully neutralized the conspiracy. Two hundred highly trained military officers were subsequently executed.

As this was unfolding in Addis Ababa and Asmara, the TPLF was busy creating an umbrella organization called the Ethiopian People's Democratic Revolutionary Front (EPDRF). It did so by bringing together major ethnic dissidents, with which they broke the back of the once-mighty 400,000-member army. The EPRDF took over Ethiopia in 1991. All major Derg leaders were soon arrested and jailed, but Mengistu fled to Zimbabwe before the rebels took over Addis Ababa. The EPRDF also allowed the Eritrean People's Liberation Front (EPLF), which had already oc-cupied Eritrea, to carry out a referendum and secede.

The EPRDF that took over the country promulgated a constitution with which nine ethnic regions were federated and given the right of secession after fulfilling certain conditions. True democracy was promised to the people of Ethiopia, as a result of which dozens of political parties registered with the national election board in order to take advantage of the promise.

To show its determination, the EPRDF ran national and regional elections from 1992 to 1995, all of which it won. The opposition charged that the ruling party won the elections through ballot rigging and intimidation. But in 2005, the EPRDF prom-ised donor nations that it would allow unfettered democratic elections. It even gave its rivals free campaign time on the government-controlled media. When the tallies came following the election, the national election board gave 63 percent of the seats to the EPRDF and 35 percent to the opposition parties. In Addis Ababa, the major opposition party, Kinijit, took all seats but one.

Soon, the EPRDF government charged opposition leaders who refused to take their seats with attempting to violently and illegally overthrow the elected govern-ment. Subsequently, all the major leaders of the opposition were arrested. The jailed opposition leaders were later given amnesty after they admitted to the charges and asked for pardon.

The once-promising opposition party Kinijit was broken up into four factions soon after its leaders were freed, but a new coalition under the name of Medrek emerged.

Ethiopian election results for 2010 were radically different from those of 2005 when the opposition garnered, even by the admission of the ruling party, about ⅓ of the seats in parliament and all but one in the capital city of Addis Ababa. By con-trast, the May 23, 2010 national election was won in a landslide by the incumbent EPRDF. The official figures, which angered the opposition parties, gave the ruling Ethiopian People's Revolutionary Democratic Front and allies 545 out of the 547 seats in parliament. Chairman of the National Electoral Board of Ethiopia, Merga Bekana, stated on June 21, 2010 that the "the board has approved the result unanimously." (Reuters, "Update 2-Ethiopia confirms win for ruling party," Jun 21, 2010.)

The European Union observation mission reported that the playing field for the 2010 election was not sufficiently balanced, leaning in favor of the ruling party in many areas. To these allegations Mr. Merga Bekana replied, "the election was peace-ful, credible, fair, free and democratic" (*Guardian*, June 21, 2010).

The coalition of eight opposition parties known as Medrek, which won only one seat and the smaller All Ethiopia Unity party, alleged widespread pre-poll intimida-tion and unfair polling practices carried out by the incumbent group. Nevertheless, both Ethiopia's supreme court and the national electoral board rejected calls from opposition parties to rerun the elections. Prime Minister Meles Zenawi has urged the international community and Ethiopian political opponents to recognize his party's overwhelming landslide election victory. In a conciliatory mood, he then told the opposition leaders that had lost the election that they would still be consulted on decisions of national concern.

REFERENCES

Abir, M. 1968. *Ethiopia: The Era of the Princes: The Challenge of Islam and the Re-Unification of the Christian Empire, 1769–1855*. New York: Praeger.

Al-Masudi and Ali ibn al-Husayn. 1841. "Meadows of Gold and Mines of Gems." Translated into English by Aloys Sprenger. El-Masudi's Historical Encyclopaeda, London: Allen.

Bahru, Zewde. 2001. *A History of Modern Ethiopia, 1855–1991*. Oxford: James Curry.

Bahru, Zewde. 2002. *Pioneers of Change in Ethiopia: The Reformist Intellectuals of the Early Twentieth Century*. Oxford: James Currey.

Barker, A. J. 1971. (1936). *Rape of Ethiopia*, 2nd ed. New York: Ballantine Books.

Barros, J. 1982. *Britain, Greece, and the Politics of Sanctions: Ethiopia, 1935–1936*. London: Swift Publishers.

Beckingham, C. F., and G. W. B. Huntingford, et al. 1967. *Some Records of Ethiopia, 1593–1646, Being Extracts from the History of High Ethiopia or Abassia*. Nendeln, Liechtenstein: Kraus Reprint.

Bekerie, Ayele. 1997. *Ethiopic, an African Writing System: Its History and Principles*. Lawrenceville, NJ: Red Sea Press.

Berhane Asfaw, W. Henry Gilbert, Tim D White, "Homo erectus, Homo ergaster, Homo cepranensis, and the Daka cranium." *Journal of Human Evolution*, Sep. 2003, Vol. 45 Issue 3, pp.1–5.

Berkeley, G. F. H. 1935. *The Campaign of Adowa and the Rise of Menelik*. London: Constable and Co.

Birkby, C. 1942. *It's a Long Way to Addis*. London: F. Muller.

British Library. 1899. *The Syriac Chronicle of Zachariah of Mitylene*. London: Methuen & Co.

Browder, Anthony. 1992. *Exploding the Myths: The Nile Valley Contributions to Civilization*. New York: Institute of Karmic Guidance.

Bruce, J., and C. F. Beckingham. 1964. *Travels to Discover the Source of the Nile*. New York: Horizon Press.

Budge, E. A. W. 1928. *A History of Ethiopia, Nubia and Abyssinia according to the Hieroglyphic Inscriptions of Egypt and Nubia, and the Ethiopian Chronicles*. London: Methuen.

Budge, E. A. W. 1932. *The Queen of Sheba and Her Only Son Menyelek I*. London: Oxford University Press.

Bunney, Sarah. 1994. "The fruits of walking on two legs." *New Scientist*, 143 (16).

Burstein, S. M. 1998. *Ancient African Civilizations: Kush and Axum*. Princeton, NJ: M. Wiener Publishers.

Cann, Rebecca L., Mark Stoneking, and Allan C. Wilson. 1987. "Mitochondrial DNA and Human Evolution." *Nature*, 325: 31–36.

Caquot, Andre and A. J. Drewes. 1955 "Les Monuments Re-cueillis a Maqalle (Tigrp)." *Annales d'Lthiopie*, 1: 18–26.

Di Lauro, Rafaei. 1949. *Come abbiamo difeso l'Impero*. Roma: Ed. L'Arnia.

Diodorus Siculus. 1653. *The History of Diodorus Siculus. Containing All that Is Most Memorable and of Greatest Antiquity in the First Ages of the World until the War of Troy*. London: John Macock.

Donham, D. L., W. James, et al. 1986. *The Southern Marches of Imperial Ethiopia: Essays in History and Social Anthropology*. Cambridge: Cambridge University Press.

Drewes, Abraham, and Roger Schneider. 1967. "Documnts epigraphiques de l'Ethiopie." *Annales d'Ethiopie*, 7: 89–102.

Fattovich, R. 1988. "Remarks on the Late Prehistory and Early History of Northern Ethiopia." *Proceedings of the 8th International Conference on Ethiopian Studies*. Addis Ababa: Institute of Ethiopian Studies, 85–104.

Fattovich, R. 2000. *The Aksum Archaeological Area: A Preliminary Assessment*. Napoli: Istituto universitario orientale, Centro interdipartimentale di servizi per l'archeologia.

Finneran, N. 2007. *The Archaeology of Ethiopia*. London; New York: Routledge.

Gadaa, M. 1999. *Oromia: An Introduction to the History of the Oromo People*. Minneapolis, MN: Kirk House Publishers.

Gebru, Tareke. 1991. *Ethiopia: Power and Protest: Peasant Revolts in the Twentieth Century*. Cambridge, MA: Cambridge University Press.

Gee, Henry. 1993. "Why We Still Love Lucy." *Nature*, 366 (6452): 207.

Gilkes, Patrick. 1975. *The Dying Lion: Feudalism and Modernization in Ethiopia*. New York: St. Martins Martin's Press.

Glover, M. 1987. *An Improvised War: The Ethiopian Campaign, 1940–1941*. London: L. Cooper.

Gould, Stephen Jay. 1992. "Eve and Her Tree." *Discover*, July, 1992.

Government of the United Kingdom. 1895–1896. *The Abyssinian Campaign*. London: Government Printing Press.

Greenfield, Richard. 1965. *Ethiopia: A New Political History*. London: Pall Mall Publishers.

Gruber, R. 1987. *Rescue: The Exodus of the Ethiopian Jews*. New York: Atheneum.

Guardian, "Ethiopian electoral board confirms PM Meles Zenawi's landslide poll victory" June 21, 2010.

Gutner, H. 2002. *Aksum: Crossroads of Ethiopia*. New York: McGraw-Hill.

Haile Selassie. 1976. *My Life and Ethiopia's Progress, 1892–1937: The Autobiography of Emperor Haile Sellassie Selassie I*. Translated by Edward Ullendorff. Oxford, England: Oxford University Press.

Haile Selassie. 1994. *My Life and Ethiopia's Progress. Vol. 2*. Translated by H.G. Marcus, et al. *Addis Abeba, 1966 E.C.* East Lansing: Michigan State University Press.

Halliday, F., and M. Molyneux. 1981. *The Ethiopian Revolution*. London: NLB.

Hammond, J. 1999. *Fire from the Ashes: A Chronicle of the Revolution in Tigray, Ethiopia, 1975–1991*. Lawrenceville, NJ: Red Sea Press.

Hansberry, W. L., and J. E. Harris. 1974. *Pillars in Ethiopian History*. Washington, DC: Howard University Press.

Hassen, M. 1990. *The Oromo of Ethiopia: A History, 1570–1860*. Cambridge, MA: Cambridge University Press.

Heliodorus and N. Tate. 1686. *The Æthiopian History of Heliodorus: In Ten Books*. London: J. L. for E. Poole.

Hess, R. L. 1970. *Ethiopia: The Modernization of Autocracy*. Ithaca, NY: Cornell University Press.

Holden, Constance. 1997. "The First Tool Kit." *Science*, January 31, 1997: p. 623.

Hoskins, G. A. 1835. *Travels in Ethiopia, Above the Second Cataract of the Nile.* London: Longman, Rees, Orme, Brown, Green, & Longman.

Hudaud al-aalam. 1980. *The Regions of the World: A Persian Geography.* Karachi: Indus Publications.

Huggins, W. N., and J. G. Jackson. 1937. *An Introduction to African Civilizations, with Main Currents in Ethiopian History.* New York: Avon House.

Huntingford, G. W. B. 1955. *The Galla of Ethiopia: The Kingdoms of Kafa and Janjero.* London: International African Institute.

Huntingford, G. W. B., P. Paez, et al. 1965. *The Glorious Victories of Amda Seyon, King of Ethiopia.* Oxford: Clarendon Press.

Ishaq, I. 1995. *The Life of Mohammed, a Translation of Ishaq's Sirat Rasul Allah with Introduction and Notes by a Guillaume.* London: University Press.

Jackson, D. R. 2007. *Jimmy Carter and the Horn of Africa: Cold War Policy in Ethiopia and Somalia.* Jefferson: McFarland & Co.

Jackson, J. G. 1939. *Ethiopia and the Origin of Civilization.* New York: Blyden Society.

James, Peter, and Nick Thorpe. 1994. *Ancient Inventions.* New York: Ballantine Books.

Jenkins, E. 1995. *A Glorious Past: Ancient Egypt, Ethiopia, and Nubia.* New York: Chelsea House Publishers.

Jesman, C. A. 1963. *The Ethiopian Paradox.* New York: Oxford University Press.

Johanson, D. C., and H. B. S. Cooke. 1978. *A New Species of the Genus Australopithecus Primates, Hominidae from the Pliocene of Eastern Africa.* Cleveland: Cleveland Museum of Natural History.

Johnson, S., and R. W. Chapman. 1927. *The History of Rasselas, Prince of Abyssinia, a Tale.* Oxford: The Clarendon Press.

Kebede, M. 2008. *Radicalism and Cultural Dislocation in Ethiopia, 1960–1974.* Rochester, NY: University of Rochester Press.

Keller, E. J. 1988. *Revolutionary Ethiopia: From Empire to People's Republic.* Bloomington: Indiana University Press.

Kendie, D. 2005. *The Five Dimensions of the Eritrean Conflict, 1941–2004: Deciphering the Geo-Political Puzzle.* Prairie View, TX: Daniel Kendie.

Kessler, D. 1996. *The Falashas: A Short History of the Ethiopian Jews.* London: Frank Cass.

Khalidi, T. 1975. *Islamic Historiography: The Histories of al-Mas'udi.* Albany: State University of New York.

Kiflu, T. 1993. *The Generation: The History of the Ethiopian People's Revolutionary Party.* Lanham, MD: University Press of America.

League of Nations. 1935. *Dispute between Ethiopia and Italy.* Geneva: League of Nations Publications.

Lefort, R. 1983. *Ethiopia: A Heretical Revolution?* London: Zed Press.

Lewis, H. S. 2001. *Jimma Abba Jifar, an Oromo Monarchy: Ethiopia, 1830–1932.* Lawrenceville, NJ: Red Sea Press.

Lobo, J., J. Le Grand, et al. 1735. *A Voyage to Abyssinia.* London: A. Bettesworth, and C. Hitch.

Lord, E. 1970. *Queen of Sheba's Heirs; Cultural Patterns of Ethiopia*. Washington, DC: Acropolis Books.

Lupke, T. V., D. Krencker, et al. 1997. *The Monuments of Aksum: An Illustrated Account*. Addis Ababa, Ethiopia: Addis Ababa University Press and in collaboration with the British Institute in Eastern Africa.

MacDonald, J. F. 1957. *Abyssinian Adventure*. London: Cassell & Company.

Mann, K. 1997. *Egypt, Kush, Aksum: Northeast Africa*. Parsippany, NJ: Dillon Press.

Marcus, H. G. 1975. *The Life and Times of Menelik II: Ethiopia 1844–1913*. Oxford: Clarendon Press.

Marcus, H. G. 1994. *A History of Ethiopia*. Berkeley: University of California Press.

Marcus, H. G. 1995. *Haile Sellassie Selassie I: The Formative Years, 1892–1936*. Lawrenceville, NJ: Red Sea Press.

Marcus, H. G. 1995. *The Politics of Empire: Ethiopia, Great Britain, and the United States, 1941–1974*. Lawrenceville, NJ: Red Sea Press.

Markakis, J., and A. Nega. 1978. *Class and Revolution in Ethiopia*. Nottingham: Spokesman Books.

Markham, C. R., and W. F. Prideaux. 1869. *A History of the Abyssinian Expedition*. London: Macmillan.

Marta Gabre-Tsadik, Marta. 1983. *Sheltered by the King*. Lincoln, VA: Chosen Books.

Medhane, T. 1999. *The Eritrean-Ethiopian War: Retrospect and Prospects: Reflections on the Making of Conflicts in the Horn of Africa, 1991–1998*. Addis Ababa, Ethiopia: Mega Printing.

Merera, G. 2003. *Ethiopia: Competing Ethnic Nationalisms and the Quest for Democracy, 1960–2000*. Addis Ababa, Ethiopia: Shaker Pub.

Michels, J. 1988. "Regional Political Organization in the Aksum-Yeha Area during the Pre-Axumite and Axumite Era." Paper read at the 10th International Conference of Ethiopian Studies, Paris.

Milkias, P. 2006. *Haile Selassie, Western Education, and Political Revolution in Ethiopia*. Youngstown, NY: Cambria Press.

Milkias, P., and M. Getachew. 2005. *The Battle of Adwa: Reflections on Ethiopia's Historic Victory against European Colonialism*. New York: Algora Pub.

Mockler, Anthony. 1984. *Haile Selassie's War*. Oxford: Oxford University Press.

Moran, J. H., A. Gode, et al. 1986. *On the Origin of Language*. Chicago, University of Chicago Press.

Munro-Hay, S. C. 1991. *Aksum: An African Civilization of Late Antiquity*. Edinburgh: Edinburgh University Press.

Munro-Hay, S. C. 2002. *Ethiopia, the Unknown Land: A Cultural and Historical Guide*. London; New York: I. B. Tauris.

Munro-Hay, S. C. 2005. *The Quest for the Ark of the Covenant: The True History of the Tablets of Moses*. London: I. B. Tauris.

Nallino, Carlo Alfonso. 1907. *Racolta di Scriti editi e inediti*, Maria Nallino (ed.), vol. 20. Roma: Instituto per l'Oriente.

Nartey, J. S. N. 1989. *Brief History of Egypt, the Sudan and Ethiopia: The Nineteenth Century*. Legon, NY: L. Cooper.

Neville, E. 1906. *The Tomb of Hotshopsitu: Her Life and Monuments*. London: Methuen.

Ottaway, M., and David Ottaway. 1978. *Ethiopia: Empire in Revolution*. New York: Africana.

Paez, P. 1905. *Historia Aethiopiae*. Romae: Excudebat C. de Luigi.

Pankhurst, E. S. 1955. *Ethiopia: A Cultural History*. Essex, England: Lalibela House.

Pankhurst, E. S. 1960. "The Genesis of the Italo-Ethiopian War, 1935–41." *Ethiopia Observer*, 3(12): 377–388.

Pankhurst, R. 1965. *Travelers in Ethiopia*. London: Oxford University Press.

Pankhurst, R. 1967a. *A Brief Note on the Economic History of Ethiopia from 1800 to 1935*. Addis Ababa, Ethiopia: Haile Selassie I University.

Pankhurst, R. 1967b. *The Ethiopian Royal Chronicles*, [extracts]. Addis Ababa, Ethiopia: Oxford University Press.

Pankhurst R. 1969. "The Ethiopian Patriots and the Collapse of Italian Rule in East Africa, 1940–1941." *Ethiopia Observer*, 12(2): 92–127.

Pankhurst, R. 2001. *The Ethiopians: A History*. Oxford: Blackwell Publishers.

Pankhurst, Richard. 1998. "The Patriotic Resistance." London: Blackwell, 1998.

Peters, G. 1986. *Antiquités*. Vol. 2, 2, 30.

Phillips, Jack. 1997. "Punt and Axum: Egypt and the Horn of Africa." *Journal of African History*. 37: 423–457.

Phillipson, D. W. 1998. *Ancient Ethiopia: Aksum, Its Antecedents and Successors*. London: British Museum Press.

Pierotti, F. 1959. *Vita in Etiopia 1940–41*. Bologna: Capelli.

Prouty, C. 1986. *Empress Taytu and Menelek II: Ethiopia, 1883–1910*. Trenton, NJ: Red Sea Press.

Quintana-Murci, Luis Omella Semino, Hans J. Bandelt, Giuseppe Passarino, Ken McElreavey, and A. Silvana Santachiara-Benerecetti. 1999. "Scientific Commons." *Genetics*. 23(4): 437, 451.

Rey, C. F. 1924. *Unconquered Abyssinia as It Is To-day*. Philadelphia: Lippincott.

Rey, C. F. 1929. *The Romance of the Portuguese in Abyssinia, an Account of the Adventurous Journeys of the Portuguese to the Empire of Prester John; Their Assistance to Ethiopia in Its Struggle against Islam and Their Subsequent Efforts to Impose Their Own Influence and Religion, 1490–1633*. London: H. F. & G. Witherby.

Rubenson, S. 1976. *The Survival of Ethiopian Independence*. London: Heinemann.

Russell, M. 1837. *Nubia and Abyssinia: Comprehending Their Civil History, Antiquities, Arts, Religion, Literature, and Natural History*. New York: Harper & Brothers.

Salt, H., and J. Bower. 1816. *A Voyage to Abyssinia, and Travels into the Interior of That Country*. London: Cass Library of African Studies.

Samatar, Said S. 1992. *In the Shadow of Conquest: Islam in Colonial Northeast Africa*. Trenton, NJ: Red Sea Press.

Scheffer, Brigette. 1995. "Dark as Hell, Strong as Death, Sweet as Love—How Coffee Conquered the World." *New Internationalist* (271): 22, 2p, 1 cartoon. AN 9510114707.

Sergew Hable, Selassie. 1972. *Ancient and Medieval Ethiopian History to 1270*. Addis Ababa, Ethiopia: United Printers.

Sergius, Moberg Axel. 1924. *The Book of the Himyarites*. Lund, Sweden: C. W. K. Gleerap.

Shinn, D. H., T. P. Ofcansky, et al. 2004. *Historical Dictionary of Ethiopia*. Lanham, MD: Scarecrow Press.

Spencer, J. H. 1984. *Ethiopia at Bay: A Personal Account of the Haile Selllassie Years*. Algonac, MI: Reference Publications.

Steer, G. L. 1942. *Sealed and Delivered: A Book on the Abyssinian Campaign*. London: Hodder and Stoughton.

Stoneking, Mark. 1994. "In Defense of 'Eve'—A Response to Templeton's Critique." *American Anthropologist* 96(1): 131–141.

Stringer, Chris. 2003. "Out of Africa" *Nature*. 423(6941): 4, 692.

Sykes, C. 1959. *Orde Wingate: A Biography*. London: Collins.

Tabarăi, Donner, and Fred McGraw. 1993. *The Conquest of Arabia*. Albany: State University of New York Press.

Taddesse Macha. 1950. *Tekur Anbessa*. Asmara: Commercial Printing Press.

Taddesse Tamirat. 1972. *Church and State in Ethiopia, 1270–1527*. Oxford: Clarendon Press.

Tiruneh, A. 1993. *The Ethiopian Revolution, 1974–1987: A Transformation from an Aristocratic to a Totalitarian Autocracy*. Cambridge, MA: Cambridge University Press.

Tubiana, J. 1980. "Modern Ethiopia: From the Accession of Menilek II to the Present." Proceedings of the Fifth International Conference of Ethiopian Studies, Nice, France, December 19–22, 1977.

Ullendorff, E. 1968. *Ethiopia and the Bible*. London: Oxford University Press.

Ullendorff, Edward. 1973. *The Ethiopians: An Introduction to Country and People*. Oxford: Oxford University Press.

U.S. Ambassador to Secretary of State, 1960. Monrovia, December 15, 1960, SD 775.11/12–1560.

Valdes Vivó, R. 1978. *Ethiopia's Revolution*. New York: International Publishers.

Vestal, T. M. 1999. *Ethiopia: A Post–Cold War African State*. Westport, CT: Praeger.

Weld-Blundell, H. J. 1922. *The Royal Chronicle of Abyssinia, 1769–1840*. Cambridge: Cambridge University Press.

Wilford, John Noble. 1995. "Believers in African Eve Think They Have Found Adam's." *New York Times* 26 May 1995.

Ydlibi, M. 2006. *With Ethiopian Rulers: A Biography of Hasib Ydlibi*. Addis Ababa, Ethiopia: Addis Ababa University Press.

Young, J. 1997. *Peasant Revolution in Ethiopia: The Tigray People's Liberation Front, 1975–1991*. Cambridge, MA: Cambridge University Press.

Zewde Gabra-Selassie. 1975. *Yohannes IV of Ethiopia: A Political Biography*. Oxford: Oxford University Press.

Zewde Gabre-Selassie. 1976. *Eritrea and Ethiopia in the Context of the Red Sea and Africa*. Washington, DC: Woodrow Wilson International Center for Scholars.

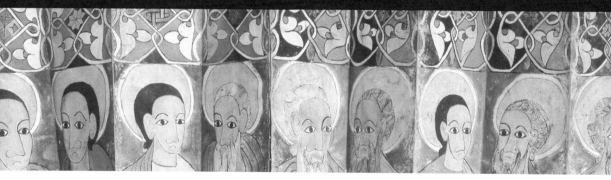

CHAPTER 3

Government and Politics

RISE OF THE RULING EPRDF

At the end of the 1980s when Mengistu's government was on the verge of collapse, the people who reviled the Derg did not put up any resistance to the march of the northern insurgents toward victory. The handpicked officers Mengistu relied on were totally inept, and demoralized soldiers threw down their guns; all flocked back to their places of origin. At that stage, the Ethiopian military dictator's power was so hopelessly corroded that there was no hope for renewal.

The Tigrayan People's Liberation Front (TPLF) moved quickly to develop a united front with the Ethiopian People's Democratic Movement (EPDM), a break-away organization of the Ethiopian People's Revolutionary Party (EPRP) consti-tuted mainly of Amharas from Gondar, Wallo, and northern Shoa. The TPLF also brought together military captives of Oromo lineage from the war with the Derg, and together with defectors form the Oromo Liberation Front (OLF), it created the Oromo People's Democratic Organization (OPDO) to claim legitimacy in Oro-mia. Later, the Southern Ethiopia People's Democratic Front (SEPDF) was added in order to expand into southern Ethiopian territories that were not populated by Oromos or Somalis. This umbrella political party was named the Ethiopian People's Revolutionary Democratic Front (EPRDF).

The EPRDF led by the TPLF continued to advance, and the EPRDF thrust drove the leaderless and demoralized central government forces from their strategic positions. At every stage of its campaign, the EPRDF's victory was so complete that the organization found it impossible to consolidate the areas it occupied for the purpose of instituting viable political structures. Within a span of six weeks, the

EPRDF wounded or captured close to 20,000 government troops and seized immense amounts of Soviet-supplied military equipment. This was facilitated in part by defections from the Derg on account of Mengistu Haile Mariam's execution of officers and men under the advice of his loyal agents and politically charged but militarily incompetent cadres, which had taken control of the conduct of the war from skilled officers. The EPRDF augmented its military capacities by amalgamating the turncoats into its own army. Soon, it expanded from Tigray, and the entire provinces of Wallo, Gondar, and Gojam; northern Shoa; and parts of Wallaga were in EPRDF's fold—Addis Ababa was ultimately surrounded.

Not waiting until the EPRDF had consolidated its control throughout the country, and seeing the weakness of the crumbling military regime, the peasantry had in the meantime abandoned the newly created villages for their old homesteads; they dismantled cooperatives and redistributed all capital goods as well as land. They drove out or disregarded party and government functionaries and in many cases took the law into their own hands and executed recalcitrant administrators.

Mengistu fled to Zimbabwe to save his skin. His replacement, General Tesfaye Gebre Kidan, called on the Ethiopian soldiers to lay down their arms and surrender to the EPRDF. He then took political asylum in the Italian embassy, where he later died. Addis Ababa thus fell without much resistance and bloodshed. Meles Zenawi,

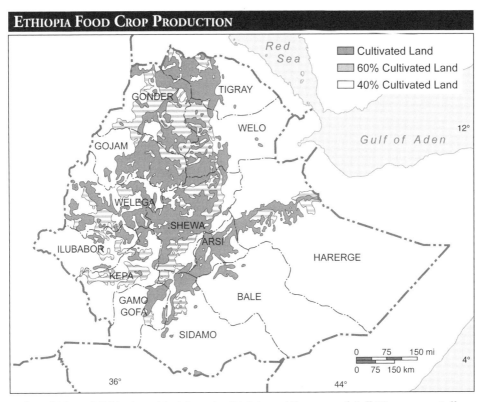

Political Map of Ethiopia—Administrative Divisions. (Courtesy of Jeff Dixon, www.jeff dixon.ca.)

who was the leader of both the TPLF and the EPRDF, then became the head of the newly established political order in Ethiopia.

THE GOVERNING TEAM

President in 2010: Girma Wolde Giorgis

Prime Minister in 2010: Meles Zenawi

The ruling party of Ethiopia, the EPRDF, is made up of three ethnic entities and one multiethnic entity. The ethnic entities are the Tigrayan People's Liberation Front, the Amhara National Democratic Movement (ANDM), the Oromo People's Democratic Organization (OPDO), and the multiethnic entity is the Southern Ethiopia People's Democratic Front (SEPDF), comprising 46 linguistic groups from southern Ethiopia. The power structure within the EPRDF stipulates that there should be equal votes for all four constituents of the umbrella organization. This is at both the

Prime Minister Meles Zenawi of Ethiopia. (Reuters/Bettmann/ Corbis.)

politburo and central committee levels, which constitute the highest political order of the governing team. The EPRDF is also the one in control of EPRDF-allied ruling parties in the remaining five *kilils*, namely Benishangul-Gumuz, Gambela, Afar, Somali, and Harari.

When the ruling party came to power, it announced the dawn of a new liberal political order. At first, a transitional government that pledged to entrench free and open elections, as well as guarantee fundamental human rights and press freedom, was set up. It is important to note that these rights were never respected under any of the previous regimes. From that point on, the task was forging a political formula that would be suitable to the rebel forces that had come to power and a plethora of political groupings that had suddenly emerged.

Though the ideological and ethnic differences among this political cluster were paramount, the government aimed to forge a long-lasting political framework that would be acceptable to all. The apparent danger, however, was that if this pragmatic formula failed to work, the country might implode and catapult Ethiopia toward an ethnic quagmire.

The democratic order that was put in place began with the adoption of a provisional charter in London in July 1991 and the subsequent establishment of the Transitional Government of Ethiopia (TGE), forged by the *primus inter pares* party, the EPRDF, the Eritrean and Oromo Liberation Fronts, and about 20 other ethnic-based organizations and political factions. However, tensions soon grew. The Oromo Liberation Front, representing an estimated 50 percent of the people of Ethiopia, exhibited the fear that the minority TPLF, representing some 6 percent of the population, might dominate political power indefinitely. After the carving up of the country into ethnic regions and the adoption of a new constitution, it found the political space getting narrower and narrower because of competition in Oromia with the OPDO, which had state support, and it withdrew from the government and started armed struggle all over again.

ETHNIC FEDERALISM

At the time a new federal structure was launched in 1994, Ethiopia was home to 84 linguistic groups. Of these, the two major ethnic assemblages, the Oromos (up to 50%) and the Amharas (35%), together represented about 75 percent of the total population of the country. Whereas the Oromos are mostly settled farmers but also have pastoralists among them, particularly in areas such as Borana, the Amhara are sedentary agriculturalists living mostly on the central plateau. The Somalis of Ethiopia, who live predominantly in the Ogaden region, are pastoralists and are numerically fourth. But Tigray, originally the center of Ethiopian civilization and with a population of only 6 percent of the total Ethiopian population, had suddenly come to dominate political power. The four ethnic groups—the Oromos, the Amharas, the Tigres, and the Somalis—constituted more than three-fourths of the population of the country.

Three other ethnic nationalities, the Sidama, the Gurage, and the Walaita, had a population of over 1 million each at the time the ethnic federal structure was put in place. Of the three, the Gurage are known for being business-oriented. In terms of demographic dispersion, the Walaita have the highest population density. The seven largest ethnic groups now constitute over 85 percent of the country's population.

Five ethnic nationalities, the Afar, Hadiya, Garno, Gedeo, and Kaffa, have between 599,000 and 1,000,000 people each. Including them, the 12 largest ethnic groups represent almost 95 percent of the people of Ethiopia.

Fourteen linguistic groups have populations ranging between 100,000 and 500,000. Twenty-eight others had a population of between 10,000 and 100,000. Twenty-three linguistic groups had a population of less than 10,000 each.

When the centralized authoritarian system under the Derg crumbled, it became clear that the centralist unitary approach to governing Ethiopia, which used coercion in controlling power and advanced a policy of assimilation, had failed inexorably. Many felt that that there should be a new approach to the country's ethnic and regional differences. But this did not mean a return to politics as it existed during the Zemene Mesafint (Era of the Princes). Thus, in July 1991, the EPRDF, with the cooperation of its surrogate fronts, the Amhara National Democratic Movement (ANDM) and the Oromo People's Democratic Organization (OPDO), prepared a national conference in which 12 divergent political factions with 400 delegates met and discussed major issues confronting the new order. The delegates prepared a provisional charter and a provisional government led by the EPRDF. At this time, there were 65 parties competing nationally and locally.

The transitional government fulfilled the charter's provisions by immediately recognizing the absolute right of all nations, nationalities, and people throughout the country to self-determination, which included the rights to self-governance and cultural and political autonomy. The charter guaranteed commitment to the protection of human rights. It explicitly prohibited inhumane treatment, proscribed the right of a person arrested to be brought before a court within 48 hours, and guaranteed freedom of religion, the right of equality and privacy, the right of assembly, and freedom of association, as well as the basic rights of women. It recognized the right to political organizations to function without obstruction.

By the time the provisional government was put in place, 65 political parties had started to compete. On December 8, 1994, a constitution that guaranteed all of the preceding was promulgated. According to the new constitution, a 550-member Council of Peoples' Representatives was to be elected from legally prescribed electoral districts based on the size of the population. It also established in article 54 that 20 (later increased to 22) of the seats would be reserved for minority nations and nationalities.

The creation of a federal arrangement involving a newly demarcated and largely ethnic-based 11 regions—namely Tigray, Afar, Amhara, Oromia, Somali, Benishangul/Gumaz, Southern Nations, Gambela, and Harari, together with the capital city of Addis Ababa and the major southeastern city of Dire Dawa, which form separate administrative units—also meant that the highly centralized system of political rule was now over.

By 2010, the 9 ethnic states were further divided into 63 zones, which are in turn subdivided into 529 *woredas* (districts). However, there are five "special woredas" listed under the Southern Nations, Nationalities, and Peoples area that do not belong to any grouping. Also, the Harari region and Dire Dawa administrative districts were not allocated zones.

The experiment put in place by the EPRDF has both strong supporters and strong opponents. Supporters argue that the problem of ethnic relations in the age-old Ethiopian empire had already reached a point of no return because the submerged ethnic complaints of those who felt they were oppressed had started a plethora of liberation movements, chief among them the Oromo Liberation Front, representing up to 50 percent of the population of the country. This information points to the possibility that the country was already on the way to implosion along ethnic lines. Thus, supporters suggest that even if the policy looked dangerous at first, it was the only one that could mollify those with grievances who had to be brought aboard in order to save the far-flung realm before it was too late.

The fact that ethnic-based liberation movements that were waging guerrilla war had been transformed into political parties ready to work with their counterparts was given as an example of this strategy's success. Furthermore, it was pointed out that the annual military expenditures of the central government had gone down from 44 percent during the time of the Derg to less than 20 percent by 1995; this was considered a dividend of the new ethnic policy of the EPRDF (Ethiopia, Statistical

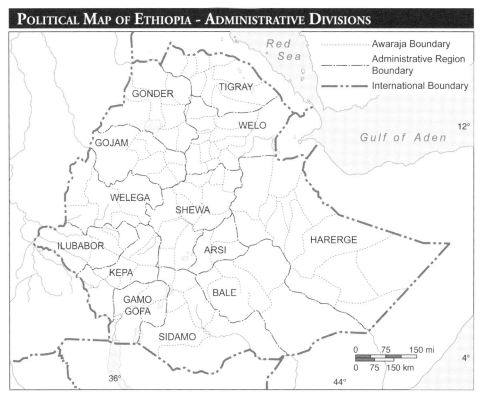

State Zones of Ethiopia. (Courtesy of Jeff Dixon, www.jeffdixon.ca.)

Abstract, 1995). Overall, economic growth in 1995–1996, when the policy was adopted, rose from negative growth in the last days of the military rule to 7.4 percent. This, it is claimed, is a spin-off from the ethnic harmony that emerged from the new type of linguistic pluralism.

In the economic sphere, as supporters point out, big strides have been made because of the proper policies put forward by the EPRDF. The government has implemented far-reaching liberalization programs. In line with the recommendations of the International Monetary Fund and the World Bank, it has devalued the birr, the national currency, in order to combat black-market currency trade. It has decontrolled most retail prices in addition to reducing import barriers.

The Ethiopian constitution of 1995 established a federal republic comprised of six regional states carved out on the basis of predominant ethnic groups, and one in the south with 46 linguistic groups. It also includes the urban areas of the capital, Addis Ababa and Dire Dawa. In Article 39, the constitution stipulated: "Every nation, nationality and people shall have the unrestricted right to self-determination up to secession." The act of secession is not automatic. It requires a two-thirds vote in the legislature of the seceding state to be followed three years later by a popular referendum of the secession-seeking region. Once a majority is garnered in the state, there is no requirement of getting approval from the federal legislature. It is argued by supporters of the present arrangement in the constitution that the right of secession has become a safety valve that averts the possibility of reverting back to cultural domination. The fact that no ethnic party has so far tried to invoke the secession clause has been pointed out by EPRDF supporters as a sign of success of the present policy.

Right from the beginning, opposition to this policy was widespread. Some scholars have actually called the experiment oxymoronic. Others who do support devolution even on an ethnic basis look at the TPLF's agenda with suspicion. Some suggest that the EPRDF, which is the umbrella organization of the TPLF, put the ethnic structure in place not because it intended to allow the people to practice democracy freely, considering that in practice it has suppressed organizations such as the OLF and the WSLF while keeping surrogates such as the OPDO that form a branch of the EPRDF.

Opponents argue that ethnic-based federalism is too drastic a formula to solve Ethiopia's need to dismantle the centralization that characterized the system under both the feudal regime and the Derg. Though they admit that addressing the problem of ethnicity is paramount, they question the EPRDF's level of commitment to protect Ethiopia's national interests. They argue that the government's first action of allowing Eritrea to secede following a referendum has made Ethiopia the largest land-locked country in the world. Even after winning the 1998–2000 war that was started by the Eritrean government, the EPRDF did not reoccupy the port of Asab for Ethiopia. This, in opponents' view, proved that the country's leaders do not have commitment to the country's long-range national interests.

The opposition fears that the EPRDF's ongoing policy may pave the way for ultimate implosion of the country under the pressure of conflict-ridden ethnicity. Thus, they vehemently criticize the ethnic policy, claiming that it simply revived

Mussolini's ethnically oriented reorganization of Ethiopia during the 1936–1941 occupation and that it is a ticking bomb that may railroad the country toward eventual balkanization.

Opponents argue that the changes announced by the ruling party are in fact window dressing and have no real depth because everything done so far has been aimed at entrenching the rule of the EPRDF led by the TPLF. Though the 1992 regional and 1994 general elections allegedly were intended to allow voters to freely choose members of a Constituent Assembly to debate and ratify a new constitution, the intimidation and harassment from government underlings forced major opposition parties to withdraw from competition, claiming that their rights were flagrantly violated by the provisional government led by the EPRDF. The groups that withdrew from the election were heavyweights such as a coalition of southern parties, the OLF, and the All Amhara People's Organization (AAPO), the three of them claiming to speak for some 90 percent of the total population of the country.

The opposition admits that Meles Zenawi's government may find solace in the fact that the country has so far remained federally united; however, they say the implosion of the once-mighty Soviet Union, from which the formula of the right of secession was borrowed, must give one pause for thought. Dangers may arise, they argue, if following the fall of the EPRDF as a monolithic organization, parties sympathetic to separatism come to power at the federal and regional levels at the same time.

CONSTITUTION AND THE FEDERAL STRUCTURE

It is clear that the political name enshrined in the Constitution of 1994, "the Federal Democratic Republic of Ethiopia," reflects the commitment of the ruling EPRDF government to advance ethnic federalism; hence, the Constitution begins by laying emphasis on the right of self-determination of nations given separate identities based on ethnicity. It stipulates that members of the federal structure may lawfully determine what vernacular they want to employ officially and at work. Nevertheless, it was also stipulated that Amharic would be the working language of the federal government. The clause in the 1931 and 1955 constitutions that made the Ethiopian Orthodox Tewahedo Church the state religion also was explicitly abrogated, with the provision that there would be separation between religion and state.

Arguably, the most controversial provision of the Constitution is article 39, which gives Ethiopian nations, nationalities, and peoples the right to secede under certain conditions. This far-reaching clause allows secession upon a three-fourths majority vote of a regional parliament bolstered by a regional referendum. Because such a right is not provided in any democratic constitution, unwritten or written, including those of Britain, the United States, India, and Canada, it has been targeted by the opposition as being most dangerous and as threatening the future existence of a united Ethiopia.

The Federal Democratic Republic of Ethiopia is bicameral, with the House of Peoples' Representatives and the House of Federation. The structure has a legislature and executive resembling the British parliamentary system, with the House of

RASTAFARIANISM

Rastafarianism is a movement that got its name from Ras Tafari, regent of Ethiopia from 1916 to 1929 and emperor with the titles "His Imperial Majesty Haile Selassie I," "Lion of the Tribe of Judah," "King of Kings," "Elect of God," and "Emperor of Ethiopia." Rastafarianism was initiated in Jamaica following the teachings of the founder of the Black Power movement, Markus Garvey, who predicted that a mighty king would soon be crowned in Africa. When Ras Tafari became emperor in 1930, many followers of Garvey in Jamaica claimed "the prophecy" had been fulfilled, and Rastafarianism was born. The Rastas (their favored moniker) approach their religion in a Talmudic fashion. They analyze and discuss doctrinal issues in sessions that are part theological debate and part prayer meeting known as "reasonings," at which they attempt to discern the truth and the will of God, whom they call JAH—a derivative of Janhoy, one of the titles of Emperor Haile Selassie, equivalent to the European "His Majesty." The Rastafarians call their Talmudic-style dialectic a way of "overstanding," as distinguished from "understanding." "Understanding" for them is the Protestant style of interpreting the Bible. The Rasta style of "over-standing" is an attempt to discern truth through divine leadership and grace. In 1960, when Rasta leaders came to Addis Ababa, the authoritative govern-ment newspaper *Addis Zemen* reported, "His Majesty, Haile Selassie I has graciously received the Elders of the Rastafarian movement who worship Him as a divine being and has informed them that He is not God." Haile Selassie was invited to pay a visit to Jamaica in 1966, and when his plane alighted in Kingston, the Rastas named it "Groundation Day," and thousands of "Dreads" in white robes received him by chanting, "Hosanna to the Son of David!" Starting in 1952, Ethiopian Orthodox Christianity succeeded in absorbing most Garvyite religious communities in Trinidad, Guyana, and New York. However, the mainstream Rasta movement remains unshaken to this day. The rapidly growing and most famous sect, "The Twelve Tribes of Israel," founded in 1968 by Vernon Carrington (known also as the Prophet Gad), hold that Haile Selassie is Jesus Christ returned in majesty as king and that therefore the Second Coming has already happened. In another difference from the Orthodox Rastafarians, the Twelve Tribes claim that Haile Selassie is divine in essence and merits "latreia," or absolute worship.

Peoples' Representatives enjoying powers of legislation in all matters assigned by the Constitution to federal jurisdiction. This organ is the highest authority of the federation. Seats in the House of Peoples' Representatives are allocated through a "first past the post" formula. The system is based on the country being divided into geographical areas known as constituencies, with a relatively equal number of constituents inhabiting them. During election time, candidates compete for seats in each constituency, either in the name of a political party or as independents. The voter chooses one among these candidates in a secret ballot. The contender in a constituency who garners most votes by simple majority count wins the seat in the parliament. The leader of the party with the most members elected to the House of Peoples' Representatives is made the head of the government, or prime minister of the country.

The upper house, known as the House of Federation, is the custodian or interpreter of the Constitution. It is a branch where all ethnic groups described as "nations, nationalities, and peoples" are proportionately and directly represented. The House of Federation is composed of at least one representative from each of the legally recognized ethnic groups of the country and one other representative for every 1 million citizens of each ethnic entity. This arrangement has made it possible for most ethnic groups to have representation in the 112-member House of Federation. Thus, the Southern Nations Nationalities and Peoples (SNNP), which is made up of 46 ethnic groups, has 54 representatives. The two largest ethnic groups, the Oromos and the Amharas, have 19 and 17 seats, respectively. Tigray, which is politically dominant, has three seats. However, the multiethnic urban administrations of Dire Dawa and Addis Ababa have no representation in the House of Federation.

The Constitution provides for an independent judiciary with two branches of court system, at the federal and regional levels, with supreme federal judicial authority being entrusted to the Federal Supreme Court. The president and vice president of the Federal Supreme Court are selected by the prime minister and approved by the House of Peoples' Representatives. With regard to federal judges, the prime minister forwards candidates chosen by the Federal Judicial Administrative Council to the House of Peoples' Representatives and seeks formal approval.

Judicial powers are enjoyed by both the federal and state levels of government. The House of Peoples' Representatives, which is akin to the British House of Commons, has the prerogative to create a federal high court as well as first-instance courts. States can establish their own supreme, high, and first-instance courts.

The House of Peoples' Representatives together with state councils have the prerogative to establish or proffer legal recognition to customary and religious courts. Nevertheless, the federal and the state supreme courts do not have the right to throw out laws legislated by either house of Parliament. The Constitution does not entrust judicial review and final arbitration concerning disagreements arising from the sharing of powers to the Supreme Court. Instead, this pivotal authority is vested on a federal council referred to as the Council of Constitutional Inquiry. According to the Constitution, judges hold office up to their age of retirement, which is determined by law, and during good behavior. No courts, it is stipulated, should be interfered with by the other branches of the government, whether federal or local.

The Constitution stipulates that states within the newly created regions will enjoy the right to form their own states. And according to article 61, a federal council composed of representatives of nations can be created as needed.

In the May 1995 national election, 108 members of this upper house were elected. Among the tasks of this council are (1) to decide on claims by nations for self-determination, including secession, (2) to settle disputes and misunderstandings between states, and (3) to determine the division of revenues derived from joint federal and state tax sources and subsidies by the federal government to states. The creation of the federal council to manage ethnic and regional relations frees up the Council of People's Representatives to deal with other pressing national issues.

DEMOCRATIZATION AND CONTEMPORARY ETHIOPIAN POLITICS

When on May 28, 1992, the EPRDF took power in Ethiopia, with the Eritrean People's Liberation Front (EPLF) in the north controlling Eritrea de facto, the new government was led by the EPRDF chairman Meles Zenawi, who previously had paid allegiance to Enver Hoxha's Albanian Communist party but who pledged he would abandon Marxism-Leninism and guide Ethiopia through a genuine recognition of the country's ethnic heterogeneity. According to the EPRDF plan, no longer would the Ethiopian union be maintained by force; rather, it would be a voluntary federation of its many ethnic groups, nations, and nationalities. And instead of authoritarianism, the country would be guided by the tenets of liberal democracy.

Supporters of the government point out that though far from being perfect, Ethiopia under the EPRDF has taken some bold steps in the right direction. State building and democratization, they point out, are slowly being applied. Independent newspapers, most of them highly critical of the powers that be, are mushrooming. The fact that there is a burgeoning free press points to the growth of a culture of tolerance and accommodation. Freedom of the press was guaranteed in 1994 in article 29 of the Constitution of the Federal Democratic Republic of Ethiopia, which provides for the "Right of Thought, Opinion and Expression," prohibits censorship, and allows for access to all information except that dealing with national security.

According to supporters, the right to civil dialogue was guaranteed, which is a new departure from the feudal and the totalitarian Derg period. By presenting divergent ideas in political debates, the private press has, in their view, advanced the culture of democracy in Ethiopia. They cite that in the 2005 elections, the private as well as state-owned press opened a new space so that political groups, whether tied to the government or opposed to it, had the chance to present their platforms. One example often quoted is the *Reporter*, a privately owned press known for its fair presentation of news. This periodical devoted almost 10 pages of its weekly paper to many ideas presented by divergent groups competing during the election. It printed discussions and hot debates conducted among the spokespeople representing various parties and did so with a professional touch. *Capital*, *Addis Fortune*, and many other major private periodicals also presented various opposing issues originating from the different parties—all in an evenhanded and just manner.

The supporters argue that since 1991, Ethiopia has had relative freedom of press and has been tolerant of nonviolent political groups. They point out that the policy of state-directed assimilation of all ethnic groups into an Amhara cultural and linguistic hegemony has been nipped in the bud. The new policies, they argue, have empowered all ethnic groups by providing them with self-governance and cultural and linguistic autonomy. Supporters claim that the new arrangement had replaced a single ethnic control on the basis of authoritarianism with a multiethnic egalitarian nation state.

Putting this arrangement in place enabled fair general lections in 1992, 1994, 1995, 2000, and 2005. A command economy also gave way to large-scale privatization.

Opponents point out many faults that they say are visible in the present rule. With regard to the structure of the EPRDF, the four ethnic and multiethnic groups as well as affiliated parties in the other regional states that together constitute the ruling coalition are, in opponents' view, satellite factions with no power of their own. It is argued that though the protection of human rights has been enshrined in the Constitution, these rights have been violated, as even the U.S. State Department has charged year after year.

The press, though free on paper, opponents argue, has been harassed, with editors being routinely jailed or exiled. Some political parties that the government considers threatening to its hegemony, such as the OLF, have been outlawed, and those allowed legally to compete have not been given a level ground to compete from. Elections have been held every four years but have been marred by irregularities, harassment, intimidation, ballot rigging, and even outright murders by supporters of the government, as attested by foreign-based observers.

The government's refusal to reorganize the election board, which was created by the ruling party, into one that is neutral is proof that it wants to continue to use the board as a tool for the control of the election process. Though all ethnic groups are said to be equal, power is monopolized by the TPLF, which represents only 6 percent of the Ethiopian population. Some call the phenomenon "the tyranny of a minority over majorities." Though separation of powers and judicial freedom are guaranteed by the Constitution, in practice, the rule of law has not been respected, and extra-judicial detentions and even killings have been reported over the years by local and international human right observers.

The economy, which is said to be arranged on the basis of Western liberal democracy, is, the opponents argue, far from being liberal or democratic. It is charged that the major economic lifeline of the nation is monopolized by TPLF-owned mega-business empires such as EFFORT. The government's adherence to revolutionary democracy is, they say, a Maoist approach, not a free-market approach. For opponents, control over the peasantry, which constitutes 85 percent of the Ethiopian population, is assured by the EPRDF in several ways. One is by the use of peasant associations and *qebele* leaders who are cadres of the governing party. These groups, critics point out, are able to use their administrative power at the local level to intimidate the rural masses because the land is in the hands of the government and fertilizers are supplied to them on loan. Those who support the opposition parties are punished through the confiscation of their farmlands and the denial of fertilizers.

Opponents argue that the process of democratization has been derailed. Prominent opposition leaders such as Judge Bertoukan Mideksa were jailed to deny them an opportunity to lead their parties into the 2010 national election. The EPRDF, through its party cadres and *qebele* underlings, critics allege, holds total control of local and district administrations to scrutinize and coerce individuals at a household level. Furthermore, the EPRDF holds a stranglehold on everything at a village level, where its minions can decide on entitlements such as schooling for children and the distribution of not only land and fertilizers but also foreign-donated food. Supporters of the ruling party are rewarded, according to the opposition, whereas others not only are denied amenities but also lose their plough oxen and their property; thus, they are driven into the urban areas, where they join the multitudes of the unemployed homeless. Near election time, the opposition parties are routinely castigated as subversives. Their constitutional right to peaceful assembly is restricted, and they are brazenly harassed.

The fledgling civil liberties of the early post-Derg era, opponents allege, have been drastically circumscribed. The press, both local and international, has been stifled. Those who are still working have to walk a tight rope. Newspapers now avoid reporting about the activities of the opposition parties or about people the government castigates as having terrorist links. Three months before the 2010 elections, the government of Ethiopia even jammed the Amharic-language broadcast of Voice of America, which is funded by the U.S. government, and Prime Minister Meles Zenawi openly admitted that he endorsed jamming the broadcast because VOA is akin to Radio Mille Collines, which promoted the Interhamawe genocide against Tutsis and moderate Hutus in 1994.

Opponents argue that it is with the privatization program that the EPRDF has won the unflagging support of the International Monetary Fund and other international donors. This, they allege, has only made the ruling party stronger because its agents, associates, organizations, and foundations such as EFFORT are being run to accumulate profit in a market climate that favors them and patently works against the interests of corporate bodies and individual entrepreneurs.

Opponents argue that control over rural land, home to more than 85 percent of the country's population, gives the governing party immense power. Local autonomy is compromised by the fact that the EPRDF, which exercises power over virtually every facet of the political process, wields undue influence over the outlying ethnic entities and urban centers by directly appointing representatives to their regional councils (as in the Gumuz-Benishangul and Afar regions) and by using the federal army and police forces to assume direct rule over turbulent regions (such as the Borena zone of Oromia, Afar, Somali, Benishangul, and the Gambella region where a bloody massacre took place in June 2004).

Opponents point out with regret that despite pronouncing during the transition period that there would be no cooperation unless the regime abided by Western-style free enterprise rules, the United States has not yet openly questioned the growing role of the EPRDF party in the private sector and its total domination of the country's economic and political landscape. This is, they claim, because the EPRDF government assists the U.S. effort to fight groups tied to Al Qaeda in the region, as exemplified by Ethiopia's armed intervention in Somalia in 2003 to neutralize the power of Somalia's Al-Shabab, which is a front for Osama Bin Laden's international anti-U.S. movement.

According to opponents, despite championing pluralism, capitalism, and civil society to appease the West, which supplies Ethiopia with economic aid, the EPRDF remains Marxist-Leninist in structure. Similar to the Bolshevik Social Democratic Party of Russia, it is run by a vanguard central committee, politburo, and secretariat. And, as Meles Zenawi tried to explain in his year 2000 treatise on "Bonapartism," a concept borrowed from Karl Marx, and "What Is to be Done," another model adopted from Vladimir Ilyich Lenin, the authority to rule is acquired by struggle not only between classes but also between elites. In the latter case, corruption might occur. But once power is garnered by the oppressed classes or their vanguard party, it has to be exercised through a hierarchical system of democratic centralism. Thus, the opposition claims, it comes as no surprise that it is the TPLF leadership, which defines itself as the vanguard of the revolution, that not only oversees the public bureaucracy but also guides and gives orders to all governing political factions.

Opponents argue that because of this pyramidal democratic centralist power structure, lack of transparency is evident at every level of the TPLF-lead government. Public communication is circumscribed and largely ritualistic. The leadership of the ruling TPLF has little interaction with those beyond an exclusive faction of political elite, most of whom are from the north. This modus operandi makes its umbrella party, the EPRDF, highly remote and distant from the everyday life of the citizens. Simultaneously, critics point out, the EPRDF continues to monopolize the parliament because it is in a position to manipulate the federal and regional elections at will. For example, a recent demand by the opposition parties, which are themselves divided, to reform the current election board, which they and independent international observers consider to be almost an organ of the EPRDF, has been spurned by the EPRDF government. But until this reform is implemented, opponents say, it is inevitable that the EPRDF will continue to perpetuate its power, as the Revolutionary Democratic Party of Mexico did for decades. Nothing short of strong pressure brought to bear by the Western countries, particularly the United States and those in the European Union that currently supply the EPRDF with billions of dollars in aid packages, can stop the trend and restore genuine democracy to post-Derg Ethiopia.

Prime Minister Meles promised donor Western nations, who provide close to 2 billion dollars a year, that he would guarantee the right of political parties to compete on a level ground. Following the 2005 general elections, however, an intense dispute arose. An opposition party, Kinijit (also known as Coalition for Unity and Democracy, or CUD), claimed it won the election. The government, supported by the election board, countered that the opposition won only one-third of the parliamentary seats. There was also a claim that Kinijit supporters in some ridings (electoral districts) had manipulated ballots. Members of the Kinijit group refused to take their seats in a parliament they claimed was rigged, and their supporters demonstrated on the streets of Addis Ababa. The government deployed police to disperse the demonstration. Shots were fired, and many demonstrators were killed or injured. A commission created to investigate the shooting claimed that 193 demonstrators were shot and killed by the government's riot squad.

Claiming to have proof that the Kinijit party was planning an orange revolution similar to that which overthrew incumbents in Ukraine, Georgia, and Kyrgyzstan, Prime Minister Meles Zenawi's government ordered the arrest of Kinijit leadership and charged them with crimes against humanity and attempted genocide. The latter charge was based on the allegation that Kinijit supporters had advocated an attack against people of Tigre origin.

After two years of incarceration, through the intercession of Professor Ephraim Isaac of Princeton University, the arrested leaders were released and their civil and political rights restored. This was achieved only after Kinijit leaders signed a document admitting to the actions they were accused of and asked for pardon. Because of the refusal of the Kinijit to participate, the 2005 parliament became 90 percent EPRDF. Despite the amnesty, the standoff continued. What is more, Kinijit was splintered into three factions, making it difficult if not impossible to repeat or better their 2005 performance.

After looking at both sides of the argument, one can conclude that, considering the authoritarian political culture of Ethiopia, the subversion of democracy through foul play cannot be surprising. After all, respect for human rights has never been the norm in Ethiopia, which had a weak civil society under both feudalism and the defunct military dictatorship. In fact, social order had always been governed by authoritarian leaders, not by the rule of law. The EPRDF, therefore, rules Ethiopia in an authoritarian manner, and its claim to the contrary has to be taken with a grain of salt.

No one, not even the supporters of the government, can deny that democratization under the EPRDF has not gone smoothly and that some unlawful actions of the ruling party forced a number of political parties, in particular the potentially power-

Insurgents of the Ethiopian People's Revolutionary Democratic Party that overthrew Mengistu and his military dictatorship. (Roger-Viollet.)

ful OLF, to boycott the 1995 elections. Neutral election observers from the United States also corroborated allegations of election irregularities in the initial regional elections. For some, however, these unfortunate developments by themselves are not sufficient reasons to castigate the new ethnic arrangement as unworkable.

Part of the problem lies in the fact that the EPRDF, in order to control power, did not dismantle urban neighborhood associations known as *qebeles* and peasant associations, both of which were created by the Derg regime with a Stalinist approach, but instead purged the leadership and installed its own cadres. This exacerbated the problem because the functionaries were intolerant of allowing pluralist political competition. To make matters worse, the opposition parties, instead of trying to cultivate their influence among the grassroots organizations, became intransigent. They boycotted the elections and started armed struggle, as did the OLF and the Western Somali Liberation Front, thus to a large extent marginalizing themselves. This left the EPRDF in total control of Ethiopian politics.

In hindsight, set against Ethiopia's turbulent past, the EPRDF regime achieved a relatively smooth transition. Furthermore, its system is characterized by noteworthy stability in comparison with other countries of the region. That is partly why the EPRDF government has won the praise of the West, which has chosen to turn a blind eye to its political shortfalls, including a wide range of human rights violations attributed to it by the Ethiopian Human Rights Commission (EHRCO), Amnesty International, Africa Watch, and even the U.S. State Department.

THE 2005 AND 2010 ELECTIONS

Ethiopia's national elections of 2005 were conducted with a single-member plurality formula that was run in all 548 districts created for the purpose. The 2005 election was a far cry from the 1995 one that was boycotted by the major opposition groups, thus allowing a clean sweep by the EPRDF, and from the 2000 election in which the EPRDF won almost all the seats—it lost only 12 of 547 seats. In 2005, to mollify Western critics, the EPRDF took courage and agreed to reform the nomination and election procedure by streamlining the candidate nomination process and dropping the requisite 500 signatures for eligibility for candidates intending to run. The government also reduced the residency requirement from five years to two. This resulted in a 71 percent increase in candidate participation from the 2000 election to the 2005 one. Taking advantage of government creation of gender quotas, the proportion of women candidates also increased from 1 percent to 14 percent, an astounding growth of 178 percent.

The National Election Board of Ethiopia, which was created by the ruling party, also established a system of shared political party forums at the national and regional levels in order to help resolve disputes arising from the ballots. Major opposition parties were given access to state-controlled newspapers and television and radio programs. Foreign and local civil society organizations were allowed to conduct civic education. Live debates were aired via the government-controlled television and radio stations. Criticism of the ruling party was tolerated by the government. Huge campaign rallies were held in support of both the ruling and opposition parties.

At the start, Prime Minister Meles Zenawi promised to make sure that the election process would be untarnished. To show his sincerity, he invited international observers from the U.S.-based Carter Center and the European Union. Thus, the May 15, 2005, national elections were run under very favorable conditions for all competitors involved. The Ethiopian people recognized this opportunity and turned out in overwhelming numbers to vote, forcing some polling stations in Addis Ababa to stay open 24 hours to accommodate those in line—voter turnout was estimated to be 90 percent.

Problems emerged when the National Election Board announced that the EPRDF and its affiliate parties had won a total of 310 seats, versus 173 for the opposition parties. This gave the ruling party 63 percent of the parliamentary seats and the opposition 35 percent. The final tally according to the national election board showed that the EPRDF, or Ethiopian People's Revolutionary Democratic Front, had won 296 seats; the Benishangul-Gumuz People's Democratic Unity Front (BGPDUF) had won 8; and the Afar National Democratic Party (ANDP) had garnered 8. In addition, it was announced that other EPRDF allies had won 6 seats. This gave the EPRDF a total of 310 out of 492 contested seats.

By contrast, the Coalition for Unity and Democracy (CUD) won 109 seats, the United Ethiopian Democratic Forces (UEDF) won 52, the Oromo Federalist Democratic Movement (OFDM) won 11 seats, and another party won 1 seat, for an opposition total of 173 out of 492 contested seats, which gave them 35 percent.

It was at this point that the major opposition parties, CUD and UEDF, claimed vast electoral fraud and challenged the results. In total, they asked for a recount of about 300 election results. Supporters of the opposition, most of them students, soon staged a massive demonstration that was met with an iron fist—193 demonstrators were shot dead by riot police, and as noted earlier in this chapter, the opposition leaders were herded to jail, accused of attempting to carry out an orange revolution similar to those in Ukraine, Georgia, and Kyrgyzstan. They were freed after admitting to the accusations leveled against them and asking for pardon, which was duly granted.

In the May 23, 2010, elections, the main coalition of opposition parties, Medrek, was sidelined, and the EPRDF swept into power in practically every region including, in all those localities where it lost the 2005 elections. This includes Addis Ababa, where the EPRDF won all the seats previously won by Kinijit. The main opposition leaders, including Hailu Shawel, Siye Abraha, Gebru Asrat, Beyene Petros, Bulcha Demeksa, and Merera Gudina, were not elected in the ridings in which they competed. Africa Watch and the European Union observation team indicated there were reports of intimidation and vote rigging. However, Prime Minster Meles Zenawi claimed that there was no way his government, which had registered double-digit growth during the preceding five years, could be voted out by the electorate.

REGIONAL GOVERNMENTS

The 1994 Constitution created a regional state system comprising nine autonomous ethnically based *kilils* (states) governed by popularly elected state councils that are recognized as the highest organs of local jurisdiction. The system has two self-governing *astadadars* (administrations), in the cities of Addis Ababa and Dire Dawa. Each *kilil* has a state president elected by a state council.

The Constitution gives significant executive, legislative, and judicial powers to *kilils*. Article 52 states, "All powers not given expressly to the Federal Government alone, or concurrently to the Federal government and the States are reserved to the States." A provision also allows regional states to have their own executive, legislative, and judiciary branches of government with law enforcement capacities. They have their own regional constitutions and their own seals and symbols such as flags. Each state has the right to choose its own working language. And most importantly, it has the right to invoke the self-determination clause in article 39 and ask for secession. States can, of their own volition, decentralize their administrative units. They have the right to organize themselves from regional state level to zonal and district (*woreda*) levels.

With regard to interstate relations, there is not much guidance in the Constitution. Nevertheless, there is significant economic interdependence, for example, involving commerce in staple foods and cash crops such as coffee, among the *kilils*. There is also some exchange in education, soil conservation, potable water and irrigation health, and environmental issues. In many of these cases, when states fail to agree on what they want to do, they resort to the mediation of the federal government.

In regard to interstate border disputes, article 48 proscribes settlement by bilateral agreement among the states in dispute. In a situation in which the parties fail to settle their differences, the House of Federation is empowered to intervene and settle the matter in a way acceptable to both and with consideration of the people of the regions in question. As for relations between the federal and state levels, article 50 only hints at the general requisite for give-and-take between the two.

An Imperial Palace in Axum (first century to sixth century AD). (Courtesy of Paulos Milkias.)

AUTONOMOUS URBAN ADMINISTRATIVE REGIONS

Addis Ababa, with a population of more than 4 million people, is the capital city of Ethiopia and one of the most important organs of the Ethiopian government. The administration of the city looks after the well-being of the citizens residing within its confines. Its city council acts as the executive body. The city is a cultural hub where most of the major ethnic groups are represented. When Emperor Haile Selassie succeeded in bringing the United Nations (UN) Economic Commission headquarters to his capital and helped create the Organization of African Unity, which has now developed into the African Union, the city became the diplomatic capital of the African continent by default.

The city has many branches looking after several services. Among them are the Acts and Civil Status branch, the Documents Record office, the Addis Ababa Road Authority, the Code Enforcement Service, the Fire and Services branch, the Houses Development Project Office, the Housing Agency, the Infrastructure and Construc-

Emperor Haile Selassie of Ethiopia pictured with Prime Minister Winston Churchill of Britain in the 1950s. (© Bettmann/CORBIS.)

tion branch, the Land Administration Authority, the Public Enterprises branch, the Sanitation and Beautification branch, the Transport Authority, and the Water and Sewerage Authority.

The mayor of Addis Ababa, who is elected directly by the people, is the head of the city government. He is assisted by members of the executive branch, including the city cabinet, the chief auditor, and the city's judicial organ.

In the 2005 general election, the opposition Kinijit won all seats in Addis Ababa except one. However, because of disagreement regarding general election issues, the party declined to take over and run the city administration.

Dire Dawa, the other of the two self-governing cities in the new Ethiopian state system, has an administrative council. It governs the city and the surrounding countryside. Though the council has no administrative zones, it has a *woreda* or district known by the name of Gurgura. The city has *kefitegnas* (subregions) and 24 *qebeles* or urban dwellers' associations. It also has 28 peasant associations.

POLITICAL PARTIES

On the eve of, and following, the fall of the Derg, political parties emerged in abundance. Among the major ones in competition were the Oromo People's Democratic Organization (OPDO); the Amhara National Democratic Movement (ANDM); the Sidama People's Democratic Organization (SPDO); the Afar National Democratic Party (ANDP); the Bench Madji People's Democratic Organization (BMPDO); the Benishangul Gumuz People's Democratic Unity Front (BGPDUF); the Ethiopian People's Revolutionary Democratic Front (EPRDF, made up of OPDO, ANDM, SEPDO, and TPLF and led by Meles Zenawi in 2010); the Gedeyo People's Revolutionary Democratic Front (GPRDF); the Guragé Nationalities Democratic Movement (GNDM); the Kafa Shaka People's Democratic Organization (KSPDO); the Kembata, Alabaa, and Tembaro (KAT) party; and the South Omo People's Democratic Movement (SOPDM). Additionally, there were the Walayta, Gamo, Gofa, Dawro, and Konta People's Democratic Organization (WGGPDO); the Afar Revolutionary Democratic Union Front (ARDUF); the Council of Alternative Forces for Peace and Democracy in Ethiopia (CAFPDE), led by Dr. Beyene Petros in 2010; Southern Ethiopia People's Democratic Coalition (SEPDC), also led by Dr. Beyene Petros in 2010; and scores of other minor parties and interest groups. Right from the start, the TPLF provided many of the parties that were its own satellites with political leadership, ideological direction, and security protection, whereas the others have had to fend for themselves in the elections conducted thus far.

Of the parties that were prominent after the EPRDF came to power, a few played prominent roles. Among them was the All Amhara People's Organization (AAPO), which was established by Emperor Haile Selassie's personal physician, Dr. Asrat Woldeyes; Hailu Shawel; and Nekea Tibeb in November 1991. This party claimed to represent the interest of the Amharas and opposed the ethnic policies of the EPRDF.

Its president, Dr. Asrat Woldeyes, was later jailed after being accused of calling for armed rebellion to overthrow the state. This party was later transformed by Ato Hailu Shawel into the All Ethiopian Unity Party.

The Council of Alternative Forces for Peace and Democracy in Ethiopia (CAFPDE) was created following the Addis Ababa conference of December 18 to 22, 1993. The meeting was led by Dr. Beyene Petros, president of the Hadiya National Democratic Organization (HNDO). The founding members of the CAFPDE were the following: the Agew People's Democratic Movement (APDO); the Ethiopian Democratic Union (EDU); the Kembata People's Congress (KPC); the National Democratic Union (NDU); the Joint Political Forum (TJPF); and the Southern Ethiopia People's Democratic Coalition (SEPDC), which included the Burji People's Democratic Organization (BPDO), the Gedeo People's Democratic Organization (GPDO), the Gurage People's Democratic Front (GPDF), the Kaffa People's Democratic Union (KPDU), the Kembata People's Congress (KPC), the Omo People's Democratic Front (OPDF), the Sidama Liberation Movement (SLM), the Wolayta People's Democratic Front (WPDF), and the Yem Nationality Democratic Movement (YNDM).

The Coalition of Ethiopian Democratic Forces (COEDF) was established in April 1991, at a conference in Washington, DC, strongly backed by exiles. The organizers were the Ethiopian People's Revolutionary Party (EPRP), the All Ethiopia Socialist Movement (Meison), the Ethiopian Democratic Union (EDU), and the Tigray Democratic People's Movement (TDPM), along with prominent civic groups and human rights and community associations. The COEDF as a party is multiethnic, and it is known for organizing the Paris Peace and Reconciliation Conference and later the Addis Ababa Conference held in December 1993.

The Coalition for Unity and Democracy (CUD), known by its Amharic name Kinijit, was a party that derived from the merging of the All Ethiopian Unity Party (AEUP), the United Ethiopian Democratic Party–Medhin (UEDP-Medhin), Kestedamena, and the Ethiopian Democratic League. When it entered the 2005 elections, Kinijit claimed to advance unity, peace, and democracy, as well as the rule of law, and said it wished to free Ethiopia from ethnic-based authoritarian rule.

After the demise of the once-powerful party Kinijit, or CUD—which splintered into three major factions, led by Hailu Shawel, Bertukan Mideksa, and Berhanu Nega, the last one advocating an armed struggle—the main opposition parties met again and created the Forum for Democratic Dialogue (FDD), known by its Amharic designation Medrek. Medkrek is made up of a dozen parties; among them are the Oromo People's Congress (OPC) and the United Ethiopian Democratic Forces (UEDF), led by Dr. Merera Gudina; Unity for Democracy and Justice (UDJ), led by Judge Bertoukan Mideksa, who is currently serving a life sentence; Arena Tigray for Democracy and Sovereignty, based in the province of Tigray and led by the former president of Tigray, Gebru Asrat, and former defense minister of Ethiopia, Siye Abraha; the Oromo Federalist Democratic Movement (OFDM), led by Bulcha Demeksa; and the Somali Democratic Alliance Forces (SDAF). There are also individual members participating in Medrek. One is the former president of Ethiopia, Dr. Negasso Gidada.

Medrek's platform asks for the reform of the electoral system and the reduction of executive powers. It promotes the creation of a new educational policy whereby the current system of general education, which ends in grade 10, would be extended to 12th grade as was the case before the EPRDF came to power.

Medrek elevates democracy and asks that decentralization take place and regions in Ethiopia be fully autonomous. Members suggest that Afan Oromo should become Ethiopia's official language, together with Amharic. The parties insist that genuine federal structure be created. They are no longer insisting that the secession clause, article 39, be rescinded immediately. Their platform asks for ending Ethiopia's status as the largest landlocked country in the world by regaining the Asab port from Eritrea. It demands that the present policy of state-owned land be replaced by privatization.

ETHIOPIAN FOREIGN POLICY

In the area of foreign policy, for over a millennium, Ethiopia remained isolationist bordering on xenophobia because Christian Ethiopia was suspicious of the surrounding political climate, which was determined by Islamic jihad and European imperialism. Both of these forces posed a direct challenge to the Christian kingdom for more than 1,000 years. That the Portuguese who came to what they called the "Land of Prester John" in the 15th century exclaimed, "the Ethiopians slept for a thousand years forgetful of the world by whom they were forgotten" (Gibbon, 1946, 51), could not be far from the truth. The status quo continued until the end of the 19th century, when Ethiopia defeated Italian imperialists at the Battle of Adwa in 1896.

In 1923, the country for the first time broke its isolationist stance and became a member of the League of Nations. But it was after its independence from Italian Fascist control in 1941 that it started to play an active role in the world and in African affairs. Ethiopia became a charter member of the United Nations early in its inception and took part in UN operations in Korea in 1951 and in the Congo conflict in 1960. Emperor Haile Selassie is considered by many as the father of the Organization of African Unity (OAU), of which Addis Ababa has become the headquarters. Addis Ababa has also become the seat for the UN Economic Commission for Africa and the OAU's successor, the African Union (AU).

From the 1950s to the mid-1970s, although it was a signatory to the non-aligned movement's protocol forged at Bandung in 1955, Haile Selassie's Ethiopia was closely allied to the United States. U.S.–Ethiopian relations were established as early as 1903, but a bona fide diplomatic, economic, political, and military relationship did not start until September 1951, when the Treaty of Amity and Economic Relations was signed. Another bilateral pact followed in 1953: the Mutual Defense Assistance Agreement, by which the United States supplied training and military hardware to the Haile Selassie regime, in return for which the imperial government allowed the United States to station a major communication facility at the Kagnew base in Asmara. Kagnew, with its 7,600-foot altitude and a spot adjacent to the relatively interference-free equatorial belt, afforded unique technical advantages in

An Ethiopian military man attached to the United Nations (UN) peacekeeping force in the Congo befriends a Katangan child in 1960. (Corel.)

the Middle East–Africa–Asia communications triad. The network linked worldwide U.S. communications facilities in the Western Hemisphere and Europe; this was extremely critical during the Cold War atmosphere of the 1950s–1970s, when the Soviet Navy was expanding into the Indian Ocean, threatening the strategic Middle East oil passage, and supporting liberation movements in mineral-rich southern and central African regions. It was due to this fact that the bond between the United States and Ethiopia became very critical and the U.S. gave more aid to Ethiopia than to the rest of the African continent combined.

Situations changed rapidly when the ancien regime was overthrown in 1974, and Mengistu Haile Mariam declared Ethiopia a Marxist-Leninist state. The Americans now hedged on supplying arms to the Addis Ababa regime, and Mengistu demanded that the United States close down the Kagnew station and all other U.S. installations in Ethiopia. By then, the first supplies of Soviet military hardware had begun to arrive, and Ethiopia had moved into a close relationship with the Soviet Union and its allies; from then on, it championed Soviet international policies and stands in Africa, the Middle East, and the rest of the world.

WHITE AND RED TERROR

After purging his Derg colleagues, Mengistu Haile Mariam, who overthrew Haile Selassie in 1974, consolidated his power as chair of the military junta. But danger was posed when the ultra-left EPRP, with the strong support of the youth, started assassinating his supporters and even attempted to kill him. The EPRP demanded that a broad-based democratic government run by civilians be instituted and that the military return back to the barracks. The Mengistu regime dubbed the assassinations by the EPRP the White Terror. Soon, the strong man of the Derg ordered tit for tat, naming his campaign the Red Terror, following the Bolsheviks' actions during the civil war that erupted following their ascent to power. The Derg's Red Terror, which started in 1977, decimated a whole generation of Ethiopian youth. By the end of that bloody carnage, over 150,000 youth had been slaughtered, and twice as many had been jailed and tortured.

ETHIOPIA AND SOMALIA

The problem between Somalia and Ethiopia is rooted in colonialism. The Ogaden province, which is populated by Somalis, was part of Ethiopia when the rest of the Somali territory was subdivided between the European colonial powers of Britain, France, and Italy. When the independent Somali Republic incorporating British and Italian Somaliland was born in 1960, Somali irredentist leaders vowed to add Ogaden to their new territory. The opportunity came when the Derg regime had purged its military leadership and was struggling against civilian dissenters and pro-monarchist fighters in northern Ethiopia. The government of Siad Barre invaded Ogaden and encroached on other non-Somali areas such as Harar, Bale, and Sidamo.

By 1976 the Soviet Union, which was allied to Somalia to counter American influence in Emperor Haile Selassie's Ethiopia, decided that the populist revolt in Ethiopian would help establish a dependable Marxist-Leninist state befitting the Cold War geopolitical realities of the day. Due to this, it concluded it would be infinitely better to shift Soviet support from Somalia to Ethiopia. So Moscow secretly promised the Derg military aid on the condition that it renounce its ties to Washington. Mengistu agreed and forced the U.S. to close down its military mission and the communications center in Asmara in April 1977. In September, Brezhneve's government cut off all military aid to Mogadishu and supplied Ethiopia with billions of dollars' worth of tanks and MiG jets. It also transferred military advisers from Somalia to Ethiopia. The Soviet foreign policy shift gained Ethiopia badly needed collaboration from North Korea, which trained its 350,000-strong People's Militia, and from Castro's Cuba and the People's Democratic Republic of Yemen, which provided infantry, armored units and mig-jet pilots. Cuba also sent a 30,000-member internationalist brigade under the command of Colonel Ochoa. With this massive support, the Derg regime crushed the Somali army at the Battle of Jijiga. Siad Barre lost some 10,000 soldiers in the war, and the country has never recovered from that loss; the situation slowly deteriorated and ended up with total anarchy following Siad Barre's ouster in 1991.

In the wake of the anarchy that gripped Somalia following the overthrow of Barre, a provisional government was created with the support of the United Nations, but because of its weakness, the country still lacked law and order. It was then that a group called the Islamic Courts Council, which follows sharia law, was organized and took over southern Somalia and the capital Mogadishu. When the Islamic courts announced that they would ultimately liberate the Ogaden province from Ethiopian control, the Ethiopian prime minister, Meles Zenawi—with the tacit approval of the United States, which suspected that some members of the Islamic militia had ties to Al Qaeda—sent an army into Somalia to shore up the provisional government based in Baidoa. Eritrea, in the meantime, provided assistance to the sectarian militia that had spent much of the year trying to pacify the country and uphold sharia law.

As Ethiopian forces drove away the Islamic militia, the latter reverted to unconventional war, using guerrilla insurgency tactics, with the aim of ejecting the Ethiopian forces and then overthrowing the provisional government itself. Meles Zenawi promised to remove his army from Somalia if a replacement was sent by the international community. The African Union found some members willing to send replacements, but, only Burundi and Uganda dispatched a token number of soldiers, not enough to replace the Ethiopian fighters in Mogadishu. Ultimately, Prime Minister Meles Zenawi made a wise decision: instead of getting bogged down in an insurgency warfare like the Americans did in Vietnam in the 1960s and 1970s, he removed his 50,000 troops completely in early 2009, leaving the protection of the Provisional government of Somalia to the 6,000 African forces from Uganda and Burundi.

The undoing of Mengistu Haile Mariam's regime came when, in 1988, Soviet leader Gorbachev told the Derg's strongman that Moscow would cease unqualified military and economic support to the military regime in Ethiopia. It was Soviet pressure that forced Mengistu to retreat at least partially from his dogmatically Stalinist approach to economic development in 1989. By 1990, the Soviet–Ethiopian alliance had ceased, and Mengistu tried to woo Israel and China for military assistance. But none of these nations were able to fill the gap, and the Derg's fall became inevitable.

In retrospect, one can certainly say that the two crucial elements in the demise of the Mengistu regime were the abortive coup d'etat of May 1989 and the loss of Soviet military aid. Mengistu, now desperate, attempted to introduce economic reforms in 1989 and 1990 and to initiate peace talks with the EPLF and EPRDF under Italian and U.S. auspices, but under the existing circumstances, there was not the slightest chance for the Derg to survive.

It should be pointed out that during the entire period of its existence, even though the Derg relied heavily on the Soviet Union and its allies for military supplies, it was just as dependent on the West for economic development and relief aid, given that the European Community was Ethiopia's major source of economic assistance. In fact, in the early 1980s, Western sources accounted for more than 90 percent of Ethiopia's economic assistance, most of which flowed from the European Community, and even though the Mengistu regime criticized the International Monetary Fund as an "imperialist" multinational organization, it received a loan of almost US$100 million from it. The Swedish International Development Authority (SIDA), the U.S. Agency for International Development (USAID), the World Bank, and other international donor agencies supplied the rest.

Also, in 1989, the lack of progress toward improved relations with Arab countries supporting the EPLF and the TPLF, along with the desperate need for arms supplies, inspired the Ethiopian regime to forge closer ties with Israel. As a result, diplomatic contact between the two nations, which had been severed during the 1973 Yom Kippur war, was reestablished. After receiving cash as well as military hardware, cluster bombs, and spare parts for old U.S.-supplied military equipment from Israel, close to 35,000 Ethiopian Jews (Beta Israel) were airlifted from Ethiopia to Israel in 1984 and 1991 in carefully planned undertakings named Operation Moses and Operation Solomon. Mengistu's government was on the verge of collapse and Operations Moses and Solomon were a way of buying American friendship, since the Soviets had already abandoned their support for his war efforts in northern Ethiopia.

BETA ISRAEL ("HOUSE OF ISRAEL")

The Beta Israel, also known as Falashas (meaning "exiles"), traditionally inhabited an area in Gondar province north of Lake Tana, which is the source of the Blue Nile. The Beta Israel claim to be descendants of the eldest sons of the 12 tribes of Israel. They maintain that their ancestors followed Menelik I, the son of the Queen of Sheba and King Solomon, to Ethiopia circa 1000 BC. There are several other explanations regarding Beta Israel's origin. One is that they were members of the Jewish contingent in Elephantine, Nubia, that rebelled against the pharaoh and, upon being defeated, trekked to Ethiopia, following the Blue Nile. The third explanation is that they are descendants of Jewish communities in Himyar who immigrated to Ethiopia between AD 525 and 600, at a time when Ethiopia ruled over South Arabia. The Beta Israel observe the laws of ritual uncleanness, offer sacrifices on Nisan 14 in the Jewish religious year, and observe other major Jewish festivals. In the 15th and 16th centuries, Ethiopia's Christian emperors attempted to convert the Beta Israel to Christianity by force. The Beta Israel got a respite following the ascension to power in Ethiopia of Emperor Fasilidas, who expelled the Jesuits and reinstated the Ethiopian Orthodox Tewahedo Church as the state religion. When a disastrous famine hit the land in 1984–1985, "Operation Solomon" was launched by Israel to shuttle some 15,000 of the Beta Israel people to Israel through the Sudan. A second wave of immigration occurred when Mengistu's dictatorship was overthrown in 1991. This was "Operation Moses," whereby an additional group of 30,000 were repatriated to Israel. There are now about 15,000 Falasha-Mura (Beta Israel converted to Christianity) who claim that their conversion was forced and that they have the right of return to Israel. In 2010, the Israeli government was trying to screen out genuine Ethiopian Jews who had converted to Christianity as a result of pressure and who thus deserved to claim the right of return according to Israeli law.

At present, Ethiopia plays an active role in the regional Intergovernmental Authority on Development (IGAD), the African Union (AU, formerly Organization of African Unity), and the New Partnership for African Development (NEPAD). Relations with Somalia have remained volatile since the Ogaden war of 1977–1978 and because of ongoing incursions of Al-Itihad Al-Islamia, a Somali Islamic fundamentalist organization that wants to seize control of the region. Also contributing to the volatility is Somalia's policy of hosting armed groups, including the OLF, the Islamic Front for the Liberation of Oromia (IFLO), and the Ogaden National Liberation Front (ONLF), and allowing them to carry out guerrilla war against the Ethiopian regime. In reprisal, Meles Zenawi's government has backed many Somali dissident groups opposed to Al-Itihad including Hussein Aideed's faction, which it actively supports with arms and finance.

Ethiopia's relations with the Sudan have been unsteady, depending on the activities of liberation fronts such as the Sudan People's Liberation Front (SPLF) and the Benishangul Democratic Liberation Movement (BPLM) and a host of other political factions taking sanctuary in one country or the other. Ethiopian–Kenyan relations have also soured recently because of cross-border armed clashes between sedentary citizens of both countries and because of OLF's attacks from across the border followed by Ethiopian security forces' incursions into Kenyan territory in pursuit of the insurgents. After the loss of its ports of Massawa and particularly Asab, Ethiopia has become heavily dependent on Djibouti for the major part of its import and export trade.

ERITREA AND ETHIOPIA: FROM WAR TO WAR

Thousands of years before Christ and after, Eritrea was the site of the major ports of Axum and was an Ethiopian province known first as Midri Bahri and later as Mereb Melash. Though the Christian highlands of Seraye, Akule Guzay, and Hamasien remained part of Ethiopia, the Muslim lowlands fell under the Ottomans in the 16th century.

Assab, near the straight of Bab El Mendeb, was taken over by Italy in 1882. Egypt took over the port of Massawa in the mid-19th century but ceded it to Italy with the tacit approval of Britain in 1885. The Treaty of Wuchale, which was signed by Emperor Menelik in 1889, recognized Italian possessions in the area, and a colony named Eritrea (derived from Mare Erythraeum—Latin for the Red Sea) was created by Italy. The colony of Eritrea extended for about 600 miles and included areas north of Cape Kasar, including the Dahlak Archipelago in the Red Sea, and south to Bab el-Mandeb Strait. Italy used Eritrea as a staging ground for its attempted invasion in 1896, but it was frustrated by an Ethiopian victory at Adwa. Benito Mussolini again launched his invasion of Ethiopia in 1935–1936 from Eritrea.

After Britain came to the region to help in the liberation of Ethiopia and expelled the Italians in 1941, the country remained in Britain's hands as a trust territory until 1952, when the United Nations decided to federate Eritrea with Ethiopia. In 1962, under pressure from Eritrean unionists and the central government of Emperor Haile Selassie, the Eritrean parliament voted to dissolve the federation and make the territory a province of Ethiopia. Guerrilla fighting to achieve independence was started under the Eritrean Liberation Front in 1961 and succeeded in achieving independence under its breakaway wing, the Eritrean People's Liberation Front, when the Derg regime crumbled in 1991.

The new government that replaced the Derg, the EPRDF led by the TPLF, which has always espoused the right of self-determination up to and including secession, allowed Eritrea to run a referendum to decide its own fate. Following a majority vote in the referendum, Eritrea became de jure independent in 1993.

Initially, the relationship was cordial between the two new governments. However, a conflict involving economic and territorial control arose between the EPRDF and the Eritrean government, led by Isayas Afeworki. A vicious conventional and trench war raged between the two from 1998 to 2000. The border war was brutal in every sense of the word: more than 70,000 soldiers died within a few months of combat. In addition, more than half a million people were uprooted from their homes, and both countries carried out expulsions and counterexpulsions. affecting close to 100,000 citizens.

Following its military victory, the Ethiopian government led by Meles Zenawi agreed to settle the territorial dispute peacefully and summoned the United Nations to send a peacekeeping force to separate the two armies. Once the peacekeeping force was in place, both countries accepted the Algiers agreement, which was to decide jurisdiction over all disputed territories, but when the village of Badme— where the war started when it was invaded by Eritrea—was given to Asmara by the arbitrators, the Ethiopian government refused to allow physical demarcation until further agreements were made between the two countries. Following the stand-off, Eritrea refused to cooperate with the UN peacekeeping force that was stationed on Eritrean soil. The force ultimately had to leave the country. Without Ethiopia's acknowledgment, the arbitrators made the demarcation on the map and gave Badme to Eritrea, but at the time of this writing, the Ethiopian government still controlled Badme.

In terms of the EPRDF's regional foreign policy, it is ironic that the first major conflict it had to face took place in relation to the EPLF party of Eritrea (renamed People's Front for Democracy and Justice, or PFDJ), with which it had cordial relations during and immediately after the liberation campaign.

When Ethiopia won the war in the year 2000, the Algiers agreement leading to cessation of hostilities was signed, and both pledged in advance to accept the verdict of a UN arbitrating body—a five-member Eritrean Ethiopia Boundary Commission (EEBC), which issued a decision in April 2002 awarding the contested Badme village and a large part of the Irob district to Eritrea. The physical demarcation of the border was is still stalled because the EPRDF, which initially agreed to accept the commission's verdict, had a change of heart because of vehement opposition from the rank and file in Tigray. So the UN Mission in Ethiopia and Eritrea (UNMEE) continues to patrol a 25-kilometer border between the two. Regardless of this standoff, however, both countries have pledged not to initiate war, and in the case of Ethiopia, the armed forces are slowly being demobilized. The 300,000-strong army that went into combat with Eritrea has been reduced to 150,000. The 2002–2003 defense budget has remained at 5 percent of the country's GDP, and Ethiopia has even contributed troops for the UN peacekeeping mission in Burundi. Nevertheless, by the beginning of 2004, Addis Ababa was busy building reserve forces to meet emergencies as the government of Isaias Afeworki, which is wary of the EPRDF regime's hostile response to the EEBC verdict regarding Badme, Irob, and other areas, continues to implement a compulsory military draft.

The United States, which was happy to see the Derg fall, accepted the promise of the TPLF and its umbrella party, the EPRDF, that they would embrace liberal democracy. Herman Cohen, former assistant secretary of state for African affairs told the leader of the newly established provisional government, Meles Zenawi, that the United States would provide help as long as they followed a democratic road. At the London Peace Conference in May 1991, Cohen specifically said, "No democracy, no aid" (All Africa News May 29).

Though they have not come to a mutual agreement acceptable to both, Ethiopia and Eritrea have pledged not to initiate war, and in the case of Ethiopia, the armed forces have been demobilized. The 300,000-strong army that went into combat with Eritrea has been reduced to 150,000. The current defense budget has remained at 5 percent of the country's GDP, and Ethiopia has even contributed troops for the UN peacekeeping mission in Burundi. Nevertheless, the government of Isayas Afeworki, which is wary of the EPRDF regime's hostile response to the EEBC's verdict regarding Badme, Irob, and other areas, continued to implement a compulsory military draft. This has forced Meles Zenawi to start military buildup again. Chances are that if one or the other fails to back down, another disastrous war is inevitable.

REFERENCES

All Africa News. May 29, 1991. http://allafrica.com/. Accessed March 12, 2000.

Babile, T., and Ethiopian People's Revolutionary Party. 1989. *To Kill a Generation: The Red Terror in Ethiopia*. Washington, DC: Free Ethiopia Press.

Baer, G. W. 1976. *Test Case: Italy, Ethiopia, and the League Of Nations*. Stanford, CA: Hoover Institution Press.

Bahru, Z., S. Pausewang, et al. 2002. *Ethiopia: The Challenge of Democracy from Below*. Uppsala, Sweden: Nordiska Afrikainstitutet; Addis Ababa, Ethiopia: Forum for Social Studies.

Bereket, H. S. 1980. *Conflict and Intervention in the Horn of Africa*. New York: Monthly Review Press.

Birkby, C. 1942. *It Is a Long Way to Addis*. London: F. Muller Ltd. 239–40.

Browder, Anthony. 1992. *Exploding the Myths: The Nile Valley Contributions to Civilization*. New York: Institute of Karmic Guidance.

Clapham, C. S. 1969. *Haile-Selassie's Government*. New York: Praeger.

Clay, J. W., and B. K. Holcomb. 1985. *Politics and the Ethiopian Famine, 1984–1985*. Cambridge, MA: Cultural Survival.

Cole, E., M. Botbol, et al. 1985. *Ethiopia, Political Power and the Military*. Paris: Banque d'information et de documentation de l'océan Indien.

Dawit Wolde, Giorgis. 1989. *Red Tears: War, Famine, and Revolution in Ethiopia*. Trenton, NJ: Red Sea Press.

De Waal, A. 1991. *Evil Days: Thirty Years of War and Famine in Ethiopia*. New York: Human Rights Watch.

Dessalegn, R., and A. Meheret 2004. *Democratic Assistance to Post-Conflict Ethiopia: Impact and Limitations*. Addis Ababa, Ethiopia: Forum for Social Studies; Roma: Bari, Laterza.

Donham, D. L. 1999. *Marxist Modern: An Ethnographic History of the Ethiopian Revolution*. Berkeley: University of California Press.

Donham, D. L., W. James, et al. 1986. *The Southern Marches of Imperial Ethiopia: Essays in History and Social Anthropology*. New York: Cambridge University Press.

Doornbos, M. R., and Institute of Social Studies Netherlands. 1992. *Beyond Conflict in the Horn: Prospects for Peace, Recovery, and Development in Ethiopia, Somalia, and the Sudan*. Trenton, NJ: Red Sea Press.

Erlich, Haggai. 1982. *Ethiopia and Eritrea during the Scramble for Africa: A Political Biography of Ras Alula, 1875–1897*. East Lansing: African Studies Center, Michigan State University.

Erlich, Haggai. 1983. *The Struggle over Eritrea, 1962–1978: War and Revolution in the Horn of Africa*. Stanford, CA: Hoover Institution Press.

Ehrlich Haggai. 1986. *Ethiopia and the Challenge of Independence*. Boulder, CO: L. Rienner.

Ehrlich Haggai, and H. Erich. 1996. *Ras Alula and the Scramble for Africa: A Political Biography: Ethiopia & Eritrea, 1875–1897*. Lawrenceville, NJ: Red Sea Press.

Ethiopia. 1974. *Declaration of the Provisional Military Government of Ethiopia*. Addis Ababa: Ethiopian Government.

Ethiopia, 1995. Statistical Abstracts. Central Statistical Agency, Addis Ababa.

Ethiopia. 1976. *Programme of the National Democratic Revolution of Ethiopia*. Addis Ababa: Provisional Military Government of Ethiopia.

Ethiopian Students Union in North America. 1976. *The National Question in Ethiopia: Proletarian Internationalism or Bourgeois Nationalism?* Toronto: Norman Bethune Institute.

Farer, T. J. 1979. *War Clouds on the Horn of Africa: The Widening Storm*. New York: Carnegie Endowment for International Peace.

Gadaa, M. 1999. *Oromia: An Introduction to the History of the Oromo People*. Minneapolis, MN: Kirk House Publishers.

Gaitachew, B., and Thomas Leiper. *The Emperor's Clothes: A Personal Viewpoint on Politics and Administration in the Imperial Ethiopian Government, 1941–1974*. East Lansing: Michigan State University Press.

Gebre-Igziabiher, E., R. K. Molvaer, et al. 1994. *Prowess, piety, and politics: the chronicle of Abeto Iyasu and Empress Zewditu of Ethiopia (1909–1930)*. Kèoln, Rèudiger Kèoppe Verlag.

Gebru, T. 1991. *Ethiopia: Power and Protest: Peasant Revolts in the Twentieth Century*. New York: Cambridge University Press.

Gershoni, I., and M. Hatina. 2008. *Narrating the Nile: Politics, Cultures, and Identities*. Boulder, CO: Lynne Rienner.

Gibbon, Edward. 1946. *History of the Decline and Fall of the Roman Empire*. Edited by J. B. Bury. London: Methuen, 1896–1900, chapter xlvii.

Gilkes, P. 1975. *The Dying Lion: Feudalism and Modernization in Ethiopia*. New York: St. Martin's Press.

Gilkes, P., M. Plaut, et al. 1999. *War in the Horn: The Conflict between Eritrea and Ethiopia*. London: Royal Institute of International Affairs.

Gill, P. 1986. *A Year in the Death of Africa: Politics, Bureaucracy, and the Famine*. London: Paladin.

Government of the United Kingdom. 1895–1896. *The Abyssinian Campaign*. London: Government Printing Press.

Government of the United Kingdom. 1943–1944. *House of Commons Debates* 55 (398): 220.

Great Britain and Ethiopia. 1952. *Exchange of Notes between the Government of the United Kingdom of Great Britain and Northern Ireland, and the Government of Ethiopia Regarding the Federation of Eritrea with Ethiopia Under the Sovereignty of the Ethiopian Crown*. London: H. M. Stationery Off.

Greenfield, Richard. 1965. *Ethiopia: A New Political History*. London: Pall Mall Publishers. 375–418.

Guleid, A. A. 2001. *The Challenges of Transformation and Demobilization: An Ethiopian Perspective*. Addis Ababa, Ethiopia: Ethiopian International Institute for Peace and Development.

Guutama, I. 2003. *Prison of Conscience: Upper Compound Maa'ikalawi, Ethiopian Terror Prison and Tradition*. New York: Gubirmans Pub.

Haile, S. 1949. *An anthology of some of the public utterances of His Imperial Majesty, Haile Selassie I*. Addis Ababa: Berhanenna Selam Printing Press.

Haile Selassie I. 1972. *Important Utterances of H. I. M. Emperor Haile Selassie I, 1963–1972*. Addis Ababa, Ethiopia: Imperial Ethiopian Ministry of Information.

Haile-Selassie, T. 1997. *The Ethiopian Revolution, 1974–91: From a Monarchical Autocracy to a Military Oligarchy*. New York: Kegan Paul International.

Halliday, F., and M. Molyneux. 1981. *The Ethiopian Revolution*. London: NLB.

Hameso, S. Y., and M. Hassen 2006. *Arrested Development in Ethiopia: Essays on Underdevelopment, Democracy, and Self-Determination*. Trenton, NJ: Red Sea Press.

Hamilton, D. 1977. *Ethiopia's Embattled Revolutionaries*. London: Institute for the Study of Conflict.

Hammond, J., and N. Druce. 1990. *Sweeter than Honey: Ethiopian Women and Revolution: Testimonies of Tigrayan Women*. Trenton, NJ: Red Sea Press.

Harbeson, J. W. 1988. *The Ethiopian Transformation: The Quest for the Post-Imperial State*. Boulder, CO: Westview Press.

Harris, J. E. 1994. *African-American Reactions to War in Ethiopia, 1936–1941*. Baton Rouge: Louisiana State University Press.

Harris, M. F. 1987. *Breakfast in Hell: A Doctor's Eyewitness Account of the Politics of Hunger in Ethiopia*. New York: Poseidon Press.

Henze, P. B. 2007. *Ethiopia in Mengistu's Final Years*. Addis Ababa, Ethiopia: Shama Books.

Hezbawi wayane harenet Tegray. 1981. *Tigray in Struggle: Information Bulletin of the Tigray People's Liberation Front*. Khartoum: Foreign Affairs Bureau.

Hiwet, A. 1975. *Ethiopia: From Autocracy to Revolution*. London: Review of African Political Economy.

Initiative Africa Ethiopia. 2005. *2005 Pre-Election Survey of Urban Areas and Towns of Major Regions of Ethiopia: Final Survey Report*. Addis Ababa, Ethiopia: Initiative Africa.

Jalata, A. 1998. *Oromo Nationalism and the Ethiopian Discourse: The Search for Freedom and Democracy*. Lawrenceville, NJ: Red Sea Press.

James, Peter, and Nick Thorpe. 1994. *Ancient Inventions*. New York: Ballantine Books. 203.

James, W., D. L. Donham, et al. 2002. *Remapping Ethiopia: Socialism & After*. Oxford, England: J. Currey.

Kassahun, B. 2007. *Electoral Politics, Decentralized Governance, and Constitutionalism in Ethiopia*. Addis Ababa, Ethiopia: Dept. of Political Science and International Relations, Addis Ababa University.

Kassahun, B., K. Yonas, et al. 2006. *Ethiopia: Politics, Policy Making, and Rural Development*. Addis Ababa, Ethiopia: Dept. of Political Science and International Relations, Addis Ababa University.

Kebbede, Tessemma. 1969. *Yetarik Mastawesha*. Addis Ababa, Ethiopia: Artistic Printing Press.

Kendie, D. 2005. *The Five Dimensions of the Eritrean Conflict, 1941–2004: Deciphering the Geo-Political Puzzle*. Prairie View, TX: Daniel Kendie.

Kiflu, T. 1993. *The Generation: The History of the Ethiopian People's Revolutionary Party*. Lanham, MD: University Press of America.

Kingma, K., V. Sayers, et al. 1995. *Demobilization in the Horn of Africa: Proceedings of the IRG Workshop, 4–7 December 1994, Addis Ababa*. Bonn, Germany: Bonn International Center for Conversion.

Korn, D. A. 1986. *Ethiopia, the United States, and the Soviet Union*. Carbondale: Southern Illinois University Press.

Leenco, Lata. 1999. *The Ethiopian State at the Crossroads: Decolonization and Democratization or Disintegration?* Lawrenceville, NJ: Red Sea Press.

Legesse, A. 2006. *Oromo Democracy: An Indigenous African Political System*. Trenton, NJ: Red Sea Press.

Legum, C. 1975. *Ethiopia: The Fall of Haile Selassie's Empire*. New York: Africana.

Legum, C., and B. Lee. 1977. *Conflict In the Horn of Africa*. New York: Africana.

Lewis, H. S. 2001. *Jimma Abba Jifar, an Oromo Monarchy: Ethiopia, 1830–1932*. Lawrenceville, NJ: Red Sea Press.

MacDonald, J. F. 1957. *Abyssinian Adventure*. London: Cassell.

Mahteme Selassie Wolde, M. 1942. *Zekra Nagar*. Addis Ababa, Ethiopia: Natsanat Matemia Bet.

Marcus, H. G. 1995. *The Politics of Empire: Ethiopia, Great Britain, and the United States, 1941–1974*. Lawrenceville, NJ: Red Sea Press.

Marein, N. 1954. *The Ethiopian Empire; Federation and Laws*. Rotterdam: Royal Netherlands Printing and Lithographing.

Markakis, J. 1974. *Ethiopia: Anatomy of a Traditional Polity*. Oxford: Clarendon Press.

Markakis, J., and A. Nega. 1978. *Class and Revolution in Ethiopia*. Nottingham: Spokesman Books for the Review of African political economy.

Mas'udi. (ca. 956) 1989. *The Meadows of Gold: The Abbasid*. Translated and edited by Paul Lunde and Caroline Stone. New York: Kegan Paul.

Meles Zenawi. 2001. "Bonapartism." Unpublished Document. Addis Ababa.

Merera, G. 2003. *Ethiopia: Competing Ethnic Nationalisms and the Quest for Democracy, 1960–2000*. Addis Ababa, Ethiopia: Shaker.

Michael, F. H. 1989. *The Roots of Nationality Problems and the Challenge to Nation-Building in Ethiopia*. Bergen, Norway: Chr. Michelsen Institute, DERAP.

Michels, J. 1988. "Regional Political Organization in the Aksum-Yeha Area during the Pre-Axumite and Axumite Era." Paper read at the 10th International Conference of Ethiopian Studies, Paris.

Milkias, Paulos. 2006. *Haile Selassie, Western Education, and Political Revolution in Ethiopia*. Youngstown, NY: Cambria Press.

Newman, E. W. P. 1936. *Ethiopian Realities*. London: G. Allen & Unwin.

Ottaway, M., and D. Ottaway 1978. *Ethiopia: Empire in Revolution*. New York: Africana.

Pankhurst, E. S., R. Pankhurst, et al. 1953. *Ethiopia and Eritrea: The Last Phase of the Reunion Struggle, 1941–1952*. Woodford Green, Essex: Lalibela House.

Pankhurst, Richard. 1965. *The Ethiopian Royal Chronicles*. London: Oxford University Press. 1–7.

Pankhurst, Richard. 1965. *Travels in Ethiopia*. London: Oxford University Press. 4–9.

Parker, B. 1995. *Ethiopia, Breaking New Ground*. Oxford, UK: Oxfam.

Pausewang, S. 1994. *The 1994 Election and Democracy in Ethiopia*. Oslo: Norwegian Institute of Human Rights.

Perham, M. 1948. *The Government of Ethiopia*. London: Faber and Faber.

Phillips, Jack. 1997. "Punt and Axum: Egypt and the Horn of Africa." *Journal of African History* 37: 423–57.

Praeg, B. 2006. *Ethiopia and Political Renaissance in Africa*. New York: Nova Science.

Richards to Secretary of State. 1960. The Abortive Coup d'etat. Addis Ababa. SD 773.11/12–1760.

Richards to Secretary of State. 1960. The Abortive Coup d'etat. Addis Ababa. SD 775.00/12–1660.

Rosenthal, E. 1941. *The Fall of Italian East Africa*. London: Hutchinson.

Sauldie, M. M. 1987. *Super Powers in the Horn of Africa*. New Delhi: Sterling.

Schwab, P. 1972. *Decision-Making in Ethiopia: A Study of the Political Process*. London: C. Hurst.

Scott, W. R. 1993. *The Sons of Sheba's Race: African-Americans and the Italo-Ethiopian War, 1935–1941.* Bloomington: Indiana University Press.

Semegn, T. B. 2007. *Seeds for Democratization in Ethiopia: Why Unity of Purpose Matters.* Bloomington, IN: Author House.

Serra-Horguelin, A. 1999. *The Federal Experiment in Ethiopia: A Socio-Political Analysis.* Pessac, Paris: Centre d'études d'Afrique noire, Institut d'études politiques de Bordeaux.

Shepherd, J. 1975. *The Politics of Starvation.* New York: Carnegie Endowment for International Peace.

Spencer, John H. 1977. *Ethiopia: The Horn of Africa, and U.S. Policy.* Cambridge, MA: Institute for Foreign Policy Analysis.

Spencer, John H. 1984. *Ethiopia at Bay: A Personal Account of the Haile Selassie Years.* Algonac, MI: Reference Publications.

Steer, G. L. 1942. *Sealed and Delivered: A Book on the Abyssinian Campaign.* London: Hodder and Stoughton.

Steffanson, B. G., R. K. Starrett, et al. 1976. *Documents on Ethiopian Politics.* Salisbury, NC: Documentary Publications.

Taye, A., G.-E. Tegegne, et al. 2007. *Decentralization in Ethiopia.* Addis Ababa, Ethiopia: Forum for Social Studies.

Tegenu, T. 1996. *The Evolution of Ethiopian Absolutism: The Genesis and the Making of the Fiscal Military State, 1696–1913.* Sweden: Uppsala University.

Tesfaye, A. 2002. *Political Power and Ethnic Federalism: The Struggle for Democracy in Ethiopia.* Lanham, MD: University Press of America.

Tiruneh, A. 1993. *The Ethiopian Revolution, 1974–1987: A Transformation from an Aristocratic to a Totalitarian Autocracy.* New York: Cambridge University Press.

Tronvoll, K., Ø. Aadland, et al. 1995. *The Process of Democratization in Ethiopia: An Expression of Popular Participation or Political Resistance?* Oslo: Norwegian Institute of Human Rights.

Turton, D. 2006. *Ethnic Federalism: The Ethiopian Experience in Comparative Perspective.* Oxford: James Currey.

U.S. Ambassador to Secretary of State, Monrovia. 1960. SD 775.11/12–1560, in Looram Report.

U.S. Congress, House Committee on Foreign Affairs, Subcommittee on Africa. 1992. *The Political Crisis in Ethiopia and the Role of the United States: Hearing.* Washington, DC: U.S. Government Printing Office.

U.S. Congress, House Committee on Foreign Affairs, Subcommittee on Africa. 1993. *Looking Back and Reaching Forward: Prospects for Democracy in Ethiopia: Hearing.* Washington, DC: U.S. Government Printing Office.

Vaughan, S. 1994. *The Addis Ababa Transitional Conference of July 1991: Its Origins, History, and Significance.* Edinburgh: Centre of African Studies, Edinburgh University.

Vestal, T. M. 1999. *Ethiopia: A Post–Cold War African State.* Westport, CT: Praeger.

Woldemariam, K. 2006. *Myths and Realities in the Distribution of Socioeconomic Resources and Political Power in Ethiopia.* Lanham, MD: University Press of America.

Work, E. 1936. *Ethiopia, a Pawn in European Diplomacy.* New York: Macmillan.

Wubneh, M., and Y. Abate. 1988. *Ethiopia: Transition and Development in the Horn of Africa.* Boulder, CO: Westview Press.

Young, J. 1997. *Peasant Revolution in Ethiopia: The Tigray People's Liberation Front, 1975–1991.* New York: Cambridge University Press.

Zegeye, A., and S. Pausewang. 1994. *Ethiopia in Change: Peasantry, Nationalism, and Democracy.* New York: British Academic Press.

Zewde, Gabra-Selassie. 1976. *Eritrea and Ethiopia in the Context of the Red Sea and Africa.* Washington, DC: Woodrow Wilson International Center for Scholars. 6–30.

Zewde, Gabre-Selassie. 1975. *Yohannes IV of Ethiopia: A Political Biography.* Oxford: Clarendon Press.

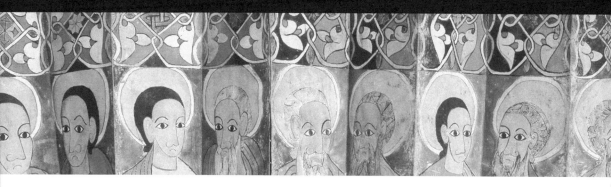

CHAPTER 4

Economy

ECONOMIC OVERVIEW

The bedrock of Ethiopia's economy is agriculture, which accounts for almost half of its gross domestic product (GDP), 60 percent of its exports, and 80 percent of its entire employment. The agricultural sector is periodically bedeviled by drought and poor cultivation practices of the rural population.

Coffee is the main commodity that keeps the Ethiopian economy going, with exports of some $412 million in 2007. Over the last few decades, low prices of coffee in the international market have forced many farmers to look for alternatives that might supplement their falling income. Many thus switched to the production of *chat* (or *qat*), a stimulant widely used in the Horn of Africa and the Near East.

The Eritrean–Ethiopian war of 1998–2000 and recurrent drought conditions have affected the economy negatively. During this period, coffee production was hit severely, leading to a significant fall in national and personal income.

The economy of Ethiopia, which found itself on a tightrope, was buoyed up by unforeseen developments. In November 2001, Ethiopia qualified for debt relief from the Highly Indebted Poor Countries (HIPC) initiative. Then in December 2005, the International Monetary Fund (IMF) voted to forgive all of Ethiopia's debt.

The Ethiopian Constitution of December 8, 1994, stipulates that all lands are the property of the state. Land use is allowed only through long-term leases. The government instituted the system with the aim of protecting the destitute peasants of the south against economically powerful persons from the urban areas. However, opposition parties and international financial bodies, including the IMF and the World Bank, as well as Western donor countries, have criticized the policy because

Woman sorting coffee in southern Ethiopia. (Transfair, USA.)

in their view it hampers growth in the industrial sector, given that entrepreneurs find it hard to use land as collateral for loans.

Adverse weather patterns had led to a 3.3 percent decline in GDP in 2003, but normal weather conditions helped agricultural and GDP growth recover during 2004–2007. In 2008 there was again a forecast for drought conditions that might affect the country's economic well-being.

HISTORICAL BACKGROUND OF THE ETHIOPIAN ECONOMY

Antiquity

Traced back to the earliest times of the nation's history, the local economy of Ethiopia was based on agricultural products, food items, and clothing and was almost exclusively conducted in neighborhood markets. The economy consisted mostly of grains, honey, butter, spices, salt, beasts of burden, livestock, handicraft items, cooking utensils, and cotton products.

Hamar Market in southern Ethiopia. (Courtesy of Paulos Milkias.)

The country's recorded history of external trade goes back to the time of the early Egyptian dynasties. From the 5th to the 2nd century BC, the Puntites (Ethiopians) exported myriads of products to Egypt.

Though the Egyptians have never given details of products they exported to Ethiopia, the *Periplus of the Eritrean Sea*, which was written by an Egyptian trader around the first century AD, mentions plenty of them.

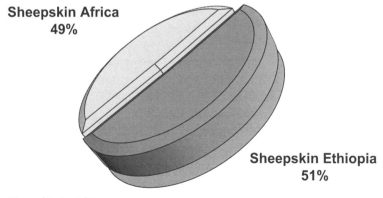

Sheepskin in Africa

From the ninth century AD on, Arabs and Armenians, and in later centuries Greeks, dominated Ethiopian commercial import and export activities. Because the Christians preferred being farmers, soldiers, or members of the clergy and were prejudiced against trade, Ethiopian Muslims became prominent in local and foreign commerce. Around the close of the 13th century, Marco Polo reported that the country was much frequented by merchants who obtained large profits. The importance of Ethiopian Muslims in import and export trade was reported in a medieval Ge'ez ecclesiastical account—the *Gadla Zena Marqos* (Pankhurst, 1990, 53; Taddesse, 1972, 85, 87–88; Cerulli, 1962), which states that the Muslim traders "did business in India, Egypt, and among the people of Greece with the money of the king," who gave them ivory and "excellent horses from Shawa [Shoa], and red pure horses from Enarya," which the merchants exchanged in Egypt, Greece, and Rome for "very rich damasks adorned with green and scarlet stones and with leaves of red gold, which they brought to the king." Many Muslim merchants also conducted business for the Christian aristocracy. Almeida, for example, recounts that the great and rich men of the Ethiopian empire all had Muslim merchants as their trade agents, who carried gold to the sea for them and brought them silks and clothing. The trends described here were characteristic the feature of Ethiopian import-export trade until the end of the 19th century.

The Ethiopian Economy under Feudalism: 1941–1974

The Ethiopian economy was based on rural production during the feudal period. Cultivators, serfs, and herdsmen possessed the means of agricultural production but had to function with varying constraints on their freedom of mobility. They worked their holdings by relying on family labor and normally belonged to a village community with certain rights to common property. They generated economic surplus above subsistence to support non-producing classes and, though subsistence-oriented, had some linkage to markets.

The land tenure structure under feudalism was known as the *gebbar* system, with two essential features. First, it was lineage-based, and individuals were allotted restricted plots. This was the subsystem of *ristegna* (property ownership). The feudal state depended on soldiers known as *Nneftegnas* (literally gunmen) who received their remuneration in grants of lands farmed by southern peasants. This was the subsystem of *chisegna*. The second feature of the *gebbar* system was the variable type of paying tribute to the state for cultivated plots from which the rulers supplied garrison towns located throughout the empire.

The landlords and the ecclesiastical personnel extracted surpluses from two basic sources, namely from tribute payments by the peasantry, which the state expropriated or handed over to its functionaries in the form of fief, and revenue from self-cultivation with, in many cases, corvée labor, which is labor exacted in lieu of paying taxes. The latter case might also involve revocable grants for administrative duties in place of salary payments. The *rist* (property) structure that constituted the main facet of the *gebbar* system in the Amhara and Tigre areas of Ethiopia was a kin-based right allotted to individuals by lineage. The plots of land each individual in the community claimed on the basis of a progenitor were of various sizes. According to available records, claim to such rights had been in place since the 13th century, when the Solomonian dynasty replaced the Zagwes. *Rist* ownership could be market-based, though in some cases it was restricted to members of an extended family. The system involved land pledges limited by time, rental payments, or sharecropping.

Gult was a nontransferable claim to state tax owed by peasants or sedentary farmers. *Gult* was connected to office and thus could not be legally transferred to another person. However, in lands taken over by force or military means, a *rist-gult* that was alienated by an official could be heritable.

In the structure just described, there was a clear class differentiation. People were classified into *gabaré* (serf), *balabat* (peer), *nagade* (trader), *wotadar* (soldier), *naft-agna* (armed colon), *kahnat* (clerics), *mesafint* (royalty), and *makwanint* (aristocracy). The system allowed mobility. But in general there was a long chain in the payment of taxes—a *ristagna* paid a levy to a landlord; a retainer to a superior; a traditional regional ruler to a monarch.

Each farmer, sedentary or otherwise, was legally required to pay a fixed tax, known as *qurt gibir*, in grains ranging in amount from one-fifth (*amisho*) to half (*ikul*) of the harvest of the season. Depending on the occupation of the individual, the tax could also be in levies, in monetary form, or in head of cattle. A peasant might be required to pay tithe to the state through a governor. He might also be obliged to provide sustenance to officials who passed through his district to carry out government duties. Failure to pay one's taxes or dues necessarily led to the loss of hereditary rights to land use, and in the case of an official, loss of a coveted government position. Regional rulers granted certain rights to their trusted retainers in the form of *madaria* land, which was temporary, or *malkagna* land, which was heritable. Such systems remained in place until Haile Selassie's ascension to the throne and then continued for many more years.

Negus Haile Selassie's centralization efforts had started to slowly erode the archaic feudal system described here, but Mussolini's occupation of the country in 1936

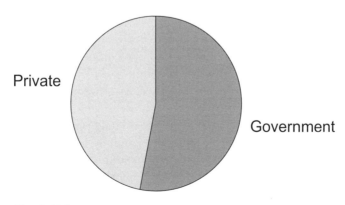

Textile Fabrics

interrupted the process. Following Fascist defeat in 1941, however, Haile Selassie's state system set its priorities on the establishment and expansion of the bureaucratic structure and ancillary services. Dependence on the rural economy continued, but trade increased, albeit at a very slow rate. Ninety percent of the Ethiopian population was engaged in subsistence agriculture and the herding of domestic animals. In some peripheral localities, nomadic lifestyle continued to be the norm. The industrial sector was, for all practical purposes, negligible.

In the early 1950s, Haile Selassie stressed in a policy speech that the nation had to transition from a subsistence economy to an agro-industrial one. For this, resources had to be allocated, and sufficient infrastructure had to be created. People's living conditions had to be improved, communication had to be expanded, and education and health services had to be in place. To administer all these changes, a central planning mechanism was formulated.

In order to enhance development, Emperor Haile Selassie established the National Economic Council. Created in 1954, it was headed by the emperor himself. Its aim was to boost productivity in agriculture and industry and to stamp out poverty, illiteracy, and ill health. To accomplish these goals, the council developed the first and second five-year plans.

The first five-year plan (1957–1961) was aimed primarily at laying down basic infrastructure for construction, transportation, and communications, so as to link the disparate regions of Ethiopia, which are naturally cut off from one another by myriad rivers and mountains. Its second aim was to create vital manpower for the emerging processing industries so that Ethiopia would not be dependent on imports of finished goods. It also encouraged the establishment of a more efficient system of agricultural production for commercial purposes. Total investment in the first five-year plan was 839.6 million birr, which was 25 percent more than the original allocation.

The second five-year plan, which was launched for 1962–1967, laid the foundation for a two-decade program to replace Ethiopia's predominantly agricultural economy with one with a modern agro-industrial base. The plan was aimed at speedy economic growth, the introduction of modern processing mechanisms, and general enhancement of the country's productive capacity. Again there was a cost overrun in the second plan—total expenditures this time were 13 percent higher than the projected 1.694 billion birr.

The third five-year plan (1968–1973), which was launched to expedite modernization, was aimed at the facilitation of Ethiopia's economic growth through the introduction and expansion of manufacturing and agro-industrial industries. It aimed at expanding educational opportunities for people and at upgrading rural farming methods. The allocation for the third five-year plan was significantly higher than for the previous two: 3.115 billion birr.

All three of Ethiopia's development plans under Haile Selassie suffered as a result of many factors. One problem was the paucity of administrative and technical wherewithal to execute the plans. Also, there were not enough established organizational structures to facilitate large-scale economic development. The planning commission, which conceived the first and second plans, also faced a severe staffing shortage. The same problem burdened the Ministry of Planning, which prepared the third one. In all cases, objectives were rarely fulfilled because of shortages of resources, including budgetary allocations, equipment, and personnel.

In the first plan, the gross national product (GNP) increased at 3.2 percent per year, falling short of the projected amount of 3.7. Growth in manufacturing, agriculture, and mining failed to meet the projected targets. Whereas imports grew at a rate of 6.4 percent per year, exports increased at only 3.5 percent. Thus, the negative balance of trade that had existed since 1951 remained.

The economic growth rate for the second and third five-year plans were 4.3 percent and 6.0 percent, respectively, but both fell short of the projected targets. Agriculture, industry, transport, and communications were anticipated to grow at 2.5, 27.3, and 6.7 percent per year during the second five-year plan and at 2.9, 14.9, and 10.9 percent per year during the third five-year plan, but the planning commission failed to assess the performance, blaming it on the shortage of qualified personnel. By all indications, targets were far from being reached.

Nevertheless, all was not bleak. Data from the Ethiopian government's Central Statistical Authority showed that during the years 1960 to 1974 a fair level of economic growth was registered. From 1960 to 1970, Ethiopia had an annual 4.4 percent average growth rate in per capita GDP. In 1960/1961, the modern sector registered double the growth rate from the previous year. The statistics show a rise from 1.9 percent to 4.4 percent in 1973/1974. During the same period, the growth rate for the wholesale, retail trade, transportation, and communications sectors also went up from 9.3 percent to 15.6 percent.

In all, compared to its neighbors, Ethiopia lagged far behind. For example, whereas between 1960 and 1973, Ethiopia's average per capita growth in GDP was 4.4 percent, Uganda's GDP grew at 5.6 percent, and Kenya registered a 6 percent annual rate of growth. What is more, from 1953 to 1974, Ethiopia's balance of trade continued to show annual deficits. Faced with this chronic problem, the government attempted to substitute locally produced industrial goods with imports. This was not

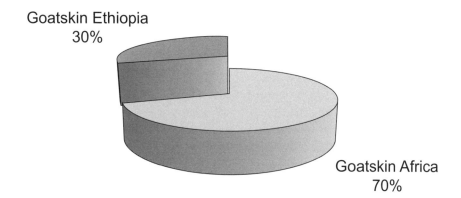

Goatskin in Africa

able to ameliorate the problem. Ethiopia had no choice but to depend on financial grants and loans from abroad to cover the balance of payments deficit.

Effects on the Economy by the Eritrean Federation and the Abortive 1960 Coup d'état

Overall, the federation of Eritrea with Ethiopia in 1952 following the United Nations (UN) decision led to a wider reach in the industrial sector, given that the former had a head start in the process under Italian colonialism for half a century and a decade-long British administration. Industrial production, public revenue and expenditure, investment and consumption, foreign trade—all benefited from the federation of traditional Ethiopia with industrializing Eritrea.

The Ethiopian economy developed from 1941 to 1960, but at a snail's pace. It was the abortive 1960 coup d'état that brought forth a rude awakening to the sluggish feudal order. The rebels directed a damning indictment at the reactionary forces for Ethiopia's backwardness compared with the newly emerging African countries that were surging forward with the spirit of freedom that had come in the wake of decaying and disappearing European colonialism. The rebellion was a clarion call for democratic governance that would pave the way for the fundamental reform that was required if the standard of living of the people were to be improved.

To make their point, the rebels executed key aristocratic leaders, ministers, and government officials who they claimed had kept modern economic development hostage before they themselves were consumed when the coup was crushed by Haile Selassie's loyalists. Ethiopia's die-hard feudalists who had somehow survived the wrath of the rebels realized that their days were numbered if economic development did not come fast enough. Thus, they gave way to reform-minded young technocrats, who catapulted the pace of economic development to a significant degree.

Feudalism was shaken by the event, but it was far from falling. So the progressive, educated Ethiopians had to warily navigate their way through its cumbersome passages. Even Haile Selassie himself realized that sluggish progress would endanger the very survival of the monarchy. Thus, he issued the Income Tax Proclamation of 1961, whereby existing and newly established manufacturing ventures would be exempted from income tax for up to five years on condition that more than 200,000 birr was invested in the project.

Haile Selassie passed another decree in 1963 that encouraged the establishment and growth of local and foreign industrial and commercial ventures. In this decree's wake came the Investment Proclamation of 1966, the most liberal edict with the most attractive investment incentives for business-minded entrepreneurs. The result was quite dramatic: foreign private investment soared to 128 million birr from the 86-million-birr base during the five years preceding the coup. This was an almost 50 percent increase between the years 1960 and 1965.

One other effect of the 1960 coup d'état was momentum for the creation of labor unions, hitherto discouraged by the feudal system that was struggling to survive the changes wrought by the newly emerging forces of economic development. Start-

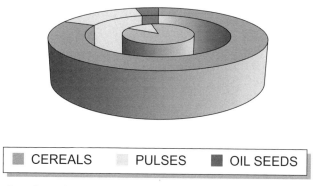

■ CEREALS   ■ PULSES   ■ OIL SEEDS

Cereals, Pulses, and Oil Seeds

ing in 1961, organized laborers boldly challenged the regime, which treated worker strikes as insurrections. The unions carried out pickets and work stoppages. Factory hands at the Dutch-owned HVA International branch, the Wonji Sugar Estate, the family-owned Darmar Shoe Factory, and the partly state-run Indo-Ethiopian Textile Factory at Aqaqi all went on strike, demanding fair wages and better working conditions.

The crowning moment for Ethiopia's workers was the creation of the Confederation of Ethiopian Labor Unions (CELU) which was duly recognized by the government through a parliamentary decree in 1963. CELU grew rapidly until it had 80,000 members by 1974. It was partly the devastating strike it called in 1974 that paralyzed the city of Addis Ababa and most urban areas of the country and brought down the feudal regime of Emperor Haile Selassie.

The abortive 1960 coup also gave impetus to student radicalism. The University College students went out in full force to support the rebels. They were almost gunned down near the Addis Ababa Railway station when they made a demonstration in support of the coup and in opposition to the feudal order then in place.

By the late 1960s, student radicalism had taken a Marxist form, particularly after the founding of the University Students' Union of Addis Ababa (USUAA), which launched the radical paper *Struggle*. The students' movement made its bold challenge against the feudal regime when it called for "land to the tiller of the soil." It also called for the right of nationalities to self-determination.

The World-Wide Federation of Ethiopian Students based in Europe and North America helped with ideological direction, and two important parties emerged from the students' movement: the All Ethiopian Socialist Movement, otherwise known by its Amharic acronym MEISON, and the Ethiopian People's Revolutionary Party (EPRP). These groups paved the way for the ideological base of the post–Haile Selassie political order through their publications *Voice of the Masses*, a political mouthpiece of MEISON, and *Democracia*, the ideological mouthpiece of the EPRP. The fact that the two groups ultimately had a falling out does not detract from their contribution to the radicalism that emerged during the Derg era.

The global economic crisis that culminated following the Yom Kippur War and the hiking of oil prices by the Organization of Petroleum Exporting Countries

(OPEC) was a bad omen for the feudal regime. Coupled with domestic problems, this added to the woes of the severely ailing feudalism still under the grip of Haile Selassie.

It is important to note that crude oil cost only US$1.7 per barrel in the 1950s and US$1.8 per barrel in the 1960s and early 1970s, but it suddenly jumped to US$9.6 per barrel in 1973, rising over 430 percent and spawning an immediate global recession. The result was that within a span of a year, Ethiopia's import bill for oil tripled, forcing the government to raise the price of oil by 50 percent. This led to a chain reaction in which the basic cost of commodities, manufactured goods, and foodstuffs spiraled upward.

At the same time, the government unveiled a World Bank–conceived Education Sector Review, which drew the wrath of the country's educators because it tried to curb their future professional growth. The hushed-up famine in Wallo and Tigray, a result of severe drought, claimed the lives of about 100,000 people. These events all fueled the general strikes of 1974, when taxi drivers, students, teachers, and public sector employees went on strike, inexorably crippling the entire system. When men in uniform complained of despicable living conditions and mutinied in their stations in southern and northern Ethiopia, it was the end of an era for Haile Selassie's feudal regime.

The Ethiopian economy under Haile Selassie's feudalism comprised fundamentally two disparate segments: an outsized subsistence sector with exceedingly small levels of productivity and yield, investment, and savings. About four-fifths of the population lived as subsistence farmers. At the time, destitution and poverty were the norm. The general picture was grim. When the rural masses produced their crops and tried to raise funds, they faced many difficulties. One issue was connected to the lack of market development for their products and was tied to three types of price differentials. Farmers had to continuously contend with the discrepancy between the retail selling and buying monetary value for farm families at the township level and wholesale cost in urban neighborhoods. Regional price differences for the same or similar goods existed, and seasonal price variations of agricultural commodities were the norm. These differentials reflected considerable transaction costs involved in the exchange, a process that substantially impoverished the peasants (Grabowski, 1991). Furthermore, those in the hapless rural multitude used most of their meager earnings to pay taxes, rents, debts, and bribes to corrupt officials.

By contrast, an inordinate amount of affluence was the norm for the moderately advanced sector tucked into the country's few urban areas, where absentee landlords, burgeoning technocrats, and prosperous businessmen lived and where modern commercial activities and fabrication of consumer goods proliferated.

Up to the mid-1960s, the subsistence sector, fundamentally reliant on outdated methods of rain-fed farming, produced cereal grains and cash crops and spawned in excess of 50 percent of the nonmonetary GDP of the country. This sector was always on a tightrope, and when nature hit it with periodic draughts and other vagaries of Ethiopia's unpredictable weather, catastrophic famines and the deaths of multitudes of peasants were the inevitable result. To make matters worse, this sector suffered from unfavorable terms of exchange, and there was huge income disparity, enormous regional differentiation, and a massive gap in access to basic services.

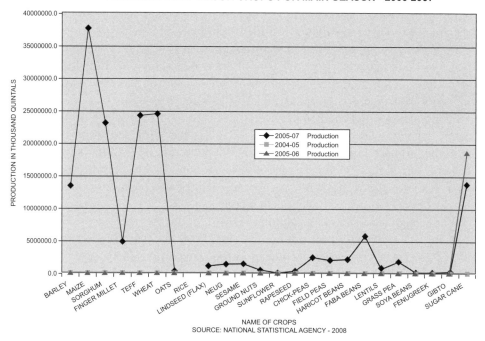

PRODUCTION OF MAJOR CROPS FOR MAIN SEASON - 2006-2007

NAME OF CROPS
SOURCE: NATIONAL STATISTICAL AGENCY - 2008

Production of Major Crops for Main Season, 2006–2007

The Ethiopian economy depended on the exports of such commodities as coffee, hides, pulses, and oil seeds and on imports of capital and intermediate goods, industrial raw materials, and consumer items. The global economy was reached by the monetized sector, which flourished by depending on surpluses generated in the subsistence sector. The monetized sector also operated as a conduit for channeling the surpluses in question toward the international market.

Foreign trade was not able to generate conditions leading to sustainable growth between 1941 and 1974. One reason for this was Ethiopia's dependence on exports of commodities and one primary item—coffee—for promoting economic development, because primary products are subject to unpredictable price fluctuations. The other reason is that the export sector failed to carry over to the other sectors of the economy.

For Ethiopia, declining terms of trade had become almost chronic. In the absence of big industries and upward pressures by trade unions that would have made the fruits of technological progress spawn higher incomes, competitive pressures in Ethiopia ensured that the gains from technical improvements in agriculture were passed on in the form of lower prices for goods consumed locally. For example, in the 1950s, after the first five-year plan had run its course, only 18 percent of Ethiopia's total produce entered the international market. The remaining 82 percent ended up as subsistence or nonmonetary product. The price of finished goods imported by Ethiopia rose relative to the price of commodities, which were the exports of Ethiopia. Thus, Ethiopia was not able to purchase enough industrial products from abroad.

For the most part, models of economic development that have been pinpointed by foreign advisers and accepted by Ethiopia's own economists traditionally have been dualistic. They have juxtaposed the traditional, subsistence agriculture–based sector with the modern, industrial sector and have advanced the assumption that as time goes on, it becomes necessary to transfer most resources from the traditional, agricultural sector to the modem, industrial sector. This means, in one way, transferring labor from where its productivity is low to where it is high.

Economic development in this conception is a mechanism by which the traditional sector, distinguished by its dependence on subsistence agricultural production, is inevitably displaced by the modern sector, characterized by manufacturing. It was further assumed that different modes of behavior would occur in the former and the latter. It was assumed that economic development by its very nature would involve the transfer of resources to the modem sector.

What characterizes modern economic growth in this view "is the presence in the economy of a systematic and continuous drive to transform production in the direction of greater efficiency. This tendency is the result of producers seeking to continuously cut costs by further specializing and accumulating their surpluses, and adopting the best available production techniques" or innovations (Grabowski, 1991). According to this view, in the modern sector, the mode of behavior dictates the emergence of capital accumulation and growth in productivity. Thus, development inevitably involves large-scale displacement of the traditional sector.

Another way of looking at this type of analysis is that development occurs as capital accumulation in the modern sector draws labor out of the traditional sector. The capital accumulation occurs as a result of the savings and investment activities of the owners of capital. Therefore, the modern sector becomes the engine of economic growth and inevitably replaces the traditional sector as a major yardstick of the process of sustainable growth.

What this approach seems to neglect is the fact that peasant farmers are no less interested in economic return than are industrial entrepreneurs or commercially oriented farmers. So it was wrong to assume there was a zero-sum game between the two sectors. Furthermore, it should not have been forgotten "that successful industrialization is, for the most part, dependent upon the rapid growth of a domestic market for manufactured goods. The development of such a market is dependent upon the expansion of rural purchasing power, which itself is dependent on expanding productivity growth in those crops that are grown by the bulk of the rural producers. The types of products usually grown by such producers are edible crops or cash crops. This will generate the widespread income growth likely to provide the foundation for successful industrialization" (Grabowski, 1991).

Economic planning in Ethiopia was based from the beginning of the period after the conclusion of the Ethiopian–Italian war on sectoral programs, mostly in the areas of manufacturing, forestry, agriculture, construction, communication, and manpower training. The initial phase of this program was launched with U.S. aid in 1945 as a 10-year industrial development program. The UN's Food and Agriculture Organization (FAO) also helped in launching development schemes in the areas of agriculture and forestry. The revamping and expansion of roads was also carried out

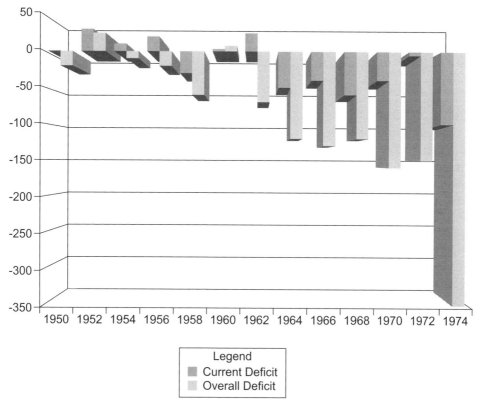

Budget Deficits, 1950–1974

through the 1952–1956 work program, and a telecommunications revamping and expansion program was carried out as part of the 10-year program. The same was done with curricular development in education.

In preparation for the launching of the first five-year plan, numerous surveys were performed to gauge the level of the country's natural resource base and development prospects. Military outlay—fueled by war preparedness; skirmishes with Somalia; and the need to suppress civil insurrections, particularly in Eritrea, where the Eritrean Liberation Front was gaining strength—accounted for one-fourth of the budget in the 1960s and early 1970s. Recurrent expenditures spawned by long-range plans in such areas as transport and communication also absorbed a large chunk of current expenditures after the projects had become operational.

Capital expenditures on agriculture, which was known to be the bedrock of the national economy, were neglected, leaving agriculture primitive by 20th-century standards. So were expenditures on health and education, which would have long-range consequences on the country's social development.

For economic expansion aimed at boosting the GDP, the country ran deficits that kept rising for the most part. Deficits increased from 2 percent of the GDP during the 1950s to 2.7 percent in the 1960s and 4 percent in the 1970s. In the 1960s, the increase in current expenditures as a ratio of GDP averaged 10 percent. This has to be compared to revenues, which went up at a rate of 9.5 percent. Between 1970 and 1974, both revenues and expenditures averaged 14 percent of GDP. During those four years, revenues grew gradually from 9.8 percent to 13 percent, and expenditures went up from 10.7 percent to 14.6 percent. In the 1960s, by contrast, expenditures as a ratio of GDP grew at a faster rate than current revenues.

The growth in budgetary deficits, which was a symptom of the country's failure to raise sufficient revenues to cover rising expenditures, made it necessary to look at other sources. Foreign borrowing was the only such source available to cover the shortfalls.

In the years 1950 to 1960, direct taxes constituted 24 percent of current revenues. The proportion of direct taxes relative to total revenue went down by 20 percent in the 1960s. But it rose once more to 25 percent in the years 1970 to 1974. Between 1950 and 1974, the proportion of direct taxes compared to total revenue was 23 percent.

With Ethiopia having a low level of per capita GDP, the proportion of direct taxes in total tax revenue was clearly high. Indirect taxes, on the other hand, increased sharply because of the escalating monetization of the economy. During the decades spanning 1950 to 1974, taxes levied on foreign trade remained the most important source of revenue because they made up of one-third of total tax revenue for 24 years following 1950. The GDP share of tax revenue rose from about 73 percent in the 1950s to 77 percent in the 1960s. Then it climbed to an average of 87.5 percent between 1970 and 1974.

The Money Factor

Ethiopians have used the silver Thaler since as far back as the time of Emperor Iyasu II of Ethiopia (1730–1755). It was minted in Austria and was widely used all over the world, including in the United States. Emperor Haile Selassie issued the Ethiopian birr, which was pegged to the U.S. dollar at a rate of exchange of 2.50 birr per U.S. dollar with the Currency and Legal Tender Proclamation of May 1945. But because of its silver value, people continued to use the Thaler even after it was legally banned. Parallel with this, barter in the form of lengths of bars of salt or lengths of cloth was used in most areas of the country.

The money supply expanded robustly during the 1960s. This was due to the growing use of modern currency, the opening up of domestic credit, and bigger earnings from exports. Growth in earnings from exports affected the money supply, which rose from 237 million birr in 1960 to 422 million birr in 1965. This was an average growth rate of 15.6 percent. Revenues from larger volumes of coffee exports and a significant rise in credits amounted to 212 million birr in 1964. There was a slowdown in 1967 when the supply of money shrank by 1.3 percent due in large measure to the fall in the price of coffee. However, it rebounded in the first half of the 1970s, when the currency supply showed tremendous growth, rising from 615 million birr in 1970 to 1.1 billion birr in 1974. This was an average yearly increase of 19 percent. Earnings from the exports of pulses and oilseeds helped to boost this huge rise.

The first central bank in Ethiopia was established after the expulsion of the fascists, and the State Bank of Ethiopia started functioning in August 1942. It was this bank that until 1963 had regulatory functions regarding money supply, credit, and the supervision of gold and foreign exchange reserves as well as the supply of currency. These functions were later transferred to the Commercial Bank of Ethiopia, which was established in 1963.

Soon, other monetary institutions were established, including the Development Bank of Ethiopia, the Agricultural and Industrial Development Bank, the Imperial Savings and Home Ownership Association, the Ethiopian Mortgage Share Company, and the Ethiopian Tourism and Hotels Investment Corporation. Nevertheless, banking services were unavailable to the rural masses who depended on loans from landlords, merchants, and usurers who charged up to 120 percent interest. This created a serious constraint on domestic savings.

Prices were relatively stable from the 1950s to the mid-1970s. From 1945 to 1954, annual changes in price indices of imports hovered between 78 and 80 points, though in 1948, they rose to 118 points.

Coffee forest in its original home, Kaffa province, where coffee grows wild. (Courtesy of Paulos Milkias.)

Between 1945 and 1954, the unit value of export price indices rose significantly from about 114 points to 190 points. Prices changes were generally stable, averaging 2.4 points between 1953 and 1960. Then they rose to 4.2 from 1963 to 1974. In 1974, the wholesale price index went up by 35 percent. Price increases were observed in cereals, which went up by about 32 percent; oilseeds, which grew by 40 percent; and pulses, which dramatically jumped by 200 percent.

Foreign Trade

As Ethiopia's economy grew starting in the 1950s, so did its foreign trade. In 1942, foreign trade was valued at 138 million birr; exports in merchandise brought revenues of 66 million birr, whereas imports cost 72 million birr. In the years between 1945 and 1950, merchandise exports brought revenues of 64 million birr; of this, coffee accounted for 20 million birr.

KALDI AND COFFEE—AN ETHIOPIAN FABLE

An old Ethiopian legend has it that once upon a time, in the southern province of Ethiopia called Kaffa (where the word *coffee* originates), there lived a young goatherd named Kaldi. Every morning, this young man would set his goats to grazing in the fertile hills near his village, and every evening, he would see his loyal goats returning home and entering their enclosure. One evening, however, Kaldi's goats failed to come home. The young man searched for his herd all through the night, but he could not find them. As he was about to give up, thinking that some bad people had probably stolen his loyal goats, at the crack of dawn, he found them, leaping and dancing with reckless abandon and perceptible merriment around a shrub with shiny green leaves and bright red berries. Kaldi watched the drama with tremendous curiosity. He then concluded that the whole spectacle had been created by the berries because he could see the goats nibbling on them from time to time as they kicked and jumped around the bush. Kaldi's impulse was to sample the berries and see if they would have an effect on his mood. Sure enough, the tiredness caused by his sleepless night disappeared, and he also started dancing merrily with his goats around the green-leaved shrubs. Kaldi gathered some of these berries and on returning home experimented with them in different ways, until he found out that at any level of their maturity, the coffee berries—fresh and red or dry and dark—can be roasted, boiled, and sipped to provide the same effect. First his family, then the neighbors, then the village and the entire country, and ultimately the whole world were thus won over to coffee drinking and coffee ceremony, which provides joy and alertness.

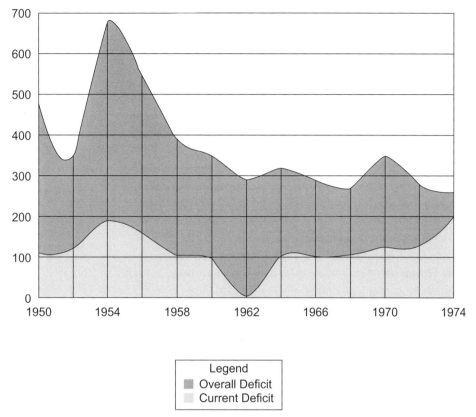

Overall Budgetary Deficit, 1950–1974

Exports

Exports increased to 71 million birr in 1950, with coffee accounting for 46 percent. During the 1950s, overall earnings from merchandise exports went up to about 143 million birr on average, with coffee again accounting for some 55 percent. Foodstuffs, consisting of cereals and pulses, brought 23 percent, and hides and skins 16 percent. Oilseeds, pulses, hides, and skins each accounted for about 9 percent of total exports during the 1950s.

Between 1960 and 1965, exports went up at an average annual rate of 10 percent, rising from 180 million birr to 290 million birr. During the 1960s, export growth averaged 5.6 percent per year. Between 1970 and 1974, exports went up at an annual average rate of 8 percent.

Merchandise exports as a share of GDP were very small. Although in 1950, exports accounted for 4.6 percent of the country's GDP, the share rose to 9.5 percent and 10.7 percent, respectively, in 1954 and 1957. Exports rose to 10 percent in 1974. This was due to major growth in non-coffee exports.

Coffee has remained the major export product of Ethiopia. Between 1945 and 1949, coffee exports constituted 30 percent of the country's overall external trade.

The average rose 55.5 percent between 1950 and 1969. The volume of coffee exports was 71,400 tons during this period from 1950 to 1968. It rose to 88,400 tons in 1969.

Coffee exports earned Ethiopia 188 million birr in 1965 when world coffee prices rose, and the volume of exports went up owing to increased production. In the years 1970 to 1974, coffee exports went down and constituted an average 51 percent of overall exports. This was because more earnings were coming from the sale of oilseeds and pulses. The worst decline was registered in 1973 and 1974, when coffee exports hit a historic low of 32 percent. By contrast, revenues from oilseeds and pulses rose to 31 percent in 1973–1974. Coffee, which had averaged 54 percent of the total export revenue between 1950 and 1974, continued to dominate the country's export earnings, making Ethiopia's economic condition totally dependent on the highly volatile nature of global coffee prices (see Chart T in the Facts and Figures section for the fluctuation in coffee prices between 1950 and 1974).

Earnings from oilseeds and pulses surpassed those from coffee by 30 percent in 1974. During the years from 1950 to 1974, exports of non-agricultural goods were less than 10 percent of total exports. Mineral exports were mostly gold, averaging about 7 million birr between 1950 and 1974. Exports of finished goods were on the whole very negligible.

Imports

In terms of imports, from 1945 to 1950, Ethiopian trade was quite low, averaging 67 million birr. Imports, however, grew starting in the 1960s, fueled by significant economic surge and increasing demand in the forms of intermediate products, raw materials, and capital. Rising income also meant more citizens were able to buy more consumer goods.

From 1945 to 1950 the value of foreign merchandise imports increased 11.6 percent, which was relatively higher than the value of exports, which stood at 9.3 percent. In the years 1960 to 1965, imports of foreign merchandise averaged 12 percent and continued to be significantly higher than exports. The high level of imports was generated by increased economic growth and investment during the second and third five-year plans. However, in the second half of the 1960s, imports decreased significantly, averaging 7.2 percent of the national economic growth. The trend was unbroken until the first half of the 1970s, when growth averaged 4.3 percent. Undoubtedly, this was to a significant degree caused by unremitting decline in the economic growth of the period.

Imports amounted to 4.7 percent of the GDP in 1950. In the 1960s, it averaged 9.5 percent of GDP. In the years 1970 to 1972, import was a bit down, registering 9.2 percent. Two-thirds of the value of imports came from capital and intermediate goods in the form of raw materials for manufacturing companies, thus showing how much Ethiopian industrial production depended on foreign sources. Trade in raw materials, intermediate goods, machinery, and equipment constituted 30 percent of total imports in 1950. However, in 1960, it doubled to 61 percent. By 1968, it had risen to 75 percent, though it went down to 61 percent again in 1974.

Capital goods imports more than tripled from a low of 9 percent of total imports in 1950 to 30 percent in 1960. Again, it grew further from 39 percent in 1964 to 44 percent in 1974, indicating marked increase in investment. Petroleum imports rose steeply in 1974, thus becoming a fuel for the revolutionary upheaval of the period. Consumer goods imports decreased from 69 percent of total imports in 1950 to 39 percent a decade later. Their share went down even further to 24 percent in 1968.

Clear in the first half of the 1970s was an upward spiral when imports of consumer goods rose from 35 percent of total imports in 1970 to 38 percent in 1974.

In analyzing Ethiopia's foreign trade, one sees clearly that the country's exports were in the main based on primary products—the greatest bulk of which was coffee, averaging 54 percent of total export earnings of the country between 1950 and 1974. One can further see that imports constituted consumer, capital, and intermediate goods and raw materials. Thus, any reverses in the global economy carried dire consequences for Ethiopia's economic well-being.

It is clear to any political economist that one of the immediate causes of the 1974 Ethiopian revolution was the tripling in price of oil exports, which led taxi drivers to call for a general strike, thus crippling all major cities, including the capital city of Addis Ababa. In addition, the rate of growth in the Ethiopian economy in relation to the rate of growth in foreign trade was such that exports and imports rose sharply in comparison with the GDP.

Starting from the mid-1940s and continuing to the fall of the Haile Selassie regime in 1974, the ratio between the average unit value of exports and the average unit value of imports had favored the developed countries that sold finished goods and bought commodities from Ethiopia. The fact that Ethiopia has always depended on a single major commodity, namely coffee, which has suffered from chronic inelasticity of demand, caused adverse global terms of trade because the ratio of the price of coffee measured in constant prices showed a consistent downward trend as compared to the finished goods Ethiopia imported, whose prices went on an upward spiral. As can be surmised, this debilitated Ethiopia's already fragile economy.

In the years 1950 to 1957, trade deficits were the exception rather than the rule. But starting in 1958, the deficit in trade balance grew rapidly. This could be attributed to the sustained growth the country was undergoing and the requirement dictated by a burgeoning economy that consumed larger amounts of imports. But with imports outstripping exports, trade balance deficit spiraled, rising to an average of 113 million birr in the late 1960s. This is in contrast to an average of 31 million birr during the early part of the decade. Though in the years 1973 and 1974 there were surpluses that averaged about 46 million birr, in large measure because of a remarkable rise in income derived from pulses and oilseeds, the rest of the early 1970s saw deficit in merchandise trade of 148 million birr.

Though current account deficits continued to bedevil Ethiopia, its fortune in the balance of payments was positive as it enjoyed significant surplus. Surplus in balance of payments doubled in the period spanning the years 1950 to 1954, when said surplus went up from 10 million birr to 20 million birr. Between 1950 and 1959, the surplus averaged 12 million birr. This was caused by the sale of coffee, the price of which doubled between 1950 and 1954. Surpluses in Ethiopia's balance of payments lasted into the 1960s, though in 1966 and 1967, there were deficits that averaged 26 million birr. This was when exports declined, when coffee prices and exports of foodstuffs fell.

Starting in 1960, private capital inflow was on a steady increase. Technical assistance, loans, and credits, as well as official grants that formed public capital inflow, increased reasonably after 1960. The country's balance of payments enjoyed lasting increase until Ethiopia's foreign reserve reached 263 million birr in 1974. Foreign exchange holdings climbed from 12 million birr in 1950, which could fund about two months' imports, to 230 million birr in 1965, when the holdings could pay for seven months' imports. During the early 1970s, Ethiopia's foreign exchange status was robust; it rose from 208 million birr in 1970 to 663 million birr at the onset of the revolution in 1974.

Foreign Aid and Debt

Foreign aid to Ethiopia started right after the Fascists were defeated in 1941, when the country's budget was augmented by the British, who came to help Ethiopia expel the invader. Subsidies from Britain amounted to 12 million birr in 1942. Then they averaged 7.6 million birr up until 1945, when subsidies were discontinued following Haile Selassie's successful rebuff of British officials' not-so-secret aim of extending protectorate status to Ethiopia. Then between 1945 and 1949, Ethiopia received 2.5 million birr in official development assistance, mainly from the United States and Sweden. By 1950, official development assistance had reached 14 million birr, which was about 0.75 cents in per capita terms.

Starting in 1958, because of paucity of domestic resources, Ethiopia started to depend to an extraordinary extent on external loans and technical assistance originating from bilateral and multilateral sources. It did so to finance its multifarious development programs dictated by the exigencies of its first five-year plan.

Up to 1974, one major source of economic and technical assistance to Ethiopia was the World Bank Group and its constituent parts, the International Bank of Reconstruction and Development (IBRD) and the International Development Association (IDA). Ethiopia was a member of the World Bank following its establishment in 1945. It also became one of the early recipients of its loans and credits.

In the years 1950 to 1955, Ethiopia was given by the World Bank three basic loans amounting to 22 million birr. Twelve million and a half birr was slated for road construction and maintenance, 5 million birr was given toward the establishment of the Development Bank of Ethiopia, and 4 million and a half birr was targeted toward the expansion and modernization of the country's telecommunications services.

The second most important source of assistance to Ethiopia was the United States. U.S. aid to Ethiopia was in the beginning tied to the exigencies of the Cold War. Responding to the overtures of the United States, Emperor Haile Selassie gave Washington permission to build a military base in Asmara. Following this development, aid allocated to the Ethiopian army alone amounted to 475 million birr up to 1974.

This was equal to half of all the military aid extended to African countries at the time.

A U.S. economic assistance agreement signed in 1951 as well as the Treaty of Amity and Economic Relations of October 1953 brought the Haile Selassie regime a total of 800 million birr. U.S. economic and technical assistance to Ethiopia continued to grow unabated.

Among bilateral sources of loans to Ethiopia, in the 1950s, the United States held the most important place. The largest volume of the aid, 35 percent, was slated for agricultural development. The second largest allotment was for education and health. The rest was invested in civil aviation—the procurement of commercial aircraft and the construction of highways and airports. Starting in the mid-1960s, U.S. help to Ethiopia emphasized technical assistance, such that out of an estimated 900 foreign technical personnel in Ethiopia in 1970, more than 40 percent were American Peace Corps volunteers.

Haile Selassie, who was always wary of dependence on only one source, approached the Soviets to provide aid to his modernizing autocracy. Thus, on his official visit in 1959, he signed an agreement with Moscow in which the Soviet Union agreed to provide Ethiopia with 100 million rubles (250 million birr). However, because of the loans' non-concessional nature, a large part of Soviet loans to Ethiopia were unutilized, such that as late as 1974, when the Haile Selassie regime fell, 200 million birr remained undisbursed.

In the early 1960s, the United States was still the largest bilateral donor to Ethiopia, with 41 percent share. The World Bank's International Development Association supplied the second-largest share, amounting to 31 percent.

In the late 1960s, however, the proportion was reversed, with the World Bank Group giving 41 percent and the United States 29 percent. In 1974, loans and credits from the World Bank rose to 44 percent, whereas those from the United States formed 31 percent. The Federal Democratic Republic of Germany (East Germany) and Italy provided 7 percent each, and Sweden gave nearly 4 percent.

In the years 1962 to 1969, aid from the Soviet Union, Czechoslovakia, and Yugoslavia had also augmented Ethiopia's total development aid. The greatest portions of the aid from these countries was slated for the building of physical and social infrastructure, which included roads and airports, power and telecommunications, education, and health.

World Bank credits and loans financed physical and social infrastructure. Aid from the Soviet Union was invested at Asab oil refinery and the Bahir Dar technical school. Aid and loans from Yugoslavia were slated for the construction and extension of Asab port and a cement plant in Addis Ababa. Czechoslovakian loans financed the establishment of the rubber and tire factories in Addis Ababa and a tannery plant at Ejersa, near the town of Mojo on the road to Adama.

Loans given by East Germany were slated for the construction of a road stretching to Moyale on the border of Kenya. They also financed a cement plant in Massawa. Italian loans were slated for the building of the Laga Dadi reservoir—a key source of water supply to the capital. Credits and grants from Sweden helped in the installation of telephone facilities and aided agricultural projects as well as the expansion

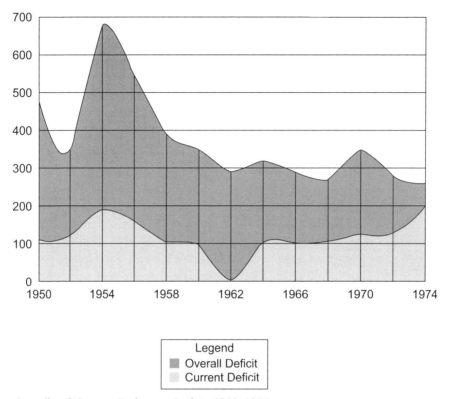

Overall and Current Budgetary Deficit, 1950–1974

of health and education. Loans from Holland helped in the purchase of ships for Ethiopia's merchant marine.

Total foreign indebtedness, including undisbursed loans and credits, made a steep climb from about 14 million birr to 827 million birr from 1950 to 1966. Undisbursed foreign loans went up from 77 million birr to 400 million birr between 1960 and 1966.

From 1970 to 1974, disbursed and undisbursed loans and credits increased in total from 1.3 billion birr to 1.8 billion birr. The large loan given by the People's Republic of China to Ethiopia in 1971, in the amount of 200 million birr, was responsible for the bulk of the increase. The amount of undisbursed loans went up from 440 million birr in 1966 (53 percent of commitments) to 654 million birr in 1970. Whereas the 1970 loans had 50 percent of commitments for usage, total disbursements increased to 52 percent, totaling 962 million birr, in 1974.

The rise in foreign indebtedness, which was rapid, was offset by the absolute volume of indebtedness, which was low in proportion to Ethiopia's exports and development stride. The debt service calculated as a percentage of income from export (debt service ratio) went up from 5.5 percent in 1954 to 6 percent in 1965. This was significantly low when compared with the statistics of other developing nations. Though a percentage of income from export climbed to 18 percent in 1970, it dropped gradually until it reached 9 percent in the year 1974.

The average for the debt service ratio was 13.5 percent from 1970 to 1974. Again, this was low by developing-country standards. In general, during the 1960s and 1970s, Ethiopia had the potential to take loans and expand its programs of economic development because its debt servicing burden was very light.

Most foreign loans extended to Ethiopia were given on moderate terms and conditions. They were characterized by low interest rates and longer maturity periods. Ethiopia generally carried low volume of debt. Because the government of Emperor Haile Selassie paid close attention to donor sensibilities, the Ethiopian nation registered an excellent record in the settlement of its international debt service obligations. This assured a high degree of creditworthiness until the revolution of 1974 suddenly changed the economic picture of the country.

Successes of Haile Selassie's Regime

Despite the overall negative assessment by specialists, quantitatively, the Ethiopian economy during the later years of Emperor Haile Selassie's imperial rule was not that poor. In fact, one can say there were some tangible positive achievements. For example, from 1950 to 1974, there was significant increase in domestic output, which went up about three and one-half times. During the same period, value-added agricultural growth was twofold. Value-added industrial production was also up 15-fold. Change in the country's infrastructure was notable. Electricity supply jumped enormously, by 24 times; mileage of all-weather roads grew 3.5 times; and the number of telephones used increased 13 times.

Improvements in public finance were also notable, as were substantial increases in revenues and expenditures. During the years 1950 to 1974, public revenues went up by over 900 percent, and expenditures multiplied by 1,000 percent.

International economic relations also rose. It is true that the ratio of imports to GDP was sluggish. But the absolute volume in imports of industrial products multiplied eight times. Imports of capital goods went up by 9 percent of total goods acquired from abroad in 1950 to over 38 percent in 1974. During the same period, imports of intermediate goods and raw materials rose from 21 percent to more than 44 percent. Total foreign debt calculated by total commitments went up from 14 million birr to 2 billion birr. Payments of foreign debt calculated as ratio of exports went up from 5.5 percent to 9 percent.

Failures of Haile Selassie's Regime

Even though these quantitative changes under Haile Selassie are impressive, they can be misleading, for in general terms, Ethiopia, which has proudly kept its independence for thousands of years by turning toward war instead of development, had a steep curve to travel in order to catch up with those who were colonized but also had

exposure to Western technological development. Thus, Ethiopia under the feudal regime of Haile Selassie remained among the least developed countries on the planet.

In 1974, Ethiopia, whose per capita income was less than 200 birr, trailed all
25 countries in Africa that the United Nations categorized as least developed. It was
not only its isolation from Western-style development that kept the country poor and
technologically backward. It was also the feudal mode of production and the archaic
system of land tenure that were in place. As long as feudalism reigned, there was
no chance of increasing economic productivity and achieving sustainable growth.
Land reform was vehemently opposed by the royal family, the powerful absentee
landlords, and the Orthodox Church, all of which controlled almost two-thirds of
the arable land in Ethiopia. The modernizing autocracy of Haile Selassie was very
conservative and resisted rapid change for fear that power would slip out of the hands
of the powers that be.

There were also other intrinsic problems. Wars to ward off would-be invaders
and continuous civil war forced the government to siphon off development funds in
order to purchase weapons. Young people who were supposed to farm were inducted
into either the government's army or the guerrilla fighters' militias. The high level
of illiteracy (estimated at 95% in 1974), chronic diseases such as malaria and yellow
fever, periodic draughts, and endemic malnutrition and hunger prevented productivity and output. Furthermore, the farming method used by 85 percent of Ethiopian
peasants living in the countryside was archaic. Physical infrastructures, particularly
roads connecting the different regions of the country, were a far cry from what was
necessary for a nation striving to develop and catch up with its fast-moving neighbors
in Africa. There was no adequate marketing system in place, and irrigated agriculture
was almost nonexistent in a country so endowed with rivers.

The Ethiopian Economy under the Derg: 1975–1991

Following the revolution of 1974, radical students' demand for "land to the tiller"
was enacted, and tenancy was legally abolished. Thus in 1975, all lands used for
farming and grazing were nationalized. The law stipulated that every farm family was
entitled to the usufructuary right to a plot not to exceed 10 hectares. This right could
be passed on to one's children as long as they used it personally. However, the land
could be neither sold nor mortgaged. The administration of the land was entrusted
to *gabaré mahbars* (peasant associations).

Despite the land reform of 1975 that removed the control of the absentee landlords, the rate of production did not improve. For example, between 1978 and 1980,
the rate of growth was only 2.4 percent.

The Derg authorized the peasant associations and women's associations, as well
as militias, to form cooperatives and gave them the power to collect taxes. Proclamation No. 31 delegated the prerogative of land redistribution and expropriation to
the peasant associations' judicial tribunals. By law, the usurious debts to landowners
that had crushed the peasants' livelihood for years were remitted.

Whereas this proclamation generally applied to the south, in the hereditary *rist*
ownership of the north, the law was applied slightly differently. It provided that

cultivators could retain the lands they worked on but could not redistribute them. It also stipulated that traditional claims to *rist* rights could not be exercised any longer.

Regarding the reform, which was initially very popular among the radical intelligentsia and the rural masses, one can clearly argue that the initial promises of the revolution were not fulfilled. When land reform was unveiled, the peasants were under the impression that they would have possessory rights over the areas they used for cultivation. They were not expecting what was applied by law: land was merely transferred from individual landlords to the state.

Furthermore, the implementation of the proclamation met with bureaucratic red tape. Multitudes of rural farmers were provided with small-scale farms not large enough to support their families. The priority of the Derg was to invest millions of dollars in machinery and fertilizers on large-scale state farms, most of which were confiscated from private owners. Because of a lack of incentives, the results were disastrous, and the huge state farms failed to generate enough revenue to justify their existence.

One other problem was that when the farmers brought their surplus production of crops to the market, they were forced to sell their produce to urban dwellers' association cooperatives at a cost below the going price. Furthermore, with the little money they made, they sought to buy basic necessities such as clothes and salt, but they found the market system to have been totally shattered—the middlemen had been systematically eliminated in favor of the cooperatives. For all practical purposes, the stores set up by the peasant associations to be used by the peasantry were empty. All this led to peasant initiative being suppressed. As a result, agricultural production all over the southern provinces plummeted.

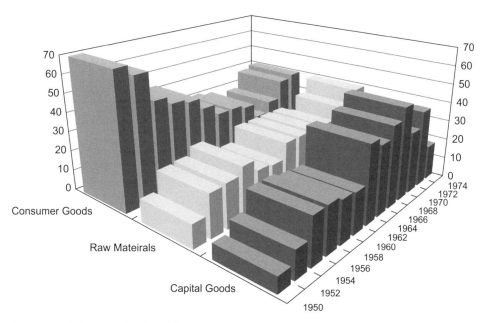

Structure of Imports, 1950–1974

Farmers' cooperatives were created extensively to help the peasants, but they did not live up to their names. First of all, they were not voluntary. In fact, peasants who refused to get in line were jailed or shot by local zealots. Furthermore, the civil war that was raging throughout the country took a toll. The recruits on both the government side and the guerrilla side were young and able-bodied men who were needed to till the land. In some rural districts, only the children, the old, and the women remained. All this contributed to the disastrous 1984–1985 famine that claimed the lives of almost a million rural inhabitants. In fact, the death rate could have jumped to 10 million had it not been for the generous and swift shipment of emergency food aid that flooded in from the Western world.

Prominent American singers recorded the bestseller album *We Are the World*, more than 16 million copies of which were sold, and gave the proceeds to the starving rural masses of northern Ethiopia. Bob Geldof of the United Kingdom and a group of U.S. rock stars also launched the Band Aid group and Live Aid concerts, which raised more than US$100 million for the cause. Even the Eskimos (Inuit) of Canada made generous contributions to help alleviate the famine. It is interesting to note that the Derg, which vehemently attacked Haile Selassie for hushing up the 1973 famine, did not publicly admit the disaster until it had lavishly celebrated the 10th anniversary of the military's ascent to power at an estimated cost of US$100 million.

In macroeconomic terms, the Derg's growth trajectory was highly uneven, even dismal. In the late 1970s and throughout the 1980s, the country's economic performance was erratic. The overall rate of growth in real terms averaged 1.7 percent. The

A British Red Cross worker assists drought victims in the Bati region of Ethiopia. (Corel.)

yearly rates of GDP growth were characterized by wide-scale fluctuations, registering a low of minus 7 percent in 1984/1985 and a high of 9.5 percent in 1986/1987. The growth in the economy fluctuated between 1980/1981 and 1986/1987 with an average growth rate of slightly over 2 percent. But between 1987/1988 and 1990/1991, it went even further down.

In 1991/1992, the country registered a negative growth rate of about 10 percent. During the last years of the Derg, the Ethiopian economy had virtually collapsed. This led to progressive decline in per capita income, which dropped by 3.6 percent in 1990/1991. By the time the military regime was overthrown, the decline in per capita income had gone down to minus 12.6 percent. This came in tandem with population growth averaging 2.8 percent during the decade of the 1980s and 3.1 percent from 1990 to 1992. The result was deterioration in the people's standard of living and rampant poverty throughout the country.

Three reasons can be given for this dismal economic performance. One cause could not be attributed to humans: the severe droughts in the mid-1980s, resulting from adverse climatic conditions.

The second cause of the economic collapse was connected to the unending civil war that raged throughout the country from Eritrea and Tigray in the north to Oromia in the south. The Derg had mobilized every aspect of Ethiopian society when it put out the slogan "all to the war front." During the 1980s, there were continuous mobilizations and states of emergency as well as war levies. This consumed material, financial, and human resources that could have helped in economic growth.

The third and most important factor that brought about economic collapse under the Derg regime was the command economy by the military junta, which controlled production, distribution, and pricing. This weakened the formal sector and forced a substantial amount of the economy to run underground in what was dubbed "Ayer Bayer" (Air to Air), where imported products exchanged hands sometimes five times before they even reached the ports.

For all practical purposes, the so-called socialist economy of the Derg brought gradual decay and total economic breakdown. By the end of 1991, when Mengistu fled to Zimbabwe, the Ethiopian GDP had registered a negative growth rate of 10 percent, per capita income had fallen by 13 percent, budgetary deficit had climbed to 16 percent of GDP, consumer prices had jumped to 36 percent, and export earnings had fallen through the floor, affected by rising imports. Furthermore, foreign exchange and essential inputs had almost disappeared, and debts and debt servicing had skyrocketed to frightening levels.

Free Market Economy—Post-1992

The Ethiopian People's Revolutionary Democratic Front (EPRDF) drove the Derg from power and assumed control of the country in May 1991, inheriting an economy in shambles as a result of 17 years of mismanagement by the Mengistu regime. The social situation was also dismal. Almost half a million Derg soldiers, numbering 1.2 million together with their families, had been demobilized and were looking for jobs that were unavailable. One hundred fifty thousand people had been displaced because of the war. Furthermore, 400,000 Ethiopian refugees who had gone to countries such as Sudan were returning back to their country, also looking for jobs that were unavailable. This situation was compounded by close to 600,000 refugees in Ethiopia who originated from Somalia and Sudan.

The World Food Program estimated that in 1992, there were 8 million malnourished and hungry people in Ethiopia who needed food aid. Homeless persons, orphans, street children, disabled soldiers, and paupers proliferated in major urban areas, particularly in Addis Ababa. This increased urban sprawl and added to the already unmanageable level of unemployment and a breakdown in the health of the people. Urban services such as water and sewerage were all in a sorry state.

The transitional government of the EPRDF aimed to solve this gigantic problem by transitioning the command economy into a market-driven system. For the nation to move forward, macroeconomic stabilization and adjustment measures had to be introduced. This was essential if Ethiopia had to attract foreign aid to carry out a program of economic recovery.

The EPRDF government introduced three basic documents to chart a new way. One was the New Economic Policy (NEP), which was promulgated in November 1991. The NEP aimed at reforming the economy by dismantling the command economy and instead strengthening the private sector.

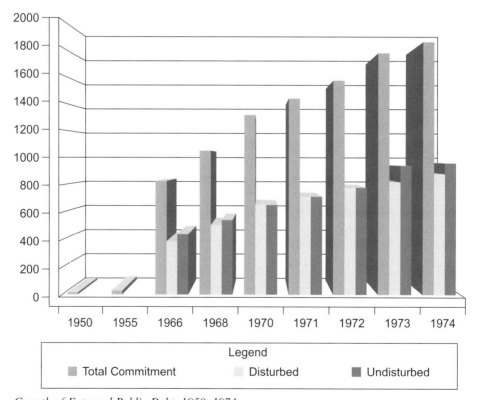

Growth of External Public Debt, 1950–1974

The second document, for emergency recovery, was put out under the title "Ethiopia's Economic Policy during the Transitional Period." To make this successful, a reconstruction program was launched in partnership with the World Bank around the end of 1991. Then in 1992, the government prepared a policy framework paper for the period from 1992 to 1995. This was put out in partnership with the World Bank and the International Monetary Fund. It was following this measure that the EPRDF government accepted the IMF's suggested structural adjustment program so as to qualify for adjustment credit.

The NEP, which went into effect in July 1992, set the short-term goals and strategies of the transitional government. Although land would remain in state hands, tenure would be secure, with farmers guaranteed unhindered use of plots as well as the ability to freely dispose of their produce. Families would have the right to inherit land but could not sell it, to avoid concentration of land in the hands of large landowners. Peasant agriculture would be accorded priority, but the nomadic population would be given due attention. Urban land would remain under public control, and urban houses would be sold to occupants, with compensation paid to former owners as appropriate. Private commercial farms would be encouraged and promoted, and state farms would be sold or redistributed to those working on them or to surrounding peasants, as the case may be, with the exception of those producing key raw materials. The manufacturing sector would be mixed, with both the public and private sectors playing their respective roles. Most industrial activities would be in the hands of the private sector, with only a few key industries—including large-scale engineering; metals; fertilizer plants; gold, copper, and potash mining; and other strategic establishments—remaining under state control or managed jointly with domestic or foreign investors. In the mining and energy industries, there would be a mix of public and private ownership. Construction would be privatized, although the public sector would also have a role to play. Insurance companies and banks would remain under public control, but private investors would be allowed to operate in the sector also. Wholesale and retail trade would be privatized, and distribution, marketing, and pricing would be liberalized.

In terms of macroeconomic development strategy, the NEP charted steps for cutting budgetary expenditures by streamlining administrative and defense expenditures, introducing reform into the taxation system, and ameliorating the situation of the decline in exports and balance of trade. To make NEP successful, the government pledged to lay down a framework for development policies; create and maintain social and economic infrastructures; forge a favorable environment for private capital; solicit international assistance; promote and strengthen popular participation in the economy; launch and give support to the role in the economy of regional administration; and reduce the role of the state, limiting it to regulatory functions, to encourage local and foreign private capital.

In cases where there were state enterprises, the policy stated that in order to make them profitable, the state should give them managerial autonomy. It also stipulated that they needed to become competitive with the private sector by streamlining their expenses and improving their operational efficiency.

Another step taken by the EPRDF was to launch, together with the World Bank and other multilateral and bilateral donors, the Emergency Recovery and Reconstruction Program (ERRP). The ERRP amounted to US$657 million and was financed by several international donors. The World Bank contributed 35 percent, USAID gave 13.2 percent, the European Economic Community contributed 17.7 percent, the African Development Bank contributed 19.2 percent, and others (mainly bilateral sources) gave 7.0 percent. A quarter of the ERRP funds were aimed at the private sector in industry, agriculture, construction, and pharmaceuticals.

The ERRP quickly lifted the economic system from its dismal state. It specifically aimed to jump-start agricultural and manufacturing production and establish economic and social infrastructures. The ERRP had three major components. The first was a production component with inputs for agriculture and public and private manufacturing, and it accounted for 45 percent of the ERRP allocation. The second was an infrastructure component spent on reconstruction of roads; water supply; telecommunications; civil aviation and power facilities; the supply of trucks, spare

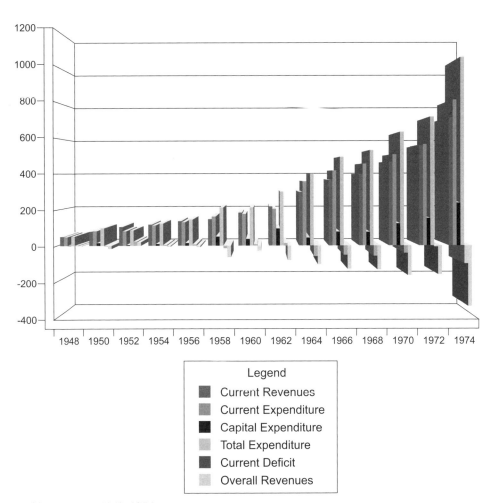

Public Revenue, 1948–1974

parts, tires, and tubes; and the supply of petroleum products; this component accounted for 35 percent of total ERRP allocation. The third component was social, aimed at the rebuilding of educational and health facilities and the acquisition of medical supplies and drugs; this component accounted for about 20 percent of the allocation.

Alongside the ERRP, the policy framework paper and the structural adjustment program (SAP) were launched with the support of the World Bank and the IMF to make Ethiopia eligible for the World Bank's structural adjustment credit and the IMF's structural adjustment facility. After the acceptance of the SAP, the EPRDF government adjusted exchange and interest rates; introduced a foreign exchange mechanism; created an auctioning scheme; reduced and ultimately aimed to eliminate price controls, including road freight tariffs; enacted a new labor code; passed a new investment law; eliminated export taxes; amended the highly progressive income tax regime; and passed regulations to encourage public enterprises' autonomy.

The most noticeable action the government took in fulfilling the SAP occurred in October 1992, when it devalued the birr by 141.5 percent. Following the adoption of SAP, the government succeeded in procuring a structural adjustment credit of about US$1.2 billion. In addition it secured a US$657 million emergency program package.

In 1992, Ethiopia owed US$660 million to foreign institutions and governments. These debts were soon either rescheduled or canceled following a meeting that took place in Paris. It is interesting to note that within two years of adopting the SAP, the EPRDF government received over US$2.5 aid from bilateral and multilateral sources. That is almost equal to the amount of aid the Derg regime received during its 17-year rule and three times as much as the Haile Selassie regime received in 33 years from the time the Italian Fascists were expelled from Ethiopia to the Emperor's overthrow in 1974.

After the adoption of the previously mentioned measures, the Ethiopian economy made noticeable recovery from the disaster of the Derg period, so much so that in recent years it has surpassed the projection of skeptics. Although there was a decline of 3.5 percent in 2002/2003, caused by a severe draught that negatively affected agricultural production, real GDP has grown remarkably, totaling a cumulative growth rate of more than 56 percent. The estimated real GDP growth in 2006/2007 was 11.4 percent. If we break that down, we find that agriculture grew by 9.4 percent, industry grew by 11.0 percent, and the service sector grew by 13.5 percent.

The sustained expansion of the Ethiopian economy in recent years has been made possible by unusually favorable weather conditions, steady expansion of governmental programs to build infrastructure, the government's encouragement of rural development, and poverty alleviation schemes. The booming urban construction projects have also added to this positive economic growth.

From 2002 to 2005, fiscal development helped stabilize the overall macroeconomic state of the nation. The government introduced what it considered key measures. The tax selection system was revamped to make it more efficient to generate more revenue; existing loopholes were closed; an incentive mechanism was built into the system; tax administration was modernized; income tax laws protecting revenue and discouraging corruption were introduced; broad-based, value-added tax and tax detection numbers were introduced; and tariff rates were rationalized. This helped tax revenue to go up by almost 14 percent of GDP in 2004/2005.

Increased external resource flows have been added to domestic revenue mobilization mechanisms. This led to an increase in investment capital from US$693.6 million in 2002/2003 to US$937.5 million and US$1055.9 million in the fiscal years 2003/2004 and 2004/2005, respectively. The EPRDF government has signed project program agreements to the tune of US$841.5 million in 2002/2003 with development partners. Furthermore, US$826.7 million was allocated for new development projects during fiscal year 2003/2004. From the total flow of external funds, the direct budget jumped from 309 million birr in 2002/2003 to 2.9 billion birr in 2004/2005. Most of the external funds were slated for the creation and improvement of infrastructure. Through training, human resource has improved. This has helped the growth of the economy as well as macroeconomic stability.

From 2002 to 2007, government expenditures increased substantially. This is because of large allocations for development and pro-poor sectors, particularly capital expenditures. During this period, the budget for defense has never exceeded 3 billion birr per year. In the meantime, total government recurrent expenditures decreased from 19.7 percent GDP in 2002/2003 to 13.5 percent of GDP in 2004/2005. But during the same period, capital expenditures went up from 9.2 percent of GDP to 11.5 percent of GDP.

On average, the share of fiscal deficit amounted to 5 percent of GDP. Of this, 2.6 percent on average was taken care of through domestic borrowing, and though opponents of the government point out many problems, World Bank and IMF specialists have judged Ethiopian fiscal management from 2000 to 2007 to be prudent.

As a strategy for poverty reduction, the EPRDF government has launched the Progress and Achievements under the Sustainable Development and Poverty Reduction Program (SDPRP), which directs government resource allocation and implementation toward investments in development and pro-poor sectors. The targets include, inter alia, improving agriculture and food security, expanding the reach of education, protecting health, tackling the problem of HIV/AIDS, and providing clean water to the populous. Infrastructure development and in particular road construction have been targeted because they help in carrying out the other plans. Of the total government expenditures, funding for poverty-oriented sectors has increased from 43 percent in 2001/2002 to 56.5 percent in 2004/2005. The progressive increase in allocations for some of the targets can be seen in Table D1. Macroeconomic indicators have also followed a positive trend

When comparing the years 2004/2005 and 2006/2007, one sees that the total nominal government revenue, including grants, increased by 26 percent. This was helped by an efficient and modernized tax collection mechanism and administration. There was also an increase in donor funding, from 3.7 million birr in 2005/2006 to 7.6 million birr in 2006/2007. Poverty reduction outlay for agriculture, food security, health, education, and roads went up 18 percent in nominal terms. By contrast, defense spending has been reduced significantly, showing a record minimum of 2 percent of

GDP. The overall balance, including grants, shows a budget deficit of 3.6 percent of GDP from 2005 to 2007.

In 2006/2007, the total value of exports went up by 18.5 percent. This was helped by several factors. One was the expansion in volume. Second was the rise in the price of coffee and a vigorous growth in other export items, such as leather products, flowers, gold, and pulses. Imports rose substantially in 2006/2007 because of the growth in private and public investment, including in machinery and transport capital goods, and the rise in demand and consumption coming on the heels of the aforementioned economic growth, coupled with escalating world oil prices.

Imports of food and live animals decreased by 17 percent owing to the remarkable performance of the agricultural sector. In 2006/2007, exports were able to finance only 23 percent of imports. As a result, by the end of the fiscal year, the trade deficit had soared to US$3.9 million, an increase of about 10 percent from 2004/2005.

There was a deficit in the balance of payments in the previous two fiscal years, but in 2006/2007, the balance of payments registered a surplus of US$85 million. Remarkably, foreign direct investments soared to US$482 million in 2006/2007. Together with an increase in official long-term loans of more than 73 percent, the surplus in capital account reached US $941 million. This has helped offset the deficit in current account balance.

As a result of significant debt relief given to Ethiopia by multilateral organizations and a decline in external loan disbursement, at the conclusion of 2006/2007, the total external outstanding debt had been reduced to US$2.3 billion, a 62.2 percent decline in comparison with the 2004/2005 fiscal year.

It is a declared aim of the EPRDF government to raise the competitiveness of the export sector. Thus, the official exchange rate of the birr has been allowed to slightly depreciate. In 2006/2007, the average official exchange rate of the birr against the U.S. dollar in the interbank foreign exchange market went down by 1.34 percent,

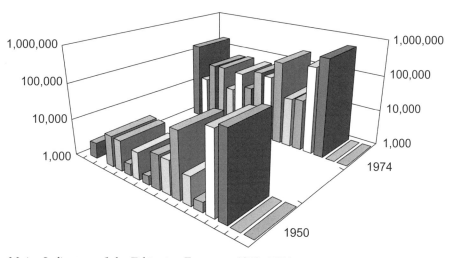

Major Indicators of the Ethiopian Economy, 1950–1974

reaching US$1 = 8.79 birr in 2006/2007 and US$1 = 8.68 birr in 2005/2006. By contrast, in the average parallel market, the birr appreciated by 0.76 percent.

Trade Liberalization

Right after the fall of the Derg, and the rise to power of the EPRDF government, Ethiopia decided to embark on trade liberalization. With its New Economic Policy, the country adopted the most comprehensive financial and structural reform in its history. The major objective was to attain economic growth with macroeconomic stability and rapid integration of Ethiopia in the global economy. To fulfill its objective, the nation needed to reduce or eliminate any form of anti-export bias, reduce import tariffs, and restrict external current account transactions.

The objectives of the government were to achieve rapid broad-based and more equitable economic growth with macroeconomic stability, to raise the level of agricultural production through productivity gains and rural development programs that help economic growth and poverty reduction, and to integrate the country's economy with the global economy by further liberalization of foreign trade. Furthermore, the external sector had several objectives of its own: building the international reserves to a significant level, cutting the current account deficits to a reasonable level (8 to 8.5% of GDP), and promoting exports by passing market-favorable laws, and laying out good institutional frameworks and building capacity in the private as well as the public sectors. What the government did to achieve these aims was declare the external value of the birr to reflect its true market price; encourage competition in the coffee export sector; change the biweekly basis of the foreign exchange auction to a weekly basis; merge the official exchange rate with the auction rate; bring about the duty drawback system; abolish the foreign exchange surrender requirement; lower the maximum tariff to 40 percent and the number of tariff bands to seven; drop all restrictions on external current-account business travel, education, and health and raise the limit on holiday travel to $1,200 per person per trip; and augment the external debt management system.

As the largest producer of coffee in Africa, and with the track record discussed here, Ethiopia took the first key steps to become the World Trade Organization's (WTO) 151st member in 2007 when it applied for membership and compiled details of its trade regime, the legislation in place, and its trade practices. Although Ethiopia will likely succeed in its bid, it has to pass some hurdles. It is going to be asked to open up the telecommunications and banking systems, which are currently off-limits to international competitors.

Privatization and Investment

Soon after coming to power in 1991, the EPRDF government, led by Prime Minister Meles Zenawi, launched a program for privatization of state-owned enterprises. To do so, it established a privatization agency. The government also laid off excess personnel in state-owned establishments, increasing the number of the unemployed and raising the wrath of the opposition parties who claimed to speak for the multitudes of jobless persons joining the ranks of the half a million demobilized soldiers of the Derg regime.

Privatization has moved a long way, but there are still many large enterprises controlled by the government. The government is in control of some manufacturing industries as well as services, including food processing, particularly of sugar; chemicals; textiles; steel; construction; telecommunications; air transport; and banking. This has required the government to look after many inefficient and even almost nonfunctional state-owned factories. The banking system has suffered greatly because it has been losing millions of dollars of loaned money to companies that go bankrupt. In many instances, the bad debts incurred by such inefficient enterprises are covered with public money.

Private-sector investment is booming, as numerous investment licensing records show. From 1992 to 2005, a total of 13,504 private investment projects mushroomed. The combined investment, both domestic and foreign, was 149 billion birr. Of the total, 86 percent was domestic, 10 percent foreign. One-half a percent was still in the public sector. In terms of investment capital, we see that 91 billion birr, or 61 percent, was domestic; 41.4 billion birr, or 27.7 percent, was foreign. The rest, about 16.7 billion birr, or 11.2 percent, was in the public sector.

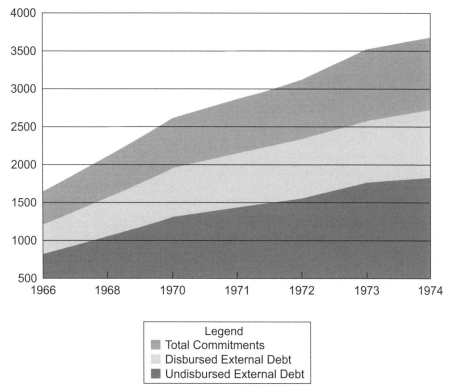

Major Indicators of the Ethiopian Economy, 1950–1974

Close to 2,872 projects involving 36.5 billion birr were given licenses in 2004/2005 alone. Of these, 672, with investment capital of 20 billion birr, were financed by foreigners. During the year 2004/2005, domestic investment constituted over 78 percent of the total projects approved by the government.

About 920 projects, or 32 percent of all projects licensed in 2004/2005, were in industry, followed by agriculture (16.1%), hotel and tourism (9.4%), education (6.1%), real estate development (5.8%), and construction (5.2%).

Owing to the EPRDF government's sustained struggles to forge an enabling regulatory environment to attract private investment both local and foreign, Ethiopia's global competitiveness has dramatically improved. According to the analysis of the World Economic Forum (2004/05; 2010/11), Ethiopia was 11th from the bottom-ranked country. However by 2010/2011 its competitiveness had surpassed 20 countries from the bottom ranks making it 119th out of 139 countries such as Nigeria, Pakistan, and Venezuela.

A SECTORAL LOOK AT THE ETHIOPIAN ECONOMY

If we take the Ethiopian economy sector by sector, agriculture is by far the largest contributor to GDP. In importance, agriculture is followed by the service and industrial sectors. The share of agriculture in total GDP averaged 46.6 percent from 2001/2002 to 2004/2005. The growth in agricultural output went up by 41 percent in 2003/2004 and by 15 percent in 2004/2005. Cereal crop production rose by 42 percent in 2002/2004 and 9.1 percent in 2004/2005. The growth in agricultural output, including cereals, was due to steady agricultural expansion through claiming more cultivable land. It was also driven by subsidiary upgrading to increase productivity though the supply of inputs.

Ethiopia's industrial sector is by and large of the cottage and handicraft type. But there are also small, medium, and large-scale modernized establishments, including construction, mining and quarrying, water, and electricity. Growth in value-added industry has been sluggish, and thus, manufacturing of textile, food, and beverages has not been competitive with countries in the same level of development. All in all, during the years 2000–2005, industrial production's average contribution to the national economy stood at 5.7 percent.

By contrast, the share of the services sector in GDP has been on a steady increase, reaching 48.6 percent in 2002/2003. This jump put it ahead of the agricultural industry's share for that year. The growth in the services industry was caused by expansion in the social sectors of health and education, which showed growths of 9 percent and 10 percent, respectively. During 2000–2005, the contribution of services to GDP averaged 39.8 percent. The growth of the sector averaged 3.9 percent. If we lump together the services sector and industry, they account for, on average, 53 percent of GDP. During the same period, agriculture accounted for the 47 percent.

Although the structure of the Ethiopian economy has fluctuated in terms of agriculture and service sector shares of real GDP, there has been slow but steady growth. However, the industrial sector has shown stagnation and needs encouragement and monetary injection in order to catch up with the rapidly developing nations of the Third World.

AGRICULTURE

Agriculture is the mainstay of Ethiopia's economy because almost 85 percent of its people depend on it, and others process and market it both nationally and internationally. Agricultural commodities provide more than 75 percent of the country's foreign exchange earnings, and 90 percent of these agricultural earnings originate from the small monetized sector of the rural economy.

Despite the distressing image of starving children that the world has come to associate with the country, Ethiopia's potential in the field of agriculture is well known among specialists. Between the late 1960s and early 1970s, production in agriculture, including commercial production, grew in real terms at about 2.6 percent per year. This almost corresponds to the rate of population growth in the country, which was 2.5 percent.

Emperor Haile Selassie's government, with substantial foreign aid, unveiled minimum package programs (MPP), which were meant to help peasant farmers boost production by providing extension services, inputs, and credits, starting in 1971.

The Chilalo Agricultural Development Unit (CADU) in Arsi province, which was almost wholly financed by Sweden, contributed to higher production by peasant

Highland massif in north central Ethiopia. (Earl & Nazima Kowall/Corbis.)

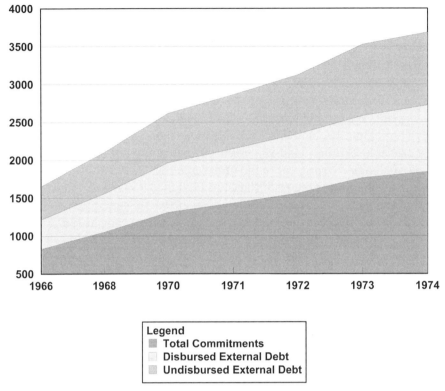

External Debt Disbursed and Undisbursed, 1966–1974

farmers, but the project's benefits were marred by landlords who extracted higher rents. The imperial regime encouraged large commercial farms and paid very little attention to the peasant sector, which encompassed the great majority of the Ethiopian population. This was evidenced by the miniscule 1 percent of total expenditures allocated for peasant agriculture in Ethiopia's third five-year development plan, which ran from 1968 through 1973.

According to a government survey of the pre-revolutionary period, 46 percent of the rural population in the south farmed lands that were wholly leased, and 9 percent cultivated partly owned and partly leased land. Of the entire cultivated land in the south, leased land composed 47 percent, and land that was partly leased and partly owned constituted 14 percent. Thus, Menelik and later other feudal rulers, including Haile Selassie, gave grants of vast southern lands to trusted retainers, public servants, and military officers who leased them to landless peasants, from whom the officials extracted exorbitant amounts of rent, sometimes amounting to 75 percent of their produce. The aim was not to carry out land reform but rather to improve government revenue collection. In the process, some serfs for the first time became freeholders in southern Ethiopia, but the general condition of the peasantry never improved.

Livestock

Ethiopia is a country where livestock are a bastion of the great majority of the population. Altogether, cattle, sheep, and goats total some 100 million. There are additionally about 10 million equine livestock (horses, mules, and donkeys) and 1 million camels. Thus, Ethiopia has the largest number of domesticated animals in the whole of Africa. Sheep and goats are exported to neighboring countries, and livestock and livestock products constitute about 15 percent of the value of the country's total exports. Forty percent of the livestock belong to nomadic pastoralists in the lowlands.

MINING

The mineral industry in Ethiopia has never had major economic importance, contributing at current factor cost an average of less than 1 percent of GDP. Traditionally, gold in Ethiopia has been mined from placers. Until the fall of the military regime, Ethiopian mining operations were run by the government. Currently, the mining industry uses a carbon-in-pulp (CIP) processing plant that produces four tons of gold per year. The government has sold the gold mine to MIDROC Ethiopia, owned by the Ethiopian-Saudi billionaire Sheik Al Amudi.

By law, the Ethiopian government can acquire 2 percent participation interest in mining ventures. Though not much by the standards of countries that have substantial amounts of known hydrocarbon sediments, there is a promising amount of gas deposit in the Ogaden region, now marred by civil war. Specialists estimate that Ogaden, which covers 217,480 square miles, contains gas reserves exceeding 4 trillion cubic feet. The federal government owns 90 percent of these reserves. The rest is allocated to regional governments and private investors. The known field's gas reserves have been estimated to be about 233 billion cubic feet.

The EPRDF government has given priority to the development of mining industries, believing that mineral exports could significantly increase Ethiopia's foreign exchange earnings and help the government diversify its coffee-based economy. It has also indicated that the production of fertilizer products could at least partially satisfy the expanding demand of the agricultural sector. Thus, through the Ethiopian Investment Authority and the Ministry of Mines and Energy, Mr. Meles's government has tried to attract foreign and local partners to develop the mineral sector. In the year 2001, the company holding a contract with the government mined and sold in the international market 66 tons and 21 tons, respectively, of tantalum and niobium pentoxide. Currently six local and foreign companies are engaged in the production of the gem. Non-gem products are also found in plenty.

Ethiopia is a country full of dormant and active volcanic activity, and it produces large reserves of good-quality mineral water. Some modern mineral water plants have gone beyond local production and have advanced to export of bottled mineral water in recent years.

INDUSTRY

Textiles and Garments

The textile industry in Ethiopia is made up of manufacturing plants that do spinning, weaving, and finishing with significant numbers of workers. The two large factories that manufacture cordage, rope, twine, and netting are government-owned. Public ownership in the textile industry is 38 percent, which is large compared with the leather industry, where ownership is only 13 percent. In the years between 2002 and 2007, of the 36 textile fabric manufacturing plants, 19 were government–owned, and 17 were private; of the 25 garment industries, 16 percent were publicly owned, and 84 percent were private.

Ethiopian textiles are mostly for domestic consumption. Problems faced by the textile industry during the previous regime, such as low-level technology, unfair competition by contraband trade, paucity of spare parts, inhibiting bank procedures and rules, mismanagement, bureaucratic sluggishness, and inadequate infrastructure, have unfortunately continued. Nevertheless, the Ethiopian textile industry has good potential. Local cotton products are available in large quantities. The fact that the industry depends on labor-intensive production in a country where there is a huge pool of working population is a plus for the growth of the sector in the future.

Leather and Footwear

Ethiopia has an estimated 36 million cattle, 12 million sheep, and 10 million goats, which gives it high production capacity for hides and skins. This gives the industry

Rates of Growth of Major Macroeconomic Variables 1980–1990 and 1991–1992

Macroeconomic Variables	1980–1990 (Averages)	1991	1992
Growth rate of GDP	2.1	–0.6	–9.6
Per Capita Income	–1.0	–3.6	–12.6
Domestic Savings	3.3	0.2	–2.7
Fixed Investment	12.8	10.4	9.1
Budgetary Deficit	18.0	15.8	11.3
Money Supply	17.6	18.7	13.3
Annual Inflation Rate	4.3	35.7	10.5
Exports (BOP)	12.0	4.2	2.3
Imports (BOP)	18.0	15.4	13.0
External Debt	19.0	53.0	56.0
Debt Service Ratio	7.0	76.0	>100

Ethiopian Economy During the Transition, 1993

a major advantage in global trade and the potential to process, manufacture, and export leather goods that will add to its monetary value in the long run. Of all animal skin products, leather and footwear production predominates.

Since the demise of the Mengistu regime, relatively rapid growth has occurred in the leather industry. When the EPRDF came to power in 1991, there were only 8 tanneries, 6 of which were owned by the government and 2 of which were privately owned. Two years later, the number had risen to 19, 15 of which were private and 4 of which were public.

The leather manufacturing plants in Ethiopia produce semi-processed as well as processed skin products for leather garments, shoe uppers, industrial gloves, and stitched upholstery and handbags as well as finished leather, mostly exported to Europe, Japan, the United States, Canada, Yemen, Nigeria, and Uganda.

Since the fall of the Derg, leather as well as semi-processed hides and skins have formed the second-largest export product of Ethiopia, generating about 20 percent of its total foreign exchange earnings. It is important to note that Ethiopia's share of Africa's export trade in skin products is by far the largest—at 51 percent for sheep products and 30 percent for goatskins.

Food Processing

In 2008, the food processing industry constituted nine industrial groups with 200 factories. Though smaller in number, public-owned food factories dominate in

A cotton plantation in the Afar region of Ethiopia. (Photo by James P. Blair/National Geographic/Getty Images.)

the amount of production as well as the number of employed personnel. All are located near major urban areas. The product lines of Ethiopian food factories include pasteurized milk, frozen and canned meats, cheese, butter, fresh and canned fruits and vegetables, edible oil, flour and bakery products such as macaroni and spaghetti, animal feeds, and confectioner's sugar and sugar.

By international standards, the quality of Ethiopian food products is average, though the factories used are relatively old. Of these, sugar processing, bakery product industries, grain mills, and meat, vegetable, and fruit-processing factories predominate.

Food security has been bleak in Ethiopia during the last four decades. As of 2011 the total production of grain is far from meeting local demands; nationwide production constitutes only 65 percent of the country's requirements. This is due to the rise in the indices of cereals, pulse, oilseeds, vegetables, fruits, potatoes and other tubers, and livestock products. Thus, the growth in this sector was in spices, livestock, and cash crops.

In general, the inability of manufacturing plants to run at full capacity, the limited amount of manufactured exports, and the decline of labor and capital productivities during the first decade of the 21st century are a reflection of technical inefficiencies among the Ethiopian manufacturing industries.

TOURISM

Foreign tourists interested in the historical, cultural, and natural attractions of Ethiopia have helped turn tourism into a major service industry in recent years. The imperial government of Emperor Haile Selassie promulgated a decree to attract private investment in the tourist sector, and there was steady growth in the industry during his regime. Under the Derg, however, heavy restrictions were imposed on the private sector's participation, there was meager investment in promotion of the industry, tourist facilities deteriorated, and an inadequate transport system discouraged growth. That was bad for foreign exchange generation and job creation.

The demise of the Derg and the rise to power of the EPRDF government in 1991 changed everything. The government gave priority to the tourism industry, knowing that it would contribute to the effort to close the balance of payments deficit. By 2000, tourism had earned the government US$57 million. New hotels were constructed, both by the government and by private companies; by 2002, there were 332 hotels with 9,676 rooms and 12,570 beds. In 2001, 2002, and 2003, the number of tourists continued to climb, bringing the government badly needed foreign currency earnings to the tune of US$136 million.

Other than wholesale and retail trade, communications, and transportation, the services sector in Ethiopia is dominated almost entirely by tourism. In 2002, more than 156,000 tourists visited the country, many of whom were Ethiopian expatriates visiting from abroad.

To maintain these positive developments in tourism, the government has invested more money in infrastructure, the building and upgrading of roads, airports,

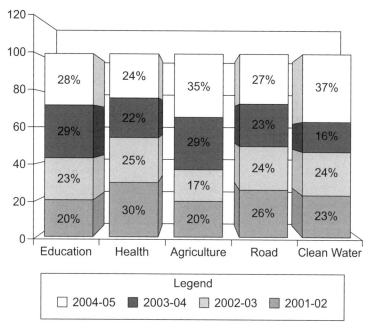

Macroeconomic Indicators, 2001–2004

and tourist-class hotels. It has also improved the capacity of local transportation systems.

Among the major problems hampering the tourist industry in Ethiopia are cumbersome visa requirements, long lines at airports due to slow customs processing, a general absence of adequate credit card facilities, unregulated hotel prices that are arbitrary once one is out of the capital city, hassling by pushy vendors, and panhandling. The government has started to take action to correct these ills, though, so tourism in Ethiopia and its contribution to GDP growth and foreign currency earnings are likely to spiral upward as the years continue.

LABOR

It is a well-known fact that 85 percent of Ethiopia's workforce consists of subsistence farmers. Those involved in wage labor are miniscule in number. Even though the EPRDF government has tried to enforce regulations against child labor within the formal industrial sector, large numbers of children of all ages grow and harvest crops in the countryside, outside of government regulatory control, where 85 percent of the Ethiopian population lives. The problem is that peasant farmers who are poor and destitute depend on the labor contributions of their offspring to guarantee their household's survival. There is no way that the government can change this without drastically altering the way of life of the Ethiopian population dependent on subsistence agriculture.

The private sector is not subject to hiring within the confines of a minimum wage, though a minimum wage in the public sector has been in effect since 1985. However, the minimum wage is far from being sufficient to provide a modest standard of living for any family in urban areas, where the costs of foodstuffs have spiraled out of control.

The average wage earner in Ethiopia works a 40-hour week. Occupational, health, and safety standards are normally negotiated among industry, unions, and the government. The 1993 labor law and the Ethiopian Constitution of 1994 provide wage laborers with the right to form and join unions. All workers are allowed the right to strike, but unions calling for a strike are required to follow detailed procedures in advance. They have to provide at least 10 days' notice to the government before the commencement of a strike. Similar restrictions apply to worker lockouts by businesses.

Workers' Unions

The first move toward recognizing the institution of labor unions was when, on the eve of Haile Selassie's silver jubilee, the 1955 Constitution guaranteed to factory hands the right to form workers' associations. But it took the government until 1962 to promulgate the Labor Relations Decree, which legitimated the creation of labor unions.

The old regime recognized the Confederation of Ethiopian Labor Unions (CELU), which represented 22 industrial labor groups in 1963. Nevertheless, the body represented only 30 percent of eligible workers in 1973. From 1972 to 1975, the union became more militant thanks to the influence of the radical student movement of the period. The latter routinely sent its clandestine cadres to join the unions disguised as ordinary workers.

The 1973 famine that claimed the lives of about 200,000 people made the CELU even more militant. In fact, one factor that hastened the overthrow of the ancient regime was the general strike called by CELU in 1974. However, the military junta that replaced the Haile Selassie regime, fearing the power of the unions, ordered that members of the CELU choose their leaders according to the aims and objectives of Ethiopia Tikdem (Ethiopian First), which was its slogan. The CELU rejected the Derg's demands and continued to agitate for democratic and civil rights. The CELU elected its leaders democratically and took decisions independently of the Derg. However, after 1978, the freedom its members had gained through their own sustained struggle was snatched away by government civil servants who had already penetrated its leadership. The government cadres manipulated not only the CELU's elections but also its policies and decisions. Instead of unions having their own defense squads as the proclamation creating them stipulated, the mass organizations started to function as defense forces of government officials and bureaucrats.

In January 1977 the All-Ethiopia Trade Union (AETU) was created and put under the watchful eyes of Derg supporters in the urban dwellers' associations. This doubled the number of the country's legally recognized labor union members overnight. The AETU claimed nine industrial groups; the largest one was based in manufacturing and constituted 29.2 percent of the entire membership. The service industry made up 15.1 percent, transportation 8.1 percent, construction 8.0 percent, trade 6.2 percent, utilities 3.7 percent, finance 2.4 percent, and mining 0.7 percent. Of the union's 313,434 members, 35.6 percent lived in Addis Ababa, and 18.0 percent lived in the province of Shoa. The AETU was again overhauled and its name changed to the Ethiopian Trade Union (ETU) in 1986.

There has clearly been a move toward democratic openness and tolerance for reasonable labor demands since the EPRDF came to power in 1991, but according to local and international observers, things have not been as smooth as expected. There are allegations that the regulation the government issued regarding labor unions does not prevent an employer from interfering and controlling the workers' activities.

Since 1991, multiple unions have been allowed in the same enterprise. Ten members is the minimum number required to organize and run a trade union. All unions have to be registered, and if the state authorities perceive that a union engaged in antigovernment activity, they can go to court and get the union's registration annulled.

For union leadership to legitimately call a work stoppage, a two-thirds membership quorum is required. The International Labour Organization (ILO), which protects labor union activism worldwide, has repeatedly requested that the government lower the quota required to take a legal strike action (Tilahun Teshome, 216–238).

Though it is generally recognized that the labor laws that came into effect after the Derg was overthrown are a positive step, the Ethiopian labor unions and the ILO have criticized the new labor law that was promulgated in February 2004 as being pro-employer. The EPRDF' creation of an industrial court has been lauded, but it is alleged by independent observers that not all workers have benefited from it. By law, there were supposed to be one court in each of the nine regions, but by 2008 there existed only four (U.S. State Department, 2008).

Tripartism in labor relations was born in May 1998 when the government provided legal license to the Ethiopian Employers' Association (EEA), which claims that it is dedicated to maintaining labor peace. The EEA has pledged to work in harmony with the ILO, CETU, and the Ministry of Labor and Social Affairs. To

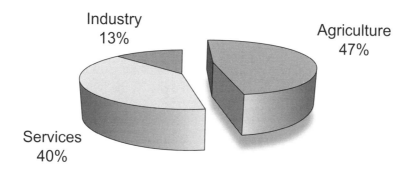

Composition of GDP by Type, 2000–2005

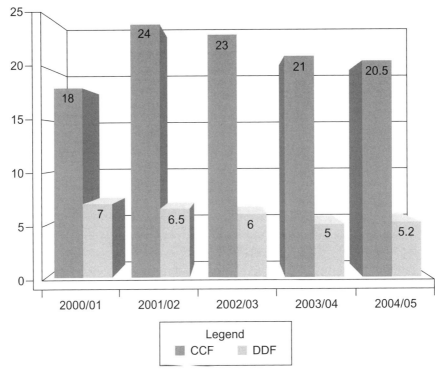

Growth of Capital Formation, GCF to DDF, 2000–2005

show its fairness in labor relations, the Ethiopian Employers' Association has vowed to respect all of the ILO's Core Labor Standards. Ethiopian entrepreneurs have repeatedly stated that cooperating with labor is in their self-interest.

FINANCE

Fiscal Policy

The Ethiopian government runs a tight ship with regard to fiscal policy because its freedom to decide its priorities is circumscribed by what the World Bank and IMF, the major contributors of foreign financing, require. If the two major international financial bodies decide that the country's fiscal policy is not prudent, they can withhold credit disbursement.

From 2000 to 2005, domestic revenue in Ethiopia rose significantly, from 12.2 billion birr to 20 billion birr, a rise of 64 percent. As a ratio of the GDP, the share of revenue showed little change, averaging 16 percent. Tax revenue as a ratio of GDP was on average 12.8 percent; no noticeable rise was shown in this regard. Non-tax revenue was on average 3.4 percent. This also showed no signifi-

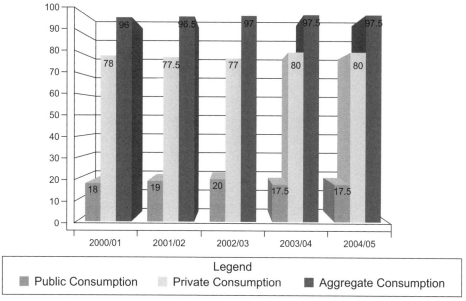

Ratio of Government and Private Consumption and Aggregate Expenditure, 2000–2005

cant increase over time. Whereas domestic revenue accounted for 77.5 percent of total government revenue, external aid contributed 22.5 percent during the fiscal year 2005.

From 2000 to 2005, total expenditures went up significantly. They rose from 15.2 billion birr in 2000 to 24.6 billion birr in 2005—a jump of 62 percent. Current expenditures increased from 10.1 billion birr to 13 billion birr, and capital expenditures more than doubled, rising from 5 billion birr in 2000/2001 to 11.4 billion birr in 2004/2005. Expenditures growth substantially outstripped revenue growth, and the fiscal deficit (not including grants) was, on average, 11.1 percent of GDP during this period.

The Ethiopian government financed the deficit through funds obtained from foreign aid and domestic borrowing. The latter constituted over 70 percent of the financing. There was a deficit of 4.7 billion birr during fiscal year 2005. To cover that, the government turned to the domestic banking system, which provided 3.2 billion birr.

Money Supply

During times of peace, the EPRDF government has tried to keep the supply of money under control. During times of war, however, it has relied on increasing the money supply to finance its soaring military expenditures. That was the case during the Ethiopian–Eritrean war of 1998–2000.

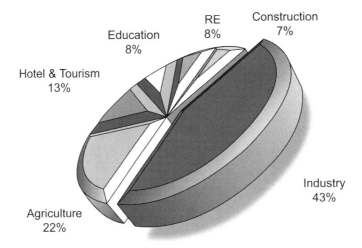

Types of Projects Licensed in 2004

Domestic liquidity, the broad money supply, grew to 30 billion birr in 2002/2003. This was a 10 percent growth rate over 2001/2002. The growth in broad money supply was attributed to growth in domestic credit of 20.7 percent. By contrast, narrow money showed a small quarterly growth of 0.4 percent until it rose to 18.1 billion birr in 2001/2002. Highly liquid assets, known as quasi-money, rose by 6 percent. Altogether, by 2007 the narrow money and quasi-money supply increased by 10 percent and 16.6 percent, respectively. This led to a 13 percent expansion in broad money supply. Under the watchful eyes of World Bank and IMF officials, the EPRDF government's policy continues to be cautious.

Prices

Unlike many developing countries, Ethiopia has succeeded in keeping inflation under control. During the 1980s, inflation was kept under 4.3 percent. However, there were periodic rises resulting from unforeseen circumstances. For example, the rate of inflation soared to 28.6 percent in 1974 following the disastrous famine of 1973, when during the same year, the price of food items rose to an astronomical level of 40 percent of what it was during the previous year. A similar rise took place in 1991/1992, following the fall of the Derg and the ensuing monetary chaos. In 2001/2002, the lowest level of inflation was registered when it fell to 7.2 percent. Economists have attributed this to favorable weather conditions, which led to an 11.5 percent increase in agricultural output. This was followed by a 13 percent decline in the food price index. Owing to an increase in food prices by 25 percent, which was caused by a severe draught, and against a drop of 13 percent the previous year, inflation jumped to 15.1 percent in 2002/2003.

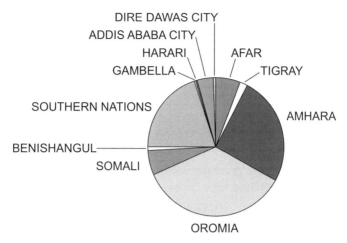

Population Census, 2007

Because Ethiopia is dependent on agricultural products for its domestic revenue and exports, adverse weather conditions can create significant hardship. When food is scarce, prices rise and inflation sets in, eroding the meager income and purchasing power of the people. The per capita income has declined in recent years on average, including a drop of 6 percent in 2002/2003. Coupled with inflation, which averaged 3.6 percent during the last five years, the decline in the standard of living of the average Ethiopian has not abated.

Exchange Rate

The liberalization of the foreign exchange regime has been one of the major macroeconomic reform policies of the EPRDF government since its takeover of power in 1991. A mechanism it has used is the hitherto nonexistent foreign exchange auctioning system. From 1991 to 2010 the Ethiopian Birr greatly depreciated against the U.S. dollar. Whereas in 1991 US$1 was equal to 2.5 Birr, by 2010 it has depreciated so much that US$1 has become equal to 17.5 Birr. One benefit of the auction system is that since the adoption of the policy, the gap between the official and parallel market rates has narrowed significantly. But every year there is a decline in the value of the birr.

Since October 24, 2001, Ethiopian exchange rates have been determined on a daily basis via interbank transactions regulated by the state's Central Bank. The decline can be seen from the following record of the birr's exchange rate with the U.S. dollar: 2003: 8.60; 2004: 8.64; 2005: 8.64; 2006: 8:69; 2007: 8.96; and 2008: 9.91. By contrast, in 2003/2004, the parallel market rate was 8.71 birr to the U.S. dollar, narrowing the gap between the official and the parallel market rates.

Savings and Capital Formation

Savings—required for investment—have been hard to come by locally in the Ethiopian context. Thus, gross domestic savings (GDS, calculated by deducting total public and private consumption expenditures from GDP) went up only slightly, from 4.9 percent in 2002/2003 to 5.5 percent of GDP in 2004/2005. Ethiopian economists attribute this to the drop in the share of total consumption expenditures from about 95 percent of GDP in 2003/2004 to 94.5 percent in 2004/2005, with GOS thus averaging 6.9 percent during 2000–2005.

During those same years, gross capital formation (GCF) averaged a little more than 21.3 percent as compared to an average of about 13 percent during the time of the Derg. The consequences are clear: lack of savings and the decline in meager domestic savings have led to dependence on external sources. One can see positive trends in gross domestic savings and investment as ratios of GDP from 2000 to 2005. As can be seen, in 2001/2002, the ratio of gross capital formation to GDP soared to 23.6 percent, the highest in 45 years.

Excessive consumption expenditures arise from low levels of savings. Lower savings and investment accrue from high consumption expenditures. From 2000/2001 to 2004/2005, government consumption expenditures per ratio of GDP were on average 16 percent, whereas private consumption expenditures were was 77.6 percent. Even though government consumption expenditures went down marginally to 14.1 percent, private consumption expenditures grew to 80.4 percent in 2004/2005. This meant that the aggregate consumption expenditures reached 94.5 percent for that year.

PRIME MINISTER MELES ZENAWI'S REPORT ON THE ECONOMY

On March 18, 2008, Prime Minister Meles Zenawi presented to Parliament a report on the state of the economy. He pointed out that the economy had made major macroeconomic gains with the GDP rising by an impressive 10.8 percent. Exports also grew, Meles pointed out, at 33 percent, though inflation rose to 17.5 percent in January 2008. He emphasized that the sustained growth of GDP in 2007/2008 was remarkable despite adverse effects of spiraling oil prices.

One should mention that because of adverse weather conditions, negative growth rates of 0.3 and 3.3 percent were registered in 2002 and 2003, respectively. Meles called attention to the record of GDP growth, which had averaged in the double digits since 2004. This impressive growth received accolades from the World Bank and the IMF.

Though opposition members dismiss the claim of economic growth under the EPRP as a myth, the Nobel laureate economist Joseph E. Stiglitz (2002) actually goes to the extent of putting Meles's economic acumen above that of the officials of the IMF who denied his government badly needed loans despite its registering of impressive economic performances since the Derg's ouster in 1991.

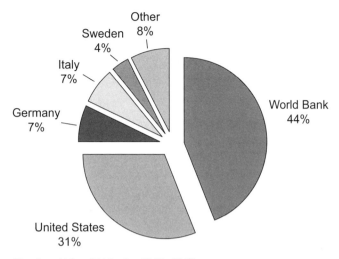

Foreign Aid to Ethiopia, 1962–1969

At the beginning of the 1990s, Ethiopia's GDP was about $6.0 billion. However, it began experiencing accelerated growth in the mid-1990s. Western economic observers point out that the country spawned a double-digit growth rate during 2008 and 2009, until by the end of 2009, its GDP had reached $33.9 Billion. That means that Ethiopia has surpassed its southern neighbor Kenya to become the region's largest economy. The 2010 World Report by the *Economist* magazine even predicted that by the beginning of the next decade, Ethiopia would be the fifth-fastest-growing economy on the entire planet.

REFERENCES

Alemayehu, S. 2005. *Proceedings of the Second International Conference on the Ethiopian Economy*. Addis Ababa: Ethiopian Economic Association.

Almeida, M. D. 1907. *Historia Aethiopiae: Liber I-IV. Romae,* C. de Luigi.

Assefa, B., and Eshetu Chole. 1969. *A Profile of the Ethiopian Economy*. Addis Ababa, Ethiopia: Oxford University Press.

Ayele, K. 2006. *The Ethiopian Economy: Principles and Practices*. Addis Ababa, Ethiopia: A. Kuris.

Baykadagn, G. 1995. *State and Economy of Early 20th Century Ethiopia Prefiguring Political Economy*. Chicago: Karnak House.

Bereket, K., T. Mekonnen, et al. 1996. *The Ethiopian Economy: Poverty and Poverty Alleviation: Proceedings of the Fifth Annual Conference on the Ethiopian Economy*. Addis Ababa: Department of Economics, Ethiopian Economic Association.

Cerulli. 1962. Gli atti di Zena Marqos, monaco etiopico del secolo (The Actions of Abuna Zena Marqos . . . Ethiopian of the Century) XIV.

Cheru, F., and S. Pausewang 1992. *Economic Reconstruction and the Peasants in Ethiopia: Two Papers Presented at the Symposium on the Ethiopian Economy, with a Postscript*. Bergen, Norway: Chr. Michelsen Institute, Development Research and Action Programme.

Economist Magazine. 2010. *World Report*, London.

Ethiopian Economic Association. 2004. *Report on the Ethiopian Economy*. Addis Ababa: Ethiopian Economic Association.

Food and Agriculture Organization and World Food Programme. 2008. *Crop and Food Security Assessment Mission to Ethiopia*, Phase 124.

Gebrehiowot, A., J. Mohammed, et al. 2002. *Policy Reform, Implementation, and Outcome in Ethiopia: Proceedings of the Eleventh Annual Conference on the Ethiopian Economy, Nov. 2–4, 2001, Nazareth, Ethiopia*. Addis Ababa: Ethiopian Economic Association and Dept. of Economics, Addis Ababa University.

Getnet, A., Y. Getachew, et al. 2007. *Proceedings of the Fourth International Conference on the Ethiopian Economy*. Addis Ababa: Ethiopian Economic Association.

Gill, G. J. 1974. *Readings on the Ethiopian Economy*. Addis Ababa, Ethiopia: Institute of Development Research, Faculty of Arts, Haile Selassie I University.

Government of Ethiopia, Ministry of Finance and Economic Development. 2006. *Ethiopia: Building on Progress, a Plan for Accelerated and Sustained Development to End Poverty (2005/06–2009/10)*. Addis Ababa, Ethiopia: Ministry of Finance and Economic Development.

Grabowski, R. 1991. "Economic Development and the Traditional Sector: A Comparison of Japanese and African Experience." *Developing Economics* 29(1) March: 5–18.

Griffin, K. B. 1992. *The Economy of Ethiopia*. New York: Macmillan.

Hansson, G. 1995. *The Ethiopian Economy, 1974–94: Ethiopia Tikdem and After*. New York: Routledge.

Henze, P. B., U.S. Office of the Under Secretary of Defense for Policy, et al. 1989. *Ethiopia, Crisis of a Marxist Economy: Analysis and Text of a Soviet Report*. Santa Monica, CA: RAND.

Hiwet, A. 1975. *Ethiopia: From Autocracy to Revolution*. London: Review of African Political Economy.

Inter Africa Group and United Nations Development Programme. 1992. *Final Report of the Symposium on Rehabilitating the Ethiopian Economy: 15–18 January 1992, Africa Hall, Addis Ababa*. Addis Ababa, Ethiopia: The Group.

James, P. O. 1973. *Ethiopian Economy*. Addis Ababa, Ethiopia: James.

McCann, J. 1983. *Household Economy, Demography, and the "Push" Factor in Northern Ethiopian History, 1916–1935*. Boston: African Studies Center, Boston University.

Mekonnen, T., K. Abdulhamid Bedri, et al. 1994. *The Ethiopian Economy: Problems of Adjustment: Proceedings of the Second Annual Conference on the Ethiopian Economy*. Addis Ababa, Ethiopia: Addis Ababa University Printing Press.

Mulugéta, T. 2006. *Atlas of the Ethiopian Rural Economy*. Addis Ababa, Ethiopia: Ya-Ma'ikalawi Statistiks.

Nelson, H. D., I. Kaplan, et al. 1981. *Ethiopia: A Country Study*. Washington, DC: U.S. Government Printing Office.

Ofcansky, T. P., L. B. Berry, et al. 1993. *Ethiopia: A Country Study*. Washington, DC: Federal Research Division, U.S. Government Printing Office.

Pankhurst, R. 1990. *A social history of Ethiopia: the northern and central highlands from early medieval times to the rise of Emperor Tewodros II*. Addis Ababa: Institute of Ethiopian Studies, Addis Ababa University.

Senait, S., S. Alemayehu, et al. 1998. *Human Resource Development in Ethiopia: Proceedings of the Seventh Annual Conference on the Ethiopian Economy: 28–30 November 1997, Nazareth, Ethiopia*. Addis Ababa: Ethiopian Economic Association and Department of Economics, Addis Ababa University.

Shiferaw Jamo. 1992. *An Overview of Macroeconomic Development in Ethiopia, 1941–1974*. Addis Ababa: Unpublished Document.

Shiferaw Jamo. 1993. *An Ethiopian Economy during the Transition*. Addis Ababa: Unpublished Document.

Shiferaw Jamo. 2008. *Prime Minister's State of the Economy Report: Somme Comments*. Addis Ababa: Unpublished Document.

Stiglitz, Joseph E. 2002. *Globalization and Its Discontents*. New York: Norton.

Taddesse Tamrat. 1972. *Church and State in Ethiopia, 1270–1527*. Oxford: Clarendon Press.

Tegegne, T., Addis Ababa University Institute of Development Research, et al. 1989. *Camel Pastoralism as Food System in Ethiopia*. Addis Ababa, Ethiopia: Institute of Development Research; Uppsala, Sweden: Scandinavian Institute of African Studies.

Tegeler, H. M. 1956. *The Agricultural Economy of Ethiopia*. Washington, DC: U.S. Government Printing Office.

Tilahun Teshome. 1993. "An Overview of the Right to Strike in Ethiopia." *Journal of Ethiopian Law* 16: 216–238.

Trivedi, U. S., and Haile Selassie I Comprehensive School. 1968. *Ethiopian Economy*. Asmara, Ethiopia: Department of Economics and Commerce.

United Nations Economic Commission for Africa. 2008. *Discussion and Guiding Principles for Africa: Land Management Information Systems in the Knowledge Economy*. Addis Ababa, Ethiopia: Economic Commission for Africa, ICT Science and Technology Division.

U.S. State Department. 2008. *Diplomacy in Action, Ethiopia*. http://www.state.gov/e/eeb/ifd/2008/100861.htm.

Wolday, A., G.H.R. Chipande, et al. 1997. *Small-Scale Enterprise Development in Ethiopia: Proceedings of the Sixth Annual Conference on the Ethiopian Economy*. Addis Ababa: Ethiopian Economic Association, Department of Economics, Addis Ababa University.

World Economic Forum. *Global Competitiveness Report*, 2004/2005; 2010/2011.

Yeshimebet, T. 1993. *The Status of Women, Women's entrepreneurship, and the Ethiopian Economy*. Addis Ababa: Private Publication.

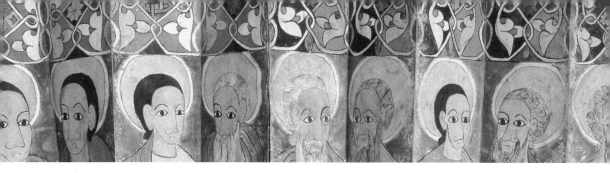

Society

Religion and Thought

PRE-MONOTHEISTIC ETHIOPIA

Both pre-Christian and post-Christian inscriptions (i.e., those before and after AD 330) indicate early serpent worship in Ethiopian mythology. The father of the Queen of Sheba was said to have been the first human king to be crowned and worshipped. He gained this status, according to age-old Ethiopian beliefs, after he killed the serpent king known by the name Arwe (Litmann, 1947). It is interesting to note that the Ethiopian term for king, *nagash* (literally "the crowned"), is similar to the Jewish term *nachash*, which means serpent. Confirming the old belief, a relief picture of a serpent can be seen on one of the fallen stelae of Axum. Just like in other societies of the Near East, the worship of the serpent was prevalent during the early period. The Persians also have a similar legend; as recounted in the holy Persian book of Avesta, ancient Persians worshipped a serpent king called Adjis Dahaka.

Judaism also has deep roots in pre-Christian Ethiopia. The first clear proof, as recounted in the biblical book of Acts, is that the Ethiopian eunuch who was converted to Christianity by Jesus's disciple Phillip was reading the book of Isaiah (circa AD 50). Furthermore, the first-century Jewish historian Josephus traces Jewish influence on Ethiopia to the time of the Queen of Sheba. He said in his writing that the Queen of Ethiopia, who also ruled Egypt, went to Jerusalem and met Solomon, from whom she acquired his wisdom.

Then later during the pre-Christian period, the worship of particular gods became widespread. This is also clearly seen on statues, pagan altars, and temples found in northern Ethiopia. The gods worshipped were many. In the ancient pagan temple of Yeha, which was built during approximately the sixth century BC, the religious

169

edifice was dedicated to a god named Almouqah. Another temple in Melazo, built circa the fifth century BC, is also dedicated to Almouqah. Other known pagan gods of the period were Astar, Baher, Medr, and Mahram, as included in one of Emperor Ezana's pre-Christian inscriptions.

The crescent and the sun were worshipped for hundreds of years. An incense burner discovered at Addi Gelemo has distinct crescent and sun symbols in its upper part. At Kaskasse, one can still see an altar with Ethiopic writings that bears the symbols of the crescent and the sun separating the letters. Emperor Ezana's scribes also used the crescent and the sun to separate letters until the monarch was converted to Christianity in AD 330, at which time the symbols were replaced by the cross (his description of himself also changed from "the son of Ares" to the servant of "the Lord of Heaven"). It is important to note that all the inscriptions of Ethiopian emperors prior to Ezana have words separated by the symbols of the crescent and the sun. All the coins of Ethiopian emperors preceding Ezana also featured words separated by the picture of the crescent and the sun.

ETHIOPIA AND THE GREEK CONNECTION

In Hellenic mythology, Ethiopia was prominently portrayed. The famous Greek poet Homer, who lived in the ninth century AD, wrote in the Iliad about "the blameless Ethiopians." He asserted that they were visited by Zeus, the king of the gods; by the goddess Iris, who traveled to their country to participate in their sacrificial rites; and by Poseidon, the sea god, who "lingered delighted" at their feasts. Later, in the first century BC, another Greek historian, Diodorus Siculus, wrote that the gods Hercules and Bacchus were both "awed by the piety" of the Ethiopians, "whose sacrifices, were the most acceptable to the gods." Clearly, the Ethiopians of antiquity were part of the religious mythology of ancient civilizations, and they worshipped gods of similar type.

ETHIOPIA AND THE JUDAIC CONNECTION

There is no doubt that Judaic influences and Old Testament reflections had reached Ethiopia long before the introduction of Christianity in AD 340 and before the Bible was translated into Ethiopic. That is why the Ethiopian eunuch was reading the book of Isaiah during the time of the apostles. There are several different explanations for this Jewish connection. One is that Jewish influences came from the direction of Egypt. Religious historians supporting this view base their argument on what the prophets in the Old Testament recorded more than 2,000 years ago with reference to Nubia and northern Abyssinia, which were then referred to together as Ethiopia. The prophet Isaiah (740–701 BC), basing his information on eyewitness accounts, mentioned the Nile tributaries that divide Ethiopia and the papyrus reed boats still used at the source of the Nile:

> Ah, the land of the rustling of wings, which is beyond the rivers of Ethiopia; that sends ambassadors by the sea, even in vessels of papyrus on the waters. Go, you

swift messengers, to a nation tall and smooth, to a people awesome from their beginning onward, a nation that measures out and treads down, whose land the rivers divide! (Isaiah 18:2)

The prophet Jeremiah (627 to 587 BC) wrote of "Jews in the country of Pathros," which was southern Egypt, adjacent to ancient Ethiopia (Jeremiah 15:8). The prophet Zephaniah (640–609 BC) referred to Jewish settlers in Cush when he wrote, "From beyond the rivers of Cush my suppliants, my dispersed community, shall bring my offering" (Zephaniah 3:10). This proves that Jews had penetrated as far as ancient Nubia and northwestern Ethiopia hundreds of years before the birth of Christ.

The Greek historian Herodotus (485–425 BC) described Egyptian garrisons believed to be of Jewish extraction who were neglected and left in Elephantine—an island in the river Nile on the borders of ancient Egypt and Ethiopia. He recounted that when they were left on duty for three years without being relieved, they revolted against the 26th-dynasty Egyptian pharaoh Psammetichos II (593–588 BC) and went to Ethiopia. Herodotus refers to the "Deserters" as *Asmach* and adds:

This word [Asmach] signifies, when translated into the tongue of the Hellenes, "those who stand on the left hand of the king." [Interestingly similar to the Ethiopian title *Gra Azmach*, which means those who stand on the left side of the king during combat!) . . . Two hundred and forty thousand Egyptians of the warrior class, . . . revolted and went over to the Ethiopians . . . from the . . . city of Elephantine. . . . The Egyptians . . . had served as outposts for three years and no one relieved them from their guard; accordingly they took counsel together, and adopting a common plan, they all in a body revolted from Psammetichos and set out for Ethiopia. . . . When they came to Ethiopia they gave themselves over to the king of the Ethiopians; and he rewarded them . . . there were certain of the Ethiopians who had come to be at variance with him; and he bade them drive these out and dwell in their land. So since these men settled in the land of the Ethiopians, the Ethiopians have come to be of milder manners, from having learnt the customs of the Egyptians. (Herodotus, Book 2)

The Aramaic papyri of the fifth century BC also mentioned the same incident. It is perfectly reasonable to assume that the Beta Israel (formerly referred to as Falashas) or Ethiopian Jews had a connection to these episodes.

In the Bible, the earliest reference to Ethiopia is found in Genesis, which refers to the River Gihon (Nile), which it says "compasseth the whole of Ethiopia," and the book of Numbers points out that "Moses married an Ethiopian woman." It is recounted in the Old Testament that around 1000 BC, the Queen of Sheba traveled to Jerusalem to visit King Solomon (1 Kings 9:1–10; 2 Chronicles 9:1-9; Matthew 12:42; Luke 11:32). Ethiopian sources have elaborations on the episode, with the Queen begetting a son from Solomon who established the Solomonian dynasty that lasted until Haile Selassie in the second half of the 20th century.

Ethiopian sources, supported by the Coptic *History of the Patriarchs of Alexandria*, have always equated Ethiopia with the kingdom of Saba. They have also claimed that Sheba and Solomon's offspring, Menelik I, brought with him to Ethiopia the Ark of the Covenant, which Ethiopian Christians believe has been preserved to present day at the Church of Zion in Axum and which is a centerpiece of the country's Christian Orthodox denomination. A detailed explanation of this was given in a book called *Kebra Nagast* (Glory of the Kings), translated from Coptic in the early 14th century, and was elaborated on by an Armenian writer named Abu Salih, who pointed out that Abyssinia (Ethiopia) is the "Kingdom of Sheba" and that "the Ethiopians possessed the Ark of the Covenant" which was looked after by "Israelites." Some old Yemeni manuscripts have portrayed the Queen of Sheba as being born to an Ethiopian mother named Azeb and a Yemeni father called Shar Habil.

The fact that Ethiopia ruled over South Arabia on and off for hundreds of years during antiquity may have something do with this, but many Eurocentric historians have depicted the Queen of Sheba as being from Yemen, not Ethiopia. However, as

---

MOSES OF ETHIOPIA

Moses of Ethiopia (AD 330–405), also known as Abba Musa (or Moses the Black), was an Ethiopian who was in the service of an Egyptian official of high authority in the early part of the Christian era. His biography, written in Coptic by Egypt's Bishop Palladius, recounts that initially, Moses lived a life of evil, which included larceny, murder, and leadership of a gang of 75 thieves. At one time, he swam across the Nile with a sword between his teeth to kill a shepherd against whom he had rancor. It was said that during this attempt to kill a rival, he saw a vision. Upon hearing of the ascetics of the Western Desert, Moses, who had now repented, entered the Monastery of Petra in the Egyptian desert of Scete. Despite constant temptations, he passed a harmonious religious life with St. Isidore and St. Macarius at the monastery. After being an ascetic, he dedicated his life to helping all those in need. Between his long fasts, he carried out manual work to feed the needy. Theophilus, Archbishop of Alexandria, heard of Moses's virtues and ordained him a Coptic Christian minister. In his old age, Moses founded a monastery on his own and led 75 disciples, all of whom followed his example. In AD 405, Moses, who was 75 years of age, and all his company of monks who refused to heed his warnings and instead remained behind to gain martyrdom like him were murdered by the Mazices, a vicious group of Barbarian burglars in the Monastery of Dais al Baramus, which Moses had founded. He was soon raised to sainthood by the Coptic see of Alexandria and is as legendary in Coptic circles as St. Jerome is among Catholics. Abba Musa is recognized as a special religious leader in the Ethiopian and Coptic Synaxarium, and his date of remembrance is 24 Sané (July 1). The well-known German scholar Otto Meinardus recently commented that Moses of Ethiopia became "the first martyr of the desert fathers." Meinardus, O. F. A. 1962. *Atlas of Christian sites in Egypt.* Le Caire: Societe d'archâeologie copte. p.31.

long ago as the first century AD, Flavius Josephus, the Jewish scholar and historian, asserted that the Queen of Sheba who visited Solomon was from Africa, not from Arabia. He specifically referred to her as the "Queen of Egypt and Ethiopia."

There are many other references that connect ancient Ethiopia with Judaism. *The Book of Amos* compares the Ethiopians with the Israelites when it cites God as asking the Jewish people, "Are you not as the children of the Ethiopians unto me?" (Amos 9:7). That is why the Abyssinian tradition developed the idea that Ethiopia had become the new Israel. It should not be surprising, therefore, that some Ethiopian emperors of antiquity engraved on their coins the title "King of Zion" (e.g., the coin of King Endybis in the third century AD). More than all these, however, the Ethiopian monarchy and the Ethiopian Orthodox Church have cherished a passage from the Psalms, where King David proclaims, "Ethiopia shall soon stretch out her hands unto God" (Psalm 68:31). Jewish and Old Testament connections through South Arabia are even more abundant, and the evidence of Jewish migration into Ethiopia from its South Arabian realm is irrefutable.

Rabbinical literature also abounds with references to Jewish connections with the Ethiopian-ruled areas of Arabia. In *Midrash Bamidbar Rabbah* and the *Talmud* (Bamidbar Rabbah Naso 9:34), there is a record by R. Aqiba, who traveled to Yemen to arouse the Jewish Diaspora against the Romans, that the "King of the Arabs" was dark-skinned. It is also revealed in the passages that an Ethiopian king ruled areas in South Arabia at the time. This was AD 130. The mention of dark complexion was undoubtedly a reference to the brown face of the Ethiopian ruler.

That a sizable number of the Jewish Diaspora with their monotheistic faith migrated to Yemen following the destruction of the first and then the second temple in 538 BC and AD 70, respectively, is clear. Ample evidence exists that there was a thriving Jewish Diaspora in Arabia. The very last Himyarite king, Dhu Nuwas, who was converted to Judaism and defeated by the Axumite general Abraha, is a well-known case. After that conquest, Ethiopia had total control over South Arabia, and during that time, a mass exodus of Jews to Ethiopia took place. The fact that they subsequently crossed over to Axum, which was one of the four most powerful kingdoms in the world and ruled South Arabia itself, cannot be disputed.

It is the Jewish connection to Ethiopia and the late migration of Jewish settlers from South Arabia that is the root of the Beta Israel (Ethiopian Jewish) phenomenon. This long historical connection going back to the time of Moses and ushering in mass migration during Ethiopia's rule over South Arabia has left a strong residue of Jewish religious tradition in Ethiopia. Some Jews stuck to their faith even under heavy persecution and at one time even succeeded in taking over power from the Axumite Christians. By the time of Ahmad Gragn's conquest in the mid-1500s, they no longer had hegemony over the state but were controlling a major province.

A sizable number of Beta Israel converted to Christianity and introduced Hebraic rites and religious elements into the Ethiopian Tewahedo Church. For all these reasons, a notion has developed among Ethiopian Church scholars that the Ethiopians have become the legitimate successors to the Jews who have failed to accept Jesus as the true Messiah. Among the royal honors of the emperors of Ethiopia up to the time of Haile Selassie was the title "Conquering Lion of the Tribe of Judah." Ethiopian Christians use the official Shield of David and seal and net of Solomon.

The Ethiopian Orthodox Tewahedo Christians believe that they have in their custody the Tabernacle of the Law of God (i.e., the Ark of the Covenant, which they refer to as the Tabot), brought from Jerusalem by Menelik, the son of Solomon and the Queen of Sheba. When Ethiopian Christians carry the Tabot out of the church during celebrations such as Epiphany, their rituals and ceremonial practices are strikingly similar to those of ancient Israel.

In many ways Ethiopian Orthodox tradition mimics a Jewish religious practice. The clergy surround the Tabot or Ark, sing in praise of God, use musical instruments such as the cestrum and the drum, and dance. This is similar to the carrying of the scroll containing the five books of Moses to the accompaniment of song and dance and the beating and rattling of musical instruments, especially during the feast of Sirnhat Torah, which commemorates the scene in the second chapter of Samuel where David and the people danced about the Ark.

Antiphonal singing, which is a major feature of the Ethiopian Orthodox mass, is another form of Jewish liturgy being practiced in Ethiopian Tewahedo Christianity. In both Ethiopian Orthodox and Jewish musical practice, there is a use of a falsetto element and trilling. Also, Ethiopian Orthodox *dabtaras* and Judaic priests make use of the staff in religious celebrations.

TIMQAT

Timqat is the Festival of Epiphany. The celebration falls on January 19, two weeks following the Ethiopian Christmas known as Ganna. It is in fact a three-day celebration, held in memory of Christ's baptism in the Jordan River. Timqat takes place during the last days of the rainy season in August, when the country starts to change dramatically. The sun glows with utmost brightness from a gleaming blue sky, and the religious carnival of Timqat always expires in this ideal weather. Everyone is well dressed for the occasion. There is even a saying, "Le Timqat yalhone qemis yibetates," which means "a vest that is not worn during the Timqat celebrations may as well be cut to pieces." All persons, whether adults or children, look shimmering for the three-day motional gala. The end of the day on January 18 is called Ketera, and at that particular time, the priests remove the Tabots (the replicas of the Ark of the Covenant) from each church and monastery and ordain the water in a pool or river to purify it, where the next day a grand festivity takes place. The priests carefully deposit the Tabots in specially prepared tents in the field, each deacon raising a lofty standard or picture portraying the church's or monastery's saint. People engage in merrymaking. The pastor sprinkles water over the converged congregation in memory of Christ's baptism in the Jordan River. Once baptism is over, the Tabots are again graciously transported back to their particular locations, followed by the devout. The procession accompanying the Tabots winds through the roads again as horsemen with alluring and garlanded attire gallop on the edges, ending the procession at the gates of the church.

In extra-religious practices, Ethiopian Orthodox *dabtaras* (church scholars) employ magical formulae similar to those used in ancient Israel. Many of the words inscribed (e.g., *elohe, adonai*) are exactly similar. Both attempt to invoke spells to disperse demons or to cure diseases. Like their Jewish counterpart, Ethiopian *dabtaras* use amulets and tefillim for presumed best effect.

In both Ethiopian Orthodox Christianity and Judaism, there is a twofold division of the priesthood. In ancient Israel, the clergy were divided into priests and Levites, the latter being responsible for conducting the ritual of hymns. Similarly, in the Ethiopian Orthodox Church, there is a division of the clergy into two: priests and *dabtaras*, the latter being responsible for choral functions.

There are many Hebrew terms associated with the temple that have been adopted in Ethiopian church circles. For example, the word for Eucharist is *Qurban* (Hebrew *Kurban*) and the tem for a high priest is *kahen* (Hebrew *kohen*). There are similarities in the garments worn by the clergy. Ethiopian Orthodox monks wear the priestly belt, the skullcap, and the scapular with 12 crosses. The latter clearly corresponds to the 12 stones on the breastplate of the Jewish high priest.

Strict adherence to Pentateuchal legal code prescribing dietary practices is another case of strong Jewish tradition in Ethiopian Orthodox Christianity. Orthodox Christians in Ethiopia follow the dictates of Leviticus regarding the consumption of

Ethiopian priest. (Carolyne Pehora | Dreamstime.com.)

MASQAL—FINDING OF THE TRUE CROSS

The Masqal feast commemorates what is believed by the Orthodox devout to be the discovery of the True Cross, the cross on which Christ was crucified. The finding was attributed to Empress Helena, mother of Constantine the Great. In Christian Ethiopia, Masqal signifies the physical presence of the True Cross at the remote mountain monastery of Gishan Mariam, located 483 kilometers north of Addis Ababa in the Wallo region. In this monastery is a massive volume called the *Tefut*, written during the reign of Emperor Zara Yaqob (1434–1468), which records the story of how the fragment of the True Cross was acquired by Ethiopia. At the time of year when Masqal is celebrated, flowers bloom on mountains and plains, and the meadows are yellow with brilliant Masqal daisies. Dancing, feasting, merrymaking, bonfires, and gun salutes mark the occasion. The festival begins with the faithful planting a green tree in a town square on the eve of the holiday. Everyone then brings a pole topped with Masqal daisies to form a towering pyramid that becomes a beacon of flame. Torches of common twigs called *chibbo* are used to light the bundle of branches called *damara*. In major cities such as Addis Ababa, Masqal celebrations start in the early afternoon, when a huge procession bearing flaming torches approaches a central square from various directions. The cavalcade includes priests and deacons in their brightly hued vestments, uniformed students, colorful brass bands, contingents of the armed forces, and bedecked floats carrying huge lit crosses. All the people in the procession circle the *damara* and fling their torches upon it. Then, they welcome the season of flowers and golden sunshine called Tseday, whereupon they sing in unison, "Iyoha-Abebaye! Meskerem Tebaye!" ("Salute my flower, spring has dawned!"). As evening darkens, the flames glow brighter. It is not until dawn that the burning pyramid consumes itself and the big tree at the center finally collapses. Then, and only then, will the euphoric Christian multitude march home, humming, "Hallelujah, praised be the Lord, my savior."

meat from mammals and birds, sometimes to the smallest detail, as for example in obeying the order in Genesis 32:33 that forbids the consumption of sinew (Ethiopian *shulluda*). Ethiopian Orthodox Christians never eat animals who do not have cloven hooves or do not chew the cud. Thus, animals such as horses are out of the question. The slaughtering and bleeding of animals is also performed in strict adherence to Pentateuchal requirements as described in Genesis 9:4 and Leviticus 3:17 and 4:6. Ethiopian Christians have added some modern prohibitions also. For example, smoking tobacco, still done by the Oromo Christian converts and widespread even among the clergy in the 16th century, has been banned by the Dersana Ragu'el, a "homily in honor of the Archangel Ragu" that calls tobacco "plant of Setatira" and asserts that it is "poisoned by the devil."

Among all Judeo-Christian people, only Jews and Ethiopians practice circumcision on the eighth day. Baptismal days for infants, as in the Jewish laws of presentation at the temple, are 40 days for male and 80 days for female.

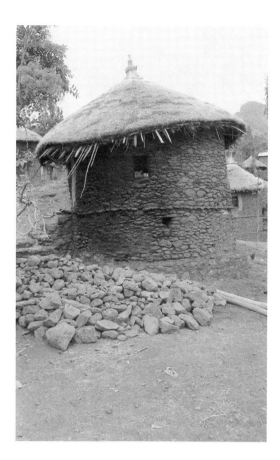

A monk's dwelling place in Lalibala, Ethiopia. (Courtesy of Paulos Milkias.)

KIKANOS

According to rabbinical extrapolations of Yashar Shemot, who compiled the *midrashim* to the Pentateuch in the 11th century, Kikanos was the king of Ethiopia during Moses's flight from Egypt. Shemot writes that when Moses arrived to take refuge after killing an Egyptian overseer, there was an intractable war between Ethiopia and the nations of the East. In time, Kikanos, with whom Moses gained great favor, died. Then the latter was chosen by the nobles of the land to marry Kikanos's widow, Adoniah, who was the Queen of Ethiopia in her own right. It should be pointed out that Moses's sister Miriam and the head priest, Aaron, disapproved of his marrying this Ethiopian woman. According to the *midrashim* of the Pentateuch, Moses soon replaced her husband as king of Ethiopia. As a king, Moses was said to have successfully removed the siege of the city and to gain victory against the eastern invaders. The *midrashim* further relates that even though Ethiopia was prospering under Moses, who ruled it for 40 years, when he reached the age of 67, the patriarch of the Jews chose to leave Ethiopia. He subsequently returned to Egypt and fulfilled his ordained mission of liberating the children of Israel from Egyptian slavery.

Beta Israel (Ethiopian Jews) praying. (AP Photo/Emilio Morenatti.)

The Ethiopian New Year celebration, which falls on September 11, is similar in religious import to the Jewish New Year. On the morning of the New Year, all Christians go to the nearest river and bathe for purification. This is similar to the immersion prescribed for the high priest in the Mishnah. As soon as the Christian flock returns from the ritual bath in the river, the head of each house-

Ancient books and church implements from the monasteries of Lake Tana. (Courtesy of Paulos Milkias.)

hold sacrifices an animal, usually a bullock, as an act of expiation. This practice clearly resembles the Jewish high priest placing his hand on a bullock prior to its slaughter. Similarly, the Ethiopian Orthodox Easter (*Fasika*) is a replication of the Jewish Passover known as *Pesach*. The observance of the Jewish Sabbath as well as Sunday—which had been a point of contention among Ethiopian monasteries as well as Orthodox Church scholars and the Jesuits who came to convert Ethiopian Orthodox Christians 500 years ago but without success—is another ancient custom in the Ethiopian Church that resembles a time-honored Jewish tradition.

The liturgy of the Ethiopian Church is remarkably similar to that of its Jewish counterpart. Ethiopian Orthodox service books contain the complete Psalter and

---

AKSUM-TSION

This is the oldest church in Ethiopia, consecrated, according to church tradition, by the first Christian co-rulers, the brothers Abraha and Atsbaha (Emperors Ezana and Saizana), in AD 330. The earliest cathedral had 12 altars, the high altar being dedicated to St. Mary of Zion. The Virgin Mary is considered "the Eternal Queen of Ethiopia." As a result, the church has always been considered the highest-ranking and holiest shrine in Ethiopia. Church tradition asserts that Emperor Ezana brought the original Ark of the Covenant from the Island of Tana Qirqos to Aksum and placed it at its present location. Ethiopian emperors received legitimacy only from this church. The original cathedral was said to have been destroyed by Yodit Gudit, a Beta Israel queen from the Dambia areas, in her quest to seize the Ark of the Covenant, which her group believed was the true Ark of the Covenant given to Moses by God. The cathedral was burned to the ground by Ahmed Ibn Ibrahim al Ghazi (Gragn), who invaded Christian Ethiopia in the 15th century. A newer though smaller church replaced the old church during the reign of Emperor Galawdewos. It was in the early 17th century that the cathedral was entirely reconstructed on a grander scale by Emperor Fasilidas. The Ark of the Covenant, which is housed in a smaller chapel nearby, is guarded by a monk who lives there and is not allowed to leave the compound. The monk stays there for life and is the only person permitted to enter and see the Ark. He appoints his own successor before he dies, and the duty is passed on to the next guardian. By tradition, St. Mary of Zion is headed by a dignitary with the title of *nibura id* who also acts as the secular governor of the town of Aksum and its environs. In feudal Ethiopia, the tile *nibura id* was equal to the title of *ras* or duke. When a *ras warq* (golden coronet) was given to the *nibura id*, his dignity outranked that of a *ras*. In 1999, by the promulgation of a Holy Synod, Aksum was elevated to the rank of archdiocese, and the title of archbishop of Aksum was reserved for the patriarch of Ethiopia, whose seat is in the capital, Addis Ababa. The Cathedral Monastery of St. Mary of Zion is referred to as the "Ri'isa Adbarat," which means first among all the churches and monasteries of Ethiopia.

are followed by the Kanan, a collection of nine odes that are similar to the Jewish *Keroba* (i.e., the poetical passages inserted into the *tefillah* (Hebrew term for prayer). Another clear adherence to Jewish practice is with regard to the Trisagion, which is a standard hymn of the Divine Liturgy of the Ethiopian Orthodox Church.

THE BETA ISRAEL

Written records detailing the life of the Ethiopian Jews, or Beta Israel, go to the period of the Middle Ages. Though the *Kebra Nagast* was said to have been translated from Arabic in the 14th century, a close historical look shows that the notion of Queen of Sheba being from northern Ethiopia was not concocted in the 14th century to legitimize the Solomonians. A 9th-century Jewish traveler named Eldad Had-Dani referred to a Jewish kingdom "beyond the rivers of Cush." He narrated that the Jewish tribe of Dan, in order to avoid the internecine wars between Judah and Israel, migrated to Cush and, finally, with the help of Naphthali, Asher, and Gad, founded an independent Jewish kingdom in the Gold Land, in the vicinity of present-day Ethiopia. Yet others suggest that the Beta Israel were Jewish émigrés who crossed the Red Sea and settled in Ethiopia during Emperor Kaleb's conquest of South Arabia in AD 525.

As these different hypotheses are advanced, material artifacts depicting ancient Jewish ceremony going to the period of antiquity have been discovered in northern Ethiopia. For example, though a pagan shrine, the Temple at Yeha in Tigray province, which was constructed in the sixth century BC, is an architectural reproduction of other Jewish synagogues found in Israel and Egypt during the pre-Babylonian era. With the influence of modern Jewry, post-exilic feasts are now being celebrated. This started only during the Jewish calendar for the year 5729 (1968–1969). Thus, the Beta Israel have at last joined the annual cycle of contemporary Jewish life.

CHRISTIANITY AS THE OFFICIAL RELIGION OF THE ETHIOPIAN REALM

There are anecdotal references to the three Magi who came to see baby Jesus being Ethiopian. But we clearly see in the New Testament (the Acts 8:26–40) a reference to a eunuch and the treasures of Queen Candace of Ethiopia (an area covering ancient Nubia and parts of the Axumite Empire), who went to Jerusalem to worship the God of Israel—another proof that monotheism was already in place in Ethiopia during Christ's early ministry. It is recounted that the Ethiopian eunuch met Philip the Deacon and was baptized by him. Ethiopian historical records assert that he returned home and evangelized Christianity in Ethiopia.

Christianity was, however, not widespread. Only a few Ethiopians and Roman merchants practiced Christianity; up to AD 330, the bulk of the people, including

THE MAGI

The magi, known as *sab'a sagal* in Ethiopia, were wise men of the East travelled to Bethlehem with gifts of myrrh, frankincense and gold, to worship the newborn Jesus. Tradition says that these gifts were presented to the Christ child by Balthasar, the dark-colored king from Ethiopia, thus fulfilling Isaiah's prophecy that gold and frankincense would be brought from the Gentiles to honor the heavenly king. Frankincense was the purest incense. When burned, it produced a white smoke that symbolized the prayers and praises of the faithful ascending to heaven. The Western tradition of the names of the Magi originate from an ancient sixth-century Greek text, translated into Latin. The description resembles a mosaic of the magi, quite possibly those found at Ravenna. A pseudo-Bedan collection of writings continued to reflect the tradition of three kings. According to one text, the oldest of the Magi was Melchoir, who was the king of Arabia. This king is said to have a long grey beard and he gave gold as a gift, symbolizing the recognition of Christ as king. Balthazar, the king of Ethiopia, was middle-aged, dark-complexioned, and bearded and gave Jesus the gift of frankincense, indicating the recognition that Christ is the High Priest. The last one, Caspar was said to be the king of Tarsus, and was in his twenties; offered myrrh, which was used in making medicines. This symbolized Christ the healer and paramount physician. All were said to have been guided by the Star of Bethlehem. The gospel of Mathew does not identify their number but Christian tradition has set their number at three, named them kings, Caspar or Gaspar, Melchior, and Balthazar. The Feast of Epiphany, January 6, commemorates their visit.

the monarch, remained pagans. It was during that time that Frumentius thought of evangelization. He brought together Christian Ethiopians and Christian merchants of Roman origin who had settled at Axum and implored them to establish religious meeting places for prayer.

Frumentius did not want to see the burgeoning Christian flock in Axum revert to the previous situation. So, he traveled to Alexandria and explained the whole affair to the newly appointed patriarch, Athanasius, whom he beseeched for the appointment of a bishop to minister to the growing Christian community in Axum that was now protected by a Christian king. After consulting a council of priests, the patriarch chose Frumentius himself to be consecrated as the first Bishop of Axum.

Frumentius, known among Ethiopian Orthodox Christians as Abba Salama, Kassate Berhan, and "Father of peace and Revealer of light," returned to Axum to carry out his ministry. Emperor Constantius—son of the first Christian Roman emperor, Constantine the Great, who had accepted the Arian creed, which was opposed to the Alexandrian creed—had written the Ethiopian emperor of the period, Ezna, to request that he oust Frumentius, but the monarch refused to do so. After Frumentius, Ethiopian Christianity spread through the intense evangelization of the Nine Saints, who came to Ethiopia in the sixth century from the Roman Empire.

St. Mary's Church of Axum, built by Emperor Haile Selassie. (Courtesy of Paulos Milkias.)

For 1,600 years, an Egyptian bishop remained the head of the Ethiopian Church. This indeed is a highly unusual phenomenon in the annals of the global Church. In practice, however, the Egyptian archbishop, who did not know the local language, could not influence imperial policies, except through providing doctrinal direction. The *etchage* (abbot of Dabra Libanos), who was of Ethiopian extraction, had wide-scale power in the imperial realm.

FIQTOR

Fiqtor (Abba, 10th century) was a Syrian impostor. Originally, he was connected to the Egyptian monastery of St. Anthony (Deir Anba Antiniyus), from where Ethiopian metropolitans (or Bishops) were usually selected. He was thrown out the monastery on account of corrupt behavior. After clandestinely traveling to Ethiopia, he falsely claimed to be a monk with connections to the patriarch in Alexandria. He produced a fake letter from the Alexandrian see bearing the signature of Patriarch Cosmas III (AD 921–933) that removed Abuna Petros and replaced him with a false monk by the name Minas. Using Minas's position, Fiqtor succeeded to get Emperor Dil Naad deposed and replaced with his brother Emperor Anbassa Wudem. Fiqtor in time quarreled with Minas, whose house he raided before fleeing to Egypt with an enormous amount of property. He subsequently converted to the Muslim religion.

When the truth was discovered by Patriarch Cosmas, Minas was deposed and then executed. But because Petros had died in the meantime, no replacement was made. The Egyptian patriarch refused to appoint another bishop, so the Ethiopian emperor appointed Petro's assistant as Ethiopia's bishop. The standoff between the Ethiopian monarchy and the Alexandrian see persisted until the devastation of Axum by the queen of Banu Hamuwiya, generally recognized to be Yodit or Judith of the Beta Israel, in the ninth century AD.

ETHIOPIAN ORTHODOX AS THE PROTECTOR
OF SOUTH ARABIAN CHRISTIANS

Ethiopian Orthodox rulers of Ethiopia acted as the protectors of Christianity in the early sixth century AD when the Hymarite king, Dhu Nuwas, persecuted the Christians of Nagran in Yemen, and Emperor Constantine of the Roman Empire implored the Axumite king to rescue those who remained. Emperor Kaleb, who had a religious zeal, dispatched a military expedition of 100,000 soldiers under the able command of Abraha, who quickly smashed Yusuf's (Dhu Nuwas's) fighting force, killed him, and put Himyar and South Arabia—which was a vassal of Axum several times through the centuries—under the control of Kaleb's chosen Viceroy: Sumyafa' Ashwa (also known as Esimiphaeus). Abraha was, for all practical purposes, an extraordinary figure in South Arabian history, ruling the realm efficiently and promoting the cause of Christianity, which had been hitherto challenged by the rapid growth of Judaism in the area and the prevalent paganism of Arabia north of Yemen.

Abraha did not pass without leaving an important imprint across the Red Sea. An inscription found at Murayghan, South Arabia, records a defeat inflicted by Abraha on the Pagan North Arabian tribe of Ma'add. But soon, the Christian houses of worship that were under the control of the Ethiopian Orthodox Tewahedo Church were swept under the rapid expansion of Islam.

TEWAHEDO CHRISTIANITY
DURING THE ZAGWE DYNASTY

Not long after Axum declined in power and fell victim to the assault of the Beta Israel queen Yodit, in the 10th century AD, the Zagwe dynasty arose in central Ethiopia. The most famous among the Zagwe monarchs was Lalibala. This emperor's enduring legacy is his building of the world-famous rock-hewn churches of Roha that now bear his name. The 11 churches were hewn out of a mountain rock below ground level; the multifaceted edifices feature flights of stairs, long channels, underground tunnels, and large inner compounds—all supplied with a water system.

The churches of Lalibala are congregated in close proximity and are connected by subterranean passageways. One assemblage is surrounded by a trench which is 11 meters long. The basilicas of Emmanuel, Marqorewos, Abba Lebanos, and Gabriel are all engraved from a single rock hill. The most conspicuous because of its shape, which is the sign of a cross, is the Basilica of Qeddus Giorgis (St. Georges), which was carved from a sloping rock terrace. The Lalibala churches were all of a different design and hold on the inside antique religious implements and several forms of cross designs as well as different patterns on the windows.

THE EPISODE OF PRESTER JOHN

With the advent of Muslim invasions that spread rapidly, not only in the Middle East and North Africa, but also across the Mediterranean into Spain and other lands,

One of the rock-hewn churches of Lalibala (10th to 13th centuries AD). (Courtesy of Paulos Milkias.)

One of the 11 rock-hewn churches of Lalibala (12th to 13th century AD). (Courtesy of Paulos Milkias.)

The Church of St. George in Lalibala, hewn in the form of the cross from a single block of rock (12th to 13th century AD) (Courtesy of Paulos Milkias.)

many Christian rulers in Europe, who were looking for allies to curb the expansion of Islam and who entertained the ambition of freeing the Holy Land from the Seljuk Turks, received reports of a legendary emperor of Ethiopia known as "Prester John" (Latin: Prete Anie). Prester John was in fact with reference to some Zagwé emperors who doubled as priests.

When a letter purportedly written by Dawit, the emperor of Ethiopia, reached major Western leaders, including Frederick Barbarossa and the Byzantine emperor Comenius I, stories circulated far and wide that contact had been established with the Prester and that with his assistance, the Crusaders could ultimately free the Holy Land. During the Fifth Crusade, which took place at the beginning of the 13th century, information about Ethiopia trickled to Europe through Crusaders in Egypt. Soon, the Christian sovereigns of Nubia and Ethiopia, always fighting to defend their faith, became famous among European Christians. From that point on, "Prester John" was clearly identified with the emperor of Ethiopia. That Ethiopian emperors

SECTS OF TEWAHEDO CHRISTIANITY

The mainstream Ethiopian Orthodox Church believes in Tewahedo (Miaphysite unity) and confesses the harmony of two natures, divine and human, in the person of Christ, without confusion and without separation. Following the Catholic/Orthodox controversy that ensued in the 17th century, a sect called Walda Qib (Children of Anointment), or unctionists, was born. The unctionists professed that Jesus Christ became perfect man and perfect God by the anointing of the Holy Spirit in the Jordan River and not upon the incarnation. There also emerged another sect called Walda-Tsagga (Children of Grace). This group supported the teaching of the "Three Births": eternal birth of the Son from the Father, genetic birth of the Son from the Virgin Mary, and His birth from the Holy Ghost after the incarnation. The Walda Qib and Tsagga sects were banned by the imperial decree of Emperor Tewodros II (1855–1868), who enforced obedience by applying severe punishment. However, they are still active in some Ethiopian monasteries.

Another sect even more radical and wide apart from mainstream Ethiopian Tewahedo Orthodoxy was a group known as Malakawuyan, a name coined by their opponents, implying that they were disciples of idolaters. The group professed two natures of God. The sect forbade the worship of the Virgin Mary as well as prostrating or genuflection before the cross. They taught that after giving birth to Jesus, Mary and her consort Joseph consummated their marriage. The group, which happened to be a branch of the Stephanite movement that broke away, encouraged free sexual relations between men and women and engaged in such practices. In other words, they did not believe in the sanctity of matrimony. Quoting Moses's teachings about leaving one's seeds for one's brother, they taught that sexual relations with one's brothers' wives, or sisters-in-law, were proper even if the brother were still alive. For these teachings, the sect members were condemned and punished. There was also strict anathema forbidding all Orthodox members from sharing prayers and the Eucharist services with them. They were not allowed to be buried in Tewahedo churchyards, and their children were not authorized to be baptized as Christians in an Orthodox shrine.

threatened to cut off the waters of the Nile from Muslim Egypt was not lost on the Crusaders.

The legends of Prester John inspired many European poets of the 16th century. The great Italian poet of the Renaissance, Ludivico Ariosto, for example, surmised that Prester John was an opulent sovereign who resided in a grand palace, whose walls and ceilings were studded with topazes pearls and sapphires. Others conjectured that the Prester bore an emerald scepter, that he was attended by hundreds of princes, and that he had an archbishop as a butler and a king as a chief cook!

THE CULT OF ZAKRISTOS

Zakristos was a 16th-century ecclesiast from the district of Gondar who claimed to be Christ; chose disciples for himself just like Jesus did; and appointed bishops, priests, and deacons. Initially, Zakristos and his close supporters survived with donations from those who could afford to give, but as the number of his followers increased, the donations dwindled proportionately. Famine among his followers emerged and forced Zakristos to order his religious followers to invade and pillage the areas below the tableland, where he set up his headquarters. Upon hearing the report, the ruler of the region Bi'ila kristos ordered a group of soldiers to storm the mountain fortress where the false prophet's followers had retreated with their loot. When the soldiers tried to scramble up the precipice, Zakristos ordered his followers to throw huge boulders down the peak, as a result of which the army found it difficult to negotiate the forbidding mountain. So instead of taking too many casualties, the solders were ordered to occupy the water source that Zakristos and his followers used. In time, thirst forced Zakristos to give himself up. After his execution, his followers scattered throughout the country, fearing that they might face the same fate. Fourteen years later, they gathered up again and started to preach that Zakristos had risen from the dead. Their doctrine was that Christ came first and was born to the Virgin Mary, who was of Jewish origin, but that after resurrection, he came back again to earth and was born to a Gentile virgin girl named Amata Wangel. They taught that the second birth, that of Zakristos, was decided on by the Lord to be fair to all peoples. In the first birth, they taught, he was called Kristos, whereas in the second, he was called Zakristos. Bishops, priests, and deacons were ordained for his sect. Their celebrations and fasting days were different. They consecrated Monday as the Sabbath. Ultimately, Ethiopian Emperor Susenyos converted to Catholicism and ordered his soldiers to round up all the followers of Zakristos and put them to the sword. That brought to an end the birth of a totally new Christian religion in the world.

ETHIOPIAN CHRISTIANITY AND THE SOLOMONIAN DYNASTY

The Solomonian dynasty took power from the Zagwes in the 13th century and continued to patronize the church. As soon as this new dynasty was established with its base south of Shoa bordering the Islamic Sultanates, it became clear that there was danger of an almost total encirclement, given that many ethnic groups in both the south and the east had embraced Islam. Another danger was posed by the Semitic-speaking kingdom established in Harar, to the east of the Christian empire. However, the powerful kingdom of Ifat was crushed in the early 14th century by Emperor Amda Siyon.

Even after this major setback, the Muslim kingdoms continued to menace the peripheries of the Christian empire. Adal (Afar) then became the most formidable force in the region because it controlled key trading routes from highland Christian Ethiopia to the port of Zeila, which was situated on the coast of the Gulf of Aden.

By the early 16th century, succession problems had weakened the Christian monarchy, and the military control of the Sultanates ceased. The status quo became one of raids and counter-raids in which neither the Christians nor the Muslims completely dominated the other.

Portuguese influence in the hitherto isolated Empire of Ethiopia continued after this episode. The Portuguese came with Catholic missionaries, who succeeded to convert some of the Ethiopian monarchs, particularly Emperor Susenyos, to Catholicism. A schism soon emerged when the Catholic convert Emperor Susenyos, under the influence of a Vatican bishop, Mendes, tried to forcibly convert Orthodox Christians to Catholicism. Civil war raged until Susenyos abdicated, and the Ethiopian Orthodox faith was reinstated.

THE ETHIOPIAN ORTHODOX SECTS

During the last several hundred years, three sects crystallized in Ethiopian monasteries and churches.

There was the main Tewahedo sect, which did not accept any new reinterpretation of Christology. This doctrine teaches the unity of two natures, divine and human, in the person of Christ, without confusion and without separation– hence the name Tewahedo, which means "unity." The second group was called Qebat, signifying "unction." This sect put more importance on the anointing of Christ and not on the incarnation of the Son. The third sect, called the Tsegga Lijoch (Sons of Grace), supported the teaching of "three births": eternal birth of the Son from the Father, genetic birth of the Son from the Virgin Mary, and Jesus's birth from the Holy Ghost after the incarnation. Though some Ethiopian emperors were swayed by the non-Orthodox sects in earlier periods, more recent sovereigns—Tewodros, Yohannes IV, Menelik, and Haile Selassie—discouraged the teachings of the Qebat and Tsegga Lijoch sects and called on all Christians to follow only the Tewahedo line.

AUTOCEPHALY

The Ethiopian Orthodox Church started to move aggressively toward autocephaly following the Italian invasion, when the Egyptian patriarch went back to Egypt while the few Ethiopian bishops such as Abuna Petros and Mikael directly confronted the invaders, refusing to accept Italian control of Ethiopia, and were martyred as a result. Ultimately, Emperor Haile Selassie convinced the Alexandrian archbishop that an Ethiopian archbishop should be appointed and that from then on, the Ethiopian church should be totally independent, though doctrinally paying allegiance to the Alexandrian Sea. Thus, the appointment of Abuna Baslios as the patriarch of Ethiopia in 1951 made the Ethiopian church totally independent.

An Ethiopian Orthodox priest. (Courtesy of Paulos Milkias.)

CATHOLICISM IN ETHIOPIA

The first Catholic missionaries came to Ethiopia with Cristóvão da Gama's Portuguese musketeers, who helped Ethiopian Christians defeat the Turkish-spearheaded forces of Ahmed Gragn, otherwise known as Ismail El Ghazi, in 1543. Mainly through the efforts of the Jesuit Peter Paez, Emperor Susenyos converted and declared Catholicism the state religion in 1622. In 1623, Pope Gregory XV appointed a Portuguese Jesuit, Affonso Mendez, as patriarch of the Ethiopian Church. Mendez imposed latinizations of the Ethiopian liturgy, and the convert Susenyos tried to enforce this change by use of the sword. This led to a civil war that claimed the lives of thousands of Ethiopians.

In 1636, Susenyos's son and successor Emperor Fasilidas expelled Mendez and ordered the restoration of Tewahedo Orthodoxy. Missionaries who tried to proselytize in Ethiopia were detained and deported and in some cases executed.

Catholic missionaries came again in 1839, led by the Lazaruses and Capuchins. Hostility toward Catholicism, however, made their work difficult. It was only after Emperor Menelik took the throne in 1889 that Catholic missionaries were given the freedom to preach their faith.

With the support of the occupying power, Catholic missionary activity expanded greatly during the Italian occupation of 1935 to 1941. Presently, the largest Catholic community is found in the capital, Addis Ababa. The Ethiopian Catholics use both the Latin and the Ethiopic rites, the latter employing the ancient Ethiopian language of Ge'ez. There were 144,000 Catholics in Ethiopia in 1967. By 2007, the national census of Ethiopia officially recorded their number at 536,827—a significant growth, but not by a large margin compared to Protestantism.

PROTESTANTISM

Protestant missions expanded into Ethiopia starting in the 19th century. There are three main groups: the Lutherans, the Sudan Interior Mission, and the Mennonites. The Lutherans founded the Mekane Yesus Church, which is strong in non-Amhara and non-Tigre areas of the south and west of Ethiopia.

The Sudan Interior Mission entered southern Ethiopia in the 1920s. The Kale Heywat church, which is a branch of the Sudan Interior Mission, has grown enormously since the overthrow of the Derg in 1991.

The Mennonites came to evangelize after the end of the Ethiopian–Italian war in 1941. Two churches emerged out of the Mennonite mission: the Meserete Kristos (meaning "Christ is the foundation") Church, which has roots in the West, and the Mulu Wengel Church, which is independent.

The Mulu Wengel Pentecostal church was outlawed in 1972, and its members joined Meserete Kristos, which they influenced to be charismatic with heavy evangelization. Meserete Kristos and Mulu Wengel churches believe in faith healing, exorcism of demons, and glossolalia. Meserete Kristos was subsequently outlawed as well,

Church painting depicting Jesus and his disciples at the Last Supper. (Courtesy of Paulos Milkias.)

and its members were led underground by the Derg in 1982. But since the fall of the Derg in 1991, it has been growing at a rate of approximately 20 percent per year.

Protestants in Ethiopia numbered a mere 250,000 in 1967. However, the national census of 2007 recorded that Protestants at that time numbered 13,746,787, which is 18.6 percent of the total population of the country. This is clearly due to the heavy evangelization and expansion drive of the Pentecostal Church.

ECUMENISM

In 1965, the heads of the Oriental Orthodox churches held a common meeting in Addis Ababa, the first time for such a gathering since the council of Ephesus in AD 431. This opened a new chapter in Eastern Orthodox Church history, and a secretariat of Oriental Orthodox churches was subsequently established in the Ethiopian capital city of Addis Ababa.

The Ethiopian Orthodox Church was a founding member of the World Council of Churches when it was established in 1948. Since then, the Church has been an active member. As of the start of the 21st century, the patriarch of the Ethiopian Orthodox Tewahedo Church, Abuna Paulos, who holds a PhD in divinity from Princeton University, was serving as the president of the World Council of Churches.

ETHIOPIA'S PLACE IN THE DIVISION BETWEEN EASTERN AND WESTERN CHURCHES TODAY

The character of the universal Church changed after the divisive argument over Christology at Chalcedon in AD 451. It was at that juncture that the Church was divided into Chalcedonian and non-Chalcedonian branches. Thus, currently, there are two different doctrines of the established Church: the Eastern branch comprising the churches of Alexandria, Armenia, Ethiopia, Syria, and Malabar in India and the Western branch comprising the Roman Catholic and the Greek Orthodox churches. The first group believes in miaphysis—the unity of Christ's divinity and his human element—whereas the second one subscribes to the doctrine of "two natures" of divinity and humanity.

ISLAM IN ETHIOPIA

Just like Christianity, Islam also has deep roots in Ethiopia. It has been recorded in the Islamic tradition that the grandfather of the prophet Mohammed saw the brunt of the Ethiopian Christian army's assault against Mecca in AD 570. A cavalry commander of the Army of Abraha, the Christian viceroy of Ethiopia in Yemen raided the neighborhood of Mecca before the final assault to destroy the Querish, as a result of which Mohammed's grandfather, Abdul Al-Mutalib, lost 200 camels. Out of compassion, the Christian General Abraha later restored the 200 camels to Mohammed's grandfather.

The first Ethiopian convert to the Muslim religion during the time when Mohammed sent his followers to Ethiopia to seek protection from the persecution of the Querish was a man called Bilal. After traveling to Mecca with Mohammed's followers, Bilal called the Muslim faithful to prayers, thus becoming the first Muezzin.

THE RISE OF POWERFUL REGIONAL MUSLIM STATES

Challenges to the Solomonian dynasty and the Ethiopian Christian Empire arose parallel to the change in dynasty in the 13th century. The Ottoman conquest of the whole region of the Middle East led to the expansion of Islam in the littoral states of the Red Sea and Indian Ocean, including the coastal areas of lowland Ethiopia. This in turn helped strong Sultanates to rise and challenge the highland-based Christian authority. Among the powerful kingdoms that arose were the Sultanate of Ifat in the northeastern Shoa, that of Adal with its capital in the port of Zeila, and the Islamic city state of Harar.

Ifat's challenge to the central Christian empire was successfully repelled by Emperor Amda Siyon in the 13th century. But at the end of the 14th century, the power of the three Sultanates coalesced under the Muslim kingdom of Adal near Harar, with its control of the port of Zeila, which was a major outlet for Ethiopia's maritime trade with the outside world. This brought about a clear threat to the Christian empire.

In the early 16th century, the Christian empire extended political supremacy over the Muslim Sultanates, but because the Sultanates were reluctant to pay taxes voluntarily, the only way the empire could collect its levy was by conducting periodic raids. But by 1529, there emerged the formidable Muslim force of Adal, which the Christian empire could not subdue.

AHMED GRAGN'S CONQUESTS

The conquest of Ethiopia's Christian empire in the 16th century by the surrogate of the Ottoman Trunks, Ahmed Ibn Ibrahim El Ghazi (known in Ethiopia as "Ahmed Gragn," meaning "the left-handed"), was one of the most destructive in Ethiopian history. Gragn was the leader of the Ethiopian vassalage of Adal, near present-day Zeila. He was responsible for the destruction of Christian churches during his invasion of the country in the early 1500s. Though initially defeated at the battle of Badiqt in eastern Shoa in September 1528, Gragn did not give up what he considered a jihad against the Christian empire. His first major triumph over the Christian forces was at the battle of Shimbira Kure, on March 23, 1529. The empire was soon laid to waste by the armies of Gragn that swept through Shoa, Amhara. and Tigray. the heartland of Ethiopian Christendom.

The Ethiopian emperor made a stiff resistance. But unperturbed by the new guerrilla-style attacks, Gragn proceeded to occupy territory after territory and emptied the fabulous treasures of the Christian monarchs that the Europeans of the Renaissance period had described as the unmatched wealth of Prester John, the king of Ethiopia.

When in 1539, the royal mountain fortress of Gishen was taken by Gragn, all the treasures deposited there by generations of Ethiopian sovereigns fell into his hands. Because of forced conversion, at the end of the campaign, 9 out of 10 Ethiopians became Muslims, though most nominally. Soon, 400 Portuguese musketeers led by Cristóvão da Gama, the son of the famous explorer Vasco da Gama, arrived, and Gragn was defeated. Skirmishes between the two forces continued for some time, but the Ethiopian Christian kingdom was never challenged on a large scale after the defeat of the Turkish-supported Muslim Adals in 1542. The task of reconstructing the churches and monasteries that were ravaged by the forces of Gragn continued for the next several hundred years.

ZARA YAQOB AND ETHIOPIAN PHILOSOPHY IN *HATATA*

Zara Yaqob was the son of a peasant farmer born in Axum in AD 1592 who attended the religious school of the day and graduated after 16 years of intense university-level education. He studied grammar and poetry as well as the sacred texts.

After the conversion of Emperor Susenyos to Catholicism, and his attempt at forced conversion of all Ethiopian Orthodox members of the church to Catholicism, there was an inquisition. Zara Yaqob found himself to be a target because he had refused to renounce his Ethiopian Tewahedo faith. To save his life, he fled from Axum and for two years lived the life of a hermit in a cave, where he meditated and developed some theological and philosophical ideas different from those of both the Catholic missionaries of the time and the Ethiopian Orthodox Tewahedo clerics he grew up with. His treatise, titled *Hatata* (Discourse), was a critique of Judaism, Christianity, and Islam.

Zara Yaqob argues in *Hatata* that intelligent human beings have the innate power to interpret the messages of the sacred texts and that nothing is to be spared from critical examinations by the inherent authority of human reasoning. For the proper exercise of rational thinking neither the sovereign nor a religious authority should have the power of manipulation and authoritarianism to intimidate people from acting their conscience and exercising their power of reasoning. It is important to point out that Zara Yaqob's rationalistic philosophy of religion and the world of man started in Ethiopia and in Europe simultaneously because he argued in the *Hatata*, "the light of reason should illuminate the dark regimes of human thought."

REFERENCES

Abir, M. 1968. *Ethiopia: The Era of the Princes: The Challenge of Islam and Re-Unification of the Christian Empire, 1769–1855*. New York: Praeger.

Al-Hashimi, M. A. A. 1987. *The Oppressed Muslims in Ethiopia*. Washington, DC: El-Hajj Malik El-Shabazz Press.

Bartels, L. 1983. *Oromo Religion: Myths and Rites of the Western Oromo of Ethiopia, an Attempt to Understand*. Berlin: D. Reimer.

Berger, N., K. K. Shelemay, et al. 1986. *The Jews of Ethiopia: A People in Transition*. Tel Aviv: Beth Hatefutsoth.

Beshah, G., M. W. Aregay, et al. 1964. *The Question of the Union of the Churches in Luso-Ethiopian Relations, 1500–1632*. Lisbon, Portugal: Junta de Investigacões do Ultramar and Centro de Estudos Históricos Ultramarinos.

Budge, E. A. W. 1932. *The Queen of Sheba and Her Only Son Menyelek*. London: Oxford University Press.

Burgess, M. 2005. *The Eastern Orthodox Churches: Consise Histories with Chronological Checklists of Their Primates*. Jefferson, NC: McFarland & Co.

Burton, K. A. 2007. *The Blessing of Africa: The Bible and African Christianity*. Downers Grove, IL: IVP Academic.

Crummey, D. 1972. *Priests and Politicians: Protestant and Catholic Missions in Orthodox Ethiopia, 1830–1868*. Oxford: Clarendon Press.

Eide, O. 1996. *Revolution and Religion in Ethiopia: A Study of Church and Politics with Special Reference to the Ethiopian Evangelical Church Mekane Yesus 1974–1985*. Uppsala, Sweden: Uppsala Universitet.

Erlikh, A. 2007. *Saudi Arabia and Ethiopia: Islam, Christianity, and Politics Entwined*. Boulder, CO: Lynne Rienner.

Erlikh, H. 2010 *Islam and Christianity in the Horn of Africa: Somalia, Ethiopia, Sudan*. Boulder, CO: Lynne Rienner.

Eshete, T. 2008. *The Evangelical Movement in Ethiopia: Resistance and Resilience*. Waco, TX: Baylor University Press.

Ethiopian Catholic Church. 2005. *The Catholic Church in Ethiopia: Working for Integral Human Development: Strengthening Partnership for United Action*. Addis Ababa: Ethiopian Catholic Secretariat.

Faqada Gurmésa, K. S. A., and E. Gebissa. 2009. *Evangelical Faith Movement in Ethiopia: The Origins and Establishment of the Ethiopian Evangelical Church Mekane Yesus*. Minneapolis, MN: Lutheran University Press.

Fargher, B. L. 1996. *The Origins of the New Churches Movement in Southern Ethiopia, 1927–1944*. New York: E. J. Brill.

Grosshans, H.-P., and Lutheran World Federation. 2009. *One Holy, Catholic and Apostolic Church: Some Lutheran and Ecumenical Perspectives*. New York: Vantage Press.

Halevy, J. 1896. "Traces d'influence inde-parsie en Abyssinie" *Revue Semitique*, Vol. 7, No. 4, 258–265.

Herodotus. Book 2: An Account of Egypt—Project Gutenberg Ebook, www.gutenberg .org.

Josephus, F. *Jewish Antiquities*. Vol. 8. Edited by J. Thacheray and R. Macus. London: Loeb Classical Library, 1961. 165–75.

Litmann, E. 1947. "La Legenda del dragone di Aksumin Lingua Tigrai." *RSE* 6: 42–45.

Pankhurst, R. 1967. *The Ethiopian Royal Chronicles*. London: Oxford University Press.

Parfitt, T., and E. Trevisan. 1999. *The Beta Israel in Ethiopia and Israel: Studies on Ethiopian Jews*. Surrey, UK: Curzon.

Rey, C. F. 1929. *The Romance of the Portuguese in Abyssinia, an Account of the Adventurous Journeys of the Portuguese to the Empire of Prester John: 1490–1633*. London: H. F. & G. Witherby.

Russell, M. 1833. *Nubia and Abyssinia: Comprehending Their Civil History, Antiquities, Arts, Religion, Literature, and Natural History*. New York: J & J Harper.

Samatar, S. S. 1992. *In the Shadow of Conquest: Islam in Colonial Northeast Africa*. Trenton, NJ: Red Sea Press.

Sumner, C. 1985. *Classical Ethiopian Philosophy*. Addis Ababa, Ethiopia: Commercial Printing Press.

Sumner, C. 1986. *The Source of African Philosophy: The Ethiopian Philosophy of Man*. Stuttgart: F. Steiner Verlag Wiesbaden.

Sumner, C. 1995. *Oromo Wisdom Literature*. Addis Ababa, Ethiopia: Gudina Tumsa Foundation.

Sumner, C. 1976. *The Treatise of Zara Yaqob and of Walda Hiywat*. Addis Ababa: Commercial Printing Press.

Trimingham, J. S. 1952. *Islam in Ethiopia*. London: Oxford University Press.

Yaqob, B. 1977. *Controversie cristologiche in Etiopia: Contributo alla storia delle correnti e della terminologia nel secolo XIX*. Naples, Italy: Istituto orientale di Napoli.

Yesehaq (Archbishop). 1997. *The Ethiopian Tewahedo Church: An Integrally African Church*. Nashville, TN: J. C. Winston.

Social Classes and Ethnicity

In traditional monarchic Ethiopia, no distinction was made between a government and a political system. The terms "mangest," "kingship," and "political system" are associated with the *negusa-nagast* (the emperor) who is at the center and the ruling gentry comprising the *gultanoch* (fief holders), the *restagnoch* (landowners), the *chika shumoch* (village headmen), and the *meslanewoch* (district prefects), scattered throughout the realm.

FEUDAL POWER STRUCTURE

Under feudalism, the institutions of the state and the head of government were fused. At the root of Ethiopian imperial authority lay the legend of the Queen of Sheba and King Solomon and the legitimizing authority of the Ethiopian Orthodox Tewahedo Church, as elaborated upon in the Feteha Nagast (laws of the kings).

The Church taught its flock that the emperor chosen by God was a supreme authority in all matters, secular and spiritual, and the people agreed with the premise without fail. In brief, he was an absolute monarch with divine right who was construed as the definitive foundation of the legislature, the judiciary, and the executive. Paradoxically, however, the emperor's power, which was generally construed as sacrosanct, could sometimes be challenged by the nobility who commanded a peasant army and by the Church, which bestowed or disallowed religious legitimacy by *qeba'a mangest* (anointing) or by *gezet* (excommunication).

CLASS STRUCTURE UNDER FEUDALISM

At the apex of the feudal class structure were the nobility, who acted like kings in their own semi-independent states. They gained their power by the use of armed retainers and by extracting all their requirements from the peasantry. There was also a class of clerics who sustained themselves by using a *tikle*, or land grant, from a lord or king. In the 19th century, the clergy and the *dabtaras* numbered a quarter of the population.

There was a merchant class mostly based on the Muslim community, given that Christians frowned on the profession of trade as menial; their preference was for military and administrative positions. Some Christians who became traders, however, had large caravans of mules or camels loaded with goods and traversed the country carrying out large-scale commerce. Though despised by the general population as *naggade* (traders, with a derogatory connotation), many of these traders, whether of Moslem or Christian background, were nevertheless rich and provided the rulers with ample tax revenue and gifts.

Handicraft workers, even more hated in the society, formed another class in the Ethiopian feudal system. Weavers, tanners, woodworkers, house builders, potters, and blacksmiths, also despised, provided all other essential services to the society.

The agricultural population during Ethiopia's feudal era was divided into three major categories: small independent peasantry, farm laborers, and rich proprietors. The small independent peasantry formed the majority, and hundreds of thousands of idlers (unsalaried feudal solders armed with guns) were quartered on the poor peasantry, making their life very miserable.

THE TRADITIONAL POLITICAL ELITE

During the period of feudalism, there was a class of Church-educated scholars known as the *dabtaras* who were given a *tikle* (free parcel of land) for their services. All were attached to the central and local power base, and the *tikle*, with its pecuniary and symbolic values, was a mechanism by which the erudite *dabtaras* were made to depend, for both their living and their status, on the monarchy and the aristocracy.

SOCIAL CLASS AND REFORM

In 1855, Emperor Tewodros revealed a series of sweeping reforms, including the establishment of a salaried standing army, a limitation on *geber* (levies) posted by local landlords, regulation of land-ownership rights of the Church, and last but not least, the establishment of a modern administrative system that was based on merit, with regional rulers and officials who were salaried, and that thus was dependent on a centralized state system with the emperor at the core. The reforms were however

---

INBAQOM

Inbaom, who died in 1470 was the 11th abbott of Dabra Libanos. He arrived in Ethiopia accompanied by a servant who was a former Ethiopian army officer captured by the Muslims of Adal during the reign of Emperor Iskender (1478–1494). Because of his knowledge of Arabic as well as the Ethiopian vernaculars, including Ge'ez, Enbaqom became a close associate of the Ethiopian metropolitan Abuna Marqos. On the orders of Emperor Lebna Dingil and in collaboration with Abuna Marqos and Michael the Egyptian, Inbaqom translated the Aragawi *manfasawi* ('*Elder Spiritual Teacher*', written by a Syrian monk named John of Saba and very revered in the Tewahedo faith) from Arabic into Ge'ez.

---

far from being applied throughout the empire. This had to wait until the end of the reign of Emperor Menelik, who laid the foundation of a modern administrative system with the trappings of Western-style ministerial framework. One can certainly say, however, that it was only during the regency of Ras Tafari (later Emperor Haile Selassie, reigned 1916–1930) that the sinews of a modern governmental and administrative system were laid down.

HAILE SELASSIE AND THE WESTERN-EDUCATED ELITE

One year after being crowned emperor, Haile Selassie, who was surrounded by a handful of young Western-educated elite bent on emulating Japanese-style modernization, started to shake up the foundations of Ethiopia's anachronistic feudal system. The apostles of modernization, now portrayed in scholarly literature as "Japanizers," were fundamentally different from the traditional elite in that they not only were scientifically oriented, dynamic, and egalitarian in outlook; they also were primarily concerned with elevating the livelihood of the average citizen, promoting democratic ideals, and advancing the educational and economic development of their country.

The emperor's promulgation of the 1931 Constitution, which provided for a bicameral parliament, with the Yeheg-Mawasagna (the Senate) appointed by the emperor and a lower house called Yeheg-Memreya (the Chamber of Deputies) manned by appointees of the different regional administrators, was an apt response to demands from this quarter.

THE NEW SOCIAL CLASS THAT EMERGED UNDER HAILE SELASSIE'S MODERNIZING FEUDALISM

The years after World War II saw the gradual growth of modern industrial and commercial activity, fairly large-scale cash-cropping in agriculture, a relatively modern military establishment, and an emerging modern bureaucracy. In some cases there were links between the old national and provincial nobility and modern entrepreneurs, bureaucrats, and the highly educated; in others there was none. Clear-cut strata replacing or encompassing the older patterns had not yet emerged. Formerly, political power (resting in part on military or other accomplishment and in part on family background) had brought or was closely associated with social status and access to wealth. By the 1960s and early 1970s, old social status did not necessarily imply political power, at least at the national level. Political power brought status, but it might be resented by the older nobility; economic entrepreneurship did not necessarily bring access to either power or status; and higher education—usually pursued in the hope of acquiring power and status—no longer guaranteed a position in the higher bureaucracy and, through it, power and the possibility of wealth. There were, then, many who were dissatisfied with the pre-revolutionary social, political, and economic orders, but the sources of their dissatisfaction were diverse, and they did not share similar perspectives.

The revolution enhanced the power and status of none of the emergent groups. Instead, it gave a limited number in the military precarious power and uncertain status. Further, the relationship of the rhetoric of peasant and proletarian power and status to actuality remained questionable.

At this juncture, one has to look at the nature of the class strata and the roles and responsibilities of the Ethiopian intelligentsia of the pre-revolutionary and post-revolutionary periods. Here the modern educated class just prior to the fall of Emperor Haile Selassie's regime is classified into four categories: (1) civilian bureaucratic intelligentsia; (2) military bureaucratic intelligentsia; (3) lumpen civilian intelligentsia; and (4) lumpen military intelligentsia.

Civilian Bureaucratic Intelligentsia

The civilian bureaucratic intelligentsia, members of which had received a college education, included higher- and middle-level civil servants, university and college professors, doctors, lawyers, bank executives, and high school directors and teachers. They were invariably professional and salaried. Their occupational aspirations were public service–oriented and not geared toward business or technical trades. Their careers were sheltered under the umbrella of the bureaucratic state apparatus.

Most civilian bureaucratic intelligentsia lived in the capital city of Addis Ababa, although there a meager number of them also lived in Asmara, Harar, Dire Dawa, Gondar, Jimma, Adama, Bishoftu, and other major towns and provincial capitals. Ethnically, the Tigrayans predominated, followed by the Amharas, Oromos, and Gurages. Their class backgrounds were diverse. Although there were a few children of workers and peasants, most came from middle- and upper-income families of civil and military officials, big and small landowners, governors, school teachers, *dabtaras*, police officers, and corporate and self-employed men and women.

The values and worldviews of the civilian bureaucratic intelligentsia were shaped in local and overseas universities and continued to be nurtured in the confines of their specific peer and social groups. Their training was mostly administrative in nature. This was true even for those few who specialized in engineering, science, and commerce.

Success in civilian bureaucratic intelligentsia occupations rarely required objective standards; nor did it demand initiative, hard work, and merit. For advancement, political patronage and imperial or aristocratic connections were more important than professional excellence or productive effort. Numerically, this group was very small—no more than 40,000 people out of an estimated population of 28 million in 1974. However, they played a critical role in running the newly created modernizing feudal structure of the ancient regime.

Military Bureaucratic Intelligentsia

The military bureaucratic intelligentsia received postsecondary education as well as professional training at one of the elite military academies in Ethiopia or abroad. Some attended universities and acquired degrees. They were inevitably career-oriented.

Competition for promotion among their ranks was very stiff. However, because of previous and current contacts with their colleagues, they shared the same peer group values as the civilian bureaucratic intelligentsia. Although their class background was basically the same as their civilian counterparts, a larger proportion of them had rural origin. Ethnically, Amharas predominated, followed by Tigrayans and Oromos. Despite the fact that those who professed the Muslim religion were roughly equal in number to the Christians in the country, the Muslims were effectively excluded from this elite group.

Almost all members of the military bureaucratic intelligentsia had traveled abroad for training purposes, and many had seen combat in Korea and the Congo (Zaire). Their salaries were about half that of their civilian counterparts, but they had other remunerations such as living expenses that compensated for the discrepancy. Some also received land grants from the emperor. In addition to purely military skills, all members of the military bureaucratic intelligentsia had acquired the expertise necessary to manage a modern military force in peacetime, and the administrative skills gained during the course of their service could be transferred to civilian life. Those who received imperial favors were later transferred to key civilian positions or were appointed as district governors.

Lumpen Civilian Intelligentsia

The third group, the lumpen civilian intelligentsia, included those still within the school system—young men and women with less than high school academic background, elementary and secondary school dropouts, autodidacts, taxi drivers, lower-level technical personnel, and office clerks and secretaries—all with an average salary of less than Eth.$250 a month.

Employment of the lumpen civilian intelligentsia was not limited to the pubic sector and government agencies; the emerging foreign-owned modern corporations whose top technocrats and managers were non-Ethiopians had absorbed a large segment of them. The rest were unemployed or underemployed. The majority came from a working-class background. Whereas ethnically they represented a cross-section the Ethiopian society, minority tribes predominated in technical trades. The lumpen civilian intelligentsia were the only group whose members were widely dispersed throughout the country, although they kept moving to Addis Ababa in search of educational opportunities and jobs. Numerically, they were the most significant among the educated, numbering no less than 100,000 strong in 1974.

Lumpen Military Intelligentsia

The fourth group was the lumpen military intelligentsia. These were noncommissioned air force, army, navy, and police officers whose class background was the same as that of the lumpen civilian intelligentsia. In terms of religion, Muslims were systematically underrepresented. Ethnically the Oromos, followed by Tigrayans and Amharas, predominated, but there were also a good number of Gurages, Sidamas, Hadiyas, Walaitas, and Kambatas among them.

Most members of this class had attended high schools, but their most important training had come after being inducted into the military, which spawned its own large educational enterprise. The noncommissioned officers were trained to handle complex military hardware as well as to perform certain administrative and technical functions. They were paid higher salaries than the officers but could not advance to military command posts, which meant that they were effectively precluded from positions of power.

Because they were permanently locked into lower-level rank positions, regardless of their qualification and training, the lumpen military intelligentsia shared one specific character with their civilian counterpart, the lumpen civilian intelligentsia: they were potentially the most revolutionary class in the military establishment, for they had nothing to lose and much to gain if the existing order were subjected to a radical change. As seen in future depositions, the most radical wing of the army, the Neus Derg, came invariably from this class.

Among the four groups of the postwar educated class, the civilian bureaucratic intelligentsia formed the most crucial link in the Haile Selassie modern intelligentsia and U.S. power triad.

A CLASS IN EMBRYO

As a group, the civilian bureaucratic intelligentsia was not monolithic. It encompassed clusters of *adirbays* (careerists), "quiescent rebels," and "die-hard revolutionaries" who did not by themselves constitute distinct social strata, but were aggregates of individuals. These were rather a class in embryo.

In terms of socioeconomic profile, whereas the *adirbays* were in better-paying positions and were in the process of being absorbed by the ruling classes, the quiescent rebels and the die-hard revolutionaries were on the periphery of the established economic structure. Irrespective of their socioeconomic profiles and their place in the production relations of Ethiopia, however, all three were antifeudal.

ADIRBAYS

In the Amharic lexicon, *adirbay* refers to the "extreme careerism" of a bureaucrat who has the propensity to pursue professional stature, advancement, or authority through any positive or negative effort in performance. Typically, adirbays had completed their studies abroad, most probably in Europe or in North America. Because of their foreign experience, their perspectives, once narrowly defined by Ethiopian tradition, had been greatly enlarged. They felt proud of the new status qualifications they had acquired—qualifications that differentiated them from the traditional Ethiopian official: residence abroad and often a university degree. They had developed a taste for a high standard of living and engaged in profit-making ventures to increase their wealth. They built lavish houses in the Western European or North American style and either lived in them or rented them out to accumulate even more wealth. They obtained satisfaction from buying every new luxury item— for example, a car or a stereo—and then soon exchanging it for other modern gadgets. They always tried to emulate the mass consumption societies of North America and Europe.

As a rule, adirbays were affected by the political socialization of the schools to which they had willingly submitted. They knew how to accommodate themselves to Haile Selassie's feudal institutions and bureaucratic structure. They were willing to be commanded, to fulfill all orders, to harmonize with the social machine without any abrasive friction. They experienced their ingenuity, critical thinking, and social "praxis" within very narrow prescriptions and took special care not to originate any reformist ideas that might raise suspicions about their loyalty to Haile Selassie and his regime. Whatever they did in their occupational endeavors was broadly demarcated by the feudal stalwarts at the top. They always attempted to appear not only to be skilled in their modern trade but also to be highly disciplined mandarins. They had just enough initiative to carry out their prescribed tasks, but not so much as to question the specific assignments given them.

The adirbays frantically competed within their own peer group and exhibited a totally servile attitude to the aristocrat by becoming traditional *dej-tegnei* (position hunters) in the imperial court. As long as they received enough regard and respect from their subordinates, as well as their peers, they would be devoid of integrity and personal dignity in front of persons of highs rank, the royal household, and particularly the emperor. One typical ritual was to kiss the feet of their superiors. Even the prime minister of Ethiopia, Aklilu Habte Wold, had to prostrate himself in full public view and kiss Haile Selassie's feet during important national celebrations. Such a scene was shown on national television on the emperor's 80th birthday in 1972.

Educated adirbays had an impassioned bent toward rules and regulations. They openly exhibited an insatiable appetite for social status and material achievement. Opportunities for using the system to achieve their goals rarely escaped their hunters' eye, for the adirbays had developed an uncanny ability to recognize the nuances of the feudal order.

In politics, the adirbays did not have a wide range to choose from, given that their platform was determined by His Imperial Majesty. Just like their expatriate teachers before them, they "waved no flag" but simply "tried to follow the leader."

Although professing antifeudal sentiments, some of the adirbays climbed the social ladder by marrying the children of the nobility, thus becoming property owners in their own right. To encourage this development, the emperor distributed to the educated youth large land holdings at government expense. He freely dispensed municipal property to loyal educated bureaucrats and generously allowed them to take out large loans from the state treasury to be paid over a long period; in fact, those exhibiting "good behavior" and fulfilling the bidding of the emperor eventually received letters from the Ministry of pen stating that they did not have to pay back their loan. This was one of the ways in which a strong bond was created between the emperor and the emerging educated class.

The same was done to co-opt the high officer corps. Because officers above the rank of colonel had so much to lose, they obviously did not play any significant role in the revolution of 1974. In fact, they were classified as oppressors, and many were executed by Mengistu, along with the feudal rulers.

At every stage of the bureaucratic hierarchy, the *negus* allowed the adirbays to help themselves to the spoils of office. Some even held the view that public office was in fact a reward from the negus for loyalty and service to the monarch, not an obligation or a national duty. Their positions were thus unabashedly employed in scheming money out of the public treasury or in practicing blatant nepotism.

Haile Selassie's aim here was very clear. It was to create a nouveau riche intelligentsia that would be grateful to him for social and economic success. He hoped that the new group would ultimately form a bulwark against the educated *balabats* (aristocrats) who might present a political challenge to his autocratic regime. The negus always encouraged rivalries between the nobility and the new breed of Western-educated officials in order to implement his policy of *divide et impera*.

QUIESCENT REBEL

The "quiescent rebel" was one who, upon return from abroad, was shocked to rediscover the plight of the average taxpayer, the common Ethiopian toiling in the fields—who lived in abject ignorance and ill health—a plight that etched in his mind deep remorse.

The young literati found it hard on their conscience to participate in the country's semi-institutionalized nepotism. For them, opting out of the system by rejecting personal benefits was a matter of principle. They would not share the spoils of office. However, they felt absolutely helpless in trying to oppose the system openly or in attempting to encourage personal or professional honesty in public service as long as Haile Selassie's overpowering influence over the populace was unchallenged. Despite the fact that they had the personal decency and professional integrity to decry graft and corruption, these quiescent rebels had not courage to challenge the system they vehemently detested.

For distraction, the quiescent rebels routinely followed developments abroad. They talked of civil rights problems in Alabama, Mississippi, and Arkansas. They continually debated the plight of the "untouchables" in India and the subordinate position of the American Indians in the Western Hemisphere. They talked of wars of liberation in Indo China, in Algeria, and in Angola and discussed the Mau Mau rebellion ad nauseam. They devised strategies for stemming the institutionalization of racism in South Africa and Rhodesia.

The quiescent rebels lived in hostels or rented apartments. Typically, they were not married, had no children, and saved no money. Their evenings were mostly spent reading novels, watching Hollywood movies, playing cards, drinking, or smoking and dancing at the big hotels or sometimes discreetly in the Dejatch Wube Bereha (Addis Ababa's red light district). In short, the quiescent rebels were silenced by total defeatism and did not act, but rather waited for others to do something to win their instant support.

DIE-HARD REVOLUTIONARIES

The third group, the die-hard revolutionaries, had both the integrity and the courage to criticize and challenge the system of corruption, oppression, and injustice in Ethiopia. They were the likes of Germame Neway, who had made tremendous sacrifices in attempting to stamp out the vestiges of feudalism, even though as the grandson of Dejazmatch Germame, he was himself from a feudal background.

Because the die-hard revolutionaries were exposed and did not have a viable political organization, whether clandestine or otherwise, they were systematically excised from the modernizing feudal power structure. In 1965 (less than a decade before the revolution), there were fewer than a dozen such individuals in the entire country. Because the strategies and fundamental beliefs of the revolutionaries were identical to those of the University College of Addis Ababa, they were ardent sympathizers and sometimes behind-the-scenes advisers to the radical Ethiopian student movement of the 1960s and 1970s.

In conclusion, it should be pointed out that the major challenge to Haile Selassie did not emanate from the die-hard revolutionaries who formed the tiny radical wing of the civilian bureaucratic intelligentsia. Nor did it stem from the military bureaucratic intelligentsia, as the Derg would have liked people to believe. Rather, as discussed as this book continues, the major challenge to Haile Selassie came from the ranks of the lumpen civilian intelligentsia, whose vanguard was the Ethiopian student movement.

Student radicalism at the university, which had the open backing of the majority of young scholars and the encouragement of the revolutionary wing of the bureaucracy, signaled the coming of a new era. And with that development, a new chapter dawned in the history of the educated youth. It also inspired the formation of a political front in a struggle against the government of Emperor Haile Selassie and by its wide-ranging magnitude precipitated the political consciousness of some the important sectors of the power structure, especially the army, the air force, and the police. Indeed, no matter its outcome, the Ethiopian Revolution was the brain child of the lumpen civilian intelligentsia and was manifestly conceived and nurtured in the cradle of the Ethiopian student movement.

THE NEW CLASS (POST-1991)

Gizeyawi sarratagna (temporary urban laborers) are former peasants and farmhands who broke off from the restrictions of peasant association and the state farm laborer status that was in vogue under the Derg and moved to the cities following the rise of the Ethiopian People's Revolutionary Democratic Front (EPRDF) in 1991 to become migrant workers in public works, factories, or service industries.

Sra-alba (jobless) are former rural inhabitants who moved to the urban areas following the breakup of peasant associations and state farms after the fall of the Derg. Finding it hard to find jobs, the *sra-alba* ended up as homeless shanty dwellers.

Taddagi-habtam (*nouveau-riche*), or the new rich, are socially conscious and hardworking rural farmers or traders who moved into the urban areas as township entrepreneurs. Some have engaged in areas such as coffee trade and have in the process become instant millionaires.

Taddagi-mehur (enterprising intellectuals) are Ethiopians of the third millennium with college or university diplomas from bachelor's degrees to PhDs. This class not only is involved in its own specific profession; it also doubles in investing. A medical doctor teaching at Addis Ababa University is, for example, more often than not an owner of a thriving multimillion-birr clinic or even hospital.

Tatari-balahabt (corporate investor) is a class of rapidly growing entrepreneurs who rose following the economic reform that was put into place by the EPRDF after the fall of the Derg in 1991. This class concentrates on joint-stock enterprises and invests lots of money in financial institutions such as banks and insurance companies and private property holdings including real estate and housing.

Wassap (the returning diaspora) are Ethiopians who made millions working abroad and returned to their country to settle and invest in myriad areas. The name *wassap* originates from their common greeting "what's up?" While abroad, they made money as small investors, shop owners, taxi drivers, and parking lot attendants. The *wassaps* are, in fact, the major force behind the booming high-rise building craze in the capital city of Addis Ababa and other large towns. A few are also investors in small-scale factories and agricultural ventures.

Gwehlawi (the shady) are the most conspicuous birr millionaires of the urban areas who do not have a particular trade. They make money benefiting from their status as underlings of corrupt officials, for whom they work as agents or clandestine partners. *Gwehlawis* are involved in every moneymaking venture, including business enterprise and brokerage. Together with retirees from international organizations with whom they associate to gain social status, this class is extremely visible. *Gwehlawis* and their associates live in exquisite mansions and drive expensive cars such as Mercedes Benz and BMW models, brand new four-wheel drives, and Hummers. Because they make their earnings without toil, *gwehlawis* do not care about the value of the money they spend; they are spendthrifts, squanderers, and compulsive shoppers who frequent five-star hotels such as the Sheraton and Hilton. Together with their cohorts, the corrupt officials, many of them have their expensive alcoholic beverages kept in luxury hotel drawers with their names inscribed on the bottles.

ETHNICITY AND LANGUAGE

It is not possible to divide the Ethiopian population strictly on the basis of ethnicity. For example, if we go by language, we are confronted by groups that belonged to one ethnic group but changed their tongue.

Some ethnic groups have been totally assimilated and have lost their identity in terms of language, though at one time they were so distinct that books were written in their language. With non-Amharas adopting Amharic names and speaking the Amharic language as fluently as the Amharas, the distinction has been blurred even further.

The census of recent years has identified at least 83 language groups, the number of speakers of each ranging from scores of millions, as in the case of the Oromos, to only a few thousand, as in the case of the Harari.

The Ethio-Semitic language group numbers about 20, but the majority speak Amharic and Tigrinya. In the Cushitic language group—which is subdivided into Highland and Lowland East Cushitic, Central Cushitic, and Northern Cushitic—Afan Oromo and Somali predominate. Members of the Nilo-Saharan language group live in the southwest and west along the border with Sudan.

The Amharas

Amhara traditionally represented a region of central Ethiopia bounded on the north by Angot and Lasta in the present-day Wallo region, on the west by the Abbay and its tributary the Bashilo River, on the east by the steep highland formation leading to the Afar Depression and to the south by the Wanchit river, which is located in Southern Wallo. The Amharas were mentioned for the first time during the early 12th century when they waged war with the Eastern nomadic tribe of Warjih. According to Tadesse Tamrat, this was recorded in an Arabic chronicle where it is mentioned that they clashed with the *Warjih* in 1128. (Tadesse Tamrat, *Church and State in Ethiopia*, p. 26.)

The importance of the Amhara people rose with the ascendance of the Solomonian dynasty, replacing the Zagwes in the late 1200s. The king from the Amhara region who established the Solomonian throne was Yekuno Amlak. The connection of the Amharas to the Solomonian dynasty was so strong that during the 14th century, Yekuno Amlak's successors referred to themselves as "negusa Amhara," meaning "kings of Amhara."

By tradition, the Amhara kings moved constantly from region to region and never showed proclivity for founding a fixed capital. The territorial designation of an Amhara nation came about only after 1632, when Gondar was established as a permanent

Amhara women carry heavy water jugs down a dirt road in the Qolla (arid zone) of Ethiopia. (Photo by Dr. Gilbert H. Grosvenor/National Geographic/Getty Images.)

capital. As Amhara kings expanded their empire, the Amharic language also spread into the occupied areas, including Begamdir, Lasta, Gojam, and Shoa, thus replacing Central Cushitic languages and other South Semitic languages such as Argobba and Gafat.

Generally, when one speaks of the Amharas, one is referring to native Amharic speakers. The foremost Ethiopian geographer, Professor Mesfin Wolde Mariam, however, vehemently argues that there is no ethnic group called Amhara and that the term simply denotes a highlander.

Other people claim that Amhara means "free people" and does not represent an ethnic group. In other contexts, Amhara has come to denote a person who has embraced Christianity. In still another interpretation, Amhara has been known to refer to ruling groups who have adopted Amharic as their main language. The Amharas are not limited to the ethnic *kilil* the government created as Amhara by amalgamating Gonder, Gojam, western Wallo, and northern Shoa into one. Through their control of the political center of Ethiopian society and through migrations, conquests, trading networks, and intermarriage, the Amharas have extended their language and their customs far beyond the borders of their primary home territory.

The Tigrayans

The Tigrayans live predominantly in areas bounded to the north by Eritrea, to the west by the Sudan, and to the east and south by the Afar and Amhara *kilils*. According to the 2007 census, 96.7 percent of the Tigrayans are Orthodox Christians, and

Muslims make up a mere 2.9 percent. Whereas 80 percent of the people in the *kilil* speak Tigrinya, the remainder are Afars, Agew, Saho, and Kunama. Most Tigrayans are plough agriculturalists.

Tigray has been under the jurisdiction of various dynasties since the establishment of the Axumite Empire before the Christian era. The Axumites spawned a very sophisticated civilization with a written script, now known as Ethiopic or Ge'ez; a numerical system called Qutir; and different forms of calendars such as Hassaba Zaman, Sir'ata Harmat, Qamar, and Awde-Warh, all of which are still employed in Ethiopia, and they advanced sophisticated architecture that can be observed in the ruins of cities and palaces and magnificent stelae. Centered on Axum, the empire extended not only all over the Ethiopian highlands and lowlands but also across the sea, stretching to Arabia. Justifiably, it is this fact that impels Tigrayans to be proud of their heritage within the family of the Ethiopian state system.

Tigrayans have some sad memories too. Being at the crossroads of local feudal wars, their land was devastated over the generations. The peasant population was forced to support one side or the other of the warring warlords and fed their predatory fighters. Furthermore, living at the edge of an empire through which invaders tried to take over the country, they carried the brunt of feeding the Ethiopian army during every war that took place.

Compounding the effects of these wars, a series of famines took their toll on the Tigrayans, thus decimating and dislocating the working population and destroying the fabric of the entire society that had been built up since the heyday of the Axumite civilization. With the soil eroded on the land they had farmed for thousands of years, total misery and impoverishment resulted. These famines claimed the lives of millions of people and drove many into refuge in other parts of Ethiopia or in the Sudan.

It was the desperation borne of this state of affairs that led to the 1942–1943 peasants' uprising in central and southern Tigray under the name "Woyane," which means "revolt." The central government's response was harsh. In order to subdue the rebels, the minister of war, Ras Abebe Aregay, with the collaboration of the British Royal Air Force, bombed and torched large areas of Tigray, including the city of Mekelle. Thousands died in the counter-offensive, and the revolt was crushed, at least for the moment. As a punishment and as a deterrent to future uprisings, the peasants of Tigray were forced to pay five times more than they had paid only three years before. Local Tigrayan leaders and civil servants at the sub-provincial and lower echelons of the administrative hierarchy were replaced by non-Tigrayans sent from Addis Ababa. This inevitably fueled resentment and ethnic nationalism.

Tigrayans as a result started to migrate to the former Italian colony of Eritrea, where they did menial work. Others moved to other areas of the country where conditions were relatively better. Many went to the capital Addis Ababa and other cities and towns in southern Ethiopia in search of work.

Before the onset of the 1974 revolution that overthrew Emperor Haile Selassie, several generations of Tigrayans had grown up with deep feelings of anguish and desperation. For thousands of years, until the fall of Axum in the 10th century, power in Ethiopia had been controlled by the Tigrayans. After the Amhara royal family came to power following the restoration of the Solomonian dynasty at the end of the 13th century, first under Menelik II and then under Haile Selassie I, Tigrayan culture gave way to Amharization, which was presented as a mainstream Ethiopian culture. Amharic was made the language of schools and courts, and the administrative machinery and even the religious orders became Amharic. There was therefore a significant amount of resentment and envy among the Tigrayans.

Tigrayan nationalists took this to a higher level and asserted that the despair that had reigned in their region and the cultural and political domination were a deliberate and systematic policy of the Shoa-Amhara ruling class to weaken and demoralize the Tigrayan people. It was in this atmosphere that Tigrayan students at Haile Selassie University created the Tigrayan National Organization (TNO), through which they discussed issues of stamping out cultural domination, massive unemployment, political marginalization, soil erosion, land degradation, and endemic famine.

When the imperial regime of Emperor Haile Selassie was replaced by a military junta that claimed to be Marxist, the Tigrayan nationalists saw an opportunity to demand self-determination, which implied administrative autonomy and a devolution of power from the center to the regions, including Tigray, and the enhancement of regional culture, language, and religion. However, the Derg was even more brutal in dealing with these basic demands of the Tigrayans and other nationalities.

That was what spurred the establishment of the Tigrayan People's Liberation Front (TPLF) in February 1975 as a small insurgency group. The TPLF ultimately expanded with training and logistical support from the Eritrean People's Liberation Front. Originally, the organization was purely nationalist, and at some stage, it even passed a resolution to achieve independence. However, as time passed, it settled on its original aim of autonomy and self-determination within greater Ethiopia. The TPLF was able to mobilize the people of Tigray and conducted a guerrilla war for 16 years until it defeated the regime of Mengistu Haile Mariam with the largest army in sub-Saharan Africa and came to power in Ethiopia in 1991, under its umbrella party the Ethiopian People's Revolutionary Democratic Front (EPRDF).

The Oromos

The Ethiopians who have always called themselves Oromo but were referred to as Galla by the Amhara constitute the largest and most widespread of the East Cushitic–speaking peoples of the Horn of Africa. They are spread north, south, east, and west through 10 of 14 former Ethiopian provinces. In the early 1990s the EPRDF amalgamated the provinces into a *kilil* called Oromia.

Almost 95 percent of the Oromos are settled agriculturalists and nomadic pastoralists, living at a subsistence level. A few live in the urban centers. The Oromo people have a distinct culture and language and are fiercely egalitarian. As such, they have lived under a complex indigenous democratic system known as *gada*—where political, military, and other leaders, including legal experts, were elected for nonrenewable eight-year terms from among males who excelled during five eight-year-long grades of continuous training.

Following the incorporation of Oromo confederacies and kingdoms by Emperor Menelik in the 19th century, the majority were reduced to tenancy, paying heavy tributes for the use of land. Under the imperial regime, written Oromo texts were disallowed, and education of Oromos was conducted only in Amharic. Place names such as Bishoftu, Ambo, and Adama were legally changed to Debre Zeit, Agere Hiywet, and Nazret. To be in harmony with the mainstream Ethiopian social system Haile Selassie had envisaged, many Oromos either changed their monikers to Amharic names or gave Amharic names to their offspring. Social advancement for Oromos was possible only by way of assimilation into the dominant Ethiopian culture. Oromo ways of life and laws such as the *gada* system were treated as pagan practices and were thus slowly abandoned. The Oromos as an ethnic group carried the brunt of the feudal oppressive system, controlled from central Ethiopia, which started during the reign of Menelik and continued until the end of the imperial era.

In 1975, the Marxist-oriented military government declared all rural land state-owned and announced the end of the feudal land tenure system. Though the Oromos received this as a positive step, much of the benefit of the reform was counteracted by compulsive collectivization, state farms, and forced resettlement programs. It is of historical interest to trace the origin of the Oromos and how they came to be predominant numerically.

Oromo Migration

Fra Mauro was the first European to locate the Cushitic Oromos of southern Ethiopia on a map, including them in his "Mappamondo" in 1460. However, their migration process started prior to the 10th century. Originally, the Oromos were pastoralists who lived between the Gulf of Aden adjacent to present-day Somaliland and the lowland areas near Bale. In the 13th century, their cousins, the Somali Cushites, who also lived as pastoralists adjacent to the Bay of Tajura, waged a vicious war to control the grazing lands hitherto used by Oromo clans. This development as well as the need for more fertile land for their cattle incited many Oromos to move southeast to the grassy plains of Banadir straddling the valleys of the Wabe Shebele and Juba rivers. Finding the Banadir area too dry for grazing, a number of Oromo clans moved into the highlands of Walabu and the rift valley as far as Abaya Lake—an area known to be extremely fertile.

Basing their advance guard at the settlement of Oda-Nabe in the early 1500's, the Oromos, divided into four clans known as Karayu, Tulama, Macha, and Wallo, expanded north into the central highlands of Ethiopia. In this campaign, the Karayus dominated a large area of Bale and then moved to Fatagar and Dawaro; the Tulamas occupied Shoa; the Macha occupied the southern territories of Enaria; and the Wallos occupied Angot, sandwiched between Tigray and present-day Amhara.

The first wave of Oromo expansion into highland Ethiopia was conducted in a systematic and well-organized way. The vanguard force of the Meliba Gada age-group belonging to the Bartuma clan made a swift invasion of southern Bale, occupied by the central government, and defeated the imperial Ethiopian forces named Batra-Amora under the command of the well-known fighter Hamalmal in 1532. Hamalmal himself died on the battlefield, and the imperial forces retreated to northern Bale. Again in 1540, more conquests were made by the Mudana Gada group. This time, the Oromos of the Bartuma and Karayu clans settled in Bale in large numbers,

*A young girl from the lower
Omo valley. (Courtesy of Paulos
Milkias.)*

WALAL

Walal is a region surrounding Tullu Walal (Mount Walal) in Qelem, Wallaga, located between Leqa Gidami and Sayyo Dambidollo, that was inhabited by people of Kafa descent known as Busase or Bushasho prior to the Oromo conquest of the area in the 14th century. A temple was then consecrated as a Christian church. Descendants of the Christian Busase who are cut off from their cousins, the Kafa's to the east and are totally sandwiched among Oromos of Sayo, Leqa and Ilubabor, are still thriving in Anfilo, not far from Tullu Walal, where just like their cousins in Kafa (the original home of coffee from which the name itself originates), they produce coffee for local consumption and for export.

and the Mudana fighters were poised to take over Fatagar and Dawaro completely. In 1545, the Kilole Gada took over the leadership of the Oromo campaign and invaded parts of Fatagar and Dawaro. The imperial forces known as Adal-Mabraq who tried to strike back, were then speedily defeated.

The battle of Adal-Mabraq was significant in one aspect. It was in this campaign that the Oromos started to use horses in battle. In 1562, the Oromos went even further and prepared a well-trained cavalry contingent under the leadership of the

---

HAMALMAL

Ras Hamalmal, [not related to Hamalmal who died in 1532] was the grandson of king Naod of Shoa. Hamalmal was a prominent king maker during the late 16th century. He was appointed Governor of the southern principalities of the Ethiopian Christian Empire by emperor Galawdewos (1540–59). Later he was recorded in the Royal Chronicles of Emperor Minas (1559–1563) as one of the Abaita Mangist (Great Lords of the Empire) and ruled Shoa. Hamalmal led a campaign against the Bahra Nagash Yisahaq (ruler of Eritrea) who tried to depose Minas and pass his crown to the latter's nephew. On the death of Minas, the latter's thirteen year old son Sartsa Dingi ascended the throne but Hamalmal forced him into exile from Shoa and followed him to Gojam where he placed him under house arrest. By receiving allegiance from all the regional kings of the Empire except for Bahra Nagash Yisahaq who refused to recognize his authority, Hamalmal became the virtual ruler of Ethiopia. When Bahra Nagash Yisahaq succeeded with his bold attempt to rescue the youthful emperor Sartsa Dingil whom he brought to Eritrea to use as a puppet emperor under his control, Hamalmal renounced the reign of Sartsa Dingil and crowned the latter's cousin, Takla Mariam as Emperor. The period of Hamalmal's governorship was marred not only by the invasions of Ahmad ibn Ibrahim al-Ghazi but also by the swift expansion of Oromo fighters. Hamalmal tried his best to check the rapid advance of the Michele Gadaa Oromo age group but was defeated in Dago near Dabra Berhan. The Oromos subsequently conquered most of the areas adjacent to Shoa, particularly Ganz, Enarya, Gafat, Damot and Maya whose inhabitants they systematically assimilated. Soon after his army's defeat in the hands of the Oromos in Southern Ethiopia, Hamalmal moved his army against Habib, the Sultan of Harar who was killed on the battlefield. In the end as he was trying to quell a rebellion in Damot near Gojam, his army which was denuded of provisions during a protracted war was defeated. Hamalmal was captured by Takla Haymanot, the ruler of Gojam but was spared serious punishment on account of his royal blood. He was in fact given a minor governorship of a district near the Blue Nile where he died in November, 1564.

Michile Gada age group. They also employed new types of weapons, including long shields that covered a fighter from head to foot, to wield off arrows from their antagonists' archers. It was with this new approach to war that they defeated the central government forces repeatedly.

The Oromos' next move was to conquer the Sultanate of Harar. The Michile Gada age group made a surprise attack at Hazalo and annihilated the forces of Sultan Ali Nur, a nephew of Gragn who avenged the death of his uncle by killing Emperor Galawdewos on the battlefield and who was marching home to prepare another campaign to reconquer Christian Ethiopia. The defeat at Hazalo was so total that the Harar that had defied so many emperors of Ethiopia never rose again. Soon, the Karayu Oromos followed up on the victory of the Michile Oromos in Harar and settled on its rich highlands of Hararge.

Oromo men and women traveling to market. (© Gallo Images/CORBIS.)

A man feeding meat to a hyena mouth-to-mouth, in Harar, Ethiopia. (Courtesy of Paulos Milkias.)

An Oromo Peasant from Bale

To protect himself from another slaughter by the Oromos, the Sultan of Harar built a wall around his capital. But the destruction wrought by the Michile fighters was followed by three years of famine and plague, which consumed not only the lives of tens of thousands of Hararis crammed within the defensive wall but also the life of Sultan Ali Nur himself, who died of plague in 1568.

Soon, the Macha clan crossed the Awash and invaded Enaria's clans Gafat and Dina, who lived in Damot (areas between the river Awash and the Blue Nile) and Bizamo (territories now occupied by Wallaga Oromos). Unlike the Spartan fighters of repute who refused to mix with the conquered and ultimately paid for it by being reduced to 10 percent of their original number and were thus speedily defeated by their enemies who were more numerous, the Oromos assimilated the people they conquered and left them alone as long as they adopted the Oromo culture and language. This helped boost their numbers as they continued to expand into the highlands.

Multitudes of Macha Oromos under the leadership of Mula'ata Lubas (1586–1594) thus engulfed the Enaria district of Damot near the Gibe River and forced the clans there to take flight across the Blue Nile to ultimately settle in Gojam province in the subprovinces of what are now known as Bure Damot and Daga Damot. The Oromos, however, did not stop their pursuit. They followed them across the Blue Nile to Gojam, until the Damots were subjugated and controlled.

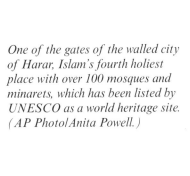

One of the gates of the walled city of Harar, Islam's fourth holiest place with over 100 mosques and minarets, which has been listed by UNESCO as a world heritage site. (AP Photo/Anita Powell.)

The Machas expanded into highland Shoa, into eastern and western Wallaga from Gibe to Tullu Walal, and from Didessa to Gojeb in Jimma and Ilubabor.

Wallo's Oromo clan had the greatest difficulty because they had to contend with the well-entrenched and well-known fighting forces of the Amharas and the Tigres. Nevertheless, during the *lubaship* (fighting age group) of Harmuffa (1562–1570), they moved from the area of Ifat, camped near Mt. Ziquala in Shoa, continued north, and invaded Angot and parts of Begamdir (Amhara), which was a base of the imperial Christian forces. They faced a formidable imperial army called Giorgis-Haile on the way north. But the strength of their infantry and particularly the Oromo cavalry was such that they achieved an easy victory at the battle of Katisino. The Oromos continued their conquest north until they took over Angot and named the area Wallo, their clan designation. The Hanrufa Gada group invaded Ganz and Saint. Soon the Azebo and Raya clans of the Wallo Oromos expanded north to the area of Tigray and occupied territories now known by their names. The Bartuma clan penetrated into Gondar but could not take over the whole area because of the fierceness of the Amhara defense.

In 1570, the Tulama Oromos made their conquest from Aba-Nabe, near Bale, north into Shoa under the leadership of the Gada age group Robale (1570–1578). The Robale fighters first defeated the imperial army under the command of Azmatch Zara Yohannes, who died on the battlefield. The Maya fighters, who were feared because they used poisoned arrows in their combat, were tackled when the Oromos, during the leadership of Birmaji Luba (1578–1586), introduced body-length shields that covered the fighters from head to feet.

Shoa was soon taken over, and Gojam was next to be invaded. A successful counteroffensive by Emperor Sertse Dingil stopped the Oromo advance at a battle near Lake Zeway, with the imperial forces confiscating large numbers of Oromo cattle and driving the Oromos back to the area of Fatagar and Dawaro, which they had already taken over. But soon, the Oromos came back in greater force, defeated the imperial army, and proceeded to eastern Shoa, Waj, Gojam, and Dambia near Lake Tana, in the Amhara stronghold of Gondar, which they occupied.

Having taken over Gondar, the capital of Ethiopia, the Oromos now played the role of kingmakers. This started when they captured and adopted the future Emperor Susenyos as a child and then helped him come to the Solomonian throne in 1605–1607. Susenyos subsequently founded the Gondarine Solomonian dynasty with the help of the Oromos. It was at this time that some Oromo groups, particularly those known by the names Yabbata, Ilma Gwozi, Basso, Jawi, and Talata, volunteered to join and bolster the imperial forces. They converted to Christianity. Many spoke Amharic in addition to their own vernacular. This phenomenon led to the cultural assimilation of most of the Oromos of Gondar, Gojam, and Wallo into the Amhara mainstream.

Following their slow cultural and linguistic assimilation, the Oromos played an important role in deciding who should be crowned emperor. For example, Emperor Iyasu was greatly aided by the Oromos in his consolidation of the imperial throne, as a result of which many Oromo nobles rose through the ranks. Liban, for example, rose to the governorship of Tigray with the title of Bitwoded. An Oromo warrior named Waragna, who aided Emperor Bakafa in his bid to consolidate his imperial power, was appointed governor of Damot in Gojam. Bakafa's son Emperor Iyassu II married Wabiti, the daughter of the Yejju Oromo chief Amiso. Emperor Iyoas, who inherited the Solomonian throne, was born from Iyassu and Wabiti. Iyoas was under the guardianship of his Oromo uncle, Waragna. Two of Iyoas's uncles, Lubo and Birale, also wielded tremendous power in the Gondarine court. As the Scottish explorer James Bruce, who spent time in Gondar, pointed out in his book written in 1798, Iyoas actually spoke only the Oromo language, making Afan Oromo the official language of the Gondarine court. This was in fact a prelude to the assimilation of the Oromo and Amhara ruling classes. It was Mika'el Seul of Tigray who brought to an end—although only for a short time—the Oromo power play in Gondar.

The Somalis

According to the 2007 national census, the Somalis are the third-largest group in Ethiopia after the Oromos and Amharas, if we take them *kilil* by *kilil* as demarcated by the federal government. However, the Somalis are concentrated in one region. Overall numerically, the Tigrayans are the third-largest ethnic group in the country because they live not only in the Tigray *kilil*, but are dispersed all over the country.

Somali clans and lineages in the Ogaden have close links with similar groups in Somalia. In general, Somali society can be identified through various traceable common patrilineal descents. The largest among them is the clan-family, where the ancestor is implicit but links are not perceptible. The clan-family can be broken down into clans. The latter are divided into lineages and sublineages. The clan-family does not have tangible economic, social, and political functions, as do other groups, that lead to economic competition and conflict between even between units of analogous type.

Ever since the Ogaden became part of Ethiopia, when Menelik expanded his control to the region in 1897, and later the British ceded territories under their control after the Italian Fascists were defeated in 1947 and 1954, the region has been highly problematic. Indeed, there were successive phases of Somali uprisings against what they referred to as Christian "Amhara" domination, as exemplified by the rebellion of Mohammed Abdullah Hassan, culminating in a full-fledged war involving the state of Somalia. Somali nationalists have charged that successive Ethiopian governments have marginalized them. A struggle of territorial control has also been exacerbated by an economic dimension. Heavy taxation of the mobile Somali pastoralists, checks on cross-border "contraband" trade with neighboring Somaliland, and the Somalia and the Ethiopian governments' concentration on the Ogaden as the future source of oil and gas deposits have caused apprehension among Somali-Ethiopians. According to highland Ethiopians, the continuous turbulence in the Ogaden has been aggravated by a series of drought conditions and severe famine that has gripped this semiarid lowland region, causing human suffering on a large scale. Thus, the Somali region has remained the most problematic of the "peripheral regions" of Ethiopia characterized by widespread political turmoil, organizational and financial dislocation at the regional government level, and endless rounds of political wrangling, dismissals, and incarceration of local political figures. According to the central Ethiopian administrators, a great amount of this is attributable to the typical "nomadic culture" of the Somali ethno-nationalist conflicts.

Ethiopian Somali nationalist narrative, however, blames the problem on the oppressive nature of the Ethiopian Christian state, which they refer to as Amhara domination, with a colonialist character not any different from the rule of the imperialist British, Italian, or French, which subdivided the Horn of Africa among themselves following the treaty of Berlin in 1885. Although many Somali-Ethiopians speak positively of the comparatively more liberal structure put up by the EPRDF, which recognizes the right of self-determination, others assert that on substance, there is not much change and that the central government still calls the shots as to who should control political power in the regional state. Harsh reprisals against the supporters of the Ogaden National Liberation Front (ONLF) are also cited.

The Afars

According to the 2007 census, the Afars, referred to as Dankali or Adal by their neighbors, number 1,411,092, and 98.1 percent of them are Muslims. Though they are relatively small in number, the Afars have held importance because of the location of their territory, which is situated between the highlands and the Red Sea, and the quasi-autonomy of a section of Afar that was ruled by the Sultan of Aussa prior to the 1974 revolution. The Afars are pastoralists who are mostly restricted in space because they need to stay in close proximity to permanent wells—the region is extremely hot and arid.

Traditional ceremony, southern Ethiopia. (Courtesy of Paulos Milkias.)

A man from the lower Omo valley. (Courtesy of Paulos Milkias.)

The Sahos

Ethiopian Saho pastoralists who live in Tigray are mostly Muslims, but a few who have been heavily influenced by the Tigray culture have become Ethiopian Orthodox Christians.

The Agaw

The Central Cushitic Agew who live in areas spread from Gojam in the west to Tigray in the north are recognized as the original inhabitants of territories now occupied by the Tigrayans and the Amharas.

SOUTHERN PEOPLES AND NATIONALITIES

Among the 45 minority ethnic groups in the newly constructed Southern Peoples and Nationalities *kilil*, the Gurages, the Sidamas, the Walaitas, the Hadiyas, the Gamos, the Kafas, and the Kambatas deserve mention. Whereas the Gurages, who

Dorze dwelling in southern Ethiopia. (Courtesy of Paulos Milkias.)

are known for their business acumen, are of the Ethiopian Semitic stock, all the remaining linguistic groups belong to Highland East Cushitic stock, also referred to as Omotic; all in this grouping are cultivators of enset and of coffee as a cash crop. In the lower areas, below 4,921 feet, however, the Sidamas herd cattle. Many of the Omotic groups retain their traditional religious practices, though some have converted to Protestantism. Others, such as the Hadiya, have embraced Islam. The Kambatas are predominantly Orthodox Christians.

Of the Nilotic groups of Ethiopia, one—the Beni Shangul–Gumuz region—has achieved statehood in the new EPRDF structure. There are five officially recognized local languages in this *kilil*: Berta, Gumuz, Shinasha, Mao, and Komo. In addition to these local nationality languages, three languages of wider communication are employed. These are Amharic, Arabic, and Afan Oromo. The resettlement policy of the Derg, which introduced Amharic speakers to the region, and a strong extension of the neighboring Oromo and ethnic ties of the Berta group with the Sudan have created some diversity of loyalty in terms of the *kilil*'s relation to the federal entity.

Other Nilotics are located in the far southwest and along the western borderlands. Here live about 20 ethnic groups speaking Nilo-Saharan languages. Major among them are the Nuer and the Anuak. Most of the Nilotics here are hoe cultivators. However, there are also significant numbers who are cattle herders.

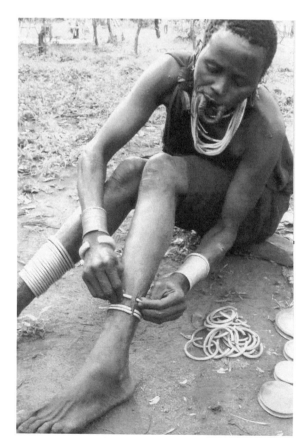

Mursi woman putting on her anklets. (Courtesy of Paulos Milkias.)

Hamer men decorating each other's bodies in southern Ethiopia. (Courtesy of Paulos Milkias.)

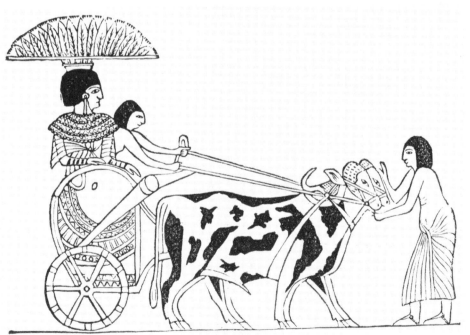

Nineteenth-century Ethiopian aristocrat's cart, drawn by oxen, 1868. (Andrea Gingerich/ iStockphoto.com.)

OBSERVABLE REALITIES ABOUT ETHNICITY IN ETHIOPIA

That ethnic groups are described here does not mean that there is a clear-cut differentiation between Ethiopia's nationalities. Indeed, there is no ethnic entity in Ethiopia that has not been influenced by others. Local wars, inter-ethnic commerce, and intermarriage have affected each and every one of them. In fact, the groups one sees in the third millennium are to a significant degree the biological and social blends of several preexisting ethnic clusters. In many cases, the differences are discernible only by conjecture, in particular if the amalgamation took place a long time ago. Thus, many Gojame Amharas simply chuckle, somewhat puzzled, when someone points out to them that the name of their sixth-generation father is Oromo. The same is true for Amharas who have been heavily mixed not only culturally but also biologically with the Agaws.

The case of Oromo-Amhara mixture is clear, especially among the ruling classes. The 17th-century Ethiopian emperor Iyoas was born to an Oromo mother, and in his capital Gondar, he made Afan Oromo the court language. Emperor Haile Selassie, born to a strong Shoan Amhara stock, had a grandfather whose name was Oromo, Guddisa. Well-known Shoan aristocrats from the time of Menelik such as Dejatch Balcha and Fitawrari Habte Giorgis were pure Oromos. And during the reign of Haile Selassie, the most powerful personalities, such as Ras Abebe Aregay and Mesfin Sileshi, were part Oromo. Even on the Tigrayan side, Emperor Yohannes IV's mother was Raya Oromo. By the time of Haile Selassie, the royal families of Shoa Amharas and Tigre had intermarried with the children of Wallaga Oromo kings such as Kumsa and Joté. The culmination of this was that the ruling families of Ethiopia before the revolution were an amalgam of several ethnic groups, though they administered the country in the name of the Amharas.

In the Facts and Figures section of this book, see Table B11, which shows the total population of Ethiopia in thousands by religion, urban–rural divide, and sex (based on the 2007 Population and Housing Census).

REFERENCES

Aklilu, K., and R. Dessalegn. 2000. *Listening to the Poor: A Study Based on Selected Rural and Urban Sites in Ethiopia*. Addis Ababa, Ethiopia: Forum for Social Studies.

Baker, J. 1986. *The Rural–Urban Dichotomy in the Developing World: A Case study from Northern Ethiopia*. New York: Norwegian University Press.

Bruce, J. (1818). *Travels between the years 1768 and 1773, through part of Africa, Syria, Egypt & Arabia, into Abyssinia, to discover the source of the Nile: comprehending an interesting narrative of the author's adventures in Abyssinia, and a circumstantial account of the manners, customs, government, religion [and] history of that country*. Glasgow: W. Falconer.

Carlson, A. J., and D. G. Carlson. 2008. *Health, Wealth, and Family in Rural Ethiopia: Kossoye, North Gondar Region, 1963–2007*. Addis Ababa, Ethiopia: Addis Ababa University Press.

Cohen, J. M., and D. Weintraub. 1975. *Land and Peasants in Imperial Ethiopia: The Social Background to a Revolution*. Assen, the Netherlands: Van Gorcum.

Crummey, D. 2000. *Land and Society in the Christian Kingdom of Ethiopia: From the Thirteenth to the Twentieth Century*. Urbana: University of Illinois Press.

Freeman, D., and A. Pankhurst. 2003. *Peripheral People: The Excluded Minorities of Ethiopia*. Lawrenceville, NJ: Red Sea Press.

Habtamu, W., B. Beit-Hallahmi, et al. 1997. *Ethnic Identity, Stereotypes, and Psychological Modernity in Ethiopian Young Adults: Identifying the Potential for Change*. Addis Ababa: Addis Ababa University Press.

Kebede, M. 2008. *Radicalism and Cultural Dislocation in Ethiopia, 1960–1974*. Rochester, NY: University of Rochester Press.

Noggo, Y. 1978. *Agrarian Reform and Class Struggle in Ethiopia*. London: Environment Training Programme.

Tegegne, G.-E. 2001. *Rural–Urban Linkages under Different Farming Systems: The Cases of Coffee and Non-Coffee Growing Regions in Ethiopia*. Addis Ababa, Ethiopia: Organization for Social Science Research

Telahun, M. 1974. *The Economic and Social Characteristics of Peasant Families at Alemaya, the Chercher Highlands of Ethiopia: Case Study of Ten Farm Families*. Alemaya, Ethiopia: Haile Selassie I University, College of Agriculture, Department of Agricultural Economics and Business.

Tesfu, B., and G. S. Seyoum. 1996. *Culture, Society, and Women in Ethiopia*. Addis Ababa, Ethiopia: n.p.

Tewodaj, M., A. Gezahegn, et al. 2008. *The Bang for the Birr: Public Expenditures and Rural Welfare in Ethiopia*. Washington, DC: International Food Policy Research Institute.

Wanna, L., and Organization for Social Science Research in Eastern Africa. 1997. *The Role of Female Potters in Household Economy: Their Work and Constraints: A Case Study of North Omo Region, Southern Ethiopia*. Addis Ababa, Ethiopia: n.p.

Woldemariam, K. 2006. *Myths and Realities in the Distribution of Socioeconomic Resources and Political Power in Ethiopia*. Lanham, MD: University Press of America.

Yared, A. 2002. *Rural Poverty in Ethiopia: Household Case Studies from North Shewa*. Addis Ababa, Ethiopia: Forum for Social Studies.

Women and Marriage

Ethiopian women face an inordinate amount of physical hardships in their lives. They carry loads of firewood and water jugs over long distances. They manually grind corn, raise children, and cook. They have fewer opportunities than men for personal advancement, education, and employment. Their worth is measured not in terms of their humanity but rather in terms of their roles as mothers and wives.

More than 85 percent of Ethiopia's women reside in rural areas, where peasant families are engaged primarily in subsistence farming. Peasant women are integrated into the rural economy, though their worth is rarely recognized, and the labor they engage in is crushing over a lifetime.

Though this does not mean that some women in Ethiopia do not have power, Ethiopian custom determines what part a women shall play in the setup of the family as well as the society. In every household, the power of the father is always paramount, and the female is in all cases dominated by males.

Before the 1974 revolution, the Ethiopian Civil Code legitimized the supremacy of the man, stating, "The husband is the head of the family and the wife owes him obedience in lawful things which he orders." Ethiopian tradition expects a woman to be totally submissive. A woman's status compared with men is always at the bottom. This situation is reinforced by women's lack of financial means. Women in all regions of the country are married young, the ideological justification being that men must be old enough to support a wife, whereas young girls only have to be good mothers to the children born after marriage.

The prevalence of armed conflicts in Ethiopia has forced many rural women to migrate to the cities, in many cases together with their children. Here they search for jobs that are hard to come by because of their lack of education and modern skills. As soon as they arrive, they are faced with lack of employment opportunities and working capital as well as paucity of food, shelter, spiraling cost of living, and dire sanitary conditions. For survival, may have no choice but to go into prostitution.

Most Ethiopian women labor in economically invisible work around the house. More poverty means more contribution needed and more hard work from female members of the family. Too often women's work is not recognized by society as productive labor because it does not generate cash. Even though girls become involved in household chores at six or seven years of age and adult women engage in intense home and farm labor, society does not view them as "breadwinners." Walking for miles and bringing back water and dry wood for fire is a woman's duty. Adult women engage in marketing. They are the ones who run the petty trade or who barter for staple foods and spices. On a market day, women carry heavy loads of woods, spices, edible crops, and butter. Women are solely responsible for brewing and selling *tella* (local beer) and *tej* (hydromale or mead).

In marriage, whether it is in relation to minimum age of spousal contract or the requirement of consent, women have literally no say. The country's age-old, patriarchal tradition has been guided by a philosophy that allows for the subjugation and exploitation of females by males. This sometimes has taken the form of violence.

Marital relationships in Ethiopia are conducted through written or oral contracts that define the spouses' obligations and privileges to each other as well as to the children they might produce. According to the civil code, there are three types of marriage: a church or religious matrimony that is harmonious with the customs of the individuals involved; civil matrimony, overseen by a civic officer; and common-law matrimony, which is acceptable to the belief systems of the couple and their families.

Church marriage is uncommon in Ethiopia because the Ethiopian Orthodox Church, like the Roman Catholic Church, has very strict laws concerning nuptials. Marriages conducted according to church traditions do not allow divorce to take place. In the case that one of the couple passes away, the surviving spouse is not allowed to marry again. He or she has to be celibate or become a monk or nun

A young girl carrying dry wood used for fire. (Courtesy of Paulos Milkias.)

unless the church provides directives otherwise. It is due to this that civil law marriage, known as *Samanya*, is the most common type people choose. *Samanya* literally means 80 and came into use because by custom, the spouse was obliged to pay a fine of 80 Maria Theresa dollars for breaching the agreed to contract. *Samanya* marriage can be conducted at home or in a municipal court. It is not uncommon for such a marriage to involve a child bride of 6 to 12 years of age.

The other type of marriage is common-law marriage, which is in reality a marriage of convenience in which the husband agrees to pay a certain stipend to the wife. The civil code calls this union "irregular union" because of its short-lived nature. Though the amount paid is a pittance even among the well-to-do (on average 30 birr, or less than US$3.00 a year), the stipend must be paid until the dissolution of the union. On the surface, this may seem fair, but the law does not entitle her to any inheritance of the estate built during the time they stay together. She is entitled only to the calculated stipend up to the end of the marriage. Women married under such an arrangement are expected to work extremely hard. They are busy seven days a week, and the hours of work are virtually unlimited. So such women are extremely exploited. Even though this practice is not common today, some widowed elderly men with offspring still prefer contract marriage to make sure that the woman cannot claim the husband's property at any time.

By tradition, there is another type of marriage known as *telefa*, "marriage by abduction." In this, a little girl is kidnapped while fetching water from the river or while collecting wood for fire or even from her parents' home while alone. Then she is taken to the prospective husband's home and declared married to the man who abducted her. The family only arranges for some form of dowry to be paid and never tries to go to court to challenge the abductor. It is interesting to note that the victims of such a marriage are only women, never men.

Young girls from the Oromia region who have been victims of a marriage called buti *(abduction). (AP Photo/Anthony Mitchell.)*

In addition to being a victim of marriage by abduction, if a woman fails to produce an heir, she can be divorced. Furthermore, rape remains a highly hushed-up crime in Ethiopia because women and girls are brought up with the attitude that female modesty and propriety are essential to protect the reputation of their family. Thus, families are forced to suppress information regarding wife beating, marital rape, and psychological abuse. Many girls simply adapt to the traumas caused by severe beating. They sometimes face murder if they fail to protect their virginity until consummation of marriage. No matter how they are treated, they are socialized to believe that they should keep up their families' honor at the cost of their own physical and psychological injury.

Ethiopian men commonly prefer younger girls who are shy and easier to manipulate. In addition, there is a general belief in Ethiopia that if a man of an older age marries a younger woman, he will be physically rejuvenated. As a result, many older men look for very young girls to marry. Under these circumstances, once an older man takes a younger woman as his wife, he automatically starts to sport a fatherly persona in relation to his wife by virtue of his age, maturity, knowledge, and experience. This paternalistic relationship leads only to male domination over females. The tendency of older men to marry younger women also has led to the prevalent situation in Ethiopia in which widows overwhelmingly outnumber widowers. The effect of an unequal matrimony in which a woman is not a direct participant only reinforces her secondary status in relation to her male spouse. Young age and lack of economic independence forces women to acquiesce to arranged marriages that may be detrimental to their future life.

Even among the educated, rarely do men marry a woman who is more experienced, self-confident, or ingenious than them. Thus, it is hard for a highly educated woman to find a husband who matches her caliber because men are fearful of her erudition and assertiveness.

On the positive side, it should be pointed out that the current constitution, issued by the EPRDF government, is clearly more gender-sensitive than previous laws. The law clearly states for the first time that in marriage, men and women are equal in status.

Under the influence of the Ethiopian Women Lawyers Association, the Federal Revised Family Code of 2000 repealed many of the most distasteful provisions of the old civil code regarding women's rights. Nevertheless, most Ethiopian marriage customs do not allow the right of consent for a girl of marrying age. Indeed, many Ethiopian women continue to be subjected to early marriage and marriage by *telefa* (abduction). Regrettably, this state of affairs is reinforced by article 34(5) of the 1995 Constitution, which gives local custom a legal status. It states that "religious and customary laws with the consent of the parties in dispute" are accepted by the state. When it says "parties in dispute," it clearly implies husbands and the families involved.

Even though the Ethiopian Orthodox Tewahedo Church objects to polygamy, it is practiced widely even today. Actually, many Orthodox Christians ignore the ban and keep mistresses or concubines whom they treat like wives. Furthermore, many married males do frequent red light districts. When they move from place to place because of their occupation, which may be civil service or commerce, they marry local women, ignoring the fact that they are engaging in polygamy, which is against the law, and keeping the matter secret from the original wife. It is interesting that the husband counts on his legal wife to remain totally faithful while this takes place. Polygamy never involves women marrying while still keeping their first, legal husband. Furthermore, any type of extramarital relationship by a woman leads to severe retribution.

Violence against women is widespread in Ethiopia. On the family level, there is domestic violence, including assault, forced labor, coerced prostitution, sexual harassment in the workplace, spousal murder, battering, incest, child marriage, female genital mutilation (FGM), marital psychological abuse, and rape. Community-wise, violence takes place in the form of rape and trafficking. On the state level, violence and abuse include beatings, custodial aggression, rape, sexual assault, and torture of women in situations of armed conflict.

By tradition, violence against the female members of the society is perceived as a regrettable but acceptable practice. Girls are socialized from the time of their childhood to take safety measures in order to stay away from violence. The family as well as the society at large is silent when it comes to such actions by men.

The law is negligent when it comes to catching and punishing culprits. The Ethiopian penal law, which was promulgated in 1957, did not provide equal treatment to women until the EPRDF government reformed it in July 1995. Based on the provisions of this law, the Ministry of Justice has increased the punishment for rape, which used to be very light.

The 1995 Constitution of Ethiopia made history in reiterating and promoting the equality of men and women as enshrined in the UN Convention on Elimination of Discrimination of Women. Nevertheless, in practice, problems still persist. Early marriage and marriage by abduction are rampant. Furthermore, the fact that article 34(5) of the 1995 Constitution suggests adherence to religious and customary laws has a retrogressive impact.

The legal system, through which recognized rights are enforced, presents its own difficulties. Members of the police force often refuse to accept and record complaints from women against their husbands or members of the family. The police treat such complaints as a private matter. To make matters worse, women who gather the courage to take husbands who battered them to court face traditional social isolation. In many communities, such women are shunned and ostracized. In all cases, the burden of proof is placed on the victim.

Ethiopian police do not consider rape a serious felony. Rape is thus not among the seven serious crimes they have on the books: attempted murder, murder, armed robbery, carjacking, general theft, robbery, and theft of car parts. Thus, lifting the logo of a Mercedes Benz to peddle it in the market for a few dollars is a more serious crime in Ethiopia than raping a woman.

Studies show that 70 percent of secondary school girls have been exposed to violence and some form of physical and sexual harassment. Violence against female students, who are routinely bullied and threatened with rape, is one important reason for low female enrollment rates. It is also one reason for the mass dropout rate among girls. This only reinforces their inferior social status in the society.

The average age at which Ethiopian girls enter their first marriage is 15.6 years. In some cases, however, marriages are arranged while the girl is as young as 9 years of age. The high prevalence in Ethiopia of fistula (a severe medical condition in which a tear develops between the vagina and rectum or bladder during childbirth) is attributed to this fact. It is said that currently, 100,000 women in Ethiopia suffer from untreated fistula, with an average of 9,000 developing the condition each year. The culprit is early marriage. Girls marrying at a tender age become pregnant with their first menses in many cases, when their bodies are far from being mature enough for childbirth. Miscarriage or fistula, or both, results because their bodies try to compete for nutrition with the fetus.

Migration abroad is one of the ways in which Ethiopian women try to get out of poverty and deprivation. The first wave of such migrants took place in the 1950s and 1960s, when many unskilled Ethiopian women went to the Sudan, Italy, Lebanon, and the United Arab Emirates where they took up unskilled work. With the money they earned, they helped and supported their families. Some even succeeded in securing education for their offspring, almost impossible to poor families in Ethiopia.

Migration of Ethiopian women to other countries has increased by leaps and bounds because of lack of job opportunities at home, lack of earnings, and lack of educational opportunities. Thousands of Ethiopian women currently do domestic work in Bahrain, Djibouti, Kenya, Lebanon, Greece, Saudi Arabia, Sudan, Tanzania, Turkey, the United Arab Emirates, and Yemen. The State Department Report on Trafficking for 2007 estimates that between 15,000 and 17,000 Ethiopian migrant

ELENI

Eleni was an empress of Ethiopia who was originally a Muslim princess from Hadiya, in southern Ethiopia, but who was given in marriage to the future emperor of Ethiopia, Atse Baeda Mariam, to cement an alliance with the Muslimized periphery and the central highland Christian kingdom. After her husband's death, Eleni exerted political influence throughout the Ethiopian empire. She played a pivotal role in choosing her son, Prince Lebna Dingil, as emperor. Because the prince was then a minor, she served as a regent. Continued Ethiopian independence was made possible only because of her foresight. She anticipated the looming menace of Turkish aggression at the coast and the need for allies to fend off the growing power of the vassal Muslim states threatening the Ethiopian Christian empire's vital trade routes to the sea. She sent an envoy—an Armenian named Matewos—to Portugal to cement a friendship. In response, the king of Portugal, Dom Manuel, sent emissaries seeking an alliance against the Ottomans, Egypt, and other Muslim powers in the Indian Ocean littoral. Eleni welcomed the emissaries and sent an ambassador to Portugal with a letter signifying her interest to carry out joint action in defense of their interests as well as her country's sovereignty and religious heritage. Meanwhile, the Ethiopians were in dire straits. They had been attacked by one of the most powerful foes that they had ever encountered, the Emir of Harar, Ahmed Ibn Ibrahim el Ghazi, known in Ethiopia as Ahmed Gragn (Ahmed the left-handed). Gragn, who was armed with muskets, drove Lebna Dingil, whose army fought only with traditional weapons such as spears, further and further to the north, conquering, destroying, and burning as he went. In this devastating war, the emperor offered a brave resistance, but the Muslim firearms and Turkish commanders of Gragn's invading force were no match for his defensive warriors armed only with conventional weapons. Thus, the forces of Gragn and Turkey devastated the country. But Eleni's foresight and her bonding of political alliance with the Portuguese paid off. The king of Portugal sent a contingent of 400 musketeers under the command of Cristóvão da Gama, son of the world-famous explorer Vasco da Gama, who helped Ethiopia turn the tide; Gragn ultimately was killed on the battlefield, and his army was destroyed. This ensured the survival of the Ethiopian Christian kingdom that empress Eleni gallantly fought for during her regency.

women are engaged in menial domestic work in just one Middle Eastern country: Lebanon. There are also an estimated 10,000 Ethiopian women doing domestic work in Yemen. Many who go to Saudi Arabia and the Gulf States become involved in low-skill forced labor. Some get trafficked into the sex trade as soon as they arrive. Many work seven days a week, from daybreak until 1:00 a.m. for a salary that amounts to about US$100/month. There are cases of Ethiopian migrant workers being locked in the house. They are denied the use of telephone and mail services. Others are physically and mentally abused. Still others are raped by the men who hire them. Thus, they also may face beating, torture, or even murder perpetrated by a jealous wife.

The agents who traffic the women or the contractors themselves deny the female workers their duly earned wages as well as access to their own passports and travel documents, to ensure that they will continue to provide services. In some extreme cases, Ethiopian women have been subjected to "starvation, coercion into prostitution, and physical and sexual abuse extreme enough that it has lead to death" (Alem Desta, 2008, 161). It is due to these disturbing reports that the EPRDF government recently took measures to uphold the rights of its citizens in Gulf States and other places. Its Private Employment Agency Proclamation No. 104/1998 aims to control illegal labor trafficking. The proclamation provides that Ethiopians be given permission to work abroad only if they are recruited by legal private employment agencies, direct recruitment by the employer being permitted only through special government permission.

ORGANIZATION OF ETHIOPIAN WOMEN

Ethiopian women have struggled to form associations to look after their welfare since before the Fascist invasion. Among these are the following:

The Ethiopian Women Humanitarian Association is the oldest Ethiopian women's organization dedicated to humanitarian work. It was organized in 1935 by prominent Ethiopian women, including Emperor Haile Selassie's consort, Empress Menen, and her daughter, Princess Tsehai Haile Selassie.

The Ethiopian Women's Welfare Organization was created to advance Ethiopian women's interests in 1935. It was founded by the well-known patriot Shewareged Gedle and another important female personality, Sinidu Gebru. However, it was overtaken by the Fascist occupation that started the same year and was never revived in the form in which it was created.

The Ethiopian Women's Voluntary Association was established in 1937. It coordinated the work of female volunteers who helped in the cause against Italian Fascist invasion. During the resistance, many of its members fought side by side with Ethiopian men.

The Ethiopian Women's Patriotic Union (EWPU) was created during the 1935–1941 occupation and served to help Ethiopian patriots who were engaged in guerrilla war against the Fascists. As members of the Central Committee of Wust Arbegnoch (Inner Patriots), many women provided intelligence information, arms caches, ammunition, sustenance, clothing, and medicine. One brave patriot, Shewareged Gedle, was captured by the Italian Fascists and suffered physical torment of enormous proportion. She refused to divulge her comrades even while being tortured with electrical currents.

Through the establishment of the EWPU, large numbers of Ethiopian women took up arms and fought in the war of liberation. Some members sounded war trumpets to alert patriots being pursued by Fascist Blackshirts and their local recruits. Others sharpened swords or they cleaned guns and shields even as bombs and mustard gas were showered upon them by Italian warplanes.

More educated women such as Sindu Gebru and Tsgie Mengesha established first aid centers where wounded patriots were cared for. Educated women such as Princess

Tsehay Haile Selassie mobilized women from every strata of society and provided clothes, rations, bandages, and gas masks to the civilians who were subjected to Fascist Italian air raids and poison gas attacks.

The Ethiopian Women's Welfare Association (EWWA) sprang up after the war was concluded with Italy's total defeat in 1941. As a traditional charity-oriented organization, EWWA catered to the interests of Ethiopian families in need. From the 1950's on, it has been dealing with health matters of the female members of the population. It provides medical care to mothers and children through its clinics. It trains local midwives. The EWWA also promotes education in elementary schools and had helped about 5,000 poor students annually up until 1974. Between 1957 and 2010, the EWWA established Ethiopian-style eateries that host large numbers of Ethiopian and international guests, including known celebrities. The Ethiopian restaurants run by the EWWA show the refined culinary art of Ethiopian women while also exhibiting antique crafts and ornaments gathered from around the country. The EWWA has opened women's training centers and kindergartens. It has established handicraft shops that sell cottage productions, with 33 local centers and 14 provincial branches all over Ethiopia.

The Ethiopian Women's Christian Association was established in the early 1960s for the purpose of offering moral guidance to Ethiopian women. It also promoted sports activities for young boys and girls, helping some of them win major contests in sports around the world.

The Revolutionary Ethiopia Women's Association (REWA) was created following the 1974 revolution, when women gained some ground in the economic and political arenas. The REWA, which had 5 million members statewide, took an active role in the education and conscientization (elevating the social consciousness) of women. The REWA was responsible for the creation of women's organizations in manufacturing establishments and the public service sector. Females for the first time became members of political organizations and urban dwellers' and peasant associations.

Thanks to the REWA's efforts, the enrollment of girls and young women in primary and secondary schools increased from about 32 percent in 1974/1975 to 39 percent in 1985/1986. There was some degree of change for urban women too. Though in far fewer numbers than men, some acquired modern education and have benefited from health care and employment outside the home environment. However, one could still see the gap 10 years into the revolution. In 1984, only one woman was a full member of the Central Committee of the Workers' Party of Ethiopia (WPE). Of the 2,000 delegates who attended the WPE's inaugural congress of 1984, and the 10th anniversary of the rise to power of the Derg, a mere 6 percent were women.

The Ethiopian Solders Wife's Association, organized by the wives of military officers, looks after the welfare of the wives and children of solders.

The Ethiopian Nurses Association, though more of a professional nature and catering to the job conditions of its members, attempts to protect the health of the general community by engaging in conscientization (elevating their social consciousness). This service is particularly crucial due to the organization's impact on curbing the HIV virus.

The Ethiopian Women's Alliance (also known as the **"Adbar" Women's Alliance**) is the first Ethiopian women's organization established in the United States. This group tries to empower Ethiopian women and their families. It provides many cultural adaptation and empowerment programs and services for newly arrived Ethiopian female refugees and immigrants.

The Ethiopian Women for Peace and Development (EWPD) is another diaspora organization established in 1991 to promote peace in war-torn Ethiopia. The organization vehemently opposes war of any kind and insists that peaceful means be used to bring about reconciliation and conflict resolution.

The International Ethiopian Women's Organization (IEWD) was established in March 2007 to reverse the feminization of poverty and to participate in private as well as government-run political, economic, and social developments in Ethiopia. The network airs concerns of Ethiopian women and children. In this it challenges not only the government but also the opposition, which it claims has not included key platforms such as violence and battery against women, child marriage, and the fight against FGM, which are crucial to the establishment of the rule of law and justice in Ethiopia. The IEWD stresses that currently Ethiopian women have very little access to training, except in activities traditionally slated for them. Women, they say, are discriminated against both at the workplace and in their own homes. They suffer from domestic violence and sexual abuse and all forms of harmful traditional practices. The IEWD makes it abundantly clear that women in Ethiopia, who constitute half the population, make up the bulk of the poor, the downtrodden, the sick, and HIV/AIDS victims. Young women, the organization points out, are forced to become prostitutes in order to survive in a society controlled by men. They become modern-day slaves in foreign countries because of the grinding poverty in which they are forced to live. The IEWD points out that one can hardly find women at the top of decision-making processes in the executive, legislative, and judicial branches of government; in religious establishments; in modern industries; or in academic institutions such as high schools, colleges, and universities.

The Ethiopian Women Lawyers Association (EWLA) was established in 1995 to ameliorate the sorry condition of Ethiopian women. The ELWA had shown its determination right from the beginning that it would inform the people at large the harm done to Ethiopian women who have been systematically subjected to organized and unorganized maltreatment. It has taken legal actions to defend them against bigotry in social, legal and administrative treatment, inequitable regulations, abductions, domestic violence, assault, battery, rape, and female genital mutilation. So far, it has provided free legal aid to 30,000 women, through its national headquarters in Addis Ababa and over ten branch offices scattered throughout the country. The beneficiaries of this generous gesture are destitute and downtrodden urban as well as peasant women folk who have no union of their own that would be vigilant in protecting their rights. The organization has made unrelenting efforts to get the government to create a human rights tribunal and the office of an ombudsman. They have also pushed for labor unions that take the special case of women as a key goal in collective bargaining. The ELWA has kept itself out of trouble with the government by steering away from sensitive human rights issues. But that has not stopped it from agitating for an increase in the political participation of women both as voters and as elected officials. In 2008, members were busy putting pressure on the government to follow the example of South Africa, Uganda, and Mozambique to set quotas for women candidates who are interested in running for elections.

The Ethiopian Media Women Association (EMWA) is a major agent for bringing about equality and security in the rapidly growing media service, which is responsible for socialization that shapes cultural attitudes. The EMWA is particularly concerned that even though Ethiopian women journalists began their work together with men more than 50 years ago, their number remains pitifully low, and where they exist, they hold only minor positions in few key departments.

Despite the struggles waged through their unions, even today, very few women with higher education have become professionals. Most are condemned to nonprofessional low-paying jobs. Almost half of the women in the urban areas are found in the service sector. They work in hotels, restaurants, and bars. Factory work, mostly in textiles and food processing, is where about a quarter of all urban women work. Those involved in sales are about 15 percent. And despite several pieces of legislation, both under the Derg and then under the EPRDF, women who work in private and public factories still earn only a little more than 25 percent of the salaries men earn doing the same job.

In 2008, of the 547 members of the federal parliament, only 116 were women (less than 22%). Also, in the 29-member Central Committee of the ruling TPLF party, there was only one female delegate—a mere 3 percent representation in a country where the number of men and women is almost equal.

The Global Gender Gap report, published by the World Economic Forum in November 2008, shows this grim reality. It analyzed 130 countries spanning the globe on how well they divide resources and opportunities among men and women, evaluating economic participation, health, education, and political empowerment. It also took into consideration national constitutions and whether or not they enshrine gender equality and ban female genital mutilation and child marriage. In the ranking, Ethiopia fell far behind the rest of the world. It slipped from a very low 113th place in 2007 to the even lower place of 122nd in 2008.

Whether under Haile Selassie, under the Derg, or under the EPRDF, most Ethiopian women have continued to work on the farms. Some are petty traders in the local markets who bring basic necessities to the family. Most keep the well-being of the household. But they have never had an independent union to protect their rights. In general, their labor has hardly been recognized for what it is worth, by the society or by the government.

REFERENCES

Alasebu Gebre, S., D. Mulumebet, et al. 1985. *Harmful Traditional Practices Affecting the Health of Women and Children in Ethiopia.* Addis Ababa: Provisional Military Government of Socialist Ethiopia, UNICEF.

Alem Desta, Candance. 2008. *Invincible Women of Ethiopia.* Addis Ababa: Ethiopian Millennium Foundation.

Asmerom, K. 1999. *Female Employment and Fertility in Selected Ethiopian Communities: A Microeconomic Analysis.* Dakar-Ponty, Senegal: Union for African Population Studies.

Asseffa, B. 1991. *Female Participation and Performance in Rural Primary Schools in Ethiopia.* Executive summary report. Addis Ababa, Ethiopia: Institute for Curriculum Development and Research of Ministry of Education.

Falola, T., and M. M. Heaton. 2006. *Endangered Bodies: Women, Children, and Health in Africa*. Trenton, NJ: Africa World Press.

Giel, R., and J. N. v. Luijk. 1968. *The Relevance of Marital Instability and a Broken Home in Ethiopian Psychiatry*. Addis Ababa, Ethiopia: Haile Selassie I University.

Habtamu, W., and Addis Ababa University Center for Research Training and Information for Women in Development. 2004. *Gender and Cross-Cultural Dynamics in Ethiopia: The Case of Eleven Ethnic Groups*. Addis Ababa, Ethiopia: Addis Ababa University.

Horrell, S. 2008. *Work, Female Empowerment and Economic Development*. New York: Routledge.

Hourihane, C. 2007. *Interactions: Artistic Interchange between the Eastern and Western Worlds in the Medieval Period*. Princeton, NJ: Princeton University.

Inter-African Committee on Traditional Practices Affecting the Health of Women and Children. November, 1997. *Newsletter*. Geneva, Switzerland: Inter-African Committee.

Kesteren, J. V. 1989. *Female Labour Force Participation and Fertility: The Case Study of One Kebele in Addis Ababa*. Addis Ababa, Ethiopia: Demographic Training and Research Centre, Institute of Development Research, Addis Ababa University.

Koohi-Kamali, F. 2008. *Intrahousehold Inequality and Child Gender Bias in Ethiopia*. Washington, DC: World Bank.

Laketch, D. 1992. *The Commoditization of the Female Sexuality: Prostitution and Socio-Economic Relations in Addis Ababa, Ethiopia*. New York: AMS Press.

Mukasa-Mugerwa, E. 1989. *A Review of Reproductive Performance of Female Bos Indicus (Zebu) Cattle*. Addis Ababa, Ethiopia: International Livestock Centre for Africa.

National Committee on Traditional Practices of Ethiopia. 1994. *NCTPE Newsletter*. Addis Ababa: National Committee on Traditional Practices of Ethiopia.

National Committee on Traditional Practices of Ethiopia. 1998. *Baseline Survey on Harmful Traditional Practices in Ethiopia*. Addis Ababa: National Committee on Traditional Practices of Ethiopia.

National Committee on Traditional Practices of Ethiopia. 1999. *Early Marriage*. Addis Ababa: National Committee on Traditional Practices of Ethiopia.

National Committee on Traditional Practices of Ethiopia. 1999. *Marriage by Abduction*. Addis Ababa: National Committee on Traditional Practices of Ethiopia.

National Committee on Traditional Practices of Ethiopia and NCTPE/EC Project Fund. 1999. *Female Genital Mutilation*. Addis Ababa: National Committee on Traditional Practices of Ethiopia/EC Project Fund.

Oduyoye, M. A., I. A. Phiri, et al. 2006. *African Women, Religion, and Health: Essays in Honor of Mercy Amba Ewudziwa Oduyoye*. Maryknoll, NY: Orbis Books.

Pathfinder International. 2006. *Report on Causes and Consequences of Early Marriage in Amhara Region*. Addis Ababa, Ethiopia: Pathfinder International.

Patterson, P., and L. Wilkins. 2005. *Media Ethics: Issues and Cases*. Dubuque, IA: McGraw-Hill Higher Education.

Quisumbing, M.A.R., Y. Yohannes, et al. 2005. *How Fair Is Workfare? Gender, Public Works, and Employment in Rural Ethiopia*. Washington, DC: World Bank.

Rubinger, D. V., and R. Corman. 2007. *Israel through My Lens: Sixty Years as a Photojournalist*. New York: Abbeville Press.

Sachikonye, L. M. 1997. *Female Workers in Agribusiness in Zimbabwe*. Addis Ababa, Ethiopia: Organization for Social Science Research in Eastern and Southern Africa.

Simala, I. K. 1998. *Sexist Overtones in Kiswahili Female Metaphors: A Critical Analysis*. Addis Ababa, Ethiopia: Organization for Social Science Research in Eastern and Southern Africa.

Singer, Norman J. 1971–1972. "Ethiopian Civil Code and the Recognition of Customary Law." *Houston Law Review* 9: 460.

Sweetman, C. 2001. *Men's Involvement in Gender and Development Policy and Practice: Beyond Rhetoric*. Oxford: Oxfam.

Thomas, F., M. Haour-Knipe, and F. Thomas. 2008. *Mobility, Sexuality and AIDS*. New York: Routledge.

United Nations Population Fund, TSD-CGHR Branch. 2007. *Global Consultation on Female Genital Mutilation/Cutting: Technical Report*. New York: Gender, Human Rights and Culture Branch, Technical Division, UNFPA.

U.S. Department of State. 2007. *Trafficking in Persons*. Report. Washington, DC: Government Printing Press.

Veale, A. 2003. *From Child Soldier to Ex-Fighter: Female Fighters, Demobilisation and Reintegration in Ethiopia*. Pretoria, South Africa: Institute for Security Studies.

Wanna, L. 1997. *The Role of Female Potters in Household Economy: Their Work and Constraints: A Case Study of Omo Region, Southern Ethiopia*. Addis Ababa, Ethiopia: Organization for Social Science Research in Eastern Africa.

World Economic Forum. 2008. *The Global Gender Gap report*. http://www.weforum.org/issues/global-gender-gap/. Accessed March 15, 2009.

Yalew, E., and W. Almaz. 1997. *Academic Achievements, Drop Out, and Repetition Rates of Female Students in Some Selected Schools of Addis Ababa*. Addis Ababa: Forum on Street Children Ethiopia.

Yelfign, W., Forum for African Women Educationalists, et al. 1995. *Study on Primary School Female Participation and Performance in Cheha District*. Addis Ababa, Ethiopia: Forum for African Women Educationalists, Ministry of Education.

Yigremew, A. 2001. *Land Redistribution and Female-Headed Households: A Study in Two Rural Communities in Northwest Ethiopia*. Addis Ababa, Ethiopia: Forum for Social Studies.

Education

Ethiopia has a profoundly unique historical background in education. Before the advent of Western influence, which was introduced by Emperor Menelik starting in 1905, the *dabtaras* and other religious clerics ran the country's time-honored schools.

TRADITIONAL EDUCATION

Traditional education in Ethiopia, which evolved during past millennia, has been under the aegis of the Ethiopian Orthodox Church. The education was imparted in Ge'ez, which is the classic Ethiopian tongue. Vernacular is spoken only by a handful of highly trained ecclesiastical scholars.

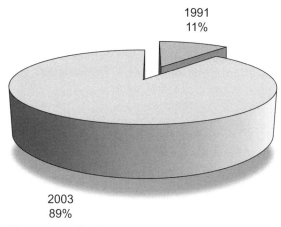

1991
11%

2003
89%

Tertiary Level Education, 1991–2003

At the primary stage of the traditional church school, the students learn the Ethiopian syllabary, with 265 characters, and then read and commit to memory the Ge'ez version of sections from the Epistle General of St. John. Students are normally introduced to numbers at this level; writing may also be attempted. He or she now becomes a primary school graduate. The intermediary level is the bare minimum required of all deacons serving the Ethiopian Orthodox Church. To acquire education at this level, students must travel to the ancient institutions of learning located in Gojam, Gondar, Tigre, and Wallo. The students hold their books and learning aids and humbly squat around him and receive oral education until midnight.

Traditional higher education in Ethiopia has three areas of specialization, which are offered at the academy of music, the academy of poetry, and the school of texts. Each of these branches of training takes at least two years of learning and exercise, with a total of eight years required to graduate as a specialist in Ethiopian church music.

Rarely will an established music scholar terminate his pedagogical pursuits at this level; he will normally proceed to the next branch of higher education, the school of poetry, where he is carefully examined and interrogated about his educational standing. For the first time, the student is expected to comprehend the Ge'ez text he is reading. Until the introduction of modern education, this coterie of traditional intelligentsia was in high demand, both at the feudal courts where members became imperial secretaries or interpreters of the law and at the church where they acted as the custodians of the Miaphysite orthodox doctrine, and as scribes, teachers, and choristers. However, traditional education is still important for those who are inclined toward the ministry. The church has built educational institutions that offer both traditional and modern curricula, at the secondary and university levels. Furthermore, preprimary education in Ethiopia is still the monopoly of the traditional learning institutions, where reading and writing are taught before the children transfer to the government-established public schools.

MEROPIUS

Meropius (also known as Metrodorus and referred to in Ethiopian ecclesiastical literature as Mérobopeyos) was an early fourth-century teacher of philosophy to two young Christian brothers called Frumentius and Aedesius in the city of Tyre who decided to make a voyage on the Red Sea Coast and offered the young boys an opportunity to travel with him. They were delighted at the invitation of their teacher, and the three of them sailed around Arabia with their crew. The year was AD 320. On their return home to Tyre, the ship docked at the famous Axumite port of Adulis, where the travelers intended to take fresh supplies. But a quarrel among the sailors and the local people led to the death of Meropius and all members of his crew. Only the two brothers, who were away from the dock studying under a tree, escaped with their lives. The officials who discovered the two surviving boys took them to the king of Axum, who gave them shelter. In AD 330, Frumentius became the king's secretary and succeeded to convert the king's son, Ezana, who took the throne after his father's death, to Christianity, thus opening a way for the mass Christian conversion in Ethiopia in the mid-fourth century.

WESTERN EDUCATION FROM 1905 TO THE END OF THE DERG ERA

The first attempt to introduce compulsory Western-style education into Ethiopia took place during the time of Emperor Menelik, who in 1905 enunciated the intent to force parents who did not send their children to school to pay stiff penalties.

The approximate age categories for different levels of institutions have been slowly evolving. Ages 2 to 7 have always been preprimary, where most students attend the traditional school system and learn the Ethiopian syllabary and the rudiments of reading and writing in their mother tongues, parallel to Amharic, which was the lingua franca (common language) of the nation until the fall of the Derg. Ages 7 to 13 received free, universal elementary education under both Haile Selassie and the Derg. Second-level education, for ages 14 to 19, run in two cycles: polytechnic, lasting four years, and academic and vocational higher secondary, completed in two.

Third-level education starts at 19. Intermediate teacher training normally runs from 19 to 21 years of age. Other university studies are arts, science, law, agriculture, public health, social work, theology, and business, which are provided to those between ages 19 and 23. Some children who have better preprimary preparation usually skip classes at the elementary or even secondary levels and finish their studies at a much younger age. Others start their education late, some in their twenties and already married, and thus obviously finish at a much older age.

During the 1973–1974 academic year, some progress was made in the area of student enrollment. The number of elementary students more than doubled, to 2,374,362; 36 percent of students were female.

At the second level, the number of registered students in 1981–1982 had more than doubled the 1974 figure, and the number of instructors had risen to more than 11,000.

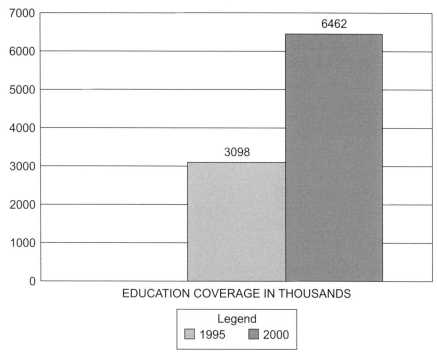

Primary Level Education, 1995–2000

Because of the intermediary polytechnic level and the newly introduced comprehensive education at the secondary stage, all students received a substantial amount of training in technical skills in addition to general academic instruction by the time they graduated from the 12th grade.

Despite this dramatic growth at the first and second levels, tertiary education languished from 1974 to 1977, due in large part to the violent confrontations and student turmoil of the 1970s.

One very important factor in the progress of Ethiopian education has been the large number of denominational private schools that were reopened by foreign mission societies after the Fascist occupation. So in one guideline it published, the Derg regime announced plans for a concerted effort to redress the discrepancies in the distribution of educational resources, which had been concentrated in the urban areas and in certain favored regions of the country such as Addis Ababa, Shoa, and Harar.

Students took general tests at the end of grades 8 through 10. The passing mark for primary and high schools was set at 50 percent; at the university level, it was set at 60 percent. By 1971, 121 primary schools, 59 secondary schools, and 10 adult education centers were participating in the program. By 1974, the mass media center, which had a new videotape machine with a 50-hour supply of tapes, had put to effective use 175 television sets that Japan and Britain had supplied to the Ministry of Education as part of their long-term technical assistance program.

After the 1941 liberation, the most important foreign source for the supply of books was Britain, which in 1944 granted the Ministry of Education and Fine Arts

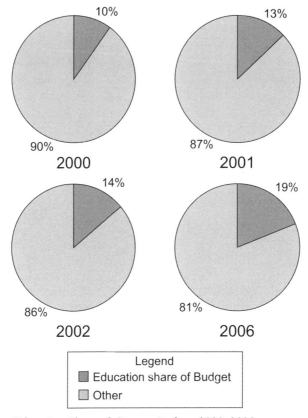

Education Share of Current Budget, 2000–2005

£200,000 for the purchase of texts and readers. This led to a long period of intense Anglo-American suzerainty via education and culture. Nevertheless, even books that were foreign to Ethiopian culture were in great demand because of the lack of viable substitutes. Since the 1960s, all Amharic materials for primary schools have been published locally by the educational material production department of the Ministry of Education. At the secondary and university levels, dependence on foreign sources, mostly American, continued until the mid-1970s.

PREPRIMARY AND PRIMARY EDUCATION

Preprimary education in Ethiopia has mostly been conducted at the traditional church schools where children are taught reading, writing, and basic Ethiopian numbers. Up to the end of the Derg regime, the primary schools ran from grades one to six, and the language of instruction at these levels was the mother tongue, later taught parallel to Amharic, with English being introduced as a special compulsory subject so that students above the sixth grade would pursue their secondary education in English. The great majority of primary school graduates went into vocational fields, and the rest into the primary teacher training programs. After 1974, a new curriculum that strongly emphasized vocational studies over academic subjects was introduced. An experimental phase of political education, history, and polytechnic training was conducted in the fifth grades in 1982 and extended to the sixth grades in 1983.

The teaching profession, particularly at the primary level, had always been plagued with problems. Another major problem plaguing the school system was overcrowding. Because the teacher–pupil ratio at the elementary level continued to climb, the newly expanded teacher training schools and colleges had to grapple with impressively rapid growth in classroom units and student enrollment.

Admittance to the next higher level of Ethiopian schools, whether academic or vocational, required a pass in national examinations given at the end of the sixth grade. Because the curriculum was primarily oriented toward preparation for the secondary level, a student who failed to pass was ill-prepared for the job market.

ACADEMIC SECONDARY SCHOOLS

The first post-elementary-level educational establishment opened after the Italo-Ethiopian War of 1935–1941 was the Haile Selassie Secondary School, which started offering regular academic training in Addis Ababa on July 23, 1943. From 1941 to 1951, seven academic secondary schools, only two of which were devoted exclusively to secondary education, were functioning in the Ethiopian empire. However, as at the primary level, the teacher–student ratio alarmed many Ethiopian educators. Officials were left with the heavy task of further expanding the country's teacher training institutes. In the secondary level was general education, the first year curriculum covered history, geography, and Amharic, with a total of three courses a week; and mathematics and science, including health, with a combined total of five courses per week.

Since 1968–1969, the curriculum of four-year senior-secondary education has been comprehensive in nature. During this period, 91 percent of the students advanced into the academic stream, and 7 percent in to the vocational program, with a minuscule 2 percent going into the primary teacher training sector.

When the modem school system was restarted following the Fascist defeat, the need for educated citizens was so overwhelming that students were propelled through the system to reach higher levels in the shortest time possible. Double promotions for bright students in primary grades sometimes cut the average year of schooling by more than half. In the late 1950s, as more and more students competed for the few available spaces, a pass in at least four ordinary-level subjects of the general certificate of education of the University of London, and in at least five subjects in the Ethiopian school-leaving certification examination, became a minimum requirement for those wishing to enroll in the two elite third-level institutions: the University College of Addis Ababa and the engineering college. This led to a heavy drain on the budget of the Ministry of Education, given that foreign teachers, other than Indians, were paid much higher salaries compared with Ethiopians of the same qualifications. At the junior-secondary level, for example, more than 93 percent of the teachers were Ethiopian nationals by the 1970s. Of the 1,697 junior-secondary teachers, 51 percent were graduates of teacher training institutes, and 1.4 percent had university degrees.

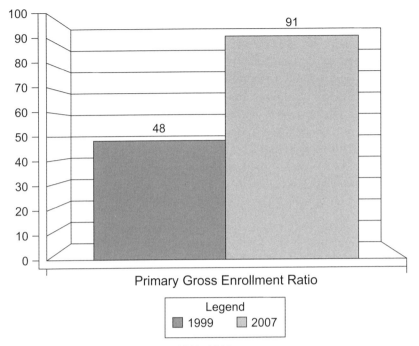

Primary Gross Enrolment Ratio, 1999–2007

HIGHER EDUCATION

The first third-level educational institution opened in Ethiopia was the French Canadian–run University College of Addis Ababa, which started operation on December 11, 1950.

During the 1960s, the second university in the country, the University of Asmara, opened. This university is now the major institution of higher learning for independent Eritrea. As time passed, due to the popularity of Western education among the common people, students who passed their ESLCE examination could not gain automatic admittance into both universities. During the formative years, students paid no fees; the state covered all the expenses, including tuition and residential costs.

Before 1991, the College of Social Sciences of Addis Ababa University encompassed nine major departments, among which were the departments of geography, history, philosophy, economics, political science and international relations, and psychology.

Enrollment at the tertiary level had grown steadily since 1950. In 1960–1961, 935 students were enrolled at a college level, of which only 56 were women. During the 1982–1983 academic year, there were 16,137 students at the tertiary level, about 10 percent of whom were female.

The number of foreign students at Ethiopian colleges rose a great deal in 1959 with the influx of young African scholars. But by 1978, at the height of the "red and white terror campaign" in which many university students perished, the number of foreign students in Ethiopian universities had dwindled to a mere 34.

Students of Addis Ababa University discussing a strategy to have a showdown with authorities and riot police in 2001. (AP Photo/Sayyid Azim.)

In 1960, there were 8,134 young Ethiopians pursuing their studies abroad, most of them in Canada and the United States. Prior to 1958, no students were sent to Eastern-bloc countries. Although there were still significant numbers of students in Western countries, more and more went to the Soviet bloc starting after the 1974 revolution when Marxism-Leninism was declared as the official ideology of the Ethiopian military regime. In 1978, for example, the Soviet Union accepted 700 scholarship students into its higher institutions of learning. During the same year, Cuba gave 280 medical scholarships to qualified Ethiopian youth, in addition to taking 1,200 primary-school-level, mostly war-orphaned children between the ages of 9 and 16. In November 1979, Cuba admitted 102 Ethiopian students into its Camagüey University.

EDUCATIONAL RESEARCH

The University of Addis Ababa has several important research centers. The Institute of Ethiopian Studies was opened in 1963 as a locus of advanced study and documentation. The Education Research Centre, located on the central campus of Addis Ababa University, serves as a research laboratory and resource place for the College of Pedagogical Sciences. The Institute of Development Research, opened within the central university campus in 1972, employs interdisciplinary approaches to study

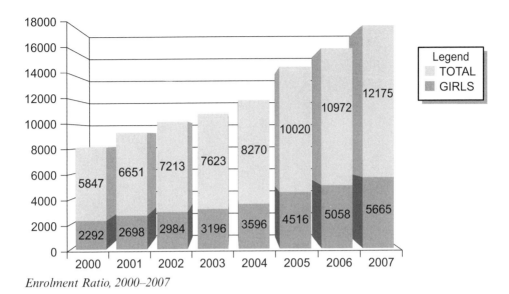

Enrolment Ratio, 2000–2007

Ethiopian and Third World development problems as well as producing social science teaching materials based on research findings by its staff.

EDUCATIONAL ADMINISTRATION AND FINANCE

After the 1941 liberation, Emperor Haile Selassie appointed a minister of education, but it was not until 1943 that a royal decree empowered the minister to guide all regulations concerning education and educational administration.

In 1947, the emperor established the Board of Education and Fine Arts, which was charged with formulating broad policy guidelines for the advancement and administration of education. Local school boards, which met twice a year to examine the progress of education throughout the country and to ensure the proper allocation of educational resources, were also created the same year. Also in place were a superintendent of education, provincial education officers, and a director of the department of provincial education, who regularly toured the different areas of the country to convene conferences and to make recommendations concerning the equitable distribution of educational supplies and the coordination of major programs. There were, in addition, 102 subprovincial educational officers who, in the majority of cases, lacked modern education and professional expertise but were nevertheless charged with very important responsibilities. In 1965, for example, only about 18 percent of Ethiopian elementary school directors had what could be considered proper training befitting their rank. The chronic shortage of qualified directors at both first and second levels, particularly at the elementary level, had been one of the longstanding problems in educational administration in Ethiopia. The instruction department, to which both the provincial and subprovincial education officers were attached, coordinated the functioning of formal and nonformal education; the design, development, and coordination of primary and high school curricula; the preparation and evaluation of national examinations and health services; and the acquisition and production of texts and teaching aids.

In 1930, when Haile Selassie ascended the throne, the minister of education was allocated 2 percent of the central government's revenue as well as an educational tax raised from rural peasants who rarely got the opportunity to send their children to school. Higher education was exclusively financed by the central government, which, after the 1941 liberation from Fascism, was desperately looking for skilled manpower at the bureaucratic level. The government tried to attract students from all strata of society by offering free room, board, and educational supplies to all college-level students and most high school and some elementary school students. Revenue for education was derived from land taxes as well as from the state treasury and from the 1950's on, was greatly boosted by technical assistance from foreign governments. From 1951 to 1962, for example, educational expenditures in Addis Ababa were more than one-half of the educational expenditures of all 14 provinces; in 1954, bilateral assistance from foreign countries, mostly the United States, constituted 12 percent of the total educational expenditures. A significant cut in such assistance could have brought the country's educational system to a virtual halt. Because Ethiopian teachers were still few in number, more foreign teachers, whose pay was several times higher than that of the Ethiopians, were hired. This drained the educational budget tremendously. However, because of internal and regional wars, in which the country had been engaged since 1975, the defense budget continued to outstrip educational expenditures and doubled between 1978–1979 and 1982–1983.

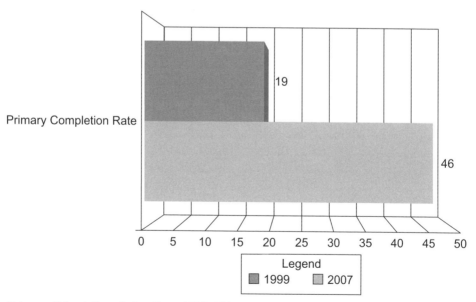

Primary School Completion Rate, 1999–2007

NONFORMAL EDUCATION

The following four types of nonformal education have coexisted in Ethiopia for a long time: pre-service training, vestibule training, in-service training, and literacy program. Vestibule training programs were similar to pre-service training except that the personnel who were hired were committed by a contract and received stipends while undergoing their apprenticeship. The major organizations that practiced vestibule training were the Telecommunications Authority, the Ethiopian Airlines, the Highway Authority, the Ethiopian Electric Light and Power Authority, the Railway Authority, the Commercial Bank of Ethiopia, the Wonji Sugar Estate, the Ethiopian Metal Tools Company, the Tourist and Hotel Association, and the Baher Dar Textile Mills.

In-service training programs, which involved receiving instruction while fully employed, had three objectives: to provide initial skill acquisition or apprenticeship; to ensure skill maintenance with refresher courses or to gain additional skills with new technology; and to effectively and consistently upgrade the performance of the employees in order to modify existing skills and positions or to train a person for another position other than the one he or she was holding. In order to consolidate the program, the Ministry of Education and Fine Arts established the Directorate of Adult Education and Literacy. Its duties included the coordination of literacy programs, the establishment of uniform standards, and the collection and analysis of literacy and adult education statistics. The directorate also produced and distributed instructional and learning manuals, follow-up readers, clip charts, and posters and set a standard syllabus, which included the learning of the Ethiopian syllabary, num-

Ethiopian children in the classroom of a school built by residents. (AP Photo/Sayyid Azim.)

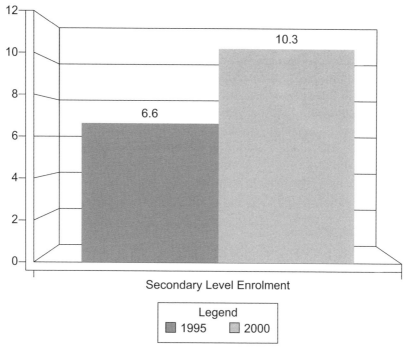

Secondary Level Enrolment, 1995–2000

bers, and civics and health education. Major organizations set up their own literacy centers, and there were also several night-school programs in regular elementary and secondary schools where literacy classes were offered. Students had to commit to heart the 27 major characters and their 7 phonetic derivatives and other symbols—a total of 235 letters—before they produced a set of words by assembling them. Since 1967, however, the ministries of education and national community development have developed teaching methods that are more logical and easier to grasp.

The first post-revolution literacy campaign was the 1975–1976 "development through cooperation" campaign known as the *zemecha* (Crusade), which involved more than 50,000 students above the 10th grade and their teachers and professors, who taught more than a quarter of a million rural inhabitants how to read and write within a span of only 18 months.

The national literacy program launched in 1979 was indeed the most far-reaching educational project the country had embarked on since the introduction of modern education at the turn of the century. The course, offered in literacy centers, each holding an average of 40 students, involved several stages of mastering the Ethiopian syllabary as well as Amharic numerals. Successful students proceeded to normal reading, the construction of simple words and sentences, and elementary arithmetical calculations. When compared with the regular school system, stages one and two of the courses brought the student to a grade two level, and the follow-up scheme to grade four.

The general aim was always to adapt the lessons to the local environment, to harness all available human and technical resources for the successful implementation of the educational program, and to make the general campaign as practical as possible.

With governmental and local contribution as well as international aid, 11 small, one-kilowatt education radio transmitters were installed in February 1981.

Ethiopia won the United Nation's 1980 International Reading Association Literacy Prize. Whereas 3 percent of the Ethiopian instructors had finished eighth grade, only a very small number of them had ever enrolled in a teacher training course.

Not only were Ethiopian teachers unqualified, but also the attrition rate was extremely alarming. In 1960, 42 percent of the community teacher-training finishers and 28 percent of the one-year teacher-training graduates quit teaching altogether to pursue other professions. The average elementary school teacher thus perceived the Ministry of Education as a nest of spies and a bastion of corruption, tribalism, and blatant nepotism. The situation was to lead to the radicalization of the teachers, which helped topple the government of Emperor Haile Selassie in 1974.

WESTERN EDUCATION SINCE THE EPRDF ASSENT TO POWER IN 1991

Since the fall of the Derg in 1991, there has been an observable trend to improve and expand the public education system in Ethiopia. Except in the Afar and Somali regions, where the predominant life style is pastoralism and opening permanent schools has become difficult, education throughout the country has shown a tremendous growth. Whereas the quality of education has deteriorated in direct proportion to this expansion in educational delivery, reports from the United Nations Educational, Scientific and Cultural Organization (UNESCO) show that it is continuously improving as the demand for qualified manpower keeps increasing.

When the present government came to power following the demise of the Derg regime, there were fewer than 3 million pupils registered at the primary level. By 2009, however, the figure had risen to 15.5 million, showing an increase of over 500 percent. Furthermore, secondary school enrollment has grown fivefold. In 1991, four or of five primary school–age children never went to school. But by 2000, over 60 percent were enrolled.

The fact that public expenditures on education, as a percentage of total outlay, had risen from a mere 10 percent during the time of the Derg to 23.6 percent in 2009 has helped in this dramatic growth. In partnership with donors, the Ministry of Education has trained teachers and administrators at a rapid pace. There has been an observable improvement in planning and participation by local governments and community groups. The fact that elementary education, which used to be conducted in Amharic, has shifted to mother tongues has enhanced service delivery and helped to attract more students. The abolition of fees for primary and lower secondary schools, increased school construction programs, expansion of education in rural areas, adoption of alternative formative education aimed at out-of-school children in remote communities, and adult literacy campaigns, coupled with school feeding programs, have all helped in the expansion of education.

Unhindered access to education has also narrowed the gender gap. Before 1991, male student enrollment was more than 50 percent higher than that for girls. How-

Boisterous elementary school children in Addis Ababa, Ethiopia. (Getty Images/Upperhall Ltd/ Robert Harding.)

Female street children learn needlework at the Goal Street Children's Project in Addis Ababa. (AP Photo/Sayyid Azim.)

ever, with an educational approach that attracts more girls with the promise of better opportunities in employment and the raising of the marriage age, which averaged 15 to 18 years of age, by 2009, gender parity has been almost achieved. Government figures show that the gap between the two has now been reduced to a mere 6 percent. If this trend continues, Ethiopia may be one of the few African countries that come near the fulfillment of the United Nations' Millennium Development Goals set for 2015.

The EPRDF government has placed great emphasis on improving the quality of education and has generally recognized it as a key component for the country's development needs. Following are problems recognized:

1. Low primary school participation.
2. Rural areas lagging behind urban areas in education.
3. Girls being deprived of equal participation in the education system;
4. low quality of education.
5. Enrollment at the secondary and tertiary levels were 15 percent and 1 percent, respectively.

The educational reform envisaged by the new system of government took a route of total departure from the previous half-century's approaches to educational development. Instead of a monolithic education system, the new policy devolved power and entrusted the administration and formulation of pedagogical services to the regional units. Overnight, education in Ethiopia became the autonomous responsibility of the nine national regional states and the two city administra-

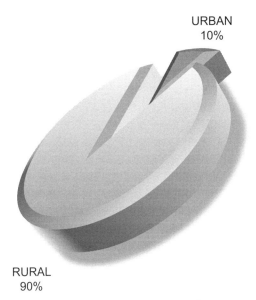

URBAN
10%

RURAL
90%

Newly Constructed Urban and Rural Primary Schools

tions, each with a bureau of education responsible for controlling and running the educational system. There were also a network of executive structures involving educational departments of each zone and *woreda* offices of education. The federal unit under the Ministry of Education of the federal government was solely responsible for tertiary-level education, but it supplied all necessary subsidies to the regional offices.

The most recent structure of the Ethiopian education system has a breakdown into formal and nonformal, with the latter providing a wide range of training both for elementary school–age boys and girls as well as adults who did not finish schooling, as well as for beginners. The formal sector is itself divided into kindergarten, general, technical-vocational, and tertiary education programs.

On the basis of the new education and Training policy, the structure of education in Ethiopia, which used to be 6 years elementary, 2 years junior high and 4 year senior high education, was changed to 8 years of primary education parceled into two cycles, and 4 years of secondary education, broken up into two 2-year cycles. The Ethiopian Federal Democratic Republic Constitution declared that education should be free of any political and religious ideology, thus making the curriculum totally secular. The New Education and Training Policy emphasized that no tuition of any kind would be paid for acquiring knowledge and skills from the general education system, though there was a proviso that at some stage, there would be a cost-sharing mechanism, starting with the second cycle of secondary education and going through the college and university levels.

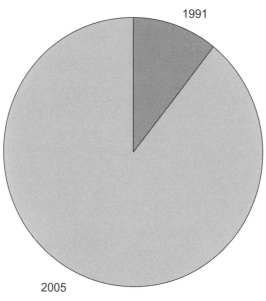

Annual Intake Rate of Tertiary Level Education, 1991–2005

A cardinal feature of the new education reform was its categorical stand that every nation and nationality has the right to learn in its own language at least at the basic education and general primary levels. That made ethnic languages a basic medium of instruction at the primary level.

Some of the points emphasized in reforming education in Ethiopia on the basis of the five years' program were the following:

- Access to quality basic education for all.
- Produce good citizenship.
- Ensure educational equity between urban and rural localities, between male and females, and among the national regional states of the Federal Democratic Republic of Ethiopia.
- Produce required middle-level skilled manpower of reasonable quality in sufficient quantities by establishing technical-vocational training system.
- Open new educational institutions, as well as expand and strengthen existing ones in order to produce professionals at a quantity and quality that match the requirement of the country.
- Enable the community to directly participate in school management and administration with a sense of ownership.
- Build manpower capacity at each level of the system to ensure successful implementation of educational management.

Furthermore, there was clear, dramatic success at the tertiary level, where enrollment in all sectors of higher education, including diploma, undergraduate, and postgraduate, increased from 18,000 in 1991 to 147,000 in 2003. From 1995 to 2000, enrollment at the primary level rose from 3,098,422 to 6,462,503—a dramatic growth by any standard.

The education share of the current budget also steadily increased from 2000 to 2005.

Rural primary education enrollment increased at a rate of 21.5 percent. Female primary-school participation also grew at a rate of 16.4 percent. Hastening the move toward parity, participation of girls in primary education in the rural sector rose by 24.8 percent compared to the urban sector, where the growth rate was 7.7 percent.

Notwithstanding this noteworthy increase in enrollment, Ethiopia remains off-track in its progress toward achieving universal primary education by the Millennium Development Goal date of 2015.

Still, it is important to note that both male and female students benefited from the increase in primary school enrollment and completion rates. Secondary-level growth was also noteworthy. During the five years following the formulation of the new education policy, urban–rural dichotomy in distribution of schools showed positive results.

Technical and vocational education has also been given priority by the EPRDF government. Industrial, commercial, skill, and manpower training have been emphasized. Furthermore, learners are encouraged through entrepreneurial education to work toward the development and creation of self-help jobs.

In order to strengthen the development of quality education, information communication technology has been introduced into the education system. At the secondary level a 9th grade to 12th grade multifaceted programs were adopted to significantly improve the quality of education. Through this medium, major subjects such as English, mathematics, physics, chemistry, biology, civics, and ethical education are currently being taught.

When the new education policy was adopted in 1994, there were only a handful of private schools in Ethiopia, and none of them were at the higher education level. Whereas when the Derg fell in 1991, there were only two universities in the country (including the University of Asmara, which is now in independent Eritrea), by 2005, seven new universities had sprung up. Equally dramatic is the annual intake rate at tertiary-level institutions, which has increased from 3,500 to 30,000.

The Ethiopian education policy since the fall of the Derg requires higher-level training at the diploma, degree, and graduate levels to be practice-oriented, enabling students to become problem-solving professional leaders in their fields of study and for overall societal needs.

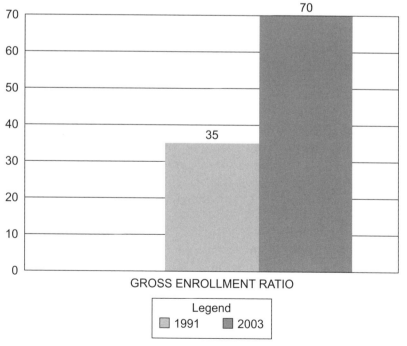

Gross Enrolment Ratio

Brain drain has been the hallmark of Ethiopia's development problems. Severe attrition has resulted from professionals' migration to other African countries as well as America and western Europe, where remunerations for their services are several-fold. Postgraduate and professional development studies are now open to many of Ethiopia's graduates who are sent abroad for a short period, but this has also led to "brain drain" because some take advantage of their travel abroad to immigrate to developed countries.

Expansion in tertiary-level education has also been dramatic. Considering that more than three-fourths of Ethiopia's major economic production is based on agriculture, which is vulnerable to variations in climate and international market forces, the EPRDF government in Ethiopia vowed to leave behind dependence on agriculture and transfer to a modern economy. Modernization needs skilled manpower that can be produced through specialized education. Thus, expansion in higher education has been the priority of the Ethiopian state.

Before the fall of the Derg regime in 1991, Ethiopia had only two universities, one in Addis Ababa and the other in Asmara, Eritrea. By 2010, 19 more universities had been opened. In addition, 26 regional teacher-training colleges and 60 government-accredited private postsecondary institutions have been opened.

At all levels, enrollment in secondary schools has increased at a very rapid pace. Many students now finish secondary schools and enroll in colleges and universities. In 2000–2001, the number of undergraduates enrolled in public universities was 34,000. Seven years later, enrollment had reached 125,000. However, gender balance is pathetically asymmetrical. Less than 30 percent of undergraduate students and 10 percent of graduate students are females. The number of teaching personnel also falls short of the need. At the beginning of the millennium, 3,400 teachers provided service at Ethiopia's universities. In 2008–2009, there were 7,500 university teachers. So as enrollment increased fourfold, training personnel only doubled. Teacher–student ratio is also problematic; it grew from 1:8 in 1995 to 1:15 in 2010 (Reisberg and Rumbley, 2010).

Qualification of teachers is another problem. Of those currently teaching in postsecondary institutions, fewer than 20 percent have earned master's degrees. Fewer than 4 percent have acquired their PhDs. The addition of classroom space, the stockpiling of library collections, the opening of computer labs, and the expansion of electronic networks have not kept pace with enrollment either.

Ethiopia currently benefits from international aid and expatriate teachers who leave their university teaching jobs abroad to help fill the crucial gap in staffing. But all these are not adequate to fulfill the need that rapid expansion has created.

There is heavy staff turnover at all levels of Ethiopian education. This is caused by the desire of the teachers to move from rural to urban areas and to earn higher salaries. Unchecked staff turnover in turn bedevils institutions' capacity. Therefore, many third-level institutions have failed to operate competently and to manage long-range plans and development policies.

By 2010, Ethiopia had increased enrollment in higher education to 3 percent of the age cohort. This is still not up to average international standards, but it is gratifying that the country has achieved a brisk 300 percent growth in enrollment. This period has proven to be an exciting time for Ethiopia's higher education system, but

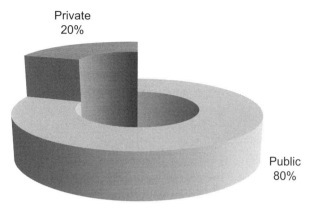

Private
20%

Public
80%

Private vs. Public Schools, 1991–2005

growing pains are evident and will continue, given such rapid expansion. At this critical stage, where much has already been accomplished, quality assurance and a commitment to appropriate and sustained infrastructure must rise to the top of the national agenda.

REFERENCES

Abdi, A. A., K. P. Puplampu, et al. 2006. *African Education and Globalization: Critical Perspectives.* Lanham, MD: Lexington Books.

Aklilu, Habte. 1967. "Brain Drain in the Elementary School: Why Teachers Leave the Profession." *Ethiopian Journal of Education* (June): 27–39.

Amare, A. 2002. *Quality of Primary Education in Ethiopia: Proceedings of the National Conference Held in Adama Ras Hotel, November 9–11, 2001.* Addis Ababa, Ethiopia: Institute of Educational Research, Addis Ababa University.

Amare, A. 1998. *Quality Education in Ethiopia: Visions for the 21st Century: Proceedings of National Conference Held in Awassa College of Teacher Education, 12–18 July 1998.* Addis Ababa, Ethiopia: Institute of Educational Research, Addis Ababa University.

Amare, A., L. Wanna, et al. 2000. *Establishing National Pedagogical Center for Higher Education in Ethiopia.* Proceedings of the National Conference Held at AAU, School of Graduate Studies, Conference Hall Amist Kilo, Addis Ababa, August 11–12, 2000. Addis Ababa, Ethiopia: Institute of Educational Research, Addis Ababa University.

Benedek, W., Austria Bundesministerium für europäische und internationale Angelegenheiten, et al. 2009. *Global Standards—Local Action: 15 Years Vienna World Conference on Human Rights: Conference Proceedings of the International Expert Conference Held in Vienna on 28 and 29 August 2008.* Mortsel, Antwerpen, Belgium.

Ethiopia. 1964. *Education in Ethiopia.* Addis Ababa: Ethiopia: Publications & Foreign Languages Press Department, Ministry of Information.

Ethiopia. 1965. *Teacher Education in Ethiopia.* Addis Ababa, Ethiopia: Department of Teacher Education.

Ethiopia. Higher Education Commission. *Higher Education in Ethiopia: Facts & Figures.* Addis Ababa, Ethiopia: Commission for Higher Education.

Ethiopia. Ministry of Information. 1967. *Education in Ethiopia*. Addis Ababa, Ethiopia: Ministry of Information, Publications and Foreign Languages Press Department.

Ethiopia. Ministry of Education. 1977. *Basic Information on Education in Ethiopia*. Addis Ababa, Ethiopia: Provisional Military Government of Socialist Ethiopia, Ministry of Education, Planning Services.

Ethiopia. Ministry of Education. 1978. *Higher Education in Ethiopia, 1978: Facts and Figures*. Addis Ababa, Ethiopia: Commission for Higher Education.

Ethiopia. International Labour Office. 1964. *Report on Workers' Education in Ethiopia*. Addis Ababa and Geneva: International Labor Organization of the United Nations.

Fisseha Tegegne. 1977. *Application of the Curve of Concentration Lorenz Curve to Distribution of Education in Ethiopia*. Addis Ababa, Ethiopia: Addis Ababa University, Department of Economics.

Fisseha Tegegne. 1977. *Finance of Education in Ethiopia, Kenya and Tanzania: A Comparative Analysis*. Addis Ababa, Ethiopia: Addis Ababa University, Department of Economics.

Girma, Amare. 1962. "Government Education in Ethiopia." *Ethiopia Observer*: 335–42.

Haile, H. G. 1980. *Contribution of Arwaja Pedagogical Centers to the Improvement of Education in Ethiopia*. Nairobi, Kenya: ACO Project.

Koohi-Kamali, F. 2008. *Intrahousehold Inequality and Child Gender Bias in Ethiopia*. Washington, DC: World Bank.

Marew, Z., D. Bridges, et al. 2000. *Secondary Teacher Education in Ethiopia*. Addis Ababa, Ethiopia: n.p.

Meinardus, O. F. A. 1962. *Atlas of Christian sites in Egypt*. Le Caire: Societe d'archâeologie copte. p.31

Milkias, Paulos, 1988. "Education in Ethiopia." *World Education Encyclopedia*. New York: Facts on File Publications.

Milkias, Paulos, and Messay Kebede. 2010. *Education, Politics and Social Change in Ethiopia*. Los Angeles: Tsehai Publishers, Loyola Marymount University.

Negash, T. 1996. *Rethinking Education in Ethiopia*. Uppsala, Sweden: Nordiska Afrikainstitutet.

Negash, T. 2006. *Education in Ethiopia: From Crisis to the Brink of Collapse*. Uppsala, Sweden: Nordiska Afrikainstitutet.

Niehoff, R. O., and B. D. Wilder. 1974. *Non-Formal Education in Ethiopia*. East Lansing: Institute for International Studies in Education, College of Education, Michigan State University.

Pankhurst, E. S. 1946. *Education in Ethiopia*. Woodford, Essex: New Times and Ethiopia News.

Pankhurst, R. 1969. *Language and Education in Ethiopia; Historical Background to the Post-War Period*. Addis Ababa, Ethiopia: H.S.I.U.

Reisberg, Liz, and Laura E. Rumbley. 2010. "Ethiopia: The Dilemmas of Expansion." *International Higher Education* 58 (Winter).

Teshome, G. Wagaw. *Education in Ethiopia*. Ann Arbor: University of Michigan Press, 1979.

Torrey, E. F. 1967. *An Introduction to Health and Health Education in Ethiopia*. Addis Ababa, Ethiopia: Artistic Printers Ltd.

United Nations Economic Commission for Africa, Economic and Social Policy Division. 1997. *Non-formal and Distance Education in Ethiopia: Lessons and Experiences.* Addis Ababa, Ethiopia: Economic Commission for Africa.

United Nations Economic Commission for Africa, Manpower Training and Manpower Section. 1972. *Occasional Report on Education and Training for Development.* Addis Ababa, Ethiopia: United Nations.

Wagaw, T. G. *Education in Ethiopia: Prospect and Retrospect.* Ann Arbor: University of Michigan Press.

Wartenberg, D. and W. Mayrhofer. (2001). *Education in Ethiopia.* Hamburg, Kovaéc.

Wondwosen, T. 2008. *The Anatomy of Private Higher Education in Ethiopia: Current Landscape, Challenges, and Prospects.* Addis Ababa, Ethiopia: St. Mary's University College.

Worku, G. 1974. *Bibliography of Theses in the Area of Education in Ethiopia.* Addis Ababa, Ethiopia: Haile Selassie I University, Faculty of Education, Research Center Library.

World Bank. 2005. *Education in Ethiopia: Strengthening the Foundation for Sustainable Progress.* Washington, DC: World Bank.

CHAPTER 6

Culture

Language

Language is the most common categorization tool in understanding the nature of Ethiopian ethnicity. Ethiopia is home to a mosaic of over 80 languages belonging to the Afro-Asiatic language group, which can be classified into four categories, the great majority of them belonging to the Semitic, Cushitic, and Omotic groups. The fourth group is Nilotic, which is part of the Nilo-Saharan language family.

The Semitic languages are widespread in the central and northern areas of the country. These include Ge'ez, Amharic, Tigrigna, Guragigna, and Harari. Ge'ez, which used to be the lingua franca of the Axumite empire, is now a dead language like Latin and is used only for religious purposes in the Ethiopian Orthodox Tewahedo Church. Amharic, which is the working language of the country today, is native to populations living in the central and northwestern areas. The country is now divided into *kilils* on the basis of linguistic classification.

Based on the 2007 census of the entire Ethiopian population of 73,918,505 people, the Amharas who speak Amharigna as their first language number 19,867,817, thus making up 26.9 percent of the inhabitants of the country; Tigrigna speakers number 4,483,776 (6.1% of the Ethiopian population); Gurages number 1,867,350 (2.5% of the Ethiopian population); and the Harari people number 183,344 (.2% of the population).

The most important Semitic language in Ethiopia, which has been the language of work since the 13th century and is still widely used in government and in the capital, is Amharic. Native Amharic speakers who live in the Gondar, Gojam, northern Showa, and western Wallo regions are 82.5 percent Ethiopian Orthodox Christian; 17.2 percent, mostly in western Wallo, are Muslim by religion with plough agricultural occupation.

The Tigrigna-speaking people who live in the province of Tigray in the north, and who became predominant in the political power structure in the post-Derg period, are almost entirely (95.6%) Orthodox Christian and are also mostly plough agriculturists. Other subgroups within the Semitic language group are much smaller than the Amharas and the Tigrayans. They also do not have a direct tie to Orthodox Christianity and the Axumite historical heritage. By and large, they are also not plough agriculturalists. The Gurage, the third-largest linguistic group among the Semites, are, for example, hoe agriculturalists who depend on a predominantly enset root, not grain, diet.

Among the Semitic-speaking Ethiopians, the Argobba are the smallest group. Some live on the slope of the Great Rift Valley escarpments. Those constituting the Southern Argobba live southwest of Harar. There are also Northern Argobba villages, scattered among Amharic- or Oromo-speaking areas, extending from Addis Ababa to southwest Wallo. The great majority of the Argobba people speak their own language as well as the language of the majority ethnic groups surrounding them (i.e., Amharic or Afaan Oromo).

In general, the Semitic languages and distinct dialects are as follows:

- Harari
- Amharic
- Argobba
- Birale
- Gafat
- Ge'ez
- Guragigna
- Chaha group (Chaha, Muher, Ezha, Gumer, Gura)
- Inor group (Inor, Enner, Endegegna, Gyesto, Mesemes)
- Silt'e group (Silt'e, Ulbareg, Enneqor, Walane)
- Soddo group (Soddo, Gogot, Galila)
- Tigrigna
- Zay

The major Cushitic languages of Ethiopia are Oromo, Somali, and Afar. Again according to the 2007 census, the Oromo speakers, who now have their own kilil of Oromia, make up 34.5 percent of the Ethiopian population, with 25,488,344 people; the Somali speakers number 4,581,793 (6.2% of the population of Ethiopia); and the Afar speakers number 1,276,372 (1.7% of the Ethiopian population). Oromo speakers (they call their language Afan Oromo) not only are the largest group but also are omnipresent in all regions of the country. Their ubiquitous presence in almost every region is the result of their rapid expansion through war from their homeland in the central southern highlands near Bale beginning in the early 16th century. Oromos share a common origin and speak varied dialectics understood by all, but they have changed with respect to social and political organization, which was originally dictated by age group and known as the *gada* system, as well as in their economic and religious affiliations as they adapted to different sociopolitical and environmental conditions.

Oromo clans, such as the Borana, are pastoralists. Some in this group still retain considerable features of their age-old social and political organization dictated by the *gada* age-group system. Some Oromo speakers lead a livelihood of mixed farming. All the rest are plough cultivators. Some Oromo speakers, such as those below the Gibe River, among which are the Jimma Limmu and the Wallaga groups, have evolved a hierarchical system of kingship. Considered on a national level, the Oromo speakers are evenly divided between Christianity and Islam: 48.2 percent of them profess Christianity (predominantly Tewahedo Orthodox, the rest being Protestants), and 47.5 percent are Muslims. The Orthodox Christians are almost wholly in southern Showa and Wallaga regions. The pastoralists who speak Afaan Oromo are either animists or Muslims. The Oromo speakers who are a majority ethnic group in Ethiopia have not succeeded in taking over political power except for a brief period during the Zemene Mesafint not only because of lack of firearms, which the Tigrayans and the Amharas acquired in abundance, but also because of inter clan wars.

Even though the wars among the Oromo groups were sometimes an outcome of competition for land, they were mostly due to the division among them—some being allied with the Amharas, but others resisting the expansion of the empire into their region. Some, like those in Wallo, changed their language to Amharic and as a result achieved a high station in the political and economic order that emerged in the last two hundred years. A very good example of Oromos from Shoa who joined the Amhara ruling class is the case of two kingmakers during and immediately after the reign of Menelik, Fitawrari Habta Giorgis and Dajach Balcha. Both played important roles in palace intrigues immediately following the death of Emperor Menelik. Dajach Balcha supported Lij Eyasu as the legitimate emperor whereas Fitaqrari Habta Giorgis helped Haile Selassie come to power as Regent and Crown Prince

Of the Somali, Afar, and Saho speakers who are almost predominantly pastoralists, the Somali predominate. Many Somali-speaking clans and lineages who live in Ethiopia's Somali kilil have close links with or are members of the same groups in Somalia, Somaliland, and Djibouti. Speakers of the Somali tongue are divided into presumed or perceptible common patrilineal descent. Largest is the clan-family, which is in turn divided into sub-clans, which are further divided still into lineages and sub-lineages. Such clan divisions entail claim to land and water holes as well as political and economic competition, which leads to a bloody conflict.

The Afar speakers, though small in number, have been important in Ethiopian history because of their proximate location on the Red Sea and their traditional status as semiautonomous under the sultan of Ausa and down to the period of the Ethiopian revolution. The Ausa community are predominantly settled cultivators. Those outside the Ausa region are nomadic and fragmented among tribes, sub-tribes, and clans. There is a clear distinction between patrician and common classes. The small Saho-speaking groups in the north, which include elements from Tigray, Afar, Tigre, and Arab stock, are almost entirely pastoralists, most being Muslims, though those living in proximity to Tigray are Ethiopian Orthodox Christians.

Highland East Cushitic language groups include Sidama speakers, which are the largest in this sector. According to the 2007 census, the Sidama speakers numbered 2,966,377 (4.0% of the Ethiopian population), Wolayta speakers numbered 1,707,074 (2.3% of the Ethiopian population), the Hadya-Libido speakers numbered 1,284,366 (1.7% of the population of Ethiopia), and the Kambata speakers numbered 630,000 (.85% of the Ethiopian population). Most of these Highland East Cushitic language groups have patrilineal clans. The groups are cultivators of enset for their staple food as well as producers of coffee, the main cash crop of the country. Those living below 4,921 feet are cattle herders. Of the Highland East Cushitic language group, only the Kambatas have adhered to Ethiopian Orthodox Christianity. Others have retained their traditional religious beliefs or have adapted the teachings of Protestant missionaries, and others still, such as the Hadya, the Timbaro, and the Alaba, have been Islamized.

The Central Cushitic speakers, known as Agaw, comprise six groups and are scattered on the central highlands, surrounded by Amharas and Tigrayans. They include the Awi, who speak Awunji; the Kunfel; the Xamtanga; and the Qimant. The Agaw groups together number 631, 566 according to the 2007 census, making up. 85 percent of the population of Ethiopia. They are the remnants of original inhabitants who were already settled when the Semitic-speaking groups arrived at the northern and central regions of the country over 4,000 years ago. As a result, it is the Agaw, more than any other group, from which present-day Tigrigna and Amharic originate. The Awi and Qimant speakers still retain their traditional religious system. But the Kunfel speakers are almost entirely Orthodox Christian. The offshoot of the Agaws, the Blen, who speak a dialect of Agawgna, live in northern Eritrea and were previously Orthodox Christian but have now to a large extent adopted Islam. Many have also started to speak the language of their neighbors—the Tigre. All Agew-speaking groups are plough agriculturists, although the Kunfel also double in hunting.

In general, there are 24 total Cushitic languages and distinct dialects:

- Afar
- Agaw
- Alaba
- Arbore
- Awngi
- Baiso
- Burji
- Bussa
- Daasanech
- Gawwada

- Gedeo
- Hadiyya
- Kambatta
- Kemant
- Konso
- Kunfal
- Libido
- Oromo
- Saho
- Sidama
- Somali
- Tsamai
- Werize
- Xamtang

Omotic is spoken in the areas between the lake regions of Ethiopia's Great Rift Valley and the Omo River. Here one finds some 80 dialects and languages. Of these, the Wolayta number 1,707,079 (2.31% of the population of Ethiopia), the Gamo number 1,107,163 (1.5% of the population), the Kaficho number 870,213 (1.18% of the population), and the Shekecho number 77,678 (.11% of the population). The Omotic speakers are limited to a special area and yet are very diverse in linguistic use, suggesting that their ancestors settled in this area several millennia ago. Their languages have been influenced by the East Cushitic language group as well as the Nilo-Saharan linguistic groups, both of which surround them. Most Omotic speakers are of the enset diet culture, with hoe cultivation. Enset is produced on the southern highlands, whereas grains are cultivated on elevations below 4,921 feet. Many also are involved in animal husbandry. Gamu highlanders are well-known artisans and expert weavers. Their artwork, particularly in the area of colorful sophisticated weaving techniques, has made them known throughout the country. In Addis Ababa, they are invariably referred to as Dorzes, the name of just one of among the several Gamo groups. The Kafa, with a long-established monarchic system, are followers of Orthodox Christianity, their penetration by this religious denomination going back to the early 16th century, but most of the rest of the Omotic speakers practice their own animistic religions. A few have converted to Catholicism or Protestantism, and some others have adopted Islam.

In general, there are 29 Omotic languages:

- Anfillo
- Ari
- Bambassi
- Banna

- Basketto
- Bench
- Boro
- Chara
- Dime
- Dizzi
- Dorze
- Gamo-Gofa
- Ganza
- Hammer
- Hozo
- Kachama-Ganjule
- Kara
- Kafa
- Kore
- Male
- Melo
- Mocha
- Nayi
- Oyda
- Skahacho
- Sheko
- Walaytta (Walamo)
- Yemsa
- Zayse-Zergulla

The Nilotics, an entirely separate linguistic group, live in the far southwest and along the country's western borders. They are distinctively recognized in Ethiopia because of their physical features; they are invariably very dark in complexion as well as slim and tall in stature. Unlike all the previously mentioned groups, they do not have connection to the Afro-Asiatic stock. Instead, they are members of the Nilo-Saharan language groups. The largest numbers of Nilotic-language speakers are the Nuer and Anuak, who belong to the East Sudanic family. Whereas most Nuers are found in Sudan, the Anuak speakers are almost limited to Ethiopia. The great majority of Nilotic speakers are both cattle herders and hoe cultivators of grains. Some, such as the Nuer, are seminomadic.

The Kunama-speaking Nilotics are settled in western Tigray. As a result of missionary influence, the Kunama speakers are mostly Protestant and Catholic Christian in religion. Within the Nilotics group, the Berta, who live in the Benishangul–Gumuz regional state of western Ethiopia, adopted Islam as their religion. The

Koman speakers constitute a number of groups residing along the Ethio-Sudan border in western Wallaga. Among them are the Gumuz, who, together with the Berta, are also called the people of Beni Shangul.

In general, the Nilo Saharan language group includes 19 languages:

- Anuak
- Berta
- Gobato
- Gumuz
- Komo
- Kunama
- Kwama
- Kwegu
- Majang
- Me'en
- Murle
- Mursi
- Nera
- Nuer
- Nyangatom
- Opuuo
- Shabo
- Suri
- Uduk

TABLE 6.1   Percentage Distribution of Major Linguistic Groups for Population Above 1 Million: 2007

Ethnic group	2007 population	%
Oromo	25,488,344	34.5
Amhara	19,867,817	26.9
Somali	4,581,793	6.2
Tigre	4,483,776	6.1
Sidama	2,966,377	4.0
Gurage	1,867,350	2.5
Wolaita	1,707,074	2.3
Hadiya	1,284,366	1.7
Afar	1,276,372	1.7
Gamo	1,107,163	1.5

Source: Central Statistical Agency of Ethiopia, 2007.

LANGUAGE POLICY

For the last several hundred years, Amharic has been used as the court language of the Ethiopian Christian state and as the language of literature. Though the language was used widely by Ethiopian rulers of the Zemene Mesafint as well as Emperor Tewodros, and even the Tigrayan-born Emperor Yohannes, Amharic got its *lettre de noblesse* under Menelik. But Haile Selassie elevated it to an official status when he specified in article 125 of the Revised Constitution of Ethiopia that "the official language of the Empire is Amharic."

Though not specified in the constitution, there was also a silent recognition of English as a second working language so as to enable the government to have a convenient means of international communication. In schools, Amharic followed by English became the medium of instruction. The former was used up to the sixth grade no matter which ethnic group the children were from. Above grade seven, however, English was the medium of instruction. The communication media, which was a monopoly of the state, used only Amharic. Newspapers and radio and television broadcasts used only Amharic and to a lesser extent English as a medium of communication. Courts, even in localities where the plaintiff, defendant, and judges did not understand Amharic, had to be carried out through the intercession of a Simabelew (Amharic interpreter) to render the process legal. Catholic and Protestant churches that tried to use the local languages in their prayer books were forced to comply with the Amharization policy. Even though English was tolerated, local languages were not.

Before this policy was unveiled, many thought that following the example of Switzerland and Canada, which had adopted multiple official languages to reflect the ethnic mosaic of their nations, Haile Selassie would recognize Afaan Oromo and Tigrigna as second and third official languages of country. The elevation of Amharic as the only official language of Ethiopia and its rigid application therefore angered many ethnic groups, especially the majority Oromos and the third-largest nationality, the Tigrayans. The latter's case became an incendiary issue, given that before Eritrea's federation with Ethiopia, the use of Tigrigna and Arabic were considered sacrosanct. The matter became politically explosive when Haile Selassie's Amharization policy went to the extent of ordering the confiscation and destruction of all materials written in languages other than Amharic. Books written by Aba Gamachis were hunted down and burned by government agents. This was one of the major grievances of the Oromo Liberation Front when it started guerrilla war in the mid-1970s. The same was true of the Eritrean People's Liberation Front, ultimately opening the way for the dismemberment of the country.

That being said, Haile Selassie's adaption of English as the second language of communication indicated Haile Selassie's great foresight. He, together with his old guard, including the prime minister, were French-speaking. However, he had recognized as early as 1941, when World War II was still raging, that because of the rise of the United States as a superpower when the former great powers were ready to decimate one another, English was going to replace French as the language of diplomacy and international communication.

A language policy change came following the fall of the Haile Selassie regime in 1974. Influenced by student radicals who were advisers to the Derg, and taking a cue from the Socialist bloc where the right of nationalities is emphasized, the Derg declared in its National Democratic Revolution Program,

> Each nationality will have regional autonomy to decide on matters concerning its internal affairs. Within its environments, it has the right to determine the contents of its political, economic and social life use its own language and elect its own leaders and administrators to head its internal organs. (Provisional Military Administrative Council, 1976)

Furthermore, in its 1987 constitution, the Derg emphasized, "The People's Democratic Republic of Ethiopia shall ensure the equality, development and respectability of the languages of nationalities." However, there was a caveat. The prominence of Amharic was to be kept. The Constitution said, "Without prejudice to Article 2 sub-article 5 of this Constitution, in the People's Democratic Republic of Ethiopia, the working language of the State shall be Amharic."

After assuring the key place of Amharic, the government passed to experts at the Ethiopian Language Academy the responsibility for the phonological and grammatical treatment of scores of tongues, the adaption of the existing alphabet or the creation of new alphabets, and the laying of groundwork for dictionaries to standardize languages and dialects. The professionals in this academy engaged in a thorough study of not only Amharic but also Afaan Oromo, Tigrigna, Sidama Walaytta, and other languages, in the fields of literature, linguistic structure, terminology, and lexicography.

The applications of the proclamations for the numerous Ethiopian languages were hampered by the great diversity that existed in the country and the uneven stages of their internal development. Other than Amharic, only Tigrigna and to a lesser extent Afaan Oromo, which had been used on previous occasions, were ready to implement the policy declaration. Thus, a detailed study of the different languages in terms of orthography and phonology became urgent. In the meantime, Amharic and English continued to be the mediums of instruction in all Ethiopian schools. But in the mass literacy campaign aimed at adults, about 15 local Ethiopian languages were employed.

The biggest hurdle was whether the Ge'ez syllabary or the Latin alphabet should be adapted, particularly for the language of the majority Oromos. It did not take long for the government to come to the conclusion that the Ge'ez alphabet was better because it would facilitate the reading and writing ability of the learners, given that many of them were already adept at the use of it in the Amharic curriculum. Additionally, the Ethiopic script, the only indigenous script in Africa, was considered a unique symbol of national identity that could not be so easily bypassed. But this was fiercely disputed by ethno-nationalists who argued that the policy was simply a political decision, not one based on utility. The argument for the Latin script came up again after the overthrow of the Derg in 1991. One of the supporters of Qube, the Latin script developed for writing Oromo, Professor Tilahun Gamta of Addis Ababa University, presented the following argument:

A priest at a Dabra Berhan church reading scriptures that are handwritten on parchment in the Ethiopic syllabary. (Photo by Three Lions/Getty Images.)

1. Whereas there are 26 characters in the Latin alphabet there are 189 characters in the "Sabean";

2. Long vowels and short consonants are hard to distinguish in the "Sabean" script;

3. Word-processors make use of the Latin script. So, as a result, the adoption of the Latin script will help Ethiopian scholars who go to the West to attend meetings and conferences. That way they need not carry "Sabean" type software or hardware;

4. It does not take long for one to learn the Latin script. The Sabean onc is clearly much harder to master in a short time.

5. The use of the "Sabean" script would require the invention of several other symbols to represent syllables, accents, and sounds. Machines or software need to be made to accommodate those, thus making it an expensive enterprise;

6. For Afaan Oromo, there are not much [material] written in the Sabean script. Thus it will not be expensive to translate the few already in existence such as the cultural and religious works of Anisimos Nesib and others.

7. The use of Latin instead of Sabean would help foreigners who are interested in learning Afaan Oromo.

8. The use of Latin will enable the Oromos to communicate with major Western countries such as the U.S and the U.K. as well as neighbors such as Kenya, Somalia, Djibouti who use the Latin script.

9. Oromo children who learn Latin at an early age would find it useful to learn English and French at a later stage.

10. Adopting Qube which is based on Latin will help readers improve their reading and writing ability. (Tilahun Gamta, 1992)

Professor Baye Yimam of Addis Ababa University argued in opposition to Professor Tilahun Gamta in the following manner:

The suggestion that the Ethiopic script is too numerous [i.e. 189] compared with the Latin script which is only 26 enabling the learner literate does not consider the fact that the Latin scripts concentrate on sound while the Ethiopic scripts represent syllables. If it is suggested that the Latin script has 26 letters, one can also suggest that Ethiopic has only 27. This is the case when one does not count the letters with vowel variations. In that sense then, again there isn't any significant difference. If we take the vowel combinations, then Latin also has 130 (26×5) scripts compared to Ethiopic which has 189 (27×7). Professor Tilahun's line of reasoning does not consider the fact that the Latin script has more than one form. For instance, the signs of the Latin script do not follow specific patterns. Each is discrete. By comparison, Ethiopic scripts can be employed in relation to one another. Recognizant the names of the Latin scripts does not simplify reading Afaan Oromo accurately. The scripts do not pose problems. What poses problems is the system one follows in teaching. Hence, a teacher who understands well how the Ethiopic scripts are formed should not have a problem to teach all the scripts in a (relatively) short period of time. The problem of the Ethiopic script not showing ong sounds and stresses can easily be ameliorated by adding a few more symbols. (Baye Yimam, 1992)

The Latin script, it is stressed, also has its own problems, similar to many of the problems mentioned in connection to Ethiopic. For example, it does not always exactly indicate a word as understood by the speaker. Amharic is now written using computer software. Even though the computer is based on the Latin script, the software is capable of converting typed Latin script to Ethiopic script. Other non-Latin writing systems such as Japanese use a similar method. Even though Mandarin has the most number of pictographs in the world, Chinese scholars have reduced its number and have adapted it to the Latin script so that one can write Mandarin on a typewriter made for the Latin script. The change is in technology, not in script. One should bear in mind that over and above its utility in conveying words, a script is also an important symbol of national identity. If there are any grounds for substituting Ethiopic for Latin, they are not based on linguistic requisites: the reasoning is strictly political.

After the fall of the Derg, the constitution of the Federal Democratic Republic of Ethiopia that was adopted in 1994 recognized equal rights for all Ethiopian languages. Article 5 declares, "All Ethiopian languages shall enjoy equal State recognition," and "each member of the Federation shall determine its own working language." However, it also added, "Amharic shall be the working language of the Federal Democratic Republic of Ethiopia." Unlike the Derg, the EPRDF government had decided to introduce local languages in the formal educational sector. It was determined that approximately 25 Ethiopian languages were to be employed as mediums of instruction in primary schooling.

Though this was an admirable step, myriad problems arose. The sudden adaption of the Latin script for almost all non-Semitic languages led to chaos. Lack of sufficient information on the distribution of the local languages and their employment as mother tongues, or second or third languages, and the degree of bilingualism in Amharic among speakers of other mother tongues also created utter confusion.

In one case, in the late 1990s, the EPRDF government took an approach that wreaked havoc in the schools in the Omotic-speaking region of Ethiopia. Even though the EPRDF government, along with its offshoot that ruled the southern states, argued that the goal was to address a real problem related to issues of language policy, managing diversity, and governance, it was a policy with an excessive top-down approach that resulted in bloodshed. The case involved the government's attempt to unite the people of North Omo by creating a brand new language called Wogagoda, which is an acronym for Wolaita, Gamo, Gofa, and Dawro, which have distinct dialects of their own. The newly invented communication medium was declared an official language of instruction for the North Omo zone. This led to mass protests by the Walaitas, the largest among the Omo states. When teachers refused to apply the policy, the local government herded them into jail. At the height of the conflict in 1999, students in Soddo broke into police stations and freed teachers imprisoned for opposing Wogagoda. They also stormed shops and torched Wogagoda textbooks. In the ensuing mêlée, 5 people were killed, 11 were shot and wounded, and 78 were detained. Schools in Wolaita were subsequently closed and were not reopened until two months later. Shaken by the development, the government was forced to backtrack on its policy by reinstating the naturally developed languages in place of Wogagoda.

ETHIOPIC ALPHABET

The Ethiopic alphabet is the second oldest alphabet in Africa. Though the original version, which was written in boustrophedon (plough) style precedes it by a millennium, the present form of the alphabet (also referred to as the Ge'ez alphabet) is traced to the third century A.D. Its structure is strictly phonetic. One writes the way the word of the language sounds. For example, there are no separate vowels. Though there are 17 basic letters or consonants in the entire syllabary, each consonant has seven variations that makes them different from one another by the vowel symbols.

For example, if you want to write Europe, you write "Yurop" with the "Yu" represented by a single symbol, and "ro" with another single letter and p with just "p." The following is the entire Ethiopic alphabet, the first letter being a consonant and the following 6 letters being variations of the first one with symbols that represent vowels.

ETHIOPIC ALPHABET

he	hu:	hi:	ha:	he:	hə	ho:		ke	ku:	ki:	ka:	ke:	kə	ko:
le	lu:	li:	la:	le:	lə	lo:		we	wu:	wi:	wa:	we:	wə	wo:
ḥe	ḥu:	ḥi:	ḥa:	ḥe:	ḥə	ḥo:		'e	'u:	'i:	'a:	'e:	'ə	'o:
me	mu:	mi:	ma:	me:	mə	mo:		ze	zu:	zi:	za:	ze:	zə	zo:
se	su:	si:	sa:	se:	sə	so:		je	ju:	ji:	ja:	je:	jə	jo:
re	ru:	ri:	ra:	re:	rə	ro:		de	du:	di:	da:	de:	də	do:
še	šu:	ši:	ša:	še:	šə	šo:		ge	gu:	gi:	ga:	ge:	gə	go:
qe	qu:	qi:	qa:	qe:	qə	qo:		ṭe	ṭu:	ṭi:	ṭa:	ṭe:	ṭə	ṭo:
be	bu:	bi:	ba:	be:	bə	bo:		p'e	p'u:	p'i:	p'a:	p'e:	p'ə	p'o:
te	tu:	ti:	ta:	te:	tə	to:		ṣe	ṣu:	ṣi:	ṣa:	ṣe:	ṣə	ṣo:
ḫe	ḫu:	ḫi:	ḫa:	ḫe:	ḫə	ḫo:		ḍe	ḍu:	ḍi:	ḍa:	ḍe:	ḍə	ḍo:
ne	nu:	ni:	na:	ne:	nə	no:		fe	fu:	fi:	fa:	fe:	fə	fo:
'e	'u:	'i:	'a:	'e:	'ə	'o:		pe	pu:	pi:	pa:	pe:	pə	po:

MEETING PEOPLE

Are you all right?—*Dahna nah?* (m) / *Dahna nash?* (f) / *Dahna nachihu?* (plural or respect)

Be patient—*Tagashee* (f) / *Tagas* (m) / *Yitagasu* (respect)

Do you speak Amharic?—*Amarigna Tichilalah?* (m) / *Amarigna Tichiyalash?* (f) / *Amarigna yichilallu?* (respect)

Do you speak English?—*Inglizigna tinagaralah?* (m) / *Englizigna Tinagerialesh?* (f) / *Englizigna Yinagaralu?* (respect, for someone in authority or older than oneself)

Do you understand?—*Gilts naw?*

Don't be afraid!—*Ayzosh!* (f) / *Ayzoh!* (m)

Excuse me—*Yeqerta*

Friend—*gwadagna*

Good day—*Malkam qan*

Good evening—*Malkam mishit*

Goodbye—*Tanaystilign*

Hello—*Salam* (formal) / *Tadiyass* (informal)

Hey, you!—*Anta!* (m) / *Anchee!* (f)

House—*bet*

How are you?—*Hiywat indet naw?*

How do you say it in Amharic?—*Bamarigna indeit yibalal?*

Hurry up!—*Tolo!*

I am fine—*Dahna nagn*

I do not understand—*Alagabagnem*

I don't know—*Alawqim*

I know—*Awqalahu*

I love you—*Iwadishalahu* (f) / *Iwadihalahu* (m)

I understand—*Gabbagn*

Let us go—*Eneheed*

Love—*fiqir*

Merry Christmas—*Malkam Ganna*

No—*aydalam*

Old man—*shimagele*

Old woman—*arogeet*

Please—*ibahkish* (f) / *ibakih* (m) / *ibakwo* (respect/plural)

Responsible—*halafee*

School—*temhirt bet*

Show me—*Istee?*

Sit down—*Qutchbal* (m) / *Qutch bayi* (f) / *Qutchbalu* (plural)

Smart/good job—*gobaz*

Son—*wand lidj*

Sorry—*Aznalahu*

Stop!—*Qoom!* (m) / *Qoomee!* (f)

Strong—*tankara*

Thank you—*Amasaginalahu*

Thank you very much—*Batam amasagenalahu*

Wait—*Qoy*

What?—*Min?*

What's your name?—*Semeh mannaw?* (m) / *Semesh mannaw?* (f)

Where are you from?—*Kayét nah?* (m) / *Kayét nash?* (f) / *Kayét nawot?* (respect)

Why?—*Lamin?*

Yes, a little bit—*Awo tenesh tenesh*

Welcome—*Enkwan dahna mattash* (f) / *Enkwan dahna mattah* (m)

Yes—*Awo*

You are welcome—*Malkam* (or *Menem-ayadalam*)

Your name?—*Semeesh?* (f) / *Semeeh?* (m) / *Semwo?* (respect)

FAMILY

Aunt: *akist*

Brother: *wandim*

Daughter: *se't lidj*

Family: *beta sab*

Father: *abbat*

Husband: *bal*

Mother: *ennat*

Relative/Cousin: *zamad*

Sister: *ehet*

Son: *wand lidj*

Uncle: *aggot*

Wife: *meest*

HOSPITALITY AND FOOD

A lot: *bezu*

Again: *indagana*

Banana: *muz*

Bathroom: *matatabya bet*

Be careful: *Tatanqaq* (m) / *Tatanqaqi* (f)

Bed: *alga*

Beef: *yebaré siga*

Beer: *birra*

Big: *tiliq*

Breakfast: *qurs*

Bring more: *Yichamar*

Cent: *santeem*

Chicken: *doro*

Clean: *netsuh*

Coffee: *bunna*

Cold: *qazqaza*

Correct: *lik*

Cost: *waga*

Dinner: *rat*

Egg: *inqulal*

Enough! *Baqqa! / Yibaqal!*

Fish: *asa*

Food: *megeb*

Fork: *shukka*

Glass: *berchekko*

Good: *tiru*

Great: *batam tiru*

Honey: *mar*

Hot: *muq*

House: *bet*

How much is it? *Sent naw?*

How much is the bill? *Hisab sintnaw?*

I am full (can't eat more): *Tagabku or baqqa*

I am hungry: *Rabagn*

I don't want it: *Alfaligem*

Juice: *chemmaqee*

Little: *tenneesh*

Luggage: *shanta*

Lunch: *mesa*

Meat: *sega*

Milk: *watat*

Money: *ganzab*

More: *chimaree*

Nice: *malkam*

No problem: *chigir yalam*

Not yet: *gana naw*

Okay? *Eshee?*

Ready: *zegeju*

Room: *kifil*

Salt: *chaw*

Shower room: *matatabya bet*

Small: *teneesh*

Soap: *samuna*

Spoon: *manka*

Swimming pool: *wanna bota*

Thank you: *amasagenalahu*

There is a problem: *chigir alla*

Toilet: *shentbeit*

Water: *wooha*

CLOTHING

Attire: *lebs*

Belt: *maqannat*

Blanket: *berd-lebs*

Blouse: *shurrab*

Hat: *barneta*

Jacket: *kot* / *kapport* (for a long jacket)

Pants: *surree*

Shirt: *shameez*

Shoe: *tchamma*

Skirt: *qamees*

Socks: *kalsee*

Underpants: *wustlebs*

TIME

Ethiopian time is calculated by 12 hours for day and night separately. For example, 7:00 a.m. in the morning is one o'clock daytime (*kaqanu and sa'at*), and 7:00 p.m. in the evening is one o'clock evening time (*kaleilitu and sa'at*).

7:00 a.m.—*and sa'at*

7:05—*and kamist*

7:10—*and kaser*

7:15—*and kasramest*

7:20—*and kahya*

7:25—*and kahayamest*

7:30—*and takul*

7:35—*lahulat hayamest gudday*

7:40—*lahulat haya gudday*

7:45—*lahulat rub gudday*

7:50—*lahulat asser gudday*

7:55—*lahulat amest gudday*

8:00—*hulat sa'at*

Afternoon: *kasa'at bahuwala*

Before: *majamarya* / *bafeet*

Evening: *mata*

Hour: *sa'at*

Just a minute: *and geezé*

Later: *bahuala*

Morning: *twat*

Night: *léileet*

Not yet: *gana naw*

Now: *ahun*

Today: *zaré*

Tomorrow: *naga*

Yesterday: *tenant*

TOURS

What time does it arrive there?—*Basent ezeya yedarsal?*

What time does it leave?—*Basent yennassal?*

Where is the airport?—*Aeroplan tabeya yet naw?*

Where is the bus going?—*Yetnaw awtobus yemeehédaw?*

USEFUL PHRASES

Excuse me—*Yeqerta*

How much does it cost?—*Wagaw sentnaw?*

Make a discount—*Waga qanis*

Where is the post office?—*Postabet yetnaw?*

What is the time?—*Sa'at sentnaw?*

What is your name? *Semesh mannaw?* (f) / *Semeh mannaw?* (m)

EVERYDAY USEFUL WORDS

And: *enna*

At: *ba*

Purse: *borsa*

Bad: *matfo*

Ball: *kwass*

Beautiful: *qonjo*

Bicycle: *bisikleit*

Bus: *awtobus*

But: *gin* (*g* as in "margin")

Car/Vehicle: *makeena*

Cart: *garee*

Cat: *demmat*

Character: *tabay*

Church: *béta kristyan*

Come: *naa* (m) / *nayee* (f)

Country (or region): *agar*

Cow: *lam*

Dirty: *qoshasha*

Doctor: *hakeem*

Dog: *wusha*

Donkey: *aheyya*

Ethiopian: *Habasha* (or *Etiopiawee*)

Far: *ruq*

Fast: *fattan*

First: *andagna*

Flower: *ababa*

Forever: *zalalam*

Go: *heed* (m) / *heejee* (f)

He: *issu*

Help me! *Irdugn!*

Here: *ezeeeh*

Horse: *faras*

Hospital: *hakim-bet*

I/me: *ené*

Insect: *tenegn*

Inside: *wust*

Island: *dassét*

Key: *qulf*

Lake: *hayeeq*

Lamb: *yabag-tebbot*

Mosque: *masgeed*

Mountain: *tarara*

Mr.: *ato*

Mrs.: *wayzaro*

Ms.: *wayzarit*

Much: *bezu*

Mutton: *yabag sega*

Near: *atagab* (or *qirb*)

New: *addis*

Newspaper: *gazeta*

Nice: *tiru*

Night: *laleet*

Now: *ahun*

Of: *ye*

Or: *waynem*

Orange: *bertukan*

Peace: *salam*

Pen: *be'er*

Petrol: *benzeen*

Pig: *asama*

Problem: *chiggir*

Quickly: *tolo*

Rain: *zenab*

Region: *bota*

Restaurant: *megeb beit*

River: *wanz*

Road: *mangad*

Sea: *baher*

She: *isswa*

Sheep: *bag*

Shop: *suq*

Short: *acher*

Sleep: *enqelf*

Slowly: *qas*

Small: *teneesh*

Sorry: *aznallahu*

Stop: *akum*

Sugar: *sukwar*

Tall: *rajem*

Tea: *shai*

There: *izia*

They: *innassu*

Today: *zarê*

Tomorrow: *naga*

Very: *batam*

Warm: *muq*

Water: *wuha*

White man: *faranj*

Yesterday: *tilant*

You: *anchee* (f) / *anta* (m)

NUMBERS

1: *and*

2: *hulat*

3: *sost*

4: *arat*

5: *amest*

6: *sedest*

7: *sabat*

8: *sement*

9: *zatagn*

10: *aser*

20: *haya*

30: *salasa*

40: *arba*

50: *hamsa*

60: *selsa*

70: *saba*

80: *samanea*

90: *zatana*

100: *mato*

1,000: *sheeh*

1,000,000: *meelyon*

DAYS OF THE WEEK

Sunday: *Ehud*

Monday: *Sagno*

Tuesday: *Maksagno*

Wednesday: *Rob*

Thursday: *Hamus*

Friday: *Arb*

Saturday: *Qedamé*

FESTIVALS

Christmas: *Ganna*

Easter: *Fasika*

Epiphany: *Timqat*

Finding of the True Cross: *Masqal*

New Year: *Addis Amat* or *Enqutatash* (falls on September 12, in the Ethiopian calendar)

Happy Birthday: *Malkam Ledat*

Happy New Year: *Malkam Addis Amat*

WORDS AND PHRASES IN TIGRIGNA

Bad: *himek*

Beautiful: *gondjo*

Black: *tsalim*

Border: *dob*

Fine: *tsebuk*

Goodbye: *daahankun* or *salamat*

Here: *hausi*

Hotel room: *madakasi*

How are you? *kamayla-hee* (f) / *kamayla-ha* (m)

How much? *kendai*

Milk: *tsaba*

Nice: *Dahan*

No: *nanai* or *yachone*

Okay: *hirai*

Red: *kaje*

Thank you: *Yakanyalay*

The coffee tastes good: *Oo oum bunna*

Today: *lomo anti*

Water: *mai*

What is your name? *Shimka man yoe?*

Where? *Lafe?*

White: *tsaada*

Yes: *ouwa*

Yesterday: *tsbah*

1: *hada*

2: *kilita*

3: *salista*

4: *arbata*

5: *hamishta*

6: *shidista*

7: *showata*

8: *shimwunta*

9: *tishiata*

10: *aseta*

WORDS AND PHRASES IN THE OROMO LANGUAGE

Again: *ammas* / *lammaffa*

Bad: *gadhé*

Black: *guracha*

Bring: *feedee*

Brother: *obbolessa*

Brown: *magala*

Buy: *beetu*

Child: *mutchaa*

Children: *ejollé*

Come: *kottu*

Cost: *gatee*

Day: *guyyaa*

Did you understand? *Esenee galéra?*

Do you speak English? *Afan Englizi betta?*

Drink: *dhuga*

Eat: *gnadhu*

Enter: *leetee*

Far: *fago*

Fast: *dafee*

Fine: *nagaa / fayyaa*

Fire: *abidda*

Girlfriend/boyfriend: *meetchu*

Go: *demee*

Going: *dému*

Good: *bayéssaa*

Goodbye: *nagatee*

Green: *magarsu*

Grey: *dalacha*

Hello: *ashamaa / attam*

Here: *asee / addanaa*

House: *manaa*

How are you? *Attam jerta / Attam jertu?* (respect)

How much is the cost? *Méqaa?*

I do not: *Lakkee*

Late: *turu*

Light: *ebsaa*

Man: *namaa*

Male: *dheeraa*

Money: *hori*

Mosquito: *boké*

Mother: *haadha*

Mountain: *tullu / gaara*

Night: *halkan*

No problem: *rakkon henjeru*

Now: *amma*

Oromo language: *Afaan Oromo*

Please: *maalo*

Red: *deemaa*

Road: *karaa*

Sister: *oboletee*

Thank you: *galatoommaa*

There: *achee*

Today: *haraa*

Tomorrow: *bor*

Village: *ganda*

Water: *beshaan*

What is your name? *Maqanké egnu?*

When: *yom*

Where is it? *Essa jeera?*

White: *adee*

Woman: *dubartee*

Yellow: *kêllo*

Yes (I do): *Éyyé*

DAYS OF THE WEEK IN AFAAN OROMO

Sunday: *Dilbata / Sanbata-Gudda*

Monday: *Dafino / Wixataa*

Tuesday: *Fatchasaa / Kibxata*

Wednesday: *Robi*

Thursday: *Kameesa*

Friday: *Jeemata*

Saturday: *Sanbata Dura*

NUMBERS IN AFAAN OROMO

1: *toko*

2: *lama*

3: *sadee*

4: *afur*

5: *shan*

6: *ja'a*

7: *torba*

8: *saddét*

9: *sagal*

10: *kudhan*

20: *diddama*

30: *soddoma*

40: *afurtama*

50: *shantama*

60: *jatama*

70: *torbatama*

80: *saddettama*

90: *sagaltama*

100: *dhibbaa*

1,000: *kumaa*

1,000,000: *meeleyonee*

REFERENCES

Ahland, M. B. 2004. *Language Death in Mesmes: A Sociolinguistic and Historical-Comparative Examination of a Disappearing Ethiopian-Semitic Language*. Dallas: University of Texas at Arlington.

Baye Yimam. 1992, March. "Wyiyit." *Dialogue*. 1(1):1–5.

Bender, M. L. 1976. *The Non-Semitic Languages of Ethiopia*. East Lansing: African Studies Center, Michigan State University.

Heine, B., and D. Nurse. 2008. *A Linguistic Geography of Africa*. Cambridge, UK: Cambridge University Press.

Kebede Hordofa, J. 1996. *A Comparative Study of Oromo Dialects: Aspects of Assimilation*. Addis Ababa: Academy of Ethiopian Languages, Ministry of Information & Culture.

Leslau, W. 1946. *Bibliography of the Semitic Languages of Ethiopia*. New York: New York Public Library.

Leslau, W. 1965. *An Annotated Bibliography of the Semitic Languages of Ethiopia*. The Hague, Netherlands: Mouton.

Leslau, W., and G. Hudson. 1996. *Essays on Gurage Language and Culture: Dedicated to Wolf Leslau on the Occasion of His 90th Birthday, November 14th, 1996*. Wiesbaden, Germany: Harrassowitz.

Littmann, E. 1904. *Bibliotheca Abessinica; Studies Concerning the Languages, Literature and History of Abyssinia*. Princeton, NJ: Princeton University Library.

Pankhurst, R. 1969. *Language and Education in Ethiopia: Historical Background to the Post-War Period.* Addis Ababa, Ethiopia: H.S.I.U.

Provisional Military Administrative Council. 1976. YeEtiopia Beherawi Democrasiawi Abiot Program (Amharic). Addis Ababa: Artistic Printing Press. Gebre, W. K. 2002. *Analysis of Culture for Planning Curriculum: The Case of Songs Produced in the Three Main Languages of Ethiopia Amharic, Oromigna and Tigrigna.* Joensuu, Finland: University of Joensuu, Faculty of Education.

Schneider-Blum, G. 2007. *A Grammar of Alaaba: A Highland East Cushitic Language of Ethiopia.* Köln, Germany: Rüdiger Köppe Verlag.

Tilahun Gamta. 1992. "Qube Afaan Oromo." Oromo Studies Conference, 1–10.

Ullendorff, E. 1955. *The Semitic Languages of Ethiopia: A Comparative Phonology.* London: Taylor's Foreign Press.

Ullendorff, E. 1995. *From Emperor Haile Selassie to H.J. Polotsky: An Ethiopian and Semitic Miscellany.* Wiesbaden: Harrassowitz Verlag.

Unseth, P. 1990. *Linguistic Bibliography of the Non-Semitic Languages of Ethiopia.* East Lansing: African Studies Center, Michigan State University.

YeEtiopia Quanquawoch Akademy. 1986. *Facts and Figures.* Addis Ababa, Ethiopia: Academy of Ethiopian Languages.

YeEtiopia Quanquawoch Akademy. 1982. *English–Amharic Glossary of Scientific and Technical Terms: Preliminary List I.* Addis Ababa, Ethiopia: The Project.

Etiquette

Ethiopians are extremely courteous individuals, and people try to stick to their age-old cultural traditions. A person coming from another culture has to know how to honor those traditions. The following are key points to remember.

GREETINGS

Ethiopia is a country of over 80 linguistic groups. So greeting and signs of respect vary. Because the Amhara culture has permeated the society, and all foreigners will have to deal with Ethiopians the Amharic way, it is better to concentrate on it. Forms of respect are expressed differently between younger and older persons, between equals, and between lower- and upper-class persons.

Whether the individuals are of a higher- or lower-class background, signs of children's respect toward their father and toward their elders can be distinguished. Up to the age of 15, a youngster kisses the feet of his or her father when the father has been absent from home for several days. The father picks up the child by the chin and kisses him or her on both cheeks. Because reciprocity of kisses is the rule, they both kiss each other three times or more. Starting from 16 years of age to the time of marriage, a son kisses not the feet but the knees of his father. Once married, the son bows his head about three feet in front of his father and then goes on to kiss his father's cheeks. The father reciprocates, and again they kiss each other on the cheeks three times or more. The Tigrayans differ a little bit. In their case, only the father kisses the son, or the elder the younger, and there is no reciprocal kissing. However, among equals, kissing is reciprocal. In the case of the Amharas, those who are equals kiss each other's cheeks in turn. Kisses are signs of respect, and the gradual advancement from feet to cheeks is a significant offering of respect by the father to the son. The general rules between father and son are applied similarly to father and daughter and mother and son, as well as elder members of the family or acquaintances. Total strangers can be treated by a youngster with a deep bow only. Kissing is not initiated unless the older stretches his hand, hinting at kissing the youngster.

Signs of respect among average individuals in mainstream Ethiopia are divided into two categories: those used outdoors and those used indoors. When two acquaintances meet each other outdoors, say, on the street, both remove any covers they may have on their heads and make a little bow with the head. They say, for example, "How have you passed the night? How have you been? Is your family doing well? Is all well?" to which the other replies, "Very good, thanks to God, and yours?" If they are mounted on horses or mules, both get off and remove their hats and ask each other's health the same way before mounting their animals again and proceeding on their travel. In all cases, men remove their hats, whereas women bow their heads a little bit and pull back the shamma or shawl that covers their head partially.

Within the house, and in relation to dining habits, the etiquette between friends and invitees is a little bit modified. When a person who is invited to dinner reaches the gate of his/her host's house, he/she sends someone, usually a servant of the host who is waiting outside, to announce his/her arrival. The host exits the house; bows his/her head low; says, "How do you do?"; and invites the guest in. When the host enters the house, everybody inside rises from his/her seat and says "yinuru," which means "live!" The guest quickly proceeds to the seat prepared for him with a bowed head while repeating the words "please sit down in the name of God!" Then he/she politely squats on a chair or a stool.

The guest is offered water to wash his hands, both before and after dinner. In each case, he must rise up and wash as a sign of respect to his hosts. When food, which is the ubiquitous *injera* and *wat*, is placed in front of the guest and the hosts, the host breaks a piece of injera and offers it to his wife. Then first the invited guest or guests followed by all adults at the table start to dip their injera in the wat, or *souse*, and eat. A woman never initiates the dinner party by proceeding to eat first. She has to wait for her husband to start the process. Her main occupation at the table in addition to eating is to bring the wat (souse), put it near the *massob* (straw table), and pour it on top of the spread injera. While the dining goes on, if a piece of injera drops on the ground, one picks it up, kisses it quickly, and places it the edge of the *massob*. Hosts and guests are supposed to dine quietly except the sporadic urgings by the hosts to the guests "Please eat!"

Children never eat with their parents. In strict observance of time-honored Ethiopian tradition, the children stand up and wait until the elders have finished their dinner. During the meal, however, the hosts or the guests may give the standing children a *gursha* (a bit of injera dipped in wat). The children come near and bow and twist their heads to receive the food, angling their neck at almost 90 degrees. It is when the adult dinner is complete that food, partly what remains and partly new, is offered to the children. At the completion of dinner, the guest blesses the hosts for their generosity and walks out of the house, bowing her head several times. She is accompanied by the hosts until she leaves the gate of the house.

When a person of lower social rank goes to the house of a superior to make a petition, he or she has to remove his or her shoes at the door. The supplicant if male, unwraps his shamma, twists the tips on both sides of the top of the toga, covers himself below the waist, bares his upper side, twists the tip on one side of the toga, and throws it up on his right shoulder. He crosses his arms at the chest and bows very low to the person of rank. He remains standing astride the wall and waits until told to sit down. When permitted to sit, he deliberately chooses a lower place. He must cross his legs as he sits and straighten his posture, with the head always bowed a little bit. He must not look at the person of rank straightforward. He must sit looking down to the floor in deference to the person of means.

The person of rank responds to the greeting from his inferior by bowing his head only a little bit. It is the supplicant not the superior who has to say the usual "ten-aystilign," which means "I wish you good health" or "How do you do?" The person in position of power always has a butler who responds to the greeting on behalf of his master. If a banquet is held while the person of lower social status is visiting, the ubiquitous *massob* is brought to the center of the dining room followed by a pot full of wat. At that point, the lower-ranked person rises and stands. He remains standing while the person of rank washes his hands. This is the procedure to be followed both before and after the meal.

As the superior washes his hands, one of the house attendants removes one end of his shamma from his shoulder and forms a curtain to shield the person of rank. This was done in archaic times to protect the master from an evil eye. A very important person may even shun himself from the remaining people at the dinner table in order to dine by himself, again to ward off the evil eye. After the superior finishes washing his hands, he dries them on a clean towel. If the towel is not ready, one of the attendants offers his or her clean shamma for the job. In the evening, because many people, even men of means, do not have electric lights in their houses, a servant or a young boy must stand holding a lit candle or lamp. The torchbearer must turn his face away from the dinner table and face the wall, the floor, the roof, or another object until the end of the meal. A person of lower rank is never allowed to sit and dine with a VIP unless the superior invites him to do so as a special favor. All the persons of lower rank sit around a separate *massob*, where they are usually served injera and wat of lower quality than that at the table of the VIP. It is unusual to eat on the street, so do not be surprised if people stare at you if you eat while walking.

When the VIP sneezes, all persons of lower rank must rise from their seats, slightly bow down, and say, "God bless you." In a situation when the person of lower rank wants to tell the VIP something important, she removes the tip of her shamma, covers her mouth lightly, bows a little bit, and speaks close to the ear in a hush-hush voice. She should remain in this position until the VIP responds in normal tone and then may return to her seat, bowing again.

When the VIP intends to speak to another person and for that purpose utters a name, the person whose name is uttered must quickly rise and say, "Abet Getaye!" which means "Yes, my lord!" If the VIP commands someone to do a chore, she must bow her head low and proceed to do it or promise to do it if it is not urgent. The lower-status person must never refuse to do a chore in front of onlookers, even if the task is impossible to do. She must always say, "Yes, sir, I shall do it!" If she has doubts about fulfilling the task, she goes to the VIP in private and explains politely why it is not possible.

For the sake of honor, the house of the VIP has to be quiet. No loud voices are allowed. Even other VIPs present must communicate with one another in whisper. If they are far apart, one of the VIPs calls a servant, or a young boy, and whispers a message to his ear so that the servant can convey it to the person it is intended for. The servant or boy goes to the other VIP, covers his mouth with his shamma, and conveys the message to the VIP's ear. He listens to the reply and then goes to tell it to the original VIP.

Before going to bed, all Ethiopians traditionally wash their legs. Most get them washed by servants or small children. In the case of a VIP, the servant or child who washes the feet of the master kisses them to prove they are clean and to show his humility.

The etiquette regarding interactions outdoors is as diverse as the etiquette used indoors. A commoner on the road traveling with someone of superior rank is not supposed to mount his mule or horse unless he is provided permission by the VIP. He keeps walking on foot, at the side of the VIP, bearing his gun on his shoulder. When the VIP mounts his mule or horse, the person of lower rank must rush and hold the stirrup for the VIP's safety. In a situation in which a person of lower rank has been offered permission to ride his mule or horse, if the VIP starts to speak to him, he has to dismount first before responding. After the answer, he has to wait for the VIP to invite him to mount his mule or horse again.

In a situation in which a person of lower rank riding a mule or horse meets a VIP she knows coming from the opposite direction, she must promptly dismount and bow down very low to the ground without uttering a word. Then she interrupts her original journey and starts to follow the VIP on foot [walking his mule if he has no servant] in the opposite direction. The moment permission is given, the lower-rank person walks fast past the VIP's mule or horse to bow down low. Then and only then can she mount her own horse or mule and continue on her original journey.

In a situation in which two VIPs on mule or horseback encounter each other on the way, both must dismount. They bow slightly to one another, ask for each other's health, remount their animals, and move on. If one of the VIPs is a younger person, he waits until the elder VIP has mounted his mule or horse before doing so himself and moving on.

If two VIPs meet at the crossroads, the younger of the two or the one who is inferior in social rank must let the superior or the elder one proceed first. It is totally forbidden for a servant to ride the mule of his master even if he is alone. He has to hold the animal by a rope and walk in front of it.

All in all, this is the etiquette that has been passed down for generations and is still respected and practiced in the countryside, where more than 85 percent of Ethiopians life. In the case of urbanized and modernized Ethiopians, who are currently a very small minority, many of the traditions mentioned here are not followed to the letter because of new developments. For example, urban people no longer travel by mules and horses; they travel by cars, buses, and trains. Urban people rarely wear the ever-present shamma of yesteryear. They are dressed in the Western fashion. They do not need servants or children holding lamps for them while they dine because they now have electric power in their houses. They do not need servants to wash their feet before they retire into bed at night because now they have modern bathrooms that they can use privately. However, they practice many of the traditions mentioned here with modifications to meet new exigencies.

GENERAL RULES OF ETHIOPIAN ETIQUETTE

On your first encounter, you should always address an Ethiopian man as "Ato" (sounds like "auto") for Mr.; an Ethiopian woman as "Woizero" (way-za-row) for Mrs.; and an unmarried Ethiopian lady as "Weizarit" (way-za-reet) for Miss. You should also use the titles "Doctor" or "Professor," as the case may be, followed by the person's first name. You should give and receive things like business cards, certificates, and bills, always showing respect. That means receiving the item with the right hand, while placing your left hand on your elbow to support your right hand.

When you find Ethiopians to be kind and generous, you ought to return the treatment in kind. Be caring and kind to them, but be careful about admiring your Ethiopian friend's possessions because he might present you with the object you admire, in which case you have no choice but to accept because refusal could be construed as disrespect.

Ethiopians kiss and shake hands, but there is a caveat. Shaking of hands is basically an informal gesture, and when done, it lingers more than in the West. It is done only between people of equal rank. But when it is done, the hands will be held throughout the health inquiry. In most cases, a handshake is accompanied by leaning toward one's counterpart and having the right shoulders touch. The touching of shoulders is a new habit; it did not exist three decades ago. Traditional and older people hug each other if they are relatives or friends of equal rank but they do not simply touch the right shoulders as young Ethiopians do.

Kissing is very common and is done regardless of the gender of one's counterpart. Friends kiss each other's cheeks—interspaced with the verbal inquiry of health. Among relatives, kisses can be on the cheeks as well as the mouth.

If the individual you meet is a very important person, you simply bow and do not attempt to shake hands unless the person stretches a hand toward you. If he does, you hold your right elbow with your left palm, bow low, and shake hands.

Young people and children, in particular, bow to older people to indicate their respect. They also avoid direct eye contact. As you exchange greetings, you repeatedly ask about the welfare and health of the person and his family and children. No matter whether the person one meets is friend, family, or stranger, an inquiry is made. Before speaking, both individuals bow low to each other, even if the encounter is among equals. Then either you or your counterpart asks, "How are you?" The appropriate answer is always "Thanks be to God, I am well. How are you?" You say this whether you are well or not because to give an actual account of one's health is indiscreet. The age-old Ethiopian Christian tradition requires that you provide positive answers, always prefaced with "thanks be to God" in order to show proper reverence to your religious convictions.

In the inquiry, each individual asks not only about the health of the other but also about family members, business, harvest, and animals. The answers are always "Thanks be to God." They are also always positive. If there is bad news, it is kept to the end. If the individuals greeting each other are in a hurry, greetings will still continue while each is walking in the opposite direction. This will be done with a high voice as long as one is within hearing distance. Besides the bow, other gestures are common during Ethiopian greetings.

When greeting a person of rank, one has to remove any head covering, and the shamma has to be unwound and its ends folded and then thrown on one's shoulders. After that, one's right hand has to touch the ground and, in supplication, the lips. Children greet their parents or older relatives and even respected strangers by prostrating themselves fully to the ground and kissing their feet.

Neighbors invite one another every morning in order to hold the traditional coffee ceremony where they also chat about matters concerning them. A coffee ceremony can go on for an hour and may be repeated soon after in another home. A guest is frequently offered coffee served in small cups. This is a key feature of Ethiopian hospitality, and to refuse is considered impolite. When elders enter a house, everybody, especially the junior members, get up until the elders are seated. You never greet a person older than you while seated because it is construed as very disrespectful and rude.

Unlike in the West, it is not inappropriate for two men to walk hand-in-hand in public. The younger generation do that more often. Men may exchange kisses on the cheek as well. These acts do not have any implication regarding their sexual preferences. Kissing on the cheeks and walking hand-in-hand are simple signs of camaraderie and friendship. Displays of affection such as kissing in public are frowned upon.

A man's elegance is judged by what he wears. Trousers are preferred to shorts and button-up shirts to t-shirts. Among modern Ethiopians, if one goes to an official meeting, collar and tie are expected. Females do not normally wear shorts and are expected to keep the length of their skirts far below the knee. Ladies are expected to cover themselves well above the waist including the shoulders.

Muslim women with scarves selling, buying, and bartering local and foreign goods in the marketplace of eastern Ethiopia. (Getty Images/Axel Fassio.)

In Ethiopia, dating is not a casual affair; it is usually considered a prelude to conjugal relations. If foreign women dating Ethiopian men do not make their intentions clear right from the beginning, confusion and unwanted behavior from the male partner may result during an attempt to end a casual relationship. When a woman accepts a man's invitation to his home, her acceptance may be mistaken as agreement to go to bed with him. Because they perceive foreign women to be liberal, Ethiopian men who are cautious with Ethiopian women may be aggressive with foreign women.

On entering a church or monastery, one needs to remove one's shoes. Some major monasteries do now allow women to enter. When invited to dinner, it is impolite to refuse. Once you arrive at the house, you have to eat a great deal as a way of courtesy. You will find that your host will press you to eat more than you really want to. Once you reach your limit, you may emphatically decline further helpings three times, after which you will be left alone and will not be pressed to eat more.

At a minimum, one has to have a taste of the food and drink and explain politely why it is enough. When water is brought to the table by older children or servants, you are expected to wash your hands, with which you eat; forks and spoons are not used in eating Ethiopian food. The housemaid or the women and the older children serve the food and stay in the background.

When calling young men or women to come, do not wiggle an index finger because this is rude and is reserved only for summoning pets. To gesture or beckon for someone to come to you, you should face your right palm toward them and make a series of downward motions with all the fingers but the thumb. Children are not supposed to speak with visitors. If they speak among themselves, they do so very quietly.

Food is first tasted by the master of the house, with prayers if he is religious, and guests follow. While eating from a common table, the previously mentioned *massob*, one should limit oneself to the food immediately in front of him or her. To try to take food from in front of another person at the same table is considered uncouth. But do not be surprised if at some stage someone, especially the wife of the host, starts to feed you from the portion in front of her. You are expected to be fed twice because feeding a guest only once is supposed to bring bad luck.

In fact, in a very traditional home, the young boys stand holding a lamp or a candle (where there is no electricity), turning their faces to the wall. Only when the diners finish their meal can they go to a corner or another room to eat their portion, a large part of which is leftovers from the adults' meal.

When you go to a restaurant, note that tips are included in the bill, so there is no need to give one once you pay. But if you offer one, do not give more than two birrs because instead of taking it as a generosity, the recipient might think that you are so rich that it does not matter how much you give. If you intend to take a common taxi that takes several people from your hotel to a restaurant or anywhere else, do not try to wait in a line as people tend to help themselves. Try to do the same and find your seat without waiting in line.

If you have an appointment with an Ethiopian, to meet at a restaurant or come over for dinner for example, do not be surprised if he or she is late by half an hour or even one hour. In the country's culture, humans and human relationships are more important than the clock. By the same token, deadlines may not work the same way they do in North America or Europe. Do not try to press that something be done by a specific date. Try to build flexibility into your timetable so that a delay will not cause your relationship to sour. In Ethiopia they say *tigist hulun yashenifal*, "patience is a virtue that wins over everything else."

Bargaining is common in every transaction, including those for market products, taxi service, and hotels, but not in modern department stores, restaurants, and public transport services. In Ethiopia, negotiators expect a counterpart to concede more on price and terms. In actual fact, Ethiopian businessmen determine the level of their success through bargaining and seeing how far they can move you down from your opening offer. The process of negotiation is considered a challenging contest, like competitive sport. So one is advised to build a large margin into an initial offer, leaving room for maneuvering. It is normal to walk away to check for a better price somewhere else or to consult with several shops before committing. Be calm, though you should feel free to show, surprise, shock, or indignation when prices seem too high. Someone who knows how the market works may buy an item or an animal such as a lamb that is initially quoted at 600 birr for only 200 birr!

Ethiopians are very proud and try their best not to ask for favors. But if they do ask, it is best to agree to do it, even if you think you might not be able to do so. The Ethiopian friend always understands if you explain that circumstances made it impossible to fulfill the promise. He will, nevertheless, greatly appreciate the fact that you agreed to try to help in the first place.

Because Ethiopians are polite, they also expect you to be polite. You should be self-effacing like them. Appearing cocky or boastful will win you only disrespect from an Ethiopian, who will report you to others as *guranga*, which means "vain."

BUSINESS ETIQUETTE IN ETHIOPIA

The language of business in Ethiopia is English. But you will make an Ethiopian feel good if you say the first time you meet him or her, "Tenaystilign!" (sounds like "ten-eyes-still-in"), which means "Good health to you!" Though many Ethiopians involved in business speak fluent English, just in case, it is useful to have an interpreter ready. A person intending to enter into a major deal is advised to hire an interpreter of his own rather than relying on the interpreter his business partner brings.

For initial contact, make sure you choose a good agent—one recommended by those with lengthy business deals in the country. Your agent must be polite and have good contacts and quick access to the right people.

Visiting businessmen need to make appointments in advance. An Ethiopian would be offended if you just dropped into his office. The right way to get an appointment with a prospective partner is to request it politely. Sending an official letter is appreciated because it gives the impression that you are serious and you respect the partner. For appointments, give a choice of several dates and times. The request ought to be made at least a month and a half before the appointment date. When a good relationship has been established, you can use the telephone to arrange a meeting.

When you meet your potential business partner, you will be offered a handshake. Reciprocate with a gentle one. Your eye contact should be strong and direct. If you see Ethiopians of the same sex sitting very close to each other, do not judge it the Western way. By culture they sit closer than many foreigners do. If they sit close to you, do not try to move away because your prospective business partner may interpret this as a sign of disrespect or coolness toward him.

You have to build a strong bond before venturing to discuss business. This is very important. In Ethiopia, it is personal contact that moves things faster. Know your counterpart well before proposing a business deal. Socializing goes a long way toward create a good business relationship.

In terms of dress code, you are advised to be on the conservative side. To show that you are somebody with means and are experienced in business deals, sport only accessories such as high-quality watches, pens, and briefcases. No matter the saying, a book is judged by its cover in Ethiopia. Your high-quality attire and dress will impress your contact and make him take you seriously.

It is common to be offered a cup of tea or coffee. This is a key feature of Ethiopian kindness and warmth. Refusing to accept it is considered indecorous. Though by tradition, Ethiopians do not expect reciprocity when they give gifts, the exchange of mutual favors is now common among modern Ethiopians.

An Ethiopian businessman may keep you waiting while he deals with people he never intended to meet in the first place. He also may have some family matters that intervene. So he may be late for the appointment he made with you. Even after you start your business discussions, it is common for your counterpart to be repeatedly interrupted by a secretary bringing papers to sign, by local or long-distance phone calls, and even by spontaneous visits by his friends and acquaintances.

Ethiopians have a social class and gender concept that is clear-cut. The way they interact always depends on their social status. For example, if they have a chauffeur, they do not eat at the same table as the chauffeur. So do not invite your driver to sit and dine with you and your host. The employee understands this archaic rule and will not be offended.

Ethiopians are not acquainted with seeing women engage in business. Therefore, they find it difficult to normally interact with female commercial partners. If you are a woman trying to strike a business relationship in Ethiopia, get introduced by a male who is older and holds high rank in society. This will smooth the way for you, and you will not have to worry about success or failure in establishing a new business contact. As a women who enters into trade negotiations, make sure that you let your technical and professional credentials be known without exhibiting arrogance or self-importance. With this careful approach, you may be accepted as a foreign business person not any different than the males with whom they are used to dealing.

Ethiopians cherish their honor, dignity, and reputation, and they want others not to transgress them. Ethiopians also put family matters before everything else. The family, not the individual, is the most important element in Ethiopia's social structure.

It is a common occurrence to see Ethiopians exhibit emotion and verbal communication filled with exaggeration that they think will attract the attention of others. Do not be surprised if Ethiopians avoid confrontation and say yes to everything you propose. In all cases you have to be modest. Never use blunt language. Work around what you want to impress on your host in a roundabout way. Accept what he or she suggests, and then present your proposal as a better alternative.

Ethiopians have many taboos, and you need to recognize and watch not to transgress them. For example, you are not expected to use your left hand while eating even if you are left-handed. You have to try to use your right hand. Many Ethiopian businessmen are Muslims, and for Muslims, the left hand is unclean. Showing the soles of one's shoes is impolite. The feet and shoes are considered impure.

When you concede to accept terms in bargaining, do not do so easily. Do it with apparent regret and reluctance. Negotiation in Ethiopia is not a quick process. Never reach a quick decision. Follow the trend your counterpart has chosen, and wait to make a decision on the basis of new developments and expectations. You are advised to get everything in writing so as to avoid legal problems if they happen to arise.

If you choose to give a gift, your gift should express something about your country. If you are a Canadian, for example, you would do better to give Canadian aboriginal art than to give an expensive product made by trendy fashion companies in North America (but make sure that at the bottom of the art, you do not see "Made in China"!). Chances are he will present you with something that represents Ethiopian culture. Under no circumstances should you decline because doing so would be construed as uncouth and boorish.

Entertainment is an important part of business conduct in Ethiopia. Eating liberally is expected when one is a guest in an Ethiopian businessperson's home. As you dine, you are continuously goaded with the words "please eat." When you hear those words, bow your head down slightly as if to say thank you for the generosity. Do not start by eating a lot in the beginning. Eat slowly and in small amounts. If you are full, continue to pretend to eat by taking a small piece and putting it into your mouth. Under no circumstances should you stop eating abruptly. The host may continue to invite you to eat even after you are full. If your host asks you to eat for a third time, say, "Thank you, I have eaten a lot" and "the food is delicious, but I am full now, thank you," and the host will understand.

REFERENCES

Amin, M., D. Willetts, et al. 2001. *Ethiopia: A Tourist Paradise*. Nairobi, Kenya: Camerapix Publishers.

Amin, Mohamed, Duncan Willets, and Alastair Matheson. 1997. *Journey through Ethiopia*. Addis Ababa, Ethiopia: Camerapics.

Briggs, P. 2006. *Ethiopia: The Bradt Travel Guide*. London: Bradt Travel Guide Ltd.

Cox, T. 1970. *Travellers' Guide to East Africa: A Concise Guide to the Wildlife and Tourist Facilities of Ethiopia, Kenya, Tanzania, and Uganda*. Elmsford, NY: London House and Maxwell.

Englebert, V. 1970. *Camera on Africa: The World of an Ethiopian Boy*. New York: Harcourt Brace Jovanovich.

Ethiopia and UNICEF. 1993. *Children and Women in Ethiopia: A Situation Report*. Addis Ababa, Ethiopia: Transitional Government of Ethiopia, UNICEF.

Ethiopian Tourist Commission. 1989. *Discovering Ethiopia*. Addis Ababa, Ethiopia: National Tour Operation.

Gozalbez, Javier, and Dulce Cerian. 2002. *Touching Ethiopia*. Addis Ababa, Ethiopia: Shama Books.

Lord, Edith. 1970. *Cultural Pattern of Ethiopia: Queen of Sheba's Heirs*. Washington, DC: Acropolis Books.

Mohammed Hakim, A., and Oromiya Kelel. 2004. *Tourist Guide to Oromoiya*. Addis Ababa, Ethiopia: Trade, Industry & Tourism Bureau of the Regional State of Oromiya.

Nichol, F. D. 1948. *Letters from Far Lands, Written during an Air Journey to 24 Lands, Describing Adventist Mission Activities and the Customs, Habits, and Daily Life of the People in Europe, the Middle East, Egypt and Ethiopia*. Washington, DC: Review and Herald Publishing Association.

Pankhurst, R. 1984. *Let's Visit Ethiopia*. Bridgeport, CT: Burke Publishing Co.

Pankhurst, R. 1990. *A Social History of Ethiopia*. Addis Ababa, Ethiopia: Addis Ababa University.

Pearce, Nathaniel. 1831. *The Life and Adventures of Nathaniel Pearce*. London: H. Colburn and R. Bentley.

Poluha, E. 2004. *The Power of Continuity: Ethiopia through the Eyes of Its Children*. Uppsala, Sweden: Nordiska Afrikainstitutet.

Poluha, E., et al. 2007. *The World of Girls and Boys in Rural and Urban Ethiopia*. Addis Ababa, Ethiopia: Forum for Social Studies in association with Save the Children Norway and Save the Children Sweden.

Rasmusson, J. 1965. *Welcome to Ethiopia: A Tourist Guide*. Addis Ababa, Ethiopia: Ethiopian Tourist Organization, printed by Artistic Printers.

Silvester, H. W. 2008. *Natural Fashion: Tribal Decoration from Africa*. London: Thames & Hudson.

Sørensen, P., and B. Selome. 2009. *Nice Children Don't Eat a Lot of Food: Strained Livelihoods and the Role of Aid in North Wollo, Ethiopia*. Addis Ababa, Ethiopia: Forum for Social Studies.

Tayetch, B., E. Poluha, et al. 1979. *Life and Play of Ethiopian Children*. Stockholm: Swedish International Development Authority, Information Division

Ullendorff, Edward. 1973. *The Ethiopians: An Introduction to Country and People*. 3rd ed. London: Oxford University Press.

Vecellio, C., M. F. Rosenthal, et al. 2008. *The Clothing of the Renaissance World: Europe, Asia, Africa, the Americas: Cesare Vecellio's Habiti Antichi et Moderni*. London: Thames & Hudson.

Waddington, G., and B. Hanbury. 1822. *Journal of a Visit to Some Parts of Ethiopia*. London: J. Murray.

Literature

HISTORICAL LITERATURE

Ethiopia is in a unique position in African history because of its long-established written language through which it produced annals (historical records) for 2,600 years. The annals are of prime importance because they have been in existence for such a long period. The original documentation of Ethiopian history was inscribed on stone. Early on, the words were written solely in consonants in the boustrophedon style, where the lines are inscribed alternately from right to left and then from left to right, plough-style. This developed into a Semitic form of right to left and much later left to right as is the practice today. After the fourth century, vowels were added to the consonants in a unique phonetic combination.

The Axumite rulers (ancient Ethiopians) developed a historical record early in their reign. They left their imprint by means of inscriptions on stone slabs. These were sometimes written in Sabean, which was a language spoken in Ethiopia as well as in South Arabia; sometimes in Ge'ez, which was a lingua franca of the empire at the time; sometimes in Greek; and in a few cases, in all three.

Although inscriptions going as far back as the seventh century BC exist, those with notable historical import start from the time of Emperor Ezana, who ruled Ethiopia from the early to mid-fourth century AD. Ezana introduced Christianity and made it the state religion of Ethiopia. The emperor's stone inscriptions can be seen in Axum to this day. The writings list the countries ruled by the emperor on both sides of the Red Sea and then proceed to recount the monarch's conquests of various peoples from the periphery to the center of the Sudan.

The second source of early Ethiopian literature is recorded in books written by *dabtaras* (scholars of theology), inscribed on parchment. During the Zagwe rule (non-Solomonian dynastic reign that was in power in Ethiopia between AD 1150 and 1270), the chronicles of emperors Lalibala, Na'akweta la-Ab, and others who were made into saints by the Tewahedo Church were described as builders of fabulous Christian shrines as well as staunch defenders of Tewahedo line. Of particular importance is that even though it was filled with fantasy, Emperor Lalibala's biography, which was written 200 years after his death in the 13th century, gives us a glimpse of the type of government that existed during the time and the way in which the famous rock-hewn churches of Lalibala were constructed.

The second chronicle of literary note is Emperor Amda Tseyon's (1314–1344) court record. Amda Tseyon, whose name means "pillar of Zion," reigned for 30 years, during which time he averted a rebellion by the Muslim leader Sabr ad-Din, the ruler of Ifat, a principality located on the lowlands east of Shoa. Sabr ad-Din torched Orthodox shrines and put to the sword thousands of Christians who refused to convert to Islam. The fighting between Amda Tseyon and Sabr ad-Din was described in detail by the imperial chronicler. Though often with apparent exaggeration of the exploits of the Christian monarch, the literature presents the Ethiopian leader as a valiant warrior who struggled gallantly against Muslim rebels and jihadist expansionists.

The third important chronicle is that of the 15th-century emperor Zara Yaqob (1434–1468). His reign represented a key period in the flourishing of Ge'ez literature of hagiographical (embellished) and realistic historical nature. An important fact about this period is that the emperor himself had become a key author of books, which was generally the work of the *dabtaras* and highly sophisticated abbots. One sees from the records that Zara Yaqob contributed to the reform of the organization of Church and State. The imperial activities inspired novel renditions of works in Arabic. Zara Yaqob's zeal led to the production of large numbers of polemical tracts and pamphlets that justified his commitment to serious secular and religious reform. Zara Yaqob authored or at least directed the production of *Matsahafa Berhan* (Book of Light), which prescribed the admonitions and regulations of the reforms, and *Matshafa Milad* (Book of the Nativity), which tried to disprove heresies that had emerged over time. The work condemns magical and pagan-style customs. The emperor's commitment to the two Sabbaths, Saturday and Sunday, was one of key features of the writings.

The emperor went to considerable extremes when he passed orders that all his Christian subjects wear amulets inscribed with the words, among others, "Of the Father, the Son and the Holy Ghost," and when he created a grand inquisitor and a nest of spies to ferret out presumed idolaters. His chronicler recorded, "Everyone trembled before the power of the King."

The emperor was not, however, able to suppress the flourishing of magical literature produced in the form of scrolls, talismans, charms, prayers, and visions. In particular, the *lefafa tsedq*, a scroll of parchment that is normally tied and buried with the body of a deceased person to lead the soul to heaven, was too much entrenched to be stamped out. Also too widespread to eliminate were the Tsalota Kepryanos (the Prayer of Cyprian) and the Tsalota Qeddus Kaleb (the Prayer of King Kaleb of Ethiopia), which prescribe means employed by *dabtara* wizards to help common citizens who believe in such practices. It was during the era of Zara Yaqob that a very original piece of literature, the *Book of the Mysteries of Heaven and Earth*, was composed. It details the secrets of the creation and the rebellion of the angels, the Apocalypse of St. John, and the mystery of the Divinity. It also contains a Jewish kabala-style computation of scriptural symbols and ciphers. The period also saw the flourishing of a new literary style that has attained a high degree of popularity in the country, concerning the *ta'amer's* (miracles) of God, saints, and angels. The *Ta'amera Marriam* (the Miracles of Mary) is the most famous among such literature.

Zara Yaqob's reign also saw the emergence of massive numbers of new and translated homilies, for large numbers of decreed celebrations of saint-days of canonized patriarchs, of Oriental Orthodoxy, and of commemorative religious feasts. Famous among these is the St. John Chrysostom's homily titled "Retu'a Haymanot" (The Orthodox).

Zara Yaqob's son, Emperor Baeda Mariam, suffered under the religious intolerance of his zealot father; he witnessed the torturing and killing of his own mother, who had been falsely accused of preparing the young prince to usurp his father's throne. As made clear in Baeda Mariam's royal chronicles, he went to great lengths to make amends for his father's excesses by freeing prisoners and allowing those in exile to return to their homes.

Emperor Lebna Dingil's chronicles describe the ruthless onslaught of Ahmed Gragn's Muslim army and the looting, destruction and torching of its churches and precious manuscripts, as well as the struggle the emperor waged to protect Christianity by seeking help from the Portuguese Christians, who responded to the call of his able mother Empress Eleni (Sabla Wangel), though the monarch died before seeing the rescue mission, which was to a large extent responsible for overcoming the invasion.

Next came the chronicles of Emperor Galawdewos. These chronicles describe how the monarch succeeded in defeating the invading Muslim armies of Adal with the aid of 400 musketeers led by Cristóvão da Gama, the son of the world-famous explorer Vasco da Gama. Da Gama and 200 of his men perished, but the remaining 200 helped Galawdewos defeat the armies of Ahmed Gragn.

After Galawdewos came Emperor Sartsa Dingil, who was a minor when he took the throne. His chronicles describe in detail the wars he had to wage against rebels in the empire that just barely survived being stamped out by the Muslim forces. Some of these were his close relatives, but he showed no mercy in suppressing them.

The next emperor was Susenyos (1607–1632), whose chronicles were filled with descriptions of a bloody civil war that ensued as a result of the emperor's conversion to Catholicism and his attempt to convert Ethiopian Tewahedo Christians to the Roman creed. Susenyos had to abdicate his throne in 1632 because even he himself was filled with remorse that many of his people had died for simple reasons of religious schism. His son and successor to the throne, Emperor Fasilidas, reversed the trend. He expelled the Portuguese Catholic preachers and reestablished Tewahedo Orthodoxy.

Chronicles were also written for emperors who ruled Ethiopia until the dawn of the Era of the Princes, when regional feudal lords enjoyed total autonomy. The chronicles describe mostly civil strife caused by succession problems, civil wars, and civil and church matters. The emperors for whom these chronicles were written include Yohannes I (1667–1682), Iyasu I (1682–1706), Bakafa (1721–1730), Iyasus II, (1730–1755), and Iyoas I (1755–1769). Complementing the royal chronicles of Ethiopian emperors are the *gedls*, or hagiographical writings regarding the lives of Ethiopia's revered saints. Among the most important are those of Gabra Manfas Qeddus, St. George, and Takla Haymanot. A large number of these writings are in the form of magnificent manuscripts embellished with strikingly colored paintings. The *gedls* have a mixture of biographical data and homiletic elements, with descriptions of miracles attributed to the particular saints. In the *gedls*, one also finds historical records of the time and place-names. There is also a record of doctrinal and power struggles during the periods in question.

Illuminated religious manuscript (ca. 13th century). (Courtesy of Paulos Milkias.)

Ancient handwritten religious books in the monastery of Lake Tana. (Courtesy of Paulos Milkias.)

Coupled with the limited amount of but refreshing secular poetry of the era of Zara Yaqob, a vast volume of religious poetry and hymnology proliferated. These works were mostly composed in honor of Christ, the Virgin Mary, the saints, and angels. Most of the hymns are dedicated to Mary, mother of Christ, the largest number of which are traced to the 15th century.

Emperor Zara Yaqob legislated over 30 feasts per year in the name of the Virgin Mary. One can imagine what that means in terms of Christians working to earn they daily living. Considering that each day of the week was dedicated to one of the various saints, there could be no time to work. The fact that Ethiopia has remained behind most Third World countries in terms of advancement can be explained in part by this phenomenon. The Church did reduce the 30 days dedicated to the Virgin

---

YARED (SAINT)

Yared, who was the learned scholar of the Ethiopian Orthodox Tewahedo Church, was a composer and musicologist in the early AD 500s. Before becoming a *dabtara* (learned church scholar) Yared was a deacon at the church of Madhané-Alam in Axum. Whereas prior to his appearance, Ethiopian liturgies and chants were murmured in a low voice, Yared introduced three modes of church music, namely, ge'ez, ezel, and araray, which are still employed in the Ethiopian Church. Yared's tome lays down the principles of the Ethiopian Orthodox church's musical education. In the end, Yared, who has since become a revered saint of the Ethiopian church, retired with many disciples into a hermitage in the Simien Mountains, where he died on Genbot 11 (May 20, AD 571).

Mary, explaining that she would prefer her devotees to work and feed themselves better. Zara Yaqob also wrote himself one praise to Mary known as "Arganona Marriam Dingil" (Organ of the Virgin Mary), which is ordered by the days of the week, just like another homily dedicated to Mary, known as *Wudase Mariam.* Zara Yaqob also wrote the homily "Egziabher Nagsa" (God Has Reigned). The most famous collection of hymns is the *Deggua,* with musical notations written by Saint Yared in the early 500s. The first break from wholly Ge'ez writing took place in the 17th century, when the Portuguese Catholics wanted to reach the ordinary people and got many of the scriptures, particularly the Psalter, Canticles, and *Wudase Marriam,* translated into Amharic.

GE'EZ LITERATURE (RELIGIOUS)

Ethiopian Church literature is quite unique in that the Church was almost totally insulated from the currents of international theological movements, given that its only connection was with Alexandria, which was controlled by Islamic people, who also surrounded Ethiopia. Many of the books are translations from Arabic, Greek, and Syriac, but they were always embellished or enlarged to fit the Ethiopian mould.

Beginning from the introduction of Christianity in AD 330 and culminating in AD 640 church literature was coupled with the heavy proselytization of Christianity, particularly after the arrival of the Nine Saints in the early sixth century in Ethiopia. This was followed by the period when Axum declined as an imperial power and no literary movement existed. A renaissance took place during the reign of Yekuno Amlak at the close of the 13th century. It continued for 150 years, reaching its zenith during the reign of Emperor Zara Yaqob and continuing for another 100 years. Then came a period of inactivity influenced by civil wars and rivalries among religious sects, which inhibited literary growth.

Monasticism played a key role in the Ethiopian literary movement. The Bible was translated during the time of the Nine Saints in the early sixth century, but the Ethiopian bible has a lot of apocryphal works not accepted by Greek, Roman, and

RUFO CHRISTIAN PAULUS LUDWIG

Rufo (1848/50–1871) was the first Oromo Bible translator of the 19th century. He was trained at the missionary center of Kornthal, Germany. After two years of translation work there, he received missionary education in Basel. He traveled to Jerusalem where he continued his studies of the scriptures and translation of the bible into Afaan Oromo. He ultimately ended up in Cairo, Egypt on his way to Oromia to preach the gospel, and died of lung disease there. Through his efforts, and his mentor, Krapf, the first Oromo translation of the New Testament reached Showan Oromos in 1877.

Protestant churches. The Ethiopian bible includes the *Book of Enoch* and the *Book of Jubilees*, which were translated from Greek to Ethiopic early during Ethiopian Christianity. Other works, such as those with Cyril's compositions and thus known as *Qerlos* (i.e., Cyril), were translated and highly popularized. *The Rules of Pachomius* and *Physiologus*, dealing with natural history, were translated from the Greek as well. Liturgical books were also produced simultaneously.

Since the church of Alexandria, which had remained the spiritual leader and the only connection of Tewahedo faith with the Christian world, its influence on the Ethiopian Orthodox Tewahedo church was very prominent. Hymn books such as the earlier-mentioned *Wudase Mariam* (Praises of Mary) were translated from Coptic. The Ge'ez *Didaskalia* with Greek overtones was also derived from the Coptic version. When Egypt fell under Islamic conquest, Greek was no longer used, and the Coptic language itself gave way to Arabic. As a result, many Ethiopian religious books from that time on were translated from Arabic to Ge'ez.

The fall of Axum came between the 7th and 10th centuries and the rise of the Zagwe dynasty gave impetus to building important shrines and the writings of the *gedls*, but a real renaissance for Ethiopian literature came with the rise to the throne of the Solomonian dynasty emperor Aste Yekuno Amlak at around 1270. It was following this epoch that books describing lives of saints and martyrs proliferated. There was *Matsahafa Sa'atat* (Book of Hours), *Matsahafa Genzat* (Book of Burials), and *Gadla Hawaryat* (the apocryphal Acts of the Apostles). An apocalyptic work known as *Fekkare Iyasus* (Interpretation of Jesus) was also produced. To con-

An antique handwritten Koran on display at a museum in Harar, Ethiopia. (AP Photo/ Anita Powell.)

front the proliferating heresies, the *Matsahafa Mestir* (Book of Mystery) was also written.

Two historical books—*Kebra Nagast* (Glory of Kings), which was composed by Ethiopians, and *Zena Ayhud*, a translation of Joseph Ben Gorion's *The History of the Jews*—became prominent starting in the 13th century AD. The first book traces history from the time of creation to the romantic legend of the Ethiopian kings, which it ties to the line of King Solomon and the Queen of Sheba. The second traces the history of the Jews from the time of Cyrus and the return back from Babylon, including an account of the fall of Jerusalem to Titus. There were also collections of ecclesiastical constitutions and canons published in eight books under the title *Sinodos*, which are included in the Ethiopian Orthodox church's New Testament. Also published were the *Didaskalia* and the *Testament of Our Lord*.

What is generally recognized as the golden age of Ethiopian literature started around 1300 and reached its zenith during the reign of Emperor Zara Yaqob between 1434 and 1468. It was a period of zealot emperors who made it their duty to fight off Islamic kingdoms that were rising on the periphery. At the same time, the emperors indulged in the production of religious tomes. Among these monarchs, Amda Tseyon was more known for his war against the Muslim sultanates south and southeast of the empire. Three of the emperors who ruled Ethiopia at that time, particularly emperors Zara Yaqob and Na'od, were authors in their own right. Zara Yaqob wrote tracts reproving the rise of occult worship. His composition *Matsahafa Berhan* (Book of Light) was a polemic against heathen tendencies, pagan ceremonies, and immoral acts of the age. But the attempt to stamp out such practices also led to the mushrooming of occult books, though they were driven underground. The production of annals (historical records) increased by leaps and bounds, and among them were those of Amda Tseyon, written in hymns and shining in their composition because of their greater length and detailed description of the events that transpired in the struggle against the Muslim sultanates. Famous church hymns were also embellished and newly produced, as was the case with the "Deggua of Yared," originally composed in the early 500s. Emperor Zara Yaqob's collection of hymns written in memory of the Saints' Days, known as *Egziabher Nagsa* (The Lord Reigneth), and the *Wudase Mariam* (Praises to Mary) (also arranged for the days of the week as *Arganona Dingil* [Organ of the Virgin] or *Arganona Wudase* [Organ of Praises]) are rooted in the period. Emperor Na'od's (1494–1508) is known for producing *Malk'a Mariam* (Likeness of Mary) and a collection of six-lined stanzas known as *Selassie* (Trinity). The Malk'a books are hymns in honor of saints in which various sections of the saint's body are recounted in an idiosyncratic stanza. The *Selassie* comprises poems to be sung in church following the readings of certain verses of the Psalter. The compositions *Antiphonary*, *Mawase'et* (Answers), and *Mi'iraf* (Chapter) are anthologies of hymns or anthems for the numerous festivals intended to be celebrated throughout the year. Emperor Lebna Dingil also commissioned the translation of John Chrysostom's *Commentary on the Epistle to the Hebrews* and the commentary on the gospels by Dionysius.

Depictions of the lives of saints, many in the form of homilies and apocryphal gospels that were produced during the previous age, also found an opportunity to be expanded in number. The lives of the national icon, Abuna Takla Haymanot; of saint Yared; and of Ne'akuto la Ab, the Zagwé emperor who relinquished the throne of his ancestors in favor of the Solomonians, were among those that were written. Other types of works that emerged during the period were "Our Lord's" compositions, which included *Matshafa Milad* (The Birth) and *Ta'amira Mariam* (The Wonders of Mary). Then comes the *Sinksar* (Synaxarium), which is the calendar of the Church. The work was originally translated from the Arabic *Synaxar* of the Coptic Church in the 1400s but was afterward embellished and enlarged with notices of Ethiopian-born saints and martyrs. The Ethiopian Synaxarium also included a short rhymed poem known as a *salam* at the conclusion of each hymn of remembrance. There was also an assemblage of tales and adages attributed to the Church Fathers referred to as *Gannat* (Paradise) and *Zenahomu La Abawu Keburani* (Stories of the Honored Fathers). It was during this period that *Giorgis Walda Amid* (Universal History of George the Egyptian) was translated into Ge'ez.

The last period of Ethiopian church literature was characterized by deterioration and destruction wrought by the revolt and jihadist war of Ibrahim El Ghazi, otherwise known in Ethiopia as Ahmed Gragn (the left-handed), who devastated the country between 1524 and 1543 and continued through the animist Oromo migration onto the highlands following the Muslim onslaught. Most original compositions disappeared when churches were sacked and torched. The Catholic interlude also came in the wake of Gragn's invasion, when doctrinal struggle ensured between the Tewahedo and Roman rites. It was then that Emperor Galawudewos wrote *Tsawana Nafs* (Refuge of the Soul), a confession justifying the practices of the Ethiopian

---

ST. TAKLA HAYMANOT

Known among Ethiopian Orthodox Christians as Abuna Takla Haymanot, he was born on December 24, 1192 and died on August 24, 1296. He remains the most revered saint of Ethiopian origin. St. Takla Haymanot was a liaison between the Church and the state. It is believed by some Church historians that he was the key person who convinced the Zagwe kings to relinquish their throne to the Solomonians, as a result of which the Church obtained one-third of the land in the highlands. Church history indicates that Takla Haymanot's lasting heritage to posterity was the institution of an enduring center of Christian scholarship and monasticism at Dabra Asbo (renamed Dabra Libanos in the 15th century). The monastery of Dabra Libanos has remained for centuries as Ethiopia's most important religious and political center. In fact, most of the monastic communities in central and south-central Ethiopia derive their origin from him and are collectively known as the House of Takla-Haymanot. Takla Haymanot's legacy became an impetus for the success of the ensuing efforts of Emperor Amda-Tsiyon (1314–1344) to centralize and expand Ethiopia's Christian empire, which was challenged by the Muslim kings of Hadiya, Ifat and Adal.

church, which has rites strikingly similar to those of the Jews. This was clearly an original work. *Fekkare Malakot* (Exposition of the Godhead) and the *Haimanota Abau* (Faith of the Fathers) were also translated from Arabic. *Fekkare Malakot* was written to defend the Tewahedo line. Then came the prodigious works of Enbaqom (Habakkuk), originally from Arabia; Enbaqom was a Muslim who converted to Christianity and became a seasoned *dabtara* (church scholar) and then was chosen to be the *etchage*, or abbot, of one of the most famous monasteries of Ethiopia—Dabra Libanos. Enbaqom authored *Anqatsa Amin* (Gate of Faith) and *Superiority of the Christian Faith.* Enbaqom also translated two other works, the *Universal History* of Abu Shaker and the *Story of Abraham and Yezvasef* (Barlaam and Josaphat), a popular religious romance originating in India. A contemporary of Enbaqom named Salik, who was also from Dabra Libanos, translated a famous theological treatise named *Matsahafa Hawi*, originally produced as the religious encyclopedia of Nicon in Greek and later translated into Arabic. It is a collection of instructions dealing with a range of subjects attributed to famous Church Fathers, stressing the necessity of understanding the commandments, the Holy Scripture, fasting, monastic life, and confessions. During the same period, Dabra Libanos scholars translated a book called *Talmid* (Pupil), which was written by an ecclesiast known as George who was a pupil of St. Anthony, the patriarch of Alexandria. The work was a refutation of the heresies of the period. Another major book translated from Arabic in 1667, instigated by Queen Sabla Wangel, mother of King Iyasu, was *Faus Manfasawi* (Spiritual Healing). In 35 chapters, the book provides precepts and recommendations on human sins, concluding with a string of instructions regarding Chrism, Baptism, Holy Communion, the Church, and discipline of the clergy. Another book translated from Arabic during the same period was the *Romance of Alexander*, originally written by Callisthenes, Greek historian and grandnephew of the famous philosopher Aristotle. The Greek version has since been lost.

The Chronicle of John, Bishop of Nikiou, which describes the Christian side of the conquest of Egypt by the Arabs, was also translated from Arabic during the period. The translation was completed by a certain Gabriel at the suggestion of Emperor Yaqob (1595–1605). The book is important because it was written by a person who witnessed the events. The Arabic original has since been lost, and the work is extant

YOHANNIS ZA SAGALA

Yohannis Za Sagala was a revered saint of the Ethiopian Orthodox Tewahedo Church who lived in the 15th century. He was one of the most productive Ge'ez spiritual scholars who lived during the reign of Emperor Dawit II. One of his important works was his Acts, whose arguments were successfully used by Ethiopian Tewahedo scholars against the Jesuits during the religious schism that arose when Catholicism was adopted by Emperor Susenyos. Yohannis of Sagala was a prolific author of Ethiopian theology.

only in the Ge'ez version. It was from 1595 to 1605 that a Tewahedo monk named Bahrey from the southern province of Gamo wrote *Zenahu Za Galla* (History of the Gallas.) Bahrey described the manner in which the Oromos fought against the Christians and the reasons that they were victorious in many of the engagements. A book titled *Ser'ata Mangest*, dealing with court proceedings, was produced at this time, as was *Fetha Nagast* (The Law of the Kings). Dealing with liturgical, civil, and criminal procedures, *Fetha Nagast* was translated from the *Nomocanon* of Abu Ishaq Ibn al 'Assal, an Egyptian writer of the 13th century. It is a collection of biblical precepts, ecclesiastical ordinances, and Roman laws. Two original philosophical works also appeared during this period. They are Zara Yaqob's *Enquiry* and his disciple Walda Hiywet's theoretical composition, *Htata*.

The 17th century brought to an end the development of Ethiopian church literature, though the imperial chroniclers continued to appear. Ge'ez had by that time become a dead language spoken only by learned church scholars. Amharic was slowly replacing the old Ethiopic, and the writers of the chronicles now started to write in Amharic, not Ge'ez. An amalgam of history writing style known as *lesana tarik* (the language of history) was also born. To accommodate Amharic words that have borrowed sounds and accents from Hamitic languages such as Agaw, new letter forms that do not exist in Ge'ez were added. In the end, the chronicles started to appear in pure Amharic.

AMHARIC LITERATURE (SECULAR)

Ethiopia's Amharic literature is unique in Africa for a variety of reasons. First, it draws on a wealth of millennia-old culture. Second, as the only country to survive foreign occupation during the scramble for Africa, Ethiopia was insulated from the currents of the outside world. Third, Ethiopia is the only country with its own indigenous writing system. For all these reasons, in both volume and quality, Ethiopia's literature surpasses any other literature written in a language that is solely African.

It was Emperor Tewodros II (1855–1868) who clearly broke away from the traditional way of writing everything in court in Ge'ez when he instructed his aides to write the court chronicles in Amharic, a language that was used even when a Tigrayan emperor took the throne under the crown name of Yohannes IV. But it was during the time of Menelik, who introduced the first printing press into his country, that Amharic became well established as a literary language. It was also during his reign that the first newspaper in Amharic under the name of *Aemiro* was launched. During Emperor Haile Selassie's reign, Amharic flourished not only in the secular domain but even in some churches; the Cathedral of the Trinity, for example, used it in songs in place of the traditional Ge'ez.

The first Amharic novel appeared in 1908 when Afeworq Gebre-Iyasus wrote a romantic fiction called *Tobia*. Then came Hiruy Wolde Selassie's monumental works, again in Amharic, 20 in total. Amharic playwriting by people such as Hadis Alemayehu began appearing not long after.

Wolde-Giorgis Wolde-Yohannes, who wrote about Ethiopian royalty, and Makonnen Endalkachew, who wrote fiction and sometimes stories based on facts known to him, were among the pioneers in those early years. The latter's first novel, *Alam Waratagna* (The Unreliable World), examines the tortured life of a woman trying to fit into intricate Ethiopian family values. His second work, a play named *Yaddam Dimts* (Adam's Voice), dramatized the martyrdom of Abuna Petros at the hands of Italian Fascists. In his novel *Yedehoch Katama*, Makonnen examined the life of a rich man divided between his dreams and good advice from another person. Makonnen also wrote an autobiography titled *Malkam Betasaboch* (Good Family).

A groundbreaking and highly sophisticated novel of world-class standard was produced by Dejazmatch Girmachew Tekle Hawaryat; *Araya* (1942), now translated into several foreign languages, is based on the life history of Tekle Hawaryat's father, Fitawrari Tekle Hawaryat, who was one of the few students Emperor Menelik sent abroad to pursue higher education in the late 1890s. Tekle Hawaryat was torn between staying abroad, where he fell in love with a Russian aristocratic girl who wanted marriage, and returning back home to Ethiopia to help his country fend off possible European colonial subjugation. After agonizing over the matter, he ultimately decided to return home, only to be frustrated by the traditional feudal system in place. Girmachew then wrote a play called *Tewodros* (1950) that tried to do justice to the much-maligned Emperor Tewodros II. Whereas Ethiopian historians emphasized the monarch's cruelty, Girmachew stressed the struggle Tewodros waged in uniting the country following the anarchy of the Zemene Mesafint that he ultimately stamped out. Late in the reign of Emperor Haile Selassie, Girmachew also wrote a book titled *Adwa*, which narrated Ethiopia's great victory against the Italian colonialists.

Kebbede Mikaél wrote plays and recorded Ethiopian folklore. He introduced European philosophers to a typically parochial Ethiopian audience. Another area in which he was interested was psychology. Kebede Mikaél's poems are didactic, noticeably woven with a rationale to impart practical knowledge or to elucidate the principles of morality. His poetic storytelling always depicts a moral point or instructs. In this, Kebede Mikaél employed personification, a form of allegory in which human behaviors such as will, forthrightness, and feeling, are ascribed to animals or inanimate objects that portray special tendency and quality. Kebede's first work was a collection of poetry titled *Berhana Helina* (Light of Conscience) (1941). He also wrote a book titled *Tariknna Mesale* (History and Metaphors, 1942) that employs a far-fetched, strained, and elaborate metaphor in which the subject is contrasted with a plain analogue, which is drawn from nature or a common circumstance.

On the orders of Emperor Haile Selassie, Kebede translated Clay's book *Beyond Pardon* (Keyiqirta Belay) but transformed it in such as way that it appealed to Ethiopian culture. His monumental contribution however, was, in the area of playwriting. Among his most well-known works are *Yetinbit Qetero* (Prophetic Appointment, 1946), a religious drama countering atheism; *Ato Belayneh Woinim Yeqitat Ma'ibal* (Mr. Belayneh or Storm of Punishment), portraying materialism and atheism as terrible evils; *Anibal* (Hannibal, 1963), which recounts the Punic wars between the

Romans and the Carthaginians as a metaphor for Ethiopian history; and *Atse Kaleb* (1963), a biography of Emperor Kaleb or Saint Elesbaan, the legendary monarch of ancient Axum who triumphed against the enemies of Christianity in South Arabia in the early sixth century. He also wrote biographies of great men of the past, including Homer, Demosthenes, Alexander the Great, and many others. Kebede Mikael translated many works into Amharic, including Shakespeare's *Romeo and Juliet*. To justify Haile Selassie's wish to follow Japan in bringing Westernization to a traditional society, Kebede Mikael also wrote *Japan Indemin Seletenech* (How Did Japan Develop?, 1953.)

Ras Emeru Haile Selassie was a traditional aristocrat turned progressive and writer. Emeru wrote *Fitawrari Belay* (1945), a historical novel; *Swunna Ewqet* (Man and Knowledge, 1959), a treatise that examines the concept of epistemology as he perceived it; and *Aleminna Tigil* (World and Struggle, 1967), which deals with man's tribulations in this universe.

Another very prominent official of the Haile Selassie period who pursued writing in addition to his administrative duties was Haddis Alemayehu. Haddis's first work was a play titled *Yehabeshanna Ye-wodahuala Gabicha* (The Marriage of an Abyssinian and the Backward, with a pun on both terms). He wrote the play when he was very young, attending elementary school, which important dignitaries attended five years before the 1935–1936 Italian occupation of Ethiopia. He wrote *Teret Teret Yemeseret* (The Fundamental Story), which retold 11 Ethiopian fables. He also published *Timhirtinna a Yetemari Bet Tergum* (Education and the Meaning of Schooling), which elaborated on the goals of education. His most famous novel was *Fiqir Eske Maqabir* (Love Till the Grave), which contains lots of satirical anecdotes that Ethiopians enjoyed, making it a best seller in the country. It was on account of this book that Haddis Alemayehu won the Haile Selassie Prize Trust Award in 1969.

Haddis wrote other novels as well, including *Wanjalagnaw Dagna* (The Criminal Judge) and *Yelm Jhat* (Sweet in Dreams). He also wrote on politics and public administration. His *Ethiopia Min Aynet Astedader Yasfeligatal* (What Kind of Administration Is Necessary for Ethiopia) was read widely by students of Ethiopian politics and public administration. His autobiography *Tezeta* (Nostalgia), which describes his life in Gojam and Addis Ababa, as well as in Mussolini's jail in Italy, quickly became a best seller among Ethiopian readers.

Abbé Gubegna was at one time the country's best-selling author and playwright. The attraction to his books was connected with his indirect criticism of the feudal regime of Emperor Haile Selassie. His first play, *Yerom Awadadaq* (The Fall of Rome, 1960), gave indirect warning to the feudal stalwarts that if they did not mend their ways, they might face the same fate as the Roman senators. In *Ye-Patrice Lumumba Asazagn Amuamuat* (Patrice Lumumba's Tragic Death), he condemned colonial and neo-colonial injustice. The most famous novel he wrote was *Aliwaladim* (I Will Not Be Born, 1962), a satirical story of a child refusing to come out of his mother's womb because of the injustices and corruption of society awaiting him. It was a stinging condemnation of the feudal order, and not surprisingly, after only 800 copies were sold, the government confiscated and burned the remaining copies. His other novel, *Melk'am Saifa Nabalbal* (Melk'am the Sword of Blaze, 1963), which sold 25,000 copies within a few weeks, vouched for a constitutional monarchy, again as a stinging rebuke to Emperor Haile Selassie's absolute monarchy. His last famous work was a play titled *Politikanna Polatikagnoch* (Politics and Politicians, 1963), which was a critique of the Marxist radicals of the 1960s and 1970s and which made him unpopular among the triumphant left movement that overthrew Emperor Haile Selassie.

Tesfaye Gessesse, a writer of dramas, modernized the archaic Ethiopian theater starting in the early 1960s. He did this through his plays, acting, direction, and instructing. Some of his stage plays were judged anti-Derg and counter-revolutionary by the Mengistu regime, on account of which Tesfaye was removed from his post as director of the Ye-Hager Fiqir Theatre and jailed by the Ethiopian military junta.

Tseggayé Gebre-Medhin, poet-laureate of Ethiopia, was arguably Ethiopia's greatest playwright. He wrote mostly in Amharic but also produced works in English. One of the latter was titled *Oda Oak Oracle*. This play was performed in theaters all over the world and still appears on reading lists in black studies departments in U.S. universities. His other English-language production, titled *Tewodros*, recounts the story of the suicide of Emperor Tewodros II after an assault by the Napier expedition in 1968. This drama was staged in many places, including at the Arts Theatre in London. Tseggayé also wrote *Ennat Alem Tenu* (Mother Courage) and *Ha Hu be Sidist Wer* (The Ethiopian Alphabet in Six Months), which analyzed the Ethiopian revolution of 1974. A sequel that came out late in his life, titled *Ha Hu Weynis Pe Pu—A or Z* (1993), was banned by the government of Ethiopia.

Teague's enduring legacy, however, was *Yekarmow Saw* (Tomorrow's Man), which won him national fame as soon as it appeared. Having been born to an Oromo father and an Amhara mother, Tseggayé was schooled in both traditional and Western schools, which taught him the dead language Ge'ez as well as English. He was equipped with several languages, and he employed them in a peculiar mixture. The style he adopted was extremely forceful and dramatic. His stories were for the most part melancholic, and his characters examined his compatriots' bitter experiences and tragedy. The writer became the youngest recipient of the Haile Selassie Prize Trust Award for Amharic Literature in 1966. He was nominated for the Nobel Prize for Literature in the year 2000, just six years before his death from kidney failure while undergoing dialysis in New York City.

A writer of two different literary traditions, the Ge'ez and the modern, poet and playwright Mengistu Lemma was known for employing comedy as a means of social criticism in theater. His work was full of allusion and allegorical narrative, intended to convey a moral truth. He explained the workings of the social system by indirect reference to things assumed to be known, such as a historical event or personage or a familiar line from traditional or modern literature, be it Ethiopian or foreign.

Mengistu's first published poem was "Yand Geta Astewaynet" (The Wisdom of a Richman), and his first book of poetry was *Yegitim Guba'e*, published in 1957. He wrote a popular drama called *Yalacha Gabicha* (Marriage of Unequals, 1964) and *Telfo Bekise* (Kidnapping, 1968), which analyzes the conflict between tradition and modernity. His play *Balakabbanna Baladabba* (The Cape Wearer and the Poorly Dressed, 1976), which dealt with the cultural conflict faced by Ethiopians who went abroad and came back, was widely read. His adaptation of John B. Priestley's *An Inspector Calls*, published under the title *Tayyaqi* (Inspector, 1979), discussed issues of class, feudalism, and capitalism. His novel *Tsara-Colonialist* (The Anti-Colonialist,

1981), which retold the struggle of Ethiopian patriots' struggle against Fascist Italy's occupation of Ethiopia and the destruction it left in its wake when they were defeated and expelled in 1941, won him a large following. Three of his plays were published under a collection named *Yetewnet Guba'e* (1982).

Mengistu Lemma's play *Shimya* (The Scramble, 1982) described the corruption and competition of the bureaucratic bourgeoisie of Ethiopia, and he wrote another play titled *Ye-Alam Negus* (The King of the World). He translated many works into Amharic, including Chekov's *The Bear*, under the title *Dandew Claude* (Tough Chebudé), and Tawfiq Al Hakim's *Lust to Kill*, under the title *Gidey Gidey Alegn* (I Have the Urge to Murder). His other notable novel is *Yabbatoch Chawata* (Ancestral Folklore, 1960), which recounts traditional stories of Ethiopia in poetic form. Mengistu also wrote "how to" books for writers, one example being *Yeteyatir Dirsat Yatsastaf Belhat* (How to Write Prose for Theatrical Production). The author also left memories from his father's days and his own autobiography, published posthumously in 1996.

Another well-known Amharic author was Dagnachew Worqu, who was a lecturer at Addis Ababa University for many years. He was interested in advancing the usage of the Amharic language. Among his major works are *YeAmarigna Felitoch* (Amharic Idioms, 1986); *Yetsihuf Tibeb Memeria* (Guide to Writing Skills); *YeAmarigna Ye-Geography Mezgebe Qalat* (Amharic Dictionary of Geographic Terms, 1986); and *Yegeletsanna Yemililis Faida BeAdefirs Yemejemeria Mi'iraf* (The Significance of Description and Dialogue in the First Chapter of Adefirs). His fiction books include *Seqeqenish Isat* (Your Love Is Like Fire, 1955); *Adefirs* (Disturber, 1969); *Imbua Belu Sawoch* (Bellow You Men, 1974); *Tibelch* (You Excel, 1965); and *Sew Ale Biye* (I Thought There Were Upright Men, 1967). The author was always philosophical in his analysis of society.

Berhanu Zerihun wrote his novels about the situation and exploitation of the oppressed, particularly women, and in his later years about the plight of the Ethiopian peasantry. In three novels, he put the exploitation of women at the center: *Hulet Ye'inba Debdabewoch* (Two Letters of Tears, 1959), a story about a bar girl who faced a tragic death after being ruthlessly exploited by others; *Yebedel Fitsame* (The Culmination of Oppression, 1964); and *Amanuel Derso Mels* (Visiting and Returning from the Madhouse, 1964). His other early novel was *Dil Kemot Behuala* (Victory after Death, 1962), which champions the struggle of the South African blacks against the apartheid system.

Berhanu also wrote historical novels, including *Yetewodros Enba* (Tears of Tewodros, 1965), which put the life of Emperor Tewodros, which had been tarnished by local historians, in good light. He also published *Chereqa Sitwata* (When the Moon Shines, 1965). Additionally, Berhanu published a collection of short stories under the title *Ber Ambar Seberelewo* (He Consummated His Marriage with a Virgin), which explores marriage customs in Ethiopia. His historical novel *Ma'ibel* (The Storm, 1975) was based on the Ethiopian Revolution of 1974 and the famine that preceded it. He wrote three plays: *Moresh* (A Call in Distressl, or SOS, 1979); *Tategnaw Tewanay* (The Disruptive Actor, 1982); and *Abba Nafso* (1982), which describes the courage of the Adwa hero Dejazmatch Balcha Abba Nafso. His last novel was *Ye-Tangut Mistir* (Tangut's Secret, 1986).

Ba'alu Girma employed his pen to expose political gridlock in the Derg system. His first novel was *Kadmas Bashager* (Beyond the Horizon, 1969), a conscientization (elevating the social consciousness) movement that struck a chord among the restless and radicalizing youth. His *Ye-Hilina Dewel* (The Bell of Conscience, 1974) describes the life of a student who had to struggle against all odds to earn a career. In the book, Bealu praised manual labor. The book was later enlarged and retitled *Haddis* (Novel, 1983). Ba'alu's *Derasiw* (The Author, 1979) adulated the Marxist revolution in Ethiopia. His two other novels revolved around the civil war raging in Eritrea: *Ye-Qey Kokeb Tiri* (Call of the Red Star, 1979) and, most famously, *Oromai* (The Pointless, 1976), in which he ridiculed many Derg members other than Mengistu Haile Mariam, on whom he showered praise. The book became his undoing because soon after, he disappeared without a trace. It has now been established that Derg members who were ridiculed had him assassinated and buried in a secret grave that to this day has not been identified.

Many other novelists also sprung up following the attempted coup of 1960, though none of them produced groundbreaking work. Among these are Taddele Gebre-Hiywet, who wrote the first Ethiopian musical, *Mannew Ityopiyawiw* (Who Is a True Ethiopian?); Aberra Lemma, who experimented with modern poetry and also produced short stories; Gebeyehu Ayele, who wrote *Tamar Tor* and *The Two-Pronged Spear*; and Debbebe Seyfu, who produced a few poems. Some, including Sahle-Selassie Berhane-Mariam and Dagnachew Worqu, shifted their medium to English in order to circumvent the hand of the censors in Ethiopia.

Following the revolution of 1974, large quantities of Amharic literature were produced. This confounded the heavy censorship that was put in place by the Derg. Lack of entertainment alternatives, given that the public media controlled by the government was used more for propaganda and dissemination of radical ideas, drove thousands of young people toward reading the Amharic novels that mushroomed from every corner. The fact that many of those books were sold at a cheap price also made them very accessible to the common man.

Though most Ethiopian Amharic literature has been geared toward utilitarianism and conscientization (elevating the social consciousness), aiming to evolve a better life for the people, other themes arose as well. For example, Yilma Habteyes concentrated on the writing of detective stories. Other authors such as Mammo Wuddineh translated spy stories from foreign languages, which became popular among Amharic literature readers.

Since Amharic was adopted as the language of instruction in schools and textbooks became written in it, Amharic literature has become widely accessible to the average urban dweller. Several high-quality Ge'ez and Amharic dictionaries have appeared since the 1950s. Among them is Kidana wold Kiflé's *Matsahafa Sewasew wo-Gis Wo-Mezgebe Qalat* (Book of Grammar, Verbs, and Terms). Two other monumental dictionaries are Desta Tekle Wold's *Yamarigna Mezgebe Qalat* (Amharic Dictionary, 1970) and Wolf Leslau's *English-Amharic Context Dictionary* (1978). A smaller but user-friendly dictionary of Amharic is Bahru Zargaw's *Zargaw Ye-Amarigna Mazgaba Qalat.*

Amharic literature has also proliferated in the fields of folklore and proverbs. Chief among the authors in this field was Balambaras Mahteme-Selassie Wolde-Mesqel, who wrote *Ye-Abbatoch Qirs* (Ancestral Legacy, 1945); *Ye-Etiopia Bahil*

Tinat Bulga (Ethiopian Culture from Bulga, 1967); *Balkan Iniweqbet Ye-Etiopia Bahil Tinat* (Let Us Know What We Possess: A Study of Ethiopian Culture, 1968); and *Sim Kemeqabir Belay* (One's Name Remains beyond the Grave, 1963).

Mahteme Selassie also produced many other works in several areas of literature, including the following: *Sile Ethiopia Ye-Meret Sirit Astedadernna Gibir Teqlala Asteyayet* (About Ethiopia's Land Tenure, Administration and Tax System); a novel titled *Etsub Dinq* (Great Miracle, 1950); *Amarigna Qine* (Amharic Poetry, 1955); *Tibebe Garahit Andagna Matsahaf* (Agrology Vol. 1); *Beila Garahit* (Agriculture, 1966); *Sawaswa Samay* (The Grammar of Heaven, 1968); *Amarigna Qine Kenemefchaw* (Amharic Poems with Explanations, 1959); *Inqilf Lemine* (Why Should I Sleep, 1959); *Yegnam Alun Iniwaqachew* (Let Us Know What Is Said to Be Ours, 1965); and *Holqu Tewlid Zanigus Sahla Selassie* (Genealogy of Negus Sahla Selassie, 1972). Over and above these works, Mahtama Selassie is more known for his huge tome (980 pages) named *Zekra Nagar*, which summarizes imperial palace documents from the Menelik era to the reign of Haile Selassie.

Several history books and biographies also form a good section of Ethiopian Amharic literature. Among them are Dabtara Zeneb's *Yetewodros Tarik* (History of Tewodros, 1870); Alaqa Taste's *Ye-Galla Tarik* (History of the Oromos, 1900); and Dabtara Wolde Mariam's *Tewodros* (1904). Hiruy Wolde Selassie's four historical books are pioneering works: *Ethiopia and Metemma: Ye-Atse Yohannes Tarik Be-Archiru* (Ethiopia and Metemma: Brief History about Yohannes, 1917); *Yehiwot Tarik Behuala Zemen leminessu Lejoch Mustawasha* (Autobiography for the Future Generation, 1922); *Ye-Haile Selassie Achir Tarik* (Brief History about Haile Selassie, 1935); and *Ye-Ethiopia Negest Tarik* (History of Ethiopian Kings, 1935). Gebre Wold Engeda Worq, one of Haile Selassie's ministers, produced *Ye-Maichaw Zemechanna Ye-Guzow Tarik* (The Campaign at Maichaw and Tales about Its Journey, 1948).

Tadesse Zewde wrote *Qarin Garamaw* (The Survivor Was Astonished, 1967), a book that describes the five years of guerrilla struggle by Ethiopian patriots against Italian Fascist occupiers. Gerima Teferra wrote *Gondare Belachew* (The Gondare with His Shield, 1956). Dagne Asemahagn wrote *Takilinna Serawitu* (Haile Selassie and His Army, 1957). A firsthand report on the history of Ethiopian patriots who carried out guerrilla warfare against the Fascist occupiers was summarized in Tadesse Mecha's *Tiqur Anbassa* (Black Lion, 1950). Makonnen Endalkachew wrote *Taytu Betul* (1957), in which Empress Taytu was praised but Emperor Tewodros was portrayed as a tyrant.

Kebede Mikaél's *Yetinbit Qetero* (Appointment with Prophesy, 1945) is part-fiction and part-history, centered on Queen Candace's eunuch, who is described in the Bible. Emperor Haile Selassie's *Autobiography* Vol. 1 (1959), both published in Amharic by Berhanenna Selam Printing Press and translated into English by Eduard Ullendorff and published by Oxford University, still remains a classic. The second volume of the same autobiography, though less important in terms of historical contribution, also was published and was later translated by Harold Marcus.

Ato Yilma Deressa wrote *Ye-Ethiopia Tarik* (1970), which for the first time since Behrey's 1953 book gave a detailed and balanced explanation of the Oromo migration into the highlands of Ethiopia. Dejazmatch Kebede Tessema's memoir *Yetarik Mastawesha* (Historical Memoir, 1969) has remained one of the most balanced Amharic books written by the Ethiopian aristocracy during the reign of Haile Selassie. In recent years, more autobiographical books with a great deal of historical interest have appeared. Among them are Fitawrari Takla Hawariat's *Ye-Hiywaté Tarik* (Story of My Life), a candid and historically rich book; Merse'é Hazan Walda Qirqos's auto-biographical book *Ye—Zemen Tarik Tizitaye Kayehutnna Ke-semmahut* (Historical Memoir—What I Saw and What I Heard); and Dejazmatch Zewde Gebre Hiwot's *Yehiywet Wutana Wurad* (The Ups and Downs of Life, 2006).

Currently, Ethiopia's most prominent writer of the contemporary-style novel is Sebhat Gebre Egziabher. This author was privileged enough to read the draft of his first novel composed in the style of Henry Miller's *Nexus, Sexus and Plexus* as long ago as 1960. The book *Letum Aynegalign* (Night Life) appeared after the fall of the Derg in 1993 in abridged form and later in unabridged version. In his prose, Sebhat is not constrained by the traditional Ethiopian writing style. Nor is his syntax orthodox. He is not verbose. His sentences are never belabored. However, even as he uses simple words and seemingly light prose, Sebhat's concepts are highly sophisticated and philosophical. He is known for employing neologism with abandon. The colloquial expressions and unconventional vocabulary he uses are not yet recognized in standard Amharic dictionaries, but chances are that whereas they were doomed to disappear from usage, they might creep into everyday parlance thanks to their popularization by Sebhat's trendy novels.

There is such a stark contrast between traditional and modern Ethiopian poets that there is no common standard between them. The former writes poetry with a relaxed attitude and ordinary tone. Their themes are to a large extent mundane and frivolous. Such poetry is intended to amuse and entertain. It clearly lacks sophistication. The main preoccupation of traditionalist Ethiopian poets is to get the right rhyme, not to haggle with complex ideas and concepts. However, this apparent weakness is compensated with the poets' wit, their ability to play with words, and their use of elegant language.

Furthermore, some types of traditional Ethiopian poetry confound tempo and rhythm. In the Bagana song mode, for instance, the artist uses blank verse, in which poetry is written without rhymes. This verse is meditative in form but very flexible, whereby the poet, typically a spiritual composer, is not hampered in the expression of thought or syntactic structure by the need to employ rhyme.

Most traditionalists compose odes in praise of a victory in war. They write serenades or lovers' songs or poems for nuptial songs. They use ambiguous words or phrases that would lend themselves to more than one interpretation. In other words, they use homonyms (i.e., two or more words that are identical in pronunciation and spelling, but different in meaning, as with the verb "deggeme," which means to read the Psalter, and "Deggeme," which means "he repeated"). In its more sophisticated form, this form of poetry is known as *seminna worq* (wax and gold), which forms the title of Donald Levine's seminal work.

Traditionalists shower praise on the powers that be. But by the same breath, when opportunities lend themselves, they also attack political figures by employing lampoons—a bitter, obnoxious satire in Ethiopian verse known as "the words of Araho"—as did an Ethiopian minstrel who was ordered beaten to death by Emperor Tewodros when the emperor found out that the singer had called him the son of a medicinal plant vendor.

Traditional Ethiopian poets use hyperbole (i.e., an audacious and calculated exaggeration). For example, the exclamation "I'd give my neck for the love of my sovereign!" is not really intended to be taken literally but is rather employed as a means of emphasizing loyalty to one's monarch. In the modern style, feelings or capacity for awareness, understanding, and sensitivity are extremely important. When one reads or listens to poets' creative verses, one gets the feeling or capacity for awareness, sensitivity, and understanding experienced by the poets themselves. Ethiopia's avant-garde poets always have the effect of balance, finality, and completeness, which leaves the listener or reader with a sense of fulfilled expectations.

Among modern Ethiopian poets, Gebre Kristos Desta, Yohannes Admasu, Tsegaye Gebre Medhin, and Solomon Deressa are the most prominent. Their style is avant-garde à la Arthur Rimbaud. They are innovating artists who promote the use of new or experimental concepts or techniques. They employ a fluid form of poetry that conforms to no set rules of traditional versification in the Ge'ez or Amharic style. Their works are free from fixed patterns of meter and rhyme, but they employ familiar poetic devices such as figures of speech, imagery, and alliteration. Their poems are filled with satires that expose and ridicule human folly or vice. Historically conceived of as leaning toward didacticism, the satire is in the main aimed at projecting moral criticism against the iniquity of social wrongs. It may also be presented with sharp humour or with rage and rancor.

The modernists' poems are not easy to read, but they are all poignant and powerful. Gebre Kristos's work, for example, is descriptive with apparent depth.

The residence of the famous French poet, Arthur Rimbaud (1880–1891). (Courtesy of Paulos Milkias.)

Yohannes is political and satirical. His creative poems are full of allegory. His stanzas in "Yegedel Sir Atint" (Skeletons under a Cliff) are allegories of oppressive feudalism and archaic religious precepts reigning over the Ethiopian society. He used controlling metaphor with symbolic stories wherein the whole poem was an allegory for the existing social and political system. In all of his poems, Yohannes presents figurative illustrations regarding the feudal stalwarts and archaic clerics of his age in poetic narratives by the use of symbolic fictional figures and actions that resemble existing circumstances. In print or in reading, he evokes strong mental images, not only of the visual sense, but of emotion and passion as well.

Tsegaye is historical and philological. He uses a mode of expression in which words are utilized out of their literal sense in order to adjoin emotional intensity or to convey his own awareness of a situation by balancing or identifying one thing with another that has a connotation familiar to the reader or listener. His poetic creations are full of figures of speech. They are peppered with seals and symbols, simile, hyperbole, personification, and metaphor. Words in Tsegaye's vernacular are mixed, given the inflectional endings of a different language, usually for satiric effect. The amalgam is used with serious intent, thus transforming what sounds like a comic verse into poetry characterized by scholarly techniques of allusion and structure. Tsegaye frequently uses figurative Language—a mix of Ge'ez, Amharic, English, and Afaan Oromo. He employs terms, idioms, symbols, and thoughts in such a way that they evoke mental images and a sense of parody. In many cases he makes syntactic departures from the usual order of literal language. One thing that stands out in Tsegaye's poetic expressions, especially in drama, is that he almost always portrays a conflict between a forceful character and a superior force such as providence ending with death or disaster.

Solomon Deressa's poems are deliberately short and simple but highly philosophical. As seen in his collection of works published under the name *Lijinat* (Childhood), his poems are characterized by the substitution of different measures to break up a rhythm. One can clearly see an act of aesthetic revolt in Solomon's deliberately brief odes which are so completely grounded in everyday life. He implicitly refuses to accept conventional poetic language. His verses express ideas and states of mind through the power of symbolism. As can be discerned from one of his verses in *Poems of Black Africa* edited by Nobel Laureate, Wole Soyinka, Solomon's epics are most radical not for turning away from lyric poetry's fixation on coherence or reference, but rather for the way the poems coerces a conventionally slanted genre into interfacing with an art form that is bona fide.

REFERENCES

Adera, T., A. J. Ahmed, et al. 1995. *Silence Is Not Golden: A Critical Anthology of Ethiopian Literature*. Lawrenceville, NJ: Red Sea Press.

Angoff, C., and J. Povey. 1969. *African Writing Today: Ethiopia, Ghana, Kenya, Nigeria, Sierra Leone, Uganda, Zambia*. New York: Manyland Books.

Asafa Dibaba Tafarraa. 2004. *Theorizing the Present: Towards a Sociology of Oromo Literature: Jaarsoo Waaqoo's Poetry*. Masters thesis, Addis Ababa University, Addis Ababa, Ethiopia.

Berzock, K. B. 2002. *The Miracles of Mary: A Seventeenth-Century Ethiopian Manuscript.* Chicago: Art Institute of Chicago.

Carnochan, W. B. 2008. *Golden Legends: Images of Abyssinia, Samuel Johnson to Bob Marley.* Stanford, CA: Stanford General Books.

Cerulli, E. 1973. *Tiberius and Pontius Pilate in Ethiopian Tradition and Poetry.* London: Oxford University Press.

Deedes, W. F. 2004. *At War with Waugh: The Real Story of Scoop.* London: Pan Books.

Faqada, A. 1998. *Unheard Voices: Drought, Famine, and God in Ethiopian Oral Poetry.* Addis Ababa, Ethiopia: Addis Ababa University Press.

Gelaye, G. 2000. *Peasants and the Ethiopian State: Agricultural Producers' Cooperatives and Their Reflections in Amharic Oral Poetry: A Case Study in Yetnora, East Gojjam, 1975– 1991.* London: Lit Verlag.

Glava, Z. A. 1937. *A Study of Heliodorus and His Romance, the Aethiopica, with a Critical Evaluation of His Work as a Serious Source of Information on Ancient Aethiopia.* New York: Graduate School of New York University.

Haberland, E. 1986. *Three Hundred Years of Ethiopian–German Academic Collaboration.* Wiesbaden, Germany: Steiner.

Huntingford, G. W. B., P. Paez, et al. 1965. *The Glorious Victories of Amda Seyon, King of Ethiopia.* Oxford: Clarendon Press.

Huntsberger, P. E. 1973. *Highland Mosaic: A Critical Anthology of Ethiopian Literature in English.* Athens: Ohio University.

Laird, E., and G. Aregawi Wolde. 1985. *The Miracle Child: A Story from Ethiopia.* New York: Holt, Rinehart, and Winston.

Leslau, W. 1965. *Ethiopians Speak: Studies in Cultural Background.* Berkeley: University of California Press.

Leslau, W. 1969. *Falasha anthology; the black Jews of Ethiopia.* New York: Schocken Books.

Leslau, W. 1982. *Gurage Folklore: Ethiopian Folktales, Proverbs, Beliefs, and Riddles.* Wiesbaden, Germany: F. Steiner.

Lifchitz, D., S. Grébaut, et al. 1940. *Textes éthiopiens magico-religieux.* Paris: Institut d'ethnologie.

Littmann, E. 1904. *Bibliotheca Abessinica.* Lyden, Germany: E. J. Brill.

Lockot, H. W., S. Uhlig, et al. 1998. *Bibliographia Aethiopica II: The Horn of Africa in English Literature.* Wiesbaden, Germany: Harrassowitz.

Nichols, L. 1973. *Menghistu Lemma of Ethiopia.* Addis Ababa, Ethiopia: Artistic Press.

Molvaer, R. K. 1980. *Tradition and Change in Ethiopia: Social and Cultural Life as Reflected in Amharic Fictional Literature ca. 1930–1974.* Leiden, the Netherlands: Brill.

Russell, M. 1833. *Nubia and Abyssinia: Comprehending Their Civil History, Antiquities, Arts, Religion, Literature, and Natural History.* Edinburgh: Oliver & Boyd.

Schuyler, G. S., and R. A. Hill 1994. *Ethiopian Stories.* Boston: Northeastern University Press.

Soyinka, W. (1975). *Poems of Black Africa.* London: Secker and Warburg.

Starkie, E. 1937. *Arthur Rimbaud in Abyssinia.* Oxford: Clarendon Press.

Stiller, J. 2002. *One People, Many Stories.* Los Angeles: JCLLA.

Uhlig, S., T. Bairu, et al. 1988. *Collectanea Aethiopica.* Stuttgart, Germany: F. Steiner.

Ullendorff, E. and 1987. *Studia Aethiopica et Semitica.* Stuttgart, Germany: F. Steiner.

Walta Hiywat. 1692. Hatata, [Ge'ez manuscript.]

Art, Architecture, and Craft

Pre-Christian art in Ethiopia was arguably unique. That can be discerned from the stelae of Axum, which date to between the second century BC and first century AD. Just like all other artistic developments, the evolution of Ethiopian art has occurred with some foreign influence, particularly Coptic, Byzantium, and Syrian, all of which entered the land through the country's intercourse with the orient and the Mediterranean world both before and after Christianity was introduced as a state religion in AD 340. For all practical purposes, Ethiopian artists blended their own African artistic tradition with those they were exposed to through religious intercourse, never allowing one to dominate over the other and always seeking balance in their style, which was syncretic. However, the artistic values and forms resulting from the blending of elements of these foreign cultures as employed by early Ethiopian artists changed so much over the years that they had become uniquely Ethiopian by the end of the mediaeval period. The architecture of the Dabra Damo from the beginning years of the Middle Ages represents the best preserved model of the Axumite building style. The monastery is built at the summit of a rock formation; it is steep on all sides and can be reached only by being dragged up with a rope. The Dabra Damo construction echoes the earliest methods of construction method in Ethiopia and exhibits similarity to the high rise, imitating stelae of the Axumites (ancient Ethiopians). The narthex of the church has a superbly paneled ceiling adorned with skillfully finished blueprints of flora and fauna, geometrical designs, and deftly engraved crosses.

The rock-hewn churches of Lalibala are the next architectural marvel of Ethiopia. In total, there are 11 churches of the type. Each church is carved out of a single rock formation, and they display an extraordinary variety in styles. The shrine of Madhane Alam, 77 feet wide and 35 feet high, is the largest. Big trenches were hollowed out on all sides of a rectangular formation, thus isolating in the center a massive block of granite. The rock was fashioned externally and internally with beautiful artistic designs. It does not take one long to realize that the adornments, carvings, and rock columns demonstrate workmanship of imposing elegance and to see why they have been dubbed one of the wonders of the world. The Genete Mariam Church has a pre-Christian temple-like appearance. The Church of St. George, which is the most photographed because of its unique shape, is carved out of rock to resemble a huge cross. St. Mary's Church is distinguished by its exceedingly intricate interior and a patio of huge dimensions. The Abba Libanos church is separated from the rock

The Great Fallen Stela of Axum (second century BC to third century AD). (Courtesy of Paulos Milkias.)

A collection of Orthodox Church crosses in Lalibala, Ethiopia. (Courtesy of Paulos Milkias.)

formation on all four sides. However, its roof remains part of the overhanging peak. The architecture of the churches of Lalibala is clearly a continuation of the Axumite style seen in other rock-hewn churches in Tigray, as specialists from Germany and Britain have come to conclude after a thorough investigation.

The palace of Fasilidas in Gondar is situated within a vast compound together with other buildings and is bounded by thick walls. The main castle is elevated, rectangular, and large and is constructed of grey stone, with four round turrets at its corners. At one time, the circumference of the precinct was one mile, and the great audience hall was 120 feet long. The latter was luxuriously furnished and covered with good-quality carpets from Persia and silks from China.

A lot has been said about this structure being of Portuguese design. It is agreed that after the Jesuit missionaries were expelled from Ethiopia in the late 1600s, the Portuguese craftsmen who remained were involved in the construction of the castles. However, the plan for the construction of the palaces and their huge enclosure was wholly Ethiopian, and the influence on the structures was not limited to Europe; they also bear similarity to the designs of South Arabia, which Ethiopia had controlled for many generations. Regarding pictorial art in Ethiopia, one finds rock carvings throughout the country that predate the Axumite civilization. Some of these are crude, whereas others are delicate color images of humans and animals etched on the faces of the rocks. These types of art are a totally distinctive art form. The mode of contemplation involved is unique compared to other types of Ethiopian pictorial drawings. Among these are the graceful rock drawings at Kohaito, drawn on perpendicular cliff faces and depicting animal scenes and slender movements. The carving of an outline of a lioness on a rock at Gobedra is so refined and lifelike that it captures the imagination at first sight.

The castles of Gondar (17th Century AD). (Courtesy of Paulos Milkias.)

The castle of Emperor Fasilides (17th century AD). (Courtesy of Paulos Milkias.)

The most illustrative and ubiquitous aspect of Ethiopian art is watercolor drawn on canvas and walls inside church buildings and on vellum in the case of manuscripts. Ethiopian artists were not limited to creating divine or secular images; they paid great attention to shapes of letters, and each scribe tried to outdo the other and thus fashioned beautiful manuscripts with even more attractive and colorful illumination. The standard of perfection that was responsible for the beautifully inscribed and illuminated religious manuscripts of the 14th and 15th centuries has never been surpassed. Church artists during the Middle Ages were found in abundance in the major religious centers such as Aksum, where coloring materials were found in great quantity. These artists specialized in religious works, but they also painted talismans that ordinary people believed would protect them against diseases and the evil eye and secular art, mostly of historical interest, such as art depicting the legend of the meeting between King Solomon and the Queen of Sheba, emperors with their entourage on march, and battle scenes. In all situations, traditional Ethiopian artistic rules are to show good persons in full face with two eyes visible, whereas evil people are to be shown in profile with only one eye visible. The method used is to draft the intended image in charcoal, outline it in black ink, and then shade them with diverse colors. Biblical personages are shown dressed in traditional Ethiopian clothing, riding mules or horses with classic Ethiopian saddles, stirrups held only by the big toe. They carry contemporary Ethiopian spears, shields, and other types of weapons.

But one thing that was characteristic was that the artists toiled anonymously; almost all of them refrained from signing their works. Among the few exceptions was a certain Fere Tseyon, who painted a picture of the Virgin Child on a panel, now preserved in the monastery of Daqa Estifanos in Lake Tana. The work was produced during the reign of Emperor Zara Yaqob (1434–1468). Alvares, a Portuguese visitor to Ethiopia in the 16th century, mentioned one remarkable artist by the name Makana Selassie, who painted a wall over the principal door of a major church with "two figures of Our Lady very well done, and two angels of the same sort, all done with the paint brush" (Pankhurst, 1990, 62).

The Ethiopian court, with panache for solemnity and ritual, was in constant need of luxury goods, most of which were made from precious metals, costly cloth, or other imported goods. Most were gold, silver, and gilt crowns; lavishly decorated mantles; apparel fashioned out of brocade; silk shirts; garlanded swords; tents; spears and shields; beautifully adorned saddles; and finely fashioned bridles and riding gear.

Traditionally, large numbers of citizens who were not peasant farmers congregated around the emperor, making any place he moved to like a mobile city. Until Gondar was made into a permanent capital in the 17th century, and even often after that period, the emperor and his lords and barons were constantly on the move from one "moving capital" to another. Craftsmen marched along with the mobile court

Religious art decorating the walls of a monastery in Lake Tana. (Courtesy of Paulos Milkias.)

and army. The artisans included skilled tailors who made sophisticated braids and tassels of fabric.

The congregation in one place of vast numbers of people, most of whom were fighters, generated a sizable demand for spears and shields, which were often lost or broken during fighting and had to be replaced. Well-to-do fighters and their families demanded carefully and beautifully adorned clothing, which required the toil of many artists. Artists, artisans, and craftsmen were in such high demand in medieval Ethiopia that sometimes the mobile emperors sought more of them from abroad. For example Emperor Lebna Dingil wrote the following to King Joao of Portugal in the 1520s:

> As brother does to brother . . . I want you to send me men, artificers, to make images, and printed books, and swords and arms of all sorts for fighting; and also masons and carpenters, and men who can make medicines, and physicians, and surgeons to cure illnesses; also artificers to beat our gold and sell it, and goldsmiths and silversmiths, and men who know how to extract gold and silver and also copper from the veins, and men who can make sheet lead and earthenware; and craftsmen of any trades which are necessary in these kingdoms, also gunsmiths. (Pankhurst, 1992, 222)

Among foreign artists who responded to such a call was a Venetian painter by the name of Nicolo Brancaleone, popularly known as "Marqorewos" by the Ethiopians. This Venetian, who came to Ethiopia in 1480 and stayed for 40 years as a captive court painter, singed his productions, a practice unknown among Ethiopian artists, as "Marqorewos, Faranj" (Marqorewos the Frank). Frank happens to be an Ethiopian designation for a white man or a person of European origin.

Sometimes, Ethiopian monarchs sent men of lower rank to be trained as artists, artisans, and performers because the average Ethiopian looked down on such professions. It is reported, for example, that at one time, Emperor Lebna Dingil (1603–1605) dispatched a special ambassador to Goa with four "slaves," two to be trained as painters and two others to be trumpeters.

Ethiopian artists of the medieval period were almost all member of the clergy. Some entered the emperor's service full-time, foregoing their spiritual vocation. Some of the foreigners who joined the emperor's court worked in cooperation with the local craftsmen. One artist who came from overseas painted the picture of the Virgin and Child for Emperor Baeda Mariam (1468–1478), but protest arose when his production was found to be at variance with that of the locals. Then in the 16th century, a Venetian artist by the name of Hieronymus Bikini was reported to have painted "many" works for the emperor of the day. For this service, he was provided with a large estate in Showa province and often traveled with the emperor, playing chess with him.

When Gondar became the permanent capital of Emperor Fasilidas, numerous people connected with art and artistic production settled down. These included parchment-makers; bookbinders; scribes; text copyists; leatherworkers; goldsmiths;

copper-workers; harness-makers; blacksmiths; millers; tailors; saddle-makers; sandal-makers; weavers; forgers of spears, swords, and knives; embroiders of women's skirts, priests' garments, and saddlecloths; makers of shields; carpenters; turners who fitted wood in rifles; and makers of drinking vessels. Whereas most of these craftsmen were men, many females also produced basketry and pottery. There were numerous jewelers who worked in gold, silver, tin, zinc, and copper, as well as by horn-workers who made sword handles from the horn of rhinoceroses. Others fashioned beautifully ornamented goblets from ox horn. Skilled tailors were by the 1840s using tools imported from Europe, with which they made ornate garments for the higher clergy, ceremonial shirts and capes for the lords and barons, top-quality burnouses for the rich and powerful, and ornately embroidered costumes for noblewomen. They also made colorful saddlecloths for the horses and mules of the nobility. Shoemakers, who were very skilled in using knives and awls, fashioned slippers for those who were economically well-off.

Carpenters from Gondar did everything from cutting down trees and squaring timber into planks to producing rifle-butts, beds, chairs, and other objects of woodwork from the kosso tree (*Hagenia abyssinica*). To do these tasks, as foreigners attested, they were quite well equipped with basic tools such as compasses, saws, gimlets, adzes, and braces.

Gondar had skilled church artisans, calligraphers, and bookbinders. Skilled leather-binding duties were handled by the *dabtaras* or lay clergy. The capital also had craftsmen who specialized in making highly prized artifacts such as small mirrors from imported raw glass and mercury.

Ancient kettles used in church services (ca. 15th century AD). (Courtesy of Paulos Milkias.)

The Beta Israel (Ethiopian Jews) formed the majority of the skilled blacksmiths and potters in Gondar. Furthermore, a great deal of the handicraft work was produced by them. The Beta Israel were judged by Plowden, the British consul in Ethiopia in the early 1900s, as "the best masons in the country." Muslims were also prominent in craftsmanship. They supplied the bulk of the city's weavers and specialized in embroidering women's dress.

Gondar was renowned for its skillfully produced tanned hides, parchments, and carpets. The capital also had a community of foreign craftsmen, mainly Italians and Greeks, who were wanted mostly for the repair of rifles, a very important service given that obtaining firearms from overseas was very difficult.

Ethiopian art can be classified into Christian and secular. The fact that Ethiopia has been a Christian nation since AD 340 means art has been shaped by the tradition developed in churches and monasteries.

For thousands of years, Ethiopia had its own artistic language. However, because the natural wealth of the country and its position along important trade routes uniting Africa, the Mediterranean, and the Orient attracted visitors, it also received a broad range of influences, particularly Byzantium, which it integrated and transformed into its own distinctive style. And because Ethiopia has its own unique writing system, its art can reliably be dated.

Konso grave marker, southern Ethiopia. (Courtesy of Paulos Milkias.)

Traditional Ethiopian religious art includes blazingly colored icons and glinting gold, silver. and bronze crosses. It represents centuries of Africa's oldest Christian culture. Cut off from the outside world for over a thousand years, the church developed distinctive belief systems, worship, and art. The most familiar of its religious objects in durable forms are crosses of gold, silver, bronze, and iron mounted on long staffs carried by priests. Meant to be gawked at in perforated silhouette against the bright African sun or candlelight, the designs of the objects became ever more elaborate and delicate. The workmanship was for the most part intricate and superb, rivaling classic pieces from Europe and the Orient.

In Ethiopian traditional art, icons, painted on wood panels or made of cloth bonded to boards, are produced in many sizes. Diminutive, closeable, pocket-size diptychs were fashioned to be portable and were sometimes worn on the body by the Christian faithful. There were also bigger and structurally more intricate versions. Most show the image of the Virgin Mary, who always takes a center place in Ethiopian Tewahedo Orthodoxy. The divine mother with the infant Jesus in her lap is always attended by wide-eyed angels and sometimes by jubilant warriors.

In the 15th century, the highlands of central and northern Ethiopia spawned magnificent paintings on wooden panels, many of which were manuscripts and processional crosses. It was in that century that the Stephanite movement emerged when a revered monk known as Estephanos was executed by Emperor Zara Yaqob for refusing to acknowledge prostration before a monarch as one would before the deity. Estephanos's followers were declared heretics, but they persisted in the teachings of their mentor and went on producing crosses and manuscripts later judged as masterpieces of Ethiopian art. There were also magic scrolls, made by *dabtaras*, or traditional scholars. These pieces of parchment, painted with Christian and magic symbols and prayers, are meant for therapeutic purposes and protection against evil spirits.

ART AND ICONOGRAPHY IN ETHIOPIA

Ethiopia has an old tradition not only in calligraphy, manuscript illumination, and iconography, which are the trademark of Ethiopian church scholars known as *dabtaras*, but also in wood carving. Strikingly handsome objects, including icons, are exhibited in tiny shops. Some are sold by street vendors. In Ethiopia specialists say that there is no real distinction between art and craft or between icons and religious art. It is important to note that the interiors of many old Tewahedo churches are entirely covered with outsized mural icons. In some churches, icons are placed on the walls. The old monasteries and churches also have numerous beautiful illuminated manuscripts. Wooden crosses, text pendants, and fold-out pieces that open out with little doors on string hinges have tiny icons inside. Icons are also painted on goat skin, some of them sporting fur on the other side.

Ethiopian ceremonial crosses like those described here are usually made of solid gold. These crosses are mounted on staffs and carried accompanying the Ark of the Covenant during processionals. When they are not being carried, they are usually displayed on altars. Such crosses are individually cast and can stand on their own without bases. The designs on the back sides are similar to those on the front.

ETHIOPIAN CROSSES AND OTHER PARAPHERNALIA

There are three forms of crosses: crosses with hollow round bases are mounted on sticks and paraded or shown displayed on altars; crosses no larger than 4 by 3 inches that have no bases are carried by hand during religious services; and the wearing of pendant neck crosses by Christians is traced to a 15th-century decree.

There are many types of Ethiopian headrests. Animal-hide shields are made by pounding the skins to wooden materials. They are put in the sun to dry and then removed to be used by soldiers. Ethiopian jewelry and usable materials are generally plain but elegant. Ethiopian icons are painted mostly on wooden materials. Such artifacts resemble classic Eastern Orthodox mode.

CROWNS OF ETHIOPIAN EMPERORS- -AXUM

The movement toward modernization of Ethiopian art started in 1887, when King Menelik of Shoa was a rising star slated to inherit the Solomonian crown thanks to the enormous amounts of weapons he had acquired from overseas. The king, together with his consort Taitu, was a patron of art. Art education, which was a

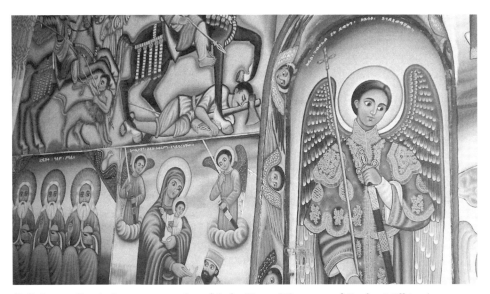

Religious wall paintings, monasteries of Lake Tana. (Courtesy of Paulos Milkias.)

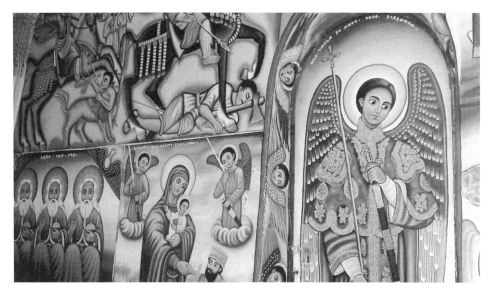

Religious wall paintings from the monasteries of Lake Tana. (Courtesy of Paulos Milkias.)

Wall painting from the monastery of Lake Tana. (Courtesy of Paulos Milkias.)

Ancient incense burner and handwritten books in the monasteries of Lake Tana (ca. 15th century AD). (Courtesy of Paulos Milkias.)

monopoly of Gondar, was slowly transferred to Entoto, overlooking the present capital Addis Ababa. Menelik's first act to modernize art found impetus when he sent a rising young Gojame artist, Afeworq Gebre Yesus, to Italy to receive training. Soon, all sorts of autodidact artists from all parts of the country were congregating around Menelik's Palace to benefit from the chance of modernization patronized by a forward-looking king. Within 25 years, the art center moved to the newly founded capital of Addis Ababa in the valley below the Entoto mountain range. Following the Fascist interlude which lasted from 1936 to 1941, the modern art movement began to flourish. The rising stars of the movement were Alefelege Selam Hirouy, Agegnehu Engeda, Abebe Wolde Giorgis, and Zerihun Dominique.

Of the postwar artists, Alefelege Selam, who was originally trained as a technician in the newly established Technical School of Addis Ababa, was noticed by Emperor Haile Selassie in the 1940's and was sent abroad to pursue Western education. It did not take long for the young man to choose his vocation in the area of art. He subsequently attended the Institute of Art of Chicago, arguably the most influential art college in the United States, from where he received his university degree. He soon returned to Addis Ababa, where he specialized in landscape and portrait painting. As an Ethiopian artist and despite his Western training, Alefelege Selam's work was of

Ancient incense burner (ca. 13th century) from the monasteries of Lake Tana. (Courtesy of Paulos Milkias.)

official court mode because he mostly decorated government buildings and churches. In that sense, his style of art was in the dominion of realism.

Soon an ultra-modern artist group sprang up in Addis Ababa and started to experiment with abstract forms. Among this coterie of artists was Gebre Kristos Desta, the painter-poet, who was an autodidact in the realm of art. After graduating from the British-run General Wingate Secondary School, he joined the University College of Addis Ababa, later to become Addis Ababa University, to study scientific agriculture. But his passion for art won out, and he started experimenting with different types of art forms. Abandoning his science education, he went to Europe and attended the Werschule fur Bildende Kunste und Gestaltung, a well-known art school in Cologne, West Germany, from 1957 to 1961. Gebre Kristos majored in painting and graphic art and excelled, graduating at the top of his class. It was here that the young artist became acquainted with European-style abstract painting, which ultimately became his specialty.

In 1962, Gebre Kristos returned back to Addis Ababa to introduce his newly adopted style of abstract expressionism, which was initially received with mixed results because his work diverged from mainstream Ethiopian art form. In time his talent earned appreciation, as a result of which he won the Haile Selassie Prize Trust

Wooden carving by Afework Tekle of Abuna of Petros, martyred in the hands of the Fascists in 1936. (Courtesy of Paulos Milkias.)

Award in Fine Arts in 1965. Gebre Kristos's artistic profession went hand-in-hand with his avant-garde poetry, which won immediate success among the rising modern educated class.

Another rising star of Ethiopian abstract painting was Skunder Boghossian, who won a scholarship to study in Europe and spent two years in London at St. Martin's School, Central School, and the Slade School of Fine Art in the 1960s. Then Skunder spent nine years as a student and teacher at the Académie de la Grande Chaumière in Paris. His formal training in Paris influenced his skill but never affected his imagination. In his abstract art, one clearly sees residues of Ethiopian culture. In 1966, the artist returned to Ethiopia and taught at the School of Fine Arts. In 1970, at the height of the student uprising that was shaking up the feudal system in Ethiopia, Skunder relocated to the United States and became a lecturer at Howard University in Washington, DC, where he taught art from 1972 to 2001. During his sojourn in the West, Skunder was touted as the most well-known African artist. He was in fact the first contemporary African artist to have a work purchased by the Museum of Modern Art in New York. Permanent collections of his work have also made it to other prestigious institutions, including the Musée d'arte Moderne in Paris and the Smithsonian Institution's National Museum of African Art in Washington, DC.

Then came other university-trained artists with an eclectic approach. At the top of this group is Maitre Afeworq Tekle. In 1947, Emperor Haile Selassie sent Afeworq Tekle to England to study mining engineering. But his interest in art worn out, and he joined the Central School of Arts and Crafts in London and later went to the famous "Slade" school, which is a branch of the Faculty of Fine Arts of the University of London. After returning to Ethiopia, he left again on a study tour of Italy, France, Spain, Portugal, and Greece. While in Europe, Afeworq made a special study of the Ethiopian illustrated manuscripts in the British Library, the Bibliotheque Nationale in Paris, and the Vatican Library, which helped him gain a deeper knowledge of his country's artistic heritage.

Afeworq was exposed to various media. However, he was never part of one specific medium. For Afeworq, realism, symbolism, and abstract art were just fields to ponder but never simply to follow. His work was rather eclectic. He chose the style that inspired his imagination and that he found to be the most appropriate to his artistic theme.

Afeworq found a breakthrough when he was commissioned by the Ethiopian government to decorate one of the capital's two most important Orthodox Tewahedo churches, the St. George's Cathedral, where he worked on murals and mosaics in the 1950s. He also worked on sculptures and was commissioned to create the equestrian stature of Ras Makonnen in Harar. But painting, not sculpting, was his major preoccupation. Afeworq's artistic status grew both locally and internationally. He produced countless murals, mosaics, drawings, paintings, stained-glass windows, and sculptures. He was commissioned to design stamps for the Ethiopian government. He also designed playing cards, posters, flags, and national ceremonial dresses. The playing cards he designed bore a series of hitherto-unknown Ethiopian motifs, many dating back thousands of years. With this endeavor, Afeworq introduced Ethiopia's artistic heritage to the general public. One of his well-known paintings, *Maskal Flower*, won him international fame when it was exhibited in the mid-1960s in the Soviet Union, the United States, and Dakar, Senegal. Afeworq won even more international fame when he produced his stained-glass windows at the entrance of Africa Hall, the headquarters of the United Nations Economic Commission for Africa, which demonstrated his talent to produce art on a gargantuan scale, covering 482 square feet. The work tries to show Africa's desolate past, present struggle, and future aspirations for grandeur. In 1964, Afeworq won the Haile Selassie Prize Trust Award for Fine Arts. In 1981, his work *Self-Portrait* was the first from the African continent to be honored for inclusion in the permanent collection of the Uffizi Museum in Florence, Italy.

In 1997, Afeworq attended the Biennale of Aquitaine, France. At the show, he presented two works: *The Chalice and the Cross in the Life of the African People*," which was a study for a stained glass window, and *The Sun of Senegal*. For this, he won the first prize. He was also nominated Laureate of the Biennale, an honor that carried with it the Grand Cordon with the Easel of Gold and membership in the French International Academy of Arts. At the 30th Anniversary of the International Congress on Science, Culture and the Arts, held in Dublin, Ireland, in 2004, Afeworq was awarded the Da Vinci Diamond "for his contribution to the wealth of human learning and advancement of modern art." The United Cultural Convention of the United States also awarded him the "Valiant Award" for "his efforts in promoting global harmony through his contribution to world art." Dr. Richard Pankhurst, OBE and fellow of the University of London, in an article he posted online, as a tribute to the artist, has this to say: "When we realize the extent of Afewerk's creative output, we can be confident that he will achieve much more in the future. His creative genius and his application to hard work have already set an example to his generation and assured his place not only as a leading Ethiopian artist but also as a figure in the art world of the twentieth century" (http://www.maitreafewerktekle.com/Biography2.html/ accessed March 20, 2011).

REFERENCES

African Training and Research Centre for Women. 1980. *Report of the Workshop on Handicrafts and Small-Scale Industries Development for Women in Francophone Countries, Held at Addis Ababa, Ethiopia, 27–30 November 1978*. Addis Ababa: United Nations, Economic Commission for Africa.

Balicka-Witakowska, E. 1997. *La crucifixion sans crucifié dans l'art éthiopien: Recherches sur la survie de l'iconographie chrétienne de l'antiquité tardive*. Warsaw, Poland: Zas Pan.

Barbieri, G., M. Di Salvo, et al. 2009. *Nigra sum sed formosa: Sacro e bellezza dell'Etiopia cristiana*. Vicenza, Italy: Terra ferma.

Berzock, K. B. 2002. *The Miracles of Mary: A Seventeenth-Century Ethiopian Manuscript*. Chicago: Art Institute of Chicago.

Bianchi Barriviera, L. 1963. *Le chiese in roccia di Lalibelà e di altri luoghi del Lasta*. Rome, Italy: Istituto per l'Oriente.

Bosc-Tiessé, C. 2008. *Les îles de la mémoire: Fabrique des images et écriture de l'histoire dans les églises du lac Tana, Éthiopie, XVIIe-XVIIIe siècle*. Paris: Publications de la Sorbonne.

Bosc-Tiessé, C., and A. Wion. 2005. *Peintures sacrées d'Ethiopie: Collection de la Mission Dakar-Djibouti*. Saint-Maur-des-Fossés, France: Sépia.

Boswell, W. P. 1987. *Bruce and the Question of Geomancy at Axum: The Evidence from the Norman Bayeux Tapestry*. Centre Island, Long Island: Winthrop Palmer Boswell.

Chojnacki, S. A. 1983. *Major Themes in Ethiopian Painting: Indigenous Developments, the Influence of Foreign Models, and Their Adaptation from the 13th to the 19th Century*. Wiesbaden, Germany: F. Steiner.

Chojnacki, S. A. 1985. *The "Kwerata Reesu," Its Iconography and Significance: An Essay in Cultural History of Ethiopia*. Naples, Italy: Istituto universitario orientale.

Chojnacki, S., and C. Gossage. 2006. *Ethiopian Crosses: A Cultural History and Chronology*. Milan, Italy: Skira.

Chojnacki, S. A., W. Raunig, et al. 2007. *Ethiopian Art: A Unique Cultural Heritage and Modern Challenge*. Lublin, Poland: Marie Curie-Skodowska University Press.

Di Salvo, M. 2006. *Crosses of Ethiopia, The Sign of Faith: Evolution and Form*. Milan, Italy: Skira.

Economic Commission for Africa. 1970. *Handicrafts and Small-Scale Industries Unit*. Addis Ababa: African Training and Research Centre for Women.

Economic Commission for Africa et al. 1979. *Women Textile Workers in Ethiopia*. Addis Ababa, Ethiopia: United Nations Economic Commission for Africa.

Economic Commission for Africa. 1980. *Report of the Workshop on the Participation of Women in Development through Co-operatives with Special Emphasis on Handicrafts and Small-Scale Industries, Khartoum, Sudan, 20–25 October 1979*. Addis Ababa, Ethiopia: United Nations, Economic Commission for Africa.

Ethiopia. YeErdata Mastababarianna Maquaquamia Komishen (Ethiopian Relief and Rehabilitation Commission) and UNICEF. 1989. *Evaluation Report and Feasibility Proposal of Menz Bana Weaving Project*. Addis Ababa: UNICEF Publications.

Ethiopia. Yemaikelawi Statistics Balasiltan. 1997. *Report on Cottage/Handicraft Manufacturing Industries Survey, March 1997*. Addis Ababa, Ethiopia: The Authority.

Ethiopia. Yemaikelawi Statistics Balasiltan. 2003. *Report on Cottage/Handicraft Manufacturing Industries Survey: November 2002*. Addis Ababa: Federal Democratic Republic of Ethiopia, Central Statistical Authority.

Ethiopia. Yestatistics Taqlay Tsihfat Bet. Business & Industry Division. 1975. *Advance Report on the 1972–73 Rural Survey of Cottage and Handicraft Industries*. Addis Ababa: Provisional Military Government of Ethiopia, Central Statistical Office, Business & Industry Division.

Ethiopian Art and Culture Chronicles Society. 1990. *The Ethiopian Art and Culture Codex*. Atascadero, CA: Atabichron Pub.

Fasil, G., and D. Gérard 2007. *The City and Its Architectural Heritage: Addis Ababa 1886–1941*. Addis Ababa, Ethiopia: Shama Books.

Fisseha, G. 2002. *Äthiopien: Christentum zwischen Orient und Afrika*. Munich, Germany: Staatliches Museum für Völkerkunde München.

Fisseha, G., and W. Raunig. 1985. *Mensch und Geschichte in Äthiopiens Volksmalerei*. Innsbruck Frankfurt/Main, Germany: Pinguin-Verlag.

Friedlander, M.-J. 2007. *Ethiopia's Hidden Treasures: A Guide to the Paintings of the Remote Churches of Ethiopia*. Addis Ababa, Ethiopia: Shama Books.

Gerster, G. 1968. *Kirchen im Fels; Entdeckungen in Äthiopien*. Stuttgart, Germany: Kohlhammer.

Gerster, G. 1970. *Churches in Rock: Early Christian Art in Ethiopia*. London: Phaidon.

Haus Völker und Kulturen Sankt Augustin Germany and A. Marx. 2001. *Katalog der Äthiopienabteilung*. Sankt Augustin, Germany: Museum Haus Völker und Kulturen.

Heldman, M. E., S. Fre, et al. 1994. *The Marian Icons of the Painter Fire Tsion A Study of Fifteenth-Century Ethiopian Art, Patronage, and Spirituality*. Wiesbaden, Germany: Harrassowitz Verlag.

Heldman, M. E., S. C. Munro-Hay, et al. 1993. *African Zion: The Sacred Art of Ethiopia*. New Haven, CT: Yale University Press.

Hespeler-Boultbee, J. J. 2006. *A Story in Stones: Portugal's Influence on Culture and Architecture in the Highlands of Ethiopia, 1493–1634*. Sooke, BC: CCB Pub.

Høgsbro, J., and B. Shiloah. 1973. *MCTC/SIDA Follow-Up Survey on Participants Trained in Courses at the Mount Carmel International Training Centre, Haifa, Israel and on Projects in Handicraft and Home Industries in Ethiopia, Kenya, Tanzania, Lesotho, Botswana, and Swaziland, 23 March-28 April 1973: Report*. Haifa, Israel: Mount Carmel International Training Centre for Community Services.

Horowitz, D. E., S. Tobin, et al. 2001. *Ethiopian Art: The Walters Art Museum*. Chailey, UK: Third Millennium.

Hourihane, C. 2007. *Interactions: Artistic Interchange between the Eastern and Western Worlds in the Medieval Period*. Princeton, NJ: Princeton University.

Isaac, E., M. LeMay, et al. 1968. *The Ethiopian Church*. Boston: H.N. Sawyer.

Istituto Italo-Africano. 1989. *Pittura etiopica tradizionale*. Roma: Istituto italo-africano.

Jenkins, E. 2008. *A Kingly Craft: Art and Leadership in Ethiopia: A Social History of Art and Visual Culture in Pre-Modern Africa*. Lanham, MD: University Press of America.

Joussaume, R. 1995. *Tiya, l'Ethiopie des mégalithes: Du biface à l'art rupestre dans la Corne de l'Afrique*. Chauvigny, France: Association des publications chauvinoises.

Juel-Jensen, B., and G. Rowell. 1975. *Rock-Hewn Churches of Eastern Tigray: An Account of the Oxford University Expedition to Ethiopia, 1974*. Oxford: Oxford University Exploration Club.

Karsten, D. 1972. *The Economics of Handicrafts in Traditional Societies: An Investigation in Sidamo and Gemu Goffa Province, Southern Ethiopia*. München, Germany: Weltforum Verlag.

Kelel 14 mastadader. YaIndusterinna edatebabat biro. 1994. *Directory of Industries and Handicrafts*. Addis Ababa, Ethiopia: The Bureau.

Kosrof, W. W., C. Clarke, et al. 2003. *My Ethiopia: Recent Paintings*. Newark, NJ: Neuberger Museum of Art.

Laird, E. 1987. *The Road to Bethlehem: An Ethiopian Nativity*. New York: H. Holt.

Lepage, C., and J. Mercier. 2005. *Art éthiopien: Les églises historiques du Tigray*. Paris: ERC.

Lepsius, R. 1849. *Denkmaeler aus Aegypten und Aethiopien nach den zeichnungen der von Seiner Majestaet dem koenige von Preussen Friedrich Wilhelm IV*. Berlin: Nicolai.

Lindahl, B. 1970. *Architectural History of Ethiopia in Pictures*. Addis Ababa, Ethiopia: Ethio-Swedish Institute of Building Technology.

Lindahl, B. 1970. *Medieval Architecture and Art in Ethiopia: Lecture Notes*. Addis Ababa, Ethiopia: College of Architecture and Building Technology.

Mammo, T. 1973. *Religiöse Kunst Äthiopiens*. Stuttgart: Institut für Auslandsbeziehungen.

Mann, G., et al. 2005. *Art of Ethiopia*. London: Sam Fogg.

Marsh, R. 1998. *Black Angels: The Art and Spirituality of Ethiopia*. Oxford: Lion Pub.

Marx, A., A. Neubauer, et al. 2007. *Steh auf und geh nach Süden: 2000 Jahre Christentum in Äthiopien*. Tübingen, Germany: Legat.

Mercier, J. 1997. *Art That Heals: The Image as Medicine in Ethiopia*. Munich, Germany: Prestel.

Mercier, Jacques. 2000. "L'Arche Ethiopienne." *Art Chrétien d'Ethiopie*. Paris: Pavillon des Arts, Musées.

Musées royaux d'art et d'histoire Belgium and J. Lafontaine-Dosogne. 1995. *L'art byzantin et chrétien d'Orient: Aux musées royaux d'art et histoire*. Bruxelles, Belgium: Les Musées.

Pankhurst, R. 1992. *A Social History of Ethiopia: The Northern and Central Highlands From Early Medieval Times to The Rise Of Emperor Tâewodros II*. Trenton, NJ: Red Sea Press.

Pankhurst, Richard. "Afewerk Tekle." http://www.maitreafewerktekle.com/Biography2. html/ Accessed March 20, 2011.

Peabody Museum of Salem, E. C. Langmuir, et al. 1978. *Ethiopia, the Christian Art of an African Nation: The Langmuir Collection, Peabody Museum of Salem*. Salem, MA: The Museum.

Perczel, C. F., M. Longenecker, et al. 1983. *Ethiopia, Folk Art of a Hidden Empire*. La Jolla, CA: Mingei International Museum of World Folk Art.

Phillipson, D. W. 2009. *Ancient Churches of Ethiopia: Fourth–Fourteenth Centuries*. New Haven, CT: Yale University Press.

Pizzi, D., and G. Muratore. 2001. *Oltremare: Itinerari di architettura in Libia, Etiopia, Eritrea*. Cagliari: Sirai.

Plant, R. 1985. *Architecture of the Tigre, Ethiopia*. Worcester, MA: Ravens Educational and Development Services.

Playne, B. 1954. *St. George for Ethiopia*. London: Constable.

Plowden, W. C. and T. C. Plowden. 1868. *Travels in Abyssinia and the Galla country: with an account of a mission to Ras Ali in 1848*. London: Longmans

Raineri, O., and T. Qes Adamu. 1996. *Santi guerrieri a cavallo: Tele etiopiche: Tele di Qes Adamu Tesfaw*. Clusone, Italy: Ferrari.

Ramos, M. J., I. Boavida, et al. 2004. *The Indigenous and the Foreign in Christian Ethiopian Art: On Portuguese-Ethiopian Contacts in the 16th–17th Centuries: Papers from the Fifth International Conference on the History of Ethiopian Art Arrabida*, November 26–30, 1999. Lisbon, Portugal.

Raunig, W., and B. Rodella. 2005. *Das christliche Äthiopien: Geschichte—Architektur—Kunst*. Regensburg, Germany: Schnell & Steiner.

Réunion des musées nationaux France and Musée national des arts d'Afrique et d'Océanie. 1992. *Le roi Salomon et les maîtres du regard: art et médecine en Ethiopie: Musée national des arts d'Afrique et d'Océanie, 20 octobre 1992–25 janvier 1993*. Paris: Réunion des musées nationaux.

Revault, P., and S. Santelli. 2004. *Harar: Une cité musulmane d'Ethiopie*. Paris: Maisonneuve et Larose.

Rigotti, G. 1939. *L'edilizia nell'Africa orientale italiana*. Torino: Editrice libraria italiana.

Rohrer, E. F. 1932. *Beiträge zur Kenntnis der materiellen Kultur der Amhara*. Schönburg-Bern: W.P. Wälchli.

Samuel P. Harn Museum of Art. 2007. *Continuity and Change: Three Generations of Ethiopian Artists*. Gainesville: Samuel P. Harn Museum of Art, University of Florida.

Scott, C., 1974. *Handicrafts of Ethiopia*. Addis Ababa: Ethiopian Tourist Organization.

Sharf, F. A., D. Northrup, et al. 2003. *Abyssinia, 1867–1868: Artists on Campaign: Watercolors and Drawings from the British Expedition under Sir Robert Napier*. Hollywood: TSE-HAI Publishers and Distributors.

Silverman, R. A., T. Qes Adamu, et al. 2005. *Painting Ethiopia: The Life and Work of Qes Adamu Tesfaw*. Los Angeles: UCLA Fowler Museum of Cultural History.

Simpson, W., and R. Pankhurst. 2002. *Diary of a Journey to Abyssinia, 1868, with the Expedition under Sir Robert Napier, K.C.S.I.: The Diary and Observations of William Simpson of the Illustrated London News*. Hollywood: Tsehai.

Sintayehu, N., T. Amelework, et al. 2007. *Lalibela: Wonders & Mystery*. Addis Ababa, Ethiopia: Addis Art and Culture.

Smallwood, C. *Librarians as Community Partners: An Outreach Handbook*. Chicago: American Library Association.

Stappen, Xavier van der. 1996. *Æthiopia: Pays, Histoire, Populations, Croyances, Art & Artisanat*. Bruxelles: Cultures Et Communications, Gordon et Breach Arts International.

Tadgell, C. 2007. *Antiquity: Origins, Classicism and the New Rome*. New York: Routledge.

UNESCO, S. Wright, et al. 1961. *Ethiopia: Illuminated Manuscripts*. Greenwich, CT: New York Graphic Society by arrangement with UNESCO.

UNICEF. 1990. *Market Survey Study of the Bana Weaving Project in Northern Shoa*. Addis Ababa, Ethiopia: Rehabilitation & Disaster Preparedness Section Emergency, UNICEF.

United Nations Economic Commission for Africa. 2002. *African Development Forum III: Defining Priorities for Regional Integration, 3–8 March 2002, Addis Ababa, Ethiopia*. Addis Ababa, Ethiopia: Economic Commission for Africa.

Van Wyk Smith, M. 2009. *The First Ethiopians: The Image of Africa and Africans in the Early Mediterranean World*. Johannesburg, South Africa: Wits University Press.

Vanderlinden, J. 1969. *The Law of Physical Persons Art. 1–393: Commentaries upon the Ethiopian Civil Code*. Addis Ababa: Faculty of Law, Haile Selassie I University.

Visonà, M. B., R. Poynor, et al. 2008. *A History of Art in Africa*. Upper Saddle River, NJ: Pearson/Prentice Hall.

YeEtiopia Tinatenna Meremer Taquam, and B. Benzing, et al. 1990. *The Hand Crosses of the IES Collection*. Addis Ababa: Institute of Ethiopian Studies, Addis Ababa University.

YeEtiopia Tinatenna Meremer Taquam, S. A. Chojnacki, et al. 2000. *Ethiopian Icons: Catalogue of the Collection of the Institute of Ethiopian Studies Addis Ababa University*. Milan, Italy: Skira, Fondazione Carlo Leone Montandon.

Yesahaq, G. I. 2005. *Dialogo introduttorio all'Eritrea archeologica*. Asmara, Eritrea: MBY Pub. & Print. Center.

Zerihun, Y., and Alliance ethio-française. 2008. *Zerihun Yetmgeta: The Magical Universe of Art*. Pretoria: University South Africa Press.

Music

The Ethiopian term *musiqa* is clearly borrowed from European languages. But it is now used in Amharic and other languages of Ethiopia as a term as legitimate as those of indigenous origin. In Ethiopia, music is closely associated with the circumstance in which it is played. For example, church songs and musical instrumentals are named on the basis of the ritual orders for which they are performed. Furthermore, music that is played in church is perceived differently than music played on secular occasions. Even the names for different kinds of music differ, and to use one for the other can create conflict. Church song is *zema*, but to refer to it as *zefen*, which is the name of secular melody, would be highly offensive to the Christians.

Church Music *Deggua* is at the base of the music of the Ethiopian Orthodox Tewahedo Church. It is a record of musical compositions, styles, and notations. Church music in Ethiopia is the specialty of the Zema Bet (Academy of Music), which has three branches. The first deals with the study of the *Deggua* (Book of Liturgical Chants), the second deals with *zemare* (Eucharist songs) and *mewaset* (songs for commemorations and funerals), and the third concentrates on *keddasse* (general liturgy). The monastery of Bethlehem in Begemder specializes in the *Deggua*, and Zurumba, in the same province, is famous for *zemare* and *mewaset*. Serekula in Wadla (Wallo) and Dabra Abbay in Tigre are also noted for *keddasse*. The school of Aquaquam (which means "styles of singing") synthesizes the three branches of music by training the student in the appropriate movement and steps of the religious dances that accompany the songs.

Of all the categories, the *Deggua* is the most important because only the best students are selected for its rigorous curriculum. The basic instruction for the students pursuing their studies at this level consists of teaching the musical notations of the Ethiopian religious hymns written in this unique Ethiopian book of liturgical chants. Even though the earliest known manuscripts to survive the devastations of Ahmed Gragn date to the 14th century, Ethiopian Orthodox Tewahedo Church history recounts that the *Deggua* chant was introduced in AD 534 by a chorister named Yared, who composed the entire body of hymns that have since been revised and that are

Religious painting depicting the famous musicologist St. Yared and the Axumite emperor Gabra-Maskal who lived in the early sixth century AD. (Courtesy of Paulos Milkias.)

found in the six books of religious chants. The notations called *melekket* consist of characters from the ancient Ethiopian language Ge'ez, in which each sign stands for a textual syllable.

According to Ephraim Isaac (1968), the *Deggua* notations called *seraye* are made up of Ge'ez syllabic characters and numbers of curving and waving signs, lines, and points. These symbols are placed above the words to be sung. Some are written in red, suggesting a particular melody and rhythm of the music. The characters provide a cue for *seraye*, which is a distinct melodic formula. Dynamic modes and tempo are shown by written signs. All indicate musical phrases, groups of notes, or rhythmic values. The mode may be *ge'ez* (*forte*), *ezel* (*legato cantabile* and *piano*), or *ararayi* (*plaintive con moto*). The tempo may be *mergd* (*largo*), *neus-mergd* (*andante*), or *abiy-tsefat* (*presto*). In the presentation of Ethiopian Orthodox Tewahedo Church chant, the musical formula is embellished with specific melodic ornaments. There are three distinct forms of chanting: *ge'ez*, in which most melodies are performed; *array*, embodying a form of "cheerful" melodies used sporadically in services; and *ezel*, used during periods of fasting and grief. Only a *dabtara*, an unordained member of the clergy, who is well versed in the Ethiopian Orthodox Tewahedo Church rituals and in aspects of the liturgy and the scriptures, and who has spent no less than 30 years at the church school, is trained to distinguish the subtleties of moods and manners of performance inscribed in the *Deggua*. Although the *dabtara* is required to copy the whole body of the *Deggua* while a student, in the final analysis, he memorizes the melodies and, while singing, improvises along the outlines of basic melodic formulas set by Yared and subsequent church scholars.

Any student of theology who has received Ethiopian Orthodox Tewahedo Church education is expected to know how to sing correctly and how to improvise using these musical notations. Ethiopian Orthodox Tewahedo Church chant and dancing consist of colorful priestly robes and elaborate ornaments that are used during each service. The most common among these are the usual cantor's praying stick known as a *monomial*, which is about five feet in length and used by the *dabtaras* as a crutch to lean on during long services or to move in concert with a melodic form during religious dances. Other musical instruments, used by the *dabtaras* during both regular services and religious parades, include the *imbilta* (hollow long reed), *bagana* (lyre or harp), bells, *masenko* (a one-stringed violin also widely used in secular music), *kabaro* (large drums), *malakat* (a long trumpet about four feet long and similar to the ancient tuba, used only in religious processions and sometimes carried before persons of rank, particularly kings, queens, and emperors), and *tsenatsel* (rattles that correspond to the ancient *cestrum* believed by some scholars to have been used in the music of pre-Christian mystical period). In general, religious dance, which is an integral part of the Ethiopian Orthodox Tewahedo Church service, is thought by many learned men to be part of Ethiopia's Jewish heritage from Biblical temple times.

The style of secular Ethiopian music is, for the most part, varied. The northern part of the country, which is mostly Semitic, has heterophonic music, whereas in the south, where Hamites and Nilotics predominate, the music is by and large polyphonic. Though some musical instruments are common among Semites and Hamites, many of the other ethnic groups have their own distinctive instruments. Each

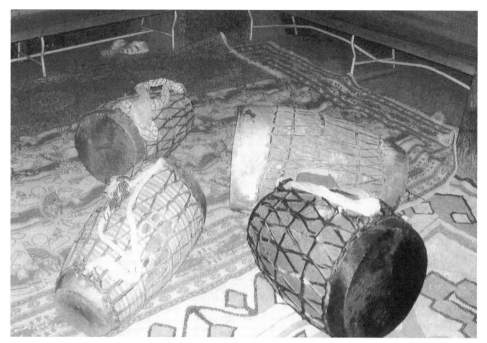

Church drums used during a religious dance. (Courtesy of Paulos Milkias.)

Church bells made of stone from the monasteries of Lake Tana. (Courtesy of Paulos Milkias.)

ethnic community also has attributes and rhythms that are unique to their own type of dance. The music of the Semitic people of the Tigray and Amhara regions and that of the Hararis basically resemble music of the Middle East and the Orient. Thus, they are monophonic or heterophonic, whether performed vocally or played with instruments. The vocal and instrumental timbre of the Semitic people is nasal. Ethiopian rhythms rarely approach the metric density typical of other areas of tropical Africa, but they are rich and wholesome to listen to and to watch in performance, which is varied and attractive, thus compensating for the repetitive beats. Dance types and rhythmic structures in Ethiopia vary from one ethnic group to another. For example, even though they are both Semitic, the Tigrayans have triple rhythms, whereas the Gurages have duple rhythms. The *eskesta* (shoulder dance) of the Amharas is strikingly different from that of the Tigrayans, which is very gentle. The *eskesta* involves springing and performing with different forms of jerking the shoulders. The jerks can be subtle or violent depending on the region from which the dance originates. The Oromos use their legs in a jumping mode and rhythmically move their heads up and down as they jump. The Amharic speakers of Minjar, perhaps as a result of Oromo influence, also use their legs. A Gurage dance that many refer to as "Wofe Lala" (a name of one of the songs used) involves a lot of hand and leg movement forward and backward.

Lalibala songs, used for begging, and mostly from the Amhara areas, are sung in two's in polyphonous manner. The pitch in the average Ethiopian music is pentatonic. Melodic categories and tuning techniques are referred to as *qegnit*, four of which are recognized universally among the Amharic speakers: *tezeta*,

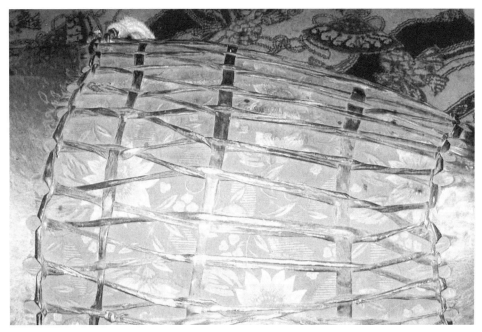

Decorated church drum known as the kabaro. (Courtesy of Paulos Milkias.)

Ceremonial dance, southern Ethiopia. (Courtesy of Paulos Milkias.)

bati, *anchihoye*, and *ambasel*. Different from the Semitic styles of the Tigrayans and the Amharas, the Omotic Dorzes have music that is characterized as being highly polyphonic. Dorze musical performance is vocal and is divided into 30 genres connected with events such as funerals, religious days, and traditional annual festivals.

Ethiopian music has a rich cultural mosaic and forms. The forms are textual or vocal, as represented by the music of the *azmaris* (griots); are mimes or expressive dances, as exemplified by the folklore of different ethnic groups such as the Anuak, the Dorze, and the Mursi; or are instrumental, performed with objects like the imbilta characterized by music stretching from and Tigray Gidole.

One early style of Ethiopian music is the *ingurguro*, which has a plain form with small ranges of rising and falling movement. The other style is *mezmur*, with a unique quality of singing, performance style, rhythmical limitations, and control of contents. Yet another style is *zefen*, which is the most widespread musical style found within all the ethnic groups. *Zefen* differs from the other two because of its asymmetrical meter. It also has isometric and heterometric modes in its performance design. Still another form is the *zema*, which, as noted previously, is reserved for church songs and hymns. There are additional secular forms to be noted:

Ingurguro is sung mostly in high falsetto vocal style by female singers and in the deep vocal range for male singers. Example: Aster Awoqe's music and Kassa Tessema's *krar* melody are good illustrations of this. Whereas Aster mixes *ingurguro* tempo with *zefen* rhythm, Kassa's krar is pure traditional Ethiopian *ingurguro*.

Mezmur is a type of song sung in a full voice—*woreb* songs and songs that follow sport games are examples.

Zefen is a song conducted in a calm manner. It goes together with a drum and a dance; *iskista* is an example.

Qualities of songs are chosen on the bases of their melismatic and loud voice. However, if they voice their songs without wavering tones in the style of *ingurguro* and *zefen* music, the singers are referred to as *chuahi* (shouter) or *gagano* (vociferous).

Singing in a deep or low rumbling voice, *zefen* style, would not win a singer a good reputation. Only a singer who recognizes and shows variety in style who sought after.

Ethiopian secular music can be categorized as follows:

Secular Music with Seven Modes

1. *Qedamai Silt (e.g. tizita)*
2. *Dagmai Silt (e.g. ambasell)*
3. *Salisai Silt (e.g. bati)*
4. *Rabai Silt* (e.g. multi-modes)
5. *Hamsai Silt (e.g. Anchihoye)*
6. *Sadisai Silt (e.g. gererso*-type music)
7. *Sabai Silt* (e.g. Adere's chromatic type)

Sacred Music with Three Modes

1. Geez
2. Izil
3. Ararray

Sacred Music Styles

1. YeQoma
2. Yebetelhem
3. Yeachabir
4. Wonchere

The basis for all Ethiopian church music is the musical composition of St. Yared. Yared's music composition is based on seasons of the year, meaning they are sung only during designated seasons:

Zemene Yohanis (Year of John): i) from Meskerem 1 to Meskerem 26 [September 11 o October 6]

ii) from Meskerem 26 to Hidar 6 (Woriha tsige) [October 6 to November 16]

Zemene Merawi (Year of Marawi): i) from Tahisas 29 to Tir 30 [January 7 to February 7]

ii) from Yekatit 1st to Miazia 29 (Woriha tsome) (Fastig Month) [February 8 to April 29]

Zemene Kremit (Year of Kremit): i) from Meazia 29 to Sene 15 (Woriha tinsae) (Month of Assension) [May 7 to June 22.]

ii) from Sene 15 to Meskerem 1 (Kiremit) [June 22 to September 11]

Ethiopian music has several singing techniques that require different techniques and forms to produce sounds. See Zenebe Bekele.

The vocal organs, which consist of lungs, larynx, pharunx, nose, and mouth as means of creating a voice, are categorized as follows:

1. *Yederet dimits* (chest)
2. *Yeguroro dimits* (larynx)
3. *Yeras dimits* (head)

Musical instruments such as lyres, aerophones, membranophones, and idiophones are found in plenty in Ethiopia. Many of these are jointly used by the different ethnic groups with minimal variation. The instruments are made to be played solo, but they can accompany singing and dancing.

We can classify Ethiopian musical instruments by the type of sound they produce: air, string, membrane, or any other self-sounding matter. Four instrumental families are recognized: aerophones, chordophones, membranophones, and idiophones. There is also now a fifth category, electrophones, because in the late 20th century, some Ethiopian musicians started to use electronically amplified instruments.

The vast ethnic diversity of Ethiopia has led to the production and use of diverse musical instruments, sometimes different only in name. Of the aerophone type of instruments, flutes are very common. One type of flute is known as *washint*, with many different names among the other ethnic groups. For example, the Oromos alone have three different names for it: *ululle*, *garri*, and *faga*. The Ethiopian flute is typically made of bamboo and has two to four finger holes.

There are also cases in which several flutes are played together, as in Western orchestras. The instrument produces a rhythmic formula on the single tone, creating a polyphony of interlocking parts. Some flutes, such as the *embelta* of the highland country, when played in orchestras can yield two sounds. The player in this case can produce many tunes by combining the resonance of the differently pitched instruments. Some ethnic groups, such as the Gawwada and the Konso, use flutes and panpipes, which are employed during rituals, entertainment, or cattle-keeping chores.

A shepherd youngster playing the flute near the Blue Nile Falls. (Courtesy of Paulos Milkias.)

The aerophone family also includes trumpets. Just like flutes, trumpets are played solo, as by the Nuer, or in orchestras, as by the Walaytta. Such instruments are made mostly of wood, bamboo, metal, or animal horn. Some trumpets produce a single sound, whereas others can produce more sounds when pitches are modulated with the hand covering the larger extremity of the instrument. The bottle-gourd *ariva* used by the Berta, which resembles a gourd rattle, is another kind of aerophone. To fashion it, a narrow tube is place into the hole at the apex of the gourd that is used as a blowing hole. This instrument produces only one note.

Chordophone musical instruments in Ethiopia include lyres, spike-fiddles, and the musical bow. Morphologically, instruments can be classified as bowl-lyre type or box-lyre type. The most conspicuous among these instruments is the *masanqo*, which is a violin-like spike-fiddle with one string, tuned by a big peg and played with a deeply arched bow. As a general rule, the sound box is diamond-shaped and is covered with parchment. Its single string is made of braided horse hair. Traditionally, this musical instrument was played by secular poet-musicians similar to the troubadours of medieval Europe. The masanqo is used by Ethiopian *azmaris* (minstrels) at secular fêtes such as carnivals and family celebrations such as weddings, as well as in bars.

MODERN ETHIOPIAN MUSIC: THE NEW WAVE

In the late 1960s and 1970s in Ethiopia came a melange of composition that borrowed not only from China and Japan but also from American jazz, blues, and soul as well, as from Latin rumba and Cha-cha. As its trademark, the newly developed tune had cross-rhythms and pentatonic melodies. This signaled the birth of a new era. As one music expert put it,

> Ethiopia's diverse blend of the traditional and the contemporary, of exotic and indigenous styles must rank as one of Africa's greatest undiscovered musical legacies, reaching its apex with the ceaselessly inventive and hypnotically funky horn-splattered sides of 'Ethiopian swing' recorded for a handful of independent labels in Addis Ababa between 1969 and 1978. (Phillip Briggs, 2006, 559–563)

Almost unheard of by the West and totally forgotten in the world, the new wave of Ethiopian music thrived only in Addis Ababa cafes and bars that hosted live bands or played tape recordings. Then came a renaissance of sorts just at the beginning of the new millennium, when a French musical expert, Francis Falceto, collected the old recordings and compiled them under the name *Ethiopiques*. Ethiopian singers such as Mahmoud Ahmud and Alemayehu Eshete, innovative composers such as Mulatu Astatke, and gifted saxophonists such as Getachew Mekuria were resurrected. And on their heels came young nationalist singers with soul, blues, and Ethiopian rhythms such as Aster Aweke, Tewodros Kassahun (Teddy Afro), Gossaye Tesfaye, and Ejigayehu Shibabaw (Gigi), whose talent has been recognized worldwide. All have been featured on BBC Television, on the *Voice of America* radio, and in major Western papers. It is interesting to note that *New York Times* music critic Jon Pareles rated Gigi's Afripop lyrics number one in a year-end roundup of the Best Obscure Albums of 2001.

Another most common instrument is the *kerar*. The *kerar* contains five or six strings. Such lyres can be plucked with the right hand with a plectrum. The left hand fingers keep the strings not played from resonating. It can also be plucked separately by the fingers of one hand. The *bagana* (harp) is the other type of lyre used by the Amhara and Tigre highlanders. The instrument is fashioned from wood to mold the pillars, yoke, decorations, sound box, tuning pegs, and bridge; skin forms the soundboard, and gut strings are plucked. The *bagana* has 10 strings and holds the highest status among the chordophones of the Amhara because of its legendary association with King David of Jerusalem.

Traditional Ethiopians believe that whereas the *begena* (lyre) was inspired by God and first played by King David who was, according to the *Fetha Negest* (Glory of the Kings), the grandfather of Menelik I, the first Ethiopian emperor of the Solomonian

Three Ethiopian musicians sit, playing their homemade stringed instruments. (© W. Robert Moore/National Geographic Society/Corbis.)

line, the *krar* is an inferior instrument because it is inspired by *seytan* (Satan) and is human-made. According to this view, the *begena* is for the praising of God, but the *krar* is used to adulate feminine beauty, to create sexual arousal, and to eulogize carnal love. The *krar* has been associated with brigands, outlaws, and wonderers. Such people, it is said, entertained men of means. Wanderers play the krar to solicit food, and outlaws play it to sing a war song called *fanno*. Today, the *krar*, which used to be the plaything of the Amharas, has become one of the most popular Ethiopian stringed instruments. One can find the *krar* in both urban and rural areas. The *krar* has six strings, extended vertically between a lower soundbox and an upper cross-bar. The crossbar is supported by two side-posts that are slot into the soundbox at their bases. The strings are attached to a strong piece of leather and fastened to the soundbox at their lower end. The tuning pegs, six in total, are tightly wrapped around and fixed to the crossbar with the strings' upper ends. A bridge is used to lift the strings from their lower base positioned on the stretched-out leather plane of the soundbox.

The soundbox of the *krar* is the key to its proper function. It has a hollow hemi-spherical mass curved out wood, or metal now, usually any tyre cup or ordinary bowl, and a membrane made from a cow's, goat's, or sheep's hide. After casing the bowl with a membrane, six holes are punctured through it. Two of the slanting holes near the edge serve to hold the side-posts, and the four round openings serve as soundmakers. The membrane is firmly stretched out over the bowl and sewn around its edge with gut. When strings are plucked, the guts vibrate and set the stretched membrane to vibrate on a different plane, producing harmonies on the tone. The bowl is normally hollow. It is arched and filled with air. Vibration is centralized, thus allowing the issuing of free resonance.

The Ethiopian *azmaris* are akin to the old European bards, skalds, and minstrels who flourished from the Middle Ages until modern times. We cannot trace exactly when they emerged, but musical specialists such as the late professor Ashanafi Kebede (1975) trace them to centuries before the Christian era.

Sacred music in Ethiopia is a branch of the of the Ethiopian Orthodox Church tradition, whereas secular music remained in the domain of the Ethiopian imperial court during the period of the monarchy. But religious and social interactions in Ethiopia regularly overlapped to the point where it is difficult to make distinctions between the two. Azmari music thrived along with the intricate style of Ethiopian religious music known as the *zema* as written in the *Deggua*. In fact, the azmari style heavily leaned on the melodic styles and other modus operandi of verse improvisation from the sacrosanct choral tradition of *zema* or *qine* and morphed them into azmari secular music. By tradition, the Ethiopian Orthodox Church influenced artistic developments. The *zema bet*, or the music school, trained young students vocally as it trained them in other areas important to the Church. The training started as young as four years old, and students graduated as deacons. Whereas some continued with religious training to become priests, a few dropped out to make a living by being azmaris. The azmaris who dropped out of the training harbored animosity against those who remained because the latter demeaned them; those who stayed looked down on the azmaris as vulgar, only a little better than beggars. To be called an azmari was actually pejorative among the Church-educated. So the azmaris attacked their critics in songs whenever they got a chance. They were also involved in social commentary via double entendre verse on very sensitive issues in society. They mocked people in high places, even emperors, if they were found to be unpopular with the public. The azmaris were the first to convey scandals in high places. One such azmari who mocked Emperor Tewodros received a capital sentence from the monarch and was beaten to death in the court.

Female azmaris flourished in feudal Ethiopia, as they do today. They are just like their male counterpart poet-musicians. Such female musicians are usually wives or lovers of male azmaris who have gradually learned the repertory of their male counterparts. Some azmaris of recent years have become extremely successful by taking advantage of modern possibilities that enable them to learn new styles of songs that combine Ethiopian and other types of music. Tilahun Gessesse, dubbed the king of Ethiopian modern music, originally had training in the Church schools in the area of sacred chant until he moved to Addis Ababa and joined the Imperial Body Guard Band, which gave him the opportunity to experiment with his voice and rise to the level he reached in his later years. It was not only Tilahun who abandoned the Church to become a stage artist. Eyoel, Frew Hailu, Getamesay Abebe, Melaku Gelaw, and Menelik Wosnachew had Church music training before they went secular as well.

In traditional Ethiopian society, attitudes toward the arts and crafts have been downbeat. Secular arts and crafts, including music, are traditionally construed as vocations that should be "left alone to the handicapped, the failures, beggars, lepers, slaves, loafers, and others that comprise the lowest stratum of the Ethiopian class society" (Kebede, 1975, 47). Being called an azmari is therefore highly derogatory. As a general rule, no parent, not even an azmari, would allow his daughter to marry an azmari because this would invite disgrace from the society.

Unlike the Sudanese *griots* and the North African *gnawas*, the Ethiopian azmaris never developed associations, brotherhoods, or guilds in order to protect or advance their mutual interests. Instead, they functioned individually. Thus, azmaris who do not have an important person to protect them can become victims of high society. As a result of lack of cooperation, the azmaris are also victims of vicious rivalries and resentfulness.

By and large, the azmaris lead an itinerant life. They go door to door, from house to house, to sing and earn money. But their major hangouts used to be *taj-bets* (mead drinking houses), which is still the case in remote villages. But since the overthrow of the monarchy, instead of taj-bets, the most common place for them to go now is *zigubigns* (nightclubs that are run within modern villas). They also go from party to party wherever there are weddings or other types of celebrations. Azmaris from the countryside move from district to district and from village to village. In olden times, some aristocrats would hire an azmari on a short-term contract to have him or her accompany him on a long journey and entertain him, so that he would not be bored while riding his mule or horse. The azmari traveled on foot, following the mule or horse together with the nobleman's servants. He then entertained the aristocrat when he camped for the night and had his regular meals. In addition to improvising their own verse, azmaris also sing lines said to them by the audience. If it is witty, there is applause. A reward for good entertainment is leftover food from the master's table and possibly a glass of *taj*, or mead.

In improvising poems and songs on the spot to fit the occasion, azmaris can be acerbic. One 19th-century European visitor to Ethiopia described this phenomenon as follows: "The Azmaris in effect . . . represent our troubadours or trouveres with astonishing fidelity. Wandering singers in the service of the princes and nobility, they come armed with their viols [the masingo]. Improvident friends of pleasure, living on their caustic or gay spirits, as . . . 'enfants terribles.' Their pointed tongues do not always spare the great lord of the manor who feeds them, especially when they consider that the gifts they receive are not fit for their devil-may-care zest" (Mondon-Viclailhct, 1922, 3182–3183).

Despite being acerbic in words, most azmaris are extremely talented. They can observe things others fail to observe and are good at mastering any language they hear. Their songs are commanding and insightful imageries of particular situations in human relationships. They are excellent at inventing metaphors to describe specific situations. The azmari is not limited to playing music. While playing music, he is also a news reporter, a social commentator, a critic, a clown, a companion, a political agitator, a religious reformer, a vagabond, a poet, a servant, and a stroller (Kebede, 1975).

Being called an azmari has gone a long way from being pejorative. With the success of the likes of Tilahun Gessese, Tedy Afro, and Gigi, the concept is changing rapidly as more and more educated young people are initiated into modern music.

The fact that Tilahun Gessese married into a family with royal connections attests to that.

With Western music such as jazz, blues, and rock permeating Ethiopian society, the azmaris who are known for instant improvisation are fast disappearing in the urban areas. That they are surviving in the villages where tradition is sacrosanct is not a consolation. Considering the rapid pace by which modern music travels through contemporary society, whether urban or rural, how long the proverbial Ethiopian azmaris can persist is anybody's guess.

Outside the central and northern regions, which are dominated by the Amhara and Tigre cultures, totally different kinds of music exist. For example, the Hamar of southern Ethiopia is the only ethnic group to use a musical bow. The instrument called *tingle* is a three-string bow. It is played by putting one end of the bow in the mouth and plucking the strings with fingers. The timbre of the sound is modulated by changing the volume and form of the mouth cavity while playing. It is an instrument usually played by an adolescent Hamar.

Membranophone musical instruments are different types of drums. In Ethiopian feudal society, drums were symbols of authority and political power. When the emperor passed an edict, a drum was sounded to emphasize its importance. When war was declared, a drum was sounded, and the people had to rally behind the monarch or leader. This type of drum is called *nagarit*. It is hemispherical with only one membrane. Some drums, known as *atamo* by many ethnic groups, are small and consist of one membrane and are played during celebrations such as weddings. Others called *kabaro*, used by priests of the Ethiopian Orthodox Tewahedo Church, are double membrane. The latter is either laid on the ground or hung from the shoulders with fabric and beaten, usually with two hands. It is the type of drum used in church music.

Idiophone musical instruments are mostly found in southwestern Ethiopia, as in Magarjgir, Nuer, and Aiiwaa, where they are known as *tum* or *tom*. Idiophones used in rhythmic accompaniment come in many shapes and forms. They include rattles made of gourds, tortoise shell, hide, or wood; miniature bells strung on cords and tied to the legs of dancers; and wooden blocks, which are common, particularly among the Oromos and the Hararis. Cow horns are another type of chordophonic instrument, used especially by sedentary ethnic groups in Ethiopia. Churches use the *dewel*, or bells of metal, stone, or wood, to call the faithful to go to church and pray. The handheld cestrum *tsanatsil*, which is fashioned out of bronze or silver, is used to emphasize rhythmic patterns of church chants or dance songs. *Dabtaras* lean on prayer sticks called maquamia, which they also use during liturgical chanting and dance. The *maquamia* moves with leg movements and strikes the ground following a set rhythm. This style of dancing requires special training in the school of Aquaquam.

Secular music in Ethiopia has always accompanied Ethiopian community life, played during work in rural and urban areas; during rite of passage at birth, puberty, weddings, and funerals; and for plain amusement. Among mainstream Ethiopian society, there is a type of music that arouses courage and incites patriotism. This type of verbal music sometimes accompanied by the *masenqo* is called *shilala* or *fukara* by the Amharas and is performed in preparation for an ensuing battle. Western influence in Ethiopian music started in 1924 when Ras Tafari (later Emperor Haile

Selassie) brought 40 Armenian orphans of the Armenian holocaust to Addis Ababa together with their Armenian music trainer. But it was starting in the second half of the 20th century that Oriental- and Western-style music penetrated the country's music scene. This was undoubtedly influenced by the wide use of radio and later television.

Commercial recordings started as long ago as the time of Emperor Menelik, when Nagadras Tasamma Eshete recorded traditional music and sold in Ethiopia. In fact, Ethiopia's adventure into modern musical recordings started with Nagadras Tasamma Eshete, who was the pioneer Ethiopian musician of modern times. He introduced Ethiopian traditional music through modern recording. Nagadras Tasamma was an outstanding individual—a troubadour singer, poet, and musician and, to top it all, minister of posts in the imperial government led by Emperor Iyasu, who succeeded his grandfather Emperor Menelik upon the latter's death in the early years of the 20th century. Tasamma was the first African artist to have a record contract cut in Germany as early as 1909.

The first record of commercial music by Negadras Tessema was one issued by the world-renowned ODEON company; it was a red-label gramophone disc released sometime between 1936 and 1941. Sixteen other ODEON red originals by Tessema are now in the possession of the Institute of Ethiopian Studies (Bender, 2006).

Tessema was the earliest African musician to record in Europe. He is also recognized as the first African to record and release a commercial disc. His mostly *semina worq* songs (double entendre tunes) were published on double-sided 78-rpm shellac discs. As Bender points out, Tessema' recordings have now become works of great interest to historians, political scientists, linguists, literary scholars, and musicologists. This is because they belong to the rare body of literary products from the start of the 20th century. Tessema's works in fact opened a new musical tradition and set the stage for the country's pop music, which uses electrical instruments as opposed to the troubador's traditional masanqo instrument.

Theater orchestra performed by saxophonist Getaccaw Maquamia in the late 1950s and later amalgamated international and Ethiopian melodies led to the "golden age" of Ethiopian popular music. It was during this period that traditional music played by famous entertainers such as Eyoel gave way to Oriental- and Western-influenced music performed by rising stars such as Tilahun Gessesse, Menelik Wossinachew, Alemayehu Eshete, and Mahmud Ahmed, to name just a few. Though most people listened to music recorded on tape, Amah Records produced many recording albums between 1969 and 1975. During the same time, the Western-trained musicologist Mulatu Astatqe started an innovative method that mixed Ethiopian, Latin, Western Jazz, and Oriental rhythms. Following the 1974 revolution, several music groups emerged and started to play in bars. Among them were the Ethio Stars and Tukul Band and the Roha Band. In the 1980s, many promising musicians moved to Washington, DC, where a large Ethiopian diaspora community is concentrated. Some won international fame, such as Aster Awake did when Columbia Records released her albums. Ethiopian music for the younger generation of the new millennium has been heavily influenced by reggae, which Tewodros Kassahun, known as Teddy Afro, popularized. Belonging to this generation is also Ejigayehu Shibabaw, known by her chosen name Gigi, who has been acclaimed by major music critics and has been exposed to a worldwide audience through international media such as the BBC. These last two musicians, who are undoubtedly avant-garde, are also very nationalistic. At a time when Ethiopian society is being remolded on the basis of ethnic nationalism, they invoke the nostalgia of the Haile Selassie years, the symbols of the Lion of Judah, the tricolor Ethiopian flag, and the courage of the Ethiopian people who defeated European colonialists at the battle of Adwa.

During the first decade of the millennium, recordings of Ethiopian music from the 1960s and 1970s have been restored and presented to a receptive international audience through the release of a compilation series titled *Ethiopiques*, originating in Paris, France. Musicians such as Mahmoud Ahmed and Alemayehu Eshete, with their hybrid music, have through these albums attained wide-scale international exposure.

REFERENCES

Discography

Admassu Wubie. *Ethio Sound*. Washington DC. 2000. CD.

Adzido Musical Group. 2005. *Ritual Songs and Dance from Africa*. ARC Music. Addis Ababa. CD.

Aga, A. 1995. *The Bägänna of Ethiopia, the Harp of King David*. Long Distance. Paris. CD.

Alamayahu Eshete, et al. 1993. *Shanachie*. Addis Records. Addis Ababa. VHS.

Alamayahu Eshete, et al. 2005. *Wanado*. Ambasal Muziqana Video. Addis Ababa. VHS.

Albatros. 1975. *Musica dell' Etiopa* (Music of Ethiopia). Distribuzione Editoriale Sciascia. Addis Ababa. Tape Recording.

Asafa, et al. 1993. *Saday Yamuziqa Qeneber*. Addis Ababa. CD.

Asalafach, B. 1998. *Yeserg Zafanoch*. Ityo Muziqa. Addis Ababa. CD.

Ašanafi, S., et al. 2006. *Temer Webat*. Salam Records. Addis Ababa. CD.

Aster Aweke. 1996. *Live in London*. Barkhanns Records. New York. VHS/DVD.

Ataxlti, et al. 1997. *Was. Qu. 4*. Soloda Muziqa Bét. Addis Ababa. CD.

Ataxlti, et al. 1999. *Enqwae Tafatarena*. Méga Audiovisual Studio. Addis Ababa. CD.

Auvidis. 1999. *Éthiopie: Musiques Des Hauts-Plateaux* (Ethiopia: High Plateaux Music). France Distribution, PlayaSound. Addis Ababa. CD.

AYO Tapes. 1982. *Afrikan Dreamland. Live at the Roots*. Nashville, TN. CD.

Baheru. 1986. *Rahél. Woy Mala*. Addis Ababa. CD.

Bahta Gebre Hiwot. 2000. *The Best of Bahta Gebre Hiwot*. Ethio Sound. Washington DC. CD.

Barchas, S., and High Haven Music. 2007. *Tonweya and the Eagles, Multicultural Folktales of Imagination and Insight*. Sonoita, AZ. CD/DVD.

Barhé, G. 1995. *Gumayé*. Ambasal Vidiyonna Muziqa. Addis Ababa. VHS.

BBC. 1989. *Under African Skies*. Music from the BBC-TV series. London. VHS/DVD.

Caprice. 1992. *Music from Ethiopia*. Stockholm. CD.

Courlander, H. 1949. *Folk Music of Ethiopia*. Folkways Records. Ethnic Folkways library. New York. Audio Recording/LP.

Cowell, H. 1961. *Music of the World's Peoples*. Vol. 5. Folkways Records. Addis Ababa. Tape Recording.

Darbabaw, et al. 1984. *Ambasal*. Marawa Demsawiyan. Ambasal Muziqana Vidiyo Madaber. Addis Ababa. Audio Recording.

Denbeshoo. 2004. *Zafan*. AFR Rec. Alexandria, VA. DVD.

Dols, N., D. Niles, et al. 1977. *Music of the World: A Selective Discography*. UCLA Music Library. Los Angeles, CA. Audio Recording.

Ellipsis Arts. 1994. *Africa: Never Stand Still*. Roslyn, NY. CD.

Enenor Alan Gana. 2005. Angel Ltd. Addis Ababa. DVD.

Endašaw, et al. 2005. *Kamešet Bahelawi Zafanoch*. Ambassel Records. Addis Ababa. CD/VCD.

Ethio Sound. 1997. *Wedding Songs of Ethiopia*. Washington DC. CD.

Ethio Sound. 2000. *Mahdara zéma*. Washington DC. CD.

Ethio Sound. 2000. *Yahagar Bahel Zafanoch*. Washington DC. CD.

Ethio Sound. 2001. *Barebada*. Washington DC. CD.

Ethio Sound. 2001. *Mishamisho*. Washington DC. CD.

Ethio Sound. 2004. *Gojjam Na Baygn*. Washington DC. CD.

Ethio Sound. 2004. *Seq Alagn*. Washington DC. DC. CD.

Ethio Sound. 2004. *Tey Atmegni*. Washington DC. CD.

Ethiopia. 1968. *Music, Dance, and Drama*. Thomas Leiper Kane Collection, Hebraic Section, Library of Congress. Washington DC. CD.

Getachew Kassa. 2000. *The Best of Getachew Kassa*. Ethio Sound. Washington DC. CD.

Hayla Eyasus Germa. 2001. *Music of Hayla Eyasus Germa*. Ethio Sound. Washington DC. CD.

Fiqaaduu, K., and G. Baqqalaa. 2005. *Biyyaa-Ambo*. Vol. 1. Mana Muziiqaa Gold Leef. Addis Ababa. CD/DVD.

Flûtes du Monde (Flutes of the World). 1996. Boulogne, France. CD.

Frystak, R. 2000. *Voici*. Los Angeles, CA. CD.

Ganat, M.A.A. 2005. *Leb weleq*. Master Sound. Addis Ababa. CD.VCD.

Germa, N.B. Manbara, et al. 1993. *Ket Demtsawiyan*. Addis Ababa. CD.

Germa Tafara and K. Abate. 2005. *Kanari Muziqa*. Addis Ababa. CD.

Gété, et al. 2005. *Ché bal Lebé*. Nile Music Center. Addis Ababa. CD.

Gillett, C. 2005. *Thirty-Seven Artists from 24 Countries Around the World*. Milwaukee, WI. CD.

Grout, P., and National Geographic Society of the United States. 2008. *The 100 Best Worldwide Vacations to Enrich Your Life*. Washington DC. CD.

Hab, et al. 2006. *Balay Balay Yawelat*. Ambasal Records. Addis Ababa. CD/VCD.

Habtu, N. 2005. *Traditional Ethiopian Instrumental Music*. Vol. 4. Addis Ababa: Master Sound Muziqa.

Hamelmal Abate. *Sedet.* 2001. Amel Productions. Washington DC. DVD.

Hampson, T., W. Rieger, et al. 2004. *Concert, 2004–12–07.* Library of Congress Music Division. Washington DC. CD.

Harrisson, R., and R. Johnson. 1975. *Musiques Ethiopiennes.* Ocora, OCR 75. Audio Recording. Addis Ababa.

Hayiluu, Getaachoo, et al. 2004. *Malli Maalii?* Mana Muziqaa Maaree. Addis Ababa. CD/ DVD.

Hebest, T., and Roha Band. 1985. *Bezu Aytanal.* Addis Ababa. CD.

Ivangadi prodakšen. 2004. *Tarik Tasara.* Addis Ababa. CD/VCD.

Jenkins, J. L. 1967. *Musique Traditionnelle d'Ethiopie.* Série Loisirs, Vogue. Paris. Audio Recording.

Jenkins, J. L. 1970. *Ethiopia: Sound Recording.* Tangent TGM 101–103. Addis Ababa. Audio Recording.

Jensen, A. E., Universität Frankfurt am Main., Frobenius-Institut., et al. 1959. *Völker Süd-Äthiopiens: Ergebnisse der Frobenius-Expeditionen 1950–52 und 1954–56.* W. Kohlhammer. Stuttgart, Germany. Audio Recording.

Johnson, R., and R. Harrison. 1973. *Ethiopian Urban and Tribal Music.* LLST 7243–7244. Lyrichord. Addis Ababa. CD.

Johnson, R., and R. Harrisson. 1999. *Mindinnaw Mistiru.* Vol. 1. Ethiopian Urban and Tribal Music. Rounder Select. Cambridge, MA. CD.

Kebede, Ashenafi. 1969. *The Music of Ethiopia: Azmari Music of the Amharas.* Anthology AST 6000. Addis Ababa. Audio Recording.

Kebede, Ashenafi. 1977. *Secular Verse and Poetry in Ethiopian Traditional Music.* International Institute for African Music. Addis Ababa. CD.

Kuyša, S. 1991. *Bali hélélé, Yanbulé.* Ityo Muziqa. Addis Ababa. CD.

Lamb, J. F. and J. Jensen. 1974. *Piano Rags.* Genesis GS 1045. Addis Ababa. Audio Recording.

Lamb, J. F., and M. Kaye. 1975. *The Classic Rags of Joe Lamb.* Vol. 2. Huntington Station. Golden Crest, NY. CD.

Lerner, L., and C. Wollner. 1974. *Folk Music and Ceremonies of Ethiopia.* Ethnic Folkways Library. Folkways Records. New York. Audio Recording.

Lerner, L., and C. Wollner. 1975. *Ethiopia the Falasha and the Adjuran Tribe.* Ethnic Folkways Library. Smithsonian Folkways Recordings. Washington DC. Audio Recording.

Lerner, L., and C. Wollner. 2001. *Folk Music and Ceremonies of Ethiopia.* Smithsonian Folkways Recordings. Washington DC. CD.

Leslau, W. 1950. *Music of the Falashas.* Ethnic Folkways Library. Folkways Records. New York. Tape Recording.

Lortat-Jacob, B. 1977. *Éthiopie: Polyphonies des Dorzé.* Le Chant du monde LDX 74646. Addis Ababa. Sound Recording.

Mabrahetu, G. Y. H. 1986. *Etiopia walala.* Addis Ababa. Audio Recording.

Madingo, et al. 2006. *Ayedaragem.* Éléktra Muziqa. Addis Ababa. CD/VCD.

Mahmud, et al. 1984. *Tezetañaw Enqu.* Etio Musiqa. Addis Ababa. Audio Recording.

Manalemosh Dibo. 2004. *Menjarigna Zefen.* AFR Rec. Baltimore, MD. VHS/DVD.

Masaka. *Qeñeta.* 2004. Masterpiece Ethio-Traditional Songs. AFR Rec. Alexandria, VA. VHS/DVD.

Masfen, et al. 1984. *Tolo Nay.* Nagarit Muziqa. Addis Ababa. Audio Recording.

Mesfin, et al. 1984. *Yemesfin Ababa Feqer Mastawasha.* Ambasal Muziqa Videyona Éléktriniks. Addis Ababa. Audio Recording.

Mitchell, J. 2003. *The Complete Geffen Recordings.* Santa Monica, CA. CD/DVD.

Mowatt, J. 1985. *Working wonders.* Ho-Ho-Kus, NJ: Shanachie Records. VHS.

Mowatt, J. 1988. *Working wonders.* Ho-Ho-Kus, NJ. Shanachie Records. Addis Ababa. VHS.

Nagarit muziqa. 2004. *Bati.* Addis Ababa. CD/VCD.

Nahom Records. 2001. *Semahenge Belew.* Corona, NY. CD/DVD.

Nahom Records. 2004. *Guadegna.* New York. CD/DVD.

Nahom Records. 2004. *Masanqo Remix. III.* Addis Ababa. CD/VCD.

Nahom Records and LC Collection Library of Congress. 2001. *Mannale!* Vol. 1. *Mert Yaamaregna.* Nahom Records. Addis Ababa. VCD.

Nalbandian, K., and L. N. Finley. 1944. *Ethiopian National Anthem.* The Boston Music Co. Boston, MA. Audio Recording.

National Theater of Ethiopia. 1989. *Krar, Appolon's Harp.* Esunikku Saundo Shirizu, 38. Tokyo, Japan. JVC/VHS.

Negesti, H. 1997. *Taadila.* Qu. 4. Art records. Addis Ababa. CD.

Ocora. 1997. *Ari polyphonies.* Radio France. Paris, France. CD.

Tiku Weldu. 2001. Ethio Sound. Washington DC. CD.

Print Resources

Bender, Wolfgang. 2003. "Initial Research into the Life and Work of Tessema Eshete: The First Ethiopian Singer to Record Commercially." In Siegbert Uhlig, ed., *Proceedings of the XVth International Conference of Ethiopian Studies, Hamburg July 20–25, 2003,* 403–408. Harrassowitz Verlag.

Combes, E., and M. Tamisier. 1838. *Voyage en Abyssinie.* Paris: L. Desessart.

Hailù, P. 1968. "Il Canto Sacro Etiopico: Conferenza Tenuta All'istituto Italiano Di Cultura Il Aprile 1968." Addis Ababa, Ethiopia: Istituto Italiano Di Cultura.

Kebede, Ashenafi. 1975, January. "The Azmari, Poet-Musician of Ethiopia." *The Musical Quarterly* 61(1): 47–57.

Lepsius, R., J. B. Horner, et al. 1853. *Letters from Egypt, Ethiopia, and the Peninsula of Sinai.* London: H.G. Bohn.

Moisala, P., and B. Diamond. 2000. *Music and Gender.* Urbana: University of Illinois Press.

Mondon-Viclailhct. 1922. "La Musiquc ethiopienne." In *Dictionnaire du Conservatoire*, 3182–83. Paris: Encyclopédie de la Musique.

Pankhurst, E. S. 1955. *Ethiopia: A Cultural History*. Lalibela House. Essex, Eng. UK.

Food

The Ethiopia that is known around the world as the land of famine has also remained for generations a land of good food and lavish feasts. In pre-Derg Ethiopia, men of means frequently held huge banquets for their followers. By tradition, the banquet was given at a lord's mansion or a king's palace. It served thousands of people with raw meat, *tella* (local beer), and *tej* (Ethiopian mead). Diners were also entertained by minstrels and clowns. So it is wrong to assume that famine was the most common experience of the average Ethiopian. Furthermore, on saints' days, it is a time-honored tradition among the nobility to hold a feast every year in the name of their patron saint. The more important saints' days such as those in the name of the Virgin Mary, Archangel Gabriel, or Michael are accompanied by colorful ceremonies. The *tabots* (replicas of the Ark of the Covenant) borne by colorfully dressed priests are carried out of the neighboring churches to honor the saints. The priests are surrounded by minstrels, and trumpeters are followed at the rear by the high-priest and other important church dignitaries, followed by the general populace. In large urban areas, the chiefs march with soldiers mounted on horseback all dressed in military apparel. The women form themselves into separate parties. They ululate, sing, and clap their hands to the beating of the drum by a young girl who carries it on a strap around her neck. Once the *tabot* retires to its holy of holies in the church, the rich people feed the multitude by slaughtering a bullock or well-fed sheep. In all cases, the banquet is similar to the one held for the soldiers and retainers in the court. Row meat, *tej*, and *tela* are served in abundance.

There is also heavy feasting when relatives of the dead hold a religious ceremony called *qurban* or *tazkar* in order to help the diseased to have his or her sins forgiven. On this occasion, a bullock or a fattened sheep or number of sheep and goats are slaughtered and offered to the community, particularly the priests and the poor. This absolution for a deceased person is a time-honored custom that even the poor try to observe within their means. But it should be borne in mind that no *qurban* is performed for a child under seven because it is assumed that a child so young could not commit a sin. No *qurban* is held for a sinner who died refusing to repent either or a person who committed suicide. These types of individuals are assumed to have sinned purposely and therefore cannot obtain absolution.

The feast of absolution is not held only one time. Such feasts are held at 40 days, 1 year, and 7 years after the burial. Those with means hold feasts at even more frequent intervals—on the 3rd, 7th, 20th, 30th, 80th, and 180th days. The feast is served the same way on each occasion, but the amount of food and drink consumed differs.

On the feast day, priests read the Psalter and hold a mass. Throughout the mass, the Christian name of the deceased is mentioned by the clergy, and some chapters from the Book of the Dead are read. In the end, the priests and the deacons recite praises to the Virgin Mary, whom the Ethiopian Orthodox believe will intercede with her son on behalf of the diseased. After the mass, all go to the house of the host and feast on row meat and drink *tala* and *tej* to their satisfaction. After the feast, the main priest says the blessings for the family, and the diners depart. If it is a poor person's absolution, and the food was not adequate, the deacons and church students who live by begging for food can be heard to murmur, "Oh, Lord, please have pity, kill a rich person for us!"

The staple food of the average Ethiopian is made of grains, particularly teff (*E. ragrostis abyssinica*), which is indigenous and is almost limited to Ethiopia alone. Other grains are wheat, barley, maize, millet, and oat. Southern people such as the Gurages, the Wolaitas, Hadiyas, and Kambatas depend on *enset* (*Ensete ventricosum*), which is a relative of the edible banana. Many types of nuts, berries, tubers, and roots as well as pulses such as beans, peas, and lentils are consumed daily also. Onions, garlic, and red peppers are mixed with a variety of spices and added to the food. Green vegetables such as collard greens and cabbage are also consumed by all sectors of the society.

Market in Addis Ababa—the largest of its kind in Africa. (AP Photo/Sayyid Azim.)

Meat is consumed by all ethnic groups, but only the well-to-do have access to it daily. Cattle, sheep, and goats are raised on a large scale by the Oromos, Somalis, and Afars. Fowl are found in the households of all rural people. Food preparation is literally a secret art in Ethiopia. Every household has its own secrets for preparing food.

Manners of dining differ from region to region in Ethiopia. For example, whereas among the Christian Amharas and Tigres, parents and children eat separately, the latter being served their portions only after the parents and their adult guests have finished eating, among the Muslims of Harar, children either are served with their parents and adult guests or are served their portions before the adults. In fact, in the age-old tradition of eating dinner among the Adares (or Hararis), a fire is lit and all the elderly men in the neighborhood sit on one side of the fire, the children sit on the next side, and next to them sit all the women, thus forming a concentric circle.

The staple food is not uniform either. For example, as noted previously, whereas the Amharas and the Tigres depend for their daily diet on injera made of teff, the people in southern Ethiopia (Sidamas, Walaitas, Gurages, Hadiyas, etc.) have a diet made *enset*, otherwise known as false banana. This crop, which is planted by men and takes seven years to fully mature, is gender-specific at the preparation stage. The art and labor of making *kotcho* (*enset* bread) out of *enset* is left to women, who extract the liquid starch of the plant by pounding it for hours on end. This requires a lot of perseverance. First, the women cut the whole plant, layer by layer. They carefully separate the nutritive part of the plant, which is found near the bottom center. As they do this, they have to work alone. Men are prohibited from looking at women while they are

A Gurage woman making dough for a bread called kotcho, which is made from the stems of the false banana known as enset. (© narvikk/iStockphoto.com.)

engaged in the elaborate preparation of *kotcho*. Breaching this rule is considered a shameful act. First, the women extract the starch. Then they bury it underground for several weeks, or even several months. The purpose is to ripen it to maturity. When it is ready, the starchy substance is removed from underground and wrapped in as many flat cakes as possible inside the leaves of a false banana. The fermented starch portions are placed inside an open fire and baked until they look like French crepe breads except that the final product is dark brown and has a caustic smell that may be repulsive to an initiate. One culinary delight of the Gurages made of minced row meat and known as *kitfo* (steak tartar) is almost invariably served with *kotcho*.

The culinary delights from the land of Pester John were once described by Shlomo-Bacharach, the editor of East Africa Forum, in the following words: "Ethiopian food is like the Ethiopians themselves: spicy, subtle, piquant and most of all, unforgettable." The range of dishes prepared is amazingly vast. A vegetarian can find solace in that multitudes of Ethiopian Tewahedo Christians are totally free of consuming animal products during most days of the year. During the fasting period, they eat only vegetarian food that their ancient traditions cultivated. Scores of their dishes are prepared during this period with vast choices of spices. Meat-eaters can also have scores of dishes, which again the Ethiopian culture has carefully evolved throughout thousands of years of history. Non-vegetarian food includes cooked beef, lamb

Meseret Lema Wondimu of Shagar Honey Wine Restaurant in Addis Ababa, conducting an Ethiopian coffee ceremony. (Courtesy of Paulos Milkias.)

or goat meat, spicy steak tartar, raw beef cubes dipped in hot peppers or the same marinated in a fiery jalapeño, and delicious beef stew made with 10 or more different spices. The only thing you might not find is pork because it is religiously forbidden by both the majority Orthodox Christians and Muslims.

Doro wat, that most ubiquitous Ethiopian culinary art, is the centerpiece of any Ethiopian banquet. It is made of salt-washed and lime-marinated chicken, with a generous amount of onions and over 15 different spices combined and cooked slowly on fire for several hours. It is served with hard-boiled eggs and injera, which is a pancake-type sour crepe that is used to hold food, in place of knives and forks.

To quench one's thirst after lunch, a person gulps *talla* (Ethiopian beer) or *taj* (honey wine). For those interested in inebriation, there are also a dozen varieties of liquor (e.g., Koso Arake) that can compete with any made in the ancient monasteries of continental Europe. It is not uncommon for Ethiopians dining at a round basket table to feed one another.

An Ethiopian meal is rarely complete without a coffee ceremony. The country is the original home of the product, and everybody expects to sip it several times after a hearty meal. A coffee ceremony is always accompanied by the captivating odor of incense, and neighbors sit around and chat about their problems, treating this everyday ritual as a group therapy.

TEFF-INJERA

Following is how to make injera from the Ethiopian cereal teff. You will need 11 pounds of teff to 14 cups of water.

1. Separate the chaff from the teff by utilizing a sieve.
2. Grind the clean teff cereal in a mill.
3. Add 14 cups of water to 11 pounds of teff flour and knead well.
4. Put your fingers in the mixture, look for lumps, and rub them out.
5. Cover the thin dough for 3 days.
6. After the fermentation is complete, pour off the water.
7. Remove 4 cups of the dough for leavening.
8. Boil 6 cups of water in a very big container.
9. Add the 4 cups of teff dough in small quantities until the mixture is well cooked and thick.
10. Add the leavening to the original teff dough and keep it undisturbed until it rises.
11. Burn a big fire underneath a clay pan (called a *mitad* Amharic).
12. When the *mitad* or clay pan is hot, grease it with crushed oil seeds.
13. Scoop a cup of the thinned dough and pour it on top of the hot *mitad* in concentric circles, starting from the edge and ending at the very center.

14. Cover it for a minute or so, until it is well cooked and the edges tend to curl up.

15. Pull the pancake-looking bread (which will look like it has sponges on the top) out of the *mitad* and into a flat-surfaced basket.

16. Make as many injera as you like and let them cool before serving.

Note that in North America today commercially made injera is plentiful at corner stores, usually near places where an Ethiopian community is found. Teff is relatively expensive so most of the injeras you find in North America may be made of teff mixed with other flours such as wheat, barley, corn, or even rice flours. You may still find plenty of pure teff injeras in cities such as Washington, DC and its surroundings where more than 100,000 Ethiopian Americans reside.

BERBERE

Red Pepper and Spice Paste

To make about 4 cups:

2 teaspoons ground ginger

1 teaspoon ground cardamom

1 teaspoon ground coriander

1 teaspoon fenugreek seeds

½ teaspoon nutmeg, preferably freshly grated

¼ teaspoon ground cloves

¼ teaspoon ground cinnamon

¼ teaspoon ground allspice

4 tablespoons finely chopped onions

2 tablespoons finely chopped garlic

4 tablespoons salt

6 tablespoons dry red wine

4 cups paprika

4 tablespoons ground hot red pepper

1 teaspoon freshly ground black pepper

3 cups water

4 tablespoons vegetable oil

In a heavy 3-quart nonstick saucepan, toast the allspice, cardamom, cinnamon, cloves, coriander, fenugreek, ginger, and nutmeg over low heat for one minute. Stir continuously until the mixture is heated all the way through. Take the pan from the heat. Allow the spices to cool for 10 minutes. Mix the toasted spices, the onions, the garlic, 2 tablespoons of the salt, and the wine or *tej* in the jar of a blender and blend at high speed. The mixture should take the form of a smooth paste. Add salt to taste. Mix the red pepper, the black pepper, and the 1 additional tablespoon of salt in a saucepan and roast over low heat for 1 minute, until the contents are all heated through. Shake the pan and stir the spices constantly. Add the water, ½ a cup at a time; add the spice-and-wine mixture; and stir forcefully and cook over very low heat for 15 minutes. Put the berbere into a jar and seal it in tightly. Allow the paste to cool at room temperature, and drip the oil over the top to make a film at least 1 inch thick. Refrigerate the prepared berbere paste until you want to use it. If you continue to add the film of oil on top every time you use the berbere, the paste can easily be kept in the refrigerator without spoiling for half a year.

NETER QEBÉ

Spiced Ghee (Butter Oil)

To make about 4 cups:

2 pounds unsalted butter, cut into small pieces

2 small onions, peeled and coarsely chopped

1 teaspoon basil

1 teaspoon savory

1 teaspoon koseret (*Lippia adoensis*—an aromatic Ethiopian herb having some similarity to basil)

3 tablespoons finely chopped garlic

4 teaspoons finely chopped fresh ginger root

½ teaspoon black cumin

1½ teaspoons turmeric

1 cardamom pod, slightly crushed with the blade of a knife, or a pinch of cardamom seeds

1 cinnamon stick, 1 inch long

1 whole clove

½ teaspoon ground nutmeg, preferably freshly grated

In a heavy 5-quart saucepan, heat the butter over moderate heat. Let it melt steadily and completely. Avoid browning. Increase heat to gradually bring it to a boil. While heating, you will see the surface become entirely covered with white foam. Mix the cardamom, cinnamon, clove, garlic, ginger, nutmeg, koseret, cumin, onion, and turmeric. Lower the heat and simmer uncovered and untouched for 5 minutes. The milk solids at the bottom of the pan will turn golden brown, and the butter on top will become translucent. Pour the clear butter oil into a bowl and strain it through a fine sieve lined with four layers of dampened cheesecloth. Dispose of the already used muddy-looking spices. If you still see some solids in the ghee or butter oil, strain it one more time to preclude rancidness at a later time. Pour the qebé (purified and spiced butter oil) into a jar that has a mouth large enough to allow a tablespoon in. Cover it firmly and store in your refrigerator or at room temperature until you use it. Qebé will solidify when refrigerated. After that, even at room temperature, it will be good for 3 months.

DORO WAT

Chicken Stew with Spices and Hot Chilies

A 2- to 3-pound chicken, cut into 12 serving pieces

2 tablespoons strained fresh lemon juice

2 teaspoons salt

2 cups finely chopped onions

2 cups neter qebé (see previous recipe)

1 tablespoon finely chopped garlic

1 teaspoon finely chopped, scraped fresh ginger root

1 tablespoon black cumin

1 teaspoon fenugreek seeds, pulverized with a mortar and pestle or in a small bowl with the back of a spoon

1 teaspoon ground cardamom

1 teaspoon ground nutmeg

1 tablespoon *nech azmud* (*ajowan* or bishop's weed), preferably freshly grated

1 cup berbere (see earlier recipe)

2 tablespoons paprika

1 cup dry white or red wine and 1 cup water

4 hard-cooked eggs

Freshly ground black pepper

Pat the chicken dry with towels and coat the pieces with lemon juice and salt. Let it rest at room temperature for half an hour. In an ungreased heavy 4-quart enameled casserole, cook the onions over moderate heat for 6 minutes, until they turn soft and dry. Stir the pan with the onions continuously. Avoid burning because this will tarnish the taste, and the burned onions will rise to the top when the sauce is done. To avoid burning, therefore, you should reduce the heat or lift the pan from the oven from time to time to let it cool for a few moments before putting it back. Stir in the neter qebé. When the sauce begins to splutter, add the cardamom, fenugreek, garlic, ginger, *nech azmud* (bishop's weed), and nutmeg, stirring well after you add each. Add the berbere and stir over low heat for 3 minutes. Now, pour in the *tej* or wine and water. Bring the sauce to a boil over high heat. Cook over moderate heat rapidly, uncovered, for about 5 minutes, or until the liquid in the pan has been condensed to the texture of heavy cream. Pat the chicken dry and put it into the seething sauce, turning the chicken pieces over with a spoon until they are covered with the spiced sauce on all sides. Decrease the heat to the lowest point possible. Cover firmly and simmer for 15 minutes.

Pierce the surface of each egg with small holes and rotate them gently within in the sauce. Cover and simmer for another 15 minutes or until the chicken is tender and shows softness when poked by a small knife. Sprinkle the sauce with pepper and taste for seasoning. Once you are satisfied with the taste, pour the entire contents of the casserole into a deep heated bowl. *Doro wat* is eaten with injera made from teff or its Western substitutes, such a mixture of barley, wheat, and rice flours. *Gomen* (boiled collard green) and cottage cheese usually accompany *doro wat*.

ZILZIL ALECHA

Beef Strips Braised in Green Pepper Sauce

Serves up to 10 people

6 medium-sized green bell peppers, seeded and de-ribbed, 2 coarsely chopped and cut into strips about 2 inches long

8 teaspoons finely chopped fresh hot chilies, preferably green

2 tablespoons finely chopped garlic

1 tablespoon scraped, finely chopped fresh ginger root

2 teaspoon turmeric

½ teaspoon ground cardamom

4 teaspoons salt

4 teaspoons white pepper

½ cup dry red or white wine

2 cups neter qebé (see earlier recipe)

4 pounds boneless sirloin steak, trimmed of excess fat, sliced, and cut into strips about 2 inches long

4 cups finely chopped onions

Combine the 4 coarsely chopped green peppers with the cardamom, chilies, garlic, ginger root, salt, white pepper, wine, and turmeric. Blend them well, until the mixture turns into a smooth puree. In a heavy 12-inch skillet, heat the 2 cups of the neter qebé over moderate heat. Brown the beef strips in the skillet, a small amount at a time. Turn them about with a large wooden spoon. Turn down the heat so that the meat is broiled uniformly on all sides. Avoid burning as you brown the meat. Then transfer the beef strips to a platter. Remove the fat in the skillet and put it aside. Clean the skillet thoroughly. Then drop in the onions and let them simmer over low heat for

6 minutes. If they become soft and dry in 5 minutes, remove them. Jiggle the pan and shift the onions about continuously to prevent them from burning. Pour in the cooking fat you set aside, and when it begins to splutter, mix in the green pepper strips. Continue to broil the mixture for 3 minutes, until the pepper becomes soft. Put in the reserved green pepper puree and, still agitating the mixture, bring to a boil. Coat the pieces of meat evenly. Then reduce your oven to the lowest level, cover in part, and simmer for 8 minutes, or until the beef is wholly cooked. Serve it with injera after spreading it on a heated platter.

ETHIOPIAN CUISINE: INJERA AND WAT

Injera is a large, spongy flat bread that looks like the French crepe but is made of a special cereal called teff that is endemic to Ethiopia. Unlike crepe, teff flour, which comes in three varieties—white, brown, and red—is kneaded and fermented for three days before being baked, as a result of which it has as an alluring flavor of sourdough. Nutritionists have only recently recognized the dietary value of this unique Ethiopian cereal grain, which has almost 3 times the iron content of other grains and 20 times more calcium than barley and wheat. Furthermore, with 82 percent complex carbohydrates, 15 percent protein, and 3 percent fat, teff provides more fiber-rich bran and nutritious germ than any other grain in the world.

Traditionally, injera is spread on top of a round basket table known as a *meson* with the *wat* or *souse* poured in the middle so that everybody sharing the meal can dip into it. The convention is for each diner to tear off a square inch piece of injera with the five fingers, scoop the *souse*, and put it in the mouth. *Wat* or *souse* is of two distinct types. The most common is called *kay wat* (red sauce) and is made red by being prepared with a spiced hot chili pepper paste known as *berbere*, which contains freshly ground onions, garlic, ginger, and several other spices. The second type of *wat* prepared for fasting days is *alicha wat* (mild sauce), which made of legumes such as peas, lentils, and broad beans, and is yellow due to the inclusion of turmeric as a coloring agent. This type of sauce is also made with onions, ginger, garlic, and other spices, minus hot peppers. Both types of *wat* come mostly in veggie varieties, but sometimes with meat, usually lamb or beef jerky. Some are also made with fish, which is allowed during fasting season. One common Ethiopian delicacy is *kitfo*, a coarsely ground raw beef kneaded in cardamom and spiced butter known as neter qebbé. *Kitfo* is now mostly known as Ethiopian steak tartar. The veggies are made from halved beans (*kik wat*), pureed beans (*shiro wat*), and lentils (*misir wat*). Arguably, the *souse* that comes most near to being called the national dish of Ethiopia is the proverbial *doro wat* (chicken stew) topped with hard-boiled whole eggs.

VEGGIE RECIPES

Ater Kik Alecha

Mild Split Pea Stew

Serves 6

2 cups split peas (yellow or green)

4½ cups water

2 cups red onion (chopped)

2 teaspoons basil

1 cup vegetable oil

2 teaspoons ginger (diced)

2 tablespoons garlic (diced)

1 teaspoon turmeric

Salt to taste

In medium-size saucepan, wash peas thoroughly and mix them in 6 cups of water. Cook peas on moderate heat until soft. In another saucepan, cook onions, ginger, turmeric, basil, garlic, and vegetable oil. Continue cooking for 10 more minutes or until the mixture becomes a thick paste. Now add 2 cups of water and bring the sauce to a boil. Let it simmer on low heat, stirring intermittently, for 45 minutes. Add salt to taste. Let it cool. Refrigerate the sauce and eat it with injera as needed.

Split Lentil Stew

Serves 6

2 cups split lentils

6 cups water

½ cups vegetable oil

2 cups red onions (chopped)

2 tablespoons ginger (diced)

2 tablespoons garlic (diced)

8 tablespoons berbere

1 tablespoon *nech azmud* (ajowan or bishop's weed)

1 tablespoon black cumin

1 tablespoon cardamom

Salt to taste

Wash the lentils thoroughly and set aside. In a large saucepan, cook onions over medium heat, stirring continuously so as to avoid burning. Add ginger, garlic, bishop's weed, black cumin, and cardamom. Cook for 2 minutes. Add vegetable oil and berbere to the mixture. Keep on cooking for 5 more minutes. As you cook, stir constantly to make sure the spices are blended well. Add the cleaned lentils and water and simmer over medium heat until the condiment is soft. This may take approximately half an hour. When done, remove, put the veggie sauce in a bowl, and refrigerate for use when needed.

Gomen Wat

Cooked Collard Greens

Serves 6

4 medium jalapeño peppers

4 cups of water

2 tablespoon garlic, diced

2 tablespoon ginger, diced

½ cup vegetable oil

2 medium red onions, chopped

2 pounds of collard greens, washed and chopped (Note: if collard greens are unavailable, you can use spinach as a substitute)

Under running cold water, wash the collard greens thoroughly so as to remove all traces of soil. Add 2 cups of water and cook the collard greens over medium heat for 40 minutes. Make sure they are soft; if after that time, they are still tough, continue cooking for 5 more minutes. Take the cooked collards from the oven and drain; cut into small pieces when cool. In a large saucepan, mix vegetable oil, onion, garlic, and ginger. Cook over moderate heat for 5 minutes, stirring often. Add 4 cups of water to the collard greens. Continue to cook until most of the water has evaporated. Then add the jalapeño pepper and cook for about 5 minutes more. Add onion mixture to the collard greens. Add salt to taste. Mix well. Cool and serve.

COFFEE CEREMONY

Coffee ceremony and consumption are an essential part of Ethiopia's cultural life. They are also central to the Ethiopian society and economic system. The growing and picking of coffee is engaged in by almost 20 percent of the entire population of the country and provides over 60 percent of the country's foreign currency earnings. Ethiopian coffee is coveted internationally and fetches a much higher price than its counterparts in countries such as Colombia and Brazil that produce most of the coffee consumed in the world. Though countries such as Brazil and Colombia produce much more coffee for the international market than Ethiopia, the latter country's product is used by coffee processors for blending the Latin American variety. It is believed the Ethiopian Mocha Arabica passes on its special aroma when blended with other types of coffee beans. Thus, premium washed Ethiopian coffee beans fetch relatively highest prices on the international market.

Coffee coming from different regions has different tastes depending on the type of soil and temperature the beans are grow in. For example, coffee coming from the Kaffa region is either harvested wild or cultivated on forested hillsides, usually at 1,500 feet above sea level, where it grows in the shadow of larger trees, which protect the plants from the hot weather of the dry season. Harar is a long-berry variety of coffee and has a unique wine-like tang and sharp acidic edge. Sidamo beans, the centerpiece of which grows in a district known as Yerga-Tchaffé, which is the name under which these beans are sold, have a very pleasant aroma liked by most Westerners.

If you are invited to attend a coffee ceremony, this is a mark of companionship and reverence. The ceremony is a social event and often performed three times a day. But in general, Ethiopians perform the ceremony at every opportunity of meeting a visitor or a guest. The ceremony is quite elaborate. It is conducted by one young lady who is dressed in the traditional garb of white *qemis* (skirt) with colorful borders.

The young woman arranges the utensils on a bed of long scented grasses. The tools used in the ceremony are the *jabana*, an elaborately decorated coffee pot, roundish at the bottom and made of clay; *seenees*, little china coffee cups; a long-handled coffee-roasting flat pan, which allows one to roast the coffee beans without getting too close to the fire; a *midija*, a miniature open roasting furnace or brazier with hot coal; a *muqecha*—coffee-grinding mortar and pestle; and a brazier with hot coal for burning incense gums that exude a fragrant smell.

The coffee lady brings and gently washes a handful of coffee beans and then puts them on the heated long-handled flat pan. She then stirs and shakes the husks away. She does that continuously so as to avoid unnecessary burning of the beans, which destroys the aroma. On a high fire, the coffee beans start to pop like popcorn. Ethiopian coffee is related to the Mocha variety of Yemen and has to be roasted carefully. If over-roasted, the composition of its subtle and stout flavor can be lost. When the coffee beans turn shiny and black, and the aromatic oil is coaxed out of the beans, they emit smells that draw in the onlookers. The coffee lady now scatters frankincense on the glowing charcoal in a special small pot, and a thick sweet grey smoke rises through the room. As if the aromatic smell of the coffee and the frankincense that spread spontaneously were not enough, the lady walks around the room with the smoky roasting beans near all the guests so that every one has a whiff. It is after this that she pours the beans into a *muqecha* (pestle) and pounds it with a long-handled mortar. The ground coffee is then put in the *jabana* (the coffee pot), which is sealed from the top with a straw cover and boiled on top of the small furnace.

When steam starts to pour out of the protruding spout of the jabana that is left open, the delightful aroma of the coffee mingles with the wafting incense, its heady scent filling the air. At this stage, the coffee is ready.

A young girl of 10 or 12 is sent out to announce this and stands ready to pass around the prepared coffee to the guests. Coffee is normally served first to the eldest

Coffee being prepared in the traditional way in Ethiopia. (© Klaas Lingbeek- van Kranen/iStockphoto. com)

person in the room and only then to the others, in order of their generations. The boiled coffee is now gracefully poured in a thin golden stream into the little cups, each of which is arranged on its own little table, from a height of about one foot without interruption, a skill that requires a lot of practice. Roasted beans or popcorn or pieces of spiced bread are distributed to the guests, and a blessing is given. Two more servings of the coffee are made, with more water being added; the coffee is allowed to brew until the color changes to from pitch black to light brown, its potency also proportionately decreasing. Traditionally, coffee is taken plain or with a little amount of salt. In modern times, sugar is substituted for salt. But no milk is added.

Coffee ceremony is conducted at least once a day by all Ethiopian households, usually before noon. In some parts of Ethiopia, it is done three times, morning, noon, and evening. In fact it is a time-honored social event within each village. It is during coffee ceremony that communities and neighborhoods discuss everything from politics to family affairs. For Ethiopian women who live under unfair gender oppression, it is the only means of discussing their own personal problems with other women. In fact, in a society where psychologists and psychiatrists are for the most part nonexistent, it is used as a group therapy.

When invited into the ceremony, it is rude to leave before three cups in the three rounds are consumed. The first serving is called *abol*, the second serving is *dagim*, and the third serving is *bereka*. Coffee is not ground for the second and third brewing. So either water is simply added to the remaining coffee sod in the pot, or a portion of coffee powder is left on purpose for two additional servings.

The third serving, the *bereka*, is a means of bestowing a blessing on all the participants, particularly the family preparing the ceremony. Foreigners who do not have an opportunity to visit Ethiopian homes where they can participate in the said ceremony can experience it at Ethiopian restaurants where coffee is taken through its full life cycle of preparation in front of the clients.

When they buy their coffee beans, Ethiopians are very discriminating. They know which type of coffee suits their palates, and they choose from many brands. Yerga-Tchaffé coffee has a strong flavor referred to as flora. Washed Yerga-Tchaffé coffee beans are considered by connoisseurs to be the best in the world. This variety has first-rate acidity and rich body. Professional roasters like its subtle flavor and are willing to pay a premium price to acquire it.

Limu coffee from near Jimma in western Oromia is famous for its piquant flavor that draws many international roasters. Its acidity is good, as is its body. Washed and dried Limu is among a family of premium Ethiopian coffees. Harar coffee is planted in the eastern highlands straddling the Rift Valley. This bean has average acidity, full body, and a very distinct mocha flavor; it is one of the varieties that fetches a high premium in world coffee prices.

Wallaga coffee, grown mostly in the regions of Qellem and Gimbi in western Oromia, is primarily recognized for its fruity tang. It has good acidity and body. Wallaga coffee is mixed with other brands for its special flavor. It is also sold separately for a special gourmet brew. Sidama coffee from southern Ethiopia is known for its sweetness, well-adjusted taste, and first-class flavor. It has fine acidity and good body. Sidamo beans are used by blenders internationally as a gourmet or specialty brand.

The cooking formula described earlier is only the tip of the iceberg. One guide titled *Exotic Ethiopian Cooking*, prepared by Daniel Jote Mesfin and introduced by Shlomo Bacharach, the editor of the East Africa Forum, offers over 100 unique recipes developed all over the country!

Ethiopia is not only the original home of *Homo sapiens sapiens* but also an age-old habitat of delicious and aromatic plant genes that were commented on with awe as long ago as the *Peripulus of the Eritrean Sea*, written by a traveler who came to Axum during the first century AD. Naturally surrounded by these spice gardens, the Ethiopians perfected blends of spices that linger long after a meal is served.

When millions of Ethiopians fled their country, which was drenched in blood by Mengistu Haile Mariam's military dictatorship, they settled in Western countries, mostly in North America, and brought with them their cooking habits. Shlomo Bacharach comments, "The few Americans who have been to Ethiopia can't believe their good luck when an Ethiopian restaurant opens nearby. A few adventurous others wander in intrigued. A few more are brought by Ethiopian friends. And so it grows. Once hooked, it's for life" (Mesfin, 1987, xvii).

REFERENCES

Abeba G. 1975. *Production and Utilization of Maize in Ethiopia*. Addis Ababa: Ethiopian Nutrition Institute.

Addis Ababa University. 1983. *Addis Ababa University Project on Post-Graduate and Under-Graduate Training and Research on Food and Nutrition*. Addis Ababa, Ethiopia: The University.

Barnett, T. 1999. *The Emergence of Food Production in Ethiopia*. Oxford, UK: Archaeopress.

Brandt, S. A. 1997. *The "Tree against Hunger": Enset-Based Agricultural System in Ethiopia*. Washington, DC: American Association for the Advancement of Science.

Christian Relief & Development Association Ethiopia. 1991. *CRDA Workshop on Nutrition and Family Health: October 15–16, 1991*. Addis Ababa, Ethiopia: CRDA.

Christian Relief & Development Association Ethiopia. 1993. *CRDA/Caritas Neerlandica Workshop on Food & Nutrition Programme in Ethiopia: June 9–11, 1993*. Addis Ababa, Ethiopia: CRDA.

Donovan, N. 1976. *Ethiopian National Food*. Addis Ababa: Ethiopian Tourist Office.

Gibson, R. S., and A. S. Kindell. 1968. *Food Composition Table of Foods Commonly Used in Ethiopia*. Addis Ababa, Ethiopia: Children's Nutrition Unit.

Mesfin, Daniel Jote. 1987. *Exotic Ethiopian Cooking*. Washington, DC: Ethiopian Cooking Enterprise.

Sørensen, P., and B. Selome. 2009. *Nice Children Don't Eat A Lot of Food: Strained Livelihoods and the Role of Aid in North Wollo, Ethiopia*. Addis Ababa, Ethiopia: Forum for Social Studies.

Tsegaye, W., and T. Degefa. 1991. *Taste of Ethiopia: A Collection of Delicious Vegetarian and Traditional Recipes and Products, including Most Popular Food and Spices*. Washington, DC: Merkato Publications International.

United States Interdepartmental Committee on Nutrition for National Development. 1961. *Ethiopia: Nutrition Survey*. Washington, DC: Government Printing Press.

Sports and Leisure

In the field of sport, Ethiopia is known more for long-distance running than for other sports. However, there are other types of sport that only those who know the country well are aware of. One is fishing. Some specialists have called the country an angler's paradise. Ethiopia offers the best sport fishing opportunity one can expect anywhere on the planet. There are plenty of fish, including trout, some of them of exceptional size. An angler has the added bonus of watching a flock of beautiful flamingos with their pink plumage near the lakeside and seeing giant hippopotamuses and crocodiles wading in the rivers.

Boat crossing a lake in Ethiopia. (Courtesy of Paulos Milkias.)

CAMPING IN ETHIOPIA:
A TRULY GREAT OUTDOORS

Camping is another venue for passing good leisure time in Ethiopia. Ethiopia has some of the most picturesque and pristine scenery one can visit. Though there are numerous Western-standard hotels at very cheap prices, one is advised to venture out to national parks and other rural areas and camp.

The Awash National Park has assigned dappled waterside campsites. However, a visitor is advised to take all equipment and supplies because there is no place one can buy them in the remote parts of Ethiopia where these campsites are located. On the way to the park, you will pass through a sunshade of tamarind and ficus on which alight a splendid assortment of birds. As you continue, Colobus monkeys and vervets will eye you from the tamarind and fig trees. Curiosity-filled Galada baboons, waterbucks, warthogs, and kudus wander nearby to sip from the cool water. At a distance, you will be able to glance at the crocodiles and large hippos.

GREATER KUDU

If you go to the Bale Mountains National Park, you will find near the Dinsho head-quarters campsites furnished with local benches and stalls. The rare Mountain Nyala, a type of antelope, that are extant to Ethiopia have become very tolerant and will

Gelada baboons from the Simien Mountain region. (Courtesy of Paulos Milkias.)

most times amble through the campsites, browsing the area. There are magnificent sites to slog through.

The Mago National Park is rather serene and dark, and the clear, cool waters streaming down the mountain are good for drinking. If you stroll away too far into the tree covering, you are advised to be accompanied by a game warden because you might suddenly encounter a buffalo or an elephant.

The Omo National Park has open campsites under massive fig trees. Here you may bathe in the pristine Mui River, but do not venture too far because you will encounter the omnipresent crocodiles.

For persons fond of high-peak terrain, the Simien Mountains National Park in Gondar is a good choice. Here again a visitor will be delighted to see the extant

A cozy tourist hotel in Axum. (Courtesy of Paulos Milkias.)

Gelada monkeys and walia ibex. The lakes are another area to visit, though on weekends there are too many visitors, and private promenades are circumscribed. Lake Langano, 672 miles south of Addis Ababa, is a very popular weekend resort. Hotels on the lake charge very moderate fees for putting up a tent on lakeside sites, positioned on sandy ground sheltered by bent acacias. Swimming in clean, greenish Lake Langano is a delight. In all these campsites, security is assured. One can enjoy a walk through the forested areas or have a peaceful night's sleep without fear because Ethiopians in the countryside are law-abiding and hospitable to strangers.

CONVENTIONAL SPORTING

Ganna

The most famous and oldest traditional game in Ethiopia is *ganna*. This sport is similar to hockey and gets its name from Christmas (Ganna in Amharic) because Ethiopian Christians had a legend that when the Virgin Mary gave birth to Jesus, shepherds were playing the game in the fields of Nazareth. It is played by boys as well as grown men during the Christmas festivities, starting a week before the festival and continuing until Timqat (Epiphany). In this game, teams from rival neighborhoods or villages try to drive a puck into their neighbor's territory.

Traditional Ethiopian field hockey called ganna *being played during the Christmas season. (Courtesy of Paulos Milkias/David Tannenbaum, An Ethiopian Album, 2008.)*

Ganna is played with set rules but with some local variations by the highlanders, including Amharas, Tigrayans, and Oromos, who refer to it as *kollé*, as well as the Gurage, the Hadiya, and the Sidama. Although no one knows when this tradition started, Christian paintings from the 17th century show the nativity with children playing *ganna* in the background. Players of *ganna* as a rule divide into what they call *budin* (teams). Each *budin* represents a specific neighborhood or region of a town. The marketplace is usually the playing field of choice. Players choose their respective captains, known as *abbat* (father). In some places, it is the captain who selects members of his team. The teams hold names such as *Baqlo* (mule) or *Faras* (horse). They may also choose a brand name of guns that are abundantly found in the country, such as Wujigra (Fusil Gras) or Sanader (Sneider). The two captains together identify a central spot they call a "house." Here they dig a small hole with a hockey stick. The hole is more often than not in the shape of a cross, denoting the game's connection to Christianity. A ball made of rounded wood or sometimes a piece of leather stitched to look round like a tennis ball—or for children, just a wad of cloth or human hair bundled together and pounded hard—is used. The two captains initiate the game playing by ritually striking each other's G-sticks three times. After that, they and the other players try to pound the ball in the direction of their opponents' section of the field. The *budin* that hits the ball as far as their adversaries' boundary, marked by a hollow spot, by a raised elevation, or as is usually the case, by a tree trunk (or in modern times, by footfall beams), scores a goal.

Gugs

Gugs is Ethiopian mock cavalry combat played partly for simple pleasure and partly as training for actual warfare. It is often played in accompaniment with rural wedding ceremonies. It is also played during major religious festivities, such as the Ethiopian New Year, Masqal, and Temqat. As a game that is customarily loosely structured, *gugs* has several variations. Mules are not used because even though they are sturdier with a lot of stamina compared to horses, they are not quick-footed.

In preparation for the game, villagers or city dwellers with trained horses divide themselves into two roughly equal groups and face each other on an open field or pasture. Riders are normally dressed in traditional white *shama* and are mounted on gaily bedecked horses. They utter *fukara*, which is bragging to intimidate the opponent and to inspire oneself for action without fear. They challenge their rivals and spur their mounts, inciting them to take off in pursuit.

Each *gugs* player is allowed to carry three thin long batons, which represent the three spears carried in real fighting. One team starts to gallop away as another team follows, ready for an offensive. When the pursuer draws close enough, he hurls a wand at his adversary, who, if necessary and possible, fends it off with a round hide shield. Each player attempts to smack one or more of his opponents on the head or on the body.

All players carry round rhinoceros shields, with which they ward off attacks from opponents. The front team members twist around and try to strike their attackers.

The tide of combat changes when they all reach one end of the field. Then the roles change, and the previously attacked group now follows the previous attackers to the opposite end of the field.

While advancing, the horsemen prod their horses forward with their thigh and instep. When they retreat, however, they simply hurtle away without touching their horses' bodies. Individuals walking or running on foot in the field gather the fallen sticks and return them to the players who threw them.

In certain types of the game, horsemen capture unlucky players by encircling their opponents with their spears. A player surrounded thus surrenders and joins the team that captured him. Serious accidents have been reported in playing *gugs* because a player or his horse may be seriously injured when hit or spiked by the point of a wand. A horseman may also fall and receive serious injuries. The plains of Sululta, along the Gojjam road on the northeast side of Entoto mountain, overlooking the city of Addis Ababa, is an ideal place to watch *gugs* on festive occasions.

For those who love horses and horse riding, Western-style show-jumping competitions and polo matches are also available at the Jan Meda playing field near the old imperial palace in Addis Ababa. Other types of horse riding can be experienced at the Equestrian center near the International School in the Old Airport area on the Jimma road in Addis Ababa and at the stables not far from the British Embassy, where one can acquire riding horses for a fee and go on a ride with a guide.

The teams continue to play all afternoon until nightfall, or as long as the players are able to see the ball on the field. The games are played repeatedly each day of the week. In some regions of the country, the last play is reserved for the bachelors and newlyweds against longtime married men. The game is generally interspaced with ritual invectives. Being very forceful and harsh, the game usually produces serious injuries. However, such injuries, even the most severe ones, are never contested because society and the courts consider them a result of voluntary play between willing individuals.

Ethiopia never had a significant number of modern upper- and middle-class people, which has hindered the expansion of up-to-date sports facilities. Sports are becoming increasingly fashionable, however, among the rising nouveau riche middle class, many of whom are returnees from the West. Private entrepreneurs have sprung up to build sizable gyms, fitness centers, and sports facilities, especially in the capital Addis Ababa.

By far the most popular sport is football (or soccer, as it is known in North America), which is played in schoolyards, on bumpy urban roads, or in rural meadows. The ball used may be the usual leather one, but players also use homemade spherical bundles of old rags or hard-squeezed human hair. Local or regional matches attract huge crowds in Addis Ababa's sports stadium.

But as noted at the start of the discussion, Ethiopia is most well known in distance race competitions, with the standard set by Abebe Bikila in the Rome and Japan Olympics in 1960 and 1964, respectively, where he won the gold. Since that time, both men and women have broken world records again and again and have become favorites in all world competitions, including the world cup and the Olympics.

ETHIOPIA IN TRACK AND FIELD

Abebe Bikila became the first African to win a gold medal in the marathon when he finished first as he ran barefoot through Rome at the 1960 Olympics. He won the gold medal again at the 1964 Tokyo Olympics. Then his compatriot from the Ethiopian highlands, Mamo Wolde, won the third gold medal in the marathon at the 1968 Olympic Games in Mexico City. A trend in African distance running was now set, and Ethiopian Miruts Yifter won two gold medals in the 16,404-foot and the 32,808-foot races at the Moscow Olympic Games in 1980. A string of gold medals came with Haile Gebrselassie and Darartu Tullu, who won the men's and women's 32,808-foot competitions at the 2000 Games in Sydney, Australia. On his own, Haile Gebrselassie has set 26 world records and won two Olympic gold medals for the 32,808-foot races. 17 world records Haile has been called by sports specialists the most versatile runner in history, and the October 30, 2010 *New York Times* refers to him as "the only person to have run 26.2 miles under 2:04 [with] a stunning, career-capping accomplishment." His compatriot, Kenenisa Bekele, also became a legend. He is arguably one of the elite distance runners of all time, with stunning records to prove it. In 2008, Kenenisa became one of only six athletes to have achieved the Olympic distance double when he set new Olympic records while winning the 16,404-foot (12:57.82) and the 32, 808-foot (27:01.17) races. He then repeated the double at the 2009 World Championships. Ethiopian women have shown the same versatility. Between 1992 and 2008, they have taken first place in three of the women's 32,808-foot races at the Olympics. Darartu Tulu became the first black African woman to win an Olympic gold medal by taking first place in the 32,808-foot race at the 1992 Barcelona Games. She won the event again at the 2000 Sydney Games. Then came Tirunesh Dibaba (cousin to Darartu Tulu), who has won the moniker "baby face destroyer," owing to her devastating finishing kick. Tirunesh won gold medals in the Athens and Beijing Olympics in the 16404-foot and 32,808-footcompetitions. She also carries eight World Championship titles in track and cross-country from 2003 through 2008. All this has made Ethiopia the greatest distance-running country at major international competitions.

SOCCER IN ETHIOPIA

Football, known in North America by the name soccer, was introduced into Ethiopia in 1923, when foreign residents of the country started to play against each other. Among the expatriates who played against each other were Armenians, Greeks, Indians, and Italians. French sailors at one time played against teams of foreign nationals in Addis Ababa and lost 3 to 1. Then the modern educational establishments in Addis Ababa, particularly the Menelik and Tafari Makonnen schools taught by expatriates from Egypt, Europe, and North America, added soccer as a sport. Poor children who did not attend school made their own balls from pieces of rugs, human hair, or sometimes inflated animal bladders or tennis balls and played soccer barefoot in the streets or in open fields. Out of these spontaneous soccer groups there came a famous team known to the present as St. George Club that started to play with the organized teams of foreign nationals (St. George because it played in the Arada area near St. George Cathedral in the heart of old Addis Ababa). The Greeks and Armenians were the particular favorites in these national-against-foreign matches. Places that sported soccer tournaments included the open spaces near Filweha and Janmeda.

During the 1939–1941 occupation, the Italian Fascists adopted an apartheid system and segregated Ethiopian players from foreign players, most of whom were white. The Ethiopians were not allowed to play outside the Addis Katama area near the large Addis Ababa bazaar. To make their mark, the Italian Fascists even forced the Ethiopians to change the names of their teams to Italian ones. Thus, the St. George became Litoria Wubé (a neighborhood near St. George), Qebéna was renamed Villa Italiano, the Sidest Kilo team was renamed Piassa Roma, and the Gulélé team was given the name Consulato.

Nevertheless, games and tournaments continued to be played among the Ethiopians short of any known soccer rules and regulations. Some experienced clubs such as the St. George and Sidest Kilo were allowed to play against the Italians. As a rule, Ethiopian teams were allowed to play only barefooted while Italian players wore sports shoes. Most of the time, it was the Ethiopian teams playing against each other for the amusement of white Italian audiences. Fights and brawls were common occurrences. One time, a minor brawl turned into a major gladiator-style fight, and the referee never called for a penalty. The Italian spectators enjoyed the bloody fight that simulated the combat between historical Roman gladiators that they knew from their ancient history. As the fight went on, the Italian audience cheered the side that showed more courage. Some injured players required hospitalization.

When an Italian club known as the Fortitido Club secured a soccer field with the right measurements and appropriate polls, the only clubs allowed to play on the field were Armenian, Greek, and other European teams. Ethiopians were barred from playing on the field. The earlier mentioned St. George team was interested in playing a game against the Italian team, the Fortitido Club, to prove that they were professionally fit to play in the international arena. At first the Italians mulled and procrastinated, fearing that such a game might incite a fight between Ethiopian and Italian players and spectators. They were also afraid of losing to a non-white team. But feeling sure that they would not lose, and also having secured proper police presence on the grounds, they agreed after two months of stalling, on the condition that the Ethiopian team come onto the soccer field with shorts only. Since the Ethiopians of the early post-Italian period wore long traditional trousers made of cotton that made them conspicuous, the Italian team that always wore shots during soccer play was afraid that the distinction would arouse more nationalism among the Ethiopian spectators who had lost so many of their kin in the hands of the Italian Fascists. When the teams played against each other after the liberation in 1942, all in shorts, St. George won 4 to 1 against the Italian team. But confounding fears, no riots arose. What followed was actually jubilation among the Ethiopian spectators at defeating the enemy once again, this time on an equal playing field. Nevertheless, one cannot tell what would have happened had the Italian team won because this was only one year after the end of the Italian occupation that decimated close to a million Ethiopians.

It was momentous in Ethiopian soccer history for an Africa team to win against a European white club and for an occupier to lose to the people it intended to rule under subjugation. It was during that year that an official sports federation was established under the auspices of Mr. Yidnekachew Tessema, a pioneer football player who later became a well-known official of the Federation of International Football Associations (FIFA); the federation then mobilized many Addis Ababa clubs to register themselves and compete with one another.

During the early period, the clubs that were recognized all over the country were the St. George (known by its Ethiopian name, Giorgis), the Armenian team named Ararat, the Italian team Fortitito, the Greek team called Olympiacos, and the English team called the Team of the Military Mission. Addis Ababa teams also played out-of-city teams. particularly the Dire Dawa club named the Teferri team (after the original name of Emperor Haile Selassie). One particular tournament between Giorgis and Teferri took place in 1945 but ended uneventfully when a dispute arose as to whether the ball the Teferri team kicked entered the net normally or slipped inside from the side as the Girogis club claimed.

From 1940 to 1960, soccer was well established in Ethiopia. The first Ethiopian championship tournament was held. Thus, the St. George Football Club played against the Ethiopian Army Football Club, the Imperial Ethiopian Body Guard Football club, the British Military Mission Football Club, and the Italian Community Football club known as Polisportiva. By 1960, there were more than 20 teams. Eight teams joined together as First Division, and another eight teams competed as Second Division. In that first tournament, victory was achieved by the Red Sea club from Eritrea. Later, the Ethiopian team joined the African championship tournament and other intercontinental contests. By the early 1970s, soccer clubs had mushroomed all over the country. Major towns and villages as well as neighborhoods established their own clubs in all the 14 provinces that existed at the time.

TRACK AND FIELD

Today, Ethiopia is best known for its achievements in track and field. The achievements of Ethiopian long-distance runners have lifted the morale of a people deeply affected by constant civil war, social turmoil, and ecological catastrophes. The country's entry into the world stage was achieved at the 1956 Melbourne Olympics. However, it was Abebe Bikila's heroic barefooted marathon gold medal triumph trudging through Rome's millennia year old thoroughfares in 1960 that catapulted Ethiopian athletes into the global competitive arena. Abebe's rise to Olympic stardom was triggered when he saw a parade of Ethiopian athletes wearing uniforms that bore the name Ethiopia. These athletes were the first Ethiopian Olympiads who participated in the Melbourne Olympics in 1956. Upon seeing them and their "Ethiopia" uniforms, Abebe asked who they were. When told that they represented their country in the international Olympics, he decided there and then that he would be one of them four years later.

Abebe Bikila of Ethiopia, running bare-foot and winning the gold medal in the Rome Olympic marathon race in 1960. He repeated the feat in the Tokyo Olympics in 1964 but this time wearing shoes. (AP Photo.)

Abebe won the national competition and was chosen to go to the 1960 Rome Olympics. When he won the gold medal in the race and broke the world record, running barefooted, he became a household name all over the world. Abebe also established himself as the first black man from the African continent to win an Olympic medal. When he was set to compete again in the Tokyo Olympics in 1964, he had a problem of appendicitis. He underwent surgery and arrived in Tokyo limping. Notwithstanding this setback, the undaunted Abebe entered the competition and won the marathon one more time, again breaking the world record. He astounded onlookers when upon finishing, he did several sit-ups and carried out gymnastic displays to show he was still fresh and powerful enough to run even longer distances. Together with his barefooted run in Rome, this feat became one of the most watched images in Olympic history. It was also the first time that any athlete had won consecutive marathon races in the Olympics game. Abebe entered a bid to compete in the Mexico Olympics in 1968 but had to withdraw eight miles into the race because he was struck by a sudden sickness. But his teammate Mamo Wolde went on to win the gold medal for Ethiopia in the marathon. Mamo had earlier competed in the Melbourne Olympics in 1956 in track and field, in every distance from 400 meters through the marathon. But he got noticed only when he won the silver medal in the 32,808 foot-race in the 1968 Mexico Olympics. Upon finding out that his compatriot the legendary Abebe Bikila had to withdraw, Mamo went on and won Ethiopia's third gold medal in the marathon.

The Olympic torch was then carried by Captain Miruts Yifter, who early in his career competed with athletes from all over the world and showed exceptional talent and stamina in the 16,404- and 32,848-foot races. His trademark was the ability to spring from the pack of runners at a distance of about 656 feet and win short-distance competition-style. Miruts's unusual burst of sprint gave him the nick-name "Yifter the Shifter." He won a bronze medal in the 1972 Munich Olympics, in the 32,808 feet competition, and went on to win two gold medals at the Moscow Olympics in 1980 in the 16,404 feet,- and 32,848-foot races. In his long career, Miruts competed in more than 252 races, out of which he won the gold medal in 221.

Starting in the 1990s, Haile Gebrselassie became an Ethiopian icon in long-distance races. Earning an extraordinary reputation as an exceptional athlete, Haile has been seen breaking records as they are made. As a schoolboy, he used to run five miles a day to go to class and return home. He attracted world-wide attention in 1992 when he won the gold medal in the 16,404- and 32,808-foot World Junior Championships. In the 1993 Stuttgart World Championships, Haile won the gold medal in the 32,848-foot race and silver in the 16,404-foot race. He set his first world record in the 16,404-foot race by clocking 12:56.96 in Hengelo, Holland, in 1994. In May 1995, Haile broke Moses Kiptanui's 2-mile world record by clocking 8:07.46. Seven days later, he broke the world record in the 32,848-foot race by clocking a new speed of 26:43.53. He achieved another victory in the World Championship 32,848-foot by earning a gold medal. His 12:44.39 record in the 16,404-foot race in Zurich in August 1995 brought the number of world records broken by Haile to four. During that year, he broke two world records: one in the indoor 16,404-foot race at 13:10.98 and another in the 3,000-foot in 7:30.72. In 1996 at the Atlanta Olympics, Haile won the gold medal.

In the 32,848-foot race of the Atlanta Olympics, Haile followed Kenyan Paul Tergat until the final lap and then sprinted past him, securing the gold medal in an Olympic record time of 27:07.34. In February 1997, in Stuttgart, Germany, Haile established a new world record in the 4,921-foot race by clocking 3:32.39. On February 20, 1997, Haile clinched another gold in the world record time of 12:59.04 in an indoor 16,404-foot race in Stockholm, Sweden. This became Haile's seventh world record. In the 1997 Million Dollar Race in Hengelo, Holland, Haile broke the record with time of 8:01.08. On July 4, 1997, in Oslo, Norway, he outdistanced and lapped all world-class athletes in the 32,848-foot race and set a new 32,848-foot world record at 26:31.32. The following month, Haile broke another world record in the 32,848-foot World Championship. This was immediately followed by another world record in Zurich in 1997, where he once again won a 16,404-foot race by setting a new world record at 12:41.86, shattering his own previous record. In 2000, Haile ushered in the new millennium with an extraordinary win another gold medal. At the 32,848-foot race in the Sydney Olympics, he clocked a winning time of 27 minutes, 18.20 seconds ahead of Paul Terget of Kenya. In a career unmatched in sports history, Haile has broken 26 world records. It is not surprising, therefore, that Haile was dubbed by the *New York Times* (2004) "the world's greatest distance runner." Haile won gold in the 32,808 foot events at both the 1996 Atlanta Games and the 2000 Sydney Games.

Also at Sydney, Million Wolde took gold in the men's 16,404-footas Ethiopia gave the rest of the world the best performance at the 2000 Sydney Games. Million, in a tactical maneuver, stayed behind Algerian Ali Saidi-Sief entering the last 200, before zooming past him to win in 13 minutes, 35.49 seconds.

Gezahegn Abera's astounding sprint finish in his bid to win the gold in the 2000 Olympic Games has also become legendary. Gezahegn was one of eight children from a peasant background. While in school, he used to run roundtrip, which strengthened his stamina. Gezahegn is married to Elfenesh Alemu, winner of the 2003 Tokyo International Women's Marathon. After getting caught among scores of runners and being tripped at 19 miles, Gezahegm surged at the 24-mile mark to win the gold. He has been handicapped by Achilles tendon mishaps that necessitated surgery. Nevertheless, he won five other international competitions in succeeding years. In fact, Gezahegn became the first man ever to win gold at both the Olympics and World Championships the same year (2001). Gezanhegn Abera also took gold medals at the Sydney Games.

Haile Gebreselassie of Ethiopia, arguably the greatest athlete of the 20th century, registering one of his more than 20 record-breaking distance runs in the 2000 Summer Olympics in Sydney, Australia. (AP Photo/ Eric Draper.)

Kenenisa Bekele, who started his track and field career as a football player and then discovered his talent in local competitions and switched to track and field, has been touted as the natural successor to his idol Haile Gebrselassie. Kenenisa's first victory came in cross-country competitions. He told *Times of London* correspondents that he was inspired to compete in the long-distance races after he watched his countryman Gebrselassie win gold at the Atlanta Olympics in 1996. In 2001, Kenenisa broke the world junior record for the 3,000 meters. From 2002 to 2006, this versatile athlete won both the long and short races at the International Cross-Country Championships.

Kenenisa began to dominate the cross-country scene, breaking Kenya's stranglehold on the sport, before winning the first of his Olympic titles in Athens in 2004. He won six successive titles in cross-country long-distance race. Kenenisa won the 2003 world title in the 32,848-foot race, but he made his mark when in 2004, he shattered the world record in both the 16,404-foot and the 32,848-foot. Kenenisa repeated this feat in 2005 and 2007. At the Athens Olympics, he tried to win the 16,404- and 31,848-foot races double, but after a win in the longest race, he lost in the 16,404-foot race y only a few seconds. In the Beijing Olympics, Kenenisa tried for a double win and easily succeeded in both events.

Kenenisa faced a personal tragedy when his Ethiopian fiancée, Alem Techale, a former World Youth Champion, collapsed and died of a heart attack while training with him. Despite the tragedy, he went on to win three world titles that year and dedicated all of them to his fiancée's memory. At this writing, Kenenisa has won 5 world titles, has broken 6 senior world records, has set the 16,404-foot world record (in 2004), and has won 11 senior world cross-country titles as well as 3 Olympic titles. He has never been beaten in the 32,808-foot race since his first win over Haile Gebrselassie in 2003. Kenenisa won the 16,404-foot and 32,808-foot double at the World Championships in Berlin in August 2009. All in all, Kenenisa has accumulated 24 Olympic and world titles. The *Times of London* (2010) has touted him as the greatest long-distance runner in history. In 2010 Kenenisa was still a young man of 27 but has indicated an interest to move into the marathon after he celebrates his 30th birthday.

Ethiopian women also enjoy an impressive record. Derartu Tulu is among them. She was 17 when she entered the track and field competition. She entered a cross-country race in Norway and won the race easily. In 1990, she broke the world record in the 32,848-foot race in Bulgaria. Derartu captured the gold medal in the 32,808 feet-meter events at both the 1992 Barcelona Games and the 2000 Sydney Games. In the latter year, she repeated her victory in Cairo, Egypt. At age 37 in 2009, Derartu was still going strong: she won the Women's New York City Marathon convincingly.

Fatuma Roba first won recognition when she won two marathons, first in January 1996 at Marakech and then in Rome, Italy, only two months later. When Fatuma joined the field of the 1996 Olympic women's marathon in Atlanta, Georgia, in July 1996, no one gave her much attention. But she won the gold medal, clocking a 2:26:05-win with a remarkable two-minute lead over her nearest competitor. In 1997, Fatuma won the gold medal in the 101st Boston Marathon. She then became the first African woman to win the famous Boston race. Fatuma again won the 1999 Boston Marathon, setting a new women's record.

Tirunesh Dibaba, who is Derartu Tulu's cousin, is another rising star in women's track and field competition. She started her winning streak when she clinched the bronze at the Athens Olympics. Since then she has shattered the outdoor and indoor 16,404-foot world records. She tied in the world 16,404-foot indoor race record. She received two gold medals at the World Cross Country Championships, becoming the first woman athlete ever to earn a gold medal at both the 16,404- and 32,848-foot world championship races. It is interesting to note that her older sister, Ejegayehu Dibaba, also received a silver medal in the 2004 32,848-foot Olympic track and field race; her little brother Genzebe Dibaba made his professional competition debut in the Reebok Grand Prix in New York City in 2007 and became the 2008 World Junior Cross Country champion.

Tirunesh Dibaba received the nickname "baby-faced-destroyer" when in 2003 she became the youngest woman athlete to win an individual gold medal in world championships. In 2008, Tirunesh earned herself a gold medal in the 26,246-foot World Cross Country competition. She was soon joined by her teammate Werknesh Kidane and became the winner of eight individual medals. All in all, Tirunesh has clinched 14 gold medals in the World Cross Country Championships, which is the most any athlete has won in the history of the sport.

In the African Championship competition, Tirunesh led an Ethiopian team that won gold, silver, and bronze in the 32,848-foot race. Her sister Ejegayehu was the one who took the silver. A month later, Tirunesh shattered the record her compatriot Meseret Defar had set in the 16,404-foot competition. In the Beijing Olympics, Tirunesh pursued Kenyan-born Dutch runner Lornah Kiplagat for the first half of the 32,648-foot race. Then she passed her and pursued Ethiopian-born Turkish runner Evlan Abeylegesse. On reaching the last lap, Tirunesh sped away from Abeylegesse to win the gold medal in a new Olympic and African record of 29:54.66. Together with her fellow Ethiopians who were running for Turkey, Tirunesh became one of the three women athletes to run the race in the shortest time ever. Tirunesh also blasted away from Abeylegesse and Defar in the 16,404-foot race and won the gold. With that she clinched a spectacular double Olympic gold, to be recognized as the only woman to achieve the feat. Because of her incredible performance, Tirunesh was named *Track & Field News*'s Athlete of the Year for the season. She married a well-known Ethiopian Olympic medalist Sileshi Sihine soon after.

Meseret Defar won the Olympic 16,404-foot gold at the Athens Games. She also won bronze in the Beijing Olympics. She triumphed in the world outdoor 16,404-foot race by winning gold in 2007. That year, Meseret broke three world records. Her Ethiopian teammate Sentayehu Ejigu also won bronze in the competition. Meseret won a record fourth successive women's world indoor 9,842-foot title on March 14, 2010, when she left behind her competitors at the final bend and produced a decisive kick to win the gold.

In international team track championships, Ethiopia and Kenya have dominated the sport, with Ethiopia leading its African neighbor, though Kenyans continues to lead in the individual marathons in cities such as Boston and New York. In the world

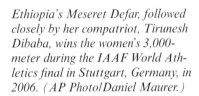

Ethiopia's Meseret Defar, followed closely by her compatriot, Tirunesh Dibaba, wins the women's 3,000-meter during the IAAF World Athletics final in Stuttgart, Germany, in 2006. (AP Photo/Daniel Maurer.)

cross-country championships in March 2004, Ethiopia lurched past its competitor Kenya by winning 14 of 18 available medals.

There are many runners training in the streets or outskirts of the Ethiopian capital. Visitors wanting to jog are advised to do it early in the morning when there are no car fumes from the numerous vehicles.

OTHER SPORTS

Many Ethiopians play basketball and volleyball, and tennis in particular is a growth industry in the capital, with tables arranged in many wayside locations. Equipments such as rackets and balls can be rented at low rate.

First-rate clay courts exist at major hotels such as the Sheraton and the Hilton hotels. Many clubs, such as the Addis Ababa Club, located near the Ghion hotel across from the Olympic stadium.

The Commercial Graduates Association, off the Bole Road near the Pilots' Club; and the International Club in the old airport area, offer coaching and court space to visitors who desire them. Visitors may avail themselves of the facilities at the major hotels such as the Sheraton, the Hilton, and the Ghion. All of the pools in these hotels are naturally warm because their source is the thermal waters of Finfine.

Lake Langano's waters, with pebble beaches, offer secure swimming where one does not have to fear getting bilharzias. There are also no crocodiles to worry about. Sailboats, mostly owned privately, offer an excellent sport in an ambiance filled with extraordinary calmness and scenic splendor, particularly in the unblemished after-noon breezes that gust down from the nearby plateau.

REFERENCES

Bazzy, C. 2008. *Sun over the Dark Continent: Fifty Four Years of Big Game Hunting in Sudan, Tanganyika, Zambia, Botswana, Ethiopia Kenya, Cameroon and Elsewhere in Africa*. Long Beach, CA: Safari Press.

Boyes, J. 1928. *The Company of Adventurers*. London: East Africa Ltd.

Cutting, S. 1940. *The Fire Ox and Other Years*. New York: C. Scribner's Sons.

Ethiopia. 1973. *Safari Ethiopia*. Addis Ababa: Imperial Ethiopian Government, Wildlife Conservation Organization.

Ethiopia Yabahelena Sport Guday Ministér. 1995. *Leyu masehét*. Special Magazine. Addis Ababa, Ethiopia: Ministry of Culture & Sports Affairs.

Green Le Roux, H. 1903. *Chasses et gens d'Abyssinie*. Paris: Calmann-Lévy.

Hindlip, C. A. 1906. *Sport and Travel: Abyssinia and British East Africa*. London: T. F. Unwin.

Hodson, A. W. 1929. *Where Lion Reign: An Account of Lion Hunting & Exploration an account of lion hunting & exploration in S. W. Abyssinia*. London: Skeffington.

Lesur, J. 2007. *Chasse et élevage dans la Corne de l'Afrique entre le Néolithique et les temps historiques*. Oxford: Archaeopress.

Longman, Jere. 2007. "Athletics: Ethiopia May Be Poor, but It's Rich in Distance Runners." *International Herald Tribune*, February 1.

Longman, Jere. 2008. "Ethiopia's Long-Distance Legacy Is Written in the Olympic Medal Standings." *New York Times*.

MacCreagh, G. 1928. *The Last of Free Africa: The Account of an Expedition into Abyssinia*. London: The Century.

Maydon, H. C. 1925. *Simen, Its Heights and Abysses: A Record of Travel and Sport in Abyssinia*. London: H. F. & G. Witherby.

Mayo, D. R. W. B., C. Whymper, et al. 1876. *Sport in Abyssinia, or, The Mareb and Tackazzee*. London: John Murray.

New York Times. 2004. "Billed as the Best. Gebrselassie Holds True to Form," May 11.

New York Times. 2010. "Despite Money, Medals and Records, Gebrselassie Remains Motivated," October 30.

Nicol, C. W. 1972. *From the Roof of Africa*. New York: Knopf.

Pease, A. E. 1902. *Travel & Sport in Africa*. London: Arthur L. Humphreys.

Powell-Cotton, P. H. G. 1902. *A Sporting Trip through Abyssiniaz: A Narrative of a Nine Months' Journey from the Plains of the Hawash to the Snows of Simien, with a Description of the Game, from Elephant to Ibex, and Notes on the Manners and Customs of the Natives*. London: R. Ward.

Rambali, P. 2006. *Barefoot Runner: The Life of Marathon Champion Abebe Bikila*. London: Serpent's Tail.

Rosen, B. 1953. *Game Animals of Ethiopia: A Short Guide for Hunters and Animal Lovers, Illustrated and Giving the Names of Each Animal in the Principal Ethiopian Languages*. Addis Ababa: Swedish-Ethiopian Co.

Sánchez-Ariño, T. 1995. *Hunting in Ethiopia*. Long Beach, CA: Safari Press.

Swayne, H. G. C. 1900. *Seventeen Trips through Somaliland and a Visit to Abyssinia: A Record of Exploration and Big Game Shooting, with Descriptive Notes on the Fauna of the Country*. London: Rowland Ward.

Thurber, Jon. 2002. "Mamo Wolde: Won Olympic Gold." *Los Angeles Times*, June 12.

Times of London. 2010. "Kenenisa Bekele Story Will Run and Run," January 8.

Tsige, A. 1996. *Triumph and Tragedy: A History of Abebe Bikila and His Marathon Career*. Addis Ababa, Ethiopia: T. Abebe.

Von Höhnel, Ludwig. 1968. *Discovery of Lakes Rudolf and Stefanie: A Narrative of Count Samuel Teleki's Exploring & Hunting Expedition in Eastern Equatorial Africa in 1887 & 1888*. London: Cass.

Yamada, K. 1984. *Abebe o oboetemasu ka*. Tokyo: Shinseisha.

YaTéwodros sport kebab Ethiopia. 1967. *YaTéwodros sport kebab masehét*. Addis Ababa, Ethiopia: Kebabu.

Popular Culture

POP MUSIC

In the 1960s and 1970s, Ethiopia was treated by the outside world on the basis of a cliché that still endures. It was considered the abode of hunger and famine. But nothing could be further from the truth. Ethiopian nightlife even during those harrowing days was one of pleasure. It was exciting and fashionable because popular culture had started to permeate the society of the rising middle class and petite bourgeoisie. The trend continued until it went into eclipse in 1974, when the Derg discouraged Western music as a symbol of capitalist decadence and instead started to patronize indigenous music through an association called *kinet*.

It should be kept in mind that by that time, like all the youth of the developed and the developing world, Ethiopian musicians were already heavily influenced by rock, jazz, and funk. To this mélange, they had added Oriental music, which captured the ear of an average Ethiopian. A final type of music penetrated the country through Ethiopian soldiers who went to Korea to fight against the armies of North Korea's Kim Il Sung that had invaded South Korea. Ethiopian soldiers on the way back were flown to Japan to see the development there, so that they could spread the news in order to enhance Haile Selassie's Japanization policy. It is from Japan that they copied some popular songs sung by Tilahun Gessesse (Eruq Mesraq Salahu, meaning "When I was in the Far East"). That particular song is almost similar to the Japanese song "Sayonara." Radio Omdurman from Khartoum also beamed Sudanese music played by artists such as Ahmed Kalifa, who had already absorbed a dose of Chinese, Japanese, and Indian music with Arabic tunes. The blend between Ethiopian, Oriental, and Western melody spawned a unique mélange that became completely Ethiopian. To the uninitiated foreigner from the West, at first encounter, it sounds strange, but soon he or she finds it irresistible, soulful, passionate, and hypnotic.

For almost half a century, modern Ethiopian music was for Ethiopians alone. That changed recently thanks to the exceptional *Ethiopiques* series. Also, Mulatu Astatke, who developed his own mix of Ethiopian, Latin, and Jazz music, gained exposure with the outside world when his creation became a centerpiece of the Jim Jarmusch film *Broken Flowers*. Mahmoud Ahmed and Alemayehu Eshete, who were not known anywhere other than in their own country, have toured the West, playing not only to the Ethiopian diaspora but also to foreigners, since the *Ethiopiques* series exposed them to the outside world. The *Ethiopiques* music became a hit the moment an LP CD was released in 1986. Music reviewers gave it generous praise. The well-known music critic John Parceles acclaimed it as one of the five best world music albums of the year in an article he wrote for the *New York Times*. But it took another 10 years for the *Ethiopiques* series, which was recorded in Paris, to be released globally. Among the Ethiopiques music two were particularly notable. One was that of Alemayehu Eshete, and another was that of Netsanet Mellesse, both of whom played with the Walias Band. The second release of the golden oldies came out in the Ethiopiques album in 1994.

Western classical music started to slowly enter Ethiopia after the 1941 liberation from Fascist Italy. When the emperor opened the Haile Selassie Theatre, the institution stated a goal to develop popular music, with singers—not *azmaris* or minstrels, as was traditional—which was something new for the country. As noted earlier, the azmaris who played for money in bars and in banquet places were looked down upon. In fact, some azmaris belonged to a low caste and followed their parents into playing music. The caste system in Ethiopia being very rigid, like in India, other people shunned them on all occasions other than the time of their performances. For average Ethiopians, marriage with them was almost unthinkable. However, the modern musicians came from mainstream society. Some, such as Mulatu Astatke, actually came from the aristocracy.

Big bands connected to the imperial bodyguard, the army, and the police force started to spring up. The singers were no longer using the traditional *krar* or *masenqo*. They were performing with the accompaniment of Western-style instrumental music. They played Ethiopian songs, arranged by music instructors with foreign training who did their best to blend Ethiopian music with Western music.

In the 1940s and 1950s, just like in the rest of the world, U.S. big band was getting popular among the Ethiopian youth. Jazz was slowly sinking in to the Ethiopian music culture through the medium of the American military base in Asmara, now the capital of Eritrea. The imperial bodyguard could use the powerful American radio there to disseminate Western-style music blended with local flavor. The U.S.

soldiers based in Asmara had everything going for them. Because of these military men, clubs and bars were booming. Young people, whether American or Ethiopian, danced boogie and rock and roll. Radio and, later, television relayed American music to the country on a daily basis. People could hear not only the jazz tunes of Louis Armstrong but also the songs of Frank Sinatra, John Coltrane, and James Brown.

Starting in the late 1950s, big civil bands with up to 20 players sprang up with very sophisticated horn sections. This gave rise to the real blend of modern Ethiopian pop music. Until the appearance of the Derg in 1974, one could clearly see the influence of the horn section, which was growing in tandem with the melodies of jazz music, blues, and big band. Ethiopian youth of the 1950s and 1960s who had no radio of their own could be seen huddled up in the city squares like the Piazza, where a big loudspeaker was installed by the government, listening to the hypnotizing horn music of Getachew Mekuria, a pure mix of Western and Ethiopian tunes.

The baby boom generation in Ethiopia that emerged after the 1941 liberation watched Hollywood movies. They listened to blues. They tried to hum the music of Little Richard or Elvis Presley and danced to their tunes. Some took up playing with electric guitars, soul music, and Latin rhythm and blues. America's music invaded not only Ethiopia, but also the rest of the world. People were, in fact, for the first time listening to the same type of music, though it was a little altered to fit local cultural tastes.

Many Ethiopian musicians soon started to act like James Brown or Elvis Presley, though always with a local blend, which made the music and performances unique. Ethiopian musicians never copied their idols. Yes, they were into rock and roll and rhythm and blues. But they were so proud of their culture that any music they played with a Western influence had to have a big dose of Ethiopian lyrics and tunes as well.

The American GIs coupled with hundreds of Peace Corps volunteers continued to popularize American music. Many had musical training and talent and played at the base or even at local nightclubs to entertain themselves and others. Foreign travelers and Ethiopian returnees frequented venues where these musicians performed.

This influence had spread to the capital like wildfire. It was actually so pervasive that many nightclubs in Addis Ababa were given names like Arizona. Some young Ethiopians who were watching Hollywood movies even created a private troop called the Texans and dressed themselves like American cowboys. Ethiopian returnees also brought back new American albums, which the local musicians copied on tapes and tried to perform in Amharic and always with an Ethiopian tang.

Seeing the potential, a rising entrepreneur called Ameha Eshete created his own record label and released recordings of modern Ethiopian music blended with that of the West. This was starting in 1968. The first album Ameha created included two songs, one on each side of a 45-minute album. It was produced in India where labor was cheap and the expertise was admirable. Alemayehu, who was featured on the record, immediately became a hit among the Ethiopian youth of the period.

DANCE

Dance is performed by Ethiopians of all ages and ethnic groups during weddings and festivities. Because Ethiopia is a country of over 80 nationalities, there are as many variations of dance, and it is hard to explain each. The concentration here is on the ethnic groups that make up close to 80 percent of the population, particularly the Oromos and the Amharas and Tigres.

Ethiopian Orthodox Tewahedo Christians dance during the major festivals of Timqat and Masqal. Dance is mostly performed in pairs among the Amharas and Gurages and in groups among the Tigrayans and Oromos. Amhara dancers face each other in twos during performance, and the Oromos usually divide up into male and female groups and stand on opposite sides and dance. The Tigrayans create a big circle with men and women mixed. All dances, regardless of origin or ethnicity, are accompanied by rhythmic drum beats, vocal melodies, and hand clappings by a non-dancing audience.

The Amhara *zafan*, which is a secular song, is pro-reactive with a solo statement followed by a harmonic rejoinder. The solo serves as a warm-up and sets the mood, whereas the choral rejoinder achieves the climax. Foot motifs involve movement and stomping and various walking rhythmic configurations.

In the Amhara *eskesta*, groups arrange themselves into small or large circles. The circle of respondents sings in chorus with instrumental accompaniment, hand clapping, and cheers. A couple, either voluntarily or nudged, enters the circle and dances, displaying individual dexterity and talent. *Eskesta* movement is interspaced by different body and foot movements, such as bending and small springing action and flexion of knees. The shoulders of the *eskesta* dancer move up and down, imitating the motion of falling rain, and there are a number of brief, sharply executed shoulder vibrations and gyrations per one foot movement.

As indicated, the Amhara *eskesta* involves shoulder movements, sometimes gentle and sometimes intense. There are variations in the manner in which the shoulders are shaken. Shoulder movements are executed in vertical, horizontal, or diagonal direction and involve jerking, shaking, and twisting. A good *eskesta* dancer stands firm on his or her feet and performs only with the shoulders, though some, like the performers of the Minjar *eskesta*, involve all parts of the body and particularly long rhythmic movements of the legs.

Eskesta dancers from Gondar are known to exhibit different variations of shoulder dance and have supreme skill in their execution. Minjar dancers use a lot of foot motifs. The Gurages do the latter so much that is it actually the foot motif that defines the character of their dance. In the Gurage dance, vocalists produce a long-lasting guttural gasp, in and out, corresponding in time with the foot motif.

Oromo dancers divide into male and female groups, face each other, and dance with the opposite sex directly in front. They pause between the rhythmic songs and walk forward and backward gently. In some cases, solo partners separate themselves from the rest of the crowd and pause to dance. In each case, the dancers make an elastic bow toward a partner of the opposite sex directly in front and return to their original position. During the bow, the head is bent forward and sways from left to right or right to left. This is particularly typical to the *shaguye* dance of the Oromos of Harar.

The Oromo dance of *kumkumé* involves quick and rhythmic neck movement up and down without involving the shoulders and other body parts, except that the whole frame rises up and down very gently in coordination with the rhythm of the drum and vocal tunes. Oromo dances of *kumkume* and *aragada* are most energetic and vehement in execution.

THEATER

Ethiopian theater started during the early years of the 20th century. The credit for the first-ever theatrical performance goes to Fitawrari Tekle Hawaryat Tekle-Mariam, who studied in Czarist Russia from the late 19th century to the early 20th century and returned back to Ethiopia but got frustrated with the feudal bureaucracy and thus went back to Europe this time to study in France. Tekle Hawaryat staged a play called *Yawurewoch Komedia* (Comedy of the Animals), a satirical adaptation of La Fontanne's Fables performed for an aristocratic audience at the Itege Hotel in Addis Ababa, between 1912 and 1916. The show was extremely powerful. It became so popular with the spectators that the aristocracy was wary it might be sending a message of double entendre regarding their rule, so they banned it. The ban continued until Haile Selassie became emperor in 1930.

The *negus*, unlike the conservative aristocracy, was not against the growth of theater. In fact he thought the best way of imparting his idea of modernization of autocracy could be using the medium as a propaganda instrument. With his support, Ethiopian theater thrived at schools between 1930 and 1935. Also, under the orders of the emperor, Minister of Education Sahle Tsedalu opened the first theatrical performance hall at the Lycée Menelik II in 1934. Other schools followed suit by opening their own theater halls. Yoftahe Nigussie staged several plays at an educational institution where he was teaching—the St. George School in Addis Ababa. Yoftahe was well versed in traditional schooling, being equipped with the *zemma* and *qine* that he had studied in Gojam. In fact, Yoftahe has been judged by many historians as a cornerstone in the foundation of Ethiopian theater. Haile Selassie soon commissioned Yoftahe and another talented young man named Melaku Begosew to create a series of plays celebrating Ethiopia's uninterrupted 3,000-year independence, Haile Selassie's efforts at modernizing Ethiopia, and the need for dedication to the Ethiopian Orthodox Tewahedo Church.

The oldest structure for dramatic performance in Ethiopia was the "Hager Fiqir Mahber" (Association for Love of Country). This theater, created in Addis Ababa in 1935 by Mekonnen Habte Wold, was the only theater in country before the Fascist occupation in 1936. In fact it is the oldest indigenous theater to appear on the entire continent of Africa.

The Hager Fiqir Theatre's original goal was to inspire the Ethiopian people to stand against the upcoming Fascist occupation. It began as a discussion group but in time developed into a modern theater. The first performance at the Hager Fiqir took place at what was then called Arada Giorgis, now Menelik Square, which is located at the heart of Addis Ababa.

Fascist occupation of Ethiopia, which lasted from 1936 to 1941, interrupted the nationalistic theme of Hager Fiqir. Then in 1942, the performance hall was constructed again from an existing structure just a few feet away from the square.

During the 25th anniversary of Haile Selassie's jubilee in 1955, the theater got a facelift. The main entrance was enlarged, and an imperial balcony and lounge were added.

At the end of the Ethiopian-Italian war, another theater company—the Municipality Theatre—was born. Whereas the Hager Fiqir was under the aegis of those Ethiopians who took exile abroad and returned back after liberation, the Municipality Theatre was run by those who stayed in the country and confronted the enemy as patriots. In time, a conflict emerged between the two, which had become rivals. Even their shows reflected this bitter division. For instance, Yoftahe Nigussie's play, staged at the Municipality Theatre, was named *Affajeshign* (You Put Me in Trouble), and as the name indicates, the play took a satirical jab at the group that left Ethiopia in the hands of the Fascists and absconded—this included not only the founder of Hager Fiqir, Mekonnen Habte, who passed the occupation years in France, but also Haile Selassie, who took exile in England. The play also obliquely criticized the way the war against Mussolini's army was conducted. It was an immediate hit among an audience that had always complained, though in a hushed-up tone, that the exiles had taken over the country and marginalized the patriots who fought against the Italians valiantly until they were finally ejected.

In 1955, the negus established the Haile Selassie Theatre, now known as the National Theatre, as an additional place for the performing arts. The emperor, who wanted to placate the patriots who held a grudge against the exiles, handed over this opulent new structure to the Municipality Theatre Group in 1956. The theater Haile Selassie built was clearly grand by Ethiopian standards and was equipped with 1,400 seats. The Hager Fiqir Theatre continued as a popular theater for the common people of the city. Its shows were not limited to its base in Addis Ababa. Its largest audience was, in fact, outside the city because it broadcast live radio shows on Ethiopian national radio. Moreover, the Hager Fiqir troupe went on tour frequently so that people from rural Ethiopia had wide access to its nationalistic productions.

The earliest directors of Ethiopia's traditional theater were Afeworq Adafre and Tesfaye Tessemma. In 1960, Tsegaye Gebre-Medhin, who had undertaken training in Europe, was assigned by the government to take over the directorship of the Haile Selassie Theatre, which had hitherto been in the hands of foreigners.

This brought about the staging of socially relevant and sophisticated shows. The leading actor, Tesfaye Gessesse, was another polished and foreign-educated intellectual who was previously sent abroad by Haile Selassie when the negus observed his talent as an amateur artist. Tesfaye was given charge of the Addis Ababa Cultural Centre, and after the 1974 revolution, he was appointed as director of the Hager Fikir Theatre. Two years later, he was appointed director of the National Theatre (formerly Haile Selassie Theatre).

Tesfaye staged a production of his own play called *Yeshi*, which brought to the fore the problem of prostitution. In 1975, Tesfaye had another well-received play, staged under the title of *Tahadiso* (Renaissance). He established a school and produced some talented actors such as Wagayehu Nigatu, Debebe Eshetu, and arguably one of the most talented actresses in Ethiopia, Alam-Tshehay Wodajo.

It was at the Hager Fiqir that modern Ethiopian music and drama were nurtured. Numerous Ethiopian performing artists of note, such as Tilahun Gessesse and Frew Hailu, began their careers on the stage of the Hager Fiqir Theatre. For more than 70 years, this important institution has hosted traditional Ethiopian plays as well as translations of classic works by William Shakespeare, Moliere, Hendrik Ibsen, and Friedrich Schiller.

The Haile Selassie, or National, Theatre emphasized history, religion, and drama. It also emerged as an entertainment place for high society. Its first show was Prime Minister Endalkachew Mekonnen's *David and Orion*. Another major play staged was *Tewodros*, written by Girmachew Tekle Hawaryat, later to become minister of information.

During the Derg regime, the Hager Fiqir and the National Theatre were set to produce socialistic plays and performances. Musicians and actors were controlled by the state's Stalinist nomenclature, and the work of the directors was censured by the government. For example, in 1975, director Tesfaye Gessesse was detained for staging a play called *Iqaw* (The Thing), which the Derg construed as counterrevolutionary. The Mengistu regime used drama as a key propaganda tool. It created the Ministry of Culture and Sport for this very purpose. All theater companies under the Derg were used for agitprop. Plays such as *Red Sickle* and *Struggle for Victory* were pure propaganda pieces. But ironically, Ethiopian theater got its *lettre de noblesse* during this period. Attendance was huge by a public that was hungry for hidden information transmitted through the Ethiopian style of Wax and Gold that was unavailable from the propaganda-pumping, state-controlled radio and television. Whether they believed it or not, people also flocked to the theaters to hear invectives against "enemies of the people." In terms of its abundance, in qualitative attributes, in bearing, in the amount of partnership of artists of various kinds, and in written works produced, this epoch was judged by specialists as "the golden age" of Ethiopian theater.

The first case of real modern theater performance in Ethiopia started in 1950 with a recital involving a gifted actor named Melaku Ashagrie (1933–1993) who had joined the Municipality Theatre group. The first play in which he was a lead performer was *Sine Siqlat* (The Crucifixion).

With demand for theater growing among the public, Matewos Bekele created the Andenet Ye Theatre Budin (Unity Theatre). He was joined by the talented actor Melaku, and they subsequently moved to Harar. After a while, Melaku came back to Addis Ababa and joined Hager Fiqir. But he left it again and joined the Imperial Body Guard band. As a member this troupe, Melaku performed in two plays, titled *Set Aredachign* (I Was Informed by a Woman) and *Seytan La Wadaju Qirb-naw* (The Devil Is Close to a Friend).

In 1972, Melaku established the Tewodros Ye-Theatre Ena Ye–Musica Budin (Tewodros Theatre and Music Group). This became the second private theater company in Ethiopia. Together with his group, Melaku performed many plays in rural and urban areas of the country. Seven years later, another independent theater group was born under the name Ras Theatre. Its first play was *Tayaqi* (The Inquisitor), which was translated by Mengistu Lemma from J. B. Priestly's original play *An Inspector Calls*.

Among the notable people who contributed to Ethiopian theater is Kebede Michael (1915–1999), who is known for introducing European works in translation to Ethiopian audiences. His most famous translated work was *Romeo Ena Juliet* (Romeo and Juliet). He translated M. Clay's *Beyond the Pardon* as *Keyikrta Belay*. Furthermore, he staged many plays written by himself, among them *Ye Tenbit Qetero* (Appointment with Prophesy), *Ye Qetat Ma'abel* (Storm of Punishment), *Kaleb*, and *Hannibal*.

Another important personage of Ethiopian theater is Tsegaye Gebremedhin (1937–2006), who studied abroad and returned back to Ethiopia to coach the actors of the Haile Selassie Theatre. As he directed the group, he also wrote plays, many of which are notable. His compositions always had social content. One very notable play he produced was *Yeshoh Aklil* (Crown of Thorns). He also created other socially relevant plays, including *Mumps* and *A Man of the Future*. His plays depicted the lives of ordinary citizens, oppression of the masses, urban sprawl, and loss of direction among today's youth. Furthermore, Tsegaye translated plays by Shakespeare, Moliere, and Berthold Brecht. He is most remembered for his plays *Hahu Be Sedest Wer* (ABC in Six Months), *Enat Alem Tenu* (Strong Mother Earth), *Melekket Wearer* (The Message of the Proletariat), *Abugida Qayso* (The Adulterated Syllabary), and *Hahu Waynem Pepu* (Hahu or Pepu).

Among the avant-garde playwrights was Mengistu Lemma, whose production *Marriage of Unequals* became a hit with the audience. This was clearly a critique of aristocratic arrogance, ignorance, and superstition that he believed governed Ethiopian society.

FILM

The first film screening in Ethiopia took place during the reign of Emperor Menelik. Ethiopia being a very conservative society and the Church having an overwhelming influence not only over the general populous but also over the court itself, hosting film shows was a hard sell. Clerics with no exposure to Western technology construed film imitating human motion as the work of a demon and not of human invention. So they protested to the emperor. In fact, when the first cinema house was opened by an enterprising aristocrat, Ras Hailu of Gojam, on the upper side of the present Churchill Boulevard, it was dubbed *Seytan Bet* (Devil's House). When the Italian Fascists occupied Ethiopia between 1936 and 1941, they used it as a medium to disseminate propaganda that adulated Mussolini and the Italian culture. Movie houses were erected in the capital Addis Ababa, as well as Dire Dawa, Gondar, Jimma and Dassie.

It was only in 1964 that a modern-style movie was locally made by Ilala Ibsa under the name *Hirut Abatewa Mannew?* (Who Is Hirut's Father?). This was a debut of an Ethiopian film history in which talents were born and talents died. As a matter of historical record, lead actress Abebech Ejegu, who played Hirut, impressed the audience and became the darling of the filmgoing crowd in Addis Ababa and other major cities throughout the country. Based on her assaying of a strong, complex Ethiopian woman in character, she proved to be an outstanding actress, one who conveyed not only unparalleled intelligence but also an unconscious elegance—a true inner beauty that radiated on screen. Abebech was a highly skilled and accomplished film actress, and her striking beauty was quickly noticed by the audience. Other films that followed in the footsteps of *Hirut Abatwa Mannew* often imitated her, but never quite so charmingly. The cautionary tale in *Hirut Abatwa Mannew* still holds one captive, propped up by compelling on-screen chemistry between Abebech and Girma (her male counterpart). In the end, the desperate young man, Girma, takes drastic measures to seize his one chance at intelligence, beauty, and bliss by marrying Abebech not only on-screen but also in real life. Many of Abebech's admirers thought that she would continue to grace the screen with her unique presence, but that was not to be. *Gumma*, another major film followed shortly after. However, Abebech did not play a part in it. For all practical purposes, professional filmmaking of a high order was not repeated in Ethiopia until decades later.

Ethiopians who hoped they would have a homemade industry that radiated their culture had no choice but to turn to Hollywood and Bollywood movies. In the meantime, the advent of VCR and the launching of the Ethiopian television programming foreshadowed the popularization of film viewing. Creative indigenous filmmaking

The first Ethiopian film actress, Abebech Ejegu. (Courtesy of Paulos Milkias.)

continued to be missing until the appearance of *Behiwot Zuria* and Solomon Bekele's full feature film *Aster*, released in 1990.

In the third millennium, film production by Ethiopians is flourishing. By 2009, reportedly one new film was being released every 15 days. The number of moviegoers has also increased by leaps and bounds. Among the recently released movies, most deal with love, but the dark regime of the past military dictatorship directly or indirectly rests in the background. Among the most recent movies are *Asra Andagna Sa'at* (Eleventh Hour), *Yewendoch Guday* (Men's Affair), *Hermela, Sekaramu Posta* (The Drunkard Post), and *Kezkaza Welafen* (Cold Flame). The reason there are so many movies coming out is that the dark Derg era that had touched practically every family in Ethiopia came to an end, and the new government that came to power—the EPRDF—has allowed free filmmaking, in keeping with the euphoria of the time. Following the fall of the Derg, everybody had a story to tell of the White and Red Terror campaign that consumed the lives of more than 150,000 young men and women in Addis Ababa alone. There were films of love stories failing during those difficult days, and there were cases of Ethiopia's Schindlers and Good Samaritans.

Arguably the most successful Ethiopian filmmaker of all time is Haile Gerima, who studied acting and directing at the Goodman Theater in Chicago and the University of California in Los Angeles. Haile, who teaches filmmaking at Howard University in Washington, DC, was influenced by his UCLA classmate and filmmaker Charles Burnett and by the celebrated African American poet and pedagogue Sterling Brown.

Haile situates his films in African and African American context, challenging the stereotype Hollywood has created over the generations. He delves into the physical, cultural, and psychological dislocation of Ethiopians and African Americans in their own milieu. He has produced many critical movies and documentaries that take a jab at misrule during his own lifetime. His 1976 film *Mirt Sost Shi Amet* (Harvest 3,000 Years) is a critique of the feudal system under Haile Selassie and his predecessors. The 2009 work *Teza* (Mist) opens the wounds of the bloody Red Terror campaign the Derg unleashed on the Ethiopian people. *Imperfect Journey* lodges a critique at the human rights record of the EPRDF government that came to power after Mengistu's overthrow.

Haile Gerima's courage to take on the film establishment in the West, his intelligence, and his creativity have paid off. At one time, when major motion picture distribution companies refused to handle his film *Sankofa*, which analyzes the tribulations of African Americans during the period of the slave trade, he used word of mouth as a publicity technique; took his film to 35 different American cities, attracting a large African American audience; and in the process grossed almost US$3 million for that film alone.

As a filmmaker, Haile Gerima has placed first among noted international competitors. He has won nine major international awards, including the Ecumenical Jury for *Mirt sost Shi Amet* at the Locarno International Film Festival in 1976, the Fipresci Price for *Ashes and Embers* in 1983, the Human Values Award for *Teza* at the Thessaloniki Film Festival in 2008, the Golden Osella Award for best screenplay in *Teza* at the Venice Film Festival in 2008, and the Dioraphte Award for *Teza* at the Rotterdam International Film Festival in 2009. His major scoop was winning Africa's top prize in the Golden Yennenga Stallion Prize for *Teza* in 2009. *Teza*, the title of which means "mist" in Amharic, takes a hard look at the horrors of the Derg's Red Terror that killed 150,000 young Ethiopians in the late 1970s.

Over and above the success of Ethiopian filmmakers such as Haile Gerima who form the large diaspora community, one can clearly see a major renaissance in Addis Ababa itself. There has been a very rapid rise in filmmaking since the fall of the Derg in 1991. This is very encouraging for Ethiopians in all walks of life. It is a sign of the society's progress. It shows that the arts are starting to bloom and that there are more film audiences than before. Most importantly, films can be a crucial medium for reversing the image of Ethiopia as the land of drought and famine.

Among the newest and most promising films produced by Ethiopians is Manyazewal Endeshaw's *The Father*—a 30 minute film directed by Ermias Wald-Amlak using a 35 mm camera. Set in Addis Ababa, it depicts the era of the Red Terror during the Derg regime. This film has won accolades from the highly discriminating movie critics. The BBC correspondent Nita Bhalla introduced it to the world with praise for "portraying the horrors of the 'Red Terror' campaign unleashed by deposed dictator Mengistu Haile Mariam" BBC. "A film about the 'Red Terror' by an Ethiopian Director." http://news.bbc.co.uk/2/hi/africa/1525300.stm/ Accessed Wednesday, 5 September, 2001. The film won the Silver Dhow at the Zanzibar Film Festival in 2001, as well as the prize for the best debut movie at the Ghanaian film festival in August 2001.

REFERENCES

Discography

Alemayehu, Eshete. 2001. *Ethiopiques*, Vol. 9. Alemayehu Eshete. Paris. CD.

Amha, E. 1969–1975. *L'age d'or de la musique ethiopienne moderne*. 2, *Golden years of modern Ethiopian music: Ethiopiques*. Buda Musique. CD.

ARC Music. 2008. *Adzido Musical Group, Africa, a Musical Journey*. East Grinstead, West Sussex, Great Britain. CD.

Asnaqètch Wèrqu. 2003. *The Lady with the Krar. Ethiopiques*, 16. Paris. CD.

Aster Aweke. 1990. *Aster*. Columbia Records. New York. VHS/DVD.

Aster Aweke. 1991. *Kabu*. Columbia Records. New York. VHS/DVD.

Aster Aweke. 1993. *World Dance Beat*. 1993. K-tel International USA. Plymouth, MN; Addis Ababa.

Aster Aweke. 1996. *Live in London*. Barkhanns Records. New York. VHS/DVD.

Baird, M. 2002. *Gongs and Bells*. St. Sharp Wood Productions. Utrecht, The Netherlands. CD.

Biniyam, K., and Master film production. 2004. *Yegetami. Tagal Seyfu, Aznagnna Massaqia film* Serawoch. Addis Ababa. Film.

Boku Aner Productions. 2000. *Balageru*. Arlington, VA. DVD.

Brown, D. 1983. *The Prophet Rides Again*. A&M. Hollywood, CA. CD.

Buda Musique. 1969–1974. *Ethio jazz and musique instrumentale*, *Ethiopiques* 4. Paris. CD.

Buda Musique. 1969–1974. *More Vintage! Ethiopiques* 22. Paris. CD.

Buda Musique. 1969–1974. *Orchestra Ethiopia*. *Ethiopiques* 23. Paris. CD.

Buda Musique. 2001. *Kirba afaa Xonso*. *Ethiopiques* 12. Distribution Mélodie Paris. CD.

Buda Musique. 2001. *Konso Music and Songs.* Paris. CD.

Buda Musique. 2004. *Asguébba! Ethiopiques* 18. Paris. CD.

Buda Musique. 2005. *Guèbrou, T.M. Ethiopiques* 21, piano solo. Paris. CD.

Chants d'amour. 1997. Maison des Cultures du Monde. Paris. CD.

Dagol, M. Sét. 2003. *Tebabu warqeyé.* Addis Ababa. CD.

Damessae, S., D. 1994. *African Odyssey*. Vol. 2. Chapel Hill, NC. CD.

Damissay, S. 1985. *Vocal and String Music of Ethiopia.* Brooklyn, NY. CD.

Embaza, et al. 2005. *Zakirayo*. Vol. 3. Soloda muziqa bét. Addis Ababa. CD.

Ethio Sound. 1998. *Habibi.* Washington DC. CD.

Gétatchèw Mèkurya. 2002. *Ethiopiques* 14. Buda Musique. Paris. CD.

Gillett, C. 2002. *37 Artists From 24 Countries Around The World.* Milwaukee, WI. CD/DVD.

Gosaye. Asafa, et al. 1993. *Gosaye: Ethiopian instrumental.* Tsaday Yemuziqa Qinibir. CD/DVD.

Guèbrou, T.-M. 2005. *Ethiopiques*, 21, piano solo. Buda Musique. Paris. CD/DVD.

Harlem Musical Group. 2006. *Sounds of the Mushroom, Bole 2 Harlem.* Vol. 1. New York. CD/DVD.

Jenkins, J.L., R. Harrison, et al. 1994. *Musiques Vocales et Instrumentals: Ethiopie*. Ocora. Paris. CD.

Joplin, S., and W. Bolcom. 1979. *Afternoon Cakewalk: Suite of Rags.* New York. CD.

K-tel International. 1993. *World Dance Beat*. Plymouth, MN. CD/DVD.

Kadiir. 2005. *Yaarabbi Amaanaa*. Mana Muziiqaa Awaash. Addis Ababa. CD/DVD.

Lion Music. 2003. *Promised Land.* Aland, Finland.

Mahari, et al. 2006. *Burbwakabawoch*. Daynamik. Addis Ababa. Audiovisual.

Manteca World Music. 2005. *Africa: The Women's Voice*. London. CD/DVD.

Masfen, B. 1998. *Menyelagnal*. Pikolo Muziqa. Addis Ababa. CD.

Master Film Production. 1994. *Lift Up Your Head*. Heartbeat Records. Cambridge, MA.

Master Film Production and Library of Congress. 2005. *Addis Taem.* Vol. 1. New Test Entertainment. Addis Ababa. CD.

Meetii, J. 2004. *Leemmittu*, 1. Adil Tango Music Center. Addis Ababa. CD.

Menelik Wossinachew. 2008. *Meqabren Liyew*. Radiofusion International. Addis Ababa. CD/VCD/DVD.

Nahom Records. 2002. *Hulé Hulé.* Corona, NY. CD/DVD.

Nahom Records. 2003. *Aneleyeym*. New York. CD/DVD.

Nahom Records. 2003. *Yeqerta.* Corona, NY. CD/DVD.

Nahom Records. 2004. *Omahire*. New York. CD/DVD.

Netsanet, M. 1992. *Spirit of Sheba*. Shanachie. CD/DVD.

New Orleans Ragtime Orchestra. 1991. *Pickles and Peppers*. Stomp Off Records. York, PA. CD.

New Orleans Ragtime Orchestra. 1994. *Creole Belles*. Arhoolie. El Cerrito, CA. CD.

Nuuhoo, G. 2005. *Obsii*. Madda Walabuu. Addis Ababa. CD/VCD.

Playa Sound. 1995. *Africa, the Music of a Continent*. Paris. CD/DVD

Rahél, Y. H. 2003. *Menelek*. AIT Records. Addis Ababa. CD/DVD.

RCA Victor Group. 2002. *Globe Trekker*. BMG. New York. CD/DVD.

Sami Video Production and Library of Congress. 2005. *Dinbi*. Smart studio. Addis Ababa. VCD.

Shanachie. 1997. *Holding up Half the Sky: Voices of African Women*. Newton, NJ. CD/DVD.

Shewankochew, F., E. Shibabaw, et al. 1997. *Éthiopie*. CD.

Shibabaw, E. 1998. *One Ethiopia*. Washington DC. CD/DVD.

Shibabaw, E. 2001. *Gigi*. Palm. New York. CD/DVD.

Shibabaw, E., and B. Laswell. 2003. *bati*. Illuminated Audio; Palm. New York. CD/DVD.

Shibabaw, E., and B. Laswell. 2003. *Zion Roots*. Frankfurt/Main, Germany. CD/DVD.

Sirucha, B., Montage Media Services., et al. 2005. *Barnootaaf*. Mana Muuziiqaa Abbaa Gadaa. Addis Ababa. CD/VCD.

Taaddalaa, G. Baallami. 2005. *Ethiopia*. Ambassel Video & Music Records. Addis Ababa. CD/VCD.

Taammiraat, S., B. Admaassuu, et al. 2002. *Qaanqee*. Vol. 1. Taphoota Fi Sirboota Oromiffa Viidiyoodhan. Addis Ababa, Mana Muuziiqaa Fi Viidiyoo Elektiraati. Addis Ababa. CD/VCD.

Tadala, G. C. 2006. *Qonnet Lafa Bahe*. Éléktra Muziqa Bét. Addis Ababa. CD/VCD.

Tadasa, A., Master Film Production, et al. 2005. *Hagaré*. Yamuziqa Clip. Quter 1. Mišamišo Muziqa. Addis Ababa. CD/VCD.

Tafara, N. A. 1984. *Yahunu Yebas*. Addis Ababa. CD/VCD.

Tait, A., S. Woolman, et al. 2007. *The Wire Tapper*. 18. The Wire. London. CD.

Taylor, S. C. 1902. *Ethiopia Saluting the Colours*. Concert March for Orchestra. Augener & Co. London. LP.

Téwodros, Kassahun. 2005. *Nayelegn*. Ambasal Muziqana Video. Addis Ababa. CD/VCD/DVD.

Téwodros Kassahun. 2005. *Yastasareyal*. Éléktra Muziqa. Addis Ababa. CD/VCD/DVD.

TigiMusic. 1993. *Qarahugn*. TJR Music. Addis Ababa. CD.

Tsegayé, S. 2004. *Ensosela Yawaré*. Walis Muziqa. Addis Ababa. CD/VCD.

Tsehai Dababa. 2002. *Central Muziqana Electronics*. Addis Ababa. CD/VCD.

Tsehai Dababa. 2006. *Makossa connection*, Vol. 2. Paris. CD/VCD.

Voice of America Music Library Collection and Library of Congress. 2005. *New Developments in Ethiopian Music*. Washington DC. CD/DVD.

Wandemu, G. A. 2004. *Gudayé Nash.* Dynamic Audio-visual. Addis Ababa. CD/VCD.

Willis, L., G. Bartz, et al. 1993. *Steal Away.* Audioquest Records. San Clemente, CA: CD/ DVD.

World Music Network. 2005. *Music: the Music Rough Guide.* African Music for Children. London. CD.

Yonas, B., 2005. *Hérméla.* EthioFilm. Addis Ababa: Film.

Zbinden, J. F. 1972. *Ethiopiques.* Paris Éditions françaises de musique. CD.

Zbinden, J. F., W. Sawallisch, et al. 1988. *Lemanic* 70 Distribution, Tudor Recording. CD.

Zulu, M. 2005. *Reggae.* Addis Ababa. Lusaka: Dread Arts. CD.

Print Resources

Briggs, Phillip. 2006. *Ethiopia: The Bradt Travel Guide* (4th Ed.) Bucks, England: Bradt's Travel Guides Ltd.

Clinton, S. 1993. *Live Aid.* Chicago: Children's Press.

Falceto, F., and K. L. Albrecht. 2001. *A Pictorial History of Modern Ethiopian Music: Abyssinie Swing.* Addis Ababa: Shama Books.

Feuillatre, E. 1966. *Études Sur Les Ethiopiques d'Héliodore, Contribution à la Connaissance du Roman Grec. Paris.* Presses Universitaires de France.

Gray, C. 1988. *Bob Geldof: The Rock Star Who Raised.* Milwaukee, WI: G. Stevens.

Heliodorus. 1943. *Les Éthiopiques.* Paris: Société d'édition les Belles Lettres.

Jacobs, V. L. 1985. *Roots of Rastafari.* San Diego, CA: Avant Books.

Jouanny, R. A. 1986. "Les Voies du Lyrisme dans Les Poèmes de Léopold Sédar Senghor: Chants d'ombre, Hosties Noires, Ethiopiques, Nocturnes." *Étude Critique Suivie d'un Lexique.* Genève: Slatkine.

Mitchell, J., and L. Klein. 1985. *Dog Eat Dog.* Los Angeles: Geffen.

Mulatu, Astatke. 2001. "Tourist of the Week: One in an Occasional Series, Tuning In to the Rhythm and Spirit of L.A." *Los Angeles Times.*

New York Times. 2001, September 5. "*Father.*" 2001.

Perry, L., A. Morrison, et al. 2000. *Stay Red.* Culture Press. Paris, France.

Pratt, H. 1980. *Les éthiopiques.* Paris: Casterman.

Senghor, L. S. 1956. *Éthiopiques: Poèmes.* Editions du Seuil: Paris.

Senghor, L. S. 1956. *Éthiopiques.* Dakar, Senegal. Fondation Léopold Sédar Senghor.

Senghor, L. S., and P. G. N'Diaye. 1974. *Éthiopiques: Poèmes.* Dakar, Sénégal: Nouvelles Éditions Africaines.

Senghor, L. S., and W. Oxley. 1981. *Poems of a Black Orpheus.* London: Menard Press.

Yohannes, Gebresellasie. 2009. "Tilahun Gessesse, An Artist Extraordinary is Simply the Best." *The Reporter.* (April 21).

Zion: La Foi des Rastas. 2003. Paris: L'Harmattan.

Contemporary Issues

DEMOCRATIZATION

For Haile Selassie, who ruled Ethiopia from the time he was regent in 1916 to his overthrow as emperor in 1974, political authority was prescriptive and divine; it was based on inheritance, which was construed as a historical mission of governance. The emperor, who was instrumental in promulgating the first Ethiopian constitution of 1931, claimed to have "given" to the Constitution to his own people "of his own free will." Nevertheless, lest someone miss how far he was willing to go, he did not forget to add, "By virtue of His Imperial Blood, as well as by the anointing which He has received, the person of the Emperor is sacred, His dignity is inviolable and His Powers indisputable."

The divine right to rule was challenged, and Haile Selassie was overthrown in 1974. At that juncture, at least for a brief period, freedom of speech was for the first time allowed; independent journals mushroomed, and people exchanged ideas through the print medium. Freedom to organize was also tolerated. As a result, in 1974, Muslim citizens, factory workers, peasants, students, civil servants, and priests staged public demonstrations in support of, or in opposition to, myriad issues. This was, however, short-lived because those who filled the vortex following Haile Selassie's fall exhibited aversion to the new development of popular self-expression.

After the 1974 revolution, a military committee called the Derg came to power and unleashed neighborhood association leaders who carried out summary executions. This led to the liquidation of hundreds of thousands of citizens, mostly school-age children. Any person found to be a dissident was herded into an overcrowded jail, from which he was often taken out for execution. In the countryside, people were forcibly relocated on the mere suspicion of having contacts with opposition parties.

When following the fall of the Derg, democratization suddenly became the buzz word in Ethiopia, the postulate that political authority derives from the will of the people was advocated. This brought about the dawning of popular participation and open deliberation. It signaled the championing of freedom of thought and expression, respect to form and join associations, and the right to create political parties and all other organizations needed in a free society.

The Ethiopian People's Revolutionary Democratic Front (EPRDF) came to power and promised multiparty democracy. The 1994 constitutional arrangement was put in place to serve as a legal basis for the 1995 elections, which formally brought to an end the transitional chapter. It also served as a basic foundation for the EPRDF coalition to form a permanent government of Ethiopia.

The 1995 elections were flawed, however; the competition was totally lopsided because the opposition parties decided to boycott the election. Thus, the incumbent EPRDF and its affiliates won nearly all the ballots cast at both the federal and regional levels.

The 2000 national and regional elections were not much better: the opposition won a mere 13 seats out of 547 seats in Parliament. What is more, the 13 seats were occupied by six different opposition parties. The small size of the group and the fragmentation meant meaningful political dialogue in Parliament was not possible.

Thanks to the EPRDF government's openness to democracy, the period immediately preceding the May 2005 elections proved to be a momentous one. For the first time in the country's history, the seeds of democracy were planted throughout Ethiopia. It was a time of optimism and the fulfillment of a shared dream.

Indeed, the planning of the 2005 parliamentary elections was unprecedented in Ethiopia's history. The EPRDF allowed genuine political competition by multitudes of political parties. It gave fair access to the government-controlled media. Full-fledged participation in free campaigns and open debate on radio and television between opposition and government leaders and supporters offered a solid background for a genuine exchange of views on the important issues affecting the Ethiopian people.

The 25,605,851 voters who registered represented 85 percent of eligible citizens. The total number of candidates running for the House of Peoples' Representatives was 1,847, and another 3,762 candidates competed for regional councils. Female candidates who competed for the House of Peoples' Representatives numbered 253, whereas those competing for regional councils numbered 700.

The EPRDF government allowed media access and established a Joint Political Party Forum at national and constituency levels. It also engaged in regular consultations with electoral authorities to resolve problems in campaign and election administration. It offered special election-related training programs for the police and the judiciary. It pledged to ensure the use of nonviolent methods to resolve disagreements between the ruling and opposition parties. The voter turnout was very high on election day, May 15, 2005. Many polls were monitored by international elections observers and political party representatives. This ensured the integrity of the votes cast at least where these observers were present. Parliamentary and municipal candidates representing the opposition won virtually all the seats in the capital, Addis Ababa. They also posted considerable gains in most of the constituencies throughout the country.

But as the ballots started to pour in, worrying that violence might break out, Prime Minister Meles Zenawi declared a state of emergency. He outlawed public gatherings. He assumed direct command of the security forces and replaced the city's local police with federal police and special forces from elite army units. Then the Elections Board announced that the Ethiopian People's Revolutionary Democratic Front had won 209 seats, and its affiliated parties an additional 12 seats. It also announced that the opposition parties had won 142 seats. Complaints were loud. There were constituencies where the opposition charged irregularities in ballots. Soon, public protest erupted all over the country, with fingers pointed at wide-scale rigging of the elections. To stop the possibility of mass insurrection, the government resorted to mass arrests of demonstrators and opposition supporters. It closed many opposition party offices. The security forces killed 193 protesters and wounded 763 more.

In November 1, 2005, leaders of the opposition party Kinijit were accused by the EPRDF of planning an Orange revolution similar to the ones that overthrew incumbents in Ukraine, Georgia, and Kyrgyzstan. Journalists and civic society leaders were arrested. The charges against Kinijit leaders and civil society leaders included

Parents and relatives of 193 student protesters who were killed by a riot squad during the 2005 demonstration, wait outside a university campus in Addis Ababa. (AP Photo/Boris Heger.)

attempted genocide and crimes against humanity. Some 40,000 supporters of Kinijit were also jailed throughout the country. The release of the jailed leaders from 20 months of incarceration came about only after they admitted to their guilt. But the most prominent among them, Ms. Bertoukan Mideksa, was rearrested and sentenced to life imprisonment when she told an audience in Sweden that the release of Kinijit leaders had been achieved through negotiations and not because they had admitted to any wrongdoing. Two years after incarceration, with the intercession of Professor Ephraim Isaac, of Princeton University, Ms. Bertoukan Mideksa admitted to breaking the terms of her release and apologized to the government of Mr. Meles Zenawi, after which she was released from jail.

That the May 23, 2010, poll was lopsided became clear when the country's electoral board announced that the ruling EPRDF and allied parties had won 534 out of 536 seats, giving the ruling group nearly every seat in the Parliament. All of the main opposition leaders, including Mr. Hailu Shawel, Dr. Beyene Petros, Professor Merera Gudina, Mr. Gebru Asrat, Ms. Aregash Adane, Mr. Siye Abraha, and former President of Ethiopia, Dr. Negaso Gidada were declared defeated. Whatever the reasons for this massive defeat, the fact that the major portion of the opposition that was united under Kinjit was hopelessly divided and bickering at it confronted the incumbent EPRDF in the 2010 election did not help. Furthermore, the European Union observer mission was quick to comment that the election had been marred by the EPRDF's use of state resources for campaigning, leaving the opposition at a disadvantage ahead of the vote. However, it emphasized that the count itself was not invalid. A U.S. National

Counting ballots in the 2005 general election when the coalition of opposition parties, Kinijit, won all the seats but one in the capital city of Addis Ababa. (AP Photo/Karel Prinsloo.)

Security Council spokesman, Mr. Mike Hammer, commented in Washington that "an environment conducive to free and fair elections was not in place even before election day." He added, "The Ethiopian government has taken steps to restrict political space for the opposition" and has "tighten[ed] its control over civil society, and curtailed the activities of independent media."

Ethiopian Prime Minister, Meles Zenawi on his part urged the international community and his country's political opponents to recognize the EPRDF's overwhelming landslide election victory. Responding to his call, the European Union and the United States emphasized their resolve to work with Mr. Meles's government because they shared common political objectives in the region. To the opposition, the prime minister offered an olive branch when he said in a victory rally in Addis Ababa, "Even if you do not have seats in parliament, we promise to consult you on issues of national concern. We consider you an important part of this renaissance!"

ETHNICITY AND ETHNIC FEDERALISM

There is a high level of ethnic diversity in Ethiopia, but because physical characteristics among the majority of the people are to a large extent the same, the best way to distinguish various groups is by language. Ethiopia is home to a mosaic of more than 80 languages classified into four groups—Semitic, Cushitic, Omotic, and Nilotic. Starting from the time of the Ethiopian–Italian war, some of the ethnic groups have rallied behind parties espousing total liberation or at least local autonomy. The present ruling group, the Tigray Peoples' Liberation Front, is just one of them. Other important groups include the Oromo Liberation Front, the Ogaden National Liberation Front, and the Afar Liberation Front

In order to solve the problem, two divergent views of Ethiopian ethnicity have emerged. One propounded mostly by Ethiopian nationalist intellectuals is that even though there are diverse ethnic groups, there is an Ethiopian nation, with an Amhara core and other ethnicities in the periphery. Mesfin Wolde Mariam (Mesfin Wolde Mariam, 2006, 1–10) argues that the linguistic group at the core, the Amhara speakers, is not really an ethnic group but a melange of ethnic nationalities speaking the Amharic language. This group does not deny that there is ethnic power asymmetry. The solution to this lopsided situation is, according to those who accept Mesfin Wolde Mariam's line, the removal of political and economic deprivation. Once that is done, they suggest, ethnic conflict is bound to wither away from the Ethiopian scene. For them, ethnic federalism is a mechanism of destroying Ethiopia as a unitary nation-state.

A second group subscribes to a "national oppression thesis" and argues that Ethiopia has been, particularly from the time of Menelik to the present, a "prison house of nationalities" and that all ethnic groups should have the right to self-determination up to and including secession.

A third group accepts the prison house thesis but calls only for the decentralization of power and resources in order to solve ethnic conflict. For this group, once accommodation is made for the different nationalities to fully take part in the political

The Secretary General of the Organization of African Unity, Salim Ahmed Salim, left, pictured with Ethiopian President Meles Zenawi, in 1995. (AP Photo/Ricardo Mazalan.)

process and to exercise self-rule, and a governing power adopts a pluralistic language policy, the ethnic separatist tendencies will dissipate. The group also argues that ethnic identity may change or adapt to new realities in reaction to a given situation, but that that does not necessarily lead to the withering away of the problem as the Ethiopian nationalists suggest.

The EPRDF, headed by prime minister Meles Zenawi, radically reformed Ethiopia's political structure when it transformed the highly centralized Ethiopian state into a federation of ethnic groups in 1995 and then employed ethnic pluralism as an organizing principle, creating multiple ethnic-based territorial units with a "right" to "secession." It in fact defined citizenship, politics, and identity on ethnic grounds. The EPRDF ruling group claims that the purpose was to create a more prosperous, just, and representative state system for all its people. EPRDF supporters argue that after Ethiopia is crafted as an egalitarian pluralist state system, the dissenting ethnic groups will not have enough grounds to ask for secession.

RELIGIOUS CONFLICT

Because the Muslim world has considered Ethiopia a land of peace where the first Muslim followers of the prophet Mohammed took shelter from their Querish opponents in Mecca, Christian Ethiopia has never seen serious religious war. The only exception was the Gragn invasion of the 1500s. But since the heavy evangelization in non-Muslim parts of the country by the Wahabist Muslims, Muslims and Christians have clashed in western Ethiopia, bringing about the death of five people. In 2008, Christians and Muslims in Desse were for the first time treating each other with suspicion. Reports have spread to Addis Ababa of Muslims training to assault Christians and Christians stockpiling weapons for an armed attack on Muslims. One incident took place near the southern Ethiopian town of Jima, where several days of violence between Muslims and Christians wrecked the area, ending with 19 people killed and 5 churches and 600 houses burned, according to Ethiopian government reports. If Lebanon is an example, this may be simply the tip of the iceberg.

HUMAN RIGHTS

The 2005 election process and the 2008 violence in the Somali region that raged between Ethiopia's security forces, local militias, and the Ogaden National Liberation Front (ONLF) raised allegations of human rights abuses. A State Department report regarding human rights in Ethiopia during the period is clearly caustic. It calls attention to

> limitations on citizens' right to change their government in local and by-elections; unlawful killings, torture, beating, abuse, and mistreatment of detainees and opposition supporters by security forces, usually with impunity; poor prison conditions; arbitrary arrest and detention, particularly of suspected sympathizers or members of opposition or insurgent groups; police and judicial corruption; detention without charge and lengthy pre-trial detention; infringement on citizens' privacy rights including illegal searches; use of excessive force by security services in an internal conflict and counterinsurgency operations; restrictions on freedom of the press; arrest, detention, and harassment of journalists; restrictions on freedom of assembly and association; violence and societal discrimination against women and abuse of children; female genital mutilation (FGM); exploitation of children for economic and sexual purposes; trafficking in persons; societal discrimination against persons with disabilities and religious and ethnic minorities; and government interference in union activities, including harassment of union leaders. (U.S. State Department, 2009, 1)

The State Department report faults not only the government but also the opposition who have reverted to violence to spread fear and violate people's rights.

The Ethiopian government's response to the assertions against it is that "the annual report of the US State Department has become an annual irritant in the otherwise excellent relations between the U.S. and Ethiopia." The government affirmed that "human Rights are a noble and an important cause; . . . it is a cause [the EPRDF leadership] fully believes in and support." The Ethiopian government argues that the report was not produced "with methodological rigor, objectivity or even-handedness." It says that the report is "a deliberately jaundiced view of Ethiopia's progress in human rights." Some points raised by the report were labeled "anecdotal," "misrepresentations," "fabrication," or "exaggerations," and others were construed as "interference in the internal affairs of Ethiopia." The government claims that many of the assertions are "unsubstantiated accusations from groups seeking to undermine Ethiopia's process of democratization."

CIVIL WAR

Oromia

The Oromos are Ethiopia's largest ethnic group, but since the mid-18th century, when their overlords ruled from the capital, Gondar, they have had little political power. So it cannot be surprising that they started armed struggle early on. The Oromo Liberation Front (OLF) grew out of two movements: the Wako Gutu–led rebellion in Bale (1963–1970) and the Mecha Tulama Organization that emerged in Addis Ababa in the late 1960s.

From its inception, the OLF set its goal as its people's liberation from "Ethiopian colonialism" and the establishment of an independent Democratic Republic of Oromia in southern, eastern, and central Ethiopia. In the beginning, the group was given moral and sometimes material support by the Eritrean People's Liberation Front (EPLF) and the Tigreyan People's Liberation Front (TPLF). In early 1988, the Ethiopian army launched an attack against the OLF forces in Wollega.

Working relations between the OLF and the EPRDF that came to power in Ethiopia in 1991 were always filled with suspicion because the latter had organized the Oromo party called the Oromo Peoples' Democratic Organization (OPDO) that took the plank away from the OLF. The OPDO demanded and received everything the OLF was asking for except secession. This weakened the OLF movement.

Since its defeat at the hands of the EPRDF forces in 2000, the Eritrean regime has been attempting to destabilize Ethiopia and has funneled money and arms to the OLF. Intermittent violence continued to erupt throughout 2002 in the Oromo region. Though proof is hard to come by, the September 12, 2002, attack on a Tigray Hotel in Addis Ababa that killed 5 people and injured 38 others was attributed to the OLF. On May 20, a bomb exploded on a public minibus in Addis Ababa, killing 6 people and wounding 5. And on May 26, bombs exploded in two hotels in Negelé Borena, which is located in the Oromia Region, killing 3 people and wounding 5. Ethiopian soldiers were among the casualties. On September 3, a bomb exploded in the Addis Ketema market region in Addis Ababa, killing 6 people and wounding 26. The Ethiopian government has been extremely vigilant and has punished suspects without mercy. The combat continues, though the OLF is now splintered and lacks its earlier puissance.

Ogaden

Ogaden National Liberation Front Fighters

The Western Somali Liberation Front (WSLF) first engaged Ethiopian government troops in 1975. In 1977, with the active support of the Somali government army, it severed the railroad bridges between Addis Ababa and Djibouti. The mantle of fighting for the liberation of the Ogaden now passed to the Ogaden National Liberation Front (ONLF).

The ONLF was established in 1984 by members of Somali liberation groups. The ONLF employs military attacks against Ethiopian government targets, sometimes using kidnappings and bombings. During its armed struggle, it has also kidnapped foreign workers, calling them agents or supporters of the Ethiopia's government. Ethiopian military convoys have been attacked and burned on many occasions. It has carried out violent acts in Dire Dawa and Addis Ababa. The ONLF has thwarted the exploration of oil and gas in the area. In its bid to fulfill this aim, the ONLF killed 74 people on April 24, 2007—65 Ethiopian and 9 Chinese oil workers. It also kidnapped 7 persons near the oil field of Abole, in the Ogaden. Whereas some experts consider the ONLF's activities terrorist, the U.S. State Department and the European Union do not keep the OLNF on their terrorist lists.

In 1991, the ONLF joined the provisional government but withdrew its support from the ruling EPRDF government when the latter failed to invoke the separation clause that would have allowed the Ogaden to secede from Ethiopia. *New York Times* reporters alleged that Ethiopian military units have in many places effectively sealed off large swaths of the Ogaden to choke off support for the rebels. It is also reported that the Addis Ababa government is preventing much of the commercial traffic and emergency food aid from entering the Somali kilil where the ONLF is deployed. The government of Mr. Meles, however, denies all of these allegations. It blames the Eritrean government for all the violence in the Ogaden. It says that the Isayas Afeworki regime is arming insurgents in Somalia and the Ogaden to destabilize the EPRDF. Although Eritrea denies Ethiopian accusations, a United Nations report has recently concluded that the Isayas regime has indeed shipped planeloads of weapons into Somalia for this very purpose.

Afar

The Afar National Liberation Front was originally known as the Afar Liberation Front (ALF). It was formed in the late 1980s by the Eritrean People's Liberation Front (EPLF) to weaken Afar nationalism from within. Later, it was dissolved by the EPLF as Afar nationalism widened within the organization. After the Afar Liberation Front resisted the Derg's land reform proclamations and as a result suffered heavy losses, it began to harass traffic on the Addis-Assab road and rail links to Djibouti. In 1989, the Afar Liberation Front attacked a military convoy on the Addis-Assab road, destroying 9 military aircraft and 120 military vehicles. In 1993, the party was renamed the Afar National Liberation Front (ANLF) to avoid confusion with Sultan Ali Mirah's Afar Liberation Front. The ANLF garnered 10 seats on the Afar Regional Council in 1995 and succeeded to place a member in the House of Peoples' Representatives. The party was officially recognized as legitimate. However, many of the party's founders, including former leaders of the Afar autonomous region under Mengistu—Habib Mohamed Yayo, Jamal Ed Din, Yusuf Yassi, and Jamal Abdulkadir Redo—have been placed under custody, accused of encouraging violence against the state.

Amhara

In the Amhara region, there is the Ethiopian People's Patriotic Front (EPPF). This movement stands not for Amhara emancipation but for pan-Ethiopian causes. Its area of activity is in the Amhara *kilil*, particularly in the localities of Gondar. It also has a contingent in the Gambella region. Just like the OLF and the ONLF, the EPPF is also supported by the government of neighboring Eritrea.

Strong support for the EPPF started following the EPRDF repression that came in the wake of the disputed 2005 elections. In March and April 2006, the EPPF claimed to have triumphed over the EPRDF fighters in the North Gondar Zone. It has strong presence in the North Gondar Zone, in the Armacheho and Belessa regions of Gondar. In some of these areas, it has set up checkpoints at highways, where it confiscates vehicles and properties that belong to the government. The government information agency, Walta, however, disputes this.

In March 2009, a bomb exploded on a public bus in Humera, near the Eritrean border, and killed 8 persons and wounded 27. The government apprehended the alleged culprits, who confirmed in court that they worked for the EPPF, which is supported by Eritrea.

Also, a UN mission in Ethiopia and Eritrea and the Mine Action Coordination Centre reported in 2009 that 10 persons, among whom were a 16-year-old girl and a 50-year-old woman, were hit by an unexploded bomb, while people were burning paper at a school in the Humera region. The bomb was attributed to the EPPF.

TERRORISM

The problem of terrorism in Ethiopia is connected to the chaos in the anarchic Somali Republic. Meles Zenawi's government sent armed forces to Somalia to oust Al-Shabab, which is a military wing of the Islamic Courts Union that took over power from the warlords in southern Somalia and was on the verge of defeating the provisional Somali government isolated in Baidoa. The provisional government is very weak and cannot survive without outside armed protection. Ethiopian government officials started rethinking the wisdom of the invasion, which only worsened violence and never made the provisional government any stronger.

The United States has supported Ethiopia's bid to send armed support, but after failing to attract African countries with the exception of Uganda and Rwanda, and after the UN members failed to send peacekeeping troops to replace the Ethiopian forces in Somalia, the Ethiopian government gave up staying put to shore up the provisional government. In early January 2009, Prime Minister Meles Zenawi ordered Ethiopian troops to withdraw from the Somali Republic. The power vacuum was quickly filled by the Islamist Courts Council fighting force. Mr. Meles's government has vowed that even though it has withdrawn from the Somali Republic, it will keep its troops in strategic positions within the borders of Ethiopia to re-enter Somalia if the ONLF, which is supported by the Islamic courts Council and Eritrea, takes advantage and increases its attacks against the central government.

DROUGHT AND FOOD SECURITY

Effect of Drought on Ethiopia

In frequency and scope of coverage, drought has remained the most common calamity in Ethiopia. The reason the country is more vulnerable than other areas of the world is Ethiopia's extreme poverty.

Drought is not new to Ethiopia: it was recorded as long ago as 250 BC. What is new is that the scale and rate of recurrence and the destructive aftermath of droughts affecting different regions of the country are totally unprecedented.

As a result of the disastrous 1973 famine that contributed to the fall of the Haile Selassie government, the Relief and Rehabilitation Commission (RRC), now the Disaster Prevention and Preparedness Commission (DPPC), was established to manage the effects of drought in Ethiopia. As a result of the DPPC's standing preparedness policy, since the famine of 1985–1986, drought-induced famine has not reached the magnitude of past disasters. The policy also involves expanding curative health services and granting land through resettlement programs.

Emphasis is being placed more on certain areas than on others, though drought affects almost all parts of the country from time to time. For example, the northern and eastern parts of the country as well as areas of the Great Rift Valley have remained the most drought-prone localities needing attention. Because large-scale storage facilities for food to be used during drought and famine have not been practical, when emergencies arise, public places such as schools are used as storage places. Regional wars, such as those that took place between Ethiopia and Eritrea in 1998–2000, and local insurgency, as is currently happening between the government and the ONLF and OLF, have displaced people and have prevented food from reaching communities that need help. The number of people needing food aid has remained large. The government of Ethiopia raised the projected number of people requiring emergency food assistance between June and December 2009 to 6.2 million people. From January to June 2009, approximately 4.9 million people required emergency food supplies.

POPULATION EXPLOSION AND FAMILY PLANNING

Though drought and famine continue to wreak havoc in Ethiopia, its population had risen to 74 million strong by 2007, making the country the second-most populous nation in Africa after Nigeria. There is clear warning that Ethiopia may not be prepared to face the consequences of such a population explosion. Demographers have projected that the Ethiopian population could reach 140 million by 2030. It has been projected by the Washington-based Population Reference Bureau that by 2050, the population of Ethiopia will have grown by an astonishing 120 percent from its base in 2006 (Catherine Maddux, 2006). That means that in 50 years, the population of Ethiopia is expected to be about 175 million. In, fact the greatest development challenge facing Ethiopia is connected to population explosion. The fertile south, which has so far remained the breadbasket of Ethiopia, is losing its potential. In the years 1980 to 2004, Ethiopia faced 15 years of drought conditions, which led to famine.

Ethiopia needs more family-planning clinics that are stocked with enough amounts and varieties of contraceptives, which should include injectables and pills, not just condoms, which many Ethiopians avoid. There also may be a possibility of providing early-term abortions on demand. Education of girls should be intensified because the more education girls have, the fewer children they are likely to have. There is a lot to be done to address Ethiopia's high fertility rate, but such efforts are in competition with many other development priorities, such as the building of infrastructure, the expansion of educational opportunities and health care, and the quest for food security.

GENDER ISSUES AND FEMALE CIRCUMCISION

The gender dynamic in Ethiopia is such that women are responsible for performing the greatest amount of labor in the home. For example, they fetch water from springs far away from home—about 20 liters at a time—in jars or jerrycans, sometimes two or three times per day.

Women are responsible for collecting firewood for cooking. Many are prevented from enrolling in schools because the family is usually unable to pay for their uniforms and for their basic fees and school materials.

In traditional as well as contemporary Ethiopia, there has always been a wide gap between male and female access to education. Female enrollment has always been very low, standing at 41 percent, in comparison with 59 percent for boys.

After they finish school, women rarely have a choice for work. For example, in the medical field, the proportion of males to females is such that women make up only 11 percent of medical doctors and 15 percent of health officers. Even in nursing, which is generally considered dominated by females, only 29 percent are women.

Ethiopian girls are vulnerable to culturally sanctioned violence, including *Telefa* (kidnapping), which is usually done by young men ambushing a lone female who goes to fetch water or collect firewood. Their mothers are vulnerable to domestic violence, sometimes taking culturally rooted forms such as the concept of a woman as a property dependent on a male protector. Female genital mutilation (FGM), which takes a severe form in the area of Somalia and eastern Oromia, is a major problem facing Ethiopian women.

Ethiopia is among many African countries where female genital mutilation is practiced. Eighty percent of all Ethiopian women undergo the ritual. It is estimated that currently, some 30,000,000 Ethiopian women have undergone this procedure. But on the positive side, a 2005 health survey reported that the practice of FGM among all women had gone down from 80 to 74 percent (Ethiopian Demographic and Health Survey, 2005). Support for FGM among women had also gone down from 60 to 29 percent.

The form of FGM known as infibulation, which involves invasive surgery and seaming of the female genitalia, is punishable by 5 to 10 years' imprisonment. However, there have not been any criminal prosecutions so far because it is the undeclared policy of the government to try to discourage the practice of FGM through education in public schools and broader mass-media campaigns rather than through legal prosecutions. Most Ethiopians still believe that without being circumcised, a girl would never find a husband. FGM sometimes results in continuous bleeding.

In general, women in Ethiopia need to have a guarantee of basic human rights as enshrined in the Universal Declaration of Human Rights. They need legal rights and entitlements equal to their male counterparts in society. Ethiopian women need sexual and reproductive safety and freedom. All these are enshrined in the laws passed by the government of Ethiopia that came to power after the demise of the Derg. However, with the overriding influence of traditionally minded male law-enforcement personnel and judges, putting such laws into practice has remained a far cry from reality.

SEX WORK

In Ethiopia, girls' transition to adulthood starts early. Family breakup is common because by tradition, men can divorce their wives for being barren or for minor reasons such as disobedience and not keeping the house in order. Polygamous and arranged marriages as well as marriage through abduction also add to the high divorce rate. Rural girls generally migrate to the large urban areas to escape unwanted pregnancy and the fear of facing stigma as a result of engaging in sex outside marriage. The fact that 84 percent of women in the rural areas have no education of any kind limits their chances of getting work that requires a certain level of literacy. That has led to a situation where many young women migrating to the cities can survive only through domestic work or sex work.

When young rural girls transfer to city life, they usually find that they can earn a living only through informal work, which includes being a housemaid, being a coffee shop attendant, panhandling or peddling, or being a bar girl. Most women are initiated into working in the informal sector through friends already established or brokers waiting at bus stations. Studies regarding sex work in Addis Ababa show that 7.1 percent of the adult female population in the capital regularly practice multi-partner sexual contact, the majority of which involves prostitution. Thirty-seven percent have experienced pregnancy, and 93 percent have been beaten while working on the streets. Many clients are drunk. They commonly abuse their temporary sex partners. Clients mostly reject the use of condoms. Others deliberately split the condoms for their own individual pleasure or because they are angry at their status as STD or HIV carriers and want to get even with a society that stigmatizes them (Ethiopia, Ministry of Health, HIV/AIDS Prevention and Control Office, 2005).

Girls working in bars (*bunna bets*) are forced to drink alcohol, which more often than not leaves them lethargic and sick. Sex workers, whether in bars or in red light districts, face stigma from society and are without legal protection against clients or sex business owners. Many also lack opportunity to learn more about the hazards of their profession, particularly ways of protecting themselves from contracting HIV.

HIV/AIDS

The rapid spread into Ethiopia of HIV/AIDS took place between the 1980s and 1990s. Its proliferation was particularly through commercial sex workers, truck drivers, and soldiers along major transportation networks crisscrossing the country. AIDS among sex workers and their clients spreads basically through lesions created by STDs, such as gonorrhea, syphilis, chancroid, and genital warts. The government of Ethiopia has come to the conclusion that a drastic action has to be taken to curb the trend. To stop this spread, therefore, it has tried to increase laboratory support, pediatric HIV/AIDS care and treatment, and infant diagnosis.

Irish rock star Bono right, shares a joke with HIV/AIDS children at Missionaries of Charity AIDS hospice in Addis Ababa, Ethiopia. (AP Photo/Sayyid Azim.)

The HIV/AIDS pandemic in Ethiopia is aggravated by chronic poverty, lack of an adequate public health system, an economy exposed to external shocks, high unemployment, perennial food shortages, multiple disease environments, and paucity of social service capacities. The 2008 Human Development Report of the United Nations Development Program ranked Ethiopia as 169 out of 177 in its Human Poverty Index and as 142 out of 144 on the Gender-Related Development Index (Ethiopian Development Research Institute, 2010).

The HIV/AIDS pandemic in Ethiopia is concentrated in the urban areas. The urban adult prevalence average is 13.7 percent. In 2007, close to 7,000 infected persons in Ethiopia received antiretroviral (ARV) treatment on a paying basis. Since 2003, when ARV drugs became available in Ethiopia, over 7,000,000 Ethiopians have received treatment, 60 percent of them male. In hospitals, the percentages of women and men coming in for testing have been about equal, but the HIV prevalence among females was 60 percent.

A new initiative to curb the spread of HIV/AIDS among women is the creation of the National Coalition for Women Against HIV/AIDS (NCWAH), which was established in October 2003 to promote women's role in controlling their condition. This important organization is led by high-profile Ethiopian women, including Prime Minister Meles Zenawi's wife, Woizero Azeb Mesfin. So far, the coalition has attempted to draw attention to the visible prevalence of gender inequality, violence against women, and the rapid expansion of HIV/AIDS among females. The group is vigorously pushing to bring about parity in treatment among men and women, to promote the prevention of HIV transmission from mother to child, and to secure equal access to antiretroviral treatment for all members of a family. It has also lobbied the government to adopt measures that would lead to the improvement of the status of women, which includes eliminating gender differentials in education and among professions, the promotion of women's economic empowerment, elimination of gender-based violence, reducing the risk factor for HIV/AIDS transmission, and providing treatment and counseling for rape and abduction victims. Other actions include the provision of adult and pediatric antiretroviral therapy services, prevention of mother-to-child transmission of HIV, tuberculosis/HIV integration services, palliative care, HIV counseling and testing, adherence support, and prevention and treatment of sexually transmitted infections, which increase the chances of the HIV virus spread

TRAFFICKING

The law in Ethiopia prohibits trafficking in persons. Nevertheless, there are reports of people being trafficked from time to time. The Ministry of Labor and Social Affairs, together with the police, is entrusted with the monitoring of trafficking in persons. The revised Proclamation 104/98 was passed to improve coordination, supervision, and control over international employment agencies and to better protect migrant workers from deceitful recruitment and debt bondage situations.

Despite the existence of protection of the law, men, women, and children are trafficked throughout the country for the purpose of forced labor. Cases of trafficking for commercial sexual exploitation are common. It was estimated that between March 2007 and March 2008 alone, 35,000 persons, almost all of them female, were trafficked internationally (U.S. State Department, 2009). The age of women trafficked ranges between 16 and 30.

Children and adults from rural areas are routinely trafficked to urban areas for domestic work and commercial sexual exploitation. Transnational trafficking in women involving women for domestic servitude, mainly to Bahrain, Kuwait, Lebanon, Saudi Arabia, Sudan, Syria, United Arab Emirates, and Yemen, is growing. Some of these women are further trafficked into the sex trade after arriving at their destinations, and others have been trafficked onward from Lebanon to Greece, Italy, and Turkey. Small numbers of adult males are trafficked into low-skilled forced labor in the Gulf States and Saudi Arabia. Brokers recruit victims at the community level. Bus and truck drivers who crisscross the country engage in the trafficking of young women and children, and brothel owners, brokers, and pimps take over at the final destination. Such persons are said to provide birth certificates, counterfeit work permits, and travel documents to the trafficked individuals. The State Department report for 2008 alleges that in 2007, it received anecdotal reports of returned trafficking victims being jailed or prosecuted in courts for violations of prostitution or immigration laws.

Trafficked individuals who have minimal education and knowledge about their own personal rights lack recourse to remedy their situation. Upon returning home, through either voluntary repatriation or deportation, many of the trafficked victims are highly traumatized and depressed. There have been reports of suicide either before or upon arrival home.

HEALTH

Modern health services reach only a small portion of the Ethiopian population. In 1993, two years after the EPRDF took over power, only 55 percent of the Ethiopian population had access to health care services.

The health system in Ethiopia is inadequate. One of the most immediate threats to life in crisis areas stems from vulnerable populations' lack of access to any form of meaningful health care. Emergency measures are still insufficient, given the vast public health threats, including adequate Emergency Public Information coverage for vulnerable populations; sufficient quantities of clean water for consumption and hygiene purposes; satisfactorily balanced, adequate, and appropriate food aid rations; and other properly conceptualized and managed nutrition interventions. Serious lack of health care means that Ethiopians of all ages succumb to preventable diseases such that the life expectancy of the people is an alarming 41 years.

The major health problem affecting Ethiopia is traced to communicable diseases and nutrition deficiencies. Drought, political turmoil, and population pressures worsen the Ethiopian health situation. In 2005, there were 600 health centers, 1662 health stations, and 4,211 health posts, mostly public-owned.

Shortage of health staff in Ethiopia has remained critical. The density of health workers to population is far below that for sub-Saharan Africa. The minimum stage of health workforce nurses and midwives density considered essential to reach the Millennium Development Goals in Africa has been estimated at 2.5 per 1,000 population. But in Ethiopia, the density is a mere 0.2 per 1,000.

In 2005 in Ethiopia, there were a total of 34,660 health workers, 776 health officers, and 18,809 nurses of all categories. A shortage of pharmacists is another problem facing the public health system. While all these problems bedevil the people of Ethiopia, health care expenditures are still under 5 percent of the country's GDP.

WATER

One of the most important sources of accessible fresh water for human consumption is river runoff. All across the world, there are 263 major river basins that cross national boundaries and are responsible for 85 percent of the planet's land water. The Nile, known to be the longest international river in the world, has been the source of political friction among the three important riparian nations of Egypt, Sudan, and Ethiopia. Both the White Nile, which flows down starting in central Africa, and the Blue Nile, which originates in Ethiopia, meet at Khartoum and then flow down to Egypt and into the Mediterranean. Ethiopia provides 86 percent of the Nile flow. The Blue Nile that starts at Lake Tana in Gondar and contributes 59 percent, the Baro-Akobo (Sobat) provides 14 percent, and the Tekezzé (Atbara) provides 13 percent. During the rainy season, the water flowing from Ethiopia constitutes some 90 percent of the Nile flow.

Blue Nile Falls. (Courtesy of Paulos Milkias.)

Blue Nile Falls. (Courtesy of Paulos Milkias.)

The Nile basin encompasses large areas in 10 countries: Rwanda, Burundi, Congo Republic, Tanzania, Kenya, Uganda, Eritrea, Ethiopia, Sudan, and Egypt, which together host 300 million people, more than half of whom are dependent on the Nile. Three of the nine riparian countries, Ethiopia, Sudan, and Egypt, are currently experiencing an alarming level of population increase.

Water shortage is the greatest threat to the food security of many riparian nations, and agriculture is responsible for 75 percent of total water withdrawal in the Nile basin. Whereas most countries in the basin use rainwater for their agricultural needs, one country, Egypt, does not have any rain and is wholly dependent on the Nile for its farming needs. To feed their continuously growing population, many nations such as Ethiopia are reverting to irrigation. Of the 10 riparian countries of the Nile basin, 3 are in the most crucial positions: Ethiopia as the major supplier and Egypt and Sudan as the key consumers.

Egypt has repeatedly proclaimed its historic right to the waters of the Nile. It contends that whereas other basin countries can depend on rainwater, it is the only one that is almost completely dependent on the Nile water for its survival.

Sudan has more rainwater than Egypt, especially in the southern areas of the country, but its dependence on the Nile is all the same critical. In fact, whereas in Egypt 50 percent of the population is dependent on farming the land, in Sudan more than 70 percent of the people are dependent on agriculture.

The United Nations Food and Agriculture Organization reports that Ethiopia cultivates about 290,000 hectares of irrigated land. This represents only 11 percent of the irrigation potential of the country. It is important to note that agriculture accounts for 40 percent of the Ethiopia's GNP and 90 percent of its export. It is also the source of 85 percent of employment.

Shepherd children near Blue Nile Falls. (Courtesy of Paulos Milkias.)

The agricultural sector of Ethiopia is almost wholly confined to the high-rainfall, mountainous areas in the north, the east, and the center, where 88 percent of the country's population resides. This constitutes 44 percent of the land area of Ethiopia. The country has suffered from serious famines, particularly in 1973 and 1984–1985, which claimed the lives of almost 2 million people.

The demographic picture in Ethiopia is even grimmer. Its population is expanding faster than Egypt's. Demographers project that Ethiopia's population will swell and surpass that of Egypt by 2025. If conflict does occur, the fact that Ethiopia is not geographically contiguous to Egypt means that Cairo's military action against Addis Ababa cannot be of an immediate threat. But if Egypt creates an alliance with Sudan, which also has a stake in the increased harnessing of the Nile, war with Ethiopia is not unlikely. In the meantime, Egypt has added to military threats the flexing of its diplomatic muscle to discourage foreign investment in Ethiopia's major irrigation projects in the Nile basin.

PRISON AND DETENTION CENTER CONDITIONS

Currently, there are 3 federal prisons and 117 regional prisons in Ethiopia. This does not include many unofficial detention centers. Reports indicate that as of September 2007, there were 52,000 prisoners. This was a decrease from 62,000 in 2006, owing to the political pardons related to Kinijit detainees.

The conditions in all the prisons are judged to be harsh by Western standards. Prisoners usually supplement their government budget with daily food deliveries from family members. In regional prisons, government services do not exist.

It is reported that in detention centers, mistreatment is common. There have been cases in which family visits to political prisoners have been restricted to a few per annum. Demands by the international community to visit police stations and federal prisons, including where opposition, civil society, and media leaders are incarcerated, have been repeatedly rejected. However, regional authorities do regularly allow official international visits where they can ask the condition of prisoners without third parties present. The local nongovernmental organization Prison Fellowship Ethiopia (JFA-PFE) also has been granted access to many prisons and detention centers, including federal prisons. Members of the diplomatic corps have often been granted access to regional prisons, so long as they have informed the authorities in advance.

CAPITAL PUNISHMENT

Ethiopian has had written laws for several hundred years. In the Fetha Negest, mutilation (such as the amputation of limbs) and the death penalty were sanctioned for high crimes such as murder and treason.

The 1930 Constitution promulgated by Emperor Haile Selassie replaced the Fetha Negest with a modern penal code. Most importantly, it retained capital punishment. So in reality, one sees both systems combined with the Ethiopian traditional law. In fact, the overriding principle in Ethiopian law is that punishment can deter wrongdoers from committing other crimes. Imprisonment and capital punishment are enforced with respect to certain crimes, but the main objective is to temporarily or permanently prevent wrongdoers from committing further crimes against society. Thus, the government set up a system of military tribunals and empowered them to impose the death penalty for a wide range of criminal and political offenses.

In the revised penal code of July 1976, the Derg amended the code to prescribe the death penalty for "antirevolutionary activities" and economic crimes.

Sentence of death shall be passed only in cases of grave crimes and on exceptionally dangerous criminals.

A sentence death shall be passed only on a criminal who, at the time of the commission of the crime, has attained the age of eighteen years.

Death sentence shall not be carried out unless confirmed by the Head of State.

Death sentence shall not be executed before ascertainment of its non-remission or non-commutation by pardon or amnesty.

A sentence of death may be commuted or remitted by way of pardon or amnesty in accordance with the provisions of the Code.

The sentence of death shall not be carried out in public by hanging or by any other inhuman means. [This was common during the previous two regimes of Haile Selassie and Mengistu Haile Mariam.]

The penalty of death shall be executed by a humane means within the precincts of the prison.

The execution of the sentence shall be carried out without any cruelties, mutilations or other physical suffering. (The Criminal Code of the Federal Democratic Republic of Ethiopia, 2004)

In 2007, the office of the special prosecutor demanded a death sentence for former Ethiopian president Mengistu Haile Mariam. Starting in 1991 when he fled from the occupying armies of the EPRDF, Mengistu has remained in exile in Harare, Zimbabwe. The Federal High Court passed a sentence of life imprisonment on Mengistu and his collaborators for genocide and crimes against humanity that they were accused of perpetrating between 1974 and 1991. But in May 2008, the Federal Supreme Court reversed the ruling and sentenced Mengistu and 18 of his senior officials to death. On April 6, 2008, a court sentenced to death five military officers in absentia. On May 21, 2007, the Federal Supreme Court sentenced eight men to death for a May 28, 2007, bombing in Jijiga in the Somali region. And on May 22, a military tribunal passed a death sentence in absentia on four Ethiopian pilots, who sought asylum while training in Israel in 2007. Most recent reports show that even though all these death sentences were imposed by courts, there were not any executions between 2007 and 2009.

URBAN SPRAWL AND STREET CHILDREN

Almost a quarter of the young men and close to 50 percent of the young women who migrate from the countryside to the cities, particularly to Addis Ababa, do so mainly to get a chance at education or to work and earn a living.

Aggravated by civil war, drought, and an ailing economy, Ethiopia's street children population has mushroomed to more than 100,000. The number of potential children who might fall through the cracks to join street life is expanding exponentially.

Ironically, about one-third of all street children in Addis Ababa are children of ex-soldiers who served in the Ethiopian army to protect Ethiopia's sovereignty and territorial integrity during the previous regime. Amputees from landmines also try to support themselves and their families through panhandling. Children of displaced slum dwellers often become breadwinners. Still others wash cars to augment their families' income. It is not surprising that Mekelé, the provincial capital of the recently war-ridden Tigray, hosts the largest population of orphaned children in Ethiopia. As much as UN agencies and nongovernmental organizations try to reunite the children with their families or relatives, 25 percent of such dislocated children in Mekelé still live on their own or in shelters. The United Nations Environmental Program estimates that in 2008, there were between 150,000 and 200,000 street children in Ethiopia (United Nations Environmental Program, 2008. P.2). Older children more often than not abuse younger ones. Some adult handlers have been found to maim or blind the children to raise their earning capacity, given that people usually feel sorry for such child beggars and give them more money.

There are some programs in place that aim to combat Ethiopia's street life for children and to rehabilitate those already leading such life. One such organization, Forum on Street Children Ethiopia (FSCE), was established just one year into the rise to power of the TPLF. In 2009, there were an estimated 800,000 high-risk children in Ethiopia, many on the brink of falling through the cracks and joining the streets.

A number of children who were helped by FSCE have secured funds from a group lending scheme administered by Save the Children and FSCE and have opened thriving shops in the bazaars.

ADOPTION

The official agency responsible for adoptions in Ethiopia is the Adoption Team located at the Children and Youth Affairs Office (CYAO), which is under the Ministry of Women's Affairs (MOWA). The head of the Adoption Team can be directly contacted for information about approved orphanages caring for children in need of permanent family placements.

ADOPTING ETHIOPIAN CHILDREN

Despite the fact that Ethiopia is known to the outside world for endemic drought, devastating famine, and unending war, it has now become a lucrative spot for international adoption. With a 2009 population of 74 million, the country has an estimated 5 million children who have lost one or both parents and are ready for adoption. In many cases, the children have lost both parents as a result of HIV/AIDS as well as malaria, tuberculosis, and famine. In 2009, the number of orphans who lost their parents to AIDS was over 750,000, and orphaned children with HIV numbered more than a quarter million. Others are from families too impoverished to feed and clothe them. There are some basic requirements for those intending to adopt children from Ethiopia. According to a set standard and law, children can be adopted only by married couples and single women. A home-study report, references, and financial documents are also required. Specialists suggest that Ethiopia has exemplary centers for orphans, run by many foreign agencies, with a very efficient adoption system that makes it possible to know the health and background of the children and complete the process at a cost of about $20,000, and all that without a bribe, as is common in many countries, and within a span of three months. The existence of transitional homes for orphans, in the countryside and in the capital, with full services and staffing and with the chance for adopting families to meet birth parents and visit the villages where the children were raised, has made Ethiopia boast of a cutting-edge practice in adoptions. A number of agencies also provide DVDs or photographs that provide details regarding the children's past. Some transitional homes have primary schools attached to them that are also open to local students. It is here that the children begin to learn English. Many have medical clinics with full-time doctors and nurses. They even have a guest house for adoptive parents. The world-famous actress Angelina Jolie had traveled to Addis Ababa and adopted an abandoned Ethiopian child whom she named Zahara Marley Jolie in July 2005. In an exclusive report, Colin Maximin writes in February 2010 that the star had decided to adopt another child from Ethiopia, because she was "deeply moved by the plight of the children in the orphanages in Addis Ababa" He quotes a person close to the actress as saying: "There she was in hospital about to give birth to two babies, and she was thinking of all the helpless kids all over the world who are alone out there and have no one to care for them. She is so caring and has a good heart" (Maximin, 2010).

In general, the Ethiopian adoption program has become very popular with prospective parents, including Hollywood celebrities, such as Angelina Jolie. Since the beginning of the millennium, foreign families have adopted thousands of children from Ethiopia. Post-placement reports are legally required on Ethiopian orphans at three months, six months, and one year after the adoption.

The Ethiopian government prefers to place prospective children with married couples who have been legally together for at least five years. Even though there is no statutory maximum age limit on the adoptive parent, the accepted practice is to limit the age of the parent to less than 40 years greater than that of the adopted child.

The sources for adoption are orphanages scattered throughout the country. It is the Ministry of Women's Affairs that routinely places abandoned or orphaned children in orphanages or foster homes. The orphans in the orphanages are identified for international adoption once it has been ascertained that they have been abandoned by their parents or have lost their parents to disease or have sick parents who cannot care for them. By law, if a child is abandoned, or if a child is found to have two HIV/AIDS-infected parents or one living HIV/AIDS-infected parent, the government declares him or her an orphan and assumes legal guardianship. There are no residency requirements for prospective adoptive parents, and adoption agencies normally advise adoptive parents of approximately how long the adoption will take.

Erin Henderson of Wyoming with two adopted children from Ethiopia, posing with others in a foster home. (AP Photo/Douglas C. Pizac.)

REFERENCES

Abara, G., and A. Hailu. 2002. *Agony in the Grand Palace: 1974–1982*. Addis Ababa, Ethiopia: Shama Books.

Addis Ababa City Administration Health Bureau. 1999. *HIV/AIDS in Addis Ababa: Background, Projections, Impacts, and Interventions* Addis Ababa, Ethiopia: Addis Ababa City Administration Health Bureau.

All Africa News Network. 2010. "Ethiopia: U.S., Europe Criticize Elections but Will Work with Meles," May 26. http://allafrica.com/stories/201005260433.html.

Appleton, J., and SCF Ethiopia Team. 1987. *Drought Relief in Ethiopia: Planning and Management of Feeding Programmes: A Practical Guide*. London: Save the Children.

Bekoe, D. A. O. 2006. *East Africa and the Horn: Confronting Challenges to Good Governance*. Boulder, CO: Lynne Rienner.

Berhanu, L., G. Davey, et al. 2005. *Young People's HIV/AIDS & Reproductive Health Needs and Utilization of Services in Selected Regions of Ethiopia*. Addis Ababa: Ethiopian Public Health Association.

Carlson, A. J., and D. G. Carlson. 2008. *Health, Wealth, and Family in Rural Ethiopia: Kossoye, North Gondar Region, 1963–2007*. Addis Ababa, Ethiopia: Addis Ababa University Press.

Children and Youth Affairs Organization and Save the Children Fund (Great Britain). 1995. *Proceedings of the Workshop on the Implementation of the Convention on the Rights of the Child: Debre Zeit, July 3–5, 1995*. Debre Zeit, Ethiopia: The Organization.

Criminal Code of the Federal Democratic Republic of Ethiopia. Proclamation No. 414/2004. http://www.ilo.org/dyn/natlex/docs/ELECTRONIC/70993/75092/F1429731028/ETH70993.pdf.

Erlikh, H. 2002. *The Cross and the River: Ethiopia, Egypt, and the Nile*. Boulder, CO: L. Rienner.

Erlikh, H. 2007. *Saudi Arabia and Ethiopia: Islam, Christianity, and Politics Entwined*. Boulder, CO: Lynne Rienner.

Ethiopia. 2005. Demographic and Health Survey, Addis Ababa.

Ethiopia, Ministry of Health, HIV/AIDS Prevention and Control Office. 2005. "The Drivers of HIV/AIDS Epidemic and Response in Ethiopia."

Ethiopia Yema'ikalawi Statistics Agency and ORC Macro. 2006. *Ethiopia Demographic and Health Survey*. Addis Ababa: Artistic Printing Press.

Ethiopian Demographic and Health Survey. 2005. *Report on FGM*. Addis Ababa: Central Statistics Agency. Ethiopian Government. "Gender-Related Development Index." 2010. Addis Ababa: Ethiopian Development Research Institute.

Ethiopia's Response to the U.S. State Department Report on the Human Rights Situation in Ethiopia. 2009. Addis Ababa, Ethiopia: Government Communication Affairs Office.

Intergovernmental Authority on Development. 2003. *The Prevention and Combating of Terrorism*. Report of the IGAD Conference, Addis Ababa, Ethiopia, June 24–27.

Lata, Leenco. 1999. *The Ethiopian State at the Crossroads: Decolonization and Democratization or Disintegration*. Lawrenceville, NJ: Red Sea Press.

Maddux, Cathernine, 2006. "Voice of America." Washington, March 8, 2006. http://radiotime. com/station/s_88023/Voice_of_America_Horn_of_Africa.aspx/ Accessed February 4, 2008.

Maximin Colin. 2010. "Angelina Jolie to Adopt Ethiopian Child—Exclusive." *Afro Saxon Heat,* 1–2.

Merera, G. 2003. *Ethiopia: Competing Ethnic Nationalisms and the Quest for Democracy, 1960–2000.* Addis Ababa, Ethiopia: Shaker Pub.

Mesfin Wolde, Mariam. 2006. *Ye'Kihdet Kulkulet* (The Precipice of Treachery). Addis Ababa: Commercial Printing Press, 2006.

Mohamed, A. 2008. *The Human Rights Provisions of the FDRE Constitution in Light of the Theoretical Foundations of Human Rights.* Addis Ababa, Ethiopia: Faculty of Law, Addis Ababa University.

National AIDS Council (Ethiopia). 2001. *Strategic Framework for the National Response to HIV/AIDS in Ethiopia (2001–2005).* Addis Ababa, Ethiopia: National AIDS Council.

Oumer, M. 2001. *Who Is Doing What on Gender Issues: A Directory of Organizations Working on Gender in Ethiopia.* Addis Ababa: Panos Ethiopia.

Pausewang, S., K. Tronvoll, et al. 2002. *Ethiopia since the Derg: A Decade of Democratic Pretension and Performance.* London: Zed Books.

Poluha, E., Yemahbarawi Tenat Medrek (Ethiopia), et al. 2007. *The World of Girls and Boys in Rural and Urban Ethiopia.* Addis Ababa, Ethiopia: Forum for Social Studies in association with Save the Children Norway and Save the Children Sweden.

Rotberg, R. I., World Peace Foundation, et al. 2005. *Battling Terrorism in the Horn of Africa.* Cambridge, MA: Brookings Institution.

Sahleyesus, Daniel Telake, and Roder Beaujot. 2009, January. "Attitudes toward Family Size Preferences in Urban Ethiopia." *Journal of Comparative Family Studies* 40(1).

Semegn, T. B. 2007. *Seeds for Democratization in Ethiopia: Why Unity of Purpose Matters.* Bloomington, IN: AuthorHouse.

Swain, Ashok. 2008. "Mission Not Yet Accomplished: Managing Water Resources in the Nile River Basin." *Journal of International Affairs* (Spring–vol. 61, No. 2, 2,201-214.

Tesfaye, A. 2002. *Political Power and Ethnic Federalism: The Struggle for Democracy in Ethiopia.* Lanham, MD: University Press of America.

Tronvoll, K., C. Schaefer, et al. 2009. *The Ethiopian Red Terror Trials: Transitional Justice Challenged.* Rochester, NY: James Currey, 2009.

Turton, D. 2006. *Ethnic Federalism: The Ethiopian Experience in Comparative Perspective.* Oxford: UNICEF.

United Nations Environmental Program. 2009. "Street Children by Country, Nairobi, Kenya."

U.S. State Department. 2009. *Human Rights Reports: Ethiopia.* Bureau of Democracy, Human Rights, and Labor. Country Reports on Human Rights Practices.

Wolde-Selassie, W. M. 2004. *International Terrorism and Its Horn of Africa Connections.* Addis Ababa: Ethiopian International Institute for Peace and Development, 2004.

Glossary

Ababa: Father (title used in addressing a priest or monk).

Abesha: Variant of Habesha; Abyssinian, Ethiopian; can refer to both Eritreans and Ethiopians; Semitic-speaking people.

Abeto: Ruler (originally an Oromo designation for king).

Abun: Bishop.

Abuna: Bishop (in title, e.g., "Abuna Baslios" for "Bishop Basilios").

Abyot: Revolution.

Abyssinia: Another name for Ethiopia, which derives from "Abasha."

Adaré: Hararis who used to live within the walled city of Harar.

Addis: New.

Addis Ababa: Name of the capital city of Ethiopia that was founded by emperor Menelik in 1880. The literal meaning of the word is "new flower."

Afaan Oromo: Oromo language.

Afanegus: Lord Chief Justice (literally, mouthpiece of the king).

Agafari: Superintendent of banquets.

Alaqa: Chief (used in both secular and religious ways).

Alga: Throne (literally, bed).

Alich'a: Mildly spiced stew made without hot chilies.

Amba: Plateau, mountain.

Ambasha: Tigrayan-style bread that looks like a pizza crust.

Amhara: Ethiopians inhabiting today's Amhara zone who speak a Semitic language. The Amharas are the second-largest ethnic group next to the Oromos.

Amharic or Amarigna: Language of the Amharas, the present working language of Ethiopia.

Arogeet: Elderly (woman).

Asa: Fish.

Askari: Native-born armed followers of European colonialists.

Assiralaqa: Corporal.

Ater: Peas.

At'mit: Cream.

Ato: Mr.

Atse: His Imperial Majesty.

Awaj: Proclamation.

Awaze: Spiced chili paste.

Awraja: Subprovince.

Ayib: Yogurt, cottage cheese.

Azazh: Commander.

Azifa: Veggie stew made of whole lentils and served cold.

Azmari: Minstrel, singer using a one-string banjo called a *masanqo*.

Bagana: Harp.

Bahr el-Ghazal: The big swamp found in southern Sudan.

Bajirond: Guardian of the royal property; noble, baron.

Balambaras: Commander of the fort.

Baldaraba: Overseer.

Balemwal: Appointee.

Barbarré: Spiced hot chilies.

Bashi-bazouk: Member of an irregular unit in the Turkish Army.

Bet: House.

Beta: House of, as in "Beta Israel" for "the House of Israel."

Birr: Ethiopian currency (in 2010, US$1 was equivalent to 16.37 birr).

Birz: Unfermented honey wine.

Blatta: Imperial officer, page.

Blattangeta: Chief administrator of the palace who was master of the pages during the imperial period.

Buda: In Ethiopian superstition, a person believed to have an evil eye.

Bunna: Coffee.

Chat or Khat: A mild drug with an amphetamine-type effect.

Chikashum: Lower-level underling in the feudal land-ownership chain.

Coptic Church: Egyptian Orthodox Church.

Dabbo: Bread.

Daber: Monastery.

Dabtara: Unordained ecclesiast with advanced-level theological training.

Dajazmatch: Commander of the fort. This is a military title equivalent to a General. During peace time, Dajazmatchs acted as civilian governors of districts, provinces, or subprovinces.

Derg: The military junta that ruled Ethiopia from the fall of Haile Selassie in 1974 to the rise to power of the EPRDF.

Dinich: Potato.

Doro Dabbo: Bread made of hot chicken stew with hard-boiled eggs.

Doro Wat: Spiced chicken stew..

Dulat: Spiced pieces of tripe, liver, and minced beef.

Duqet: Powder.

Echa'at: One of the parties that emerged during the fall of the imperial regime and that catered to the interest of oppressed nationalities, particularly the Oromos.

Eder: Self-help community association.

Egziabher: God.

Elfegn: Royal apartment.

Emaledih: Pre-party formation; Union of Ethiopian Marxist Leninist Organizations, 1977–1979.

Enset: False banana whose roots are used as a staple food by southern Ethiopians.

Etchagé: Administrative head of the Ethiopian Orthodox Tewahedo Church whose title was originally reserved for the abbot of Libanos Monastery. The title of Etchagé is now vested in the patriarch of the Ethiopian Orthodox Tewahedo Church.

Falasha: Ethiopian Jews now commonly referred to as Beta Israel.

Faranj: A person who is of European origin; white person; white people.

Fitawrari: Commander of the advanced guard. The Fitawrari acted as an overall commander of the imperial forces during war. In peace time, the title was held by a high-level dignitary just below the rank of a dajazmatch, who is a governor during peace time.

Fukkera: Boasting to inspire oneself and others during wartime.

Gabbar: Serf.

Gabi: A blanket-like toga made of cotton.

Gadam: Monastery.

Galla: Another name for Oromo. This term, which was originally associated with animism, is now out of use.

Gari: Horse-drawn cart.

Gasha: Land measuring 98.84 acres or 40 hectares.

Geber: Tax.

Ge'ez: An old Semitic language of Ethiopia that is dead but that, like Latin, is still being used in the Ethiopian Orthodox Tewahedo Church.

Gesho: Hops.

Ghibbi: Compound; imperial courtyard.

Gomen: Collard green.

Grazrmatch: Commander of the Left Wing. This was a title bestowed on a military leader who led the imperial army on the left flank of the fighting formation. In peace time, the Grazrmatch, whose rank is just below the Fitawrari, administered a smaller territory than the latter.

Gult: Land grant belonging to an armed retainer.

Gush: Premature beer.

Habesha: Abyssinian; Ethiopian; south Semitic–speaking peoples.

Hail: Power.

Haile: Power of (as in, for example, Haile Selassie, meaning "Power of the Trinity").

Hamsaleqa: Sergeant.

Hawult: Statue; stela.

Hulat Lidat: Faction of Ethiopian Orthodox Christianity that subscribes to the idea of "two births" in Christology.

Igzi'abher: God.

Injera: Spongy, slightly sour pancake or crepe-like bread usually made of teff.

Itégé: Her Majesty (title used in addressing the wife of a monarch).

Janhoy: His Imperial Majesty.

Jantrar: Ruler of Ambasel district in Wallo.

Kahin: Pastor; Priest.

Kantiba: Mayor.

Kebra Nagast: Literally "glory of the kings," which describes the Ethiopian Church version of the visit of the Queen of Sheba to Solomon whereby she had a son called Menelik, who, it is claimed, founded the Solomonian dynasty.

Kefetagna: An urban administrative district larger than a *qebele*.

Kitfo: Spiced Ethiopian-style steak tartar.

Lebashai: Thief finder.

Legaba: Chancellor of the court.

Leul: Highness (for a prince).

Lidet: Birthday.

Lielt: Highness (for a princess).

Lij: Honorific title reserved for men born to a family of nobility.

Liq: Learned, erudite.

Liqamakwas: King's double.

Liqawint: Scholars.

Mahabar: Association.

Mahal Safari: Imperial guard stationed near the palace.

Mahbar: Social club where drinks are served and held on special saint's days.

Makwanent: Nobility.

Malerid: Marxist Leninist Revolutionary Organization, 1974–1978.

Mamher: Teacher.

Mana: House in Afan Oromo.

Mar: Honey.

Markato: Marketplace.

Masafint: Aristocrats.

Masfin: Noble.

Masob: Round dining basket made of straw.

Masqal: The finding of the True Cross.

Matab: Neck cord to signify that one is a Christian.

Matoalaqa: Lieutenant.

Meezé: Best man of a wedding.

Meison: All Ethiopian Socialist Party.

Mered Azmatch: Honorific title given to the Crown Prince of Ethiopian emperors.

Misir: Lentils.

Mit'meett'a: Very hot chilies.

Monotheism/Monotheistic: Belief in one God.

Naftagna: Retainer of feudal rulers who carried firearms.

Nagast: Monarchs.

Naggadras: Customs chief.

Na'ib Turkish: Title for deputy rulers of the Ethiopian port of Massawa.

Nebura'id: Secular and spiritual ruler of Aksum.

Negest: Queen.

Negus: King.

Negusa-nagast: King of kings, emperor.

Neter Qebé: Ghee, spiced and purified butter.

Oromo: Singular of Oromos.

Oromos: The largest Ethiopian ethnic group, comprising about half of the population of the country.

Papas: Archbishop.

Qagnazmatch: Commander of the right flank. This was a title bestowed on a military leader who led the imperial army on the right flank of the fighting formation. In peace time, the Qagnazmatch, whose rank is just below the Fitawrari, administered a smaller territory than the latter.

Qébélé: Urban neighborhood association.

Qeddus: Holy.

Qés: Priest.

Qoch'o: Bread made of false banana roots.

Qolo: Roasted grain.

Querban: Eucharist, Communion, mass.

Querban Gabitcha [Ye]:   Church marriage.

Ras: In military terms, head of an army; in civilian terms, the highest-ranking feudal potentate.

Ras-Bidwoded: A title above *ras* and below king.

Re'es: Head.

Re'esa Dabr: Abbot, monastic head.

Re'esa Mamakert: Head of a council.

Re'esa Maqwanent: Leader of the nobility.

Rist: Land, property.

Ruz: Rice.

Samania Gabitcha [Ye]:   Civil marriage.

Sambar or Tchagwarra: Tripe.

Samuna: Soap.

Sanafitch: Mustard.

Seded: A political party during the time of the Derg that was led by Colonel Mengistu.

Sega: Meat.

Selassie: Trinity.

Sendé: Wheat.

Shai: Tea.

Shalaqa: Major.

Shambal: Captain.

Shamma: White toga made of cotton.

Shango: Ethiopian Parliament during the time of the Derg.

Shibbirtegna: Terrorist.

Shifta: Rebel, outlaw, bandit.

Shimagille: Elderly (male).

Shimbra: Chickpeas.

Shiro: Powdered peas.

Shum: Appointee.

Shum Agame: Ruler of Agame subprovince in Tigray.

Somalis: One of the four major ethnic groups found in the north, next to Djibouti, the Republic of Somalia, and Somaliland.

Suff: Sunflower.

Tabot: Ark, copy of the Ark of the Covenant.

Talba: Flax.

Talla: Local Ethiopian beer.

Tankwa: A boat made of Papyrus reeds.

Tarik: History.

Tazkar: A church ceremony and feast held in memory of the dead.

Teemateem: Tomatoes.

Teff: A cereal endemic to Ethiopia from which injera is made.

Tej: Hydromel, mead, honey wine.

Thaler: Austrian minted silver currency used in Ethiopia and the Middle East during the 19th and early 20th centuries.

Tigrés: One of the four major ethnic groups found in the north, next to Eritrea.

Timqat: Epiphany.

Tsa'ha'fé Te'ezaz: Minister of Pen.

Tsagga Lijoch [Ye]:   One of the factions of the Ethiopian Orthodox Tewahedo denomination that subscribes to a Christological idea that Christ's divinity was achieved not at birth but upon baptism.

Tukul: Hut.

Wagshum: Ruler of Wag subprovince in Wallo who was the descendant of the Zagwe kings.

Waizarit: Miss, Ms.

Wat: Spiced stew.

Wazleague: One of the political parties during the time of the Derg.

Woreda: District.

Zamana Masafint: Era of the princes in the 19th century when regional feudal lords were acting like sovereign rulers of states.

Zar: Possession by a demon.

Zemene: Era of.

Zenjebel: Ginger.

Zigni: Tigrayan-style ground beef stew.

Facts and Figures

Tables A.1–6 below present basic facts about Ethiopia, as well as demographics (including population, ethnicity, and religion), geography, economy, communications and transportation, and military. Subsequent charts present further statistics on economic indicators and demographics.

BASIC FACTS AND FIGURES

TABLE A.1   Country Information

Location:	Northeastern Africa, bounded by Somalia to the east and south, Djibouti to the east, Eritrea to the north and east, Sudan to the west, and Kenya to the south
Local Name:	Ityop'iya Federalawi Demokrasiyawi Ripeblik (Amharic)
Government:	Federal republic
Capital:	Addis Ababa
Head of State:	Girma Woldegiorgis
Head of Government:	Meles Zenawi
National Holiday:	National Day, May 28 (1991)
Major Political Parties:	Ethiopian People's Revolutionary Democratic Front (EPRDF), Coalition for Unity and Democracy (CUD)

Source: CIA Factbook, United Nations, Ethiopian government

This table features information about the people of Ethiopia, encompassing statistics on population, religion, language, and literacy, among others categories.

TABLE A.2 Demographics

Population:	85,237,338 (2010 est.)
Population by age:	
0–14	46.1%
15–64	51.2%
65+	2.7% (2010 est.)
Median Age:	16.8 (2010 est.)
Population Growth Rate:	2.6 (2005–2010 average annual)
Population Density:	221 people per sq. mile
Infant Mortality Rate:	80.8 deaths per 1,000 live births (2010 est.)
Ethnic Groups:	Oromo, Amara, Tigraway, Somalie, Guragie, Sidama, Welaita
Religions:	Orthodox Christian, Protestant, Muslim, traditional
Language:	Amarigna, Oromigna, Tigrigna, Somaligna, Guaragigna, Sidamigna, English
Voting Age:	18 years
Voter Participation:	n/a
Literacy:	43%
Life Expectancy (Average):	55.41
Fertility Rate:	6.07 children per woman (2010 est.)

Source: CIA Factbook, United Nations, Ethiopian government

The following table provides general facts and figures on Ethiopian geography.

TABLE A.3 Geography

Land Area:	426,373 sq. miles
Arable Land:	10%
Irrigated Land:	1,154 sq.miles (2009)
Natural Hazards:	droughts, Great Rift Valley subject to earthquakes and volcanic eruptions
Environmental Problems:	deforestation, desertification, soil erosion, overgrazing, water shortages in some areas
Major Agricultural Products:	cereals, pulses, coffee, oilseed, cotton, sugarcane, potatoes, qat, cut flowers, hides, cattle, sheep, goats
Natural Resources:	small reserves of gold, platinum, copper, potash, natural gas, hydropower

Source: CIA Factbook, United Nations, Ethiopian government

This table offers basic economic information on Ethiopia, including financial, labor, and trade statistics.

TABLE A.4   Economy

GDP:	$33.92 billion (2009 est.)
GDP Per Capita:	$900 (2009 est.)
GDP By Sector:	agriculture 43.8%; industry 13.2%; services 43% (2009 est.)
Labor Force:	agriculture 85%; industry 5%; services 10% (2005)
Unemployment:	n/a
People Below Poverty Line:	38.7% (2009 est.)
Major Industries:	food processing, beverages, textiles, leather, chemicals, metals processing, cement
Exports:	$1.608 billion (2009 est.)
Imports:	$7.315 billion (2009 est.)
Export Goods:	coffee, qat, gold, leather products, live animals, oilseeds
Import Goods:	Food and live animals, petroleum and petroleum products, chemicals, machinery, motor vehicles, cereals, textiles

Source: CIA Factbook, United Nations, Ethiopian government

The following table features facts and figures on Ethiopia's communications networks (such as telephone users) along with the country's transportation statistics (such as roads).

TABLE A.5   Communications and Transportation

Electricity Production:	3.46 billion kWh (2007 est.)
Electricity Consumption:	3.13 billion kWh (2007 est.)
Telephone Lines:	908,900 (2008)
Mobile Phones:	3.168 million (2008)
Internet Users:	360,000 (2008)
Roads:	22,660 miles (2004)
Railroads:	423 miles (2008)
Airports:	63 (2009)

Source: CIA Factbook, United Nations, Ethiopian government

The following table outlines basic statistics on Ethiopia's military.

TABLE A.6   Military

Defense Spending (% of GDP):	1.2% (2010)
Armed Forces:	138,000 active (2009)
Manpower Fit for Military Service:	11,446,713 males; 12,444,706 females (2010 est.)

Source: CIA Factbook, United Nations, Ethiopian government

Charts A–E present information on population trends and factors influencing population growth. Ethiopia has one of the highest fertility rates and population growth rates in the world.

Facts and Figures

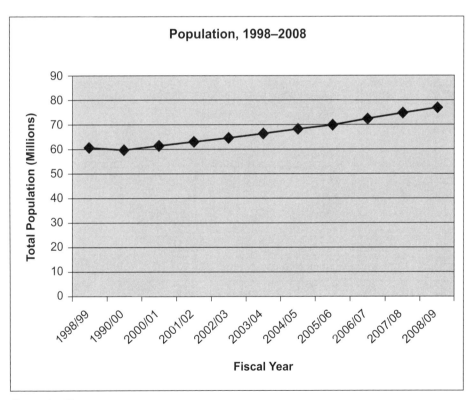

CHART A   POPULATION

Source: National Bank of Ethiopia Annual Report 2008/2009

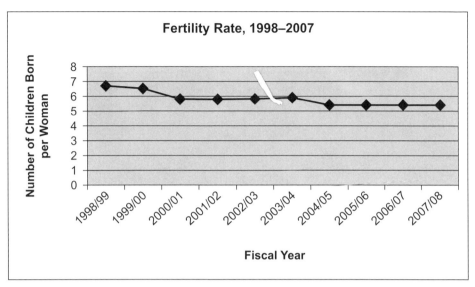

CHART B   FERTILITY RATE

Source: National Bank of Ethiopia Annual Report 2008/2009

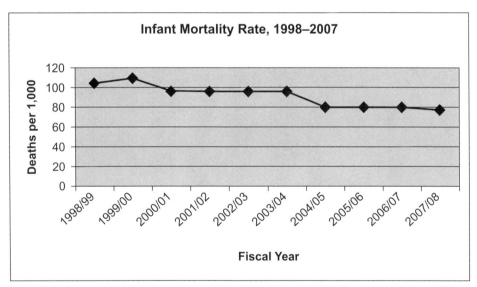

CHART C   INFANT MORTALITY RATE

Source: National Bank of Ethiopia Annual Report 2008/2009

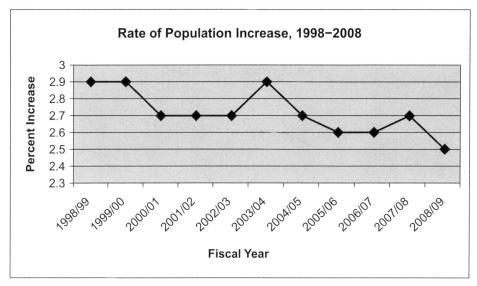

CHART D   RATE OF POPULATION INCREASE

Source: National Bank of Ethiopia Annual Report 2008/2009

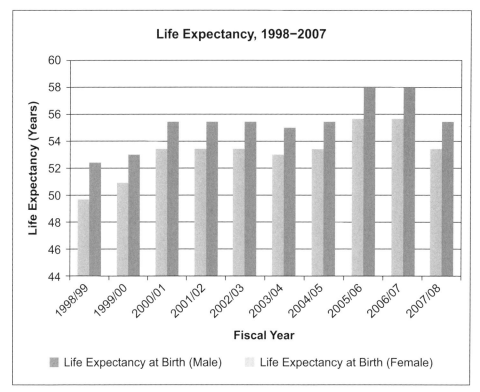

CHART E   LIFE EXPECTANCY

Source: National Bank of Ethiopia Annual Report 2008/2009

This chart compares the urban and rural working-age populations of Ethiopia. Altogether more than 80 percent of the country's population is in rural areas.

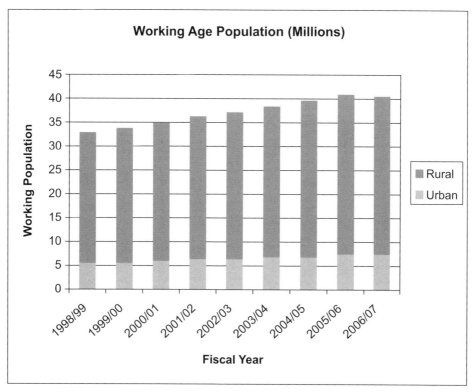

CHART F   WORKING-AGE POPULATION

Source: National Bank of Ethiopia Annual Report 2008/2009

Charts G–I shows the rise of Gross Domestic Product (GDP), a measure of the country's output. Ethiopia is heavily dependent on agriculture, which accounts for nearly half of GDP. A war with Eritrea from 1998–2000 and subsequent droughts hampered production, which later rebounded.

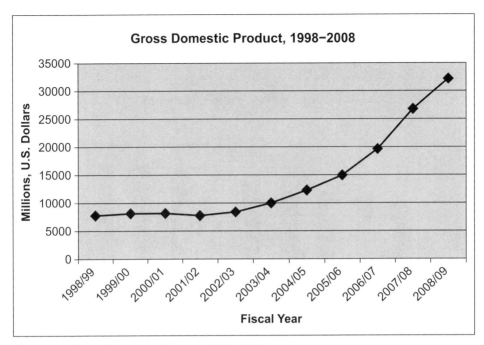

CHART G   GROSS DOMESTIC PRODUCT, 1998–2008

Source: National Bank of Ethiopia Annual Report 2008/2009

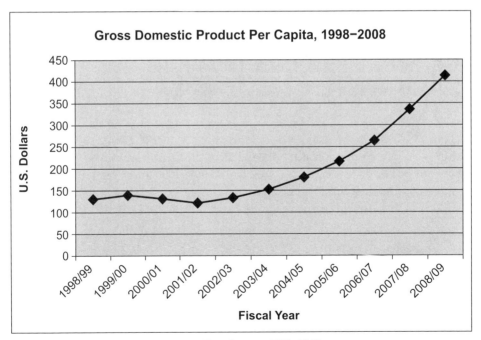

CHART H   GROSS DOMESTIC PRODUCT PER CAPITA, 1998–2008

Source: National Bank of Ethiopia Annual Report 2008/2009

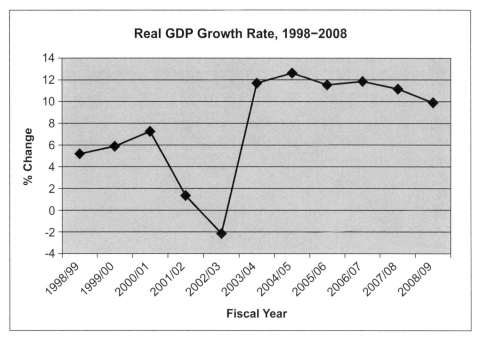

Real GDP Growth Rate, 1998–2008

CHART I   REAL GDP GROWTH RATE, 1998–2008

Source: National Bank of Ethiopia Annual Report 2008/2009

Charts J and K show levels of consumption by the private and government sectors, respectively, and Chart L shows government revenues and expenditures. The Ethiopian government for many years has controlled the economy and owned all land (which citizens lease); only in the 21st century has the government gradually introduced modest reforms toward privatization.

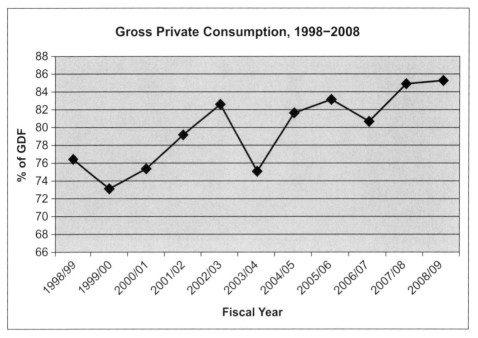

CHART J GROSS PRIVATE CONSUMPTION, 1998–2008

Source: National Bank of Ethiopia Annual Report 2008/2009

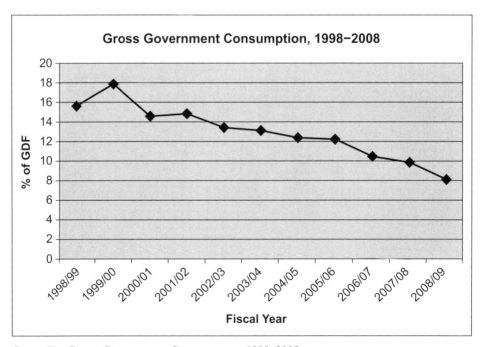

CHART K GROSS GOVERNMENT CONSUMPTION, 1998–2008

Source: National Bank of Ethiopia Annual Report 2008/2009

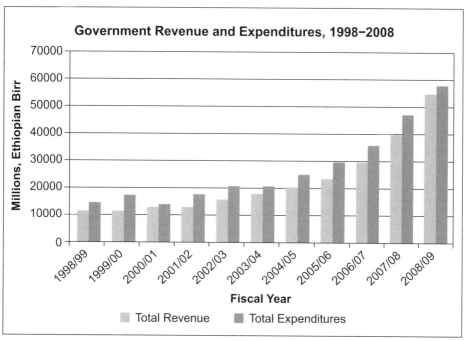

CHART L   GOVERNMENT REVENUE AND EXPENDITURE, 1998–2008

Source: National Bank of Ethiopia Annual Report 2008/2009

Charts M and N compare inflation figures for food and non-food items, in the country overall (Chart M) and in the capital and largest city, Addis Ababa (Chart N). As measures have been taken to improve economic performance, the country has battled high inflation.

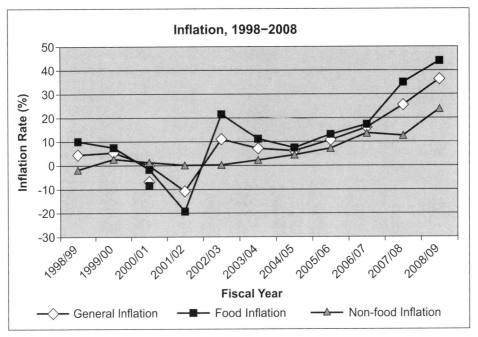

CHART M INFLATION, 1998–2008

Source: National Bank of Ethiopia Annual Report 2008/2009

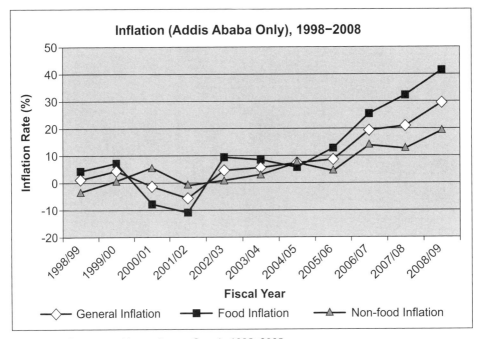

CHART N INFLATION (ADDIS ABABA ONLY), 1998–2008

Source: National Bank of Ethiopia Annual Report 2008/2009

Charts O and P show the relative values of exports and imports. Ethiopia has for decades incurred a large trade deficit. Exports are primarily agricultural products; coffee alone accounts for more than a quarter of Ethiopia's total foreign exchange earnings.

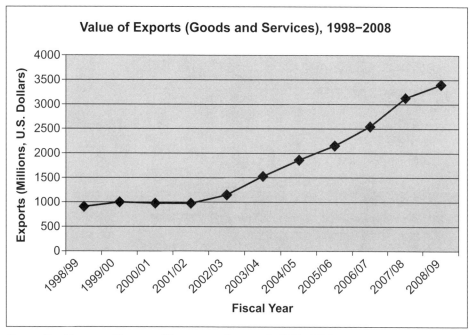

CHART O   VALUE OF EXPORTS (GOODS AND SERVICES), 1998–2008

Source: National Bank of Ethiopia Annual Report 2008/2009

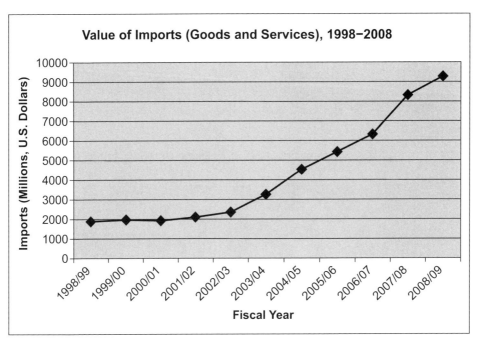

CHART P   VALUE OF IMPORTS (GOODS AND SERVICES), 1998–2008

Source: National Bank of Ethiopia Annual Report 2008/2009

Foreign investment was hampered for many years by a government-controlled economy, as well as such factors as a lack of infrastructure and political instability. As those factors have lessened, foreign investment has improved.

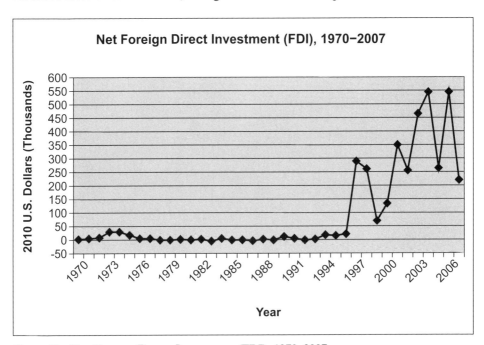

CHART Q   NET FOREIGN DIRECT INVESTMENT (FDI), 1970–2007

Source: World Bank, World DataBank African Development Indicators, 2010

Charts R and S illustrate the growing importance of tourism as a source of income. The government has made investments in tourism infrastructure, such as hotels, to help develop this sector. Attractions include national parks and historic sites.

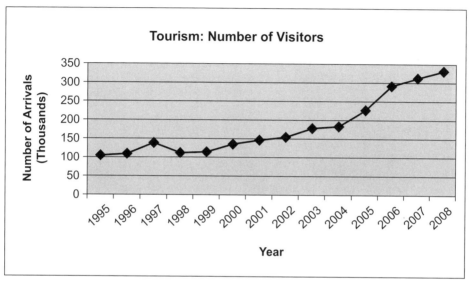

CHART R   TOURISM: NUMBER OF VISITORS, 1995–2008

Source: World Bank

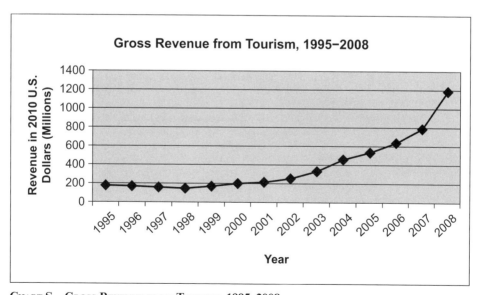

CHART S   GROSS REVENUE FROM TOURISM, 1995–2008

Source: World Bank

Chart T shows production levels for coffee, Ethiopia's most important crop. Ethiopia is the fifth-largest producer in the world, behind Brazil, Vietnam, Indonesia, and Colombia.

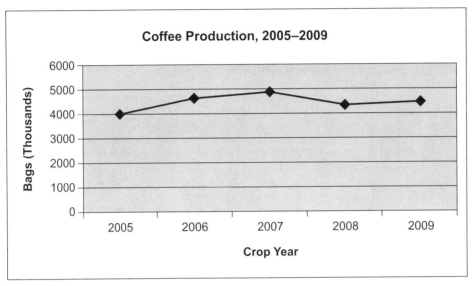

CHART T   COFFEE PRODUCTION, 2005–2009

Note: One bag contains 132 pounds
Source: International Coffee Organization

Holiday Chart

Date	Type of Holiday
Jan 6	*Timket (Epiphany, signifying Christ's baptism)
Jan 7	Ethiopian Christmas, known as Ganna
Feb 15	Mawlid al-Nabi (birth of the Prophet Mohammed)
Mar 2	Victory of Ethiopia at the battle of Adwa
Apr 21	*Ethiopian Easter
May 1	Labor Day
May 5	Patriots Victory Day
May 28	Downfall of the Derg
Aug 30	Eid al-Fitr (end of Ramadan)
Sep 11	*Ethiopian New Year (Addis Amat)
Sep 27	*Meskel (Finding of the True Cross)
Nov 6	Eid-al Adha (Arafat)

Note: Ethiopia employs the Julian calendar with 12 months of exactly 30 days each and a 13th month called Pagumen of 5 days (6 days on a leap year). The Ethiopian year starts on September 11 and is 7 to 8 years behind the Gregorian calendar between January 7 and September 10 and 7 years behind between September 11 and January 8. Holidays given here are for 2010 and 2011. Those shown with an asterisk (*) are movable Ethiopian Orthodox Tewahedo church holidays. Muslim holidays are set according to local sightings of various phases of the moon. Thus, these dates are simply approximations.

Country-Related Organizations

ADDIS ABABA CULTURE AND TOURISM BUREAU

Addis Ababa
Tel: 011 111 6053
Tel: 011 111 6143
Fax: 011 111 6238
Web site: www.tourismaddis.org

The Addis Ababa Tourism Commission provides details about life in Addis Ababa. It directs you to the city's tourist attractions, night clubs, tours, and tourist facilities.

Addis Ababa, which hosts the headquarters of both the African Union and the Economic Commission for Africa, has numerous world-standard hotel accommodations that vary from top-class luxury hotels such as Sheraton Addis, which has been rated one of the top 10 hotels in the world, to many fair-priced but well-equipped hotels and motels. The city's modern conference facilities are fully booked most months. The city's selling points are its rich culture, wide global connections, fine cuisine, and terrace cafes. Addis Ababa's nightlife hosts traditional folk dance. Its discos and bars provides lavish entertainment until the wee hours of the night. The Addis Ababa Culture and Tourism Bureau provides valuable sightseer information regarding Addis Ababa and its environs.

DRUG ADMINISTRATION AND CONTROL AUTHORITY OF ETHIOPIA

Addis Ababa
Tel: 011 552 4122
Fax: 011 552 1392
Web site: www.daca.gov.et

The Drug Administration and Control Authority of Ethiopia is a federal agency promoting and protecting people's health as well as their animals. Its mission is to ensure the well-being and health by ensuring the safety, efficiency, and value of drugs, prescribed or unprescribed.

EASTERN AFRICA POWER POOL

Addis Ababa
Tel: 011 618 3194 or 011 618 3694
Fax: 011 618 3387

The East Africa Power Pool is a regional organization that promotes a common market among East African and southern African countries. Its mission is to promote regional economically integrated nations by eliminating all duties and tariffs. One of its immediate objectives is to develop crucial electrical-power generation among its members.

ETHIOPIAN AIRPORTS ENTERPRISE

Addis Ababa
Tel: 011 665 0400
Fax: 011 665 0686

The Ethiopian Airports Enterprise is aimed at developing the aviation industry in Ethiopia and as well as the continent of Africa. It has so far helped to forge the growth of air transport connecting all East African nations through its outlay for the creation of new facilities as well as the upgrading of existing ones. It is for this reason it won the much-coveted Corporate Achievement Award for excellence given to the aviation industry.

ETHIOPIAN CIVIL AVIATION AUTHORITY

Addis Ababa
Tel: 011 665 0200
Fax: 011 665 0281
Web site: www.ecaa.gov.et

The Ethiopian Civil Aviation Authority (ECAA) is a legal entity created by the government of Ethiopia to administer the air-transport sector in the country. It coordinates all technical and economic transport regulations.

ETHIOPIAN CUSTOMS AUTHORITY

Addis Ababa
Tel: 011 551 3100
Fax: 011 551 8
E-mail: Min.of.reve@ethionet.et355
Web site: http://www.erca.gov.et/about.php

The Ethiopian Customs Authority is aimed at raising revenue for the federal government and prohibiting black market trade and contraband.

ETHIOPIAN INFORMATION AND COMMUNICATION TECHNOLOGY DEVELOPMENT AGENCY

Addis Ababa
Tel: 011 554 3363 (Ext. 151 and 152)
Tel: 011 552 1381
Fax: 011 550 3974
Web site: www.eictda.gov.et

The Ethiopian Information and Communication Technology Development Agency (EICTDA) was created to foster a conducive environment for the growth of information and communication technology and its application for national development to contribute to the socioeconomic development of the country and the building of democratic governance.

ETHIOPIAN INSTITUTE OF AGRICULTURAL RESEARCH

Addis Ababa
Tel: 011 646 2633
Fax: 011 646 1294
Web site: www.eiar.gov.et

The Ethiopian Institute of Agricultural Research conducts research as a nationally coordinated agricultural research system in Ethiopia. The EARS grew out of agricultural institutions in Ambo and Jimma starting in the 1940s and is now very active in promoting new ideas, which it disseminates to the ever-growing rural population.

ETHIOPIAN SCIENCE AND
TECHNOLOGY AGENCY

Addis Ababa
Tel: 011 551 1344
Fax: 011 551 8829
Web site: www.estc.gov.et

The Ethiopian Science and Technology Agency is a federal government institution empowered with responsibilities to plan, advance, coordinate, finance, and supervise all sexually transmitted infections activities of Ethiopia. It helps in formulating government policies regarding science and technologies and screens projects that apply for grants.

ETHIOPIAN SCIENTIFIC
EQUIPMENT CENTER

Addis Ababa
Tel: 011 646 3033
Fax: 011 646 3028
Web site: www.estc.gov.et/NSEC/htm

The Ethiopian Scientific Equipment Center is aimed at developing national capacity in the choice, acquisition, establishment, and maintenance of scientific and medical equipment, and it advises government agencies created in different departments on matters pertaining to the acquisition, establishment, upgrading, and fashioning of medical and scientific equipment and the training required thereof.

MINISTRY OF EDUCATION

Addis Ababa
Tel: 011 155 2922
Fax: 011 155 0877
Web site: http://www.moe.gov.et/

The Ethiopian Ministry of Education is aimed at providing high-quality education for students at all levels of pedagogical endeavor. Right from its inception, curricular development created a huge challenge because the ministry had to haggle with the choice of Amharic as the language of instruction for the entire primary school system, creating a handicap for children with a different primary language. The ministry has a Higher Education Institutions Board that plans and reviews budgetary allocations. Each university and college also has an academic commission that provides proposals for new programs. The ministry allows higher education institutions to recruit their own staff following certain criteria. Teachers must receive from colleagues and students an above average rating to keep their employment status.

MINISTRY OF INFORMATION

Addis Ababa
Tel: 011 551 6538
Tel: 011 515 3380
Fax: 011 554 2586
Web site: www.moinfo.gov.et

The Ministry of Information is an institution of state with the power to produce and disseminate information such that any information that is put out by the ministry is treated as official. The ministry also screens and issues press certificates to nongovernmental organizations

PASTORAL COMMUNITY DEVELOPMENT PROJECT

Addis Ababa
Tel: 011 550 4548
Fax: 011 550 4596
Web site: www.pcdp.org.et

The Pastoral Community Development Project (PCDP) is aimed at forging effective models of public service delivery, investment, and disaster management in pastoral and agro-pastoral areas of the country. It aims to empower rural communities and local administrations to manage local development in pastoral regions of Ethiopia.

PROCUREMENT SERVICES ENTERPRISE

Addis Ababa
Tel: 011 440 3613
Fax: 011 440 3579
Web site: www.pse-eth.com

The Procurement Services Enterprise is a government-created and funded enterprise that enables one to acquire economical and right types of goods. It helps not only in procurement but also in consultancy and training. It also provides necessary market information on suppliers, sources of supply and prices of goods, specifications, and so on to the public.

THE ETHIOPIAN DEVELOPMENT RESEARCH INSTITUTE

2479
Addis Ababa,
Tel: 011 550 6066
Fax: 011 550 5588
Web site: www.edri.org.et

This is a semiautonomous institution with research activities focusing on macroeconomics, agriculture and rural development, industrial growth, international economics, and human resources activities. It works in partnership with the World Bank, the World Bank Institute, the African Capacity Building Foundation, the International Food Policy Research Institute, the University of Reading, the University of Götenborg in Sweden, the Ethiopian Agricultural Research Organization, and the University of Addis Ababa.

THE NATIONAL URBAN PLANNING INSTITUTE

Addis Ababa
Tel: 011 552 5994
Fax: 011 551 0545
Web site: www.nupi.gov.et

The National Urban Planning Institute aims to contribute to the design and development of a national urban development policy. As such, it helps the government to design a comprehensive urban development policy and to ensure that the policy design process incorporates views and opinions of the stakeholders in the national urban development priorities.

TRADE AND INDUSTRY DEVELOPMENT BUREAU

Addis Ababa
Tel: 011 155 0161
Tel: 011 155 3676
Tel: 011 155 8576
Fax: 011 155 3755

The Trade and Industry Development Bureau was created to promote and develop micro and small enterprises and to foster the growth of medium- and large-scale industries, which would ultimately reduce unemployment and poverty in Addis Ababa. Its focus is in the areas of textiles and garments, wood and metal works, food processing, construction, and municipal activities.

ETHIOPIAN MISSIONS ABROAD

Australia
Consulate General
Chancery Address: 38 Johnson Street
Fitzroy, Victoria, Australia 3065
Tel: +61 3 9417 3419
Fax: +61 3 9417 3219
E-mail: ethiopia@consul.com.au
Web site: http://www.consul.com.au
PO Box: 2088, 38 Johnson Street
Fitzroy, VIC 3065 Australia
Residence Address: 222 Barkly Street
Brunswick, Victoria, Australia 3056

Austria
Embassy
Chancery Address: Wagramer Strasse 14½
A-1220 Vienna, Austria
Chancery Tel: 0043-1-71 02 168
Chancery Fax: 0043-1-71 02 171
Residence Address: Biraghigasse 43 A-1130 Vienna, Austria
Residence Tel: 0043-1-804 57 20 and 804 58 27
E-Mail: office@ethiopianembassy.at
Web site: www.ethiopianembassy.at

Bangladesh
Ethiopian Consulate in Dhaka, Bangladesh
Honorary Consulate of Ethiopia in Bangladesh
9/A, Toyenbee Circular Road (2nd Floor)
Maximization, Motijheel C/A
Dhaka-1000, Bangladesh
Phone: 0880-29551477
Fax: 0880-2-9551477
Email: maxim@msnbd.net

Bangladesh
Office Tel: 0880-29551477
Residence Address: 618 North Shajahanpur
Dhaka, Bangladesh
Residence Tel: 0880-2-9338352
Tel: 0189412754
Fax: 0880-2-9551477
P.O. Box: Nirala Bhavan 9/A
Toyenbee Circular Road (2nd Floor)

Maximization
Motijheel C/A
Dhaka-1000
E-mail: maxim@msnbd.net

Belgium
Embassy
Chancery Address: Avenue de Tervuren 231
1150 Brussels
Chancery Tel: 0032-2-771 32 94
Residence Address: Avenue des Sorbiers 24
1180 Uccle
Residence Tel: 0032-2-374 92 62
Fax: 0032-2-771 49 14
E-mail: etebru@brutele.be
Web site: http://www.ethiopianembassy.be

Canada
Consulate General
Chancery Address: 3080 Yonge St. suite 5080
Toronto, Ontario
M4N 3N1
Tel: 416-482-6637
E-mail: infoethi@magi.com
Fax: 416-4869175
Web site: http://www.ethiopia.ottawa.on.ca

China
Embassy of the Federal Democratic Republic of Ethiopia in
Beijing
No. 3, Xiu Shui Nan Jie, Jian Guo Men Wai 100600
Tel: (+86)10 6532 5258
(+86)10 6532 1972 (for Visa Office)
Fax: (+86)10 6532 5591
Email: ethiochina@ethiopiaemb.org.cn, ethchina@public3.bta.net.cn
Web site: http://www.ethiopiaemb.org.cn

Congo Democratic Republic
Embassy
Chancery Address: Off Kira Road
Plot No. 3L
P.O. Box: 7745
Kampala, Uganda
Tel: +256-41-348340 / +256-41-341881
Fax: +256-41-341885
E-mail: ethiokam@starcom.co.ug.

Côte d'Ivoire
Embassy
Chancery Address: Immeuble Nour Al Hayat, 8ème Etage
Residence: Cocody Deux Plateaux Vallon,
P.O. Box: 01.B.P. 3712 - Abidjan 01, Côte d'Ivoire
Telephone Res.: (225) 22 41 44 90
Telephone Off.: (225) 20 21 33 65
Fax: (225) 20 21 37 09
E-mail: ambethio@gmail.com

Cuba
Embassy
Chancery Address: 5ta Ave. No. 6604
apto 3 e/66 y 68
Miramar, C. Havana, Cuba.
Chancery Tel: 0053 7 206 9905
Fax: 0053 7 206 9907
E-mail: info@embaethi.co.cu

Denmark
Honorary Consulate
Chancery Address: Groennemosevej 6
DK-5700 Svendborg, Denmark
Office Tel: 45 62 199100
Residence Address: Groennemosevej 6
DK-5700 Svendborg, Denmark
Residence Tel: 45 40 164111
Fax: 45 62 22 44 22
P.O. Box: Groennemosevej 6
DK-5700 Svendborg, Denmark
E-mail: info@kjaergroup.com
Web site: http://www.kjaergroup.com

Djibouti
Embassy
Chancery Address: Bvld. Marechal Foch
Chancery Tel: (00253) 350718
Residence Address: Bvld. Marechal Foch
Residence Tel: (00253) 353519
Fax: (00253) 354803
P.O. Box: 230
E-mail: ye_ethemb@intnet.dj

Egypt
Embassy
Chancery Address: Mesaha Square
Villa 11
Dokki-Cairo, Egypt
Chancery Tel: (00202) 3353693 or (00202) 3353696
Residence Address: 12 Midan Bahlawi—Dokki
Residence Tel: (00202)–7616269
Fax: (00202)–3353699
E-mail: ethio@ethioembassy.org.eg
Web site: http://www.ethioembassy.org.eg

Finland
Honorary Consulate
Chancery Address: Saboure Int. Trading Co.
Apollonkatu 3C, FI-00100 Helsinki
Office Tel: 358 (0) 968712780
Residence Tel: 358 (0) 405020490 (Cellular)
Fax: 358 (0) 968712781
P.O. Box: Saboure Int. Trading Co.
Apollonkatu 3C, FI-00100 Helsinki
E-mail: ethiopia@saboure.com

France
Embassy
Chancery Address: 35 Avenue Charles Floquet 75007 Paris
Chancery Tel: 0033147838395 / 0033147832339
Residence Tel: 0033147833710 / 0033142190233
Fax: 0033143065214
E-mail: embeth@free.fr
Web site: http://embeth.free.fr

Germany
Embassy
Chancery Address: Boothstrsse 20a
12207 Berlin
Chancery Tel: (0049 30) 77 206-0
Residence Address: Goldfinkweg 46
14195 Berlin
Residence Tel: (0049 30) 89 72 99 24
Fax: (0049 30) 77 206-24/26
E-mail: Emb.ethiopia@t-online.de
Web site: http://aethiopien-botschaft.de

Honorary Consulate
Chancery Address: Kasernenstr. 1 B
40213 Düsseldorf, Germany
Tel: 0049 211 84800
Fax: 0049 211 329000
E-mail: renka@xyndet.de
P.O. Box: Kasernenstr. 1 B
40213 Duesseldorf, Germany
Residence Address: Grunerstr. 64
40239 Duesseldorf, Germany
Tel: 0049 211 633243

Consulate General (Trade Affairs) Frankfurt
Residence Address: 100-Morgenring 91
64546 Moerfelden-Walldorf, Germany
Residence Tel: 0049-61 05-96 86 30
Fax: 0049-69 97-26 96 33
E-mail: Consul.eth@t-online.de / consulfrankfurt.eth@t-online.de.

Ghana
Embassy
Chancery Address: No. 2 Milne Close Off Dr. Amilcar Cabral Road
Airport Residential Area, Accra
Chancery Tel: 00-233-30-2775928 / 00-233-30-2765682
Residence Address: H/No. 6
Roman Ridge Ambassadorial Estate Extension, Accra
Residence Tel: 00233-21-77 23 35 or 00233-21-77 29 78
Fax: 00-233-30-2776807
P.O. Box: 1646
Accra
E-mail: ethiopianemb@4u.com.gh

Greece
Embassy
Chancery Address: 253 Sigrou Avenue
171 22 Athens, Greece
Chancery Tel: 0030210-9403483 / 0030210-9430922
Fax: 0030210-9426050
E-mail: ethembath@ath.forthnet.gr

Hungary
Honorary Consulate General
Chancery Address: P.O. Box: H-1056
Budapest Havas V-3
Tel No: 00363 03731977 / 00361267-2992
Fax: 00361 318 2396
E-mail: asheber.wanna@chello.hu
Residence Address: H-1048 Budapest Szekapatk U. 24
Tel: 00361 3808654

India
Embassy
Chancery Address: 7/50-G
Satya Marg, Chanakyapuri
New Delhi—110 021
Chancery Tel: 009111-6119513, 009111-6119514, or
009111-24675366/67
Residence Tel: (0091 11) 26888225
Fax: (0091 11) 26875731
E-mail: delethem@yahoo.com

Israel
Embassy
Chancery Address: 48 Menahem Begin St.
Tel Aviv 66184
Chancery Tel: 972-3-6397831 / 972-3-6397832
Chancery Fax: 972-3-6397837
Residence Address: 49 Havatzelet Hasharon St.
Herzliya Pituah
Residence Tel: 972-9-9566510
Fax: 972-9-9561437
E-mail: ethembis@netvision.net.il
Web site: http://www.ethioemb.org.il

Italy
Embassy
Chancery Address: Via Andrea Vesalio
16-18 00161 Rome, Italy
Chancery Tel: 0039 (06) 44 161 6307 / 0039 (06) 44 161 6312
Residence Address: Via Viggiano 70
00178 Rome, Italy
Residence Tel: 0039 (06) 50 40 521
Fax: 0039 (06) 44 03 676
E-mail: info@ethiopianembassy.it

Honorary Consulate
Chancery Address: Via G. Leopardi 28
20123
Italy
Office Tel: 0039 (02) 439 01 93
Fax: 0039 (02) 439 04 88
E-mail: consular@ethiopianembassy.it

Ireland
Embassy
Chancery Address: 1-3 Merrion House
Fitzwilliam Street Lower, Dublin 2
Chancery Tel: 003531 6787062
003531 6787063
003531 6787067
Fax: 0035301 6787065
E-mail: info@ethiopianembassy.ie

Japan
Embassy
Chancery Address: 3-4-1
Takanawa, Minato-Ku
Takanawa Kaisei Bldg. 2FL
Tokyo 108-0074
Chancery Tel: 0081 3 5420-6860/1 / 0081 3 5420-4806
Chancery Fax: 0081 3 5420-6866
Residence Address: Mita House 1-25-14 Fukazawa
Setagaya-ku, Tokyo
Residence Tel: 0081 3 3701 4055 / 0081 3 3701 4066
Fax: 0081 3 3701 4077
E-mail: info@ethiopia.emb.or.jp
Web site: http://www.ethiopia-emb.or.jp

Lebanon
Consulate General
Chancery Address: Badaro, Sami el Solah Highway
Manhaton Bldg. 2nd Floor
Chancery Tel: (00961) 1388786
1388923
1389821
Residence Address: Badaro, Beirut
Fax: (00961) 1388787
P.O. Box: 165905
Lebanon, Beirut
E-mail: eth_con_leb8@hotmail.com

Kenya
Embassy
Chancery Address: State House Avenue
Chancery Tel: 00254-2-2732057
Residence Address: State House Avenue
Residence Tel: 00254-2-2732054
Fax: 254-2-2732054
P.O. Box: 45198-00100
E-mail: executive@ethiopianembassy.or.ke

Kuwait
Embassy
Chancery Address: Jabriya
Block 10, St. No. 107, Villa No. 30
Chancery Tel: 00965-5330128 / 00965-5334291
Residence Address: Jabriya
Block 9, St. No. 11, Villa No. 16
Residence Tel: 00965-5315416
Fax: 00965-5331179
P.O. Box: 939 Code 45710
E-mail: ethiokwt@qualitynet.net

Malaysia
Consulate General
Chancery Address: Menara KLH
Business Center
No. 2
Jalan Kasipillai
off Jalan 1 Poh
51200
Kuala Lumpur
Chancery Tel: 00603-23811170
Fax: 00603-23811176

Mexico
Honorary Consulate
Office Address: Priv. de Manchester No. 12 Col. juare
06600 Mexico D.F., Mexico
Office Tel: 52 55 55 33 14 40
Residence Address: Monte Libano No. 840
Col. Lomas de Chapultepec
11000 Mexico D.F.
Residence Tel: 52 55 52 02 98 20 / 52 55 18 00 11 31 (Cellular)
Fax: 52 55 55 33 12 81
E-mail: cabezut@ethiopiaconsulmex.org

Nigeria
Embassy
Chancery Address: Plot No 332 Cadastral Zone AO
Mission Road, Central District
Garki, Abuja
Chancery Tel: 00234-9-2349202
Residence Address: Plot No 932 Pope John Paul II Street
Off Gana Street
Maitama, Abuja
Residence Tel: 00234-9-4131627
Fax: 00234-9-2340817
P.O. Box: P.M.B 5178
E-mail: etembabuja@yahoo.com

Netherlands
General Consulate
Chancery Address: Dr. Kuyperstraat 11
2514BA The Hague, The Netherlands
Chancery Tel: 0031(0) 70-358-69-44
Fax: 0031(0) 70-358-44-05
E-mail: Cons01@xs4all.nl

Norway
Ethiopian Consulate in Oslo, Norway
Strandvn. 20, Postboks. 33
1324 Lysaker, Norway
Tel.: (47) 67 58 45
Telefax: (47) 67 58 45
Email: erik.nes@barwil.com

Pakistan
Honorary Consulate
Chancery Address: D3 KDA Scheme No. 1
Karachi-75730, Pakistan
Chancery Tel: 00-92-21-4316361
7008558
8396271
8396270
Cellular Tel: 00-92-300-8232235
Residence Address: D3 KDA Scheme No. 1
Karachi-75730, Pakistan
Residence Tel: 00-92-21-4316361
Fax: +0092-21-4381960 / +0092-21-5206086 / +0092-21-4316361
P.O. Box: s/31
S.I.T.E. Maurinur Road

Karachi-75730, Pakistan
E-mail: info@consulate.com.pk
Web site: http://www.consulate.com.pk

Portugal
Honorary Consulate
Office Address: Av. D. vasco da Gama
n 0 29
1400 Lisbon, Portugal
Office Tel: 00351-1-303 13 80
Residence Address: Av. Barboso do bocage
n 0 109-10 D
1650 Lisboa
Residence Tel: 351-96-801 86 49 (Cellular)
Fax: 358 (0) 968712781
E-mail: general.ccp@netcabo.pt
Web site: www.ccp.pt

Russian Federation
Embassy
Chancery Address: Russia
129041 Moscow
Orlovo-Davydovsky Per. 6
Chancery Tel: 095-6801616/ 6801676
Residence Address: 129041 Moscow
Orlovo-Davydovsky Per. 6
Residence Tel: 095-6801616 / 6801676
Fax: 095-6806608
P.O. Box: 129041
Moscow
E-mail: eth-emb@col.ru

Saudi Arabia
Embassy
Chancery Address: Diplomatic Quarter
Chancery Tel: 009661-4823919 / 4824055 / 4824056
4803762 / 4803752
Residence Address: Diplomatic Quarter
Residence Tel: 009661-4823712
Fax: 009661-4823821
E-mail: ethiopian@awalnet.net.sa

Saudi Arabia
General Consulate
Chancery Address: Al Andlous Dist. Soliman Mosque St. Villa No. 18

Chancery Tel: (009662) 6653444
6653320
6650450
6650520
6653539
6653622
Residence Address: Al-Rawda
Residence Tel: (009662) 6913243
Fax: (009662) 6653443
E-mail: jedethcons@icc.net.sa

Senegal
Embassy
Chancery Address: Boulevard de la Républic No. 18-ler Etage
Chancery Tel: (221) 821-98-96
Ambassador office Tel: (221) 821-98-94 (Direct Line)
Residence Address: 46 Boulevard Martin Luther King-Dakar
Residence Tel: (221) 824-37-08
Fax: (221) 821-98-95
P.O. Box: 379-Dakar-République du Sénégal
E-mail: ethembas@sentoo.sn

Singapore
Honorary Consulate
Office Address: 23 chin Bee Avenue
Singapore 619943
Office Tel: (65) 2621233
Residence Address: 1 Namely Close
Singapore 267588
Fax: (0065) 62612800
E-mail: amocan@pacific.net.sg

Somaliland
Trade Office
Chancery Address: Sha'abka area (near the Presidency)
Tel No. 00252-2-518685 / 00252-2-518684
Residence Address: Jigjiga Yaar.
Fax: 00252-2-518663
E-mail: Etohargeisa@yahoo.com

South Africa
Embassy
Chancery Address: 47 Charles St. Bailey's Muckleneuk

Chancery Tel: (002712) 3463542
Residence Address: 26 Farmers Folly
Lynwood, South Africa
Residence Tel: (002712) 3489242
Fax: (002712) 3463867
P.O. Box: 11469 Hatfield 0028
E-mail: ethiopia@sentechsa.com

Sri Lanka
Honorary Consulate
Chancery Address: 139 Mihindu Mawatha
Colombo-12, Sri Lanka
Tel: 421685 / 435876
Fax: 330734 / 331485

Sudan
Embassy
Chancery Address: Near Farouq Cemetery
Plot No. 04
Block 384BC
Khartoum South
Chancery Tel: (00249-11) 47-11-56/47-13-79
Residence Address: Kober
Residence Tel: (00249-13) 34 91 51/34 91 52
Fax: (00249-11) 47 11 41
P.O. Box: 844
Khartoum, Sudan
E-mail: eekrt@hotmail.com

Sweden
Embassy
Chancery Address: Lojtnantsgatan 17
115 50 Stockholm
Chancery Tel: 0046-8-6656030
Residence Address: Inverness Strand 1
182 76 Stocksund
Residence Tel: 0046-8-857202
Fax: 0046-8-6608177
P.O. Box: 10148
100 55 Stockholm
E-mail: ethio.embassy@telia.com
Web site: http://www.ethemb.se

Sweden
Honorary Consulate
Office Address: Master Nilsgatan 1

Box: 6172
SE-200 11 malmo
Sweden
Office Tel: +46 40 233024
Residence Address: Master Nilsgatan 1
SE-200 11 malmo, Sweden
Residence Tel: +46 40 302216 / +46 705 828262 (Cellular)
Fax: +46 40 18 3456 / +46 40 302214
P.O. Box: Box: 6172
SE-200 11 malmo, Sweden
E-mail: lars.haraldson@rabeco.se

Switzerland
Permanent Mission to the United Nations Office and other International Organizations
Chancery Address: 56 rue de Moillebeau
1211 Geneva 19, Switzerland
Chancery Tel: (41-22) 919 70 10/16
Residence Address: 6 chemin du Vengeron
1292 Chambésy, Switzerland
Residence Tel: (41-22) 758 25 71
Fax: (41-22) 919 70 29
P.O. Box: 338
E-mail: mission.ethiopia@ties.itu.int
Web site: http://www.ethiopianmission.ch

Honorary Consulate
Office Address: Neugut 89
8304
Wallisellen, Switzerland
Office Tel: 00141-1-839 41 41
Fax: 0041-1-839 41 44

Tanzania
Embassy
State House Avenue
P.O. Box: 45198
Nairobi, Kenya
Tel: +254-20-723053 / +254-20-723035 / +254-20-723027
Fax: +254-20-723401
E-mail: ethermbna@sers.africaonline.co.ke

Thailand
Honorary Consulate
Chancery Address: 954/32 Suite 406 Prannok Plaza

Bangkok 10700 Thailand
Tel: 0-2583 3993 / 0-2583 5995
Fax: 0-2583 3993
E-mail: Vorasakdi@yahoo.com
P.O. Box: 39/68 Nichada Thani
Samak-kee Road
Pak-kret, Nonthaburi
11120 Thailand
Residence Address: 39/68 Nichada Thani
Samak-kee Road, Pak-kret
Nonthaburi, 11120 Thailand

Turkey
Embassy
Chancery Address: Ugur Mumcunum Sokagi No: 74/1-2
06700 Gaziosmanpasa Cankaya / Ankara
Chancery Tel: 0090312 436 04 00 / 0090312 448 19 38
Residence Address: Funda Beyezavler Sites 629
Villa No. 7 Oran 06450 Cankaya / Ankara
Residence Tel: 0090312 490 85 85
Fax: 0090312 490 84 85
E-mail: ethembank@ttnet.net.tr

United Arab Emirates
Consulate General
Chancery Address: Bur Dubai
Al Mankhool St
Sharaf Bldg Flat # 222/2, 6th floor
Chancery Tel: +971-4-3516868 / +971-4-3513550 (Direct)
Residence Address: Ibrahim & Mohd Obaidullah 124/22B Street DM.44 Reqqa
East Flat/25
Fax: 971-4-3516328
P.O. Box: 115353
E-mail: ethcodu@ethcongen.ae

Uganda
Embassy
Chancery Address: Off Kira Road
Plot No. 3L
Kampala
Chancery Tel: 00256-41-348340 / 00256-41-341881
Residence Address: Kololo Hill Drive
Plot No. 27
Residence Tel: 00256-41-254311
Fax: 00256-41-341885

P.O. Box: 7745
Kampala
E-mail: ethiokam@starcom.co.ug

United Kingdom of Great Britain and Northern Ireland
Chancery Address: 17 Princes Gate
London
SW7 1PZ
Tel: 44 (0)20 7589 7212
Fax: 44 (0)20 7584 7054
Email: info@ethioembassy.org.uk
Web site: www.ethioembassy.org.uk

United Nations
Permanent Mission
Chancery Address: 866 Second Avenue
Third Floor New York, NY 10017
Chancery Tel: (212) 421-1830
Residence Address: 29 Hereford Road
Bronxville, NY 10708
Residence Tel: (914) 961-4192
Fax: (212) 754-0360
P.O. Box: 866 Second Avenue
3rd Floor
New York, NY 10017
E-mail: ethiopia@un.int or ethiopianmission2002@yahoo.com

United States
Embassy
Chancery Address: 3506 International Drive NW
Washington, D.C. 20008
Chancery Tel: 011 (202) 364-1200
Residence Address: 2209 Wyaoming Ave.
Washington, D.C. 20008
Residence Tel: 011 (202) 986-3500
Fax: 011 (202) 587 0195
P.O. Box: 3506 International Drive NW
Washington, D.C. 20008
E-mail: ethiopia@ethiopianembassy.org
Web site: http://www.ethiopianembassy.org

United States
Honorary Consulate
Chancery Address: 9301 Southwest Freeway, Suite 250
Houston, TX 77074
Chancery Tel: 713-271-7567

Fax: 713-772-3858
E-mail: gezahgen@juno.com
Residence Address: 8306 Furlong Lane
Houston, TX 77071
Residence Tel: 713-779-5439
Cellular Telephone: 832-788-5439

United States
Consulate
Chancery Address: Consulate General of Ethiopia
3460 Wilshire Blvd. Suite 308
Los Angles, CA 90010
Chancery Tel: (213) 365-6651
Fax: (213) 365-6670
E-mail: info@ethioconsulate-la.org
Web site: www.ethioconsulate-la.org

Honorary Consulate
Office Address: World Trade Center
2200 Alaskan Way, Suite 200
Seattle, WA 98121
Office Tel: 206-364-6401
Residence Address: 12612 Blakely Place NW
Seattle, WA 98177
Residence Tel: 206-364-9215 / 206-595-6595 (Cellular)
Fax: 206-224-4344

Yemen
Embassy
Chancery Address: Al-Hamadani St. Sana'a
Chancery Tel: (009671) 208833
211208
Residence Address: 14th of October St. Sana'a
Residence Tel: (009671) 417478
415879
Fax: (009671) 213780
P.O. Box: 234
E-mail: ethoembs@y.net.ye

Zambia
Embassy
14 Lanark Road
P.O. Box: 2745
Belgravia, Harare, Zimbabwe
Phone: +263-4-701514 / +263-4-701515

Fax: +263-4-701516
E-mail: emb@ecoweb.co.zw

Zimbabwe
Embassy
Chancery Address: 14
Lanark Road Belgravia
Chancery Tel: (263-4) 70 15 14 / (263-4) 70 15 15
Residence Address: 20 Woodholme
Emerald Hill
Residence Tel: (263-4) 33 64 53 / 091 232703 (Cellular)
Fax: (263-4) 70 15 16
P.O. Box: 2745
E-mail: emb@ecoweb.co.zw

EMBASSIES OF AFRICAN UNION MEMBER STATES IN ADDIS ABABA, ETHIOPIA

Algeria
L'Ambassade de la République Algérienne Démocratique et Populaire
P.O. Box: 5740
E-mail: algemb@telecom.net.et
Tel: 011371 96 66-20 57 57
Fax: 719668
Chancery Address:
Nefas Silk Lafto Sub City–K. 03

Angola
The Embassy of the Republic of Angola
P.O. Box: 2962
E-mail: Angola.embassy@telecom.net
Chancery: Bole Kifle Ketema, Kebele 05, House No. 114
Wireless Telephone No. 011-6519009 (Ambassador Office Direct line)
011-6519010 (Minister Counsellor Office Direct Line)
011-6518831 (Ambassador's Secretary Office)
011-6519011 (Administration)
011-6518824 (PABX)
Tel: 0115 51 00 85
Fax: 0115-51 49 22 or
0115-52 89 09

Benin
L'Ambassade de la République du Bénin
P.O. Box: 200084
Tel: 710187, 727924, 728727
09/24 03 44

09/40 29 82
Fax: 72 87 31

Botswana
The Embassy of the Republic of Botswana
P.O. Box: 22282 Code 1000
E-mail: boteh@telecom.net.et
Tel: 0113 715422/23
Fax: 71 40 49

Burkina Faso
L'Ambassade du Burkina Faso
P.O. Box: 19685
E-mail: ambfet@telecom.net.et
Chancery
Bole Sub-City
Kebele 03, House No. 138
Tel: 011-6615863/64
Fax: 011-6615857

Burundi
L'Ambassade de la République du Burundi
P.O. Box: 3641
E-mail: burundi.emb@ethionet.et
Tel: 011-4651300/4655547
Fax: 011-4650299
L'Ambassade de la République du Cameroun
P.O. Box: 1026
E-mail: ambcamaa@telecom.net.et
Tel: 0115 504487/88/89
Fax: 528458
0910693754 (M. Maule, Section Consulaire)

Cape Verde
L'Ambassade de la République du Cap Vert
P.O. Box: 200093
E-mail: embcv@telecom.net.et
Tel: +251 11 618 48 53 or
+251 116518890
Cellular phone:
+251 911 213880
Fax: +251 11 6635466

Congo Republic
L'Ambassade de la République du Congo
P.O. Box: 5639
E-mail: Prpropoch@yahoo.fr

Tel. 0116 633 200/638 621/638 623
Fax: 0116 638622
Bole K/K,
Kebele 03,
House No. 407

Congo Democratic Republic
L'Ambassade de la République Démocratique du Congo
P.O. Box: 2723
E-mail: rdcaddis2@telecom.net.et
Tel: 710111-713466
Fax: 713466
Chancery: Nifas Silk Lafto Kifle Ketema, Kebele 05,
House No. 1779

Côte d'Ivoire
L'Ambassade de la République de Côte d'Ivoire
P.O. Box: 3668
E-mail: cotedivoire_a@yahoo.fr
Standard: 15 98 66
Premier Conseiller: 15 36 46
Attaché Défense: 15 98 53
Fax: 15 98 67
Chancellerie Bole Central
Woreda 18, Kebelé 36, No. 766

Djibouti
L'Ambassade de la République de Djibouti
P.O. Box: 1022
Tel: 0116 613200 / 0116 613006
Fax: 612786
The Embassy of the Arab Republic of Egypt
P.O. Box: 1611
E-mail: Egyptian.emb@ethionet.et
Tel: 0111-226422
0111-226434
(visa section)
Fax: 0011-226432

Ethiopia
The Ministry of Foreign Affairs of the Federal Democratic Republic of Ethiopia
P.O. Box: 393
E-mail: MFA.Addis@telecom.net.et
Web site: www.mfa.gov.et
Tel: 011-5517345
Fax: 011-5514300

Gabon
L'Ambassade de la République Gabonaise
P.O. Box: 1256
Tel: + (251) 0116 611075/90
Fax: 0116 613700
The Embassy of the Republic of the Gambia
P.O. Box: 60083
E-mail: gambia@ethionet.net
Tel: 0116 613 874
Fax: 0116 627 895
Bole Kifle Ketema,
Kebele 03, House No. 218

Ghana
The Embassy of the Republic of Ghana
P.O. Box: 3173
E-mail: ghmfa@telecom.net.et
Tel. 0113 711402 / 0113 720676
Fax: 0113 712349
Lideta Kifle Ketema, Keble 01
H.No. 103, Off Jimma Road

Guinea Republic
L'Ambassade de la République de Guinée
P.O. Box: 1190
Tel: 0114 65 13 08

Equatorial Guinea Republic
L'Ambassade de la République de Guinée Equatoriale
P.O. Box: 246
E-mail: embarge@telecom.net.et
Chancery:
Kifle Ketema: Bole
Kebele: 03, House No. 162
Tel: 011-6626278 &
0116-637424
Fax: 0116-633525
or 0116-61 59 73

Kenya
The Embassy of the Republic of Kenya
P.O. Box: 3301
E-mail: kenigad@telecom.net.et
Tel: 0116 610033
Fax: 0116 611433

Chancery address:
Yeka Kifle Ketema, Kebele 01

Lesotho
The Embassy of the Kingdom of Lesotho
P.O. Box: 7483
E-mail: lesoaddis@telecom.net.et
Tel. 011-6614368/9 and
0116-612828
Fax: 011-6612837
Bole Kifle Ketema, Kebele 03
House No. 2116/K

Liberia
The Embassy of the Republic of Liberia
P.O. Box: 3116
Tel: 0115 513655, 513791/0911237799
0911 70 2227 (Ambassador)
Fax: 0115 51 36 15

Libya
The People's Bureau of the Great Socialist People's Libyan
Arab Jamahiriya
P.O. Box: 5728
E-mail:
Libyan Embassy@telecom.net.et
Tel: 0115 511077/78
Fax: 0115 511383

Madagascar
L'Ambassade de la République de Madagascar
P.O. Box: 60004
E-mail: emb.mad@telecom.net.et
Tel: 0116 61 25 55
Tel: 0116 63 75 61
Fax: 0116 61 01 27

Malawi
The Embassy of the Republic of Malawi
P.O. Box: 2316
E-mail: malemb@ethionet.et
Tel: 0113 71 12 80

Fax: 0113 719742
Nifas Silk Lafto, Kebele 03, H.No. 1021

Mali
L'Ambassade de la République du Mali
P.O. Box: 4561
E-mail: keitamoone@yahoo.fr
Tel: 011-4168990/91/92
Fax: 011-416 28 38

Mauritanian Islamic Republic
L'Ambassade de la République Islamique de Mauritanie
P.O. Box: 200015
Tel: 0113 72 91 65
Fax: 0113 72 91 66

Mauritanian Republic
The Embassy of the Republic of Mauritius
P.O. Box: 200222
E-mail:
mmaddis@telecom.net.et
Tel: 0116 615997
Fax: 0116 614704
Chancery: Bole Kifle Ketema,
Kebele 03, House No. 750
Until further notice the following telephone and fax lines could be used
Tel. No. 251 0234
Tel. No. 251 0236
Fax No. 251 1131

Mozambique
The Embassy of the Republic of Mozambique
P.O. Box: 5671
E-mail:
embamoc-add@ethionet.et
Tel: +251 116 63 38 11/12
Fax: +251 116 62 15 40
Chancery: Bole Road,
Bole Sub City,
Kebele 05, House No. 477

Namibia
The Embassy of the Republic of Namibia
P.O. Box: 1443
E-mail: nam.emb@ethionet.et

Tel: 0116 611966
0116 612055 (Ambassador)
Tele/Fax: 0116 612677
Chancery: Bole Road, Woreda 17, Kebele 19,
House No. 002

Niger
L'Ambassade de la République du Niger
P.O. Box: 5791
E-mail: ambniger@telecom.net.et
Tel: 65 13 05, 65 11 75
Fax: 651296

Nigeria
The Embassy of the Federal Republic of Nigeria
P.O. Box: 1019
E-mail: nea@nigerianembassy-et.org
addis_nigeria@yahoo.com
Tel:0111 550644
Fax: 011 552307
Cell (Ambassador)
0911 210526

Rwanda
L'Ambassade de la République du Rwanda
P.O. Box: 5618
E-mail: rwanda.emb@telecom.net.et / Ambaddis@minaffet.gov.rw
Tel. 0116 61 03/0116 61 03 57
Fax: 0116 61 04 11

Saharawi Arab Democratic Republic
The Embassy of the Sahrawi Arab Democratic Republic
P.O. Box: 3008
E-mail: sadrem@telecom.net.et
Tel: 718666
Fax: 718668

Senegal
L'Ambassade de la République du Sénégal
P.O. Box: 2581

E-mail:
ambassene-addis@telecom.net.et
Tel: 0116 611376
Fax. 0116 610020

Seychelles
The Embassy of the Republic of Seychelles
Global House, 296 Glenwood Drive
Lynwood Park 0081, Pretoria, South Africa

Sierra Leone
The Embassy of the Republic of Sierra Leone
P.O. Box: 5619
E-mail: salonbadd@yahoo.com
Jimma Road, Sub-City Nifasilk/Lafto, kebele 04/12, House No. 591,
Next to Umma Hotel
Tel: 0113 710033
Fax: 0113 711911

Somali Federal Republic
The Embassy of Somali Federal Republic
P.O. Box: 1643
Tel: 0115
Fax: 0115 505150

South Africa
The Embassy of the Republic of South Africa
P.O. Box: 1091
E-mail: sa.embassy.addis@telecom.net.et
Tel: 0113 724 761/62/63

Sudan
The Embassy of the Republic of the Sudan
P.O. Box: 1110
E-mail: sudan.embassy@telecom.net.et
Tel: 0115 516477
Fax: 0115 51 99 89
Chancery: Kirkos Kifle Ketema, Kebele 10,
House No. 543

Swaziland
Embassy of the Kingdom of Swaziland
P.O. Box: 416, Code 1250
E-mail: swaziaddis@telecom.net.et

Tel: 26 21 25 or 26 17 78
Fax: 26 21 52
Chancery address:
Bole Kifle Ketema Kebele 01, House No. 1185

Tanzania
The Embassy of the United Republic of Tanzania
P.O. Box: 1077
E-mail: tz@telecom.net.et
Tel: 251 116634353
Fax: 251 116627882
Chancery address:
Bole Kifle Ketema, Kebele 03/05, House No. 2213

Tchad
L'Ambassade de la République du Tchad
P.O. Box: 5119
E-mail: amtchad@ethionet.et
Chancery Old Airport
N/S/L/Sub-City
Kebele 03
House No. 1896/a
Tel./Fax (Temporary)
011 371 04 85

Togo
L'Ambassade de la République Togolaise
P.O. Box: 25523 (code 1000)
E-mail: togo.emb@telecom.net.et
Tel: 721912
Fax: 729722

Tunisia
L'Ambassade de la République Tunisienne
P.O. Box: 100069
E-mail:
a.t.addisabeba@telecom.net.et
Tel: 0116 612063, 621840
Fax: 614568 & 621841

Uganda
The Embassy of the Republic of Uganda
P.O. Box: 5644
E-mail: uganda.emb@ethionet.et

Tel: 011-5513114/513088
Fax: 011-5514355

Zambia
The Embassy of the Republic of Zambia
P.O. Box: 1909
E-mail zam.emb@telecom.net.et
Tel: 0113 711302
Fax: 0113 711566
Chancery: Kifle Ketema 23, Kebele 12

Zimbabwe
The Embassy of the Republic of Zimbabwe
P.O. Box 5624
E-mail: Zimbabwe.embassy@telecom.net.et
Tel: 011-661 38 77
011-663 37 67/8
Fax: 011-661 34 76
fax No. 613045
The Ambassador's mobile No. 09 203926 and the Minister Counsellor's
mobile No.
0911 203925

FOREIGN EMBASSIES AND MISSIONS IN ETHIOPIA

Algerian Embassy
Nifas Silk Lafto K. Ketema
05 Addis Ababa, Ethiopia
Tel: 251 1 71 96 66 / 251 1 20 57 57
Fax: 251 1 71 96 68.

Angolan Embassy
Rue Bole Road Wrada 18
Kebele 26 House No 006 CP 2962
Addis Ababa, Ethiopia
Tel: 251 1 710118
251 1 711528
Fax: 251 1 514922
E-mail: angola.embassy@telecom.net.et

Austrian Embassy
Old Airport Area, Addis Ababa, Ethiopia
P.O.B. 1219

Addis Ababa, Ethiopia
Tel: (+251) (11) 371 21 44
(+251) (11) 371 24 45
(+251) (11) 371 0052
Fax: (+251) (1) 371 21 40
Web site: http://www.aussenministerium.at/addisabeba/
E-mail: addis-abeba-ob@bmaa.gv.at

Belgian Embassy
Kebena District
Comoros Street
Kebele 08
P.O. Box: 1239
 Addis Ababa, Ethiopia
Tel: + (251) (11) 662.12.91
+ (251) (11) 662.34.20
+ (251) (11) 661.16.43
+ (251) (11) 661.18.13
Fax: + (251) (11) 661.36.46
Web site: http://www.diplomatie.be/addisababa
E-mail: AddisAbaba@diplobel.org

Botswana Embassy
P.O. Box: 22282
Addis Ababa, Ethiopia
Tel: (2511) 715422
Fax: (2511) 714099

Brazilian Embassy
Kebele 02 Bole Sub-City
House Nr. 2830
P.O. Box: 2458 Code 1250
Addis Ababa, Ethiopia
Tel: (25111) 662-0401 or 662-0403
Fax: (25111) 662-0412
E-mail: embradisadm@ethionet.et

Bulgarian Embassy
Bole Kifle Ketema Sub City
Kebele 06
Haile G/Selassie Road
Addis Ababa, Ethiopia
Tel: (0025 11) 661 00 32
Fax: (0025 11) 661 62 70
E-mail: bul.addis@gmail.com

Canadian Embassy
Old Airport Area, Nefas Silk Lafto Sub City
Kebele 04, House No. 122
Addis Ababa, Ethiopia
Tel: +251-11-371-3022
Fax: +251-11-371-3033
Web site: http://www.ethiopia.gc.ca
E-mail: addis@international.gc.ca

Chinese Embassy
Jimma Road, Higher24, Kebele 13, House No.792
P.O. Box: 5643
Addis Ababa, Ethiopia
Tel: 002511-711960
Fax: 002511-712457
Web site: http://et.china-embassy.org
E-mail: chinaemb_et@mfa.gov.cn,chineseembassy@telecom.net.et

Cuban Embassy
Woreda 17, Kebele 19
Casa 197 (Bole area)
Addis Ababa, Ethiopia
Tel: (251-1) 62 0459
(251-1) 62 0461
(251-1) 62 0462
Fax: (251-1) 62 0460
E-mail: etcubemb@telecom.net.et

Czech Embassy
Kirkos Kifle Ketema Rd.
Kebele 15
House No. 289, Addis Ababa, Ethiopia
PO Box 3108
Addis Ababa, Ethiopia
Tel: 00251/11/5516382
00251/11/5516132
Fax: 00251/11/5513471
Web site: http://www.mzv.cz/addisababa
E-mail: addisabeba@embassy.mzv.cz

Danish Consulate
c/o Royal Norwegian Embassy
Buna Road
Mekanisa
P.O. Box: 12955
Addis Ababa, Ethiopia

Tel: +251 (1) 711 399
Fax: +251 (1) 711 399
E-mail: gkl.addis@telecom.net.et

Danish Embassy
Bole Ketema, Kebele 03
H. No. 'New'
P.O. Box: 12955
Addis Ababa, Ethiopia
Tel: +251 (0)116 187 075
Fax: +251 (0)116 187 057
Web site: http://www.ambaddisababa.um.dk
E-mail: addamb@um.dk

Salvadoran Embassy
SIDIST KILO, Gulele Sub-City
Kebele 02 Addis Ababa, Ethiopia
Tel: (002511) 1226422
Fax: (2511) 1226432

Finnish Embassy
Mauritania Street
Nifas Silk Lafto Kifle Ketema (Old Airport Area)
Kebele 12
House No 1431
P.O. Box: 1017
Addis Ababa, Ethiopia
Tel: +251-11-320 5920
Fax: +251-11-320 5923
Web site: http://www.finland.org.et
E-mail: sanomat.add@formin.fi

French Embassy
Quartier Kabana
PO Box 1464
Addis Ababa, Ethiopia
Tel: [251] (11) 140 00 00
Fax: [251] (11) 140 00 40
Web site: http://www.ambafrance-et.org
E-mail: presse@france-ethiopie.org

Gabonese Embassy
Bole Road H-17
House 269
Addis Ababa, Ethiopia
Tel: (251-1) 61 10 75
Fax: (251-1) 61

German Embassy
German Embassy
Khabana, Woreda 12
Kabele 20
Addis Ababa, Ethiopia
Tel: 251 1 55 04 33
Fax: 251 1 55 13 11
Web site: http://www.addis-abeba.diplo.de
E-mail: german.emb.addis@telecom.net.et

Ghanaian Embassy
P.O. Box 3173
Addis Ababa, Ethiopia
Tel: 71-14-02, Telex: 21249 GhanaEmb ET

Greek Embassy
Off Debre Zeit Road, P.O. Box 1168
Addis Ababa, Ethiopia
Tel: (002511) 654911-2
Fax: (002511) 654883
Web site: http://www.telecom.net.et/~greekemb/
E-mail: greekembassy@telecom.net.et

Greenlandic Embassy
Royal Danish Embassy
Bole Ketema, Kebele 03
H. No. 'New'
P.O. Box: 12955
Addis Ababa, Ethiopia
Tel: +251 (0)116 18 70 75
Fax: +251 (0)116 18 70 57
Web site: http://www.ambaddisababa.um.dk
E-mail: addamb@um.dk

Greenlandic Consulate
Royal Danish Consulate General
c/o Royal Norwegian Embassy
Buna Road
Mekanisa
P.O. Box 12955
Addis Ababa, Ethiopia
Tel: +251 (1) 711 399
Fax: +251 (1) 711 399
E-mail: gkl.addis@ethionet.et

Hungarian Consulate
Honorary Consulate of Hungary
P.O. Box: 11127, Addis Ababa, Ethiopia
(22 Mazoria, next to Nazreth Building)
Addis Ababa, Ethiopia
Tel: 11-621-133
Fax: 11-615-494
E-mail: haimanot54@yahoo.com

Indian Embassy
Arada District, Kebele-14
[Next to Bel Air Hotel]
H.No 224, Around Aware
Post Box No. 528
Tel: 00-251-11-1235538/39/40/ 41
Fax: 00-251-11-1235547/1235548
Web site: http://www.indianembassy.gov.et/
E-mail: bharat@ethionet.et

Indonesian Embassy
Mekanissa Road Higher 23
Kebele 13, House No. 1816
Addis Ababa, Ethiopia
Tel: (251-1) 712-104, 712-185
Fax: (251-1) 710-873
Web site: http://www.indonesia-addis.org.et
E-mail: kbriadis@telecom.net.et

Iranian Embassy
P.O. Box: 70488
Addis Ababa, Ethiopia
Ethiopia
Tel: 200794-712012
Web site: http://www.telecom.net.et/~iranet/

Irish Embassy
Kirkos Sub-city, Kebele 06
Sierra Leone St. (Debre Zeit road)
House No. 021
P.O Box 9585, Addis Ababa, Ethiopia
Tel: +251 (11) 466 5050
Fax: +251 (11) 466 5020
Web site: http://www.embassyofireland.org.et/
E-mail: addisababaembassy@dfa.ie

Israeli Embassy
Higher 16, Kebele 22
House no. 283, Addis Ababa, Ethiopia
Ethiopia
Tel: +251-11-646 09 99
Fax: +251-11-646 19 61
Web site: http://addisababa.mfa.gov.il
E-mail: embassy@addisababa.mfa.gov.il

Italian Embassy
Villa Italia–Kebenà–P.O. Box 1105
Addis Ababa, Ethiopia
Tel: 00251111235717, 1235685
Fax: 1235689
Web site: http://www.ambaddisabeba.esteri.it
E-mail: ambasciata.addisabeba@esteri.it

Jamaican Consulate
Jamaican Consulate
Debrezeit Road
Higher 20, Kebele 45
House # 921, P.O. Box 5633
Addis Ababa, Ethiopia
Tel: 251-1-6543-22
Fax: 251-114-654-747

Japanese Embassy
House No.653, Kebele 7
Woreda 18
P.O. Box: 5650
Addis Ababa, Ethiopia
Tel: +251-1-51-10-88
Fax: +251-1-51-13-50

Kenyan Consulate
High Commission of the Republic of Kenya
Fikre Mariam Road
High 16 Kebelle 01
P.O. Box 3301
Addis Ababa, Ethiopia
Tel: +251 11 6610033
Fax: + 251 11 6611433
E-mail: kengad@telecom.net.et

Kuwaiti Embassy
Bole Road, Nouse 128
Addis Ababa, Ethiopia
Tel: (+251-11) 6615411, 6615412
Fax: (+251-11) 6612621

Basotho Embassy in Kebele, Ethiopia
P.O. Box 7483 Wereda
17 Kebele 23 H.2116/K
Addis Ababa, Ethiopia
Tel: +2511 612828/614368/9
Fax: +2511 612837
E-mail: mscaya@hotmail.com

Malagasy Embassy
Kefetagna 17, Kebele 19
House Nr. 629
Bole, Addis Ababa, Ethiopia
Tel: 251 1 61 25 55
Fax: 251 1 63 75 62
Web site: http://www.madagascar-consulate.org/embassies-world.html
E-mail: amba.mad.addis@telecom.net.et

Malawian Embassy
Malawian Embassy in Ethiopia
Woreda 23, Kebele 13, House. No. 1021
P.O. Box: 2316
Addis Ababa, Ethiopia
Tel: (+251-11) 3711280
Fax: (+251-11) 3719742
E-mail: malemb@ethionet.et, malemb@telecom.net.et

Malian Embassy
Tel: (+251-11) 2712601
Fax: (+251-11) 2712601 Addis Ababa, Ethiopia
E-mail: addismali.addis@telecom.net.com

Mauritian Embassy
P.O Box 200222, Addis Ababa, Ethiopia
Tel: 002511615997
Fax: 00 25 11 614704
E-mail: mmaddis@telecom.net.et

Mexican Embassy
Shola Axion (to former Jacross Compound)
Bole Kifle Ketema

Kebele: 14
House Number: New Block: B5/6
P.O. Box 21021 Code 1000
Addis Ababa, Ethiopia
Tel: (251-116) 479-333
Fax: (251-116) 479-333

Moroccan Embassy
P.O. Box: 60033,
Addis Ababa, Ethiopia
Tel: (+251-11) 5531700
Fax: (+251-11) 5512818

Mozambican Embassy
P.O. Box 5671
Addis Ababa, Ethiopia
Tel: (+251-11) 3728622/3, 3718593
E-mail: embamoc-add@ethionet.et

Namibian Embassy
Bole Road W. 17, Kebel 19
House No. 002, P.O. Box 1443
Addis Ababa, Ethiopia
Tel: +251-1-611966 or 612055
Fax: +251-1-612677

Dutch Embassy
Royal Netherlands Embassy
P.O. Box: 1241
Old Airport Zone
H24, K13, House 001
Addis Ababa, Ethiopia
Tel: 251-1-711100
Fax: +251 (0)1 711577
Web site: http://www.mfa.nl/add/
E-mail: add@minbuza.nl

Nigerien Embassy
W.9, K.23
PO Box 5791
Addis Ababa, Ethiopia
Tel: (+251-1) 651305, 550644
Fax: (+251-1) 651296

Nigerian Embassy
P.O. Box 1019
Addis Ababa, Ethiopia
Tel: (+251-11) 1550644
Fax: (+251-11) 1552307

Norwegian Embassy
Buna Board Road, Mekanissa
PO Box 8383
Addis Ababa, Ethiopia
Tel: +251-11-3710799
Fax: +251-11-3711255 / 3713605
Web site: http://www.norway.org.et/
E-mail: emb.addisabeba@mfa.no

Pakistani Embassy
House No. 2038,
Kebele 03, K.K. Bole,
P.O. Box: No. 19795,
Addis Ababa, Ethiopia

Palestinian Embassy
PO Box 5800
Addis Ababa, Ethiopia
Tel: 251 1-610811 / 251 1-610672
Fax: 251 1-611199
E-mail: pal.emb.et@telecom.net.et

Polish Embassy
Bole Sub-City, Kebele 03, House No. 2111
P.O. Box 27207, 1000
Addis Ababa, Ethiopia
Tel: (+255-1) 185401, 637635
Fax: (+255-1) 610000
E-mail: polemb@telecom.net.et

Portuguese Embassy
"Dembel" City Centre 8th Floor Bole Road
Addis Ababa, Ethiopia
Tel: +251.11.552.6899
Fax: +251.11.552.6885
E-mail: embportaddis@gmail.com

Romanian Embassy
Woreda 17, Kebele 19, Houses No. 0910, Bole Road
or P.O. Box: 2478

Addis Ababa, Ethiopia
Tel: (00) (251) (1) 610156
Fax: (00) (251) (1) 611196
E-mail: roembaddis@telecom.net.et

Russian Embassy
P.O. Box: 1500, Yeka Kifle-Ketema, Kebele 08,
Fikre-Mariam Street,
Addis Ababa, Ethiopia
Tel: +2511 612-060, 611-828
Fax: +2511 613-795
E-mail: russemb@telecom.net.et

Rwandan Embassy
Africa Avenue H-17K-20
P.O. Box: 5618
Addis Ababa, Ethiopia
Tel: (+251-11) 6610300, 6610357, 6610387
Fax: (+251-11) 6610411
E-mail: ambaddis@minaffet.gov.rw

Saudi Arabian Embassy
Saudi Arabia Embassy, Ethiopia
W24, K13, House No. 002
PO Box 1104
Jimma Rd. Old Airport Zone
Addis Ababa, Ethiopia
Tel: 251-1-710303
Fax: 251-1-711799
Web site: http://www.mofa.gov.sa/detail.asp?InServiceID=367&
intemplatekey=MainPage

Senegalese Embassy
Senegal Embassy, Ethiopia
Africa Avenue, W17, K20, House No. 777
PO Box 2581
Addis Ababa, Ethiopia
Tel: +251-1-611376
Fax: +251-1-610020

Serbian Embassy
W15, K26, House No. 923
PO Box 1341
Addis Ababa, Ethiopia
Tel: +251-1-517804

Fax: +251-1-516763 / +251-1-514192
E-mail: yugoslav.embassy@telecom.net.et

Sierra Leonean Embassy
Nafas Silk Sub-City Kebele
05 House no 2629,
Addis Ababa, Ethiopia
Tel: 251113710033
Fax: 251113711911
E-mail: saloneembadd@yahoo.co.uk

South African Embassy
Alexander Pushkin Street
Higher 23, Kebele 10
House 1885, Old Airport Area
Addis Ababa, Ethiopia
Tel: + 251 11 371 1002 / + 251 11 371 1017 / + 251 11 371 7186
Fax: + 251 11 371 3035
E-mail: sa.embassy.addis@telecom.net.et

Spanish Embassy
Entoto Av. P.O. Box: 2312
Addis Ababa, Ethiopia
Tel: 55 02 22
Fax: 55 11 31
E-mail: ethiopia@ethiopianembassy.org

Sudanese Embassy
Tel: +251-1-515-241
Fax: +251-1-517-030 / +251-1-518-141
Addis Ababa, Ethiopia
E-mail: sudan.embassy@telecom.net.et

Swedish Embassy
Lideta subcity
Kebele 07/14, House No. 891
P.O. Box 1142
Addis Abeba, Ethiopia
Tel: +251 (11) 518 0000
Fax: +251 (11) 518 0030
Web site: http://www.swedenabroad.com/Start____38838.aspx
E-mail: ambassaden.addis.abeba@sida.se

Swiss Embassy
Old Airport, W24, K13
Tel: (+251-1) 711107, 710577, 711608

Fax: (+251-1) 712177
Addis Ababa, Ethiopia
E-mail: vertretung@add.rep.admin.ch

Tanzanian Embassy
P.O. Box 1077, Addis Ababa, Ethiopia,
Addis Ababa, Ethiopia
Tel: (251-1) 511063, 612904, 518155

Togolese Embassy
Tel: +251 152-26-75 / +251 152-35-22
Addis Ababa, Ethiopia

Tunisian Embassy
Africa Avenue
Woreda 17
Kebele 19
House No. 0008
100069
Addis Ababa, Ethiopia
Tel: +251-1-612063 / +251-1-621-840 / +251-1-621-841
Fax: +251-1-650233

Turkish Embassy
Africa Avenue, W17, K19, House No. 018
Addis Ababa, Ethiopia
Tel: +251-1-612321
Fax: +251-1-611688

Ugandan Embassy
Kirkos Kifle Ketema, Kebele 35, H. No. 031
Addis Ababa, Ethiopia
Tel: +251-1-5513114 / +251-1-5513088
Fax: +251-1-5514355
E-mail: uganda.emb@ethionet.et, uganda.emb@telecom.net.et

Ukrainian Embassy
Woreda 17, Kebele 23
House 2111
Addis Ababa, Ethiopia
Tel: +251-1-611698
Fax: +251-1-621288

Web site: http://www.mfa.gov.ua/mfa/en/509.htm
E-mail: emb_et@mfa.gov.ua / ukremb@ethionet.et

Sahrawian, Sahraouian Consulate
Mission of the Sahrawi Arab Democratic Republic
P.O. Box: 3008
Addis Ababa, Ethiopia
Tel: (+251-11) 271 8666
Fax: (+251-11) 271 8667
E-mail: sadrem@telecom.net.et

United States Embassy
Entoto Street
P.O. Box 1014
Addis Ababa, Ethiopia
Tel: 251-1-550666
Fax: 251-1-174001
Web site: http://addisababa.usembassy.gov/
E-mail: usemaddis@state.gov

Yemeni Embassy
P.O. Box: 664
Addis Ababa, Ethiopia
Tel: (+251-1) 711811 / 712204 / 710990
Fax: (+251-1) 710991

Zambian Embassy
P.O. Box: 1909
Addis Ababa, Ethiopia
Tel: (+251-11) 371 1302
Fax: (+251-11) 371 1566
E-mail: zam.emb@ethionet.et

Zimbabwean Embassy
W17, k19, house No. 007
PO Box 5624,
Addis Ababa, Ethiopia
Tel: (+251-1) 61 38 77 / 2
Fax: (+251-1) 61 34 76
E-mail: zimbabweembassy@telecom.net.et

Annotated Bibliography of Ethiopia

GEOGRAPHY

Briggs, Philip. 2005. *Ethiopia*. London: Bradt. 596 pp.

Philip Briggs introduces Ethiopia, whose engaging people and rich traditions surpass conventional expectations of drought and famine, with infectious enthusiasm. In this travel book with 76 maps and 29 descriptive chapters, the author provides a pile of comprehensive background information and full details of mostly ignored but very important geographic locations in Ethiopia. A comment on the monograph by the *Daily Telegraph* sums it all: "Thorough and reassuring, this guide provides all the practical and background information to make readers leap from their armchairs and visit this vast magical country."

De Waal, Alex. 1991. *Evil Days: Thirty Years of War and Famine in Ethiopia*. New York: Human Rights Watch. 386 pp.

The author chronicles in this prodigious work the war crimes and crimes against humanity perpetrated against the Ethiopian people by Mengistu Haile Mariam's Derg regime between 1974 and 1991. The book argues convincingly that food was deliberately withheld by the Derg from insurgent-controlled areas to starve the inhabitants, with the aim of destroying the protagonists' economic base.

Ethiopian Mapping Agency, Geography Division. 1981. *National Atlas of Ethiopia*. Addis Ababa: Ethiopian Mapping Agency.

The National Atlas of Ethiopia is an information tool with over sevenscore detailed maps and synthesized information made for administration, planning, education, and research purposes. It is a useful reference tool and was made to help different national and interna-

497

tional agencies that needed to keep abreast of development of Ethiopia up to the medium period of the Derg regime.

Gozálbez, Javier, and Dulce Cebrian. 2008. *Touching Ethiopia*. Addis Ababa: Shama Books. 403 pp.

This book was prepared as a coffee table book. Printed in an elegant fashion on superbly thick, glossy paper and strongly trussed by Spanish binders, it has a pile of information and numerous photographs of extremely high quality. Though begging for copyediting in some sections, it is a thoroughly well-researched almanac about contemporary Ethiopia, its geography, its land, and its people. This book is highly recommended to anybody who is interested in visiting Ethiopia and not being a stranger to its age-old traditions or its natural habitat.

Hancock, Graham, Richard Pankhurst, and Duncan Willetts. 1987. *Under Ethiopian Skies*. London: H&L Communications. 200 pp.

This fascinating travel book came out less than a decade before Graham Hancock's runaway best seller *The Sign and the Seal* catapulted him to the top of the charts. Though dated, it is a required reading for any individual interested in Ethiopian geography.

Mesfin, Wolde Mariam. 1972. *An Introductory Geography of Ethiopia*. Addis Ababa: Haile Selassie University. 215 pp.

For 2010 this is dated, but technically speaking, for a basic understanding of Ethiopian geography, this is still a definitive scholarly rendering and most informative tool.

Schultz, Sam. 2009. *Ethiopia in Pictures*. New York: Lerner Publishing Group. 80 pp.

This visual geography of Ethiopia, first published in 2004 and then reissued with a revised edition in 2009, presents a capsule of historical and current information on Ethiopia. It discusses the land, the government, the culture, the people, and the economy and presents Ethiopia as one of Africa's oldest nations. The book shows Ethiopia as a diverse country, with 80 different ethnic groups who speak more than 200 dialects. Any newcomer to Ethiopian geography will benefit greatly by reading this brief but highly informative book.

Tannenbaum, David. 2008. *An Ethiopian Album: Photographic Journey through Nature and Culture*. San Francisco: Blurb Creative Publishing. 233 pp.

With 400 beautiful color photographs, this is another table book–style guide. The album covers Ethiopian geography from wilderness to fertile highlands, from primeval relics to contemporary cities. The author portrays in rich detail all the splendor and pomp that makes Ethiopia unique in every aspect, including in its varied landmass, its lakes, its wildlife, and its people's traditions. This photographic guide is highly recommended to any visitor of Ethiopia.

HISTORY

Bahru, Zewde. 1991. *A History of Modern Ethiopia, 1855–1974*. Addis Ababa: Addis Ababa University Press. 244 pp.

This is an account of the history of modern Ethiopia, from 1855 to 1974. The book starts with the first half of the 19th century, including the anarchy that existed prior to 1855. It then deals with European and Egyptian challenge to Ethiopian sovereignty, the success of the battle of Adwa and political developments up to 1935, the Italian occupation from 1936 to 1941, and finally historical events between the1941 liberation and the 1974 revolution. The book is a must-read for those who are unfamiliar with Ethiopian history from the rise of Tewodros to the ascendancy of the Derg regime.

Bierman, J., and C. Smith 1999. *Fire in the Night: Wingate of Burma, Ethiopia, and Zion.* New York: Random House. 434 pp.

The English general Orde Wingate is revered in Ethiopia and Israel. Wingate is treated like Lawrence of Arabia, and his exploits in Ethiopia and Burma, where he fought the Italian Fascists and the Japanese invaders until his death in a plane crash in March 1943, are well narrated here. It is an interesting book on an eccentric person who was always on the side of the underdog.

Burstein, S. M. 2009. *Ancient African Civilizations: Kush and Axum.* Princeton, NJ: Markus Wiener. 190 pp.

The civilizations of Kush in Nubia and Axum in Ethiopia are generally overshadowed by the great accomplishments of Egypt. The book draws on 27 diverse source texts in all, found in Greek, Ge'ez, Coptic, and Arabic. This book is very useful for students and teachers of African history.

Frederick, Myatt. 1970. *The March to Magdala: the Abyssinian War of 1868.* London: Leo Cooper. 431 pp.

This book, which was written as part of a project to document 19th-century military campaigns, describes the sorry episode of Ethiopian Emperor Tewodros' unsuccessful struggle to hold on to power against Britain and local lords that rebelled against him in all regions of the country.

Greenfield, R. 1969. *Ethiopia: A New Political History.* London: Pall Mall Press. 515 pp.

This book, which tries to cover Ethiopian history from antiquity to 1960, is very important for readers who are interested in the abortive 1960 coup d'etat staged by the brothers Germame and Mengistu Neway against the feudal regime of Emperor Haile Selassie.

Hilton, A., and W. F. Deedes. 2007. *The Ethiopian Patriots: Forgotten Voices of the Italo-Abyssinian War, 1935–41.* Gloucestershire: Spellmount.

This book revisits the generally forgotten guerrilla struggle Ethiopian patriots waged against Italian Fascists during the 1936–1941 occupation. It is important to read this work to dispel the notion that had Britain not come to the rescue of Ethiopia, the Italian occupation would have continued indefinitely.

Milkias, Paulos, and Getachew Metaferia. 2005. *The Battle of Adwa: Reflections on Ethiopia's Historic Victory against European Colonialism.* New York: Algora. 320 pp.

This book, with articles contributed by eminent scholars, including Richard Pankhurst, O.B.E.; Zewde Gabre-Selassie, D.Phil. Oxon and former Ethiopian deputy prime minister; and Harold Marcus, distinguished professor of history at the State University of Michigan, is a must-read to understand all aspects of this battle that registered Africa's historic victory over Europe since the Battle of Canne in 216 BC.

Pankhurst, Richard. 1998. *The Ethiopians.* Malden: Blackwell. 299 pp.

This is an absorbing account of Ethiopia. The author delves into the history of ancient Ethiopia as the land of Punt. He explores Ethiopia's relations with the Egyptian pharaohs and the Greeks. The book also gives major biblical references to the country and people and the Axumite civilization. Pankhurst's *The Ethiopians* is a must-read for all interested in Ethiopia, whether individually or organizationally.

Rubenson, Sven. 1978. *The Survival of Ethiopian Independence*. London: Heinemann. 437 pp.

Sven Rubensen documents in this seminal work how Ethiopia alone among all African countries preserved its independence throughout the era of the European scramble for the continent. He proves with ample evidence that it was not its intractable geographic location or the lack of determination by imperial powers to colonize Ethiopia that preserved its sovereignty against all odds. This tome is without doubt one of the most meticulously researched contributions to Ethiopian history. The detail, authority, and assiduous research that Sven Rubenson put into the book are stupendous. The work is highly recommended.

Sergew, Hable Selassie. 1972. *Ancient and Medieval Ethiopian History to 1270*. Addis Ababa: United Printers. 370 pp.

This is a well-researched book on the ancient history of Ethiopia not including the period after the Solomonic restoration in 1270. It provides a good background to the history of Ethiopia in subsequent centuries up to the present.

Ullendorff, Edward. 1973. *The Ethiopians: An Introduction to Country and People*. London: Oxford University Press. 235 pp.

Though dated, for those who are totally unfamiliar with Ethiopia, this book is still an excellent introduction. Because of the fact that Ullenforff is by training a linguist and a noted literary figure in the area of Semitic vernacular, the chapters on languages and literature are particularly revealing. The little book is highly recommended to all interested in Ethiopian history and people.

GOVERNMENT AND POLITICS

Amnesty International. 2005. *Ethiopia: The 15 May 2005 Elections and Human Rights: Recommendations to the Government, Election Observers and Political Parties*. London: Amnesty International, International Secretariat.

This report concludes by making key recommendations to the government, election observers, and political parties. The work is a must-read for all, particularly foreign embassies and agencies.

Clapham, Christopher. 1968. *Haile Selassie's Government*. New York: Praeger. 218 pp.

This book tells the evolution, structure, and functions of the different organs of the Ethiopian government and is a good expose of Ethiopian politics, in addition to Margery Perham's classic work, *The Government of Ethiopia*, which appeared in 1948. An important read for all African political pundits.

Clapham, Christopher, Siegfried Pausewang, and Paulos Milkias. 2001. "Government." In *Encyclopaedia Aethiopica*, Vol. 2., pp. 863–869. Edited by Siegbert Uhlig. Wiesbaden: Harrassowitz.

This brief expose by three scholars, one British, one Norwegian, and one Ethiopian, provides the basics of Ethiopian government and politics from the traditional to the modern. A must for one who is in need of a quick reference to Ethiopian government and politics.

Dessalegn, Rahmato, et al. 1994. *Land Tenure and Land Policy in Ethiopia after the Derg: Proceedings of the Second Workshop of the Land Tenure Project.* Dragvoll: University of Trondheim Land Tenure Project and Institute of Development Research, Addis Ababa University.

Edited by an Ethiopian scholar who is arguably the most informed about agrarian issues in the region, this document needs to be read by all who are interested in understanding the complicated land tenure issue in Ethiopia.

Ethiopia. 1994. *The Constitution of the Federal Democratic Republic of Addis Ababa.* Addis Ababa: Government of Ethiopia.

This constitution is unique in Ethiopian history. It is the only one that enshrines the right of secession in one of its clauses. All political scientists need to read it carefully.

Haile Selassie. *My Life and Ethiopia's Progress 1892–1937.* Oxford: Oxford University Press. 337 pp.

This book describes Haile Selassie's life as recorded by him in exile in Bath, England, during the Italian occupation of 1836–1941. The Amharic original appeared in 1973, just a year before his government's overthrow. Of more interest to political scientists is his chapter dealing with ordinance and proclamation of internal administration and his promulgation of the first parliament and constitution in Ethiopia. A must-read for all interested in Ethiopian governance.

International Human Rights Law Group. 1994. *Ethiopia in Transition: A Report on the Judiciary and the Legal Profession.* Washington, D.C.: International Human Rights Law Group. 200 pp.

A must-read for all because it is the most informed view of highly qualified scholars from around the world.

Jackson, D. R. 2007. *Jimmy Carter and the Horn of Africa: Cold War Policy in Ethiopia and Somalia.* Jefferson, NC: McFarland. 230 pp.

This is a balanced look at U.S. foreign policy toward Ethiopia, particularly the Cold War–influenced policy shift by Washington during the Carter administration when the Ethiopian dictator Mengistu Haile Mariam clearly went over to the side of the Soviets.

Lata, L. 1999. *The Ethiopian State at the Crossroads: Decolonization and Democratization or Disintegration?* Lawrenceville, NJ: Red Sea Press. 270 pp.

In this book, Lenco Lata, one of the key leaders of the Oromo Liberation Front, for the first time clearly accepts accommodation with a reformed and fair Ethiopian state, quite contrary to the long-standing policy position of his party to settle for nothing but secession. The book should be read by all policy makers and organizations who strive to bring peace to Ethiopia.

Lefort, Rene. 1981. *Ethiopia: An Heretical Revolution?* London: Zed Press. 306 pp.

This is a well-researched description of the great upheavals that rocked Ethiopia following the overthrow of the feudal regime in 1974. The book is recommended to all those who want to grasp the nature of the Ethiopian revolution.

Medhanie, Tesfatsion. 1986. *Eritrea: Dynamics of a National Question*. Amsterdam: B.R. Gruner. 347 pp.

A classic work on Eritrean nationalism, written by a scholar of Eritrean extraction. This seminal work, which is written with apparent evenhandedness, should be read by all interested in the civil war that led to the current situation.

Perham, Margery. 1948. *The Government of Ethiopia*. Harmondsworth: Penguin. 247 pp.

For contemporary Ethiopian politics, this is clearly dated, but no one can fully understand the evolution of the Ethiopian political system by the beginning of he third millennium without perusing this landmark book.

Tesfaye, A. 2002. *Political Power and Ethnic Federalism: The Struggle for Democracy in Ethiopia*. Lanham, MD: University Press of America. 192 pp.

This is one of a plethora of books that came out in recent years to suggest the best way of making federalism in Ethiopia fair and functional. All political scientists need to read it.

Tiruneh, A. 1993. *The Ethiopian Revolution, 1974–1987: A Transformation from an Aristocratic to a Totalitarian Autocracy*. Cambridge: Cambridge University Press. 435 pp.

This is a well-written book that describes Ethiopia's historic jump from feudalism to Marxist military rule. Tiruneh analyzes the decimation of Haile Selassie's feudal autocracy and the rise to power of Mengistu Haile Mariam's Derg. He documents the hard ball the Derg had to play in foreign policy and the failure of its pan-Ethiopian nationalism. This is a book that is recommended to those who want to understand the genesis of the Ethiopian revolution.

Tronvoll, K., C. Schaefer, et al. 2009. *The Ethiopian Red Terror Trials: Transitional Justice Challenged*. Rochester, NY: James Currey. 158 pp.

The authors and their contributors look at the legal issues surrounding this long political trial that took 15 years.

Ye-Etiopia Public Service Institute. 1969. *Organization of the Imperial Ethiopian Government*. Addis Ababa: Berhanenna Selam. 650 pp.

This is a synopsis of the way in which Haile Selassie restructured his government and should be read by all who are interested in Ethiopian politics.

ECONOMICS

Alemayehu, S., and Ethiopian Economic Association. 2005. *Proceedings of the Second International Conference on the Ethiopian Economy*. Addis Ababa, Ethiopia: Ethiopian Economic Association. 230 pp.

This important study presented by many scholars at the forum of the Ethiopian Economic Association in 2003 covers diverse subjects, including the country's economic conditions, policies, agricultural potential, poverty reduction issues, and social conditions. For specialists as well as casual readers of the Ethiopian economic situation, this is useful and informative.

Ayele, K. 2006. *The Ethiopian Economy: Principles and Practices*. Addis Ababa: A. Kuris. 249 pp.

An important book for all those who are interested in understanding problems and prospects as well as short-term and long-term economic policies of the EPRDF government.

Collier, P. 1992. *The Macroeconomics of the Transition to Peace in Ethiopia.* Paris: DIAL. 49 pp.

This brief scholarly study came out to survey Ethiopia's bold move away from the Marxist command system of the Derg toward a market-oriented economy after the ascendancy into power of the EPRDF. The author provides suggestions for future modification of economic policies in Ethiopia.

Gelawdewos, Araia. 1995. *Ethiopia: The Political Economy of Transition.* Lanham, MD: University Press of America. 246 pp.

This is an important book that traces the genesis of the modern Ethiopian state system from its early beginnings under Tewodros to the present. This is a necessary read for those interested in the introduction of modernity to Ethiopia.

Hansson, Göte. 1993. "Ethiopia: Away from Socialism. In *Economic Crisis in Africa. Perspectives on Policy Responses*, pp. 288–343. Edited by Magnus Blomström and Mats Lundahl. London: Routledge.

This is part of a general work that analyzes the intense economic crises facing the entire African continent. In this essay's narrower focus, Hansen presents the analysis in the context of the specific urgency of reform in Ethiopia.

Hiwet, A. 1975. *Ethiopia: From Autocracy to Revolution.* London: Review of African Political Economy. 115 pp.

A timeless and classic analysis of the Ethiopian economy under feudalism. This book is still the most important contribution to our understanding of the Ethiopian economic system under the ancien regime and deserves to be read by all in its entirety.

Jamo, Shiferaw. 1992. "An Overview of Macroeconomic Development in Ethiopia, 1941–1974." Addis Ababa, mimiographed material. 70 pp. (Part of Author's Collection.)

Jamo, Shiferaw. 1993. "An Ethiopian Economy during the Transition." Addis Ababa, mimiographed material. 20 pp. (Part of Author's Collection.)

Jamo, Shiferaw. 2006. "An Overview of the Ethiopian Economy." Addis Ababa, mimiographed material. 19 pp. (Part of Author's Collection.)

Jamo, Shiferaw. 2008. "Prime Minister's State of the Economy Report: Somme Comments." Addis Ababa, mimiographed material. 5 pp. (Part of Author's Collection.)

All these works that dissect the Ethiopian economy during the last half century with sharp intellect are important because the author has been arguably one of the most respected and highly qualified Ethiopian-born economists whose service has passed through the period of Haile Selassie's feudal autocracy, the Derg regime, and the present state structure. He has during the last several decades served as minister of planning in the Ethiopian government, deputy regional representative of the World Bank, and director of the African Development Bank. Because of this rich background experience and his deep insight, any work he has put his pen to is extremely important and should be read by policy analysts as well as international organizations.

United Nations Industrial Development Organization. 1996. *Ethiopia: Accelerating Industrial Growth through Market Reforms.* New York: United Nations Industrial Development Organization. 111 pp.

This is an industrial development survey on trends in mid-1990s Ethiopia regarding macroeconomic market information. It provides statistics concerning the industrial sector and the country's production capacity. It employs input-output analysis to figure out manpower needs in education, skills, gender parity, and labor productivity. An important piece to read by generalists as well as specialists.

SOCIETY

Bahru, Zewde. 2002. *Pioneers of Change in Ethiopia: The Reformist Intellectuals of the Early Twentieth Century*. Oxford: J. Currey. 228 pp.

Bahru Zewde deals mainly with two generations of intellectuals. The book shows that both groups were by and large faithful followers of the modernization efforts Emperor Haile Selassie, under whose reign they obtained important political offices. This is a novel work that deserves to be read by all interested in Ethiopia's westernization struggle.

Baxter, P. T. W., J. Hultin, et al. 1996. *Being and Becoming Oromo: Historical and Anthropological Enquiries*. Uppsala Lawrenceville, NJ: Red Sea Press. 310 pp.

This work recounts the Oromos' struggle for national identity and recognition and suggests a model for emerging late 20th-century ethnic nationalism. This book lays bare contemporary problems of the Oromo, who number more than 20 million and are thus one of the largest ethnic groups in Africa.

Erlikh, H. 2007. *Saudi Arabia and Ethiopia: Islam, Christianity, and Politics Entwined*. Boulder, CO: Lynne Rienner. 249 pp.

This book surveys the establishment of both Ethiopia and Saudi Arabia as states dominated by religious elites based on Christianity and Islam. The author offers a valuable insight into the political conditions that shaped the salience of religious tensions in Ethiopia. This is a must-read for all scholars of Ethiopian studies.

Eshete, T. 2009. *The Evangelical Movement in Ethiopia: Resistance and Resilience*. Waco, TX: Baylor University Press. 480 pp.

This book's importance lies in that it documents early Church–State relations under Mengistu Haile Mariam's communist order and the southern evangelical response to the persecution, through an "underground" Christian movement. The book provides an important societal episode of the rapid growth of the Pentecostal movement in Ethiopia.

Fargher, B. L. 1996. *The Origins of the New Churches Movement in Southern Ethiopia, 1927–1944*. New York: E. J. Brill. 329 pp.

It is common knowledge that Christianity has been in Ethiopia since AD 340. The Ethiopian Tewahedo Orthodox Church has always remained a manifestation of Ethiopian culture. But new missionaries brought a notion of the Church completely different from that of the age-old national Church. This book documents a story that is essential for religious scholars.

Hassen, M. 1994. *The Oromo Of Ethiopia: A History, 1570–1860*. Trenton, NJ: Red Sea Press. 253 pp.

Mohammed Hassen's book is a commendable scholarly study that documents Oromo history in general and that of the Oromos of the Gibe Confederacy in particular. These very important ethnic groups who were subdued by the firearms using northerners have in recent decades become important due to their numerical strength, constituting over 40 percent of the total population of Ethiopia. This is a must-read for all politicians and historians and Ethiopianists of all categories.

Hosken, Fran P. 1979. *The Hosken Report: Genital and Sexual Mutilation of Females*. 2nd enlarged rev. ed. Lexington, MA: Women's International Network News. 368 pp.

Showing obvious abhorrence of the widespread practice of female genital mutilation (FGM), the author at the same time tries to show that in order to stamp it out, a novel approach is required. Evidence is presented that often it is women themselves who are most insistent upon the retention of FGM. It is emphasized that "customs" are very important to consider. The book is a key tool in understanding reasons that this abominable practice has persisted for so long.

Jalata, A. 1993. *Oromia and Ethiopia: State Formation and Ethno-National Conflict, 1868–1992*. Boulder, CO: L. Rienner. 320 pp.

The emphasis of the author is on the idea that the Oromos are the historical victims of past and present rulers of Ethiopia. It is almost a political manifesto of radical Oromo nationalists against the Ethiopian state system and needs to be read to fathom the resentment they have and why many of them ask for sovereign independence.

Jolly, Alison. 1999. *Lucy's Legacy: Sex and Intelligence in Human Evolution*. Boston: Harvard University Press. 416 pp.

Lucy the Australopithecine, a human ancestor discovered in Ethiopia in 1974, is discussed in this interesting scholarly analysis. The author mentions Lucy's legacy of food sharing, development of the facility for language, and migration—spheres of human accomplishment where women aced men. But Jolly's evolutionary heroine is not in competition with her hero. This remarkable story should be read by everybody to see how *Homo sapiens sapiens* became what they are today.

Lyon, Len. 2007. *The Ethiopian Jews of Israel*. New York: Jewish Lights Publishing. 240 pp.

The Falashas, meaning in Ethiopic "immigrants," or Beta Israel, meaning "House of Israel," is the term by which Ethiopian Jews prefer to be called. The book reports that more than 100,000 of them were repatriated to Israel between 1977 and 1993. It provides readers a well-balanced account of the Ethiopian Jews' exodus from Ethiopia to Israel.

Thesiger, Wilfred. 1996. *The Danakil Diary: Journeys through Abyssinia, 1930–34*. New York: HarperCollins. 214 pp.

It was in 1930 that Wilfred Thesiger went hunting alone in the hostile Danakil desert of Ethiopia. He describes his dangerous journey among the fierce Afars which is still one of the best descriptions of the territory and its people. The book is a good source for understanding the lifestyle of the Afars of the period.

CULTURE

Adera, T., A. J. Ahmed, et al. 1995. *Silence Is Not Golden: A Critical Anthology of Ethiopian Literature*. Lawrenceville, NJ: Red Sea Press. 214 pp.

This is an anthology of critical articles on Ethiopian literature and provides a valuable introduction to a national tradition.

Cerulli, E. 1917. *Folk-Literature of the Galla of Southern Abyssinia*. 228 pp.

This book is still the best source for folk tales, history, legends, and culture of the Oromo people, which is the majority cultural group in Ethiopia. The texts are presented in the original Oromo, with translations and detailed notes and explanations. Specialists of Ethiopian languages have to consult this book.

Cotter, G. 1992. *Proverbs and Sayings of the Oromo People of Ethiopia and Kenya with English Translations*. Lewiston, NY: E. Mellen Press. 591 pp.

A very rich ethnic wisdom that has been collected before it is swamped under the powerful onslaught of the Semitic and English vernaculars. A very important read for people interested in the age-old sayings of northeast Africa's not only numerous but also very resourceful people.

Ethiopia Publications and Foreign Languages Press Department. 1968. *Music, Dance, and Drama*. Addis Ababa, Ethiopia: Ministry of Information, Publications & Foreign Languages Press Department. 110 pp.

A succinct description of the art of music as well as dance and drama in Ethiopia during the Haile Selassie period. A good background for specialists and enthusiasts of Ethiopian culture before the fall of the feudal regime.

Leslau, W. 1979. *Falasha Anthology*. New Haven, CT: Yale University Press. 222 pp.

This book was translated by W. Leslau from the original Ge'ez . This is based on the Ethiopic *Apocalypse of Baruch* (*5 Baruch*), extant only in Ethiopic and thus a must-read for Semitic scholars.

Lindahl, B. 1970. *Medieval Architecture and Art in Ethiopia*. Addis Ababa: College of Architecture and Building Technology. 171 pp.

A very important and informed description and analysis of Ethiopian architecture. Important to read for those interested in Ethiopian civilization.

Lovett, Charlie. 1997. *Olympic Marathon: A Centennial History of the Games Most Storied Race*. New York: Praeger. 192 pp.

This book is the first complete history of the Olympic Games' most storied race. It starts from ancient Greece and covers Atlanta in 1996. Abebe Bikila's and Mamo Wolde's interesting episodes are covered. An interesting read for its own sake.

Mesfin, Daniel Jote Mesfin. 1987. *Exotic Ethiopian Cooking: Society, Culture, Hospitality and Traditions*, with introduction by the Famous Environmentalist Shlomo Bachrach. Falls Church, VA: Ethiopinan Cookbook Enterprises, 258 pp.

This cookbook, with clear-cut vegetarian and non-vegetarian sections, comes with 178 tested recipes and food composition tables. With Daniel's instructive recipes, you can concoct, with apparent ease, your own spiced chicken stew, *shiro wat*, and gourmet veggies made with spiced pea sauce.

Plastow, Jane. 1996. *African Theatre and Politics: The Evolution of Theatre in Ethiopia, Tanzania, and Zimbabwe*. Amsterdam: Rodopi, 1996. 300 pp.

This is a comparative study of theater in Africa based on the author's rich experience as a teacher of English and drama in African schools. The book, which is a landmark for the history of drama in Africa, can be a good guide for people in the field.

Powne, M. 1968. *Ethiopian Music, an Introduction: A Survey of Ecclesiastical and Secular Ethiopian Music and Instruments*. London: Oxford University Press. 156 pp.

This book provides a mass of information regarding traditional Ethiopian music. Its discussion is primarily of the music of the Hamito-Semitic plateau people and is divided into three sections: musical instruments, secular music, and ecclesiastical music. This is a must-read for all music lovers.

Rushby, K. 1999. *Eating the Flowers of Paradise: A Journey through the Drug Fields of Ethiopia and Yemen*. New York: St. Martin's Press. 322 pp.

This work deals with *qat* (also referred to as *tchat* in Ethiopia), a leaf with the natural ingredient of amphetamine. The book describes the ceremony involved with *qat* and its place in both Ethiopia and Yemen. It is recommended to those who are interested in cultural traditions in the region.

Samuelsson, Marcus. 2006. *The Soul of a New Cuisine*. New York: Wiley. 300 pp.

Marcus Samuelsson, born in Ethiopia and raised in Sweden, is an accomplished cookbook author and the winner of two major awards for his refined art of cooking. To write this book, Samuelsson made many trips to Ethiopia and other regions of the African continent. He has collected 200 recipes tested by him and informed by his knowledge of African tastes and techniques. Almost half of these are totally unknown to Westerners. This book is a must for all connoisseurs regardless of their origin.

Selinus, R. 1971. *The Traditional Foods of the Central Ethiopian Highlands*. Uppsala, Sweden: Scandinavian Institute of African Studies. 341 pp.

This book describes the staple crop and food items of the Ethiopian highlanders, mainly Amharas. It is an instructive work for those interested in the food habits in highland culture.

Sumner, Claude. 1995. *Oromo Wisdom Literature: Proverbs Collections and Analysis*. Addis Ababa: Gudina Tumsa Foundation. 240 pp.

Sumner, Claude. 1996. *Proverbs, Songs, Folktales: An Anthology of Oromo Literature*. Addis Ababa: Gudina Tumsa Foundation. 482 pp.

As the name indicates, this is a very rich collection of Oromo cultural heritage and needs to be read by all sociologists interested in Ethiopia and the Horn of Africa.

Thematic Index

HISTORY

GOVERNMENT AND POLITICS

Index